Get the eBook FREE!

(PDF, ePub, Kindle, and liveBook all included)

We believe that once you buy a book from us, you should be able to read it in any format we have available. To get electronic versions of this book at no additional cost to you, purchase and then register this book at the Manning website.

Go to https://www.manning.com/freebook and follow the instructions to complete your pBook registration.

That's it!
Thanks from Manning!

Fighting Churn with Data

Fighting Churn with Data

THE SCIENCE AND STRATEGY OF CUSTOMER RETENTION

CARL GOLD
FOREWORD BY TIEN TZUO

MANNING

SHELTER ISLAND

	Development editor: Toni Arritola
	Technical development editor: Mike Shepard
	Review editor: Ivan Martinović
Manning Publications Co.	Production editor: Deirdre S. Hiam
20 Baldwin Road	Copy editor: Frances Buran/Tiffany Taylor/
PO Box 761	Keir Simpson
Shelter Island, NY 11964	Proofreader: Pamela Hunt
	Technical proofreader: Al Krinker
	Typesetter: Dennis Dalinnik
	Cover designer: Marija Tudor

ISBN: 9781617296529
Printed in the United States of America

brief contents

contents

PART 3   SPECIAL WEAPONS AND TACTICS 315

8 *Forecasting churn   317*

9 *Forecast accuracy and machine learning   367*

foreword

This book is a rarity. Although it's intended primarily for technically oriented people with some familiarity with coding and data, it also happens to be lucid, compelling, and occasionally even (gasp!) funny. The first chapter in particular should be mandatory reading for anyone who's interested in running a successful subscription-based business. Buy a copy for your boss.

It's exciting to think about all the different companies that will benefit from the sharp analysis in these pages. Data folks from all sectors of the global economy, from streaming-media services to industrial manufacturers, will be paying close attention to Carl's book. Today, the whole world runs "as a service": transportation, education, media, health care, software, retail, manufacturing, you name it.

All these new digital services are generating vast amounts of data, resulting in a huge signal-to-noise challenge, which is why this book is so important. I study this topic for a living, and no one has written such a practical and authoritative guide to effectively filtering through all that information to reduce churn and keep subscribers happy. When it comes to running a subscription business, churn rates are a matter of life and death!

Thousands of entrepreneurs are already deeply familiar with Carl Gold's work. He is the author of the Subscription Economy Index, a biannual benchmark study that reflects the growth metrics of hundreds of subscription companies spread across a variety of industries. As Zuora's chief data scientist, Carl works with the most timely and accurate dataset in the subscription economy. He's a big part of why Zuora is not only a successful software company but also a respected thought leader.

If you're reading this book, you will soon have the ability to make immediate and material contributions to the success of your company. But as Carl discusses extensively throughout the book, it's not enough to do the analysis; you also need to be able to communicate your results to the business at large.

So by all means, use this book to learn how to conduct the proper analysis, but also use it to learn how to share, execute, and basically excel at your job. There are examples and case studies and tips and benchmarks galore. How lucky are we? We get to work in the early days of the subscription economy, and we get to read the first landmark book on churn.

—Tien Tzuo, founder and CEO, Zuora

preface

Customer churn (cancelations) and engagement are life-and-death issues for every company that offers an online product or service. Coinciding with the wide adoption of data science and analytics, it is now standard to call in data professionals to help in the effort to reduce churn. But understanding churn has many challenges and pitfalls not common to other data applications, and until now, there has not been a book to help a data professional (or student) get started in this area.

Over the past six years, I have worked on churn for dozens of products and services, and served as the chief data scientist at a company called Zuora. Zuora provides a platform for subscription companies to manage their products, operations, and finances, and you will see some Zuora customers in case studies throughout the book. During that time, I experimented with different ways to analyze churn and feed the results back to people at companies that were fighting churn. The truth is that I made a lot of mistakes in the early years, and I was inspired to write this book to save other people from making the same mistakes that I made.

The book is written from the point of view of a data person: whoever is expected to take the raw data and come up with useful findings to help in the fight against churn. That person may have the title of data scientist, data analyst, or machine learning engineer. Or they may be someone else who knows a bit about data and code and is being asked to fill those shoes. The book uses Python and SQL, so it does assume that the data person is a coder. Although I advocate spreadsheets for presentation and sharing data (as I detail in the book), I do not recommend attempting the main analytic tasks of churn fighting in spreadsheets: many tasks must be performed in sequence, and some of these tasks are nontrivial. Also, there is a need to "rinse and repeat" the process multiple times. That kind of workflow is well suited to short programs but difficult in spreadsheets and graphical tools.

Because the book is written for a data person, it does not go into details on the churn-reducing actions that products and services can take. So this book does not contain details on how to do things like run email and call campaigns, create churn-save playbooks, and design pricing and packaging. Instead, this book is strategic in that it teaches a data-driven approach to devising your battle plan against churn: picking which churn-reducing activities to pursue, which customers to target, and what kinds of results to expect. That said, I will introduce various churn-reducing tactics at a high level as is necessary to understand the context for using the data.

acknowledgments

There are many people without whom it would not have been possible for me to create this book for you.

Starting at the beginning, I thank Ben Rigby for bringing me to my first churn case study and everyone who worked at Sparked (Chris Purvis, Chris Mielke, Cody Chapman, Collin Wu, David Nevin, Jamie Doornboss, Jeff Nickerson, Jordan Snodgrass, Joseph Pigato, Mark Nelson, Morag Scrimgoeur, Rabih Saliba, and Val Ornay) and all the customers of Retention Radar. Next, I have Tien Tzuo and Marc Aronson to thank for bringing me to Zuora, and thanks to Tom Krackeler, Karl Goldstein, and everyone from Frontleaf (Amanda Olsen, Greg McGuire, Marcelo Rinesi, and Rachel English) for welcoming me to their team. Continuing in chronological order, I also thank everyone who worked on or with the Zuora Insights team (Azucena Araujo, Caleb Saunders, Gail Jimenez, Jessica Hartog, Kevin Postlewaite, Kevin Suer, Matt Darrow, Michael Lawson, Patrick Kelly, Pushkala Pattabhiraman, Shalaka Sindkar, and Steve Lotito), the data scientist on my team who worked on churn (Dashiell Stander), and all the Zuora Insights customers. All these people were part of the projects on which I learned what I now know about churn; in that way, they made it possible for me to write this book for you. And I want to thank everyone at Zuora who either helped promote or edit the book: Amy Konary, Gabe Weisert, Helena Zhang, Jayne Gonzalez, Kasey Radley, Lauren Glish, Peishan Li, and Sierra Dowling.

Next comes my publisher, Manning, where I thank my first acquisitions editor, Stephen Soehnlen, for bringing me on board; my main development editor, Toni Arritola, and my temporary DE, Becky Whitney, for patiently teaching me how to write

xix

a Manning-style book; and my second AE, Michael Stephens, for getting the book across the finish line. I also thank my technical and code editors—Mike Shepard, Charles Feduke, and Al Krinkler—and everyone who commented on the liveBook forum during the early access period. My thanks also go to Deirdre Hiam, my project editor; Pamela Hunt, my proofreader; and Frances Buran, Tiffany Taylor, and Keir Simpson, my copyeditors. I would also like to thank all the reviewers: Aditya Kaushik, Al Krinker, Alex Saez, Amlan Chatterjee, Burhan Ul Haq, Emanuele Piccinelli, George Thomas, Graham Wheeler, Jasmine Alkin, Julien Pohie, Kelum Senanayake, Lalit Narayana Surampudi, Malgorzata Rodacka, Michael Jensen, Milorad Imbra, Nahid Alam, Obiamaka Agbaneje, Prabhuti Prakash, Raushan Jha, Simone Sguazza, Stefano Ongarello, Stijn Vanderlooy, Tiklu Ganguly, Vaughn DiMarco, and Vijay Kodam. Your suggestions helped make this book better.

Special thanks go to the three companies that allowed me to present a selection of their case study data to bring the material in the book to life: Matt Baker and everyone at Broadly; Yan Kong and everyone at Klipfolio; and Jonathan Moody, Tyler Cooper, and everyone at Versature.

Finally, I thank my wife, Anna, and children, Clive and Skylar, for their support and patience during a challenging but fruitful time.

about this book

This book was written to enable anyone with a little background in coding and data to make a game-changing analysis of customer churn for an online product or service. And if you are experienced in programming and data analysis, the book contains tips and tricks for churn and customer engagement that you won't find anywhere else.

Who should read this book

The primary audience for this book is data scientists, data analysts, and machine learning engineers. You will want this book when you are tasked with helping understand and fight churn for an online product or service. Also, the book is absolutely suitable for students of computer science and data science, or anyone who knows how to code and wants to learn more about an important area of data science at a typical modern company. Because the book begins with raw data and provides the necessary background on every analytic task described, it reads as a complete hands-on course in data science, taught on a consistent project: analyzing churn for a small company. (A sample dataset is provided.)

That said, chapters 8 and 9 in part 3 of the book, on forecasting and machine learning for churn, may entail a steep learning curve for someone who does not have some experience on the subjects it covers. If you don't have that background, I think you can still learn everything you need to know in chapters 8 and 9, but you may have to spend extra time to read some of the recommended online resources.

This book should also be read by noncoding business professionals. The book includes a unique set of case study observations about churn at real companies. The book explains the data typically available for analyzing churn, the practices used to turn that data into actionable intelligence, and the most typical findings. One emphasis of the book is how to communicate data results to businesspeople; consequently, *all the important takeaways are explained in plain English* (no jargon!). So if you care about churn but aren't a coder, you should skim the book for the takeaways (clearly labeled) and skip the coding and math. Then share the book with one of your developers to get help putting the concepts into action.

How this book is organized: A road map

The book is organized to take you step-by-step through a specific process: the process a data person at an online company should go through when they harness raw data to drive the fight against churn. As such, the book is best read in order, chapter by chapter. That said, the material in the book is front-loaded in the following two senses:

- In every chapter, the most important topics are taught first, and details about less common scenarios come at the end of the chapter.
- The most important lessons come in the earliest chapters, and the topics in later chapters are more specialized.

So if you find yourself near the end of a chapter that doesn't seem to be relevant to your scenario, there usually is no harm in skipping to the next chapter. Also, if you are pressed for time and need to master the basics, you can try to take one of these abbreviated reading paths:

- To get the foundations, read chapters 1–3 plus section 4.5, which corresponds to reading almost all of part 1 (skipping all but one section of chapter 4).
- To get an advanced course without the most specialized subjects, read chapters 1–7, which corresponds to reading parts 1 and 2.

More details on these abbreviated courses of reading and how to apply the learnings are given in chapter 11.

The book is divided into three parts. Part 1 explains what churn is and how to measure it, what data companies typically have available to help them understand and reduce churn, and how to prepare the data to make it useful:

- Chapter 1 is a general introduction to the field and includes an introduction to the case studies, highlighting the type of intelligence the book will help you achieve for your own product and service.
- Chapter 2 explains how to identify churned customers and measure churn in a variety of ways. SQL code begins in this chapter.
- Chapter 3 introduces the creation of customer metrics from the event data that most online companies collect about their users.
- Chapter 4 explains how to combine the churn data from chapter 2 with the metrics from chapter 3 to create an analytic dataset for understanding and fighting churn.

Part 2, which contains the core techniques in the book, is devoted to understanding how customer behavior relates to churn and retention and using that knowledge to drive churn-reducing strategies:

- Chapter 5 teaches a form of cohort analysis, which is the primary method for understanding and explaining the relationship between behaviors and churn. Chapter 5 also includes many case study examples, and the code is in Python.
- Chapter 6 looks at how to deal with data that is big in an undesirable way: most company datasets have closely related measurements of the same underlying behavior. How you deal with this somewhat-redundant information is important.
- Chapter 7 returns to the subject of metric creation and uses the information from chapters 5 and 6 to design advanced metrics, which help explain complex customer behaviors such as price sensitivity and efficiency.

Part 3 covers forecasting with regression and machine learning. When it comes to reducing churn, forecasting is less important than having a good set of metrics, but it can still be useful, and some special techniques are needed to get it right:

- Chapter 8 teaches how to forecast customer churn probabilities with a regression and how to interpret the results of those forecasts, including calculating customer lifetime value.
- Chapter 9 is about machine learning and measuring and optimizing the accuracy of churn forecasts.
- Chapter 10 covers analyzing demographic or firmographic data in the context of churn and finding lookalikes for your best customers.

Most readers should start at the beginning and read parts 1 and 2. If, after learning and applying those techniques, you need to make forecasts or find lookalike customers, continue to part 3. If you are already using advanced analytics, you may be able to skip part 1 and start in part 2 and/or 3. For purposes of this book, being advanced in analytics means that you already have a good set of customer metrics and can identify and measure churned customers. Otherwise, start with part 1.

About the code

The book contains code listings in SQL and Python. Each listing represents one small step in the process of preparing data, understanding why customers churn, and reducing churn:

- All the code from the book is available in the author's GitHub repository at https://github.com/carl24k/fight-churn.
- The GitHub repository also provides a Python wrapper program to run both SQL and Python listings. That program is the recommended way to run the code.
- The book contains examples you can run on a simulated set of customer data, designed to look like the data that would be generated by users of a small online service: a social network with 10,000 customers.

- The README file of the GitHub repository contains instructions for setting up the programming environment and running the simulation to create the sample data for the examples.

liveBook discussion forum

The purchase of *Fighting Chum with Data: The Science and Strategy of Keeping Your Customers* includes free access to a private web forum run by Manning Publications, where you can make comments about the book, ask technical questions, and receive help from the author and from other users. To access the forum, go to https://livebook .manning.com/#!/book/fighting-chum-with-data/discussion. You can also learn more about Manning's forums and the rules of conduct at https://livebook.manning.com/ #!/discussion.

Manning's commitment to our readers is to provide a venue where a meaningful dialogue between individual readers and between readers and the author can take place. It is not a commitment to any specific amount of participation on the part of the author, whose contribution to the forum remains voluntary (and unpaid). We suggest that you try asking him some challenging questions, lest his interest stray! The forum and the archives of previous discussions will be accessible from the publisher's website as long as the book is in print.

Other online resources

I maintain a website, https://fightchurnwithdata.com, that hosts my blog and links to other resources and information.

about the author

 CARL GOLD is Chief Data Scientist at Zuora, Inc. (NYSE: ZUO). Zuora is a comprehensive subscription management platform and newly public Silicon Valley unicorn with more than 1,000 customers worldwide. Zuora's clients come from a wide range of industries, including software (Software as a Service, or SaaS), media, travel services, consumer packaged goods, cloud services, Internet of Things (IoT), and telecommunications. Zuora is widely recognized as a leader in all things pertaining to subscriptions and recurring revenue. Carl joined Zuora in 2015 as Chief Data Scientist and created the predictive analytics system for Zuora's subscriber analysis product, Zuora Insights.

about the cover illustration

The figure on the cover of *Fighting Chum with Data: The Science and Strategy of Keeping Your Customers* is captioned "Paysanne du canton de Zurich," or "Farmer's wife from the canton of Zurich." The illustration is by the French artist Hippolyte Lecomte (1781–1857) and was published in 1817. The illustration is finely drawn and colored by hand and reminds us vividly of how culturally apart the world's regions, towns, villages, and neighborhoods were only 200 years ago. Isolated from one another, people spoke different dialects and languages. In the streets or in the countryside, it was easy to identify where they lived and what their trade or station in life was by their dress alone.

Dress codes have changed since then, and the diversity by region, so rich at the time, has faded away. It is now hard to tell apart the inhabitants of different continents, let alone different towns or regions. Perhaps we have traded cultural diversity for a more varied personal life—certainly for a more varied and fast-paced technological life.

At a time when it is hard to tell one computer book from another, Manning celebrates the inventiveness and initiative of the computer business with book covers based on the rich diversity of regional life of two centuries ago, brought back to life by pictures from collections such as this one.

Part 1

Building your arsenal

Before you can fight churn with data, you need to prepare the data. Knowledge is going to be your weapon in the fight against churn, but for most products and services, the raw data is useless. Although you will never stop building and honing your data, this part teaches you how to lay the foundations. The goal of this part is to show you how to accomplish a few foundational tasks: measuring churn, creating metrics for your customers, and combining your customer data into datasets for performing further analysis and sharing with your business colleagues.

Chapter 1 contains background information about the industry of online products and services. This chapter also introduces the company case studies and demonstrates the type of results the book will teach you to create. Finally, the first chapter introduces the simulated data case study that will be used in examples throughout the book.

Chapter 2 teaches the calculation of churn rates using SQL. This skill is necessary so you can measure churn properly before starting to fight it. This chapter also lays the foundation for some advanced SQL techniques later in the book.

Chapter 3 is the first chapter on the calculation of customer metrics, which is one of the main themes of the book. As you will see, carefully designed customer metrics are the main weapon you will use in the fight against churn.

Chapter 4 introduces the concept of a dataset and shows you how to create a dataset for understanding churn from your own raw data. This chapter combines the techniques from chapters 2 and 3 and is the foundation for the techniques in part 2.

The world of churn

What is churn? Why do we fight it? And how can data help? In short, why are you reading this book? If you are reading this book, you are probably

- A data analyst, data scientist, or machine learning engineer
- Working for an organization that offers a product or service with repeat customers or users

Or maybe you are studying to get one of those jobs or filling such a role even though it's not your job.

Such services are often sold by subscription, but your organization does not need to sell subscriptions in order to take advantage of this book. All you need is a product with repeat customers or users and a desire to keep them coming back. This book teaches a lot of techniques related to subscriptions, but in every case, I show how the same concepts apply to retail and other nonsubscription scenarios.

To get the most out of this book, you should have a background in data analysis and programming. If that is you, then get ready for a game-changing breakthrough in the way you think about customers and data. This is not your usual book about data analysis and data science because, as you will learn, the usual approach doesn't work for churn. But you don't need a degree in data science to take advantage of this book: I will review enough of the basics so that anyone with a little programming experience can get great results. With that in mind, I refer to you, the reader, as a *data person* because this book is written from the point of view of the person who works with the data. That said, this book is packed with business insights from real-world case studies, so even if you don't program, you can still get a lot from reading the book and then give the book to your developer when it comes time to put theory into practice. This book provides a hands-on approach to the subjects of churn and data.

If you work with an organization that offers a live service, you probably know all about churn and want to get on with the fight to prevent it. But I need to provide context for those who are just starting out; and even if you already know about churn, I need to dispel a few common misconceptions before we begin.

This chapter is organized as follows:

- Sections 1.1–1.3 provide the context for the rest of the book: what churn is, how to fight it, why fighting churn is hard, and why I have selected the topics for the book.
- Sections 1.4–1.6 make the theory concrete. I describe the business contexts where these strategies apply and what data different companies have to work with.
- Sections 1.7–1.8 bring the theory to life by looking at case studies that are featured throughout the book. By the end of the book, you will be ready to create those kinds of results for your own product or service.

1.1 *Why you are reading this book*

A primary goal for any service is to grow by adding customers or users through marketing and sales. (This is true for both for-profit and nonprofit enterprises.) When customers leave, it counteracts the company's growth and can even lead to contraction.

> **DEFINITION**   *Churn*—When a customer quits using a service or cancels their subscription.

Most service providers focus on acquisitions. But to be successful, a service must also work to minimize churn. If churn is not addressed in an ongoing, proactive way, the product or service won't reach its full potential.

The word *churn* originated with the term *churn rate*, which refers to the proportion of customers departing in a given period, as we will discuss in more detail later. This leads to the customer or user population changing over time, which is why the term *churn* makes sense. The word originally meant "to move about vigorously" (as in churning butter). In the business context, *churn* is now used as both a verb—"the customer is churning" or "the customer churned"—and as a noun—"the customer is a churn" or "make a report on last quarter's churns."

Customers not churning from a service can also be framed in a positive sense, if you prefer to see the glass as half full. In that case, people talk about customer retention.

> **DEFINITION**   *Customer retention*—Keeping customers using a service and renewing their subscriptions (if there are subscriptions). Customer retention is the opposite of churn.

Reducing churn is equivalent to increasing customer retention, and the terms are interchangeable to a large degree. When a goal is stated as retaining more customers longer, then in addition to saving customers who are at risk of churning, there should also be a focus on keeping customers engaged. There is even the possibility of upselling the most engaged customers more advanced versions of the service, typically for more money. Saving churns, increasing engagement, and upsells are all important goals for services with repeated customer interactions. The difference between these is a matter of focus and not a difference in the intention.

> **TAKEAWAY** Despite the wide variety of products and services with repeat customers, there is a single set of techniques for using data to fight churn and increase engagement, retention, and upsell.

This book gives you the skills to address engagement and upsells and to fight churn effectively using data in any kind of recurring user interaction scenario.

1.1.1 The typical churn scenario

If you work in an organization that creates a subscription product, your situation probably looks something like the one shown in the top of figure 1.1. The key ingredients are as follows:

- A product or service is offered and used on a recurring basis.
- Customers interact with the product.
- Customers may have subscriptions to receive the product or service. Subscriptions often (but not always) cost money.
- Subscriptions can be ended or canceled, which is known as *churn*. If there are no subscriptions, a customer churns when they stop using the product.
- The timing, prices, and payments for the customers and subscriptions (if any) are captured in a database, typically a transactional database.
- When customers use or interact with the product or service, these events are often tracked and stored in a data warehouse.

In section 1.4, we'll look at a wide variety of products that fit this description. If your scenario is not quite like this but has some of the elements, that's fine. As described in section 1.5, the techniques in this book also apply to related situations. What is described is simply the most common situation.

Throughout the book, I interchange the terms *subscriber, customer,* and *user.* These have slightly different connotations, but in general, the same ideas apply (a subscriber has a subscription, a customer pays, and a user may not do either but you still want them coming back). The techniques in this book apply regardless of your relationship with your customers. If I present an example using a persona that is not relevant to you, then you should mentally substitute one that is appropriate for your product.

1.1.2 What this book is about

Figure 1.1 shows how the techniques in this book work together. The following describes each step in the process:

1. *Churn measurement*—Uses subscription data to identify churns and create churn metrics. The churn rate is an example of a churn metric. The subscription

database also allows identification of customers who churned and who renewed and exactly when they did; this data is needed for further analysis.

2 *Behavioral measurement*—Uses the event data warehouse to create behavioral metrics that summarize the events pertaining to each subscriber. Creating behavioral metrics is a crucial step that allows the events in the data warehouse to be interpreted.

3 *Churn analysis*—Uses behavioral metrics for identified churns and renewals. The churn analysis identifies which subscriber behaviors are predictive of renewal and which are predictive of churn and can create a churn risk prediction for every subscriber.

At this stage, sources of information in addition to the subscriber database and event data warehouse can also be brought into the analysis (not shown in

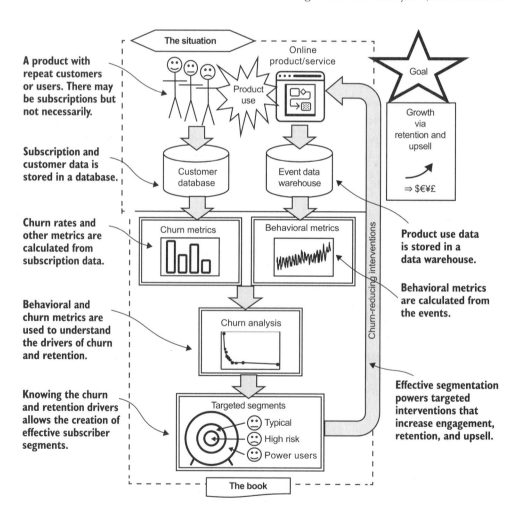

Figure 1.1 Mental model for fighting churn with data

figure 1.1). These include *demographic* information about customers or users who are individual consumers (age, education, etc.) and *firmographic* information about subscribers that are businesses (industry, number of employees, etc.).

4 *Segmentation*—Based on their characteristics and risks, divides customers into groups or *segments* that combine aspects of their risk level, their behaviors, and any other significant characteristics. These segments target customers for interventions designed to maximize subscriber lifetime and engagement with the service.

5 *Intervention*—Using the insights and subscriber segmentation rules derived from the churn analysis, plans and executes churn-reducing interventions, including email marketing, call campaigns, and training. Another long-term intervention makes changes to the product or service, and the information from the churn analysis is useful for this too.

This is the crucial step that drives the desired outcome (growth!). More information about types of interventions begins in the next section and is provided throughout the book, but I cover interventions only in a general way. This is why figure 1.1 shows interventions as partly outside the scope of this book.

I will refer back to figure 1.1 in each chapter to make it clear which part of the process the chapter covers.

1.2 Fighting churn

One motivation for writing this book stems from the challenges of trying to reduce churn. That said, my motto is to underpromise and overdeliver. I will begin with warnings about how hard reducing churn can be. Later, I will show that the imperfect options available can still lead to a material impact on your churn and user engagement.

1.2.1 Interventions that reduce churn

Companies use five main strategies to reduce churn. I summarize them here and will discuss them more throughout the book:

- *Product improvement*—Product managers and engineers (for software) and producers, talent, and other content creators (for media) reduce churn by changing product features or content, which improves the utility or enjoyment that customers receive. This can include adding new features and content or repackaging to ensure that users find the best parts of the product or service. This is the primary, most direct method of reducing churn.

  Another (software) method is to increase *stickiness*, which roughly means modifying the product to increase the cost for a customer to switch to an alternative. Switching cost is increased by providing valuable features that are hard to reproduce or difficult to transfer from one system to another.

- *Engagement campaigns*—Marketers reduce churn with mass communications that direct subscribers to the most popular content and features. This is more of an educational function for marketing than a traditional type of marketing. Remember, subscribers already have access and know what the service is like, so promises won't help. Still, marketers often use this function because they are skilled in crafting effective mass communications.

- *One-on-one customer interactions*—Customer success and support representatives prevent churn by making sure customers adopt the product and helping them if they can't. Whereas Customer Support is the department that traditionally helps customers, Customer Success is a new, separate function in many organizations: it's explicitly designed to be more proactive. Customer Support helps customers when the customers ask for help; Customer Success tries to detect customers who need help and reach out to them *before* they ask for it. Customer Success is also responsible for *onboarding* customers and making sure they do everything necessary to take advantage of the product.

- *Rightsizing pricing*—The Sales department (if there is one) may be the last resort in stopping churn, assuming the service is not free. Account managers can reduce the price or change subscription terms, managing the process through which a customer can down-sell to a less expensive version. For consumer products without a Sales department, Customer Support representatives who have similar authority usually take on this role. A more proactive approach is to right-size sales in the first place: do a better job of selling the product version that is optimal for the customer rather than selling the most expensive version possible. This can hurt short-term gains from each sale; but if done correctly, it reduces churn and ultimately improves the lifetime value of the customer.

- *Targeting acquisitions*—Different channels where you acquire customers may produce customers with different retention and churn quality. If that's the case, it makes sense to focus on the best channels. Rather than trying to keep the customers you have longer, you try to find better customers to replace them. This is the least direct method to reduce churn and is limited because most products cannot get unlimited customers from their preferred channels. Still, it is an important tool, and you should take advantage of it if you can.

All of these methods are most effective when they are *data driven*, meaning your organization picks the targets and tailors the tactics based on the correct reading of available data. Being data driven does not require that you have a certain amount or type of data or a particular technology. The emphasis in this book is on using the available data correctly, regardless of what type of product you work on or what type of intervention you ultimately employ to reduce churn.

> **TAKEAWAY** Being *data driven* when fighting churn means designing product changes, customer interventions, and acquisition strategies based on a sound reading of available data.

One thing to note: interventions and service modifications are the final crucial step to achieving the goal of lower churn and longer retention. How to execute interventions is beyond the scope of this book, however. Unlike data analysis techniques, *interventions to influence subscriber behavior are generally specific to the type of subscription service.* There is no one-size-fits-all intervention. Also, in general, people other than the data person make those interventions (product designers or marketers, for example).

> **TAKEAWAY** There are some general principles for churn-reducing interventions, but these require customization for each product's circumstances.

The circumstances that shape interventions include not only the particular features of the product or content but also the technology and resources available for making the interventions. To give adequate coverage to interventions would be another book (or even a separate book per industry), and it would be a book aimed at business managers, not a technical book like this one. Interested readers should look for titles on "Customer Success" in the business section, or more specifically, under product design, marketing, customer support, and so on. The tools and techniques in *this* book will revolutionize your products' performance in every one of those areas, but don't expect the data person to do it all!

1.2.2 Why churn is hard to fight

Now that you know the goal and the available strategies, I will introduce you to the difficulties you will face. These motivate my recommendations (in the next section) for how to use data to fight churn.

CHURN IS HARD TO PREVENT

The bad news is that people are (mostly) rational and self-interested, and your customers already know your product. In order to reduce churn long term, and in a reliable way, you have to either improve the value delivered by your product or reduce the cost. Remembering the last time you churned, what would have prevented you from churning? Better content and features? Maybe. A lower price? Perhaps. How about an improved user interface? Probably not, unless the user interface was terrible to begin with. And would more frequent email notifications about the product stop you from churning? Again, probably not, unless they contained information that you found valuable. (There's that *value* word again!)

To reduce churn, you need to increase value, but doing so is harder than getting people to sign up in the first place. Because your customers already know what the service is like, promises made by marketing or sales representatives won't get much traction. As the data person, you may be asked for "silver bullets" to reduce churn, but here is the bad news.

> **TAKEAWAY** If a *silver bullet* means a low cost and reliable method, there are no silver bullets to reduce churn!

In the words of the famous startup CEO and venture capitalist Ben Horowitz, "There are no silver bullets for this, only lead bullets." He was talking about delivering competitive software features in his startup memoir, *The Hard Thing About Hard Things* (Harper Business, 2014), but I think this applies equally to fighting churn. It means there are usually no quick "once and done" fixes; you continuously have to do the hard work of increasing the value you provide to subscribers. I'm not saying simple fixes for problems with subscription services never exist. But these types of issues are usually addressed by people like product managers and content producers. When the service turns to a data person for help reducing churn, the low-hanging fruit have usually been picked already. If a data person *does* discover easy fixes, it is a sign that those who created the service have not been doing their jobs well. (It's possible you will find easy fixes, but you *shouldn't*.)

The alternative, of course, is to reduce the cost of the service. But reducing the monetary cost is the nuclear option for a paid service; revenue churn or down sells may be better than a complete and total churn, but it's still churn.

> **WARNING** Price reduction is a "diamond bullet" against churn: it always works, but you can't afford it.

As you will see in the next chapter, most services consider down sells just another form of churn.

PREDICTING CHURN DOESN'T WORK (WELL)

Now let's talk about the usual tool in the data scientists' toolkit: prediction with a machine learning system. There are two reasons predicting churn doesn't work well. First, and most important, predicting churn risk doesn't help with most churn-reducing interventions. Because there is no such thing as a one-size-fits-all intervention, churn interventions need to be targeted based on factors other than the likelihood of churn. This is different from other areas like spam email or fraud detection where yes/no predictions tell you enough to choose an action. If you classify an email as spam, you put it in the spam folder—done! But if you predict a customer is at risk for churn, then what?

To reduce churn, you can run an email campaign to promote the use of a product feature. But a campaign like that should be targeted at users who don't use the feature, not sent to *all* users who are churn risks for any reason. Clogging users' inboxes with inappropriate content is going to drive them away, not save them! Churn-risk prediction can be a useful variable in choosing customers for one-on-one interventions by Customer Success teams, but even then, it is only one variable defining the targets.

This may disappoint you. To reduce churn, it isn't sufficient to deploy an AI system that can win a data science competition. If you deliver an analysis that predicts churn without providing more actionable information, the business will not be able to use it easily, if at all. Believe me when I tell you that predicting churn is not the focus of fighting churn with data. This is one of the most important lessons I had to learn when I started working in this area.

TAKEAWAY A one-size-fits-all churn intervention doesn't exist, so predicting customers at risk of churn is only a little helpful for reducing churn.

The second reason predicting churn doesn't work well is that churn is hard to predict with high accuracy, even with the best machine learning. It's easy to see why, if you recall your behavior the last time you churned: you probably were not taking full advantage of the product, but it took you a long time to cancel because you were too busy or you spent some time researching alternatives. Perhaps you couldn't make up your mind, or you forgot. If a predictive system were observing your behavior during that time, it would have flagged you as at risk and been wrong during all the time it took you to make up your mind and find the time to cancel. The moment of churn was shaped by too many extraneous factors to be predicted.

Apart from extraneous factors influencing timing, churn is hard to predict because utility or enjoyment is a fundamentally subjective experience. The likelihood of churn varies from individual to individual, even under the same circumstances. This is especially important for consumer services, where churn is usually hardest to predict. For business products, customers tend to be rational. But neither the customer nor you have enough information to do a precise cost-benefit analysis on their use of the product.

Finally, churn is normally rare in comparison with retention; it has to be, for any paid subscription that remains in business. Because churn is rare, false positive predictions are common no matter how you make predictions.

Given all these things, churn predictions are inevitably relatively crude. If you worked on a project where you predicted churn in the past and found it easy to predict with high accuracy, you might have been predicting churn too late, when it was not actionable (see chapter 4). I will provide data on churn prediction accuracy and what constitutes accurate versus inaccurate churn prediction in chapter 9. For now, I hope I've given you enough anecdotal arguments to show why highly accurate prediction usually is not possible.

TAKEAWAY Extraneous factors, subjectivity, incomplete information, and rarity make it hard to predict churn accurately.

REDUCING CHURN IS A TEAM EFFORT

One of the hardest things about preventing churn is that it is no one's job, in the sense that no one person or job function can do it alone. Consider the strategies for churn reduction described in the last section: product improvement, engagement campaigns, customer success and support, sales, and pricing. Those functions span more than half the departments in a typical organization! That means churn reduction is going to suffer from problems of communication and coordination. If left unchecked, there will be a tendency for different teams to come up with uncoordinated approaches to reduce churn. It would be counterproductive, for example, for the product and marketing teams to decide to focus on driving the use of different features or content. And those approaches may be based on limited or flawed information. Because they aren't the data experts (that's you, remember?), there's no guarantee that choices made by independent teams will be properly data driven.

> **TAKEAWAY** Churn-reduction efforts are at risk of miscommunication and lack of coordination between the multiple teams involved.

Also, in a typical situation, the data person can't do anything to reduce churn on their own. Reducing churn depends on actions taken by specialists in different parts of the business, not by a person who is wrangling the data. These coworkers are diverse, and I will refer to them as the *businesspeople* for lack of a better term. I'm not implying that the data person is not part of the business; but data people usually have no *direct* responsibility for concrete business outcomes (like revenue), whereas the people in those other roles usually do. From the data person's point of view, the business is the end user of the data analysis results.

> **TAKEAWAY** The data person's goal is to make businesspeople more effective at churn-reducing interventions.

1.2.3   *Great customer metrics: Weapons in the fight against churn*

Churn is hard to fight because different parts of the business are responsible for reducing churn in different ways. All of these teams have different tools and methods, and they may not align on the situation and strategies. Also, every method to reduce churn requires businesses to target interventions to the customers most likely to respond. As a result, to fight churn, businesses need a shared set of facts or rules for understanding customers and their engagement with the product.

   The best way to make data into a weapon in the fight against churn is to use the data to produce effective customer measurements and get those measurements into the hands of the business's churn fighters. As we will explore fully in chapter 3, a measurement of customers is called a *metric*.

> **DEFINITION** *Customer metric*—Any measurement you make on all customers individually.

As a simple example, a metric can be something like how many times per month each customer uses a software feature or watches episodes from a certain series. But not every metric is great for fighting churn.

> **TAKEAWAY** For a customer metric to be great for fighting churn, it should have the following characteristics: (1) easily understood by the business; (2) clearly associated with churn and retention, so it is obvious what a healthy customer looks like; (3) segments customers in a way that's useful for targeted interventions that increase engagement; and (4) useful to multiple functions of the business (product, marketing, support, etc.).

To continue the simple example, you may discover business rules like "customers who use (view) the product feature more than five times a month churn at half the rate of customers who use it only once a month or less." Something like using or viewing more of a particular feature is not very complicated, and the finding about churn makes it obvious what a healthy customer is. Each part of the business can use a fact like that differently. Product creators will know the feature is providing value and can either replicate it or make it easier to find. Marketing can design a campaign to drive users to the feature. And when Customer Success/Support people talk to a customer, they can ask if the customer is using that feature and encourage them to try it if not.

That may sound easy, but coming up with actionable findings that *appear* simple is harder than it sounds. Some findings can be misleading (see section 1.8.2 for an example), and the more common problem is that there are too many potential metrics and rules. The challenge then is to find a *concise* set of metrics for the business to follow. So just because you are looking for easy-to-understand facts and rules doesn't mean your job will be easy!

I arrived at this focus on delivering great customer metrics by experiencing situations where the metrics were *not* great. When I was starting out, the situation usually went like this: Before we began analyzing churn, the company chose customer metrics, and we used them as inputs for a predictive model. I often found that the customer metrics were poorly designed and weren't good for predicting and understanding churn, so the predictive model gave poor results, and no one used it. But they continued using the mediocre metrics because they needed measurements for segmenting. That's when the light bulb went on for me. Data analysis should focus on making sure the metrics are great for churn because that's what people will use to do their job. I knew that as a data expert, I could do a better job of creating customer metrics than the businesspeople—and so can you.

The approach I will teach you is like traditional statistical or scientific analysis. Data people trained as statisticians will likely find this approach more natural than computer scientists will. The process is to iteratively test different customer metrics, analyze their relationship to churn and to each other, and evaluate them for interpretability and how useful they are for segmenting and making interventions. You find the best set of metrics, and that is the main deliverable to the business. You will also be in a good position to run predictive models for additional use cases, as described in later chapters.

TAKEAWAY The main deliverable to the business from the data analysis project is a set of customer metrics.

1.3   *Why this book is different*

You might suspect by now that this is not your usual book about data science or data analysis. I will explain these differences now, so you know what to expect.

1.3.1   *Practical and in-depth*

Table 1.1 summarizes some ways this book differs from a typical book in this field.

Table 1.1   **How this book compares to other data analysis books**

This book	Most books about data analysis
One scenario from start to finish, including applications	Helicopter into many different scenarios but omit practical details
Focuses on understanding the data and designing metrics (aka feature engineering)	Focus on algorithms
Creates datasets from raw data in an iterative process	Use datasets that are fixed benchmarks
Emphasizes interpretability, parsimony, and agility	Emphasize maximizing accuracy or other technical metrics

This book focuses on one thing: a *practical* approach to using your data to fight churn. In contrast, most books on data analysis cover a wide variety of use cases, emphasizing statistical and computer science algorithms. That said, section 1.5 explains that there is a whole family of use cases that are similar to churn, and the same techniques apply. But this *book* stays focused on churn to make the learning easy; once you are an expert, it won't be hard to modify the techniques to related scenarios.

In typical data analysis books, the focus is on teaching algorithms. The datasets used to demonstrate the techniques are given and are known as *benchmark datasets*. This book starts with raw data and creates an analytical dataset, which is a large part of the work. I explain several statistical/machine learning algorithms at the level required to use them, but I will not teach a lot of theory. Instead, the focus is on teaching the entire process, including application of the results in a real-world scenario.

An important way in which real-world data problems differ from training is that in the real world, the job never ends: as soon as one analysis of churn is complete, new product features or content are created, requiring reanalysis. Or an entirely new type of data to enhance the original may become available. Also, there are constant changes in the business environment, such as competition and changing economic conditions. Such changes can require reanalysis, even if the product isn't modified.

To succeed in this environment, the process of using the data must be *parsimonious* and *agile*. *Parsimony* means using the minimum amount of data and the fewest analytic steps required to get the job done. *Agility* means responding to change quickly and efficiently. Achieving parsimony and agility has important consequences. I will return to these themes throughout the book but, for now, here are two key takeaways.

TAKEAWAY Your goal is to deliver actionable knowledge to the businesspeople. Listen to them, and try to answer their questions first. Do not exhaustively test every hypothesis or evaluation metric.

TAKEAWAY Write code to automate the process. This makes it much easier to accommodate the inevitable corrections or requests for changes.

Because of the need to communicate with businesspeople to fight churn, a data person's analysis achieves maximum impact when it provides actionable knowledge. For this reason, this book tells you how to communicate the analysis results in a way that nontechnical people understand. This means using relatively simple visualizations and avoiding technical jargon in favor of a common language. I even recommend making simplifications when explaining the analysis (but not cutting corners in doing the analysis). Throughout the book, I give specific examples of explanation strategies I have found to work.

The importance of data and metric design (aka feature engineering)

Many people who take academic classes on data science or data analysis get a surprise when they start working at a company or on a real research project: the data they need is not waiting for them in a CSV file or a database table, ready to run through an algorithm. Most real-world projects involve locating and merging data from multiple databases or systems, and this process is a large part (usually more than half) of the work on the project. In academic data science, this is referred to as *feature engineering*, but I will stick to the term *metric design* because of the need to communicate with businesspeople (more about this in chapter 3).

Another common misconception is that the choice of algorithm or analytic method is the most important thing contributing to model accuracy. The design of the summary metrics (aka *data features* to academics) that allow the data to be analyzed is the most important part of the process, even where accuracy is concerned.

Some data people who are academically inclined may see it as inefficient or even unworthy of them to prepare their data, viewing it as drudgery. But many small decisions must be made when preparing the data, some of which can have huge consequences for the results, especially if those decisions are not made correctly or not in the way the data person expects.

> **WARNING** It is extremely risky to delegate data-preparation tasks to another team.

Finally, I want to add that in my own experience, understanding the data and designing the metrics is the most fun, creative part of the entire process! In my opinion, this is the true "science" in data science: learning from your data through experimentation, not just running someone else's algorithm. It's not drudgery in my book!

1.3.2   *Simulated case study*

To meet its goals, this book revolves around an in-depth case study. You will start with a database of customer and event data and use it to perform all the steps in a real churn-fighting process: calculating the customer churn rate, understanding customer behavior by creating and analyzing metrics, discovering how customer behavior relates to churn, and using all that knowledge to design segments that you can use for targeted interventions (or to make targeted interventions, if it really were your company).

Because customer data is sensitive, I can't distribute real customer and product data to support your learning. Instead, this book includes a highly realistic customer simulation that you can use to generate your own data. I will also make frequent comparisons to case studies made on real companies (described in section 1.7). You will see that the results you get from your simulation are surprisingly similar to the real thing. The code for the simulation and instructions to set it up and run it are on the book's website (www.manning.com/books/fighting-churn-with-data) and in the book's GitHub repository (https://github.com/carl24k/fight-churn).

> **NOTE**   The most up-to-date instructions to set up the development environment and run the simulation and code will always be in the README page at the root of the book's GitHub repository. *The instructions for setup are not included in this book.*

I'll tell you more about the company you are going to simulate and study in section 1.7.4, after I introduce the real case studies. But first, to put the case studies in context, I want to talk more broadly about the kinds of companies and data to which this book applies.

1.4   *Products with recurring user interactions*

For those not already familiar with this area, I'm going to summarize the current state of the world of products that have recurring user interactions or subscriptions. Subscription and recurring payment business models are definitely not new; subscription news services have existed since at least the sixteenth century, and the recurring payment of insurance premiums was established in the seventeenth century. The twentieth century saw the rise of ubiquitous recurring payment services for a wide range of utilities made available by the second industrial revolution: first water, gas, electricity, and telephone service; and, in the late twentieth century, cable television, mobile phone service, and, of course, internet service. These services are all based around recurring payment relationships between consumer and provider. All such relationships can be referred to as *subscriptions*.

When we think of subscriptions, we usually think of a fixed fee paid periodically, although subscription services can collect three types of payments between the consumer and provider:

- *Recurring payments*—Fixed payments of the same amount for each period of service
- *Usage-based payments*—Payments for the amount of service used, based on some unit of measure

- *One-time payments*—Usually fees for setup but also for temporary (nonrecurring) upgrades to service or one-time (*in-app*) purchases

The services are sometimes paid for in advance (at the start of each service period) and sometimes in arrears (after the service is provided). But common to all of these services is the continuing relationship between consumer and service provider.

The twenty-first century has seen a new explosion in subscription services, largely delivered over the internet and created (or at least managed) using cloud computing platforms. One important characteristic that sets them apart from most of their predecessors is that the new products are usually of a more discretionary nature. While twentieth-century recurring payment services had few or no options (many utilities are still regulated monopolies), we have a variety of options when it comes to twenty-first-century subscriptions. There are usually alternative services to choose from, like switching from one streaming music service to another. Also, there can be alternative means of achieving the same ends, such as a business developing its own software rather than buying it with a subscription. And finally, many modern subscriptions are things we can live without (do you need that food delivery subscription when you could shop in a store?).

In the following sections, I will describe some of the wide variety of subscriptions that exist today. We will consider these business models in the rest of the book.

1.4.1 Paid consumer products

Most people are familiar with consumer subscription services. These products typically cost a modest amount each month (less than a fancy meal), and the price typically ends with "99" (9.99, 49.99, 99.99, etc.). These days, most consumers get a lot of their entertainment this way, and a variety of additional products have become available:

- Desktop software (word processors, spreadsheets, graphics creation tools, antivirus programs, etc.), formerly sold through perpetual licenses
- New types of software as a service (identity-theft protection, cloud storage, home security video monitoring, etc.)
- Boxes of physical products (shaving and personal grooming items, meals, crafts, gifts, etc.)
- Personal apparel items (including clothing and watches)

These products are often referred to as business-to-consumer services (B2C). Another related term is direct to consumer (D2C), which usually refers to selling video entertainment to consumers without bundling it with other channels in a cable or satellite entertainment package. (At the time of this writing, many television channels are available only through cable or satellite subscription, but a streaming service is D2C.)

1.4.2 Business-to-business services

In terms of market value, subscription services for businesses are an enormous market segment. These are commonly known as business-to-business (B2B) products. Starting with Salesforce, which created the first cloud-based customer relationship management

(CRM) system in the 2000s, this market has exploded. Now nearly all new software products for businesses are offered as a service (software as a service, also known as SaaS). At the same time, existing on-premises software products have started to shift to a new model due to the efficiency of cloud deployment and upgrades. These products exhibit a dizzying variety of payment terms because business products do not shy away from complex contracts (indeed, they often seem to favor them). The best-known categories of B2B subscriptions include

- *CRM*—SaaS to coordinate sales team and marketing interactions
- *Enterprise resource planning (ERP)*—SaaS for accounting, logistics, and production
- *Subscription business management (SBM)*—SaaS to manage subscriptions (also sold on a subscription basis)
- *Human resource management (HR)*—SaaS for managing employees, including hiring
- *Support issue tracking systems (ITS)*—SaaS for tracking and managing customer support interactions or *tickets*
- *Desktop software*—Spreadsheets, word processors, email, illustration programs, and so forth, sold through multiuser subscriptions
- *Cloud computing resources*—Cloud servers, storage, databases, and content distribution networks (CDNs)
- *Business intelligence (BI)*—Tools to query and visualize data of a variety of types
- *Security products*—Virus protection, password managers, network monitoring, and other tools for ensuring individual computer and corporate system security

This short list does not do justice to the wide variety of SaaS products used by businesses today. Nearly every modern SaaS company is dependent on a wide array of other SaaS products to provide the software running the noncore portions of the operation. A typical SaaS company uses in-house software engineers only to create what is unique about the service; almost every other part of the operation is run using software provided by another SaaS venture and paid on a subscription basis. These include the standard applications listed previously, as well as SaaS products designed for use by companies in specific verticals:

- Most online news or media services use software to manage comments and discussions, but that service is not created by those companies—they focus on creating content.
- Information services supporting specific verticals used to be common only in the finance and legal industries, but now industries like real estate, energy, manufacturing, and agriculture also have vertical-specific information services.
- Services are available to manage invoices and accounts payable functions that are specific to a single industry or vertical.

These are just a few examples from a very large and heterogeneous category.

1.4.3   Ad-supported media and apps

Since the early days of the internet, one of the most common business models (if not *the* most common) is to provide free media content (reading material, videos, music, etc.) but with ads displayed before, during, and/or after. There is no formal subscription to use such a product, so the scenario has some important differences from those in figure 1.1. There is no subscription database, although another database probably tracks user profile information for the purpose of selecting ads. While the means of capturing value from the consumer is different, these services share the same discretionary nature as regular paid consumer services and the same obvious concern with churn: services want their users (ad viewers) to keep coming back.

As I will explain, without a subscription, *churn* can be defined to simply mean that a customer disappears for an extended period of time. This type of product can also benefit from the churn analysis techniques taught in this book, as long as some form of event data warehouse tracks users across multiple sessions.

> **TAKEAWAY**   Tracking user events across multiple sessions is the one minimum requirement to use the techniques in this book.

1.4.4   Consumer feed subscriptions

Another novel type of subscription delivers free information in a feed, such as YouTube subscriptions or email updates. This is a variant of the ad-supported media model in which content is still advertising supported, but the provider creates the option to upgrade the experience by subscribing for free. This subscription usually means the consumer consents to product updates via new information pushed to their inbox or video feed. In this case, the structure of the relationship fits the typical scenario in figure 1.1, but there are no fixed payments on the subscription; instead, advertising revenue is derived from events.

1.4.5   Freemium business models

A *freemium* offering refers to any subscription service that has both a free version and a paid, or premium, level of service. For some services, the free version may be time-limited, giving users a chance to "try before you buy." For other services, it may be possible to use the free level of service in perpetuity. Another common variety is to have a free version with advertisements (as described in section 1.4.3) and a paid version that is ad-free.

As far as churn is concerned, freemium services are just like services without a free level, but there are two distinct types of churn: churn from the premium service and churn from the free level of service. The free level is analyzed using techniques described for nonsubscription, activity-based churn analysis. There is also the transition from the free to the paid service level, known as *free trial conversion*, which can be analyzed with the same techniques as churn (see section 1.5).

1.4.6   *In-app purchase models*

A variant on the freemium model are products that are free to use in perpetuity (or which require only a relatively small one-time payment to use in perpetuity) but that offer a variety of ways to upgrade the experience by making one-time payments during use. This is becoming the predominant model in online gaming. To play the game is free, but if you want a cool-looking skin for your avatar, a better weapon, or a shortcut to a higher level, it's going to cost you!

This is another type of scenario that fits the model of figure 1.1 but without subscriptions. Instead, a transactional database tracks the one-time purchases (and the original purchase of the app, if there is an initial fee). *Churn* can be defined as a user (customer) going inactive; all of the usual techniques in this book apply as long as user behavior can be tracked across sessions of use.

1.5   *Nonsubscription churn scenarios*

The focus of this book is on explicit churns from subscriptions, but the same approach works in a variety of other common business scenarios. I'll briefly explain those here but—for simplicity—teach the techniques focusing mainly on churn from subscriptions. After you master the techniques, you should have no trouble repurposing what you have learned for other scenarios.

1.5.1   *Inactivity as churn*

User inactivity can be seen as churn for the free tier of a freemium service, and the same applies for apps or ad-supported products with no explicit subscription. You choose a time window in which a user must engage with the service (such as one month or three months). *Churn* is then defined as users who go inactive for that long. In contrast to the typical scenario in figure 1.1, there is no subscription transaction database, only an event data warehouse. But the techniques in the book can be used as long as one key requirement is satisfied: user behaviors must be tracked consistently across different episodes or sessions of activity.

1.5.2   *Free trial conversion*

As described in section 1.4.5, a freemium model offers both free and paid levels of service. Because similar behavioral data is available at the free level as in the paid subscription, it is just as easy to analyze the *conversion* of subscribers from the free service to the paid service as it is to analyze churn from the paid service. This is essentially the opposite of churn, but the scenario looks like that in figure 1.1, so the same analytic techniques can be used.

1.5.3   *Upsell/down sell*

Adding new services or moving to a higher-cost plan is known as an *upsell*, while removing services or moving to a lower-cost plan (without churning) is known as a *down sell*. As with churn, behavioral data and user characteristics can be analyzed to determine what scenarios are most likely to lead to an upsell or a down sell. The additional challenge is that there may be different possible upsell/down sell options to analyze. In practice, however, additional analysis for upsell/down sell is often unnecessary. Most of the time, the customers who are most likely to purchase some form of upsell are those who are the best customers identified by the churn analysis, while those customers most likely to move to a lower-cost plan (down sell) are also those most likely to churn.

Upsells are also often related to crossing a specific usage threshold, such as the number of users (seats) sold for an enterprise software license or the number of gigabytes of data in a mobile phone service. In that case, an in-depth analysis is unnecessary: you know who is a candidate for an upsell simply by looking at a single relevant usage metric.

1.5.4   Other yes/no (binary) customer predictions

Customer churn is an example of a prediction problem where there is a yes or no answer. In statistics and data science, this is referred to as a *binary outcome* in reference to the two possibilities. The methods in this book can be applied without modification to virtually any situation involving predicting a future customer state that can be framed as a yes/no question. Examples include whether any kind of insurance policy will result in a claim (medical, auto, and so on) and whether a borrower will default on a loan. The one caveat here is that this book tends to focus on *rare* outcomes (which also happen to be the case for insurance claims and loan defaults). Slightly different methods can be used if yes and no outcomes are equally common, mainly in the measurement of accuracy (see chapter 9).

1.5.5   Customer activity predictions

Assuming a subscriber continues a service, it is reasonable to want to analyze what a subscriber is likely to do in the future. This is especially important for behaviors that are revenue generating, such as how much the subscriber will use a pay-as-you-go feature; or how much content the user will consume, and the resulting ad revenue generated for an ad-supported service.

Most of the techniques in this book also work for this sort of analysis, but with the major caveat that for churn, we use techniques for modeling two-state or binary outcomes (churn vs. continue), and for activity prediction, we use techniques for modeling numeric outcomes. If you have already trained in data science or statistics, it's not too hard to adapt the methods in this book to forecast real values, but such extensions won't be covered.

1.5.6   Use cases that are not like churn

One use case that is very different from churn and will not be covered in this book is product recommendation systems. Those are scenarios with a wide variety of products or content to choose from, where the goal is to recommend the most suitable ones based on previous choices. The techniques in this book, however, do apply for customers choosing among a small number of products like basic, standard, and premium plans for a subscription. For large catalogs of physical or media products, you should consult a book or resources specifically about recommender systems.

1.6 *Customer behavior data*

Given the huge variety of products and services that include recurring customer/user interactions, there is an even larger variety of possible forms those interactions can take. One section in one chapter cannot possibly give an exhaustive listing of all the possibilities, so consider this only an introduction. Almost anything that happens in software or that can be tracked by software can be considered an interaction or event.

> **DEFINITION**   *Event*—In the context of fighting churn, any user interaction or result that the data warehouse tracks. Events are time-stamped and pertain to a single account or user.

1.6.1 *Customer events in common product categories*

I'll make the discussion of data concrete by listing typical customer events for common product categories. What these all have in common is that they refer to individual events that can happen to one customer or user at any time. For some events, the simple fact that the event took place for a certain user at a certain time might be the only information available; for other events, details are tracked along with the event. Some typical customer events follow:

- *Software*—Refers to any software product (SaaS) but can also refer to other types of products with software interfaces:
  - *Logins*—Logging in to the application is usually tracked as an event.
  - *User interface (UI) interaction*—Almost any click or typing in the user interface can be tracked as an event. The event usually includes a detailed reference to the part of the UI.
  - *Document/record actions*—Includes creating, editing, updating, and deleting records or documents, which are tracked in the application database. The event can include information about what type of document and specifically what document field, when appropriate.
  - *Batch processing*—Many applications include processes that users run periodically. Every item processed can be seen as an event, or the batch job can be the event.
- *Social networks*—Dedicated social networks and also products that have social functions:
  - *Liking*—Indicating that the user likes something they see is one of the most ubiquitous interactions with a social network.
  - *Posting*—Sharing any type of media supported by the network.
  - *Sharing*—Usually a specialized post that refers to another user's post.

- *Connecting*—Connecting with other users is usually the most important form of engagement, as it enriches future user experience.
- *Telecommunications (telco for short)*—Providers of mobile or fixed-location telecommunication products and services:
  - *Calling*—Making a voice or video call. Typically, call events are tracked with the duration and the type of call.
  - *Data*—Data usage is usually tracked with the amount of data.
  - *App*—Using an application and specifically which one.
  - *Adding/removing a device*—Updating devices is an important event in the lifecycle of using the service.
- *Internet of Things (IoT)*—Products consisting of connected devices:
  - *Geospatial*—Events about device movement, including location and speed.
  - *Sensor*—Data received by a sensor can include almost any type of additional information received from the sensor.
  - *Device*—As with sensors, device activity can refer to almost any kind of activity and includes device-specific information.
- *Media*—Any product that provides any type of prerecorded or live-streamed media including video, audio, images, and text, not only for enjoyment but also for educational and professional training:
  - *Viewing/playing*—Playing media is the most common event on a media-specific service and usually includes details about what media was played and how much was played. This includes articles or pages read for news and books.
  - *Dwell time*—Viewing a page or other content and explicitly capturing the time spent.
  - *Liking*—Indicating media preferences by liking (or giving a thumbs down) is an important event for media.
- *Gaming*—Any product that is a game:
  - *Playing*—Many events are typically generated during playing a game and can include information about exactly what parts were played, for how long, and so on.
  - *Levels and score*—Many games include points or other forms of "leveling," and achieving these is often tracked as an event.
- *Retail*—Shopping websites or services that allow purchase of individually selected items, which can be either physical or digital products:
  - *Viewing*—Viewing products can be tracked as an event, along with details of what product is viewed.
  - *Searching*—Searching a product catalog can be tracked as an event, along with keywords used for the search.
  - *Adding to cart*—Adding products to a shopping cart can be tracked as an event.
  - *Returns*—Returning products is also tracked as an event, along with product details.

- *Box delivery*—Services where curated selections of (usually physical) products are delivered to customers periodically:
  - *Delivery*—Successful delivery of each box is an important event, as well as any failures or difficulties in delivery. Tracked information typically includes the type of box (when there is more than one) and the time it takes to arrive.
  - *Returns*—Many box services allow items to be returned, an important event indicating user dissatisfaction.
  - *Retail*—Most box delivery products also include retail options, so all retail events are also relevant.

Some categories of events occur across a variety of kinds of products and services. Here are some examples:

- *Financial*—Financial events occur on all products and services that are not free:
  - *Recurring payments*—These are so common they are often nonevents, but they are tracked and often are more important when they don't occur than when they do.
  - *Nonrecurring purchases*—All sales on retail sites, including any extra or in-app purchases made on games or subscription services.
  - *Overage charges*—Charges that apply when users exceed a threshold.
- *Support*—Whenever the customer turns to the service for help, whether through a call, email, chat, or searching support/help documentation:
  - *Ticket*—A support ticket or case, usually tracked with an opening and closing time and a wide variety of details.
  - *Call/email/chat*—Any kind of interaction between the customer and support representatives, possibly including the full text of the interaction.
  - *Documentation*—Use of online documentation resources can be tracked as UI events.
- *Plan*—Subscription-plan-related events occur for any product or service that has an actual subscription:
  - *Plan change*—The time/date of plan changes can be tracked as events.
  - *Billing change*—Events like changing the credit card or other payment method, as well as switching billing details, such as monthly versus annual billing.
  - *Canceling*—Yes, canceling the product or service is also tracked as an event. But note that when we talk about cancellations as events, we are talking about the date and time the cancellation change is entered into the system, not necessarily the time the service contract ends when the user has time remaining. *For this reason, a cancellation event is not the same as a churn.* The churn occurs when the subscriber completes the current term without signing up for a new one, often allowing a short grace period. Consequently, *a cancellation event does not necessarily mean a churn will occur, because the customer still might re-sign before much time has passed.* This happens often enough that

the act of cancellation should be considered an event that suggests churn is likely, but it is still not a certain conclusion.

Note that many products or services contain events from multiple categories; for example, any product with a software UI will collect software events, while many products have social network features (for example, games) even if they are not exclusively or primarily social network products.

1.6.2 *The most important events*

With all this discussion of types of events, you are probably wondering which types are the most important, and with good reason. With so much variety, it's important to stay focused. There are no hard rules for this, but I can give some general guidelines to frame the discussion for the rest of the book. And to be clear, figuring out which events are the most important is one of the main points of doing the analyses in this book because it is different for every product or service. This is just a preview of things we will look at in depth later.

The bottom line is that the most important events are those that are closest to the customer achieving the goal or purpose of the service. That's vague, but some examples should make it clear:

- Software products usually have a goal (for example, writing documents). Creating documents, therefore, is more important than just logging in. In general, login events are much less important than events that are directly involved with achieving the goals of the product.
- Many B2B software products are used for making money, so if there is any way to measure how much money is likely to be made from the events, then those are the most important. For example, if a product is a CRM system used to track sales, then closed deals and their value is probably the most important type of event. Often a product is not that close to the money business customers make, but you should still focus on events associated with commercial success. For example, if the product is an email marketing tool, opened emails are important events.
- For most media services, the purpose is to enjoy the media, so playing content is generally important as are, more specifically, indicators of enjoying the content such as watching the whole thing, giving it a like, or sharing it. But you can never directly measure enjoyment because it's a subjective state.
- For a dating service, the purpose is to go on dates, so actual meetings are probably more important than things like searching, viewing profiles, or online interactions. That presents a challenge because success on the service is well defined, but the events occur offline.
- For gaming, the purpose is to have fun. As with media, subjective feelings are hard to measure, so the most important events may be things like achieving scores and levels or social interactions with friends.

There are many important caveats that go along with the takeaway, and I have only noted a few, but the fact remains.

> **TAKEAWAY**   Look for events that are as close as possible to the value created by using the service, even when that value cannot be measured directly.

The rest of the book is about bringing rigor to this simple intuition.

1.7   *Case studies in fighting churn*

A few companies appear in the case studies throughout the book. They all used data to address their churn problem in a way that made a difference. This section introduces them and provides examples to make the data discussion of the last section more concrete.

1.7.1   *Klipfolio*

Klipfolio is a data analytics cloud app for building and sharing real-time business dashboards and reports on web browsers, TV monitors, and mobile devices. Klipfolio helps companies stay in-the-know and in control of their business by giving visibility into the key performance indicators (KPIs) and metrics that matter most. Klipfolio believes in empowering people to use and understand their data anytime and anywhere, eliminating the unknown, and making them more competitive. Subscriptions to Klipfolio's online app are sold to businesses. Like most B2B SaaS products, the price depends on the number of users and a variety of extra features. Most subscriptions bill either monthly or annually and continue until the subscriber cancels.

As an extremely data-driven company (its products are all about data!), Klipfolio was enthusiastic in using data to fight churn and increase customer engagement. It learned early on that luring customers to stay with down sells and discounts was not worth it—customers tended to churn anyway as soon as the discount expired. By analyzing usage and churn patterns, Klipfolio discovered that customers were at risk of churn if only one person in an organization used the product, so a key metric became the number of active users per account. The company also found there was a high risk of churn early in the subscription if the customer did not fully adopt the product, so it instituted onboarding calls by its support group and free support for the first three months. Klipfolio also realized that the lifetime value of some customers was too low to justify. To address the situation, it reconfigured its pricing and packaging to reflect the more profitable versions of its plan and features.

You will see more about how Klipfolio uses their data to achieve those outcomes throughout the book. For now, we start by taking a quick look at some of the company's event data. As the product allows for making Klips and dashboards, the most common events are viewing the dashboard, editing a Klip, and saving a Klip. Also, there are events around social features, like sharing, that are related to the Klips.

More than 80 different events are captured; the most common are listed in table 1.2. Klipfolio's events also identify individual users within each company, and some of the events, like session duration, contain additional data.

Table 1.2 Most common Klipfolio customer events

View dashboard	Switch orientation
Switch tab	Account active today
Klip editor	Exit Klip editor
Edit Klip from dashboard	Add Klip overlay
Save Klip in editor	Reconfigure data source

1.7.2 *Broadly*

Broadly changes the way local service businesses grow. It helps thousands of local service businesses attract, retain, and "wow" their customers every day through powerful customer experiences. The company is on a mission to bridge local businesses to modern consumers by helping them attract and capture leads, streamline their communications by email and text, monitor their online presence, and gather reviews, all through one app. Like most B2B SaaS companies, Broadly sells subscriptions with different plans, depending on the size of the buyer and things like the number of users. Subscriptions are sold on either a monthly or annual basis and include a variety of add-on products.

Because Broadly's products facilitate communications and connections with customers, it appreciates the importance of engaging with its customers. Broadly has a team of customer success managers (CSMs) who reach out to customers struggling with the product. The CSMs use metrics to guide their conversation with customers: strengths and weaknesses suggested by the metrics become talking points. Another tactic Broadly uses is to focus on customers in the midrange of customer engagement and risk: the company doesn't try to help customers who haven't logged in, but instead focuses on customers showing some signs of usage but below target usage levels. Broadly also found that one of the most important factors in influencing customer retention was a customer integrating Broadly with their company booking systems. Now the CSMs help with integrations whenever possible. Broadly also uses email campaigns to drive interest and adoption of new product features.

One of the most important aspects of Broadly's product is finding customers and persuading customers to review the business. As such, customer data includes events for adding customers, asking customers to review, and whether customers review positively or negatively. More than 60 different events from the SaaS product are captured, and the 10 most common are listed in table 1.3.

Table 1.3   Most common Broadly customer events

Transaction added	Follow-up email sent
Ask presented	Review ask decision
Customer added	Customer promoter
Thank-you email sent	Ask fulfilled
Affinity updated	Page view (path: /add_customer)

1.7.3   *Versature*

Versature is disrupting the Canadian telecom industry with cloud-based unified communication solutions for businesses. Trusted by clients and partners across the country, Versature is an award-winning company that is raising the bar with superior, cost-effective technology and Canadian-based support. Businesses take advantage of Versature's unified communication packages with plans that depend on the number of users, volume of calls, and other online communications services. Most customers are subscribed to monthly renewing services.

The systematic study and fight against churn started at telecommunication companies back in the late twentieth century, following deregulation. As a telecommunications provider born into the deregulated market, Versature focused on customer success from day one, with an emphasis on churn prevention. It has experienced steady growth thanks to negative net churn year after year. The ability to identify at-risk customers early in their lifecycle dramatically reduced controllable churn and allows Versature's CSMs to have value-driven conversations before the customer reaches the point of no return.

Versature's service combines traditional telecommunications call features with additional digital features such as a client-accessible administrative portal known as Sonar, a call data management offering known as Insights, and integration with digital products like Google Chrome and Salesforce. Customer events are a combination of traditional telco calls with software events like logins and page views. Versature's top 10 most common events are listed in table 1.4.

Table 1.4   Most common Versature customer events

Local call	Sonar login
Sonar page view	International call
Canada call	Sonar call center support
Toll-free call	Conference phone number
US call	Conference call

Churn case studies and privacy protection

The companies described in this book have all generously allowed themselves to be profiled and have made their data available for demonstrating techniques. However, these companies are all in business at the time of this writing and have a strategic need to protect information about their operations. For that reason, detailed information that might have been interesting to many readers is nevertheless withheld. In particular, *no churn rates of actual companies are reported anywhere in this book*:

- All numeric examples of churn calculation (like those in chapter 2) use randomly generated data for illustrative purposes.
- All figures showing relationships with churn found through analysis (like those in the next section and later chapters) show relative, not actual, churn rates.

Other types of information that are obscured throughout the book include facts and figures that portray or can be used to derive information about the customer base or pricing of the case study companies when such information is not already available through other public sources of information.

Also note, no personally identifiable information (PII) about the case study companies' customers was accessed *at any point* in the production of this book. The book's emphasis is on anonymous behavioral analysis that does not involve PII. Although some PII like geographic information can be useful in some churn analysis (see chapter 10), those parts of this book are illustrated using only simulated data.

1.7.4 Social network simulation

It is best to learn a new technology by example, so this book is organized around a series of examples that will guide you through a churn case study. But real churn case studies involve sensitive data about products and customers, so it was not possible to find a real set of data for examples in the book. Instead, you will learn the techniques for fighting churn with data through a case study on a *simulated* set of customer and product data.

The simulated product is a simple social network. Eight events are in the simulation, and they are listed in table 1.5. These include the most common events that you would find in any ad-supported social networking service: making friends, posting, liking, disliking, and so forth—and, of course, viewing ads. The simulation is designed so that there are realistic relationships between the occurrence of these events for the simulated customers and the customers' simulated churn and renewal. You will discover these relationships throughout the book.

Table 1.5 Events in the social network simulation

Ad view	New friend
Dislike	Post
Like	Reply
Message	Unfriend

WARNING   Do not take any results in this book from the social network simulation as a guide to what you can expect from your own product or service. The examples use a realistic-looking set of data for the purpose of demonstrating the method to use on real data, but nothing more. They cannot be expected to predict the results for any real product or service.

More information about how to run the simulation that generates the social network case study data can be found in the README page of the GitHub repository for this book: https://github.com/carl24k/fight-churn.

1.8   *Case studies in great customer metrics*

Before getting into technical details in chapter 2, I'm going to show you a few examples of results from using the techniques in this book. I need to warn you that you will not be able to make findings like this immediately; you have to learn the techniques to prepare your data (chapters 2–4) before you start doing churn analysis in chapter 5.

As I mentioned in the discussion of events, the behaviors that are most closely related to the value delivered by the service are most important. But choosing the measurement to make is also crucial. Here are three metrics that I have found to be especially effective in the fight against churn:

- *Utilization*—Metrics that show how much of the service the customer uses. If the service imposes limits on some types of use, a utilization metric shows what percentage of the allowed amount the customer took advantage of.
- *Success*—Metrics that show how successful a user is in activities that have different outcomes.
- *Unit cost*—Metrics that relate to the price the customer pays for the quantity of the service consumed or used.

Don't worry if you don't follow every detail in these case study examples; this is a quick preview of what the rest of the book is about! The details are presented in later chapters.

1.8.1   *Utilization*

Introduced in the last section, Klipfolio is a data analytics cloud app for building and sharing real-time business dashboards. These dashboards can be created by multiple users, and a common metric for any product that allows multiple users on one subscription is the number of users who are active. Figure 1.2 shows how the number of active users per month at a Klipfolio customer is related to churn.

Figure 1.2 uses a technique called *metric cohorts* to show the relationship between a behavior and churn. You will see a lot of these plots in this book and learn how to create them, but for now, I will give a brief explanation of how this technique works.

Given a pool of customers and a metric like the number of active users per month, the customers are organized into cohorts by their measurements on the metric. Typically, 10 cohorts are used, so the first cohort contains the bottom 10% of customers in

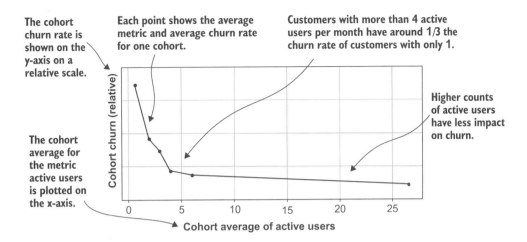

The cohort churn rate is shown on the y-axis on a relative scale.

Each point shows the average metric and average churn rate for one cohort.

Customers with more than 4 active users per month have around 1/3 the churn rate of customers with only 1.

Higher counts of active users have less impact on churn.

The cohort average for the metric active users is plotted on the x-axis.

Figure 1.2   Klipfolio churn versus active users

terms of the metric, the second cohort contains the next 10%, up to the final cohort, which contains the top 10% of customers on the metric. Once the cohorts are formed, you calculate what percentage of customers in each cohort churned. The result is displayed in a plot like that shown in figure 1.2. Each point in the plot corresponds to one cohort, with the x-value of the point given by the average value of the metric for the customers in the cohort, and the y-value of the point given by the percentage of churns (the churn rate) in the cohort.

As mentioned in the sidebar on privacy protections, the case study churn plots in this book don't show actual churn rates, only the relative difference between the cohorts. However, the bottom of the metric cohort plots is always set to zero churn rate so the distance of the points from the bottom of the plot can be used to compare *relative* churn rates. For example, if one point is half as far from the bottom of the plot as another, that means the churn rate in that cohort is half of the other's.

Turning to the details and what they mean, figure 1.2 shows that the lowest cohort has less than 1 active user per month (an average over multiple months), and the highest cohort has an average of more than 25 active users per month. In terms of churn, the churn rate on the cohort with the lowest active users per month is around 8 times greater than churn in the cohort with the highest number of active users. At the same time, most of the differences in churn rates occur between around 1 and 5 active users per month.

While measuring the number of active users is a good metric for fighting churn, an even better one is shown in figure 1.3. This is the license utilization metric calculated by dividing the number of active users by the number of seats the user has purchased. Many SaaS products are sold "by the seat," meaning the number of users allowed (this is called the *licensed number of seats*). If the number of active users is divided by the number of licensed seats, the resulting metric measures the percentage utilization of the seat license by the customer.

The result in figure 1.3 shows that license utilization is an effective metric for fighting churn. The lowest cohort in license utilization has an average utilization just above 0, and the highest cohort has a license utilization around 1.0. The lowest cohort has around 7 times the churn rate as the highest cohort, and the churn rate varies more or less continuously across the cohorts. In contrast to figure 1.2 (showing churn and the number of active users per month), there is not a level at which having higher utilization no longer makes a difference. This makes license utilization more effective for understanding customer health than active users alone.

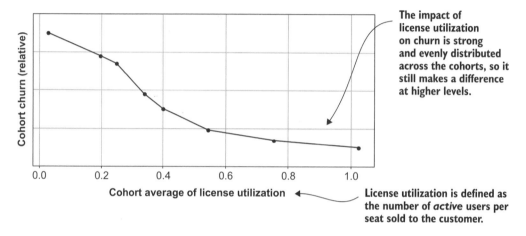

Figure 1.3   Klipfolio churn versus license utilization

As will be explained further in later chapters, active users per month is less effective for distinguishing churn risk because it conflates two different underlying factors related to churn: how many seats were sold to the customer and how often a typical user is active. Utilization is a measure of how active the users are on a relative basis, which is independent of the number of seats sold. License utilization is generally useful for segmenting customers with respect to their engagement and churn risk.

1.8.2   Success rates

Introduced in the last section, Broadly is an online service that helps businesses manage their online presence, including reviews. An important metric for Broadly's customers is the number of times the business is reviewed positively, or *promoted*. Figure 1.4 shows the relationship between churn and the number of promoters per month that a Broadly customer has. In the figure, the cohort with the fewest promoters per month (just above zero promoters on average) has a churn rate that is around 4 times higher

The lowest cohort, with no promoters, has a churn rate that is around 3.5 times higher than the churn rate on cohorts with more than around 20 promoters per month.

A customer promoter is one who leaves a good review. The metric is customer promoters per month.

The churn rate does not get lower after around 20 promoters per month.

Cohort churn (relative)

Cohort average of customer promoters

Figure 1.4 Broadly churn versus customer promoters

than the cohorts with the most promoters; most of the reduction in churn happens between 0 and 20 promoters per month. This is a clear relationship for an important event, and it is easy to understand why customers who have promoters are more likely to stay with the Broadly service: receiving positive reviews is one of the main goals for a business using Broadly!

Another important event for Broadly's customers related to the number of promoters is the number of *detractors*, or the number of times the business is reviewed negatively. Figure 1.5 shows the relationship between churn and the number of detractors per month that a Broadly customer has. The cohort with the fewest detractors per month (just above zero) has a churn rate that is around 2 times higher than the

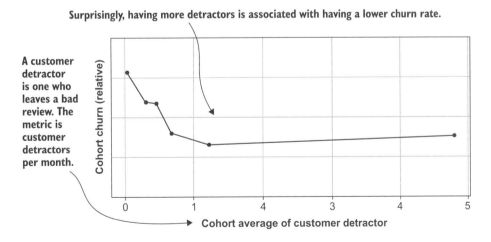

Surprisingly, having more detractors is associated with having a lower churn rate.

A customer detractor is one who leaves a bad review. The metric is customer detractors per month.

Cohort churn (relative)

Cohort average of customer detractor

Figure 1.5 Broadly churn versus customer detractors

cohorts with the most detractors (average of just under 5 detractors per month); most of the reduction in churn happens between 0 and 1 detractor per month.

While this relationship looks a lot like the one for customer promoters shown in figure 1.4, doesn't it seem like something is wrong? Getting negative reviews is a bad thing and presumably not the result that Broadly's customers are looking for, so why is having negative reviews associated with reduced churn?

To understand why more of a bad thing (like detractors) can be associated with *less* churn, it helps to look at another, better metric for Broadly's customers. If you take the number of detractors and divide it by the total number of reviews (promoters plus detractors), then the result is the percentage of detractors, which I call the *detractor rate*. Figure 1.6 shows the relationship between churn and the detractor rate. This is probably more the kind of relationship you were expecting for a product event that is negative for the customer: the higher the detractor rate, the higher the churn, and in a very significant way.

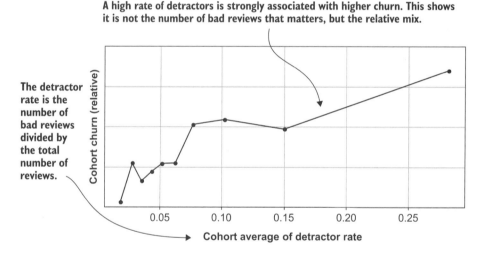

Figure 1.6   Broadly churn versus detractor rate

So why does the relationship to churn show that more detractors are good when you look at the detractor count in figure 1.5, and that more detractors are bad when you look at the detractor rate in figure 1.6? The answer is that the *total* number of detractors in figure 1.5 is related to the total number of promoters shown in figure 1.4 because Broadly customers who receive a lot of reviews overall are likely to receive more of both good and bad reviews. When you look at the impact on the relationship between the number of detractors and churn in the simple way in figure 1.5, it conflates two underlying factors driving the metric: having a lot of reviews (which is good) and having a high proportion of bad reviews (which is bad). When the proportion of bad reviews is analyzed alone, you get the more useful result shown in figure 1.6. This illustrates why success and failure rates can be so effective for understanding churn.

1.8.3 Unit cost

Versature, introduced in the last section, provides telecommunication services for businesses. As a unified communications provider, many of its most important events are voice calls that have a duration stored in a field attached to each event. Figure 1.7 shows the relationship between the total time spent on voice calls and churn for Versature customers. The lowest cohort in terms of local calls has practically zero calls and a churn rate that is around three times higher than cohorts of customers with local call times per month in the thousands.

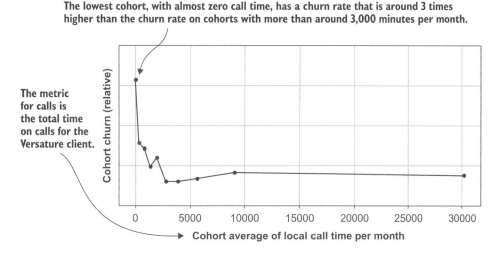

Figure 1.7 Versature churn versus local calls

When trying to understand churn, it is important to consider not only the amount of service that customers use but also how much they pay. Monthly recurring revenue (MRR) is a standard metric for calculating the amount a customer pays to use a subscription service: it is the recurring amount a customer pays each month to use a service, but not including any setup fees or irregular charges. (I will say more about MRR and how to calculate it in chapter 3.) The amount customers pay can also be analyzed with a metric cohort approach to look for a relationship with churn, which is shown for Versature in figure 1.8.

The metric cohort plot in figure 1.8 does something new. Rather than displaying the average MRR of the cohorts directly, it shows the average after every MRR

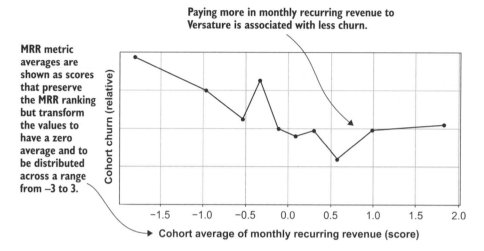

MRR metric averages are shown as scores that preserve the MRR ranking but transform the values to have a zero average and to be distributed across a range from –3 to 3.

Figure 1.8   Versature churn versus monthly recurring revenue (price) scores

measurement is converted to a *score.* If you are familiar with the concept of grading on a curve, metric scores are the same idea: the measurements are converted from one scale to another, but the ordering remains the same. A given cohort like the bottom 10% on the metric is still the same set of customers if the metric is converted into a score, and the cohort has the exact same churn rate. That means converting a metric into a score affects only how the cohorts are placed along the horizontal axis of the cohort plot but not the vertical position of the points, which is the churn rate. Metrics are converted to scores when rescaling on the horizontal axis makes the result easier to understand. I will say more about metric scores and teach you how to calculate them in chapter 3.

The cohort churn rates in figure 1.8 show that MRR is also related to churn, although not as strongly as making calls. The churn rates in the different cohorts do not vary in a totally consistent way, and the lowest cohort churn rates are only about one-half or one-third less than the highest churn cohorts. But this is another case that makes you stop and think about what the plot shows: people who pay more, churn less. Is that what you expected? This may be surprising, but it's actually quite common, especially in business products. That's because business products are sold with higher prices for bigger customers, and bigger customers churn less for interrelated reasons. They have more employees, so when it comes to product use like making calls or using software, customers who pay more for a product generally use it more, too. The lower churn for customers paying higher MRR (shown in figure 1.8) is related to the lower churn for customers with more calls (shown in figure 1.7).

Figure 1.9 shows a different metric for looking at how the amount customers pay relates to churn: the MRR metric is divided by the metric for the number of calls per month. This results in a metric that is the cost per call the customer makes. I call this a *unit cost metric* because it explains how much of the service the customer receives for their money.

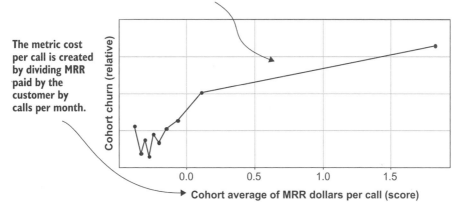

A high cost per call is strongly associated with higher churn. So, paying a lot *relative* to usage drives customers to churn, but paying a lot when the product is used appropriately does not.

The metric cost per call is created by dividing MRR paid by the customer by calls per month.

Figure 1.9   Versature churn versus monthly price per call

As in figure 1.8, figure 1.9 shows the cohort average as a score rather than in dollars. The metric cohort churn plot for cost per call shows that customers who pay more really do churn more when the payment is measured in relation to the amount of the service used. The highest cohort in cost per call has a churn rate that is around six times higher than the cohorts with the lowest cost per call. Value metrics like this are key for understanding why customers churn and an important subject that will be explored fully in later chapters.

These examples should give you an idea of where the book is going. In the next chapter, you will start with the basics and learn how to identify churns and calculate churn rates.

Summary

- The term *churn* arose in the context of subscription products and means users quitting or canceling a service.
- Churn also applies to all products and services where customers or users repeatedly interact with the product over long periods of time, whether or not there is a formal subscription or any form of payment.
- Recent years have seen an explosion in the number of discretionary online services for consumers and businesses. The discretionary nature of these services means churn is a constant problem that needs to be addressed.

- People skilled in data analysis are frequently called in to help understand what causes churn and what can be done to reduce it.
- Online products and services track a wide variety of user interactions with the service, generically referred to as *events*. The history of such events is one of the primary sources of data for fighting churn.
- Churn is not a situation where a predictive model alone helps to achieve the goal (churn reduction) because churn-reducing interventions depend on knowing the causes for churn.
- To help reduce churn, the data person should create the best possible customer metrics.
- Great customer metrics have the following characteristics:
  - Easily understood by the business
  - Clearly associated with churn and retention, so it is obvious what a healthy customer looks like
  - Segment customers in a way that's useful for targeted interventions, which increase engagement
  - Useful in multiple functions of the business (i.e., product, marketing, support, and so on)

Measuring churn

This chapter covers

- Identifying churned accounts and calculating the churn rate
- Calculating the net retention rate and churn rates based on monthly recurring revenue
- Converting churn rates between monthly and annual measurements

You have already learned that the churn rate is a measurement of the proportion of customers who quit every month or year. If you don't measure churn correctly, it's that much harder to do anything about it. This chapter teaches you multiple definitions of churn that are suitable for different business scenarios and how to calculate them efficiently from a subscription database. Recalling the overall book scenario introduced in chapter 1, this chapter focuses on the process highlighted in figure 2.1.

Calculating the churn rate really is not rocket science, but you do need to know some intermediate SQL and a couple of algebraic equations. There are a few things that make calculating churn rates nontrivial. Part of the challenge is complexity, and another is logistical. The complexity in calculating churn is that an account can have multiple subscriptions over its lifetime, including the following:

- Accounts can churn and sign up again any number of times. This is true for all subscription products and services.
- For many subscription services, accounts can hold multiple subscriptions for different products simultaneously. This is especially common for B2B products and services.

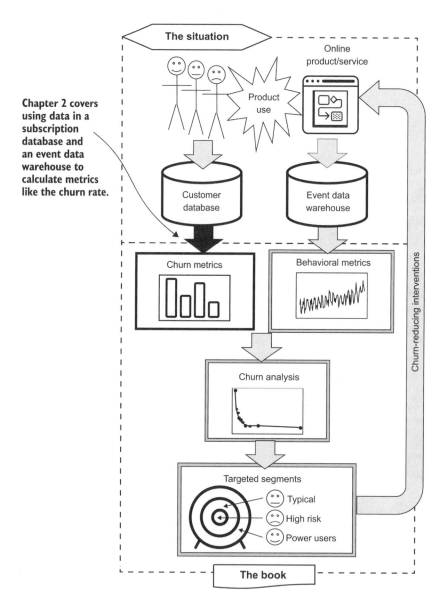

Figure 2.1   The subjects of this chapter in the process of fighting churn with data

Normally, there isn't a field or flag on a subscription or account saying, "This is a churn." Rather, churn is a dynamic state for each account that must be determined at a given point in time. For that matter, if there *is* a field or flag on an account or subscription that says it's a churn, you are probably the person who has to calculate it, because you're the data person—right?

There is also a logistical challenge in calculating churn: first, the data is sensitive. For any subscription product or service, the subscription database is one of its most valuable assets. The subscription database usually contains *personally identifiable information* (PII) for the subscribers and sensitive financial information for the company. This is not data you want to extract and leave lying around in unsecure locations. The second pitfall is one that comes with success: if your product or service is successful, this data is big. For both of these reasons, taking the data out of the database for processing is not a good idea.

The problem then is that dynamic logic is necessary to calculate churn, but you're better off doing what needs to be done in the database without extracting the data. For that reason, I will show you how to calculate churn using multipart SQL statements that return the result as the output of a SELECT statement (to be fair, I call these *SQL programs*). This is a best practice that recurs throughout the book: do as much of the work as possible in the database or data warehouse, and extract reduced data only when necessary. This may seem foreign or even frustrating if you are used to doing this sort of logic and calculation in a procedural language like Python. Although it is possible to do these tasks in Python, that approach doesn't scale nearly as well as the in-database approach taught in this book. Once you get used to processing data in the database with multipart SQL programs, you will wonder how you ever got by without it!

Here's how this chapter is organized:

- Section 2.1 shows you the concept of churn in a diagram and a few equations before you do any coding.
- Section 2.2 shows you what a typical subscription database looks like; you will use that sample database structure in churn calculations.
- Section 2.3 begins the churn calculations with net retention, which is a common metric related to churn. (There is a related net churn measurement—but as I will explain, people don't use it much.) Net retention comes first because it is straightforward conceptually, the easiest to calculate, and sufficient for simple subscription scenarios.
- Section 2.4 teaches you the standard churn rate calculation, which is more generally applicable but a little more complicated than net retention.
- Section 2.5 considers the case of churn calculations when there are not subscriptions but customers have repeated use of a product or service. These techniques are suitable for advertising or in-app purchase products.
- Section 2.6 covers revenue churn measurement, known as monthly recurring revenue (MRR) churn; it is suitable for complex subscription services.
- Section 2.7 explains how to convert a one-year churn rate into a monthly churn rate and vice versa.

Code for fighting churn with data

All of the source code for this book is available on the book's website (www.manning
.com/books/fighting-churn-with-data) and in the book's GitHub repository (https://
github.com/carl24k/fight-churn). Listings from the book are in the folder /listings.
See the repository README page for detailed setup instructions. In summary, you
need to perform the following steps to run the code listings in this book:

1 Install Python and Postgres. I also recommend installing the free GUI tools to
   work with them. If you are already an expert with these tools, then use your
   favorites; but if not, follow the setup instructions in the README precisely.
2 Create a database schema with `fight-churn/data-generation/churndb.py`.
3 Generate simulation data and save it into the Postgres schema with `fight-
   churn/data-generation/churnsim.py`.

The simulation typically runs for around 10 minutes, generating approximately
15,000 customers for an imaginary social network over 6 months. The simulation
creates all of their subscriptions and events such as making friends, making posts,
viewing ads, and liking and disliking posts. More details about the simulation are provided throughout the book.

After creating the database and generating data, there is a Python wrapper program,
`run_churn_listing.py`, that you can use to run all the listings in the book. This is
helpful for the SQL listings in chapters 2–4 because the script takes care of details
like variables and connecting to the database; the wrapper program is also used for
the Python functions beginning in chapter 5. Command-line parameters control what
listing is run. For example, to run listing 2.1, you use this program:

```
fight-churn/listings/run_churn_listing.py --chapter 2 --listing 1
```

Alternatively, if you want to run the listings with another method, all the listings are
organized by chapter in folders under fight-churn/listings/. For example, listing 2.1 is
in the file fight-churn/listings/chap2/listing_2_1_net_retention.sql. The SQL listings
are all stored as templates containing bind variables beginning with %; they do not
contain specific parameters like dates or event names. You will need to substitute
the values for these variables before you run the queries. The wrapper script
`run_churn_listing.py` takes care of this for you.

Bind variables are used in the SQL listings so that they can be easily reconfigured to
run on datasets other than the provided simulation. If you want to use your own data
instead of the simulation, first do the following (after you install Python and Postgres
as explained in the README):

1 Create a schema with `fight-churn/data-generation/churndb.py`. Set the
   schema name by editing that executable and setting the variable `schema_name`
   near the top of the file.
2 Load your subscriptions, events, and schema event tables. (Details of how to
   do this are beyond the scope of this book, but a variety of free tools make it
   pretty easy to load data into Postgres databases.)

> **3** The listing wrapper program works from parameters stored in a JSON file, fight-churn/listings/conf/churnsim_listings.json. To run the listings with different parameters, you must make your own version of that JSON file. For each chapter and listing, there are parameter blocks, with parameters stored as key-value pairs. You can set these to the appropriate values for your own dataset.
> **4** Run the listings with the wrapper program and the additional parameter `--schema <your_schema>`.
>
> More details for installation and use are in the README.

2.1 Definition of the churn rate

Figure 2.2 illustrates the idea of churn: the two circles represents the subscriber pool at different points in time. The area of each circle represents either the number of subscribers or the total amount they pay; the latter is used when subscribers pay different amounts. But whether churn is based on the number of subscribers or the amount of revenue, the concept is the same. The churn is the downward-facing crescent at the top: the part of the start circle that does not overlap the bottom (end) circle, which is those subscribers who are no longer with the service. To complete the picture, the overlap between the two circles is the retained subscribers, and the upward-facing crescent at the bottom of the end circle (that doesn't overlap the top circle) represents newly acquired subscribers. Note that, in general, the size of the two circles is not exactly the same.

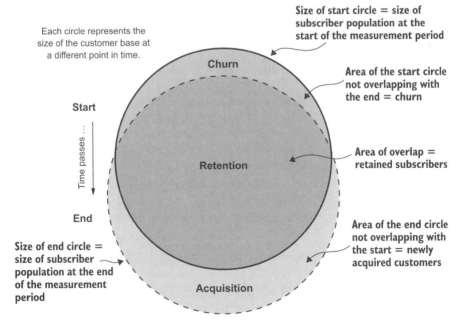

Figure 2.2   Churn Venn diagram showing a growing subscription service where acquisition is larger than churn

2.1.1   *Calculating the churn rate and retention rate*

Next I show you how to turn the qualitative picture in figure 2.2 into a formula. The *churn rate* is defined as the proportion of the start subscribers (start circle) who leave the service (top crescent). In an equation, this is

$$ChurnRate = \frac{\#ChurnedCustomers}{\#StartCustomers}$$

(Equation 2.1)

where *#StartCustomers* means the area of the start circle, and *#ChurnedCustomers* means the area of the churn crescent. Figure 2.3 shows a simple example.

The customer list is shown for January 1 and February 1.

Every customer renews every month, on the same day of the month as when they signed up.

Customers on 1-January			Changes	Customers on 1-February		
AccntID	Start	Next renewal		AccntID	Start	Next renewal
1	3-October	3-January		1	3-October	3-January
2	17-October	17-January	X	2		
3	2-November	2-January		3	2-November	2-January
4	11-November	11-January		4	11-November	11-January
5	7-December	7-January		5	7-December	7-January
			+	6	3-January	3-February
			+	7	15-January	15-February

In January, one customer does not renew (a churn, shown by the X) and two new customers sign up (+). But the two new signups do not influence the churn calculation.

The churn rate is the number who churned (1) divided by the number who were on the service at the start (5), or 1/5 = 20%.

Figure 2.3   A simplified example of a churn rate calculation

The product has only five customers in January, and all customers have a monthly renewal on the same day of the month as when they started. During January, one customer does not renew and two new customers sign up, so in February, there are six customers.

Equation 2.2 shows the churn rate calculation measured over the month of January:

$$ChurnRate_{Figure\ 2.3} = \frac{\#ChurnedCustomers}{\#StartCustomers} = \frac{1}{5} = 20\%$$

(Equation 2.2)

Note that the churn rate does not use the total subscribers at the end or the subscribers acquired. Look at figure 2.2 to understand why: the churn rate is the portion of the start circle that is not covered by the end circle, but the size of the end circle depends on both the retention and the number of new subscriber acquisitions. The acquisition of new subscribers is an incredibly important subject, but it is a separate matter from the churns because it results from a different set of processes, so it is not covered in this book. So, the churn rate is based only on churn in relation to the subscribers at the start. If the churn were instead divided by the area of the end subscriber pool, it would be incoherent because that would mix parts of two pools and confuse the contributions of acquisition and retention with the size of the subscriber pool.

The retention rate is defined in equation 2.3:

$$RetentionRate = \frac{\#RetainedCustomers}{\#StartCustomers} \qquad \textbf{(Equation 2.3)}$$

Using the example in figure 2.3, the retention rate is

$$RetentionRate_{Figure\ 2.3} = \frac{\#RetainedCustomers}{\#StartCustomers} = \frac{4}{5} = 80\% \qquad \textbf{(Equation 2.4)}$$

2.1.2 The relationship between churn rate and retention rate

Here is an important fact about churn rate and retention rate: they are related in a very precise way and are two sides of the same coin. Look at the parts of the start circle in figure 2.2. The entire start circle is either the churn portion or the retention portion, represented by this equation:

$$Start = Churn + Retention \qquad \textbf{(Equation 2.5)}$$

Now come a few algebra manipulations. If you divide both sides of equation 2.5 by the start subscribers, you get

$$\frac{Start}{Start} = \frac{Churn}{Start} + \frac{Retention}{Start} \qquad \textbf{(Equation 2.6)}$$

Next, substitute into equation 2.6 the definitions from equations 2.1 and 2.3 for the churn and retention rates, and remember that any number divided by itself is 1, or 100%. This equation shows the relationship:

$$100\% = ChurnRate + RetentionRate$$

Finally, those terms can be rearranged to show the conclusion:

$$RetentionRate = 100\% - ChurnRate$$

$$ChurnRate = 100\% - RetentionRate \qquad \textbf{(Equation 2.7)}$$

Equation 2.7 can also be understood by looking at figure 2.2. Churn and retention together make up the start circle, so the sum of the two proportions must add up to the whole circle, or 100%.

TAKEAWAY   Retention rate can be easily calculated from the churn rate and vice versa. Which measurement you look at is a matter of preference.

Most organizations use the churn rate for internal discussions around reducing churn. The retention rate is usually used to report to outsiders (for example, investors) when the emphasis is meant to be positive ("the glass is half full").

2.2   *Subscription databases*

As I described in chapter 1, subscription products or services usually have a database that tracks when subscriptions begin and end, and the examples in this book generally assume a subscription database is in use. If your business does not have a subscription database because it is a free or ad-supported product, section 2.5 shows how to calculate churn rates without subscriptions, but I advise that you read this section and the ones that follow because they build the necessary concepts and techniques.

Table 2.1 shows the key elements of a typical subscription database table.

Table 2.1   A typical subscription data table

Column	Data type	Required?
subscription_id	integer or char	Yes
account_id	integer or char	Yes
product_id	integer or char	Yes
start_date	date	Yes
end_date	date	No
mrr	double precision	Maybe

In practice, there are usually more fields than this, but for purposes of illustration, this subscription data model consists of some core fields you might expect to find in a production environment:

- *Subscription ID*—A unique identifier for each subscription.
- *Account ID*—An identifier for the account holder or user. These are unique at the account level but are not assumed to be unique in the subscription table. In general, accounts can hold multiple subscriptions.
- *Product ID*—An identifier for the unique product that is subscribed to. This data model uses one product per subscription, but as mentioned, accounts can hold multiple products. If a subscription service offers only a single product, there might not be a product field; but it is fair to consider this a required

field because single-product services that plan to grow normally come up with new offerings.

- *Start date*—Every subscription must start on some date. These are simple dates without times.
- *End date*—Subscriptions may or may not have end dates. If there is no end date, the subscription is assumed to last until explicitly canceled.
- *Monthly recurring revenue (MRR)*—Paid subscriptions have an associated amount of recurring monthly revenue.

In summary, a subscription is a product sold to a customer, which begins on a specific start date and for a specified recurring cost. As discussed, there may be an end date, or there may not.

> **NOTE** Subscriptions with end dates are usually referred to as *termed subscriptions*, and the time between the start and the end dates is called the *term*. Subscriptions that last forever (until canceled) are usually called *evergreen subscriptions*.

Note that the database table(s) that contains this information might not be called `Subscriptions`. If you work at a B2B company that uses a *customer relationship management* (CRM) system to track deals, your company might store this information as `Opportunities`; alternatively, if your company uses a *subscription business management* (SBM) product designed to track multiproduct subscription offerings, the table might be called `Product Rate Plan`. But as long as all the required data elements are available, you have what you need to calculate churn. Note also that for any company that sells paid subscription services, MRR can be considered a required field, although it can be zero if there is a discount or a free trial (for example, a freemium subscription at the basic level).

Messy subscription databases

One theme you will see repeatedly throughout this book is that algorithms are designed to handle irregularities in the subscriptions saved in the database, also called *messy* or *unclean* subscription data. Messy subscription data can come in many forms: duplicates for the same account, entries for accounts that are not real, inconsistency in what are supposedly consistent subscription terms (like the duration and price), unexpected gaps between subscriptions, and end dates that come before start dates, to name a few.

If you are still a student or have never worked in a corporate environment, then this might surprise and even annoy you, because some of the algorithms I use are more complicated than you may expect or think necessary. But I can assure you that these complications are necessary most of the time.

In the real world, clean subscription databases are rare; messy subscription databases are the norm. One problem you might not appreciate yet is that it takes only a small amount of messy data to throw off some algorithms, and the blast radius can be larger than just the accounts with the bad data.

2.3   *Basic churn calculation: Net retention*

I begin with net retention because it is the easiest churn measure to calculate, although I will also show you that it is not always the most useful. Figure 2.2 shows the retention rate when the circles represent revenue. Like all churn and retention measurements, net retention is measured over a specific period (usually a year). The *net retention rate* (NRR) is the proportion of recurring revenue that your company still receives at the end of the period *from the subscribers who were present at the start.*

> **NOTE**   If your subscription product is free (has no paid recurring revenue), you should still read this section. The net retention calculation can be used to calculate regular (account-based) churn, and it's a simpler formula than the more general churn formula presented in section 2.4.

Like all churn measures, net retention ignores new revenue acquired from signups during the time period. On the other hand, an important fact about net retention is that it includes changes in revenue from subscribers who are retained if this occurs. This can occur for any product or service with multiple product plans, temporary discounts, or pricing plan changes (most paid subscriptions). I will ignore these details and focus on teaching the calculation of net retention and churn; you will learn about these different cases in the following sections.

2.3.1   *Net retention calculation*

Net retention is defined in equation 2.8:

$$NetRetention = \frac{MRR_{retained\_account}}{MRR_{start}}$$ **(Equation 2.8)**

That's a slightly different definition of retention than the one in equation 2.2. Figure 2.4 extends the example in figure 2.3 to include two different plan types with different MRRs: a Standard plan for $9.99 a month and a Premier plan for $29.99 a month. In the figure, one customer on the Premier plan churns, two new customers sign up, and one customer changes from Standard to Premier. This example shows important differences from the count-based churn calculation in figure 2.3:

- Because the churn calculation is based on MRR, customers who pay more have a bigger impact on the rate when they churn.
- Changes in MRR for customers who don't churn also impact the rate.

Every customer has either the Standard plan for $9.99 or the Premier plan for $29.99 and renews monthly on the same day of the month as when they signed up.

In January, one customer on the Premier plan does not renew (a churn, X), two new customers sign up (+)—one on the Standard plan and one on the Premier plan—and one customer switches from Standard to Premier (^).

Customers on 1-January

Customers on 1-February

ID	Start	Next renewal	Plan	MRR	Changes	ID	Start	Next renewal	Plan	MRR
1	3-October	3-January	Standard	9.99		1	3-October	3-January	Standard	9.99
2	17-October	17-January	Premier	29.99	X					
3	2-November	2-January	Standard	9.99		3	2-November	2-January	Standard	9.99
4	11-November	11-January	Premier	29.99		4	11-November	11-January	Premier	29.99
5	7-December	7-January	Standard	9.99	^	5	7-December	7-January	Premier	29.99
				89.95	+	6	3-January	3-February	Standard	9.99
					+	7	15-January	15-February	Premier	29.99
										119.94

The net retention rate is the MRR of the customers who stayed (the total of customers 1, 3, 4, and 5 on 1-Feb, or 79.96) divided by the MRR of those who were on the service at the start (89.95), or 79.96/89.95 = 89%.

Note that the two new signups do not influence the net retention calculation, but the upgrade from the Standard plan to the Premier plan does.

Figure 2.4 A simplified example of a net retention calculation

Look at the example in figure 2.4 and equation 2.8: the numerator for the net retention rate is the MRR of all the remaining customers, including the customer who switched to the Premier plan, or $79.96. The MRR of all the customers at the start is $89.95, so the net retention is given by

$$RetentionRate_{Figure\ 2.4} = \frac{MRR_{retained\_account}}{MRR_{start}} = \frac{79.96}{89.95} = 89\% \qquad \textbf{(Equation 2.9)}$$

There is also a churn measure related to net retention, defined as 100% minus the net retention rate. Equation 2.10 shows the definition of net churn from net retention:

$$NetChurn = 100\% - \frac{MRR_{retained\_account}}{MRR_{start}} \qquad \textbf{(Equation 2.10)}$$

Net retention is the only churn-related measurement that is more commonly quoted as a retention rate and not a churn rate. This is due in part to the scenarios that arise in multiprice subscriptions, particularly the possibility of negative net churn (net retention, on the other hand, is always positive). In the next section, you will learn how to calculate the net retention rate with SQL, as well as more details about the use of PostgreSQL in this book.

2.3.2 *SQL net retention calculation*

As this is the first SQL program in the book, I am going to briefly introduce *common table expressions* (CTEs). This SQL program and all the others in the book use CTEs, which are a relatively new extension to ANSI SQL. CTEs allow the definition of intermediate, temporary tables in a query, in the order they appear. Compared to other syntaxes for temporary tables, CTEs are clean and concise. Temporary tables in a database are the results of SELECT statements that are persisted in the database and can be used in further SELECTs that are part of the same overall SQL statement or program. The temporary result, however, is not persisted outside of the current execution.

I use CTEs to teach these techniques because they allow a clear, step-by-step presentation of the program logic. (I refer to these as *SQL programs* and not the common term, *SQL statements*, which implies a shorter and simpler logic.) The following is a high-level overview of listing 2.1, which presents our first SQL program, described in relation to the churn diagram in figure 2.2:

1. Set the start and end times for the measurement.
2. Identify the subscribers and total revenue at the start (top circle in figure 2.2).
3. Identify the subscribers and total revenue at the end (bottom circle in figure 2.2).
4. Identify the retained subscribers and their revenue (intersection of the two circles in figure 2.2).
5. Divide the retained subscriber revenue by the start subscriber revenue (equation 2.2).

Another note about this program (which goes for all the others) is that, in general, I look at the *hardest* or most complex use case you might encounter. This also means it might be overpowered for some scenarios, but I would prefer to let some users simplify the program at their own discretion rather than omit guidance that will be helpful to many others. In particular, the program assumes that subscribers can hold multiple subscription products with different recurring revenue. If your subscription has only a single product and price and/or no paid recurring revenue, you can use the same SQL but replace sums of MRRs with the count of accounts. If your service has only termed subscriptions, you can remove the cases for null end dates. (As described in section 2.2, a *termed subscription* has a defined end date at the time the subscription is created.) The SQL for the program is shown in listing 2.1.

> **NOTE** The date variables in listing 2.1 are set with a configuration parameter, so in the book's downloadable code, they appear as bind variables starting with %. The listing shows the SQL after the variables are bound. The same is true for all SQL listings in the book.

Listing 2.1   Net retention SQL program

Criteria for being active on a given date: The
start date is on or before the date, and the
end date is after the date or null.

Sets the period for which the
program will calculate churn

```
WITH
date_range AS (
    SELECT '2020-03-01'::date AS start_date, '2020-04-01'::date AS end_date
),
start_accounts AS
(
    SELECT  account_id, SUM(mrr) AS total_mrr
    FROM subscription s INNER JOIN date_range d ON
        s.start_date<= d.start_date
        AND (s.end_date>d.start_date or s.end_date is null)
    GROUP BY account_id
),
end_accounts AS
(
    SELECT account_id, SUM(mrr) AS total_mrr
    FROM subscription s INNER JOIN date_range d ON
        s.start_date<= d.end_date
        AND (s.end_date>d.end_date or s.end_date is null)
    GROUP BY account_id
),
retained_accounts AS
(
    SELECT s.account_id, SUM(e.total_mrr) AS total_mrr
    FROM start_accounts s
    INNER JOIN end_accounts e ON s.account_id=e.account_id
    GROUP BY s.account_id
),
start_mrr AS (
    SELECT SUM (start_accounts.total_mrr) AS start_mrr
    FROM start_accounts
),
retain_mrr AS (
    SELECT SUM(retained_accounts.total_mrr) AS retain_mrr
    FROM retained_accounts
)
SELECT
retain_mrr /start_mrr  AS net_mrr_retention_rate,
    1.0 - retain_mrr /start_mrr AS net_mrr_churn_rate,
start_mrr,
retain_mrr
FROM start_mrr, retain_mrr
```

CTE containing all the account IDs active at the
start and their total MRR on the start date

Uses the aggregate
sum so that when
there are multiple
subscriptions, the
SELECT returns
the total

CTE containing all the account IDs active at
the end and their total MRR on the end date

Uses the
aggregate
GROUP BY
function,
so the
SELECT
sums the
total MRR
for each
account

Criteria for being active
on a given date: The start
date is on or before the
date, and the end date is
after the date or null.

CTE containing all the accounts
that did not churn (were retained)

Uses the aggregate sum
so that when there are
multiple subscriptions,
the SELECT returns the
total

The inner join results
in this containing
accounts that were
active at both the
beginning and the
end, meaning they
were retained.

Sums
the total
MRR of all
accounts
active on
the start

Sums the total MRR of all
accounts that were retained

Net MRR churn
formula: 1.0 minus
net retention

Net retention
formula: MRR of
retained accounts
divided by MRR at
the start

Includes the components of the result
to show how the MRR was produced

The following list describes each CTE in the program and the final SELECT statement
and what role each CTE plays in the calculation, numbered according to the calculation strategy steps outlined before listing 2.1:

1   `date_range`—A table with one row that holds the start and end dates for the calculation.

2   `start_accounts`—A table with one row for each account active at the start. This table is created by selecting from the subscription table based on the condition that the account is active at the start of the churn measurement, meaning it holds a subscription (where the subscription start date is before the churn measurement start date, and the subscription end date is after the churn start date, or there is no subscription end date).

3   `end_accounts`—A table with one row for each account active at the end of the churn measurement. The condition for being considered active is the same as for the start accounts, using the churn measurement end date for the criteria.

4   `retained_accounts`—A table with one row for each account that is active at both the start and the end. This table is created by a standard join on account IDs between the `start_accounts` table and the `end_accounts` table.

5   `start_mrr`—A one-row table that sums the total MRR at the start of the churn measurement, for clarity.

6   `retained_mrr`—A one-row table that sums the total MRR of all of the retained accounts, for clarity.

7   *Final* `SELECT` *statement*—Takes the results from the `start_mrr` and `retained_mrr` tables and calculates the final results by plugging the values into equations 2.2 and 2.3.

That is how net retention and net churn (described by equations 2.5 and 2.6) can be calculated from a typical subscription database in SQL.

This SQL program was tested on the simulated dataset produced by the code on the book's website (www.manning.com/books/fighting-churn-with-data) and in the book's GitHub repository (https://github.com/carl24k/fight-churn) and generated the result shown in figure 2.5. You should run listing 2.1 by following the README instructions. If you don't have data from your own product or service, you can run the code on a simulated dataset; instructions are in the README at the root of the repository. If you have generated the simulated data, then run listing 2.1 by executing the wrapper program `run_churn_listing.py` with parameters like so:

```
fight-churn/listings/run_churn_listing.py --chapter 2 --listing 1
```

The wrapper program prints the SQL it is running, and the final result looks similar to figure 2.5. This figure and all the SQL outputs in this chapter show the result in a tabular format as it would appear if the query were run in a SQL tool. If you run listing 2.1 using the Python framework provided on GitHub, the result is printed as a line of text. Also note that your results will differ slightly because the underlying data is randomly simulated.

Typical result returned by the net retention SQL (listing 2.1). Your result
will not be exactly the same because the data is randomly simulated.

net_mrr_retention_rate	net_mrr_churn_rate	start_mrr	retain_mrr
0.9424	0.0576	$103,336.56	$97,382.52

Net rate of retention and churn
(retention + churn = 1.0)

Monthly recurring revenue (MRR)
from the net retention calculation

Figure 2.5   Result of running listing 2.1 on the simulated dataset

Use of PostgreSQL (aka Postgres) in this book

This book presents all the examples using code that was tested and run on Postgre-
SQL 11. I chose PostgreSQL 11 because it is the latest version of PostgreSQL at the
time of writing this book, and it is a popular open source database that has modern
features that make it easy to demonstrate the concepts being taught. If you are working at a company with another database, it shouldn't be too hard to convert the SQL
in this book into a version that works for you. The main issue may be the CTEs, which
will have to be converted to temporary tables or subqueries. If you are a student or
just learning these techniques and can choose your database, I strongly recommend
that you use PostgreSQL to simplify using the book code as you are learning.

PostgreSQL, of course, does not have the capability of a big data warehouse; and
while common table expressions are easy to read, they can be computationally
expensive. So this arrangement is suitable for use only on services and products with
relatively small numbers of customers. The company case studies in this book all had
tens of thousands to around 100,000 customers, and PostgreSQL was easily adequate. Depending on the hardware you use and the amount of effort you put into performance tuning, PostgreSQL should scale up well to an analysis of millions of
customers. If you have 10 million customers or more, you will probably end up using
a data warehouse product architected specifically for big data. Fortunately, most
modern data warehouses (like Redshift and Presto) support SQL with common table
expressions, so the techniques in this book should translate directly. Nevertheless,
if you are learning techniques like those in this book for the first time, I strongly recommend you do your learning on a PostgreSQL database that fits on your laptop.

2.3.3   *Interpreting net retention*

The following scenarios can occur and affect how you interpret net retention:

- All subscriptions pay the same, including free.
- Multiple subscription prices with two cases:
    - *Standard case*—Churns and down sells outweigh upsells.
    - *Negative churn case*—Upsells outweigh churns and down sells.

If all subscribers pay exactly the same and no subscribers ever change the amount they pay, the MRR churn and retention calculated in this section are exactly the same as the subscriber count-based churn and retention described in section 2.1. Look at the circles in figure 2.2: if everyone pays exactly the same, then the area of a circle based on the MRR of subscribers is exactly proportional to the area of a circle based on the number of subscribers, and this proportionality is the same at both the start and the end. It's the same thing if the service is free and the MRR is zero: the net retention and derived churn are the same as calculating the subscriber-count-based churn, although in this case, you would have to modify the SQL in listing 2.1 to use a count aggregation instead of the sum of MRR.

On the other hand, when the amount subscribers pay varies, then net retention and churn based on revenue are not the same as the retention and churn (based on subscriber count). That's because, over time, the amount that individual subscribers pay can change, so if the circles in figure 2.2 represent revenue, there are four ways for the size of the circle to change. This more complex scenario is illustrated in figure 2.6, which illustrates MRR retention and churn with upsells and down sells. The four ways the subscriber revenue can change are

- Subscriber acquisitions
- Subscriber churns
- Upsells (retained subscribers change to a higher recurring revenue)
- Down sells (retained subscribers change to a lower recurring revenue)

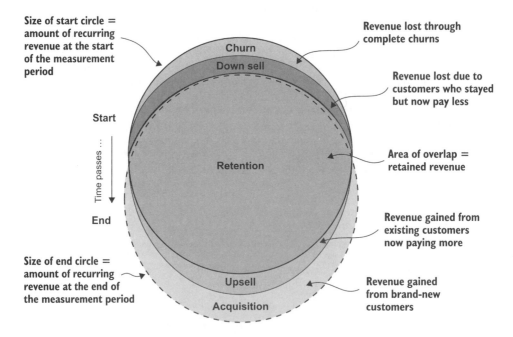

Figure 2.6   Revenue retention and churn with upsell and down sell

Net retention and net churn based on revenue are different from the (standard) churn based on the subscriber count. The impacts of upsells in retained subscribers can effectively offset churn, and down sells among the retained subscribers can effectively increase churn.

> **TAKEAWAY** *Net retention* is known as *net* because it combines the effects of churns, upsells, and down sells.

This netting property of net retention makes it somewhat less useful for fighting churn than the other definitions of churn. This is because including down sells and upsells are not the same, and conflating them confuses the issue. It is logical to include down sells in the churn calculation because that is the part of revenue that was present at the start but was lost from customer disengagement. The upsell revenue comes from a "different pie"—the end revenue circle in figure 2.6—so the net retention measure is no longer a ratio between parts of a whole. Also, the expiration of discounts is a contracted change in price and not related to customer satisfaction.

> **WARNING** Upsells and the expiration of discounts reduce the apparent churn rate in net retention, which makes it a less specific measurement of churn and less useful for fighting churn. The standard (count-based) churn and the MRR churn described in the following sections are more specific measures of churn and are preferred.

Net retention is not the most useful measure for fighting churn, but it is nevertheless remarkable because of the following fact about churn-reporting practice.

> **TIP** Net retention is the preferred measure of churn to report to outside investors in subscription companies.

Why the preference for net retention in reporting? There are two reasons: a benign reason is that as an operational metric, net retention summarizes churn, upsell, and down sell into one convenient number that is, arguably, the most important to outside investors. A slightly more contrived reason is that whenever upsells are higher than down sells, the net churn (derived from 100% minus net retention) is less than the standard (count-based) churn that ignores revenue changes. As I just explained, the net revenue changes (upsells and discount expiration minus down sells) effectively hide the true underlying churn rate. For many companies, reporting net retention rather than one of the more specific churn measurements is a matter of better investor relations and a slight obfuscation of the business fundamentals. In extreme cases, the increase in the revenue pool from upsells can be greater than the combined negative effect of down sells and churns reducing the revenue pool. This is a rare but highly desirable scenario known as *negative churn*.

> **DEFINITION** *Negative churn*—When the increase in revenue from upsells is greater than the combined negative effect of down sells and churns.

This means the revenue of the retained subscribers is greater than the revenue of the subscribers at the start, even after allowing for churn and down sells. As a result, net retention is greater than 100%. If net churn is calculated according to equation 2.6 in section 2.1.2, the result is a negative number. Note that this is not truly a negative value for the standard churn rate—the standard churn rate can only be a positive number (or possibly zero, for services with no subscriber cancellations). As described earlier, this is not the most useful churn measurement for fighting churn with data because it obscures how much churn is really going on, but it is very impressive to report to investors!

2.4   *Standard account-based churn*

The standard account-based churn rate has the simplest meaning because it is unaffected by upsells, down sells, and expiration of discounts. It always simply refers to the proportion of customers who completely cancel the service.

> **DEFINITION**   *Standard churn*—Churn measurement based on the customer count. Also known simply as the *churn rate*.

The standard churn rate is often called the *account churn rate* because it refers to the complete churn of an account holder who may hold multiple subscriptions. So for the standard churn rate, an account holder who cancels one subscription but keeps another subscription is not considered a churn. (This would be considered a down sell, which I will revisit in the next section.) In the B2B space, the standard churn rate is also referred to as *logo churn* because each account holder is a company (a logo).

In this section, I demonstrate how to calculate the churn rate directly rather than calculating it from retention. Direct calculation requires the SQL feature known as an *outer join*. It is true that the churn rate could be calculated from account retention using an inner join like the one used for net retention, but being able to identify churned accounts with an outer join is a skill you will need later. Because outer joins are not a basic SQL feature, I will review outer joins in section 2.4.2, after I outline the query in section 2.4.1.

2.4.1   *Standard churn rate definition*

Before considering the details, let's first review the steps to calculate the standard churn rate based on figure 2.2 and equation 2.1:

1   Set the start and end times for the measurement.
2   Identify and count the subscribers at the start (top circle in figure 2.2).
3   Identify the subscribers at the end (bottom circle in figure 2.2).
4   Identify and count the churned subscribers (upper downward-facing crescent in figure 2.2).
5   Divide the number of churns by the number of accounts at the start (equation 2.1).

2.4.2   *Outer joins for churn calculation*

The churned accounts are selected from the start and end accounts using an outer join. I will review outer joins briefly for readers who are not familiar with them.

An *inner join* is the more common type of join, like the join on `account_id` to create the `retained_accounts` CTE in listing 2.1. It returns all matching rows (according to the join field) and returns the desired fields from both tables for the matches. An *outer join* is different because instead of returning only the matches, it returns all the rows in one table. The join returns matching rows from a second table, but it fills fields from the second table with nulls for rows from the first table where there is *no matching row in the second table*. This is known as a *left outer join* because all the rows from the first table are always selected, which is on the left side of the `join` statement. (There is also a right outer join that behaves in the opposite way as far as which table keeps all its rows, and even a full outer join that returns all rows from *both* tables. But left outer joins suffice for churn.)

An outer join is used to find churned accounts because the point is to find the accounts present at the start that are *not* present at the end. If you do an inner join, it matches those present at both the start and the end, and those are precisely the ones to remove. A left outer join returns *all* the accounts present at the start, not just the ones that churned, and that's why the CTE to select churned accounts also needs a `WHERE` clause. It selects only those accounts from the join *where the* account _id *from the end accounts is null*, meaning it chooses only those rows from the join that were in the `start_accounts` CTE for which the matching `account_id` is not in the `end_account` CTE.

> **TAKEAWAY**   Outer joins can be used to find rows that do not match a join criterion, which makes them useful for identifying churns.

Look again at the churn diagram in figure 2.2: it also provides an illustration of the logic of inner and outer joins (this is shown in figure 2.7). The retained accounts are the intersection of the start and end accounts, which are selected by an inner join. The churned accounts, the left outer join, are found from the starting accounts by removing all records that have a match at the end with the `WHERE` clause, selecting where the end `account_id` IS NULL. (It follows that the acquired accounts would be the right outer join with a `WHERE` clause selecting for a null start `account_id`, but this is not needed for the techniques in this book.)

2.4.3   *Standard churn calculation with SQL*

The SQL for the standard churn calculation is shown in listing 2.2. It is identical to the net retention query from listing 2.1 for the first three CTEs, in which it creates temporary tables containing the accounts for the start and end of the measurement. But after finding the accounts, it creates a table of churned accounts rather than a table of retained accounts.

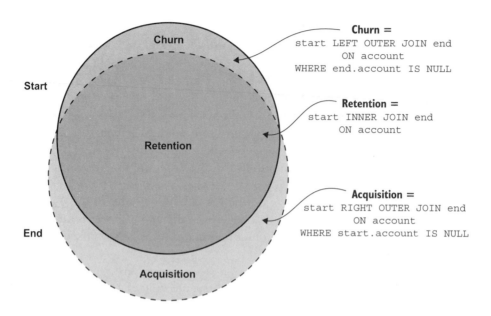

Figure 2.7   Customer calculations showing inner and outer joins

---

Listing 2.2   Standard (account-based) churn SQL program

**Criteria for being active on a given date: the
start date is on or before the date, and the
end date is after the date or null.**

```
WITH                                    Sets the period for which the
date_range AS (                         SQL will calculate churn
    SELECT  '2020-03-01'::date AS start_date, '2020-04-01'::date AS end_date
),
start_accounts AS                    CTE containing all the account
(                                    IDs active at the start

    SELECT DISTINCT account_id
    FROM subscription s INNER JOIN date_range d ON          Uses a distinct
        s.start_date<= d.start_date                         query because
        AND (s.end_date>d.start_date or s.end_date is null) you cannot
),                                                          assume every
end_accounts AS                      CTE containing all the           account has just
(                                    account IDs active at the end    one subscription

    SELECT DISTINCT account_id
    FROM subscription s INNER JOIN date_range d ON
        s.start_date<= d.end_date
        AND (s.end_date>d.end_date or s.end_date is null)
),
churned_accounts AS              CTE containing all the account IDs for
(                                accounts that churned: those that were
    SELECT s.account_id          active at the start but not active at the end
    FROM start_accounts s
```

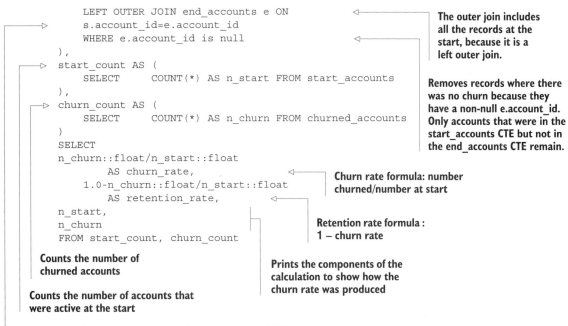

```
        LEFT OUTER JOIN end_accounts e ON
        s.account_id=e.account_id
        WHERE e.account_id is null
    ),
    start_count AS (
        SELECT      COUNT(*) AS n_start FROM start_accounts
    ),
    churn_count AS (
        SELECT      COUNT(*) AS n_churn FROM churned_accounts
    )
    SELECT
    n_churn::float/n_start::float
            AS churn_rate,
        1.0-n_churn::float/n_start::float
            AS retention_rate,
    n_start,
    n_churn
    FROM start_count, churn_count
```

The outer join includes all the records at the start, because it is a left outer join.

Removes records where there was no churn because they have a non-null e.account_id. Only accounts that were in the start_accounts CTE but not in the end_accounts CTE remain.

Churn rate formula: number churned/number at start

Retention rate formula: 1 – churn rate

Counts the number of churned accounts

Prints the components of the calculation to show how the churn rate was produced

Counts the number of accounts that were active at the start

The join looks for records that match by account ID and fills them with NULLs for the end accounts where there is no match.

The following describes each CTE in the program and the final SELECT statement and what role each CTE plays in the calculation in relation to the steps described in section 2.4.1:

1 date_range—A table with one row that holds the start and end dates for the calculation. This is step 1.

2 start_accounts—A table with one row for each account active at the start. This table is created by selecting from the subscription table based on the condition that the account is active at the start of the churn measurement. This is step 2.

3 end_accounts—A table with one row for each account active at the end of the churn measurement. The condition for being considered active is the same as for the start accounts, using the churn measurement end date for the criteria. This is step 3.

4 churned_accounts—A table with one row for each account that is active at the start but not active at the end. This table is created by the outer join on account IDs between the start_accounts table and the end_accounts table, and the WHERE clause that removes accounts where the end account_id is not null. This is step 4.

5 start_count—A table with one row that sums the total number of accounts at the start of the churn measurement, for clarity.

6 churn_count—A table with one row that sums the total number of accounts that churned during the measurement period, for clarity.

7 *Final* SELECT *statement*—Takes the results from the start_count and churn_count tables and calculates the final results by plugging the values into equations 2.1 and 2.2. This is step 5, the final step in the program.

Now you know how the churn rate and retention rate described by equations 2.1 and 2.2 can be calculated from a typical subscription database in SQL. Listing 2.2 was tested on the simulated dataset produced by the code on the book's website (www.manning.com/books/fighting-churn-with-data) and in the GitHub repository (https://github.com/carl24k/fight-churn) and generated the result shown in figure 2.7. You should run listing 2.2 by following the instructions in the README. After setting up your environment (detailed in the README), run the listing with this command:

```
fight-churn/listings/run_churn_listing.py --chapter 2 --listing 2
```

In comparison to figure 2.5, which shows the result for net retention calculated with listing 2.1, the result in figure 2.8 shows the same churn rate, but instead of revenue, it was calculated from accounts. This is to be expected because the simulation uses the same MRR for every customer.

Typical result returned by the churn rate SQL (listing 2.2): churn_rate = n_churn/n_start

churn_rate	retention_rate	n_start	n_churn
0.0534	0.9466	10331	552

Churn rate and retention rate   **Number of customers at the**
(retention + churn = 1.0)   **start and number who churned**

Figure 2.8   Result of running listing 2.2 on the simulated dataset

2.4.4   *When to use the standard churn rate*

The standard churn rate is used as the main operational metric when all subscribers pay similar amounts or the subscription is free. If all subscribers pay *exactly* the same (meaning no discounts or any variation, or the product is free), standard churn can be calculated with either a net retention query or the standard churn rate query. But if there is a *modest* amount of pricing variation, or if there are temporary discounts, then you should use the standard churn calculation method given in this section.

As you will see later, the standard churn rate also has a special role in churn analysis. Because churn analysis uses a model designed to predict customer (subscription holder) churn, a correctly calibrated predictive churn model should reproduce the standard account churn rate. However, for subscriptions with a significant amount of variation in the amount customers pay or those with extensive use of discounts, the standard churn rate is not the best churn rate; for those scenarios, you should use MRR churn, which is taught in section 2.6.

TAKEAWAY   If there is a moderate amount of pricing variety, including discounts, then you should use the standard churn calculation method. For this purpose, moderate pricing variety means most customers pay close to the same price, but there may be some customers on older plans, discounts, or currency conversion effects.

2.5 Activity (event-based) churn for nonsubscription products

In chapter 1, I told you that fighting churn is not just for subscription services; it is for any product or service with repeat customers. Now you will learn the main technique specifically for nonsubscription scenarios: calculating churn based on customer activity.

The concept of event-based or activity churn is the same as with standard subscription churn, but you need an informal definition of what defines a customer as active versus churned. To use these techniques, you need only a data warehouse of *events*, which are time-stamped facts about customer use of the product. I will say more about event data in chapter 3, but for the sake of simplicity, a data model with an event time-stamp is assumed for the examples in this section.

2.5.1 Defining an active account and churn from events

The most common definition of an *active* customer for nonsubscription products is simply a customer who has used the product within a recent time window, typically, one or two months. The concept is illustrated in figure 2.9. User activity tends to be clustered, so it is natural to think of an active period as a sequence of events without a large gap between any two successive events. If the maximum time limit is exceeded, that is considered a churn. Such a time limit should be set long enough that most customers who exceed the limit don't come back, at least for a while.

Other criteria for an active customer based on events can be things like these:

- A customer is considered active only if they have certain specific events.
- A customer is considered active only if they have a minimum number of events.

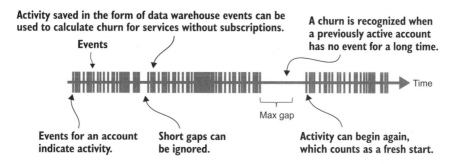

Figure 2.9   Event recency defines active periods and churn.

- A customer is considered active only if they have specific metrics calculated on events within the recent time period. Examples of specific metrics to make a customer active (and churn when they fail the test) would be a minimum (or any) spend on retail purchases or a minimum amount of revenue generated from ads.

These different choices don't change the SQL program that much.

2.5.2 *Activity churn calculations with SQL*

The SQL program for calculating churn from events is shown in listing 2.3. It is almost identical to listing 2.2, except it makes no use of the subscription table. Instead, the CTEs for the accounts at the start of the measurement and end of the measurement are based on a table of events (a table named event). As described previously, the criterion for an account to be considered active is simply having some recent event. As in listing 2.2, the parameters controlling the date range are in a CTE.

Because products without subscriptions are usually used for a shorter length of time, listing 2.3 demonstrates churn over a one-month period (monthly churn). Another difference in this case is that there is another parameter controlling the recency threshold. Other than those changes, the main logic of the program is the same as listing 2.2, so here I just summarize it:

1. Find accounts active at the start of the churn measurement. Accounts that are active at the start are those that had an event within a window of time ending at the (nominal) start time for the churn measurement.
2. Find accounts active at the end of the churn measurement. These are accounts that had an event within a window of time, which ends at the end for the churn measurement.
3. Outer join the two sets of accounts to find those accounts that were active at the start and no longer active at the end. These are the churned accounts.
4. Divide the number of churned accounts by the number of accounts active at the start to calculate the churn rate.

Listing 2.3 was tested on the simulated dataset produced by the code on the book's website (www.manning.com/books/fighting-churn-with-data) and in the GitHub repository (https://github.com/carl24k/fight-churn) and generated the result shown in figure 2.10. After setting up your environment, run the listing with this command:

```
fight-churn/listings/run_churn_listing.py --chapter 2 --listing 3
```

In comparison to figure 2.7, which shows the result for the standard churn calculated with listing 2.2, this result shows a similar churn rate but not exactly the same. That's to be expected because these are the same customers churning, but listing 2.3 uses slightly different criteria for determining when the churn takes place.

Typical result returned by the activity churn rate SQL (listing 2.3)

churn_rate	retention_rate	n_start	n_churn
0.0463	0.9537	14604	676

Number of customers active at the start and those who churned by becoming inactive

Figure 2.10 Result of running listing 2.3 on the simulated dataset

Listing 2.3 Activity (event-based) churn SQL program

```
WITH
date_range AS (                    Sets the time period for which
                                   the SQL calculates churn
    SELECT  '2020-03-01'::TIMESTAMP AS start_date,      Uses a timestamp for the dates
        '2020-04-01'::TIMESTAMP AS end_date,            because events use timestamps
        interval '1 months' AS inactivity_interval
),
start_accounts AS              This CTE is similar to the
(                              same CTE in listing 2.2.
                                                        Picks accounts with
    SELECT DISTINCT account_id                          events within the time
    FROM event e INNER JOIN date_range d ON             limit of the start date
        e.event_time>start_date-inactivity_interval
        AND e.event_time<= start_date)          This CTE is identical to the
start_count AS (                                same CTE in listing 2.2.
    SELECT      COUNT(start_accounts.*) AS n_start FROM start_accounts
),
end_accounts AS            This CTE is similar to the
(                         same CTE in listing 2.2.
                                                   Picks accounts with
    SELECT DISTINCT account_id                     events within the time
    FROM event e INNER JOIN date_range d ON        limit of the end date
        e.event_time>end_date-inactivity_interval
        AND e.event_time<= end_date
),                                          The rest of the code is
end_count AS (                              identical to listing 2.2.
    SELECT COUNT(end_accounts.*) AS n_end FROM end_accounts
),
churned_accounts AS
(
    SELECT DISTINCT s.account_id
    FROM start_accounts s
    LEFT OUTER JOIN end_accounts e ON s.account_id=e.account_id
    WHERE e.account_id is null
),
churn_count AS (
    SELECT      COUNT(churned_accounts.*) AS n_churn
    FROM churned_accounts
)
SELECT
n_churn::float/n_start::float AS churn_rate,
```

```
    1.0-n_churn::float/n_start::float AS retention_rate,
n_start,
n_churn
FROM start_count, end_count, churn_count
```

One important difference between churn based on subscriptions and churn based on activity is that activity-based churn requires a wait time for every customer to know whether they have churned. On a subscription, you know a churn is a churn the day after the subscription ends without a replacement; but for users on a system without a subscription, you never know if an event is the last event defining a churn until some time later. That said, in chapter 4, you will see that the same logic can also apply with subscriptions if you allow short gaps between subscriptions (typically a few days) without counting a churn.

> **TAKEAWAY** You can calculate the churn rate on nonsubscription products based on the recency of activity.

2.6 *Advanced churn: Monthly recurring revenue (MRR) churn*

In the previous sections, you learned that the standard churn rate can have a problem with multiprice subscription products. The standard churn rate ignores down sells, which should be considered part of churn, while net retention includes down sells but also includes upsells, which should not be considered churn. There is another churn measure made for this situation: MRR churn. This is the most complex calculation for churn, but it is the most accurate when there are multiple subscription products and prices.

> **TIP** Use MRR churn if you have customers who pay a wide range of prices: that is, your most valued customers pay twice your least valuable rate or more. In enterprise B2B software, the most valuable customers may pay more like 100 times the least valuable, and MRR churn is an absolute necessity in such scenarios.

2.6.1 *MRR churn definition and calculation*

MRR churn is once again a ratio of losses to the starting state, but now the numerator of the churn rate is the total losses from both churn *and* down sells, while the denominator is the revenue of the customers at the start. Referring to figure 2.6, which illustrates churn calculations with upsells and down sells, the MRR churn includes outright loss of MRR from complete churns (the top downward-facing crescent in figure 2.6) as well as losses due to down sells (the second downward-facing crescent in figure 2.6) as the numerator. It includes the retained MRR as the denominator but not the upsell MRR. For this reason, it is the most accurate measure of churn for multiprice subscription products.

In an equation, MRR churn is defined as shown in equation 2.11, and MRR retention is shown in equation 2.12.

$$MRRChurn = \frac{MRR_{churned\_accounts} + MRR_{downsell}}{MRR_{start}}$$ **(Equation 2.11)**

$$MRRRetention = 100\% - \frac{MRR_{churned\_accounts} + MRR_{downsell}}{MRR_{start}}$$ **(Equation 2.12)**

In the equations, $MRR_{churned\_accounts}$ means the total MRR of all accounts that churned, and $MRR_{downsell}$ means the total reduction in MRR of all accounts that were down sold.

Figure 2.11 shows an example of an MRR churn calculation by extending the example from figure 2.4 in section 2.3.1. In the figure, one customer on the Premier plan churns, two new customers sign up, and two customers change their plans. One customer upgrades from Standard to Premier, and one downgrades from Premier to Standard. The example shows an important difference between MRR churn and net retention: down sells enter into MRR churn, but upsells do not.

Using equation 2.11 and filling in the values from the example shown in figure 2.11 gives equation 2.13:

$$MRRChurn_{Figure\ 2.11} = \frac{MRR_{churned\_accounts} + MRR_{downsell}}{MRR_{start}}$$

$$= \frac{29.99 + 20}{89.95} = 56\%$$ **(Equation 2.13)**

In January, one customer on the Premier plan does not renew (a churn, X), a customer on the Premier plan downgrades to Standard (v), one customer upgrades from Standard to Premier (^), and two new customers sign up (+).

	Customers on 1-January				Changes		Customers on 1-February			
ID	Start	Next renewal	Plan	MRR		ID	Start	Next renewal	Plan	MRR
1	3-October	3-January	Standard	9.99		1	3-October	3-January	Standard	9.99
2	17-October	17-January	Premier	29.99	X					
3	2-November	2-January	Standard	9.99		3	2-November	2-January	Standard	9.99
4	11-November	11-January	Premier	29.99	v	4	11-November	11-January	Standard	9.99
5	7-December	7-January	Standard	9.99	^	5	7-December	7-January	Premier	29.99
				89.95	+	6	3-January	3-February	Standard	9.99
					+	7	15-January	15-February	Premier	29.99
										99.94

The MRR churn rate is the MRR of the customers who left or now pay less (29.99 from customer 2, who churned, and a 20 change from customer 4, who downgraded, for a total of 49.99) divided by the MRR of all the customers at the start (89.95), or 49.99/89.95 = 56%.

Note that the two new signups and the upgrade do not influence the MRR churn calculation, but the downgrade from the Premier plan to the Standard plan does.

Figure 2.11   MRR churn calculation dataset

2.6.2 *MRR churn calculation with SQL*

The SQL for MRR churn calculation is shown in listing 2.4. It includes elements from both the net retention SQL and the standard churn SQL calculations. First, I outline the steps in the calculation and how they relate to the MRR churn equation (equation 2.7) and the down sell/upsell revenue diagram (figure 2.6). After that, I go through how these are implemented in the SQL program's CTEs. The steps in the calculation are as follows:

1 Set the start and end times for the measurement.
2 Identify the subscribers and the total revenue at the start (the top circle in figure 2.6).
3 Identify the subscribers at the end (the bottom circle in figure 2.6).
4 Identify the churned subscribers and their revenue (the top downward-facing crescent in figure 2.6).
5 Identify the subscribers who were down sells and the amount of the down sell (the second downward-facing crescent in figure 2.6).
6 Divide the total of churned revenue and down sell subscriber revenue by the start subscriber revenue (equation 2.11).

Those steps are implemented in the SQL program (listing 2.4) as the following CTEs:

1 `date_range`—A table with one row that holds the start and end dates for the calculation. This is step 1.
2 `start_accounts`—A table with one row for each account active at the start. This table is created by selecting from the subscription table based on the condition that the account is active at the start of the churn measurement. This is step 2.
3 `end_accounts`—A table with one row for each account active at the end of the churn measurement. The condition for being considered active is the same as for the start accounts, using the churn measurement end date for the criteria. This is step 3.
4 `churned_accounts`—A table with one row for each account that is active at the start but not active at the end. This table is created by the outer join on account IDs between the `start_accounts` table and the `end_accounts` table, and the WHERE clause that removes accounts where the end `account_id` is not null. This is step 4.
5 `downsell_accounts`—A table with one row for each account that is active at both the start and the end but that has a lower MRR at the end than at the start. This is created by a join on account IDs between the `start_accounts` table and the `end_accounts` table and a WHERE clause that selects only those records where the end MRR is less than the start MRR. This is step 5.
6 `start_mrr`—A one-row table that sums the total MRR at the start of the churn measurement.
7 `churn_mrr`—A one-row table that sums the total MRR of the churned accounts.

8 `downsell_mrr`—A one-row table that sums the total MRR of all the retained accounts.

9 *Final* `SELECT` *statement*—Takes the results from the one-row result tables `start_mrr`, `churn_mrr`, and `downsell_mrr` and calculates the final results by plugging the values into equation 2.7. This is step 6, the final step in the program.

Listing 2.4 MRR churn SQL program

```
WITH                                            Sets the time period for which
date_range AS (                                 the SQL calculates churn
    SELECT '2020-03-01'::date AS start_date, '2020-04-01'::date AS end_date
),
start_accounts AS                                           CTE containing active
(                                                           accounts and their
    SELECT account_id, SUM(mrr) AS total_mrr               MRR at the start
    FROM subscription s INNER JOIN date_range d ON
        s.start_date<= d.start_date                        Uses the aggregate
        AND (s.end_date>d.start_date or s.end_date is null) sum in the case of
    GROUP BY account_id                                     multiple subscriptions
),
end_accounts AS          CTE containing active accounts      Aggregates GROUP
(                        and their MRR at the end            BY for the sum
    SELECT account_id, SUM(mrr) AS total_mrr
    FROM subscription s INNER JOIN date_range d ON
        s.start_date<= d.end_date                          Uses the aggregate
        AND (s.end_date>d.end_date or s.end_date is null)  sum in case of
    GROUP BY account_id                                    multiple subscriptions
),
churned_accounts AS          CTE containing all IDs for
(                            accounts that churned
    SELECT s.account_id, SUM(s.total_mrr)
        AS total_mrr                   The join matches records
    FROM start_accounts s              by account ID and fills in
    LEFT OUTER JOIN end_accounts e ON  nulls on no match.
    s.account_id=e.account_id
    WHERE e.account_id is null
    GROUP BY s.account_id        Removes records where there
),                               is a non-null e.account_id
downsell_accounts AS
(
    SELECT s.account_id, s.total_mrr-e.total_mrr
        AS downsell_amount            The down sell amount
    FROM start_accounts s             is positive by definition.
    INNER JOIN end_accounts e ON s.account_id=e.account_id
    WHERE e.total_mrr<s.total_mrr    Sums the total MRR of all the
),                                   accounts active at the start
start_mrr AS (
    SELECT SUM (start_accounts.total_mrr) AS start_mrr
    FROM start_accounts
),                               Sums the total MRR of all
churn_mrr AS (                   the churned accounts
    SELECT    SUM(churned_accounts.total_mrr) AS churn_mrr
    FROM churned_accounts
),
```

Annotations (left margin):
- **The criteria for being active on a given date**
- **Aggregates GROUP BY for the sum**
- **Sums the total MRR in the case there are multiple subscriptions**
- **CTE containing all the accounts that down sold**
- **The WHERE condition selects accounts paying less at the end.**

<table>
<tr><td>

CTE
containing
the total
reduction
in MRR
from
down sell

</td><td>

```
downsell_mrr AS (
    SELECT coalesce(SUM(downsell_accounts.downsell_amount),0.0)
        AS downsell_mrr
    FROM downsell_accounts
)
SELECT
    (churn_mrr+downsell_mrr) /start_mrr AS mrr_churn_rate,
    start_mrr,
    churn_mrr,
    downsell_mrr
FROM start_mrr, churn_mrr, downsell_mrr
```

</td></tr>
</table>

← **Coalesce fills with zeros in case there are no down sells.**

← **MRR churn formula**

← **Prints the components of the calculation**

Listing 2.4 was tested on the simulated dataset produced by the code on the book's website (www.manning.com/books/fighting-churn-with-data) and in the book's GitHub repository (https://github.com/carl24k/fight-churn) and generated the result shown in figure 2.12. You should run listing 2.4 by following the README instructions on GitHub. After setting up your environment (detailed in the README), run the listing with this command:

```
fight-churn/listings/run_churn_listing.py --chapter 2 --listing 4
```

In comparison to figure 2.7, which shows the result for the standard churn rate calculated with listing 2.2, this result shows the same churn rate. This is to be expected because the simulation uses the exact same MRR for every customer, so the simulation has no down sells or reason for this to differ from the standard calculation. That said, the simulation code can be extended to include the variable MRR, and that would make this exercise more interesting. I encourage you to do so as an exercise.

Typical result returned by the MRR churn rate SQL (listing 2.4)

mrr_churn_rate	n_start_mrr	churn_mrr	downsell_mrr
0.0534	$103,206.69	$5,514.49	$0.0

MRR of churned customers and MRR at the start

The simulation does not include down sells.

Figure 2.12 Result of running listing 2.4 on the simulated dataset

2.6.3 *MRR churn vs. account churn vs. net (retention) churn*

At this point, you have learned about three different churn formulas:

- Net churn, calculated from net retention
- Standard (account-based) churn
- MRR churn

You have also learned where each is usually appropriate:

- *Net retention and churn*—For reporting as an operational metric to investors. Net-retention-based churn is equivalent to standard churn when all subscribers pay the same (or all subscribers pay nothing).
- *Standard churn*—For fighting churn when subscribers pay more or less the same, but there can be some variety in pricing and discounting that would complicate the interpretation of net retention.
- *MRR churn*—For fighting churn when there is a large variety in the amounts different subscribers pay.

One fairly common situation where it is *not* appropriate to use MRR churn is for subscriptions that have an annual plan with lower MRR than the monthly plan. Subscribers can lock in a low rate but commit to a whole year by paying up front. This is usually good for the subscription business because if done correctly, it leads to higher lifetime value for the subscriber, as will be explained in chapter 8. However, it would be considered a down sell when a subscriber switches from the monthly plan to the annual plan, and such changes would have a negative impact on the reported churn rate. In such a situation, it is probably better to use the standard churn rate.

MRR churn is most appropriate when there is a truly great difference between MRR of different types of accounts: in B2B software sales, big accounts can easily pay 10 times or more the amount of small accounts. For companies that do have such variety in their pricing, there is usually a consistent relationship between the three churn measures.

TAKEAWAY Standard churn > MRR churn > Net churn

You might expect that MRR churn would normally be higher than the standard churn measure because MRR churn includes the impact of down sells, but standard churn does not. However, as I will discuss in later chapters, it is almost always the case that accounts that pay more churn less often than accounts that pay less for multiprice products. The subscribers paying the least almost always churn more. This can seem paradoxical if you do not work on such a product, according to the logic that paying more should make a customer more unhappy. However, in B2B products, higher prices go to larger company subscribers that use the product more (have more users), and larger companies are almost always more stable than smaller companies. Also, larger companies paying more tend to be more committed to using the product for a longer time because they have had a longer deliberative process before making the purchase and have more invested in the setup and operation of the subscription product. As a result, the standard churn rate that counts all subscribers equally is almost always higher than the MRR churn rate for a B2B product.

Net churn calculated from net retention is almost always the least of all the churn measures. This is because, in addition to reflecting the low churn rate of large company subscribers, it also counts upsells in retained accounts against the churn rate. As mentioned previously, it is even possible for the net churn calculated from net retention to be negative when upsells outweigh down sells and churns.

2.7   *Churn rate measurement conversion*

So far, the calculations have assumed you want to calculate the churn rate over one month. As I mentioned, it is possible to calculate churn over any time period, and most B2B product subscriptions calculate churn as an annual number to better reflect the typical length of a subscription. That's fine because the calculation is the same, and using the same code to calculate annual churn is as easy as changing the start and end to suitable dates one year apart. But what if a company wants to calculate an annual churn rate but has been in operation for less than a year or has less than a year's data in the database for some other reason? This is not a problem because you can convert a churn rate from a shorter period (like a month) to a longer period (like a year). But the relationship between churn measured over one month and churn measured over one year is not completely straightforward.

Spoiler: annual churn is not 12 times monthly churn. This section shows how churn measurements made over different time frames are related and how to convert a churn measurement made over a month into an annual churn rate and vice versa.

2.7.1   *Survivor analysis (advanced)*

Note that this section contains a lot of equations. If you don't like math, you can skip to the answer, which is shown at the start of the next section.

The key to understanding the relationship between monthly and annual churn is to think about retained customers as survivors and look at how many survive over many months. The term *survivor* comes from population studies in biology, which is where this kind of analysis originates, but it is perfectly reasonable to think of retained customers as survivors in a process where churn is like death. This is illustrated in figure 2.13, which shows what happens to an initial pool of subscribers if there is a monthly churn rate and, equivalently, a monthly retention rate of one minus the churn rate, as explained earlier in this chapter. Figure 2.13 shows both a simple concrete example (on the left) and the same process in terms of algebraic equations (on the right).

Here is how a churn process evolves over a year, starting with 100 accounts and a 10% (0.1) churn rate, which is depicted on the left side of figure 2.13:

1 At the beginning of the first month, there are 100 subscribers. During the first month, $100 \times 0.1 = 10$ customers churn, leaving 90. This is equivalent to 100 times the retention rate of 0.9.

2 At the beginning of the second month, there are 90 subscribers, and during the second month, $90 \times 0.1 = 9$ customers churn, leaving 81. This is equivalent to the original 100 multiplied by the retention rate squared because $81 = 100 \times 0.81 = 100 \times 0.9^2$.

Note that because the churn rate is the percent of accounts that churn, if there are fewer accounts to begin with, then fewer will churn, although the *rate* of churn is the same.

3   At the beginning of the third month, there are 81 subscribers, and during the third month, $81 \times 0.1 \approx 8$ customers churn, leaving 73. This is equivalent to the original 100 multiplied by the retention rate cubed because $73 = 100 \times 0.73 \approx 100 \times 0.9^3$.

4   The pattern that continues in subsequent months is that after 12 months, there are $100 \times 0.9^{12} = 28$ customers remaining.

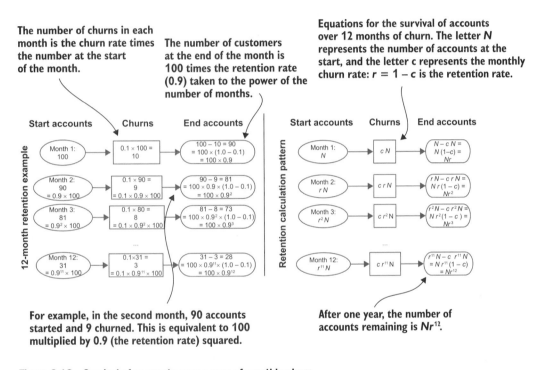

Figure 2.13   Survival of accounts over a year of monthly churn

In terms of equations (the right side of figure 2.13), this is the process month by month for the first few months and then showing this general pattern:

1   At the beginning of the first month, there are N subscribers, but during the first month, cN churn according to the definition of the churn rate. At the end of the month $(1 - c)N$ or rN subscribers remain.

2   At the beginning of the second month, there are $rN = (1 - c)N$ accounts, and $c(1 - c)N$ churn during the month. The number of accounts remaining after month two is $(1 - c)N$, the starting number, minus $c(1 - c)N$, the number that churn, or $(1 - c)N - c(1 - c)N$.

It is not too hard to work out the algebra and show that from the definition of the retention rate

$$(1 - c)N - [c(1 - c)]N = (1 - c)N \times (1 - c) = (1 - c)^2N$$

and

$$(1 - c)^2N = r^2N$$

3 At the beginning of the third month, there are $r^2N = (1 - c)^2N$, and $c(1 - c)^2N$ churn during the month. The number of accounts remaining after month three is $(1 - c)^2N$, the starting number, minus $c(1 - c)^2N$, the number that churn, or $(1 - c)^2N - c(1 - c)^2N$.

It is not too hard to work out the algebra and show that from the definition of the retention rate

$$(1 - c)^2N - [c(1 - c)^2]N = (1 - c)2N \times (1 - c) = (1 - c)^3N$$

and

$$(1 - c)^3N = r^3N$$

4 The pattern that continues in subsequent months is that after x months, there are

$$r^xN = (1 - c)^xN$$

This shows that the number of retained accounts over many months is equal to the retention rate to the power of the number of months multiplied by the number of accounts at the start.

2.7.2   *Churn rate conversions*

The multimonth relationship for retention rates is the key to converting monthly churn rates to an annual measurement. In the previous section, I showed you that the number of retained customers after one year in which the month churn rate is c and the monthly retention rate is $r = (1 - c)$ is

$$N_{year} = r^{12}N$$

It follows that the one-year retention rate, which is denoted by R, is

$$R = r^{12}$$ (Equation 2.14)

Equation 2.14 shows how to convert from monthly retention rate r to an annual retention rate R. This follows directly from the definition because the number of customers retained after a year must be equal to the number at the start times the annual retention rate. Also, from the definition, you know that the annual churn rate, which I denote as C, must be equal to 100% minus the annual retention rate. It follows that the annual churn rate C must be equal to

$$C = 100\% - R$$

$$C = 100\% - r^{12}$$

$$C = 100\% - (1 - c)^{12} \qquad \text{(Equation 2.15)}$$

In a few words, the annual churn rate is equal to one *minus* one minus the monthly churn rate to the twelfth power. That sounds complicated, but it's pretty easy to understand in terms of the retention rate. The annual retention rate is the monthly retention rate to the twelfth power.

> **TAKEAWAY**   To convert monthly churn rate to annual, use the fact that annual retention is monthly retention to the twelfth power, and retention is one minus churn.

Note that the annual retention rate is less than the monthly retention rate because taking a number less than one to any power reduces it further. This makes sense as more must churn in a year than in a month: the subscribers have 12 times longer to churn. The annual churn rate, on the other hand, must be greater than the monthly churn rate, again because there is more time to churn.

What about converting the annual measurement of the churn rate to monthly? I won't go into all the details, but the same relationship holds in reverse. If you refer back to equation 2.14 and take the twelfth root of both sides, you get

$$r = \sqrt[12]{R} = R^{1/12} \qquad \text{(Equation 2.16)}$$

Equation 2.16 shows how to convert from an annual churn R to a monthly churn rate r. I use the notation that the twelfth root of a number is implemented by taking the number to the twelfth (1/12) power. If you are not familiar with root operations, recall that the square root of a number x is that number which when squared gives x. The twelfth root is defined similarly: the twelfth root of x is the number that when taken to the twelfth power gives x. Don't worry. No one calculates twelfth roots and powers in their head, but it's a piece of cake in any programming language. Taking the twelfth root is the same as raising a number to the one-twelfth (1/12) power, and this is how such roots are implemented in most programming languages.

The equivalent monthly retention rate for an annual retention measurement is just the twelfth root of the annual measurement. Similarly, this equation calculates an equivalent monthly churn rate from an annual measurement:

$$c = 100\% - \sqrt[12]{1-C} = 100\% - (1-C)^{1/12} \qquad \textbf{(Equation 2.17)}$$

Equation 2.17 shows how to convert from an annual churn rate C to a monthly churn rate c.

TAKEAWAY   To convert annual churn rate to monthly, use the fact that monthly retention is the twelfth root of annual retention, and retention is one minus churn.

2.7.3   *Converting any churn measurement window in SQL*

You can easily convert any churn measurement window into an equivalent churn rate for any other measurement window. This is a good trick to use if you need to measure churn for a company with less than one year of data in the subscription database. You would calculate a churn rate with as much data as is available (whether it is 2, 6, or 10 months) and then convert the result into an annual churn rate. I won't go into details, but for any churn measurement, c' made over any time period of p days is the equivalent annual churn rate C:

$$C = 100\% - (1 - c')^{\,365/p} \qquad \textbf{(Equation 2.18)}$$

In this case, the power to which the measured retention rate $(1 - c')$ is taken to is 365 divided by the length of the time period p. If p were 1 month, this would reduce to (approximately) 12. Similarly, the monthly churn rate c can be calculated from a churn rate c' made over any period of p days with equation 2.19:

$$c = 100\% - (1 - c')^{\,(365/12)p} \qquad \textbf{(Equation 2.19)}$$

Returning to the calculation of churn rates from a subscription database with SQL, it's easy to calculate both monthly and annual churn rates from one measurement of churn made over any time period. Listing 2.5 shows the necessary SQL SELECT statement, assuming the same common table expression as the regular churn rate calculation in listing 2.2, except that the start and end dates in the date_range CTE can be any dates (any dates where the end date is after the start date, that is). This SQL implements equations 2.13 and 2.14 as part of the SELECT statement by calculating the time period p on the fly.

> **Listing 2.5   Churn SQL `SELECT` statement for uneven time periods**

Number of subscribers at the start, as in listing 2.2

Number of subscribers that churned, as in listing 2.2

Standard churn rate calculation (equation 2.1)

Displays the difference in days between the start and end dates

```
SELECT
    n_start,
    n_churn,
    n_churn::float/n_start::float AS measured_churn,
    end_date-start_date AS period_days,
    1.0-POWER(1.0-n_churn::float/n_start::float,365.0/(end_date-start_date)::float)
        AS annual_churn,
    1.0-POWER(1.0-n_churn::float/n_start::float,(365.0/12.0)/(end_date-start_date)
        ::float)
        AS monthly_churn
```

Equation 2.13

Equation 2.14

An example of the result of using the `SELECT` statement in listing 2.5 is shown in figure 2.14. In this case, because the measurement period is between one month and one year, the equivalent annual churn rate is more than the measured churn rate, and the equivalent monthly churn rate is less than the measured churn rate.

Listing 2.5 was tested on the simulated dataset produced with the code on the book's website (www.manning.com/books/fighting-churn-with-data) and in the GitHub repository (https://github.com/carl24k/fight-churn) and generated the result shown in figure 2.14. You should run listing 2.5 by using this listing wrapper script (the same command as early in the chapter), changing the listing parameter to `--listing 5`:

```
fight-churn/listings/run_churn_listing.py --chapter 2 --listing 5
```

In comparison to figure 2.8, which shows the result for the standard churn rate calculated with listing 2.2, this result measures the churn rate over 92 days (a hypothetical example assuming there is 92 days' worth of data available to calculate an annual churn rate). The result includes a monthly version of the churn rate and an annualized version of the churn rate. The monthly churn rate is similar but not exactly the same as the result in figure 2.8—this monthly churn rate is an average monthly rate over the entire 92 days.

Typical result returned by the time-scaled churn rate SQL (listing 2.5)

n_start	n_churn	measured_churn	period_days	annual_churn	monthly_churn
10393	1394	0.13412	92	0.43525	0.04649

Churn can be measured for an arbitrary time period: in this case, 92 days.

The resulting churn rate is scaled to an equivalent annual and monthly rate.

Figure 2.14   Result of running listing 2.5 on the simulated dataset

2.7.4 *Picking the churn measurement window*

Given that you have a choice, you might be wondering what time frame you should choose to measure churn. In general, you should measure the churn rate for a time frame that is close to the typical subscription renewal term (if there are subscriptions). Then you can use the methods in this section to scale the measurement if you need to report churn another way.

> **TAKEAWAY**   Churn on consumer subscriptions is usually measured as a monthly rate, and churn on business subscriptions is measured as an annual rate.

Problems can arise if you measure churn in a time frame that is different from your typical subscriptions. The issues are a bit different if your subscriptions are mostly monthly or mostly annual.

First consider the case of annual subscriptions. If your subscriptions are mostly annual, and you measure churn over one month, you have to make sure the month you choose has approximately one-twelfth of your annual renewals. Otherwise, the churn measurement will be biased. For many businesses, most renewals come in a particular season; if this is the case, and you measure churn over any other time of year, you will see an artificially low churn rate. Conversely, if you measure churn over a month that happens to have a large number of the annual customers up for renewal, you can end up calculating an artificially high churn rate by seeing much of the year's churns in a short time.

If your subscriptions are mostly monthly, and you measure churn over a year, then the churn calculation will miss accounts that start and churn in between the two dates. To see this, note that all the churn calculations in this chapter check the accounts on just two dates, and accounts that are active in between the two dates would be ignored. This results in an underestimate of the churn rate. This is a problem, in general, if you measure churn with a time period that is longer than the shortest subscriptions.

> **WARNING**   Measuring churn over a time window that is different from the typical subscription length (or typical customer active lifetime) can result in errors in the churn rate.

2.7.5 *Seasonality and churn rates*

In the previous section, I warned you that calculating churn using a time frame that is different from the typical subscription length can cause problems. There is one other type of problem to beware of when calculating churn rates, and it applies mainly to monthly churn calculations: seasonality.

> **DEFINITION**   *Seasonality*—Variations that occur at particular times of the year.

Many subscription businesses have seasonal variations in the churn rate, and if you are measuring churn with monthly time windows, you may find the churn rate moves up and down throughout the year due to seasonal effects. The challenge is that when you start trying to reduce churn, if you do not correct for seasonality, it can be hard to know if changes you see in the churn rate are due to your churn-fighting efforts or seasonal variation.

> **WARNING** If you use monthly churn rates, seasonality can make it hard to assess the impact of churn-reduction efforts.

Seasonality is less of a problem for annual measurement because an annual churn measurement always includes every season of the year. If you make one annual churn measurement in January and another annual churn measurement in February, both churn measurements include every season: the difference between two annual churn measurements made a month apart reflects the difference between the churns in that month and the same month one year earlier, so the change in churn rate is already controlled for seasonality. (If many annual renewals occur in one season, then that season can be a time when the churn rate changes significantly; the rest of the year, changes in the churn rate are smaller because fewer renewals occur. But having a critical season in the business when contracts renew is not the same as seasonality.)

What do you do if you use monthly churn rates? First, measure monthly churn rates over as many years as possible, and try to determine if there is a significant seasonal pattern. You will need at least two years of history to see if there are seasonal patterns; with just one year of data, you can't tell if a pattern is seasonal or if it has some other cause.

If you do have a seasonal pattern, then you have a couple of choices to correct for it. An ad hoc approach to dealing with seasonality is just to be aware of the seasonal trends and look for other changes in churn rate, resulting from churn-reduction efforts or changes in the business environment that are significantly bigger than the usual seasonal variation. If you are trained in statistics, you can do this rigorously by using appropriate techniques for time series analysis. Such advanced statistics is beyond the scope of this book, but see *Analysis of Financial Time Series* by Ruey S. Tsay (3rd ed., Wiley, 2010) if you are interested. There are a few ways to handle seasonality in churn rates that don't require advanced statistics, but they involve a slightly more complicated churn calculation and at least two years of data. Going into a lot of detail on these is too much to put in this book, but I can give you a few ideas here.

One way to calculate a churn rate that controls for seasonality is to make an annual churn calculation on month-to-month subscriptions but fix the problems using annual churn on monthly subscriptions. Recall that in the previous section, you learned that if you make an annual churn calculation on monthly subscriptions, you miss accounts that signed up and churned midyear. One solution is that instead of looking at all the accounts active on each date two years apart, you look at *all the accounts that were active within a year prior* of each date. The process is as follows:

1 Find all accounts active any time in year 1.
2 Find all accounts active any time in year 2.

3 Find churned accounts by comparing the two sets with an outer join.

4 Divide the lost accounts by the number in year 1.

The churn calculated that way is an annual churn rate that does not miss midyear churns and includes all seasons. If you repeat the calculation one month (or one quarter) later, the change in the churn rate reflects the difference between churn in that month (or that quarter) and the same time one year earlier. It is controlled for seasonality.

One downside of this approach is that it allows a new signup any time within a year, and the customer won't be counted as a churn. If you have many accounts that churn and sign up again later, you should stick with the regular monthly churn calculation and handle seasonality differently.

Another relatively simple way to handle seasonality with monthly churn rates is to calculate monthly churn rates every calendar month and then make averages over quarters (or a year) for comparison purposes. Rather than comparing one month's churn rate to the next, which can be influenced by seasonality, compare the average of 12 monthly churn rates from the last year to the average of 12 monthly churn rates from the previous year. Or compare the average churn rate from the last three months to the average churn rate *from the same three months one year earlier*. Then you can see if anything you have done to improve churn in the last year made a difference in the churn rate from the same quarter one year ago. Because you are comparing to the same quarter, you are controlling seasonality. You can take this approach with one month and compare one month *to the same month one year earlier*, which also controls seasonality. Also note that comparing one calendar month's churn rate to the churn rate in the same period one year earlier requires only 13 months of data, so this is probably the best option for new companies.

Summary

- Churn rates measure how many subscribers and/or how much revenue churns from a service over a period of time.
- The churn rate and retention rate are interchangeable according to the relationship retention plus churn equals 100%.
- Different versions of the churn rates can be calculated on a subscription database using SQL.
- Outer joins are used to identify churned accounts in SQL.
- The standard churn rate measures the number of account holders who cancel their subscriptions and is unaffected by upsells and down sells. The standard churn rate is most useful for subscription products where there are a few prices that are not far apart or possibly some discounts.
- Net retention includes the impact of both upsells and down sells, which makes it less useful for fighting churn, but it is a popular reporting metric.

- If all subscribers pay the same (or pay nothing), net retention equals the standard retention, and net churn equals standard churn.
- MRR churn includes the impact of down sells but not upsells and is the best metric for measuring churn when subscribers pay a wide variety of prices, as is typical for B2B products.
- For nonsubscription products, churn can be measured based on event data by defining customers as active whenever they have had an event within a recent time period. Churn is then calculated as the difference between the sets of accounts that are active on two different dates.
- Churn measured over any time period can be converted into an equivalent churn rate for any other time period.
- Churn rates are converted from one time period to another by survivor analysis on retention rates, which are then converted back to churn rates.
- To convert a churn rate, the corresponding retention rate is taken to a power to increase the time period; a root of the retention rate is used to decrease the time period.
- Churn is usually measured as a monthly rate for consumer products and an annual rate for business products.
- Problems may arise if you measure churn on a time scale that is different from the typical subscription length.
- For monthly churn rates, seasonality can be an issue when interpreting changes in the churn rate.

Measuring customers

If you are operating a product or service with repeated interactions with users or customers, then you should be collecting data about those interactions in a data warehouse. *Interactions* in this context means interactions between the user and the product, service, or platform. (It can also include interactions with other users, mediated by the platform.) It is common to refer to such interactions as *events* for short, because interactions tracked in a data warehouse invariably have a timestamp telling you when they happened.

> **DEFINITION** *Event*—Any fact about user behavior, stored in the data warehouse with a specific timestamp.

I am not going to teach you how to collect that data, but I *am* going to teach you how to put that data to good use. The first step in using raw data to fight churn is to turn the event data into a set of measurements that summarize the events and collectively produce a profile of the users' behaviors. These measurements are often called *behavioral metrics*, or just *metrics*, for short.

> **DEFINITION** *Metric*—Any summary measurement of user behavior. Metrics also have a timestamp, although they summarize behavior over more than just one point in time.

Turning related events into measurements is necessary because each event is like one tiny dot in a big picture: by itself, one event usually doesn't mean much. But while we need to zoom out from each individual interaction, we are not going to zoom out very far. Each measurement is made individually for each customer, and it is made repeatedly over their lifetime as a customer. That's because user engagement and churn are dynamic processes for each individual, and you need to watch how those metrics change over the subscriber's lifetime to understand subscriber engagement.

To teach this subject, I assume you have collected events but have not done behavioral measurements on them. If you don't have your own data, there is a simulation program in this book's downloadable code that creates artificial data for you to run the code on. See the code at www.manning.com/books/fighting-churn-with-data and https://github.com/carl24k/fight-churn/tree/master/data-generation and the detailed instructions in the README file. Run the script to install the schema (`fight-churn/data-generation/churndb.py`), and then run the simulation that generates customers, subscriptions, and events on an imaginary social network (`fight-churn/data-generation/churnsim.py`). If you already generated data to run the examples in chapter 2, you're good!

If you work with a live product or service and are already making behavioral measurements, you are going to learn some new ideas for metrics and techniques to check the quality of your data; it will not be hard to use your existing measurements in the analysis. If you work at a live service and are not collecting data yet, you will achieve an excellent understanding of what kind of data to collect. In relation to the book's overall scenario, this chapter covers calculating behavioral metrics from an event data warehouse (figure 3.1, explained in chapter 1).

This is a big chapter, and not only in terms of length: good behavioral metrics are the most important step in a successful churn analysis, and this chapter explains a lot of the pitfalls that can prevent you from getting the best results:

- In section 3.1, we start with a brief overview of the concept behind making behavioral metrics from events.
- Section 3.2 introduces a typical or minimal database schema for an event data warehouse, which is used in the SQL programs for the rest of the book.
- Beginning in section 3.3, you learn the most universally useful behavioral metrics: counts, averages, and totals measured over specific windows in time. I also

teach you some best practices regarding measuring behaviors that follow weekly cycles and timestamping metric measurements.

- In sections 3.4–3.6, you learn more practical details about how to calculate the metrics introduced in section 3.3.

Along with learning about calculating metrics, it is only appropriate that you learn to check the results by running quality assurance (QA) tests. This is necessary because customer event data in data warehouses is often unreliable. This unreliability can manifest in different ways; for example, events can be lost on the network before they

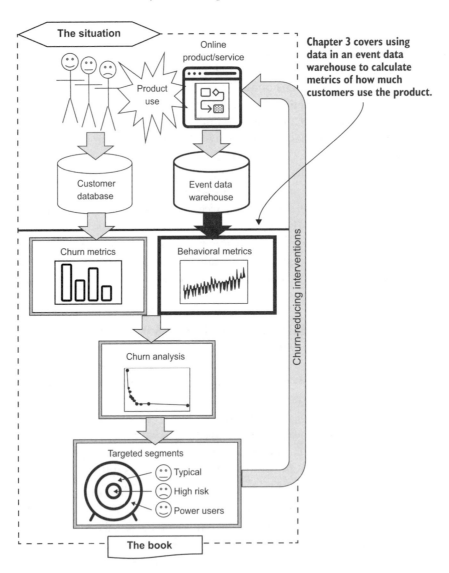

Figure 3.1   This chapter's place in the process of fighting churn with data

reach the data warehouse. In general, event data does not receive a lot of scrutiny, so the data person doing a churn analysis might be the first person to check if event data fields are correct.

- Section 3.7 introduces time-series QA tests for metrics. The QA reveals a common challenge: not all events are equally frequent, so no single time frame works well for all types of events.
- Section 3.8 shows some basic QA on the events that helps to clarify the situation as far as event frequency.
- In section 3.9, I show you how to use the event QA to solve the problem of selecting a metric time frame.

NOTE This discussion is out of order from real-world practice. Normally, you do event QA first and then calculate metrics, but I want to dive in and show you what the metrics look like before getting into the details of QA.

At the end of the chapter, we change gears:

- In section 3.10, you learn how to make an important measurement of each customer: how long they have been customers on the current subscription (or the current engagement, when there is not a subscription). This is called the customer or account *tenure* (not age) so that it is not confused with the customer's actual age.
- Section 3.11 presents a technique to take data from subscriptions and turn it into metrics that are comparable with other behavioral metrics.

Feature engineering vs. metric design

People trained in data science, machine learning, or statistics call the topic I just described *feature engineering*. The problem with the term *feature engineering* is that it is easily confused with software product features and creating such features through software engineering. Instead, I'll stick to language business users understand and call this process *metric design*.

WARNING The term *feature engineering* can be confusing to people not trained in data science, machine learning, or statistics. Avoid it when talking to your business colleagues; use *metric design* instead. This is especially true at software companies.

3.1 From events to metrics

In this section, I first introduce the concept of turning events into metrics without any code, and then I show you the SQL. Imagine you are collecting login events in your data warehouse, and you want to turn them into usable information. For each user, you have a series of events, as illustrated in the top half of figure 3.2. To start, we focus on only the series for a single event: logins. In typical online product scenarios, there are many types of events, and the events can occur at any time. For some types of events, there can even be multiple events at the same time. To find subscribers' comparable metrics, use a time period to make the measurements, as illustrated in the bottom half of figure 3.2.

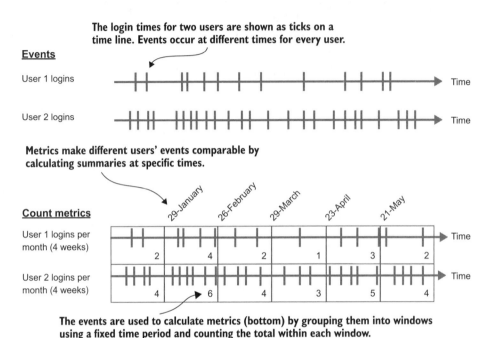

Figure 3.2   Events transformed into time-windowed metrics

A *time period* in this context means a range of time (a start time and an end time) in which to measure data. But these periods are defined *relative* to the observation time of each measurement, so a time period is usually described by its duration or length.

> **DEFINITION**   *Time period*—In an event-based metric calculation, the window of time within which events are used for the measurement. Time periods are described by their duration because the specific window for each measurement (the start and end times) is determined relative to the measurement date.

For example, a metric with a four-week period like the one in figure 3.2 makes repeated measurements within windows that are four weeks long. The metric calculation may be to count the number of events in each resulting window, or more complex measurements can be used, as described later in the chapter. I define all my metric periods as an even number of weeks; I explain why in section 3.4.1.

Also note that these metrics are calculated on the day after the period ends, so the observation of events is complete. For example, on January 29, you can calculate the number of logins per subscriber in the four weeks covering January 1–28. Then, on February 26, you can measure the number of logins for the four weeks from January 29–February 25, and so on. I return to this discussion in detail in section 3.4.2.

3.2 *Event data warehouse schema*

This chapter examines how to calculate metrics with code; but to lay the groundwork, I need to explain how events are stored in a data warehouse. There are many types of data warehouses, and I assume you can query the data warehouse with SQL. You can use a transactional SQL database as your event data warehouse as long as the data is not too big. The examples in this book were generated in Postgres (or PostgreSQL).

Table 3.1 shows the key elements of a typical event data schema. This schema is used for all the SQL code listings related to events. (See the book's downloadable code for detailed instructions on how to set up a database with this schema and populate it with simulated data.) The following is the typical minimum set of fields for this kind of table:

- `account_id`—An identifier for the account holder or user, required to track events back to the customer who created them.
- `event_type_id`—Because events generally have many types, this is the foreign key to a separate table describing the types.
- `event_time`—A timestamp, which every event must have.

Table 3.2 shows an associated event type table so the string names for events are not duplicated (for performance reasons, as is standard practice in a database or data warehouse). In summary, an event is something (the event type ID) that happens to someone (the account ID) at some time (the event time). The following additional fields can also be included in such a table but are not required:

- `event_id`—Unique identifiers for events may or may not be included in a data warehouse. It's not relevant for the analysis because there is normally no uniqueness constraint on events.
- `user_id`—A user ID can be present (in addition to an account ID), especially in services where there are multiple individuals associated with a single account.
- `event_data`—Events often have a large number of optional data fields that provide additional information about the events. These are most often numeric but can include textual information as well.

If you are familiar with data warehouses, you can see that the schema for events is pretty typical of any *fact table*, except that numeric data fields for events are optional (they are often required for some types of data warehouses).

Table 3.1   Typical event data schema

Column	Type	Notes
account_id	integer or char	
event_type_id	integer or char	Key for event_type_name
event_time	timestamp	
event_id	integer or char	Optional
user_id	integer or char	Optional
event_data_1	float or char	Optional
. . .		
event_data_n	float or char	Optional

Table 3.2   Typical event type data schema

Column	Type	Notes
event_type_name	char	Unique
event_type_id	integer or char	Key for event_type_name

3.3   *Counting events in one time period*

Figure 3.3 is a continuation of the scenario illustrated in figure 3.2: it shows the details of calculating a metric for one account and one event based on the event schema in table 3.1. Each event in the table is mapped to a corresponding time period, and the total count is the result for that period. Because the periods do not overlap, each event is counted only once. The calculation is repeated for every event and account, which would be tedious if you were planning to do this by hand or even in a spreadsheet. Fortunately, SQL offers a concise language for expressing and implementing this type of calculation.

Performing these calculations at scale involves a challenge you saw in chapter 2: this data is likely to be big. Just like calculating churn rates, we do all the work in the data warehouse with SQL, rather than extracting data and then working on it in a programming language like Python.

> **NOTE**   This is another place where you may be used to performing such computations in a procedural language, but I ask that you reserve judgment and learn what a powerful tool SQL can be for this kind of calculation.

Listing 3.1 shows the SQL to count the number of events within a single time frame (like that illustrated in figure 3.2). The main steps in the query are as follows:

1 Set the date to make the measurement, using a common table expression (CTE, introduced in chapter 2).

2   Select all the events in the time frame with the correct type.

3   Aggregate-count the events by account.

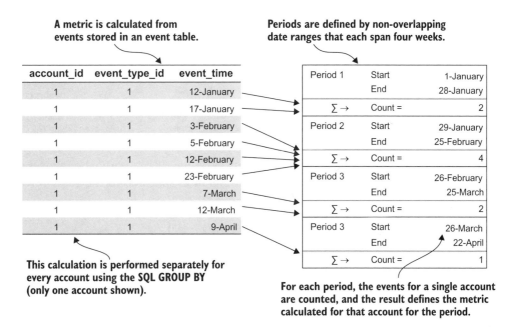

Figure 3.3   Metric calculation from an event schema

If you created the simulated social network dataset, it includes an event for users liking posts. Listing 3.1 shows the query for counting these events, and figure 3.4 illustrates the result. For each account that made any *likes* within 28 days prior to the
metric calculation rate, there is one count.

account_id	n_like_perMonth
0	1396
2	119
3	54
4	496
5	23
...	...

The first column is
the account ID, and the
second column is the
number of events in
the last 28 days.

Figure 3.4   Result of the event
count SQL (listing 3.1) on the
simulated social network dataset-
like event. Your results will differ
because the data was randomly
simulated.

Your result will not be exactly the same
because the data is randomly simulated.

Listing 3.1   Counting the number of events in a time window

```
WITH calc_date AS (
    SELECT '2020-05-06'::timestamp  AS the_date
)
SELECT account_id, COUNT(*) AS n_like_permonth
FROM event e INNER JOIN calc_date d ON
    e.event_time <= d.the_date
    AND e.event_time > d.the_date - interval '28 day'
INNER JOIN event_type t ON t.event_type_id=e.event_type_id
WHERE t.event_type_name='like'
GROUP BY account_id;
```

This CTE sets the date used to calculate the measurement.

Selects the account, the date, and the count

Using "greater than but not equal to" avoids double counting.

Sets the period for which the measurement is made

The GROUP BY aggregation yields one measurement per account.

Selects the event we are making the measurement for

Run listing 3.1 to see the result on your own data. If you have generated the default simulated dataset and set up the environment as specified in the README, you can run the listing with this command:

```
fight-churn/listings/run_churn_listing.py --chapter 3 --listing 1
```

The wrapper program prints the SQL before it connects to the database, executes the query, and prints some of the results. If you don't want to use the wrapper program, the source code for listing 3.1 can be found in fight-churn/listings/chap3 in the book's code. Note that the listing code is stored as a template with bind variables (beginning with %); you can modify the bind variables and run the query with the SQL tool of your choice. Your result will look similar to figure 3.4, but not exactly the same, because the data is randomly simulated.

If you are familiar with SQL, you might have some questions about that query: why do I use the date condition "less than or equal to" for the end of the window but "greater than and not equal to" at the end of the query? Why not use the "between" syntax? This is to avoid double-counting any events on the boundary if you make repeated measurements. A related question might be why I don't use SQL window functions to calculate the results. The reason is that SQL window functions usually operate on a fixed number of records, but the number of events within a given date range is not fixed. The boundary for the window is set by the date condition, not the number of events in the window.

3.4   *Details of metric period definitions*

Now that you know how to calculate a metric, I'll discuss choosing metric periods. These details may seem trivial, but you would be surprised how much they can impact the effectiveness of your analysis.

3.4.1   *Weekly behavioral cycles*

You are probably wondering why I have used metric measurements calculated over four-week periods and not calendar months. To understand this, you need to realize that human activities follow a weekly cycle, so it is likely that the events in your data warehouse also follow a weekly cycle. If your product is something that people use for work, then most events will occur on Monday through Friday, and Saturday and Sunday will have fewer events. On the other hand, if your product is something people use for leisure, like watching videos or playing a game, then the heaviest use will be on Friday through Sunday, and Monday through Thursday may be relatively slow.

The reason to use metrics with periods defined as an even number of weeks is that every measurement window used to make a calculation has the same number of high- and low-usage days. For example, imagine a consumer product with peak usage on the weekend. Months that have five weekends will appear to have around 20% more events than months with only four weekends. But it would be a mistake to think this represents a real increase in usage because it is an artifact of the fact that the measuring windows are not even.

> **TIP** Most human behaviors follow weekly cycles. Consequently, for metrics using a period of one month or less, it is best to measure using time windows that are multiples of seven days.

The user behavior on Klipfolio is a perfect example of weekly behavioral cycles. Klipfolio is a software as a service (SaaS) company that allows businesses to create online dashboards of their key metrics (introduced in chapter 1). The weekly cycle of business-to-business (B2B) software use is illustrated in figure 3.5, which shows the number of dashboard views per day for Klipfolio. It is obvious that usage is significantly higher on weekdays and much slower on the weekend: on average, weekdays have 40% more dashboard views than weekends.

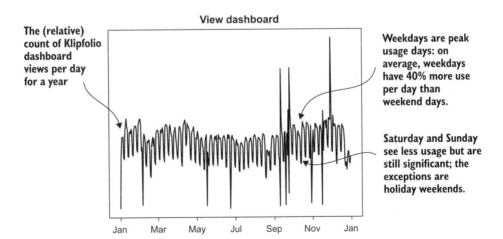

Figure 3.5 Klipfolio's total dashboard views per day

That said, note that making measurements in even numbers of weeks is important for small measurement windows: if the measurement period is more than around 12 weeks, then adding or subtracting one weekend will not make much difference. For example, for one-year measurements, there is no reason to choose 52 weeks, or 364 days, rather than 365 days.

3.4.2   *Timestamps for metric measurements*

Another important issue is how measurements are timestamped.

> **DEFINITION**   *Timestamp*—A *single* date and time to represent the metric, which is a calculation made on events in a time window.

Measurements like this need to have a timestamp representing the period they cover because you make the measurements repeatedly and analyze how they change over time. A seemingly trivial but actually subtle point is as follows. Suppose you measure the number of logins:

- You measure all events from January 1 through January 28 (inclusive).
- You make the measurement on January 29.

Which date do you timestamp that measurement with?

1 January 1
2 January 28
3 January 29
4 Some other option

Best practice is to timestamp the metric with the date/time immediately after the measurement period: in this case, January 29 at midnight for the January 1–28 measurement. This is a convention, and it may seem arbitrary, but the wrong choice leads to undesirable complications. There are a few reasons you will need to synchronize the measurements to make a snapshot of a customer at a single point in time. Making a synchronized snapshot is easiest if you timestamp at the end of the observation window because then you just select all the metrics for the same timestamp.

> **TAKEAWAY**   The best choice for the timestamp on behavioral metrics is the date and time on which the measurement of the customer would be made, assuming it was calculated in real time, at the earliest time possible. This is true even if the measurement is calculated at a later date.

The problems with the alternatives are these:

- Using the start date of the window as the timestamp causes problems if you use windows of different lengths in a single analysis. In that case, you need to calculate the synchronization date from the timestamp plus the time period.
- The time you make the measurement is not a good timestamp because it could be days or months after the fact, which introduces uncertainty.

- Using the last day (at midnight) of the measurement period as a timestamp is subtly misleading in that it implies you could observe the full period measurement when there is still one day remaining. If you timestamp the measurement 24 hours before it is complete and then need to sync the measurements with other data sources, it can introduce subtle errors.

This day-after period timestamp convention may be a bit confusing at first because many people timestamp measurements for a calendar month with the first of the month, even though the measurement is not made until the first of the next month. (It might confuse other people in your organization who are used to that way of thinking.) The same goes for using four-week periods rather than calendar months. But four-week "months" and day-after timestamping facilitate the analysis, and I recommend them as best practice.

3.5 *Making measurements at different points in time*

To understand churn, you need to compare measurements of subscriber behavior at different points in their life cycle. This requires a slightly more advanced metric calculation technique than the one you just learned.

3.5.1 *Overlapping measurement windows*

To compare customer behavioral measurements as they change over the customer life cycle, you need to repeat the metric calculation at regularly spaced points in time. However, there is a problem with the simple approach shown in figure 3.2: if you literally followed that approach, you would update the metric only once every four weeks. Four-week intervals between measurements are not very dynamic. A lot can happen in four weeks, and you might have to check on your customers' behavior more often. Figure 3.6 illustrates the solution. The answer is to repeat the four-week measurements at more frequent intervals: in this case, weekly.

As shown in figure 3.6, the resulting four-week windows overlap. You can also see that the measurement gradually tracks between the monthly measurements shown in figure 3.2. For subscriber 1, the first four-week, non-overlapping measurements are 2, 4, 2. The overlapping measurements include intermediate points where the value was 3: 2, 3, 4, 3, 2, representing the transition period.

Details of the calculation illustrated in figure 3.6 are shown in figure 3.7 for the first four periods. Because the calculation windows overlap, the fourth period has an end date that is just four weeks after the end date of the first period. Also, each event is part of the count in multiple periods. With a four-week window staggered one week apart, every event will be counted in four periods, although this fact is not apparent from the abbreviated example in figure 3.7. But as in the example calculation with non-overlapping periods (figure 3.7), each event is mapped into the time periods based on the beginning and end dates (of the periods), and the result for each period is the total count. Even more so than for the non-overlapping periods, this is not a calculation you would want to do by hand! But, remarkably, the SQL that does this

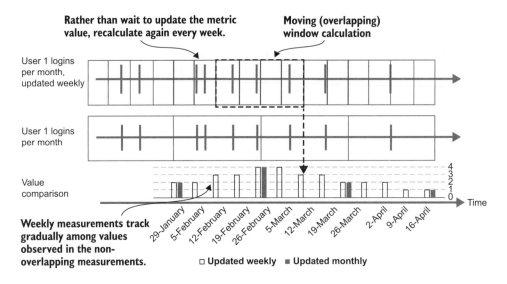

Figure 3.6   Calculating metrics with overlapping time windows

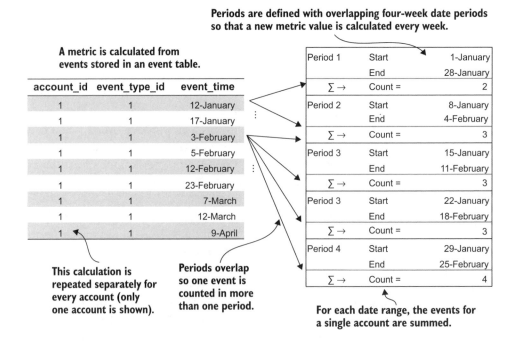

Figure 3.7   Simple metric calculation with overlapping time windows

metric calculation for overlapping periods is no more complex than for calculating non-overlapping periods.

Listing 3.2 shows the SQL that implements such measurements, and a sample result for the simulated churn dataset is shown in figure 3.8. Unlike the result of the single-day query (listing 3.1 and figure 3.4), there are now multiple results for each account, but only the first few are shown. Also, each measurement is timestamped with the time at the end of the measurement period.

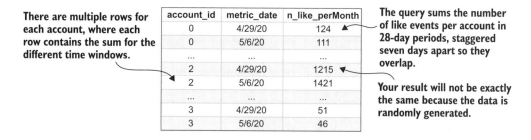

There are multiple rows for each account, where each row contains the sum for the different time windows.

account_id	metric_date	n_like_perMonth
0	4/29/20	124
0	5/6/20	111
...	...	...
2	4/29/20	1215
2	5/6/20	1421
...	...	...
3	4/29/20	51
3	5/6/20	46

The query sums the number of like events per account in 28-day periods, staggered seven days apart so they overlap.

Your result will not be exactly the same because the data is randomly generated.

Figure 3.8   Result of a multidate event count with SQL (listing 3.2) on the simulated social network dataset-like event

The main steps in listing 3.2 are basically the same as in listing 3.1, but now the SQL works on a range of dates:

1   Choose the sequence of dates to make the measurement. These dates are closer to each other than the intended period size.
2   For each measurement date, select the events within the time period associated with that measurement.
3   Aggregate-count the events by account and measurement date.

For step 1, the SQL in listing 3.2 uses the generate_series function to create a CTE containing a list of the calculation dates. With this list of metric dates included in the join with the event table, you calculate the count for every account and every measurement date by including the measurement date in both the SELECT and GROUP BY statements. As a result, the query calculates the metrics for an entire sequence of measurement dates at once.

Listing 3.2   Calculating metrics with overlapping windows

```
WITH date_vals AS (
    SELECT i::timestamp AS metric_date
    FROM generate_series('2020-01-29', '2020-04-16',
    '7 day'::interval) i
)
```

CTE for the end dates of the windows for metric calculation

Postgres function to generate a series of values

```
SELECT account_id, metric_date, COUNT(*)
    AS n_like_per_month
FROM event e INNER JOIN date_vals d
    ON e.event_time < metric_date
    AND e.event_time >= metric_date - interval '28 day'
INNER JOIN event_type t ON t.event_type_id=e.event_type_id
WHERE t.event_type_name='like'
GROUP BY account_id, metric_date
ORDER BY account_id, metric_date;
```

Events are within four weeks of the measurement date.

Both the account ID and the date are in the GROUP BY clause.

Joins on date_vals CTE to set the dates

Sorts the results for readability

Selects the account, time, and measurement

Run listing 3.2 to see the result. If you are using the simulated churn data and the Python wrapper program, run this command:

```
fight-churn/listings/run_churn_listing.py --chapter 3 --listing 2
```

The result of running listing 3.2 should be similar to figure 3.8, but not exactly the same, due to randomness in the simulation.

Alternatives to the generate_series function

In the code examples in this book, I use the Postgres function `generate_series` to create sequences of dates that are equally spaced. However, other database systems do not support this function. The same goal can be achieved by creating a regular (permanent) table and filling it with the desired date sequence in a one-time load. Also, if you search the internet for "alternatives to generate_series on *XXX*" where *XXX* is the database or data warehouse of your choice, you might find system-specific implementations. I apologize to non-Postgres users for the lack of generality, but the `generate_series` function is useful for teaching because one short line of code is all it takes.

3.5.2   *Timing metric measurements*

In this book, I generally demonstrate techniques using weekly updated measurements for the same reason mentioned in section 3.4: human behavior generally follows weekly cycles. But for products where the typical customer lifetime is very short (less than a few months), it might be necessary to update the measurements more frequently.

> **TIP**   For products where a typical customer lifetime is a few months or less, you may need to update metrics every day. But for products where a customer's typical lifetime is several months or more, it is usually adequate to calculate metrics once a week.

For products where customer lifetime is even longer, maybe many years, it might be adequate to update the measurements only once a month (or at four-week intervals).

This is a judgment call you need to make based on the dynamism of your situation; it has to do with how long it takes a typical customer to see value from your product (or fail to see value) and decide to churn (or not). In any event, all the same analytic techniques apply, just on different time scales. Most people overestimate the need for real-time (frequent) updates to measurements like these. Usually, retention and churn is a war waged over weeks, months, or years; it is not common for it to come down to rapid up-to-the-minute information and interventions.

Another important issue is when to make your measurements. As mentioned previously, consumer products are usually used most heavily on the weekends, while business products are used most heavily during the week. So, it is usually best to make consumer product measurements at the beginning of the week on Monday or midnight Tuesday, so they capture the most recent weekend's activity. For business products, it is best to measure on the weekend, either Saturday or Sunday, so the measurement reflects the most recent complete work week.

> **TIP** Measure products used for entertainment once a week on Monday or Tuesday at midnight to capture the entire previous weekend's activity. Measure products used for work on Friday or Saturday at midnight to capture the entire previous five-day work week.

3.5.3 Saving metric measurements

Looking at listing 3.2 and the result of the query in figure 3.8, you might be thinking this type of measurement could produce a lot of data. No problem! You have a data warehouse, right? Metric calculations should be inserted back into the data warehouse for storage until later analysis. A typical schema for storing metrics is illustrated in table 3.3. The SQL code listings related to metrics use this schema. (See the book's code for detailed instructions on how to set up a database with this schema and populate it with simulated data.) The following are the typical fields:

- `account_id`—An identifier for the account holder or user. Account IDs are required to track metrics back to the customers who created them. This is the first part of the composite primary key.
- `metric_name_id`—Metrics generally have many types, and there is typically a foreign key to a separate table describing the types. This is the second part of the composite primary key.
- `metric_time`—Every metric must have a timestamp, as described in section 3.5.1. This is the third and final part of the composite primary key.
- `value`—A numeric value for the metric.
- `user_id`—In addition to account IDs, user IDs may be present in services where multiple individuals are associated with a single account.

There is also an associated metric name table (shown in table 3.4) so that the string names of the metrics are not duplicated (for performance reasons, as is standard practice in a database or data warehouse). The schema for metrics is similar to the schema for events (table 3.1), which makes sense because both are *fact tables* in a data warehouse.

One important difference between metrics and events is that metrics should have a *composite primary key* consisting of the `account_id`, `metric_name_id`, and `metric_time` fields. That means the combination of the account, the metric, and the time of measurement must be unique: only one measurement for each account at any given time. Another difference between the metric and event schemas is that while an event can have no data fields or an arbitrary assortment of data fields associated with each action, a metric always has exactly one data field: the metric value.

Table 3.3   Typical metric data schema

Column	Type	Notes
account_id	integer or char	Composite primary key 1
metric_name_id	integer or char	Composite primary key 2; foreign key for metric_name
metric_time	timestamp	Composite primary key 3
value	float	
user_id	integer or char	Optional

If your data warehouse supports inserting `SELECT` statement results directly back into the data warehouse, then saving the metric results is easy, as illustrated in listing 3.3. The code in listing 3.3 is just the same as that in listing 3.2 but with the `INSERT` keyword that turns it into an SQL `INSERT` statement. If your database does not support `INSERT SELECT` statements, then the normal practice is to save the result from a query like listing 3.2 in a delimited (comma-separated values) text file and then load that back into the data warehouse using whatever mechanism the data warehouse provides.

Table 3.4   Associated metric name data schema

Column	Type	Notes
metric_name	char	Unique
metric_name_id	integer or char	Key for metric_name

Listing 3.3   Inserting metric calculations into the data warehouse

This CTE contains the
dates for the calculation.

```
WITH date_vals AS (
    SELECT i::timestamp AS metric_date
    FROM generate_series('2020-01-29', '2020-04-16', '7 day'::interval) i
)
INSERT INTO metric
    (account_id,metric_time,metric_name_id,metric_value)
```

Inserts the result of
the SELECT into the
metric table

```
SELECT account_id, metric_date, 0,
    COUNT(*) AS metric_value
FROM event e INNER JOIN date_vals d
    ON e.event_time < metric_date
    AND e.event_time >= metric_date - interval '28 day'
INNER JOIN event_type t ON t.event_type_id=e.event_type_id
WHERE t.event_type_name='post'
GROUP BY account_id, metric_date;
```

> **Includes the ID for the metric, which we assume is 0**
>
> **The rest of the SELECT statement is the same as listing 3.2.**

Run listing 3.3 and see that it writes to your own database schema. If you are using the simulated data and the Python wrapper program, use the command

```
fight-churn/listings/run_churn_listing.py --chapter 3 --listing 3
```

Note that there is no output other than the line printed by the Python wrapper program. The result is that data is saved in the database. You should select the result from the database with a query against the metric table: for example, SELECT * FROM metric limit 10;. The result of such a query should look like the sample in figure 3.8.

Remember that you can run this listing only once, unless you change the configuration or clean the results out of the database. After you have inserted results for one metric for particular accounts on particular dates, you can't reinsert new results for the same accounts and dates. If you insert values for a new metric, you also need to make a *one-time* insert into the metric name table (table 3.4). This statement is short and well known to anyone with basic SQL knowledge, but sample code is shown in listing 3.4 for the sake of completeness.

If you inserted a metric with listing 3.3, you must also insert the name by running listing 3.4 to run later listings in this chapter. Run listing 3.4 using the Python wrapper program and the parameter --listing 4, or make an equivalent insert through an SQL tool of your choice. Note that you should never insert the same metric name or ID twice. (In a relational database, a key constraint should prevent this. The best practice in a relational database is to insert the metric name first and use a foreign key constraint on the metric table to prevent loading metrics with no name.)

Listing 3.4 Inserting a metric name into the data warehouse

```
INSERT INTO metric_name ('like_permonth',0) ON CONFLICT DO NOTHING;
```

Before moving on, I want to call your attention to the fact that the metric calculation in listing 3.3 does not insert zeros for accounts with no events. This is a natural product of the inner join on events, and you might not have paid attention to it. It is not much more difficult to define a count metric that produces zeros for accounts with no events, but storing zero-count metrics scales badly when the number of accounts is large, and events can be rare. You could even end up storing mostly zeros! The approach I take is to not store the zeros on counts in the data warehouse; then, during the analysis phase (beginning in the next chapter), I generate zeros when needed to analyze accounts with no events.

3.5.4   *Saving metrics for the simulation examples*

By running listings 3.3 and 3.4, you should have inserted one event count metric for the number of likes into the database and a name in the metric_name table: likes _permonth. There are seven more events in the simulated social network dataset: dis-like, post, new friend, unfriend, adview, message, and reply. The metrics on these events are used for examples in the rest of this chapter and the book, so you should insert them into your own database before moving on. To make it easy to do, the list-ing wrapper program includes the required alternative versions of listings 3.3 and 3.4. To run them, add the --version flag and a list of version numbers to the execution command. Also, you can run listings 3.3 and 3.4 together by listing both numbers after the --listing flag. To run listings 3.3 and 3.4 and insert the next seven count metrics for the simulation, use this command with the wrapper script:

```
fight-churn/listings/run_churn_listing.py --chap 3 --listing 3 4
    --version 2 3 4 5 6 7 8
```

To insert so many metrics will take at least 10 minutes on most systems, so this is a good time to take a coffee break. (You might want to run just one first, to see how long it takes on your system.) Note that the prior runs of listings 3.3 and 3.4 were consid-ered version 1, so the additional metrics start at version 2. More instructions for run-ning the listings are in the README file at the root of the GitHub repository.

3.6   *Measuring totals and averages of event properties*

So far, we've looked only at metrics that are simple counts of events; but when events have data in additional fields, you will probably want to summarize that data in the metric. The most typical case is when an event has a numeric value associated with it. Some of the most typical cases are as follows:

- The event has a duration in time such as the length of a session or playback of some media.
- The event has a monetary value such as a retail purchase or an overage charge.

In such scenarios, the most common metrics are one of these:

- The total value of all the events
- The average value per event

Either one of these (and many others) can be calculated with similar SQL, shown in listing 3.5 for the case of a total, assuming the events have a field called time_spent. The metric represents the total time each user spends in this type of session during a four-week period. The steps in the metric calculation are as follows:

1. Choose the sequence of dates to make the measurement.
2. For each measurement date, select the events within the time window associ-ated with that measurement.
3. Sum the time-spent field from the events grouped by account and measure-ment date.

The SQL is almost identical to listing 3.2 for the event count metric. The only difference is in the SELECT statement, where rather than counting the number of events with the COUNT(*) aggregate function, the SQL sums the total of the time_spent field with the aggregate function SUM(time_spent).

Versature (introduced in chapter 1) is a provider of unified telecommunication services for businesses. As a unified communications provider, one of its most important events is voice calls that have a duration stored in a field attached to each event. A few lines of example output from running listing 3.5 on Versature's local-call event are shown in figure 3.9. The result in figure 3.9 appears similar to the output of count metrics in figure 3.8, but the metric value is not the count of events in the time window: it is the total of the time-spent quantity field in those events.

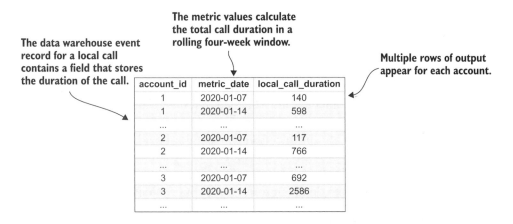

Figure 3.9   Result of total duration SQL listing 3.5 for Versature's local-call event

At the time of this writing, the default simulated data does not include event properties, so you can't run this on simulated data out of the box. That said, the simulation code can be extended to include event properties. I encourage you to do so and then make a pull request to share your work. Although you cannot run listing 3.5 on the simulation, it is provided as an example to use with your own data that includes event properties.

Listing 3.5   Measuring a sum of an event property

```
WITH date_vals AS (                          ⊲─┤ This CTE contains the
    SELECT i::timestamp AS metric_date           dates for the calculation.
    FROM generate_series('2020-01-08', '2020-12-31', '7 day'::interval) i
)
SELECT account_id, metric_date::date,
```

```
          SUM(duration) AS local_call_duration
  FROM event e INNER JOIN date_vals d
      ON e.event_time < metric_date
      AND e.event_time >= metric_date - interval '28 day'
  INNER JOIN event_type t ON t.event_type_id=e.event_type_id
  WHERE t.event_type_name='call'
  GROUP BY account_id, metric_date
  ORDER BY account_id, metric_date;
```

The date criterion is the same as in listing 3.2.

Otherwise the SELECT statement is the same as for the count metric.

Assumes the event has a duration data field, and SUMs over events

3.7　*Metric quality assurance*

Now that you've learned how to calculate a few metrics, I need to take a step back and teach you some basic techniques to check the results. In the previous sections, I have shown you only a few examples of the output results, but spot-checking a few lines of results is not an adequate method for assuring the quality of behavioral metrics. In case you didn't catch the last sentence, let me repeat.

> **WARNING**　Spot-checking a few rows of results is not an adequate method of assuring the quality of behavioral metrics.

Why? You can see from a few lines of code that the formula is correct, right? But your concern is not just the correctness of the code, as in an ordinary programming project. Your concern is also problems like missing or bad data in some accounts but not others, which you would miss by just spot-checking a few rows. There are many ways to assure the quality of behavioral metrics, and I will present a few right here, along with suggestions for what to do about some common problems.

3.7.1　*Testing how metrics change over time*

One important way to check metrics for problems is to look at how the results change over time. This can be done with an aggregate query that selects the count, average, minimum, and maximum separately for each date. This doesn't tell you everything about the values of the metric, but it should alert you to any major issues because such problems usually result in unusual movements in one of these summary statistics. An example of a plot of this result is shown in figure 3.10, which was created for the like_per_month metric from the simulated social network. The random simulation data shows less variability than a real churn dataset, so I'll show you real examples from case studies after a quick look at the code in listings 3.6 and 3.7. As you will see, one listing is a SQL SELECT statement to get the data from the database, and the other is a short Python listing to make the plot.

Listing 3.6 shows a query to select the count and average value of one metric over the entire range of dates calculated. Note that listing 3.6 takes a slightly indirect approach:

1　Create a CTE of the dates to check.
2　Create a CTE of the metric being tested.
3　Use an outer join to calculate the result.

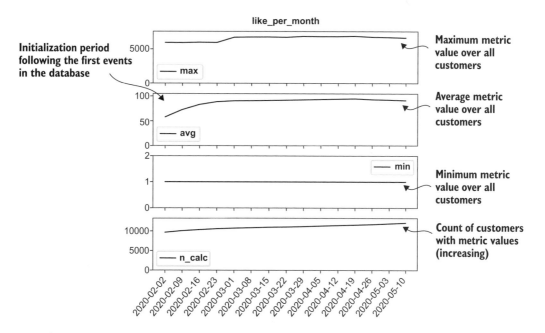

Figure 3.10   Metric quality assurance using time-series statistics

It might seem like there is a simpler alternative, which is to make a single aggregate SELECT statement on the metric table, grouping by the metric_time column. The reason for the indirect approach is that it gives a result even for days when no metrics were calculated: for a date with no metrics, the result is null for the average and zero for the count. Rows like that in the result make it easy to detect days when no metrics at all were calculated. In contrast, if an aggregate query were made on the metric table alone, there would be no result at all for days when there were no metrics. When missing days don't produce rows in the result, it is easy to miss days when no metrics were calculated.

> **TIP**   When you quality-check metric results, always use methods that make it obvious when results are not produced in addition to when bad results are produced. That means picking the dates to check independently from the data being checked.

Run listing 3.6 on the simulated data using the Python wrapper program with these arguments:

```
--chapter 3 --listing 6
```

Listing 3.6   Measuring the average, min, max, and count of a metric over time

```
WITH
date_range AS (
```
This CTE contains the
dates for the calculation.

```
        SELECT i::timestamp AS calc_date
        FROM generate_series('2020-04-01', '2020-05-06', '7 day'::interval) i
), the_metric AS (
        SELECT * FROM metric m
        INNER JOIN metric_name n ON m.metric_name_id = n.metric_name_id
        WHERE n.metric_name = 'like_per_month'
)
SELECT calc_date,  AVG(metric_value), COUNT(the_metric.*) AS n_calc,
        MIN(metric_value), MAX(metric_value)
FROM date_range LEFT OUTER JOIN the_metric
    ON calc_date=metric_time
GROUP BY calc_date
ORDER BY calc_date
```

Selects the average and number calculated with aggregate functions

Left outer join so the query has a result for every day

Orders by calc_date to make the result more readable

Groups by calc_date

Selects the metrics into a CTE for the final SELECT

The code to make the metric QA plot in figure 3.10 is in listing 3.7. To begin, listing 3.7 loads the result of the query (listing 3.6) into a Pandas `DataFrame`. After that, the listing uses the `matplotlib.pyplot` package to draw and save the plot. Because there are four nearly identical subplots, a helper function is used to make each one.

Listing 3.7   Plotting the metric QA stats over time

```
import pandas as pd
import matplotlib.pyplot as plt
from math import ceil

def metric_qa_plot(qa_data_path, metric_name,**kwargs):
    metric_data_path = qa_data_path + '_'
        + metric_name + '.csv'
    qa_data_df=pd.read_csv(metric_data_path)
    plt.figure(figsize=(6, 6))
    qa_subplot(qa_data_df,'max',1,None)
    qa_subplot(qa_data_df,'avg',2,'--')
    qa_subplot(qa_data_df,'min',3,'-.')
    qa_subplot(qa_data_df,'n_calc',4,':')
    plt.title(metric_name)
    plt.gca().figure.autofmt_xdate()

    save_to_path=metric_data_path.replace('.csv','.png')
    print('Saving metric qa plot to ' + save_to_path)
    plt.savefig(save_to_path)
    plt.close()

def qa_subplot(qa_data_df, field, number, linestyle):
    plt.subplot(4, 1, number)
    plt.plot('calc_date', field, data=qa_data_df, marker='',
        linestyle=linestyle, color='black', linewidth=2, label=field)
    plt.ylim(0, ceil(1.1 * qa_data_df[field].dropna().max()))
    plt.legend()
```

Takes kwargs for default arguments from the SQL listings

Loads the data file into a DataFrame

Opens a figure

This is the file saved by listing 3.6.

Uses the helper function to make subplots

Annotates the plots

Saves the plots

Note that you run the Python listing the same way as the SQL listings. To run listing 3.7, use the following command to the Python wrapper program:

```
fight-churn/listings/run_churn_listing.py --chap 3 --listing 7
```

The program makes a printout showing the location of the figure it saved. For example:

```
Saving metric qa plot to ../../../fight-churn-output/socialnet7/
socialnet7_metric_stats_over_time_like_per_month.png
```

It should be equivalent to figure 3.10. If you want to run the QA on the other metrics, there are other prepared versions of the command configuration for you to use. First, use this command to extract the data for all the metrics:

```
run_churn_listing.py --chap 3 --listing 6 --version 2 3 4 5 6 7 8
```

The following command makes the plots for the other metrics:

```
run_churn_listing.py --chap 3 --listing 7 --version 2 3 4 5 6 7 8
```

3.7.2 *Metric quality assurance (QA) case studies*

Figure 3.11 illustrates the result of running the metric QA query shown in listing 3.6 on one of the Klipfolio application metrics: the count of Klip overlay events per month (when a user has applied a layer over a Klip). Figure 3.11 shows that for real metrics, the results for the average and maximum aren't as smooth as for the simulation.

Figure 3.12 illustrates one example of a QA result when something is wrong: missing data was simulated by deleting one month of data for an event. (For an explanation of a regular metric QA, see figure 3.11.) Broadly (introduced in chapter 1) is a mobile-first communications platform that ensures businesses looks great online. A customer-promoter event occurs when a customer writes a positive review, and customer-promoters per month is an important metric of customer success for the product. Normally, the average and number calculated for the metric are mildly variable over the year, but when data is missing, both of these QA measurements fall. They continue to fall until the metric calculation window passes the period of missing data. The maximum value of the metric is normally more varied, but in this case, the fall due to the missing data is even greater.

When data for an event is missing, the maximum, average, and number calculated for a metric all decline. If the missing period were longer, those values would reach zero when there are no events in the metric measurement window; as it is, the period used to calculate the metric is longer than the period of the missing data, so the metrics do not all go to zero.

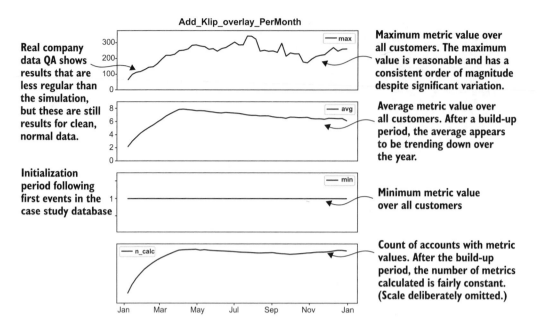

Real company data QA shows results that are less regular than the simulation, but these are still results for clean, normal data.

Maximum metric value over all customers. The maximum value is reasonable and has a consistent order of magnitude despite significant variation.

Average metric value over all customers. After a build-up period, the average appears to be trending down over the year.

Initialization period following first events in the case study database

Minimum metric value over all customers

Count of accounts with metric values. After the build-up period, the number of metrics calculated is fairly constant. (Scale deliberately omitted.)

Figure 3.11   Results of a time-series QA on a healthy metric for Klipfolio

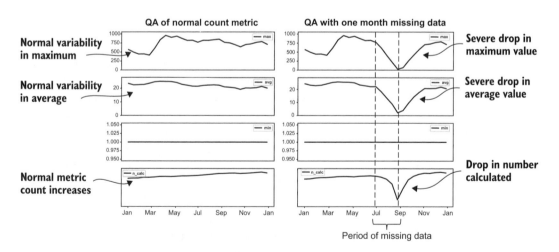

Normal variability in maximum

Normal variability in average

Severe drop in maximum value

Severe drop in average value

Normal metric count increases

Drop in number calculated

Period of missing data

Figure 3.12   Results of a time-series QA on a metric with missing event data for Broadly

Figure 3.13 illustrates a second example of a QA result for Versature, where something is actually wrong: extreme values were inserted into an event property field. As mentioned earlier, a local-call event is logged in the database when a customer places a local call, and the total local-call time summed over a three-month period is an important metric for Versature's accounts. Normally, the average and maximum for the metric are pretty constant over the year, with an increase during the end of the year. But when there are extreme values in the duration field, both QA measurements jump. The impact of the bad data is greatest in the maximum values and more muted in the average. The impact on the average value could almost be mistaken for normal variability, except for the sudden and discontinuous nature of the change. The extreme field values have no impact on either the number calculated or the minimum values. If the extreme values were negative, then the impact would show up as a minimum rather than a maximum value.

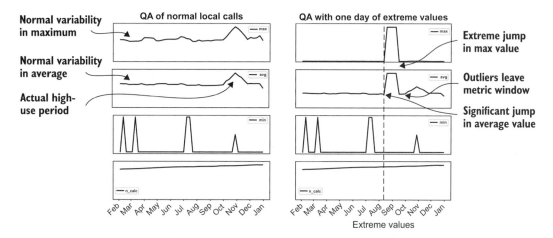

Figure 3.13   Example results of time-series QA on a metric with extreme values for Versature

Figure 3.13 illustrates the impact of erroneous extreme values on a metric calculation by showing the QA result (on the left) before and after several extreme amounts in the local-call duration data are inserted into the event database (on the right). When there are extreme (positive) values in an event data field, the biggest impact is on the maximum value, and there is more of a muted impact on the average value. If the extreme outliers were negative, the impact would be on the minimum value, which is unaffected in this case. The jump in the metric values lasts as long as the outliers are in the metric calculation window.

3.7.3   *Checking how many accounts receive metrics*

Another important question for QA is what *percentage* of the total population of active accounts has each metric. Listing 3.6 looks at the number of accounts with the metric over time, which can show temporal anomalies, but it would not detect an error where some accounts *never* have events for a metric. Checking the fraction of customers that receive a metric value and seeing whether it is lower or higher than you expect is an important test.

The SQL in listing 3.8 calculates what percentage of all active accounts received a result for each metric in a given time range. The average, minimum, and maximum values are also calculated. An example of the result for running listing 3.8 for the simulated social network is shown in figure 3.14. Most metrics cover nearly all accounts (90%+), except for unfriend_permonth, which only 59% of accounts have received. Does that seem correct, or is it more likely a data problem? It might be correct because you expect most people to post and view ads every day but not to unfriend people frequently.

metric_name	count_with _metric	n_account	pcnt_with _metric	avg_ value	min_ value	max_ value	earliest_ metric	last_ metric
account_tenure	13714	13747	100%	58.86	0	130	2/2/20	5/10/20
adview_per_month	13684	13747	100%	175.75	1	9545	2/2/20	5/10/20
dislike_per_month	13659	13747	99%	75.38	1	5403	2/2/20	5/10/20
like_per_month	13693	13747	100%	411.11	1	30401	2/2/20	5/10/20
message_per_month	13683	13747	100%	224.71	1	18009	2/2/20	5/10/20
newfriend_per_month	13366	13747	97%	12.69	1	271	2/2/20	5/10/20
post_per_month	13686	13747	100%	184.40	1	8663	2/2/20	5/10/20
reply_per_month	13598	13747	99%	75.82	1	6820	2/2/20	5/10/20
unfriend_per_month	8109	13747	59%	1.16	1	5	2/2/20	5/10/20

Almost all metrics were calculated for all accounts, but only 59% of accounts had the metric for unfriend per month.

Other summary stats are shown for QA purposes.

Figure 3.14   Result of counting the percent of accounts with a metric (listing 3.8) for the simulated dataset

The steps in calculating the percentage of accounts with the metric are as follows:

1. Pick a time frame. The query makes one overall measurement for this window (not a day-by-day calculation like listing 3.6).
2. Count the number of accounts that had active subscriptions in the time window.
3. Count the number of accounts that had each type of metric in the time window.
4. Calculate the percent of accounts that had each type of metric by dividing the result of step 3 by the result of step 2.
5. Measure other statistics of the metrics in the time window.

The SQL in listing 3.8 uses two common table expressions (CTEs):

- `date_range`—Sets the start and end date for the calculation
- `account_count`—Calculates the total number of accounts active within the time frame

The final result is calculated by an aggregation to count the number of accounts with events and divide that by the result of the `account_count` CTE to get the percentage.

Listing 3.8 Measuring the percent of accounts with metrics (metric coverage)

```
WITH date_range AS (                          ← This CTE sets the start and end for the QA.
    SELECT  '2020-04-01'::timestamp AS start_date,
        '2020-05-06'::timestamp AS end_date
), account_count AS (                          ← This CTE counts the number of accounts.
    SELECT COUNT(distinct account_id) AS n_account    ← Counts the number of accounts with subscriptions
    FROM subscription s INNER JOIN date_range d ON
    s.start_date <= d.end_date                 ← Selects all accounts that were active
    and (s.end_date >= d.start_date
        or s.end_date is null)                 ←
)
SELECT metric_name,
    COUNT(distinct m.account_id) AS count_with_metric,    ← Counts the number of accounts that had values for the metric
    n_account AS n_account,
    (COUNT(distinct m.account_id))::float/n_account::float
        AS pcnt_with_metric,                   ← Divides the count of the metric by the count of subscribers
    AVG(metric_value) AS avg_value,
    MIN(metric_value) AS min_value,            ← The standard aggregate function for the min
    MAX(metric_value) AS max_value,            ← The standard aggregate function for the max
    MIN(metric_time)  AS earliest_metric,
    MAX(metric_time) AS last_metric
FROM metric m CROSS JOIN account_count
INNER JOIN date_range ON                       ← Limits to the time period specified by the date-range CTE
    metric_time >= start_date
    and metric_time <= end_date
INNER JOIN metric_name  n ON m.metric_name_id = n.metric_name_id
INNER JOIN subscription s
    ON s.account_id = m.account_id             ← Sets a join on subscriptions
    AND s.start_date <= m.metric_time
    AND (s.end_date >= m.metric_time or s.end_date is null)
GROUP BY metric_name,n_account
ORDER BY metric_name;
```

From the account _count CTE → `n_account AS n_account,`

The standard aggregate function for the average → `AVG(metric_value) AS avg_value,`

→ `FROM metric m CROSS JOIN account_count`

Cross-join that duplicates the account count on every row

Run listing 3.8 to confirm the result and check that all your metrics have calculated properly. If you are using the Python wrapper program, run it with the arguments `--chapter 3 --listing 8`. The result is saved in a CSV file and should look similar to figure 3.14.

3.8   *Event QA*

In the last section, I showed you how to QA metrics and the percentage of accounts with a metric, but what about the events? If you check the events first, you have a better idea of what you are going to get with the metrics, and it might even change the way you decide to calculate the metrics. (I show some techniques to do this in the next section.) You've seen how to calculate a few metrics, but I am teaching this out of order from the way you would do it in practice.

> **TIP**   Spend some time checking the quality of your event data before you dive into calculating metrics. This book teaches the steps in a mixed-up order to show you the end result first. The correct order is (1) event QA (this section), (2) calculate metrics (sections 3.5 and 3.6), and (3) metric QA (section 3.7).

3.8.1   *Checking how events change over time*

Figure 3.15 demonstrates a simple time-series summary QA on an event: counting the total number of events per day over all accounts. You already saw that most real events follow weekly cycles (figure 3.5), and the simulation was designed to reproduce that kind of behavior. In a moment, I'll show you the results from more case studies, but first let's look at the code that produces such figures (listing 3.9).

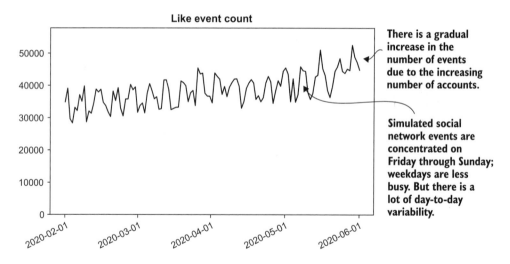

Figure 3.15   Result of counting like events per day (listing 3.9) on the simulated dataset

Listing 3.9 takes advantage of the techniques you saw in earlier sections. A CTE with a sequence of generated dates (described in section 3.4) is used in an outer join with event data to ensure that every date has a result from the QA query, even if there are no events.

Listing 3.9 QA check of events per day

Casts event times to dates ─────┐

This CTE contains the dates for the calculation.

```
WITH
date_range AS (
    SELECT i::timestamp AS calc_date
    FROM generate_series('2020-01-01', '2020-12-31', '1 day'::interval) i
)
SELECT event_time::date AS event_date,
    COUNT(*) AS n_event
    /*, SUM(optional_field) AS total _field */
FROM date_range LEFT OUTER JOIN event e
    ON calc_date=event_time::date
INNER JOIN event_type t ON t.event_type_id=e.event_type_id
WHERE t.event_type_name='like'
GROUP BY event_date
ORDER BY event_date
```

Sums the number of events

If the events have numeric properties, sums the properties

Selects the event that is being checked

A left join on the date series ensures a result for every date.

Groups by calculation date

Run listing 3.9 on the simulated dataset to confirm that it works with your data. Doing so makes a CSV file with one event count per row. The program prints a line saying what it has done:

```
Saving: ../../../fight-churn-output/socialnet7/socialnet7_events_per_day_like.csv
```

The script to make the plot (like figure 3.15) is shown in listing 3.10. This listing uses a Pandas `DataFrame` to load the data and a standard `matplotlib.pyplot` plot. To make the dates on the x-axis readable, a filter is created using a lambda that selects dates ending in 01, which are the first of each month (2020-02-01, 2020-03-01, etc.). That list of filtered dates is passed to the `matplotlib.pyplot` `xticks` function.

Listing 3.10 Plotting the number of events per day

```python
import pandas as pd
import matplotlib.pyplot as plt
from math import ceil

def event_count_plot(qa_data_path, event_name,**kwargs):
    event_data_path = qa_data_path +
        '_' + event_name + '.csv'
    qa_data_df=pd.read_csv(event_data_path)
    plt.figure(figsize=(6, 4))
    plt.plot('event_date', 'n_event', data=qa_data_df,
        marker='', color='black', linewidth=2)
    plt.ylim(0,
        ceil(1.1*qa_data_df['n_event'].dropna().max()))
    plt.title('{} event count'.format(event_name))
    plt.gca().figure.autofmt_xdate()
    plt.xticks(list(filter(lambda x:x.endswith(("01")),
        qa_data_df['event_date'].tolist())))
```

Reads the data into a DataFrame

The path to the data saved by listing 3.9

Plots the number of events vs. the date

Sets a y-axis limit based on the maximum

Rotates the x-axis date labels

Makes a list of first-of-month dates for x-axis labels

```
plt.tight_layout()
plt.savefig(event_data_path.replace('.csv',
    '_' + event_name + '_event_qa.png'))
plt.close()
```

◁———— **Ensures that all axis labels are visible**

◁———— **Saves the result**

If you are using the Python wrapper program, you can run listings 3.9 and 3.10 together to create the data and the plot with one command:

```
fight-churn/listings/run_churn_listing.py --chap 3 --listing 9 10
```

The program prints the location of the figure it saved; it should be equivalent to figure 3.10. If you want to run the QA on the other metrics, there are other prepared versions of the command configuration for you to use. First use this command to create the counts for all of the events:

```
run_churn_listing.py --chap 3 --listing 9 --version 2 3 4 5 6 7 8
```

Note that this might take a little longer than the QA on the metrics because it has to aggregate events for every day. The following commands will make the plots for the other metrics:

```
run_churn_listing.py --chap 3 --listing 10 --version 2 3 4 5 6 7 8
```

To illustrate how you can discover missing events, figure 3.16 shows a real case study (from Broadly) of the output from running the QA query in listing 3.9 on the true customer-promoter events (when a customer writes a positive review) and also when one month of events was deliberately deleted (the same deletions used in figure 3.12). It is usually easy to notice such problems if you take the time to look, although it can

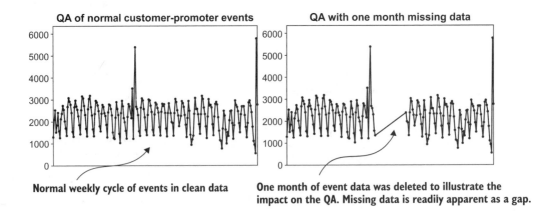

Figure 3.16   Counting events per day for Broadly customer-promoter events

be more of a challenge to recognize the problem if data is missing for a short amount of time.

To illustrate how you can discover outlier values in an event field, figure 3.17 shows a second example (for Versature) of the output of running the QA query in listing 3.9 with data in its true state and also after extreme values were deliberately added. These are the same changes used to make the example in figure 3.13. A local-call event is logged in the database when a customer places a local call, and the database has a field that stores the duration of the call. Extreme values in an event field don't affect the count of events but are usually obvious if you plot the sum of the event field (the total call duration) or some other aggregate function of the event field.

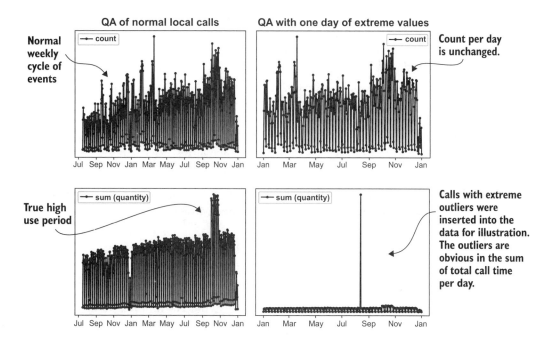

Figure 3.17 QA of events per day for Versature local calls

3.8.2 Checking events per account

Another important check on events is to look at the overall number of events and how many there are per account. You should do this to assess the overall number and type of events. This is similar to checking the percent of accounts with metrics, as shown in the previous section.

An example of the output of this check is shown in figure 3.18 for the social network simulation. The figure shows that the average account has around 75 like events per month but fewer than one unfriend event. This explains why there were fewer accounts with unfriend-per-month metrics (figure 3.13). Only around one-third of the accounts had a nonzero value for the metric, which is consistent with the events per account per month.

event_type_name	n_event	n_account	events_per _account	n_months	events_per _account_ per_month	
like	3,586,812	13,723	261.4	3.5	74.7	**Typical accounts have dozens of these events per month.**
message	2,484,742	13,723	181.1	3.5	51.7	
post	1,535,130	13,723	111.9	3.5	32.0	
adview	1,522,256	13,723	110.9	3.5	31.7	**Typical accounts have less than one unfriend per month.**
reply	915,902	13,723	66.7	3.5	19.1	
dislike	598,919	13,723	43.6	3.5	12.5	
newfriend	256,631	13,723	18.7	3.5	5.3	
unfriend	11,747	13,723	0.9	3.5	0.2	

Figure 3.18   Result of counting events per account per month with listing 3.11 for the simulated social network

Listing 3.11 contains the SQL to calculate the number of events per account and convert it into a count per month. The steps in the calculation are as follows:

1 Pick a time window.
2 Count the number of accounts that had active subscriptions in the time window.
3 Count the total number of events in the time window.
4 Divide the total number of events twice:
   a Divide the total number of events by the number of accounts.
   b Divide the total number of events by the number of months that were measured.

This procedure results in an average count of events per account per month. The start of the calculation is the same as that in listing 3.8, which calculated metrics per account. The only new trick here is in the final SELECT statement that makes the measurement: it also selects the number of months in the time frame and divides the result by that.

Listing 3.11   Measuring the average number of events per account

```
WITH                                    This CTE sets the start
date_range AS (                         and end date for the QA.
    SELECT  '2020-01-01'::timestamp AS start_date,
        '2020-12-31'::timestamp AS end_date       This CTE determines the
), account_count AS (                             number of accounts.
    SELECT COUNT(distinct account_id) AS n_account
    FROM subscription s INNER JOIN date_range d ON
    s.start_date <= d.end_date
```

```
                AND (s.end_date >= d.start_date or s.end_date is null)
        )
        SELECT event_type_name,
            COUNT(*) AS n_event,
            n_account AS n_account,
            COUNT(*)::float/n_account::float
                AS events_per_account,
            extract(days FROM end_date-start_date)::float/28
                AS n_months,
            (COUNT(*)::float/n_account::float)/
                (extract(days FROM end_date-start_date)::float/28.0)
                    AS events_per_account_per_month
        FROM event e cross join account_count
        INNER JOIN event_type t ON t.event_type_id=e.event_type_id
        INNER JOIN date_range ON
            event_time >= start_date
            AND event_time <= end_date
        GROUP BY e.event_type_id,n_account,end_date,
            start_date, event_type_name
        ORDER BY events_per_account_per_month desc;
```

Divides events by accounts to get events per account

Counts the total number of events

Number of accounts from the account_count CTE

Divides the number of days to get the count of four-week months

Divides the events per account by the number of months

Limits the measurement to the chosen date range

GROUP BY that includes all nonaggregated terms in the SELECT

Cross join that duplicates the account count on every row

Orders events so the most common appear at the top of the list

This section is about QA, which means checking for problems; but in this case, considering the number of unfriend events from the example, it seems there is no problem. Maybe it's just that people don't unfriend their friends that much.

When you see a low number of events per account per month, you need to use your knowledge of the product to know whether it is a problem. There is no absolute standard across all products, because there are many products that should see near-constant user interaction, while there are others where you would expect interactions with the product only a few times a year. If you don't have the expertise to judge whether the number of events per account is low or high, then you need to talk to other people in your organization and get them to help. That might not be advice that some data people want to hear, so let me repeat it.

TIP If your knowledge of the business is not good enough to judge whether the observed counts of events per month is reasonable, then you must get help from someone in your organization who does. Do this before you spend a lot of time calculating behavioral metrics and doing churn analysis.

A table like that in figure 3.18 is usually sufficient to communicate this information to the business. If there are a lot of events, you should sort them by frequency to show the most frequent events at the top, because those are the ones your audience is most likely to be familiar with. Even someone who is familiar with their product might not know about rare events. This is doubly true if the events do not have intuitive type names, which is often the case for software and internet services where the event can be a user hitting a particular URL.

Run listing 3.11 to confirm the result on your own data. If you are using the Python wrapper program, do this by changing the argument to `--chapter 3 --listing 11`. The result will look similar to figure 3.18 but not exactly the same, due to the randomness in the simulation.

Automatic anomaly detection for QA

It's worth pointing out that there are methods to automatically detect data quality problems like those mentioned in this section. Automatic detection of data problems is a field known as *anomaly detection*. My approach of generating a bunch of plots and viewing them manually is pretty inefficient in comparison! But the truth is, I never bother with automatic anomaly detection for a typical churn analysis. For one thing, if there are dozens of events and metrics (fewer than 100), it doesn't take long to look at all of them. I script the generation of a set of plots like the ones shown in this section, and then I flip through them quickly with an image viewer.

It's easy to detect anomalies visually—arguably more effective than almost any algorithm. The other reason I recommend the manual approach is that it's a good way to get to know your data. You might discover useful patterns or relationships that you would miss if you relied on an algorithm. That said, if you have more than around 100 events or metrics, you might need to use a fully automated approach, but automatic anomaly detection is beyond the scope of this book.

3.9   *Selecting the measurement period for behavioral measurements*

Let's say you know this business, and you know that an event like unfriend is rare, so seeing a small number of events per account per month like the unfriend event in figure 3.18 is okay. Does that mean everything is okay with having only 59% of accounts getting a value for the metric in any given month? (That result is in figure 3.14.) Not quite. There isn't anything wrong with the data, but there is something that could be better about the measurement.

Here's the idea: if an event is rare, use a longer period in the metric definition. That way, you can catch more customers in the measurement and can compare more accounts on that behavior. Remember that the metric calculation in listing 3.2 uses only a 28-day (four-week) period. As it stands, all accounts that had no events of a rare type in the last 28 days have 0 in the metric. On the other hand, if you measure the metric with a longer period, there might be some accounts that have the event only every couple of months, which were missed with the 28-day period but will be picked up with the longer period. At the same time, there might be some accounts that have the rare event every month, and they will have an even higher count of the metric if you use the longer period.

TAKEAWAY   Use longer measurement periods when making metrics on rare events.

What's a good period to choose? Like many things in fighting churn with data, there is no strict rule; there are only guidelines. Choosing the measurement period is a trade-off between the *responsiveness* of the behavioral metric to changes in time and the *sensitivity* of the behavioral metric at picking up accounts with rare events. Responsiveness of the behavioral metric means the metric for an account changes rapidly if that account's event level decreases or increases. For example, if you use a one-year (365-day) period for calculating a metric and update it every day, then each day, only 1/365 of the data going into the metric has changed. As a result, if someone has a high level of the event in the earlier part of the year but the level has fallen off to zero, it will take a long time before the person has a low value of the metric. To summarize:

- Behavioral metrics with short time periods are more responsive to changes in behavior but less sensitive at picking up accounts with low event levels.
- Behavioral metrics with long time periods are less responsive to changes in behavior but more sensitive at picking up accounts with low event levels.

Which should you choose? Based on the frequency of events, I use a rule of thumb for the *minimum* time period you should observe events to make a behavioral metric: pick the period to be at least twice the time it takes for an average account to have one event. But due to the weekly behavioral cycle that I mentioned in section 3.4, the period should never be less than a week, no matter how frequent the events. And (usually) you should never take a behavioral measurement longer than a year (more about this in the moment). For example, if there is one event per account per month, use at least two months for measurement. If there are two events per account per month, it's okay to go down to one month. By following this guideline, it's likely that most accounts have at least one event in the time period.

TIP The minimum time period for a metric should be at least twice the time it takes an average account to have one event.

The minimum observation periods recommended by the rule of thumb are summarized in table 3.5.

Table 3.5 Minimum behavioral measurement period (rules of thumb)

Events per account per month	Number of months: one event	Minimum measurement period
>8	< 0.1	1 week
8	0.125	1 week
4	0.25	2 weeks
2	0.5	1 month
1	1	2 months

Table 3.5 Minimum behavioral measurement period (rules of thumb) *(continued)*

Events per account per month	Number of months: one event	Minimum measurement period
0.5	2	4 months
0.333	3	6 months
0.25	4	8 months
0.1666	6	12 months
< 0.1666	> 6	12 months

The behavioral measurement rules of thumb in table 3.5 set a minimum, and in general, you shouldn't measure behavior with longer than a one-year period. But what is a good trade-off between responsiveness and sensitivity within that range?

For subscriptions with a fixed term like a month or a year, behavioral measurements should be similar in time scale to the term of the subscription. If you sell one-year subscriptions, you should probably use a one-year time period for behavioral measurements; and if you sell a one-month subscription, you should use a one-month time period for behavioral measurements. The reason for this is to make your behavioral measurements reflect the experience that the customer received from the service over the term of the subscription. That said, the experience of the service may be most important near the end of the term, because that will be more immediate in the customer's mind when it is time for renewal. If you want to use something like three to six months to measure behavior on a one-year subscription, that makes sense, but don't use a one-month metric for one-year subscriptions.

What if the product has no fixed-term subscriptions? Then you should aim to make your behavioral measurements using a period that is around one-quarter to one-half of the typical time a subscriber remains active. If customers typically stick around for six months, use a one- or two-month behavioral measurement. If a customer usually stays only one month, then make behavioral measurements over just a week or two, subject to the minimum shown in table 3.5. The rationale here is that you should make measurements on a short enough time scale that you have completed the measurement period before the average customer might consider churning.

You should scale the measurement period based on the frequency of the event. That's good advice, but it has one problem: if you choose different measurement periods for different events, it's going to be confusing. This is especially true if you have a lot of events. Do you have to set your observation period to be suitable for the rarest event you are interested in? A problem with this approach is that if you use a lengthy period to measure behavior, it takes a long time before you have a valid measurement for a new account. In chapter 7, I show that you can have the best of both worlds: measure some behaviors over long time periods and others over shorter periods and still present them in an interpretable way as averages.

3.10   *Measuring account tenure*

So far, we have considered behavioral measurements based only on events. But there are important measurements of customers that are based not on events but instead on subscriptions. The length of time an account has been a customer or active user is one such measurement. I refer to the length of time an account has been a customer as the *account tenure* rather than something along the lines of account age because age can be confused with the actual age of a person (or company).

Account tenure is important in analyzing churn because it can relate to churn in significant ways: there can be particular points in the customer life cycle when churn is most (or least) likely, or churn can generally decrease (or increase) with longer account tenure. I show you how to do those analyses in chapter 5; for now, you will learn how to calculate account tenure.

3.10.1   *Account tenure definition*

Account tenure would be easy to calculate if every account had only one subscription (or period of activity, if there are no formal subscriptions). This is the duration of time from the start of the subscription to the time the tenure measurement is made. But tenure calculations are more complicated in the multisubscription context (or in "messy" subscriptions). You don't just want the time since the current subscription started, because the customer might have had earlier subscriptions in an uninterrupted sequence. In that case, it makes sense to consider them all as one big subscription for the tenure measurement. If the account was active in the distant past and then churned, that would not count as an "old" customer because they have not been active the whole time. If an old customer signs up anew after an extended absence, they are more like a new customer, so tenure should measure only the current subscription. Figure 3.19 shows an account tenure definition for a hypothetical case of multiple subscriptions.

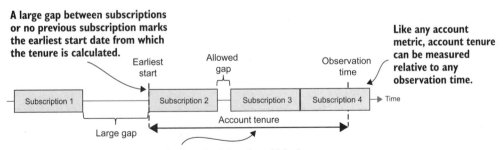

Figure 3.19   Account tenure with multiple subscriptions

At the same time, it is often a good idea to allow *small* gaps between subscriptions and still consider it a continuous subscription for the tenure measurement. For example, suppose an account fails to renew because the credit card on file was out-of-date; the account subsequently updates the card and signs up again a few days later. A few days or a one-week gap in the subscription probably should not alter the tenure measurement because they are not really a newly signed-up customer. On the other hand, if there is a multimonth gap (or longer) in the subscription, it is fairer to consider the new subscription as being a fresh start for the customer and for the tenure calculation.

The exact amount of gap required to consider an account new for tenure calculation depends on the business. For monthly subscriptions, a gap of up to a month is usually acceptable. For annual subscriptions, gaps of a month or two or even up to four can be considered short enough lapses in the subscription to still be ignored for tenure calculation purposes.

> **DEFINITION**   *Account tenure*—The length of time a customer uses a product on their current, uninterrupted sequence of subscriptions or their current uninterrupted period of activity, possibly including a relatively short time gap between subscriptions or activity.

Figure 3.19 shows that at some observation time, the account is in the middle of its fourth subscription. There is no gap between subscription 3 and subscription 4, a small (allowable) gap between subscription 2 and subscription 3, and a large gap between subscription 1 and subscription 2. The tenure is the time from the start of subscription 2 up to the time when the observation is made.

More details of a tenure calculation based on the illustration in figure 3.19 are shown in figure 3.20. The tenure starts at 0 on the start of the first subscription and

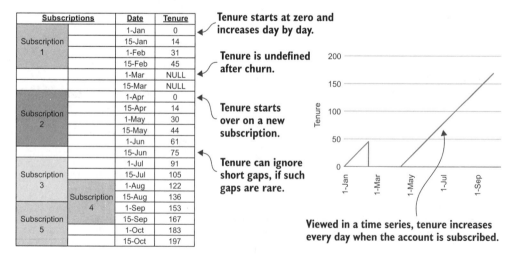

Figure 3.20   Example of an account tenure calculation

increases by one each day until the first subscription ends in churn. After churn, the tenure is not defined at all; it is not even zero. Tenure is defined and begins accumulating again only when a new subscription starts. The calculation on any given date counts the number of days since the relevant subscription start date. As with most metric calculations, this calculation would be tedious or impossible to perform by hand for every account. But, again, SQL provides a way to perform the calculation for arbitrarily complex subscription scenarios.

3.10.2 *Recursive table expressions for account tenure*

Calculating account tenure in the multisubscription case requires an advanced feature of SQL known as *recursive common table expressions* (recursive CTEs). As the name implies, recursive CTEs allow SELECT statements to run recursively when building a result set. Recursive CTEs are similar to standard CTEs but differ in that they have two parts:

- A main or "anchor" SELECT statement that defines the columns of the CTE and fills the table with an initial result set.
- A recursive SELECT statement that adds more rows to the CTE by running repeatedly until no more rows are produced. The recursive SELECT statement can reference both the current result set in the CTE and other tables that are available in the schema.

That might sound abstract, but the problem of calculating account tenure from multiple subscriptions will make a recursive SQL calculation concrete. Here is the recursive strategy for finding the earliest start date of any subscription that is in an uninterrupted sequence with the current subscription, up to an allowed gap of one month:

1. Create the CTE by selecting the currently active subscription with the minimum start date (if there are multiple currently active subscriptions) for every account.
2. Select any other subscriptions for the same account with earlier start dates and end dates that are up to one month before the current earliest start date for the same account.

If step 2 is repeated until there are no earlier subscription start dates, then the subscription with the earliest start date in the CTE is the one you are looking for: the earliest start date of any subscription that forms an uninterrupted sequence of subscriptions with the current subscription. Finding the earliest subscription start date fits easily into the framework of recursive CTEs.

Figure 3.21 shows an example of how the recursive approach operates on the hypothetical multisubscription scenario in figures 3.19 and 3.20. The following are the steps for finding the earliest start date through recursion:

1. On initialization, the start date of subscription 5 (1-Sep) is entered into the CTE table for this account, which is current because it starts before the current date and has an end date after the current date.

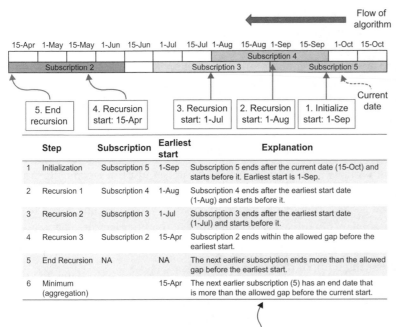

The initialization (1) of the common table expression captures the start date of subscriptions that are currently active (start date before the current date, end date after the current date, or no end date).

Recursive steps walk backward through the subscriptions for this account until there are no more subscriptions that meet the criteria. The end date must be after or within the allowed gap before the earliest start date.

Step	Subscription	Earliest start	Explanation
1	Initialization	Subscription 5	1-Sep	Subscription 5 ends after the current date (15-Oct) and starts before it. Earliest start is 1-Sep.
2	Recursion 1	Subscription 4	1-Aug	Subscription 4 ends after the earliest start date (1-Aug) and starts before it.
3	Recursion 2	Subscription 3	1-Jul	Subscription 3 ends after the earliest start date (1-Jul) and starts before it.
4	Recursion 3	Subscription 2	15-Apr	Subscription 2 ends within the allowed gap before the earliest start.
5	End Recursion	NA	NA	The next earlier subscription ends more than the allowed gap before the earliest start.
6	Minimum (aggregation)		15-Apr	The next earlier subscription (5) has an end date that is more than the allowed gap before the current start.

When the recursion is complete, a minimum aggregation returns the earliest start and the difference between the earliest start and the current date, which is the account tenure. For the example, on 15 Oct, the account tenure is 183 days.

Figure 3.21 Account tenure recursion calculation example

2 On the first iteration of the recursive step, the start date (1-Aug) of subscription 4 is entered into the CTE because its end date is after the start date of subscription 5, but the start date is earlier.

3 On the second iteration of the recursive step, the start date of subscription 3 (1-Jul) is entered into the CTE because its end date is after the start date of subscription 4, but the start date is earlier.

4 On the third iteration of the recursive step, the start date of subscription 2 (15-Apr) is entered into the CTE because the gap is small and the end date of subscription 2 is still close enough to the start date of subscription 3.

5 On the fourth iteration of the recursive step, no more rows are entered into the table for this account because the end date of subscription 1 is too far from the start of subscription 2. The recursive SELECT statement can make additional results for other accounts, but this account is finished.

6 After the recursion completes, the minimum start date in the CTE for the hypothetical account is the start date of subscription 2.

The time from that earliest date to the present is the account tenure. This process of identifying current subscriptions and working backward to the corresponding earliest start date with a recursive SQL program allows the account tenure calculation to be performed efficiently for any number of accounts and subscriptions.

3.10.3 *Account tenure SQL program*

Listing 3.12 shows the SQL that performs the account tenure measurements. Now that you know the computation strategy, I will explain a few more details about the recursive CTE with reference to the listing. First a note about recursive CTEs in general.

NOTE The RECURSIVE keyword appears after the WITH keyword for all CTEs even though the first CTE might not be the recursive one.

Turning to the details of listing 3.12:

1 The first CTE, date_range, sets the date of the tenure calculation.
2 The second CTE, earlier_starts, is the recursive one. I chose the name earlier_starts for it because it recursively finds earlier start dates for subscriptions on the same account.
   a The first half of earlier_starts selects the minimum start date of any currently active subscription from the subscription table. To select active subscriptions, the query uses the usual check that a subscription is active if it starts before the calculation date and ends on some future date (or has no defined end).
   b After the first part of earlier_starts are some important SQL keywords.

NOTE Between the two parts of the recursive CTE is the UNION keyword. It specifies that the results from the recursive query are merged *without duplicates* with the results already in the CTE. The alternative, which is not used, is UNION ALL, which preserves duplicates.

   c The second, recursive part of earlier_starts finds subscriptions starting earlier that also meet the end-date condition. To do so, it uses an inner join between the subscription table and the current CTE result set. The recursive part of the CTE joins on account IDs because the search for earlier start dates is performed separately for each account.
3 The final query after all the CTEs is an aggregation over the result in the recursive CTE, selecting the earliest start date as well as calculating the days since the earliest start in the current CTE.

Listing 3.12 Measuring account tenure with a recursive CTE

The RECURSIVE keyword goes at the beginning.

Initializes with start_dates of current subscriptions

```
WITH RECURSIVE date_range AS (
    SELECT '2020-07-01'::date AS calc_date
),  earlier_starts AS (
    SELECT account_id, MIN(start_date) AS start_date
```

This CTE sets the date for which to calculate.

Adds results to the CTE without duplication

```
FROM subscription INNER JOIN date_range
    ON start_date <= calc_date
    AND (end_date > calc_date or end_date is null)
GROUP BY account_id
UNION                                          Inserts new account
SELECT s.account_id, s.start_date              IDs and start dates
FROM subscription s INNER JOIN earlier_starts e
    ON s.account_id=e.account_id
    AND s.start_date < e.start_date            New records must have an end
    AND s.end_date >= (e.start_date-31)        date that is within a short gap.

) SELECT account_id, MIN(start_date)           For each account, selects
    AS earliest_start,                         the earliest start date
    calc_date-MIN(start_date)
        AS subscriber_tenure_days              The time from the earliest
FROM earlier_starts cross join date_range      start to the calculation date
GROUP BY account_id, calc_date
ORDER BY account_id;                           Cross join that duplicates
                                               the calc_date on every row
```

Subscriptions that start before the one that was already entered

GROUP BY of all the nonaggregate terms in the SELECT

The new records must be for the same account.

Figure 3.22 shows an example of the result of running listing 3.12. The output shows SELECTs from different ranges of accounts and their tenure. The calculation is made for May 6, 2020, and at that point, the oldest subscribers go back to January 2020 and have tenure of around 100 days. For more recent dates, there are new accounts that have tenures of just a few days.

Run listing 3.12 and see that you get a similar result on your own data. If you are using the simulated data and the Python wrapper program, then you need to update the parameter to listing 3.12. The result will look similar to figure 3.22.

Listing 3.12 and figure 3.22 show the earliest start date to illustrate the tenure calculation. In fact, the goal is to run the calculation like a metric and insert it into the metric table so that the tenure calculations for a range of dates are available for use in further metric calculations and analysis (discussed in later chapters). To insert the

Typical result of running the account tenure calculation SQL (listing 3.10)

account_id	earliest_start	subscriber_tenure_days
0	2020-01-24	103
2	2020-01-06	121
...	...	...
11541	2020-03-01	66
11543	2020-03-20	47
...	...	...
16604	2020-05-01	5
16605	2020-05-02	4

Your result will not be exactly the same because the data is randomly simulated.

Figure 3.22   Result of running the account tenure calculation

account tenure calculation into the metric schema, a few changes are needed to make listing 3.12 more like the other metric calculations:

- Make the calculation for a sequence of dates instead of just one calculation date by using a sequence of dates in the `calc_date` CTE.
- The calculation date must go in the recursive CTE `SELECT` statements and joins. Otherwise, the recursive CTE is unchanged.
- Do not select the earliest start in the final `SELECT`; rather, select the calculation date. This is the measurement observation timestamp for insertion into the metric table.
- If your data warehouse supports `INSERT SELECT`s, the appropriate `INSERT` statements are also needed (see listing 3.3).

A SQL program that has these modifications and that calculates the metric and inserts it into the database is shown in listing 3.13. Run listing 3.13 to insert the metric (we analyze it with the others in later chapters). If you are using the wrapper program to run the listings, the command is

```
fight-churn/listings/run_churn_listing.py --chap 3 --listing 13
```

This inserts the account tenure measurement into your local database; you'll have to use a SQL query (or the metric QA query in listing 3.6) to check the result. Note that as with listing 3.3, you can run this listing only once, unless you change the configuration or clean the results from the database. Finally, insert the name for the new metric (`account_tenure`) in the metric name table. To do that, you need to reuse listing 3.4. To make this easier to do, the code that runs the listings has another version of the listing 3.4 parameters that are already set up for you: rerun listing 3.4, but add the parameter `--version 11` to the executable command:

```
fight-churn/listings/run_churn_listing.py --chap 3 --listing 4 --version 11
```

Listing 3.13 `INSERT SELECT` SQL to calculate and save account tenure as a metric

```
                              The RECURSIVE keyword
                              goes at the beginning.          This CTE contains
                                                              the dates for the
WITH RECURSIVE date_vals AS (        ←─────┘                  calculation.
    SELECT i::timestamp AS metric_date     ←─────┘
    FROM generate_series('2020-02-02', '2020-05-10', '7 day'::interval) i
),                            │ This CTE is mostly the
earlier_starts AS      ←─┤ same as in listing 3.12.      Starts an entry in
(                                                        the recursive CTE
    SELECT account_id, metric_date,                      for every date
        MIN(start_date) AS start_date    ←
    FROM subscription INNER JOIN date_vals               Applies the subscription activity
        ON start_date <= metric_date     ←               condition separately per date
        AND (end_date > metric_date or end_date is null)
    GROUP BY account_id, metric_date
```

Metric dates have to be included in the recursive SELECT.

```
    UNION

    SELECT s.account_id, metric_date, s.start_date
    FROM subscription s INNER JOIN earlier_starts e
        ON s.account_id=e.account_id
        AND s.start_date < e.start_date
        AND s.end_date >= (e.start_date-31)
)
INSERT INTO metric
(account_id,metric_time,metric_name_id,metric_value)
SELECT account_id, metric_date, 8 AS metric_name_id,
    extract(days FROM metric_date-MIN(start_date))
        AS metric_value
FROM earlier_starts
GROUP BY account_id, metric_date
ORDER BY account_id, metric_date
```

The INSERT statement is mostly the same as for earlier metrics.

Enters the account tenure metric as the metric ID 8

The value of the tenure is calculated separately for each metric date.

Calculating account tenure for nonsubscription products and services

If you are working on a product without subscriptions (ad-supported, retail, nonprofit, and others), it is still important to analyze and understand how account tenure relates to churn. The only difference is that, rather than working from subscriptions to measure tenure, you work from events to determine how long someone has been with the product. If you are thinking that something like the tenure calculation described here should work for events, you are correct; the program is shown in the next chapter (section 4.3). The account tenure algorithm described here is an important part of creating churn analysis datasets for nonsubscription products.

If your product doesn't have subscriptions, this would be a good time to skip ahead to chapter 4 and learn more, because the next section is on metrics that are specific to subscription products. But start at the beginning in chapter 4: the techniques in section 4.3 build on sections 4.1 and 4.2.

3.11 *Measuring MRR and other subscription metrics*

Other important measurements of customers are made from their subscriptions, like account tenure, but depend on the details of the subscriptions, not only on the subscription start and end dates. Like the account tenure measurement, these measurements are conceptually straightforward and don't require much calculation if every customer has one (and only one) subscription. However, as usual, things become complicated when customers can have more than one subscription over time or more than one subscription at the same time. I will demonstrate general techniques that work with any kind of "messy" subscription data you might encounter, and you can choose to simplify the approach if the condition of your data warrants.

3.11.1 *Calculating MRR as a metric*

When customers pay for subscriptions, the total monthly recurring revenue (MRR) is an important measurement. You might not think of MRR as a measurement but see it instead as a simple fact. Figure 3.23 illustrates that whenever there is a possibility of multiple subscriptions with potentially different prices, MRR is something you need to measure at different points in time, just like a regular behavioral measurement.

Because you have no guarantee of what subscription(s) an account has at any given time, the MRR at every point you are interested in must be computed separately. And because the cost of multiple subscriptions adds up, the calculation sums the total MRR for all subscriptions active on any given date. The example in figure 3.23 illustrates how changes in MRR can occur when an old subscription ends or a new subscription begins.

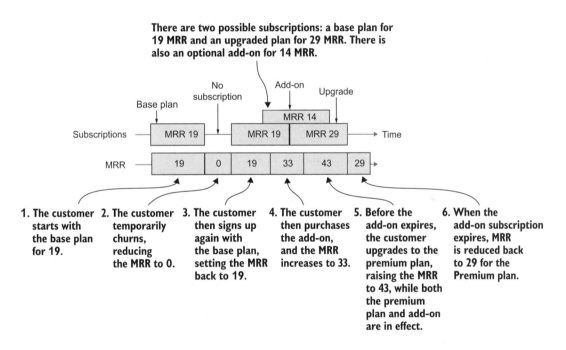

Figure 3.23 Monthly recurring revenue (MRR) metric calculation

The figure illustrates how the MRR changes over time:

1. The customer starts with the base plan (MRR = 19).
2. The customer temporarily churns (MRR = 0).
3. The customer signs up again with the base plan (MRR = 19).
4. The customer purchases the add-on (MRR = 33).

5 Before the add-on expires, the customer upgrades to the premium plan (MRR = 43).

6 The add-on subscription expires (MRR = 29).

Although MRR can change at any time, if you are calculating all the other behavioral measurements on a weekly basis (as advised in section 3.5.1), it is sufficient to calculate the MRR for all accounts on those dates when you are making the other metric calculations. Listing 3.14 shows the SQL query that calculates the total MRR for all accounts on a sequence of dates defined like any other metric. The strategy to calculate the MRR is as follows:

1 Define a fixed sequence of measurement dates using generate_series (see the sidebar on alternatives to generate the series function in section 3.4 if you are using a database other than Postgres).

2 Join the subscriptions with the dates to find all subscriptions active on each date. A subscription is active if the start date is on or before the measurement date and if the end date is after the measurement date (or there is no end date).

3 Use a standard aggregation to sum the total MRR for all the subscriptions on each date.

Listing 3.14   SQL to calculate MRR as a metric

This CTE contains the dates for the calculation.

```
WITH date_vals AS (
    SELECT i::timestamp as metric_date
    FROM generate_series('2020-04-02', '2020-04-09', '7 day'::interval) i
)
SELECT account_id, metric_date, SUM(mrr)as total_mrr
FROM subscription INNER JOIN date_vals
    ON start_date <= metric_date
    AND (end_date > metric_date or end_date is null)
GROUP BY account_id, metric_date
```

For each account and date, sums the total MRR

Limits to subscriptions that end after the measurement date

Aggregates the total on each account and date

Limits to subscriptions that begin by the measurement date

There is no sample output for listing 3.14. By now, you know there would be an MRR result for each account and date. At the time of this writing, the default simulated data includes only one subscription per account and only one MRR (price). So you can run listing 3.14, but if you are using the default simulated data, the results will not be very interesting. For real companies, MRR often varies across accounts, and it is rare to see changes in the MRR of individual accounts. Such changes occur only when the subscription plan(s) for the account changes in between the two measurement dates.

While this approach to calculating MRR may seem excessively complex or expensive to compute, it is much faster than calculating event-based metrics because customers usually have fewer subscriptions than events. It also might seem inefficient to store MRR that doesn't change often in a table with weekly (or daily) updates. This is a fair criticism, but in practice, it's just one more metric stored in a data warehouse that typically houses dozens (or more) of metrics throughout the analysis process. The benefit of storing the MRR metric in a common format with the other behavioral metrics outweighs any downside. It makes it much easier to integrate MRR with the other behavioral metrics, as demonstrated in the next two chapters.

3.11.2 *Subscriptions for specific amounts*

So far, while discussing subscriptions, I have not talked about the details of what the subscriptions are for. Or rather, the subscriptions have been presented as being for products that have names but no other facts or distinguishing details. But many subscriptions are for something specific, in the sense that the subscription entitles the user to a fixed allowance of a certain type of product usage.

For example, in SaaS, it is common that a subscription is for a certain number of seats, meaning the maximum allowed number of users. For telecommunications and the Internet of Things (IoT), there is often a set number of handsets or devices, or possibly data or bandwidth allowances. To refer to such properties of subscriptions generically, it is common to call what the subscription is for the *unit* of the subscription, and the number of units is the *quantity*.

> **DEFINITIONS** *Unit*—For a subscription, a specific type of entitlement offered by the subscription. *Quantity*—How many units a subscriber is entitled to.

Table 3.6 shows an expanded subscription table schema that you can use when subscriptions have associated units and quantities. This schema for subscriptions adds a text field to describe the units and a numeric field to represent the quantity. Note that in this schema, each subscription is for only a single type of unit, but in practice, multiple types of units can be sold together. If multiple types of units are sold together, it usually makes sense to enter them as separate subscriptions in the schema with the same start and end date. In the terminology of subscription business management software systems, each individual sale of some number of units for a specific time period is often referred to as a *charge segment*, a *rate plan charge*, or just a *charge*.

> **DEFINITION** *Charge segment*—A single recurring contract for a certain quantity of some units. Also referred to as a *rate plan charge* or just a *charge*.

If *charge segment* terminology is used, then a subscription is defined as a set of related charge segments. For simplicity and consistency, in this book I will refer to each such entry in the subscription table as a subscription but with the understanding that customers can have multiple subscriptions at any point in time. This is largely a matter of semantics concerning the parts and the whole of the various recurring products sold to the customer.

Table 3.6 Subscription table schema with units, quantity, and billing period

Column	Type	Notes
subscription_id	integer or char	Standard subscription fields introduced in chapter 2
account_id	integer or char	
product_id	integer or char	
start_date	date	
end_date	date	
mrr	double precision	
quantity	integer or double	How many units this subscription is for
units	char or text	Units of this subscription
billing_period_(months)	integer	How many months apart the customer is invoiced

3.11.3 *Calculating subscription unit quantities as metrics*

The point of introducing subscriptions with a number of units now is that the quantity a customer has subscribed to for each type of unit is an important metric, just like the MRR. Calculating unit quantity metrics relies on almost the same calculation.

   One difference with the MRR calculation is that instead of summing the MRR field, the quantity field is summed. And when there is more than one type of unit, there must be an additional constraint to select the right unit: there should be one metric for each type of unit sold. The strategy to calculate subscription unit quantities is as follows:

1   Define a fixed sequence of measurement dates using generate_series (see the sidebar on alternatives to generate the series function in section 3.5.1 if you are using a database other than Postgres).
2   Join the subscriptions with the dates to find all the subscriptions active on each date. A subscription is active if the start date is on or before the measurement date and if the end date is after the measurement date or if there is no end date.
3   Limit the subscriptions to those with the correct type of units.
4   Use a standard aggregation to sum the total quantity for all matching subscriptions on each date.

The SQL to calculate subscription unit quantities is shown in listing 3.15. As promised, it is similar to the MRR metric calculation in listing 3.14. You might wonder why, when summing the unit quantities, I use aggregate SQL that sums the total if there are multiple subscriptions. Shouldn't there be only one subscription for each type of unit? Actually, a quantity increase is a very common type of add-on subscription. If a customer needs more units, and they are midway through an existing subscription, rather than end-dating the original subscription and entering a new one, it is often easier to make a second subscription for the additional units with its own price and start and end date. This is what motivates calculating unit quantities as metrics that can vary over time and calculating the metric with an aggregation.

Listing 3.15 SQL to calculate total unit quantity as a metric

```
WITH date_vals AS (                                        This CTE contains the
    SELECT i::timestamp as metric_date                     dates for the calculation.
    FROM generate_series('2020-04-02', '2020-04-09', '7 day'::interval) i
)
SELECT account_id, metric_date, SUM(quantity)              Sums the total quantity
    AS total_seats                                         for the subscription
FROM subscription INNER JOIN date_vals
    ON start_date <= metric_date                           Limits to subscriptions
    AND (end_date > metric_date or end_date is null)       that begin by the
                                                           measurement date
WHERE units = 'Seat'
GROUP BY account_id, metric_date                           Limits to units of Seat
```

Limits to subscriptions that end after the measurement date

Totals each account and date

The default simulated data does not include subscription units or quantities, so you can't run this on simulated data. This example is just meant to show you how to do it when you have your own data that includes unit quantities. But the simulation code can be extended to include these kinds of details: I encourage you to do so as an exercise.

3.11.4 *Calculating the billing period as a metric*

Table 3.5 shows an expanded subscription table schema. In the last section, we looked at making metrics from the subscription unit quantity. Table 3.5 has one more element that is often relevant when looking at churn: the billing period for the subscription.

> **DEFINITION** *Billing period*—Measures how often the customer is billed. Billing every month is defined as a billing period of 1; annual billing (billing every 12 months) is a billing period of 12; and so on.

The billing period can be important because subscribers with different payment frequencies can churn at different rates. It is often (but not always) the case that people on longer payment cycles (annual, for example) churn less than people on shorter payment cycles (monthly, for example). This is especially true when payment is made in advance of service, and it can be difficult or impossible for customers to obtain a refund, so they are less likely to churn midterm. Annual billing usually comes with a discount to entice customers to make the large payment in advance: the question for the subscription business is whether the discount offered is justified by the lower churn rate. You will learn how to answer this question when we look at the impact of the billing period on churn in the next chapter and customer lifetime value in chapter 8.

The billing period can and should be treated like any metric based on subscriptions. It should be calculated from an aggregation on the subscriptions at the same interval as behavioral metrics so that it can be easily combined with other metrics in a churn analysis. The SQL for calculating the billing period as a metric is shown in listing 3.16. It has a lot in common with the subscription metrics shown earlier in this section (MRR and unit quantities). One novel point regarding the billing period metric is that the aggregation to combine multiple billing periods on different subscriptions is not a sum. This is because having two 12-month (annual) billing periods, for example, at the same time does not make a 24-month billing period; billing periods on different subscriptions are not additive.

Having multiple subscriptions on different billing cycles is rare. Most customers pay on the same billing cycle with a single invoice even when they have multiple subscription products. That is definitely the best practice because customers prefer simpler billing! But some kind of aggregation is necessary in the metric calculation to guarantee that there is one result per account per measurement date, even if there is more than one subscription active. The choices for the aggregation are the minimum billing period, the average billing period, or the maximum billing period. All of these choices return the single correct billing period when all subscriptions have the same period, and they return a number bounded by the minimum and maximum billing period in use. In listing 3.16, I choose the minimum because if a customer gets a bill every month (billing period 1), they are probably going to behave like a customer who gets a bill every month even if they also have other products that bill on a longer cycle.

Listing 3.16 SQL to calculate billing period as a metric

```
WITH date_vals AS (                                         ◁─┤ This CTE contains the
    SELECT i::timestamp as metric_date                           dates for the calculation.
    FROM generate_series('2020-04-02', '2020-04-09', '7 day'::interval) i
)
SELECT account_id, metric_date, MIN(bill_period_months)     ◁─┤ For each account and
    AS billing_period                                            date, sums the total
FROM subscription INNER JOIN date_vals                           quantity
    ON start_date <= metric_date
    AND (end_date > metric_date or end_date is null)        ◁─┤ Limits to subscriptions
GROUP BY account_id, metric_date        ◁─┤ Totals on            that end after the
                                             each account        measurement date
Limits to subscriptions that                 and date
begin by the measurement date
```

You can run listing 3.14 by following the instructions in the book's code, but if you are using the default simulated data, then the results might not be very interesting. At the time of this writing, the default simulated data includes only one billing period (monthly), but it will show you that every account always has a billing period of one month. That said, the simulation code can be extended to include details like varied billing periods. I encourage you to do so as an exercise and then make a pull request to share your work.

Software frameworks for automating metric calculation

If it's not obvious already, I have to give you some bad news: generating and saving a lot of metrics that are counts, averages, and totals of customer events gets tedious pretty quickly. If you have more than a few types of events, use software to automate as much of this process as possible. If you haven't already worked on this kind of project, I should warn you that it's usually much more work than you imagine because invariably, you don't just calculate metrics once. You end up calculating them many times as you and other people in your organization consider different choices and correct problems found by QA tests. For the simulation, you don't have to deal with all that because it's just a simple simulation and I have set up reasonable metrics for you.

> **WARNING** In a real-life case study, you will probably calculate your metrics many times as you test and fix multiple versions.

> **TAKEAWAY** Automation is key to successfully iterating on a variety of metrics over the lifetime of an effort to fight churn with data.

The Python script that runs the listings is an example of such an automated framework, but it's not optimized for the task of calculating metrics. A metric calculation software framework should include the following features, at a minimum:

- Storing metric SQL programs generically so the same SQL can be used to calculate metrics on many different events by binding event IDs as the variables and parameterizing options like the time period in the metric calculation
- Handling the details of inserting generated metrics, including names, into the data warehouse
- Removing old results when a metric is recalculated

The program wrapper was written to demonstrate a wide variety of listings, and it accomplishes the first goal but not the second. More advanced metric-calculation frameworks might include features like controlling date ranges for metric calculations and automatically updating metrics when new event data arrives in the data warehouse.

How to design and implement better metric-calculation frameworks is beyond the scope of this book because that is a software engineering exercise that depends on the particular use case. This book is about data analytics and data science. But I have posted another example of a metric-calculation framework written in Python in the GitHub repository that goes with this book: https://github.com/carl24k/fight-churn/tree/master/metric-framework. I used that framework for the customer case studies before I decided what the book listings would be, and it is more specialized for metrics.

Summary

- Behavioral measurements, also known as metrics, summarize each customer's events at a point in time or at many points in time.
- Metrics make customer accounts comparable by providing a behavioral profile. This is necessary because the events for different accounts occur at different rates and disparate times.
- Common metrics are measured over time periods ranging from weeks to a year.
- For measurements using a time period of one month or less, it is best to use multiples of seven days because nearly all human activities follow weekly cycles.
- Common metrics include
  - Count of events
  - Averages of event properties like duration, dollar value, or size
  - Totals (sums) of event properties like duration, dollar value, or size
- All the common metrics can be calculated with aggregate SQL SELECT statements.
- All events and metrics need to be tested for quality assurance (QA) because event data is not always reliable and metric calculations can contain bugs.
- The correct procedure for calculating metrics is as follows:
  a Run QA tests on the event data.
  b Calculate metrics.
  c Run QA tests on the metrics.
- An important QA test on metrics is how the number of metrics calculated and the average, minimum, and maximum values change over time.
- Another important QA test on metrics is what percent of active accounts have nonzero values for the metric and what average, minimum, and maximum measurements are found for all customers.
- An important QA test on events is to calculate the average number of events per account per month and confirm this agrees with the opinion of experts in the business.
- The time period of observation for making event measurements needs to be longer when events are rare.
- Account tenure measures how long an account has been a customer in its current period of subscription or activity, ignoring older periods of subscription or activity that are not continuous with the present one.
- When accounts can have multiple subscriptions (or churn and re-sign up), then account tenure should be calculated with a recursive common table expression (CTE).
- When accounts can have multiple subscriptions at different prices, then the monthly recurring revenue should be calculated as a metric based on subscriptions at the same frequency as event-based metrics.

- Subscriptions can entitle a user to a specific amount of a product or feature. The amount is known as the quantity, and the product or feature is known as the unit of the subscription.
- When subscriptions can have different quantities and/or units, then the unit quantities for each customer should be calculated as a metric based on subscriptions at the same frequency as event-based metrics.
- Subscriptions can have different billing periods, meaning the length of time between payments (monthly, annual, and so on).
- When subscriptions can have different billing periods, then the billing period of each customer should be calculated as a metric based on the subscriptions at the same frequency as event-based metrics.

Observing renewal and churn

This chapter covers

- Picking a lead time in advance of churns for observation
- Picking observation dates from subscriptions or activity
- Creating an analytic dataset by flattening metric data
- Exporting a current customer list for segmentation

The essence of fighting churn with data is learning from the *natural experiments* that occur every time a customer chooses to stay with or churn from the service. A natural experiment in this context means a situation that tests an outcome you are interested in, but you didn't set it up like a formal experiment. These experiments are the churns and renewals that have already occurred, and the results are waiting for you in your data warehouse. Why aren't you learning from the results already? Actually, observing these experiments and reading the results can be a little tricky if you've never done it before. This chapter teaches you the right way to observe the customer experiments that have already taken place in your own data.

The scenario in this chapter assumes you have already produced behavioral metrics (as described in chapter 3) and calculated some kind of churn rate measurement (chapter 2). This chapter is a preparation step for the churn analysis. You are going to collect observations of customer metrics at known times when customers churned or continued with the service. In relation to the overall book scenario introduced in chapter 1, this chapter focuses on the processes highlighted in figure 4.1.

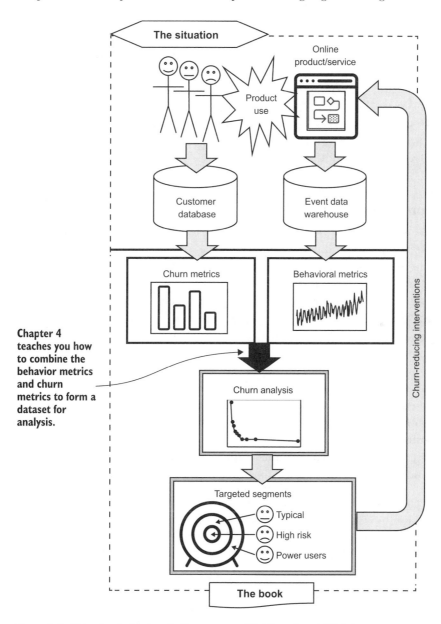

Figure 4.1 This chapter's place in the process of fighting churn with data

The chapter is organized as follows:

- In section 4.1, I introduce the idea of using a dataset to learn from your customers.
- Section 4.2 discusses how to choose the observations at a conceptual level and introduces the concept of lead time.
- Section 4.3 shows how to simplify the data where there are multiple overlapping subscriptions or gaps between subscriptions. This greatly simplifies the process of choosing the observation dates.
- Section 4.4 adapts these techniques for products where there are no actual subscriptions and instead uses customer event data by merging the activity and then applying the techniques from section 4.3.
- Section 4.5 teaches you how to generate a set of observation dates for customers, having prepared the data using the techniques in sections 4.2 and 4.3.
- Section 4.6 brings it all together by teaching you how to combine the observation dates with the metrics from chapter 3 to form a dataset for the analysis of churn.
- Section 4.7 adds a related technique: exporting the current, or most recent, customer snapshot to use for segmentation.

4.1   Introduction to datasets

As in most of these scenarios, the challenge in learning from your customers is partly due to complexity and partly due to logistical considerations. What makes observing a lot of customers complex is that they are all at different points in their journey with your product. It doesn't make sense to just look at all your customers right now or at any single fixed point in time. You want to observe them all at the same point (or points) relative to their life cycle with the product, which makes them comparable. If you do this incorrectly and observe at the wrong times, it may distort your analysis and be counterproductive in the fight against churn. This chapter teaches you how to pick appropriate observation points in the customer life cycle.

Then, at all the observation points for all the customers, you take a snapshot of all the metrics as they were measured at those times. (The metric calculations in the last chapter were all run at sequences of times to make this possible.) This combined set of customer snapshots is called a *dataset* of customer observations, or simply *the dataset*. In case you are not already familiar with the term, a dataset is used in data science and statistics for a collection of data assembled for a particular analysis.

> **DEFINITION**   *Dataset*—A concise summary of a set of situations (facts) and outcomes that you are interested in analyzing. Usually, a dataset is a single table (or file) with the same number of columns for every row and in which every row contains complete information for one situation and outcome.

When a collection of data is called a dataset, it implies that the data is organized in a table having the same number of columns for every row. Every row contains complete information for one instance or observation of the phenomena in question (meaning separate rows are separate observations), and every column corresponds to one type of fact about the situation (typically a measurement or a metric). When you create a dataset, you ensure that there are no missing fields or null (empty) values. You have to either come up with sensible defaults for missing measurements or exclude the observations that contain the missing data.

> **DEFINITION** *Churn analysis dataset*—A dataset in which every row represents a customer facing the decision to churn or stay. The outcome is what they do. The facts about these situations are the customer's behavioral metric measurements (and possibly other data you have about them).

The logistical challenges in creating this dataset are the same two as in chapters 2 and 3: the data is sensitive and it can be large, so you are better off if you can do all the data processing in your database or data warehouse. The way to make this work, as in earlier chapters, is to write short programs in SQL and save key results in the data warehouse. In the end, a concise dataset with only the minimum possible amount of sensitive information can be efficiently extracted for further analysis.

4.2 How to observe customers

To observe the natural experiments that occur when customers churn or continue to use a product, you need to start by asking *when* to make the observation. First we consider the question at an abstract level (code is coming in later sections).

4.2.1 Observation lead time

When to observe customers is an easy question, right? Observe a customer when they have churned, isn't that the point? Not quite. Think about it this way: what will a customer's behavioral metrics for a media-sharing app look like when the customer has churned? Logins? Zero. Downloads? Zero. Likes? Zero. Because they've churned, all their behaviors on the product should have stopped. Observing a customer when they have already churned is not very helpful. Also, after someone has churned, you don't have much chance of getting them to sign up again: you have a better chance of influencing them before they have made up their mind.

> **TAKEAWAY** It is easier to convince customers to stay before they churn than to sign up anew after they churn. The period before churn, therefore, is the focus of the analysis.

Observe customers before they churn. Right! I call this observing customers with a *lead time* in making the observation, which means making the observations before the thing you are really interested in (the renewal or churn). How long before the churn should you observe a customer: a day before they churned? Maybe, but most likely you should observe what customers were doing even longer before they churned. That's because, often, the customer's behavior changes in the time immediately before they churn. This is illustrated in figure 4.2, with a hypothetical example for a media-sharing service.

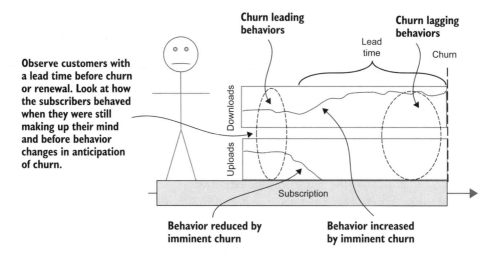

Figure 4.2   **Lead time and customer behavior before churn**

If someone is planning to churn, some behaviors are likely to be reduced in the period right before the churn, whereas others may increase. In the example of a hypothetical file-sharing service, uploads might completely stop before churning because the customer doesn't want to waste time contributing anything else. Instead, they focus on downloading content before their access to the service ends. As another example, logins can increase in the period before churn, before going to zero.

For some products, these kinds of changes in behavior can make likely churners easy to spot in the period before churn. But behaviors brought on by imminent churn are still not what you want to observe because that's not going to tell you why the customer chose to churn in the first place. You want to observe what the customer was like in the time *before* they decided to churn, because then you are observing what a customer looks like when they are still making up their mind. This is important because when the customer is still making up their mind, you have the best chance to influence them! I will emphasize the point again.

> **TAKEAWAY**   The goal of the analysis is to identify and understand customers who are still making up their minds about churn, because that is when you have the best chance of influencing them.

How do you know when customers are still making up their minds about churning or continuing to use the product? You can't know exactly, unless you are psychic. You have to observe customers at a time when it is reasonable to expect them to be thinking about their next renewal, not immediately after the last renewal, and not right before the upcoming renewal where they might churn. The amount of time depends on the service, but generally, the longer the commitment and the more expensive the service, the longer the lead time should be:

- For monthly subscriptions, observe customers one to two weeks before the monthly renewal or about one-half to three-quarters of the way through the current month.
- For annual subscriptions with consumers or small businesses, observe customers about one month before the annual renewal.
- For annual subscriptions with large businesses, observe customers anywhere from two to four months before renewal; 90 days is typical.

For nonsubscription products, you don't pick a lead time. You pick a sequence of regularly spaced observation dates, just like for a subscription product. But since there are no renewals, you have no guide as to when someone might be considering canceling.

4.2.2 *Observing sequences of renewals and a churn*

When you create a dataset, you don't want to observe just customers who churn. You also want to observe customers who renew. That way, you can compare churns and renewals and see the difference in your analysis. And you don't want to choose just a few renewals: for the purpose of the analysis, you want to pick enough renewals to observe that the renewal observations in your dataset *are in proportion to the true retention rate*.

> **TAKEAWAY** For a churn analysis dataset, try to make the renewals in your dataset in proportion to the true retention rate. Churns should be in your dataset in proportion to the true churn rate.

For example, if you have a 5% churn rate and a 95% retention rate, you want to make a set of observations that is also around 5% churns and 95% renewals. That might sound complicated to arrange, but it's straightforward: you just observe every renewal for every account as well as the churns. This results in about the same proportion of renewals and churns in your observations as your true churn rate.

   If the subscription does not have a fixed term or it automatically renews, observations should be made based on when each payment is due. Payments are typically due at fixed periods after the subscription begins: every month, for most consumer subscriptions. For consistency with the churn observations that have a lead time, you should also apply the same lead time before each renewal or payment. Figure 4.3 illustrates this scenario.

   A subscription has periodic payments (for example, monthly) and continues until canceled. The observation dates selected are the lead time before each payment is due. The subscription finally ends after the last paid month ends, and the churn observation is made in the lead time before the end of that month; that was when the customer was making the final determination to churn or renew. This is why the title of this section is "Observing sequences of renewals and *a* churn." Typically, you observe each account many times as they renew and then only once when they churn.

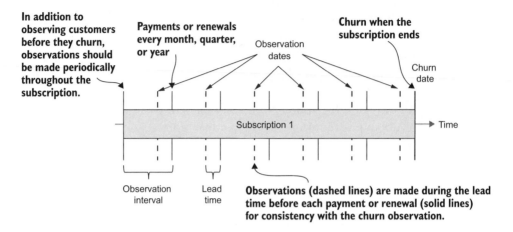

Figure 4.3   Payment cycle dates, lead time, and observation sequences

What if your product has subscriptions that are on different renewal or payment cycles? For example, many products have both monthly and annual plans. There are multiple ways to handle this, but my advice is to observe all customers at the same frequency by assuming they are all on the same renewal or payment cycle. The observation frequency to choose is the payment or renewal cycle that is the most common. Usually this is the period that you use to quote your churn, so the choice should be obvious:

- For a consumer subscription that reports a monthly churn rate, observe customers every month even if some renew or pay on annual contracts.
- For a business subscription that reports an annual churn rate, observe customers every year, even if some pay or renew on monthly and quarterly schedules.

Remember: when in doubt, if it makes the most sense to quote your churn based on a particular period (monthly, quarterly, or annual), then that is probably the right period to use when observing subscribers throughout their lifetime on the product.

If you think about it, in a way, it doesn't make sense to observe an annual customer midway through the year because they don't have a chance to churn at that point, and they are probably not thinking about it. But if you observe the annual customers only once a year, it complicates reproducing the churn and renewal rate in your data and also makes it harder to interpret the impact of being on the annual plan versus being on the monthly plan. (I will explain further when you learn how to analyze the churn impact of plans in chapter 5.)

4.2.3   *Overview of creating a dataset from subscriptions*

Now I'll go over the procedure to create a dataset for the case of having actual subscriptions; the process for when there are no subscriptions is covered in section 4.4. An overview of the entire process is shown in figure 4.4. The starting point of the process is the subscription data described in chapter 2 and the metrics you created in chapter 3 and saved in the data warehouse.

The main steps shown in figure 4.4 are as follows:

1 Identify periods when customers are subscribed to one or more subscriptions that are ongoing at the present time (no churn, yet). These are called *active periods that are ongoing.*

2 Identify periods when each customer is subscribed to one or more subscriptions and when these periods end in churn. These are called *active periods ending in churn.*

3 Using these active periods, pick sequences of observation dates for each customer using the payment or renewal cycle and lead times as described in the last section. Keep track of which of these observations are made in the lead time before an actual churn.

4 Use the sequences of observation dates to choose metrics saved in the data warehouse. The metric values, along with the churn and observation details, are selected in a single dataset, one observation per customer per row of the dataset.

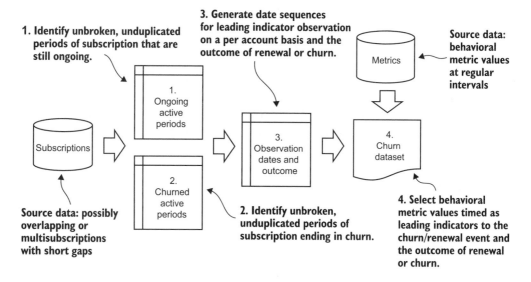

Figure 4.4   Process for creating a dataset from subscriptions in four steps

I just mentioned an important new concept that will be used throughout the process.

> **DEFINITION**   *Active period*—A span of time when a subscriber has *at least one* active subscription. There can be small gaps between subscriptions without disrupting the active period.

Section 4.3 provides details on steps 1 and 2 of this process: creating the active periods. Section 4.4 takes a detour to explain how this process differs for products where there is not an actual subscription. Section 4.5 picks up and explains step 3 in this process: selecting observation dates. Finally, section 4.6 discusses the final step: merging the metric data with the observation dates and exporting the dataset.

4.3   *Identifying active periods from subscriptions*

The goal in this phase of the process is to make regular observations of your subscribers at appropriate times to understand why they churn. The first step is to handle problems caused by redundancy or irregularity in the subscriptions. These are the same issues encountered in chapter 3 when you learned how to calculate account tenure. There can be multiple subscriptions for some customers so that the effective period the customer is active is longer than any single subscription, and there can be short gaps between the individual subscriptions that you might not want to consider churns. Also, some customers have multiple subscriptions at the same time when there is more than one product or if there is a base product and add-ons. The dates for these additional subscriptions may not align with the main subscription.

If your subscription product does not have any of the complexities that this step is designed to handle, you can skip to section 4.5. To be clear, skip this section only if your product's subscriptions are already guaranteed to consist of single, non-overlapping periods for each account, with no unintentional gaps.

4.3.1   *Active periods*

An *active period*, illustrated in figure 4.5, is a period of time when an account is continuously subscribed, through one or more individual subscriptions. In figure 4.5, there are a total of seven separate subscriptions, numbered sequentially by their start time. An active period differs from a subscription in that the active period merges any multiple subscriptions and ignores short gaps. Each account can be in only one active period at a time, and any gaps between active periods represent genuine churn followed by resubscribing at a later date.

> **NOTE**   If an account is not in an active period, the end of the last active period was a churn.

In figure 4.5, the first active period is a simple one: a single subscription. Period 2 in the figure is an example of a complex active period made of three main subscriptions (numbers 2, 3, and 5). Between subscriptions 2 and 3 is a short gap—short enough that it should not be considered a churn. Subscriptions 3 and 5 align, so there is no gap; and another subscription, an add-on (number 4), begins in the middle of subscription 3 and ends in the middle of subscription 5. All of these meet the condition that they make up one active period. Period 3 is an example of an active period that is ongoing; this is when the subscription has no end date or an end date in the future at the time the analysis is done.

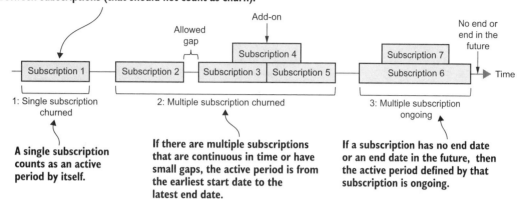

Figure 4.5 Determining active periods from multiple subscriptions

4.3.2   Schema for storing active periods

The active periods are just one step in the process of forming the dataset, and it is convenient to store them in the database. Alternatively, you might choose to combine all the short programs in this chapter into one large program that produces the dataset without any permanent storage. Because this book teaches each step in a short program, I store the results in a table. The schema required to store the active periods is shown in table 4.1. It has some similarities to the schema for storing subscriptions (chapter 2, table 2.1) in that each record has an account ID and a start date, which are required, and another date that is the churn date, which is nullable like the end date on the subscription. But an active period record has some important differences from a subscription:

- The combination of `account_id` and `start_date` must be unique for an active period, so they should be implemented as a compound key or index on the table.
- Active periods have none of the details associated with a subscription, like the product or MRR.

(If you need a reminder about how to calculate metrics like the MRR in the context of multiple subscriptions, see section 3.10.)

> **NOTE**   The constraint on `account_id` and `start_date` can be implemented as a constraint on the table, but there is another implied constraint that must be implemented by the application logic. For each account, the start dates and churn dates of active periods must define non-overlapping time periods, and there can be only one active period without a churn date for each account: the currently active period.

Table 4.1   Active period table schema

Column	Type	Notes
account_id	integer or char	Not null; compound key
start_date	date	Not null; compound key
churn_date	date	Nullable

4.3.3   Finding active periods that are ongoing

I show you how to find active periods that are still ongoing first because it's easier than finding active periods that ended in churn. For ongoing active periods, you don't need to find churn dates because you know they don't end in churn: it's just a matter of finding the start date. Look at figure 4.5, and think back to the account tenure calculation you learned in section 3.10 (see figures 3.19–3.21). Finding the start date of an active period that is ongoing is basically the same as finding the tenure of every account (the tenure of every account as of today, that is). The only difference is that the desired result is the start date of the period when customers were actively subscribed rather than how long they have been an active subscriber. As with calculating account tenure, you need to find the start of not just the current subscription but the oldest subscription that overlaps or forms a contiguous series up to the present.

Listing 4.1 shows a short SQL program that calculates the currently ongoing active periods. Again, note that the result is simply a list of all accounts that are currently in the middle of an active subscription and the earliest start date when they entered into any active subscription that is continuous at present. This is the same as the account tenure calculation using a recursive common table expression (CTE), described in the last chapter, but I will go through it again as a quick review. The process is implemented with the following SELECT statements:

1. A CTE holds parameters controlling when and how active periods are found.
2. A recursive CTE in two parts finds sequences of active subscriptions.
   - The initialization SELECT statement finds all accounts that are currently active.
   - The recursive SELECT statement finds earlier subscriptions that overlap with or are continuous with but older than the subscriptions currently found.
3. An aggregate SELECT statement finds the earliest start date of any subscriptions for each account.

Because this result is saved and combined with the results for active periods ending in churn, the final SELECT statement includes an INSERT statement to save the result in the table named active_period.

> **Listing 4.1 Active periods that are currently ongoing**

```
WITH RECURSIVE active_period_params AS
(
    SELECT interval 7  AS allowed_gap,
    '2020-05-10'::date AS calc_date
),
active AS
(
    SELECT distinct account_id, min(start_date)
        AS start_date
    FROM subscription INNER JOIN active_period_params
        ON start_date <= calc_date
        AND (end_date > calc_date or end_date is null)
    GROUP BY account_id

    UNION

    SELECT s.account_id, s.start_date
    FROM subscription s
    CROSS JOIN active_period_params
    INNER JOIN active e ON s.account_id=e.account_id
        AND s.start_date < e.start_date
        AND s.end_date >= (e.start_date-allowed_gap)::date
)
INSERT INTO active_period (account_id, start_date, churn_date)
SELECT account_id, min(start_date) AS start_date, NULL::date AS churn_date
FROM active
GROUP BY account_id, churn_date
```

Latest date to consider

This CTE holds constant parameters.

This is the same as calculating account tenure (chapter 3).

The maximum time without subscription before churn

Initializes recursive CTE with the start of every current subscription

Inserts new account IDs and start dates during recursion

The new records are for subscriptions that start earlier.

The new records must be for the same account.

New records must have an end date within the allowed gap.

Saves the result to the active_period table

Groups by account_id; churn_date must be in the GROUP BY

Selects the earliest start date and null for the churn date

Run listing 4.1 by following the instructions in the book's downloadable code at www.manning.com/books/fighting-churn-with-data or https://github.com/carl24k/ fight-churn. It is preconfigured to run on the default simulated dataset. (Instructions for the data simulation are in the README page.) After setting up your environment, run listing 4.1 with this command:

```
fight-churn/listings/run_churn_listing.py --chapter 4 --listing 1
```

The wrapper program run_churn_listing prints the SQL it is running. But note that listing 4.1 performs an insert into the database, so it does not produce any output. To see the result, run a query using a SQL query method of your choice (see the README for suggestions); for example:

```
SELECT * FROM active_period ORDER BY account_id, start_date;
```

Figure 4.6 shows the results of running listing 4.1 on the default simulated dataset and then viewing the results with a SELECT statement like the previous one. Use a LIMIT clause if you have a large amount of data, but you shouldn't need it for the default simulation. The result contains accounts that began near the start of the simulation, as well as accounts that were added at the end of the simulation. Due to the constraint on the active_period table, you can run listing 7.1 only once without deleting the data already in the table.

There is one record for each account and active period, regardless of how many subscriptions are in that period. (Your result will not be exactly the same—the underlying data is randomly simulated.)

account_id	start_date	churn_date
0	2020-01-15	NULL
3	2020-01-23	NULL
7	2020-01-05	NULL
...	...	...
3480	2020-05-05	NULL
3493	2020-05-05	NULL
3498	2020-05-03	NULL

The churn dates are NULL because these are the ongoing active periods; the column is required for inserting in the table that also holds churned periods.

Figure 4.6 Result of running listing 4.1 for active periods that are ongoing

4.3.4 *Finding active periods ending in churn*

Finding active periods ending in churn is probably the most advanced SQL program in this book. But this program is not harder than anything you've seen; it just combines other techniques you have already mastered: the outer join technique from chapter 2 used to calculate churn, and the recursive CTE from chapter 3 (and reviewed in the last section) to find the earliest start of any subscription continuously up to another subscription.

The algorithm for finding all the churns is based on the outer join method demonstrated in chapter 2 for calculating the churn rate, but it is not exactly the same. It starts with the observation that every churn must correspond to an end date of a subscription. Further, an end date on a subscription is a churn if there was no other extension through a new subscription by the same account.

DEFINITION *Extension*—Another subscription that begins either before a previous subscription ends or within the allowed gap period and that has a future end date. An extension extends an active period. This definition of *extension* is specific to the discussion of the current algorithm and is not a term generally used in the trade.

An extension is so named because it extends the end date of a prior subscription and prevents that end date from being churn. The key is that a churn is an end date with no extension. Figure 4.7 provides an example of finding churns by considering end

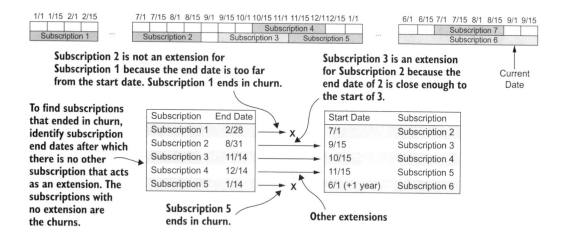

Figure 4.7 Finding churns from end dates and extensions

dates and extensions. It's based on the sequence of subscriptions illustrated in figure 4.5. To identify churns of one account, you use the following steps:

1 Identify all the end dates of subscriptions for that account. (Subscriptions with no end dates cannot be churns, so ignore them.) This is limited to end dates within a time period that ends at the current date and can start as far back as you are interested in when looking for churns.

2 Identify all extensions that extend those end dates. These are subscriptions that begin before the other subscriptions' end date or within the allowed gap time and end later in the future.

3 Select the end dates *that do not have an extension.* These are the churns. In SQL, use an outer join for the end dates with the extensions and select those subscriptions from step 1 with null on the outer join and the extension subscriptions from step 2. These end dates correspond to active periods ending in churn.

Figure 4.8 shows the complete process for finding churns and their corresponding start dates. It consists of first finding churns by considering end dates and extensions and then finding the start dates of the active periods that ended with a churn. This takes place in two additional steps (4 and 5):

4 The start dates are found in the same way as the start dates for ongoing active periods (and for account tenure calculations): using a recursive CTE that searches for progressively earlier start dates.

5 Take the minimum of the start dates from the subscriptions that precede the subscription ending in churn (if any).

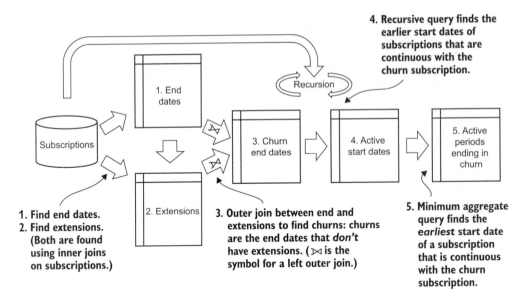

Figure 4.8   Process for finding churns and the corresponding active period start dates

Listing 4.2 is the SQL program that finds the active periods ending in churn. It includes four CTEs:

- `active_period_params`—Contains the fixed constants that define when the program will find churns and the maximum allowed gap between subscriptions that is not considered a churn.

- `end_dates`—Contains all subscriptions that have end dates within the desired periods. As a convenience for the next step, it also calculates the maximum date for which an extension could occur to extend this end date: the end date plus the allowed gap defined in the parameters.

- `extensions`—Contains every subscription end date that has another subscription that extends it (an extension). This is any subscription for a matching account that begins before the maximum extension date (calculated in the `end_dates` CTE) and has an end date in the future or a `null` end date.

- `churns`—A recursive CTE that performs the key calculation of the algorithm:
  - The initializing `SELECT` statement is an outer join between the end dates and the extensions, which selects only end dates *that don't have an extension*. These are the churns.
  - The recursive `SELECT` statement finds earlier start dates for subscriptions that come before the churn for the same account; the earliest of these is the beginning of the active period.

The final SELECT statement in listing 4.2 finds the minimum start date corresponding to every end date that is a churn the same way as in listing 4.1 for active periods that are still active. It also contains the INSERT statement to save this result along with the ongoing active periods in the active_period table. Crucially, the end dates of the subscriptions that had no extension are the churn dates.

Listing 4.2 Active periods that end in churn

This CTE holds constant parameters.

```
WITH RECURSIVE active_period_params AS
(
```
Maximum time without a subscription before churn

```
    SELECT INTERVAL '14 day' AS allowed_gap,
           '2020-05-10'::date AS observe_end,
           '2020-02-09'::date AS observe_start
```
Latest date to consider for finding churns

Earliest date to consider for finding churns

This CTE contains unique start and end dates for every account.
```
),
end_dates AS
(
```
Uses DISTINCT in case multiple subscriptions have the same end

```
    SELECT distinct account_id, start_date, end_date,
        (end_date + allowed_gap)::date AS extension_max
    FROM subscription INNER JOIN active_period_params
        ON end_date between observe_start
        AND observe_end
```
Date by which the account should be re-signed up to avoid churn

Limit to end dates within the period being checked for churns
```
),
extensions AS
(
```
Uses DISTINCT in case multiple subscriptions have the same date

```
    SELECT distinct e.account_id, e.end_date
    FROM end_dates e INNER JOIN subscription s
        ON e.account_id = s.account_id
        AND s.start_date <= e.extension_max
        AND (s.end_date > e.end_date
            OR s.end_date is null)
```
Other subscription must start by the date the extension period ends.

This CTE identifies churns and finds the period start dates.
```
),
churns AS
(
```
Other subscription must have an end date after the original.

The end date of the subscription is the churn date.

```
    SELECT e.account_id, e.start_date,
        e.end_date AS churn_date
    FROM end_dates e LEFT OUTER JOIN extensions x
    ON e.account_id = x.account_id
        AND e.end_date = x.end_date
    WHERE x.end_date is null
```
Identifies churns with an outer join

Joins the end dates and extensions

```
    UNION
```

This CTE contains subscriptions that extend the end dates.

Identifies churns that don't have extensions

```
    SELECT s.account_id, s.start_date, e.churn_date       ←┐   The recursive
    FROM subscription s                                        SELECT finds the
    CROSS JOIN active_period_params                            earliest start date.
    INNER JOIN churns e ON s.account_id=e.account_id
        AND s.start_date < e.start_date
        AND s.end_date >= (e.start_date-allowed_gap)::date

)                                                             ┐   Inserts the result in the
INSERT INTO active_period                                     │   active_periods table
    (account_id, start_date, churn_date)              ←┘
SELECT account_id, min(start_date) AS start_date,
    churn_date                              ←┐
FROM churns                                   │   Selects the minimum start
GROUP BY account_id, churn_date                   date for each churn
```

Run listing 4.2 by following the instructions in this book's downloadable code. If you ran the other listings, then by now you know how to do this by changing the parameters of the wrapper program to --chapter 4 --listing 2. Note that listing 4.2 performs an insert into the database, just like listing 4.1. It does not produce any output (the code that runs the listing prints the SQL that is being run). To see the result after you have run listing 4.2, run a query like this:

```
SELECT * FROM active_period WHERE churn_date is not null ORDER BY account_id,
    start_date;
```

Figure 4.9 shows the results of running listing 4.2 on the default simulated dataset and then viewing the results with a SELECT statement like the previous one. Use a LIMIT clause if you have a large amount of data, but you shouldn't need it for the default simulation. Active periods ending in churn begin in all parts of the simulation times and have a variety of lengths. Due to the constraint on the active_period table, you can run this SQL only once without deleting the data already in the table.

account_id	start_date	churn_date
2	2020-01-10	2020-03-10
4	2020-01-08	2020-03-08
6	2020-01-06	2020-03-06
17	2020-01-06	2020-05-06
...	...	...
2923	2020-04-03	2020-05-03
2977	2020-04-01	2020-05-01
2995	2020-04-03	2020-05-03

Typical result for active periods ending in churn (Your result will not be the same because the underlying data is simulated.)

Figure 4.9   Result of running listing 4.2 for the active periods ending in churn

4.4 Identifying active periods for nonsubscription products

Since chapter 1, I have been telling you that the techniques for analyzing churn in this book apply to products without actual subscriptions, like ad-supported media, apps with in-app purchases, and retail websites. Now I will (finally) explain how to calculate the active periods for those accounts. I waited until now because, at this point, you have learned the necessary techniques.

4.4.1 Active period definition

In chapter 2, I mentioned that the key to understanding churn in nonsubscription products is to calculate active periods that reflect the periods when an individual account was live on the product, similar to a subscription. In this context, a *churn* is defined to be whenever an account goes inactive for more than some maximum allowed time, typically one month or a few months. You should choose this time limit so that most people who go inactive don't come back, or if they do, it would be fair to consider it a fresh start.

Figure 4.10 presents the idea of active periods derived from events. The point is to find, for each account, groups of events in which no events are farther apart than the allowed gap. Once such active periods are calculated, the churn rate can be calculated as if these were subscriptions. Also, all the analytic techniques described in the rest of the book can be applied without any other modifications.

> **DEFINITION**   *Active period derived from events*—A span of time when a user has had *at least* one event. There can be gaps between events up to the limit, without disrupting the active period. The definition of active periods from events is similar to the definition of active periods from multiple subscriptions.

Here's the basic idea: in the last section, I demonstrated algorithms in SQL to handle scenarios where accounts can have multiple subscriptions over time. It's necessary to

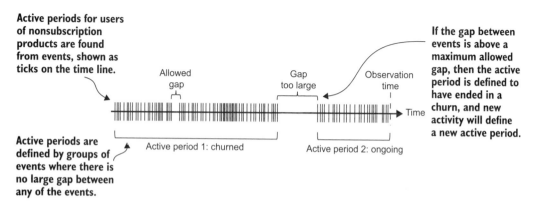

Active periods for users of nonsubscription products are found from events, shown as ticks on the time line.

Allowed gap

Gap too large

Observation time

If the gap between events is above a maximum allowed gap, then the active period is defined to have ended in a churn, and new activity will define a new active period.

Time

Active periods are defined by groups of events where there is no large gap between any of the events.

Active period 1: churned

Active period 2: ongoing

Figure 4.10   Active periods from events

find the earliest start date of any of those subscriptions and to find when sequences of subscriptions end. All those calculations on subscriptions also include an allowed gap, in case customers have short periods of time without a subscription. If you think about it, that's exactly the calculation that needs to happen with events to determine periods when accounts are active. The subscriptions and events both have to be grouped so that no subscription/event in the group is further apart than an allowed gap. The only difference is that a subscription has a duration (a subscription has an end date that comes after the start date), but an event is at a single point in time. An algorithm similar to the one used to find active periods from subscriptions will work to find active periods from events.

But there is one important difference between subscriptions and events that impacts the performance of this algorithm, if not the logic: accounts typically have only one or a few subscriptions at a time, but accounts can have a very large number of events. To put it another way, subscriptions are usually small data, whereas events are often big data. It might not be a good idea, therefore, to apply the active period algorithms from the last section directly to the events. Instead, make a simplification: define an active week as seven days during which an account has any event.

DEFINITION   *Active week*—A seven-day period when an account has at least one event.

The first step is to calculate which weeks are active for all accounts. This can be done by using an aggregation query and saving the result. This simple first step reduces the size of the data for the steps that follow. If your users typically have 100 events per week (for example), then after aggregation, the data representing the activity is one-hundredth the size. And if customers have 1,000 events per week . . . (you get the drift).

Of course, such active periods allow accuracy in identifying churn dates only up to the weekly interval defined for measuring activity in the aggregation step. These active periods do not tell you the *precise* date or time the user became active or churned. If you think the weekly period is not accurate enough for finding the start and end of the active periods, switch to daily aggregation. Then you can have daily precision in the computation, which is seven times as much. If that works for the size of your data and the system you use to run the process, no problem. It's a trade-off between the accuracy you want in timing churns versus the size of the data you have and the available computing resources. I will continue with the examples assuming weekly aggregation periods, because this is usually the best compromise between accuracy and computational cost.

4.4.2   *Process for forming datasets from events*

After the active weeks are calculated, you can use the ongoing active period algorithms (listing 4.1) and the churned active period algorithms (listing 4.2) on active weeks instead of subscriptions to create the churn analysis dataset. Because those algorithms are designed to merge sequential subscriptions, they can also merge active weeks, and you can choose to allow no gaps (or gaps consisting of any number of weeks) in forming active weeks. (If you choose to work with active days, instead, you can run the same algorithm in terms of days with an allowed gap defined as a number of days.) The results of running listings 4.1 and 4.2 on the week are what you are looking for: the dates of continuous periods of time when accounts had events (at least one per week). Those active periods are known to either have ended in churn in the past or continue up to the present. Figure 4.11 illustrates the complete process for forming a churn dataset from events.

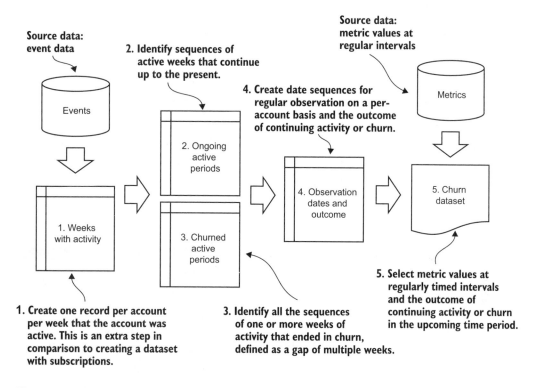

Figure 4.11   Process for finding event-based periods of activity

If you compare the process for forming a dataset from events without subscriptions (figure 4.11) to the process of forming a dataset from subscriptions in the last section, the only difference is one extra step at the beginning: grouping events into weeks of activity. Because the rest of the process is the same, the weekly grouping is the only new code necessary.

4.4.3   SQL for calculating active weeks

Because the weeks with activity are stored, you need to create a database table to hold them, using the schema shown in table 4.2. This is similar to the schemas you have seen for subscriptions and active periods. For active weeks, the end date is redundant with the start date because the start date uniquely identifies the end date for a fixed-length period. But including the end date allows the SQL programs used for subscriptions in the last section to work with the active weeks without changing the logic of the queries.

Table 4.2   Active weeks table schema

Column	Type	Notes
account_id	integer or char	Not null; compound key
start_date	date	Not null; compound key
end_date	date	Not null

Listing 4.3 provides the SQL for grouping events into weeks with activity. This technique is known to anyone who knows aggregate GROUP BY queries because the main logic of the query is to make groups of events defined by one-week periods. The only remarkable technique in listing 4.3 is using a generated series function to pick the dates.

Listing 4.3   Grouping events into weeks of activity

```
WITH periods AS                                    This CTE holds a sequence
(                                                  of weekly intervals.
    SELECT i::timestamp AS period_start,
        i::timestamp + '7 day'::interval AS period_end
    FROM generate_series('2020-02-09', '2020-05-10', '7 day'::interval) i
)
INSERT INTO active_week                            Inserts the result into the
    (account_id, start_date, end_date)             active_periods table
SELECT account_id,
period_start::date,                 The start and end of each
period_end::date                    period from the sequence
FROM event INNER JOIN periods
    ON event_time>=period_start                    Event time must be strictly
    AND event_time < period_end                    less than the period end.
GROUP BY account_id, period_start, period_end      GROUP BY account
                                                   ID and period dates
Event time is greater than or
equal to the period start.
```

Run listing 4.3 by following the instructions in the book's downloadable code. Using the wrapper program, change the parameters to --chapter 4 --listing 3. Note that listing 4.3 performs an insert into the database, just like listings 4.1 and 4.2, so it does not produce any output. (The code that runs the listing prints the SQL that is being run.) To see the result after you have run listing 4.3, run a query like this:

```
SELECT * FROM active_week ORDER BY account_id, start_date;
```

Figure 4.12 shows the results of running listing 4.3 on the default simulated dataset and then viewing the results with a SELECT statement like the previous one. Use a LIMIT clause if you have a large amount of data, but you shouldn't need it for the default simulation. Note that the code saved in the GitHub repository is not set up to calculate active periods from the active weeks. I encourage you to make those modifications yourself.

account_id	start_date	end_date
0	2020-03-04	2020-03-11
0	2020-03-11	2020-03-18
0	2020-03-18	2020-03-25
...	...	...
3497	2020-05-06	2020-05-13
3498	2020-04-29	2020-05-06
3498	2020-05-06	2020-05-13

Typical result for active weeks derived from events (Your result will not be the same because the underlying data is simulated.)

Figure 4.12   Example output from running listing 4.3

After calculating active weeks and saving them in a table, you can use the same programs as in listings 4.1 and 4.2 to find active periods. Modify these to use the active_week table (table 4.2) instead of the subscription table (table 2.1). Once you calculate active periods from the active weeks, these can be used in place of subscriptions in the standard churn calculation in chapter 2 (listing 2.2).

> **NOTE**   To use the programs in listings 4.1 and 4.2 with active weeks derived from activity instead of subscriptions, modify the code by replacing the subscription table in the joins with the active_period table; no other changes are required.

> **NOTE**   To use the program in listing 2.2 to calculate the churn rate from activity instead of subscriptions, modify the code by replacing the subscription table in the joins with the active_period table; also, the churn_date column in active_period replaces the end_date column from the subscription table.

4.5   Picking observation dates

Your goal is to make regular observations of your subscribers at appropriate times to understand why they churn. Once the subscriptions (or events) have been divided into active periods (whether from subscriptions or activity), the next step is to pick the actual observation dates for each account.

4.5.1   Balancing churn and nonchurn observations

As I described in section 4.2, the idea is not only to observe accounts when they churn but also to take snapshots of accounts when they don't churn. The churn analysis works best when the churn and nonchurn observations in the dataset are in the same proportion as the churn rate and renewal rates. The way to accomplish that is to observe every account on the same periodic cycle that you use when calculating your churn rate. Also recall that the observations are offset by a lead time. As described in section 4.2, the lead time is designed so the observation is made at a point before the customer has probably made up their mind about churning or staying. This process was illustrated previously in figure 4.3 and is reproduced in figure 4.13.

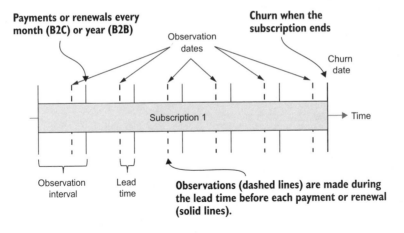

Figure 4.13   Reprise: payment cycle dates, lead time, and observation sequences

As shown, in addition to observing customers before they churn, observations should be made periodically throughout the subscription. These observations should be made at the same frequency that the organization measures its churn, which is normally the same frequency with which customers renew (for termed subscriptions) or pay their bills (for evergreen subscriptions): annual frequency for B2B (business) products and monthly frequency for B2C (consumer) or SMB (small and medium businesses) products. For consistency with churn observations, these observations are made with a lead time before each payment or renewal.

4.5.2 Observation date-picking algorithm

Considering figure 4.13, the detailed algorithm for picking the observation dates is as follows:

1. Begin with the start date of every active period for each account.
2. For the first observation:
    a. Add the periodic time interval at which you will be making observations (for example, a month) to the start date separately for all accounts and active periods. For subscriptions, this is usually the next payment or renewal date.
    b. Subtract the lead time to find the first observation date in each active period.
    c. If this observation date is followed by a churn, flag it as a churn observation, meaning if the active period ends in churn between this observation and one observation period later, then this is the last observation before the churn.
3. For the second observation on each account:
    a. Add *two times* the observation period to the start dates for each account.
    b. Subtract the lead time.
    c. If this observation date is followed by a churn, flag it as a churn observation.
4. Repeat step 3 for each account, incrementing the number of periods added to the start (and always subtracting the lead time) until the next observation date is beyond the active period.

An example of running the algorithm for picking monthly observation dates with a seven-day lead time for two accounts is shown in figure 4.14. It demonstrates that after some initial calculation, each account is repeatedly observed on the same day of the month. If there are monthly payments or subscription renewals, the date is timed to be

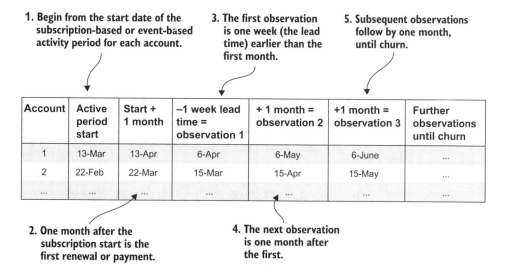

1. Begin from the start date of the subscription-based or event-based activity period for each account.

3. The first observation is one week (the lead time) earlier than the first month.

5. Subsequent observations follow by one month, until churn.

Account	Active period start	Start + 1 month	−1 week lead time = observation 1	+ 1 month = observation 2	+1 month = observation 3	Further observations until churn
1	13-Mar	13-Apr	6-Apr	6-May	6-June	...
2	22-Feb	22-Mar	15-Mar	15-Apr	15-May	...
...	...	...	...	...	...	...

2. One month after the subscription start is the first renewal or payment.

4. The next observation is one month after the first.

Figure 4.14 Illustration of the observation date-picking algorithm

one week before the monthly payment. If this were a product with an annual subscription, the observation dates would be on the same day every year. Again, the observations would be timed to have a lead time before the annual renewal (or payment), and the lead time would be longer—one to three months, as described in section 4.2—but the idea is the same.

To pick observation dates for each account, begin with the start date for each active period and add the observation period (one month, in this example) less the lead time (one week) to get the first observation date. To get the second observation date, add two times the observation period, less the lead time, to the start date. To get the third observation date, add three times the observation period, less the lead time, and so on.

4.5.3 *Observation date SQL program*

Because the observation dates are stored, at least temporarily, you need to create another table for them. Table 4.3 shows the schema to hold the observation dates. This table contains the account ID and observation date, which together define a compound primary key on the table, and one additional column: a logical value that tracks whether the observation is the last observation in an active period ending in churn.

Table 4.3 Observation dates table schema

Column	Type	Notes
account_id	integer or char	Not null; compound key
observation_date	date	Not null; compound key
is_churn	logical	Not null

Listing 4.4 provides the SQL program to produce the observation dates. It assumes there is a table `active_period` with periods defined from subscriptions. The SQL program for generating observation dates uses a recursive CTE, and the strategy for creating the observation dates recursively is as follows:

1 Initialize the recursive CTE with one observation for every `active_period`:
   a Pick the first observation date to be one observation interval after the start date, less the lead time.
   b Set a counter to 1 on the observation. This is used to calculate the time of later observations.
   c Set a Boolean indicating whether the churn date is between that observation date and the next observation date, which will be the observation interval after this observation date.
2 Recursively insert additional observation dates into the CTE for each active period:
   a Increment the counter by one.
   b The new observation date is calculated from the start date plus the new counter value multiplied by the observation period, less the lead time.

c Set a Boolean indicator on every observation so that an observation that immediately precedes the end of the active period (the churn) is set to true.

d Exit recursion when one of the following conditions is met:

  – The next observation date is after the end of the active period.

  – The next observation date is after the end of the overall period being considered.

The SQL program for the observation dates uses just two CTEs: one to set the constant parameters and one for the recursion. After this recursive procedure, the results are inserted into the observation table. The SQL program in listing 4.4 uses a one-month observation interval and one week of lead time.

Listing 4.4 SQL for observation dates

The **RECURSIVE** keyword goes at the beginning.

This CTE holds constant parameters.

```
WITH RECURSIVE observation_params AS
(
```

Observations are made with a lead time of seven days prior.

Observations are one calendar month apart.

```
    SELECT interval '1 month' AS obs_interval,
           interval '1 week'  AS lead_time,
           '2020-02-09'::date AS obs_start,
           '2020-05-10'::date AS obs_end
```

Observations are made between these dates.

This recursive CTE holds the sequences of observation dates.

```
),
observations AS
(
```

Initializes with a record for the first observation of each account

Counter to determine the later observation dates

```
    SELECT account_id,
    start_date,
    1 AS obs_count,
    (start_date+obs_interval-lead_time)::date
      AS obs_date,
    CASE
```

The observation is one period after the start, less the lead time.

```
        WHEN churn_date >= (start_date +   obs_interval-lead_time)::date
           AND churn_date < (start_date + 2*obs_interval-lead_time)::date
        THEN true
        ELSE false
    END AS is_churn
    FROM active_period INNER JOIN observation_params
    ON (churn_date > (obs_start+obs_interval-lead_time)::date
        OR churn_date is null)
```

Sets is_churn to true if churn is between the observation and the next period

Skips cases where churn comes before the first observation

The recursive SELECT adds additional observations.

```
    UNION
```

Starts plus the counter times the interval, less the lead time

```
SELECT o.account_id,
    o.start_date,
    obs_count+1 AS obs_count,
    (o.start_date+(obs_count+1)*obs_interval-lead_time)::date
      AS obs_date,
```

Increments the counter by one with each new observation

```
CASE
    WHEN churn_date >= (o.start_date +
                        (obs_count+1)*obs_interval-lead_time)::date
    AND churn_date <   (o.start_date +
                        (obs_count+2)*obs_interval-lead_time)::date
    THEN true
    ELSE false
    END AS is_churn
FROM observations o INNER JOIN observation_params
ON  ( o.start_date+(obs_count+1)*obs_interval-lead_time)::date
    <= obs_end
INNER JOIN active_period s
    ON s.account_id=o.account_id
    AND ( o.start_date+(obs_count+1)* obs_interval-lead_time)::date
        >= s.start_date
    AND ((o.start_date+(obs_count+1)*obs_interval-lead_time)::date
        < s.churn_date or churn_date is null)
)
INSERT INTO observation (account_id, observation_date, is_churn)
SELECT distinct account_id, obs_date, is_churn
FROM observations
INNER JOIN observation_params ON obs_date BETWEEN obs_start AND obs_end
```

- Sets is_churn to true if the churn is between the observation and the next period
- Joins with the previous result by account
- Don't add an observation if it would go past the date limit.
- Adds new observations for subscription periods that continue

Run listing 4.4 by following the instructions in the book's downloadable code. Using the wrapper program, change the parameters to --chapter 4 --listing 4. Note that like listings 4.1–4.3, listing 4.4 performs an insert into the database, so it does not produce any output. (The code that runs the listing prints the SQL that is being run.) To see the result after you have run listing 4.4, run a query like this:

```
SELECT * FROM observation ORDER BY account_id, observation_date;
```

Figure 4.15 shows the results of running listing 4.4 on the default simulated dataset and then viewing the results with a SELECT statement like the previous one. Use a LIMIT clause if you have a large amount of data, but you shouldn't need it for the default

account_id	observation_date	is_churn
0	2020-03-10	FALSE
0	2020-04-10	FALSE
...	...	...
17	2020-04-01	FALSE
17	2020-05-01	TRUE
...	...	..
3040	2020-05-03	FALSE
3041	2020-05-03	FALSE

Observation date sequence ending in churn (Your result will not be exactly the same.)

Figure 4.15 Example output of running listing 4.4

simulation. The observations where is_churn = TRUE are those that occur immediately before the churn date. For each account, the observation dates are spaced one month apart, as specified by the observation interval.

You might wonder why the SQL program in listing 4.4 keeps a counter and multiplies it by the observation period duration to calculate each observation date. This leads to the following expression appearing repeatedly in the code:

```
(o.start_date+(obs_count+1)*obs_interval-lead_time)::date
```

An alternative would be to add the observation period to the last observation date. Although it would be simpler to add the observation period to dates in sequence, doing so would lead to poor handling for dates around the month's end: for example, if the start date is the 31st. Then when February comes around, the day of the month would become the 28th. This is how the database defines the result when you add a month to January 31. But when the next month rolls around, if the algorithm simply adds the observation period, it does not shift the date back to the 31st; it would use March 28 and continue to use the 28th in subsequent months. In non-leap years, all end-of-month renewals would be shifted to the 28th after February.

By multiplying the observation period and adding it to the start date anew on each observation, a renewal on the 31st is treated as the 31st in every month with 31 days. Although it shifts as necessary in a month with fewer days, it does not change the result in subsequent months.

4.6   Exporting a churn dataset

The final step in creating the dataset is to select all the metrics for the accounts on the dates of their observations. In principle, this is simple, but as usual, there are a few complications.

An important part of extracting the dataset is to transform the data from the convention of database tables to the convention of analytic datasets, which is illustrated in figure 4.16. In an analytic dataset, you have to arrange the data so that each row corresponds to a single observation of an account (that churned or didn't), and each column corresponds to one behavioral metric. In the database table, though, the data is normalized so the values of all metrics are in a single column, and another column identifies which metrics are on a given row. In the database, the behavioral snapshot for a single account on a single date is spread over many rows. This is often referred to as *wide data* versus *tall data*. An analytic dataset is wide because it has many columns for all the different variables; a database table is tall because the data is all stacked up in one column. Converting data from tall to wide is often known as *flattening* the data, and that is what you must do to create the churn dataset. (It is also referred to as *pivoting* the data by those who have seen this done with the Pivot function in a spreadsheet.)

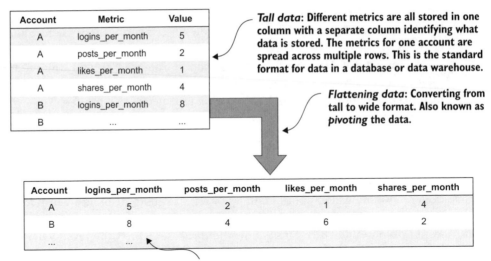

Figure 4.16   Flattening tall data into wide data

4.6.1   *Dataset creation SQL program*

There is a trick to pivoting data in standard SQL; if you know it, feel free to skip ahead. If you don't, get ready to either love it or hate it, but I promise you will find yourself using this trick again!

You can flatten a tall table like the metric table illustrated in figure 4.16 into a wide dataset with a GROUP BY aggregation, where you group all the separate rows of metrics for each account into one row for each date. You have probably seen the use of aggregation to merge multiple rows into one with a function like a sum or an average that combines the values. Aggregate functions can also be used to *choose* specific values from among multiple rows and put each in a specific column, which is the transformation needed for flattening.

Listing 4.5 shows the trick to flatten data. It uses multiple SUM aggregate functions, one for each metric that you want to flatten from the tall table to the wide table. To take the desired value from the column (and not add anything to it), you put a CASE statement inside each SUM that selects just one type of metric value from the tall table. A series of such SELECT statements inside a GROUP BY aggregation effectively flattens the tall data to wide. It isn't pretty, but it works!

Another complication is that you might not have calculated metrics for your accounts every single day. I have encouraged you to calculate metrics just once a week. If you follow my advice and do not calculate the metrics every day, then when you create the dataset, you need to select metrics that are not necessarily on the exact day of the observation. This leads to using a date range for picking the metrics in the SELECT.

One last trick in listing 4.5 is handling cases where a metric was not calculated for an account around the observation date at all. Recall that in chapter 3, the count and average value metrics were defined so that when an account had no events, no metric value was stored. This means for such metrics, there might not be any value for the JOIN statement in listing 4.5. But one metric always has a value, regardless of the events for an account: the account tenure.

The account tenure must always have a value for a user who has active subscriptions or is in an active period of usage. The fact that account tenure always has a value means the JOIN in listing 4.5 always finds at least one metric around the observation date for every account. What about the other metrics? The logic of the CASE statement means any other metrics being flattened are filled with zero, which effectively handles the problem of filling missing values for these kinds of metrics.

> **WARNING** If you do not use the account tenure metric or at least one metric that is guaranteed to have a value for every account every time you calculate it, then the query in listing 4.5 might drop account observations with no metrics. This problem can be solved with an outer join between the metrics and the observations, but my recommendation is to include the account tenure in your analysis.

Listing 4.5 uses a CTE to hold constant parameters, including one that is the metric calculation interval. The INNER JOIN statement uses the metric interval to select the last metric calculated within the seven days before the observation date.

> **NOTE** The output of listing 4.5 also includes the account ID and the observation date. Although not necessary for the analysis, this kind of descriptive data is often useful for quality-checking the data.

In the next chapter, you'll spend more time looking at how to check the quality of datasets extracted in this manner.

Listing 4.5 SQL for dataset creation

```
                          This CTE holds
                       constant parameters.
WITH observation_params AS      ⟵           The frequency at which
(                                           metrics were calculated:
    SELECT interval  interval '7 day'       every seven days
        AS metric_period,          ⟵
        '2020-02-09'::timestamp AS obs_start,    Forms observations     One observation
        '2020-05-10'::timestamp AS obs_end       over this date range   per account per
)                                                                        date; includes
SELECT m.account_id, o.observation_date, is_churn,    ⟵                  the churn flag
SUM(CASE WHEN metric_name_id=0 THEN metric_value ELSE 0 END)
    AS like_per_month,                                      ⟵
SUM(CASE WHEN metric_name_id=1 THEN metric_value ELSE 0 END)    Sums the
    AS newfriend_per_month,                                     result of a CASE
SUM(CASE WHEN metric_name_id=2 THEN metric_value ELSE 0 END)    statement to
    AS post_per_month,                                          flatten the data
```

```
SUM(CASE WHEN metric_name_id=3 THEN metric_value ELSE 0 END)
    AS adview_feed_per_month,
SUM(CASE WHEN metric_name_id=4 THEN metric_value ELSE 0 END)
    AS dislike_per_month,
SUM(CASE WHEN metric_name_id=5 THEN metric_value ELSE 0 END)
    AS unfriend_per_month,
SUM(CASE WHEN metric_name_id=6 THEN metric_value ELSE 0 END)
    AS message_per_month,
SUM(CASE WHEN metric_name_id=7 THEN metric_value ELSE 0 END)
    AS reply_per_month,
SUM(CASE WHEN metric_name_id=8 THEN metric_value ELSE 0 END)
    AS account_tenure,
FROM metric m INNER JOIN observation_params
    ON metric_time between obs_start and obs_end
INNER JOIN observation o ON m.account_id = o.account_id
    AND m.metric_time > (o.observation_date - metric_period)::timestamp
    AND m.metric_time <= o.observation_date::timestamp
GROUP BY m.account_id, metric_time,
    observation_date, is_churn
ORDER BY observation_date, m.account_id
```

> Joins on observation parameters to limit the overall date range

> GROUP BY for the SUM/CASE aggregation pattern

> Joins on the observations, selecting the most recent metric

Run listing 4.5 by following the instructions in the book's downloadable code. Using the wrapper program, change the parameters to `--chapter 4 --listing 5`. Listing 4.5 ends with a `SELECT` statement containing the result. If you run it using the code in the GitHub repository, it saves the result in a CSV file for you. The wrapper program prints the path to the file; for example:

```
Saving: ../../../fight-churn-output/socialnet/socialnet_dataset.csv
```

Figure 4.17 shows an example of the result of running listing 4.5. It skips rows to follow a few accounts through the dataset; the dataset observations are arranged by date, so records for a single account are dispersed throughout.

account_ id	observation _date	is_churn	like_per _month	newfriend _per_ month	post _per _month	adview _per_ month	dislike _per_ month	unfriend _per_ month	message _per_ month	reply _per_ month	account _tenure
11	2/18/20	FALSE	318	4	571	235	40	0	29	7	24
...	...		...	...	...	...	...	...	...	...	...
15	3/2/20	FALSE	54	7	42	26	5	1	65	20	54
...	...	...	...	...	...	...	...	...	...	...	...
11	3/18/20	FALSE	362	10	589	280	44	0	43	7	52
...	...	...	...	...	...	...	...	...	...	...	...
15	4/2/20	FALSE	69	10	37	41	11	2	62	16	82
...	...	...	...	...	...	...	...	...	...	...	...
11	4/18/20	TRUE	345	3	613	288	44	2	37	12	80
...	...	...	...	...	...	...	...	...	...	...	...
15	5/2/20	FALSE	54	8	42	41	7	0	45	16	110

Figure 4.17   Example output of running listing 4.5

Note that listing 4.5 is hardcoded to a fixed number of metrics with predefined names, so listing 4.5 works *only* for the default simulated dataset. If you want to run listing 4.5 on your own data, you need to modify it so that it reflects the specific metrics you have created. However, a better option is to automate this step with a script that generates the right SQL based on whatever metrics are in the database. A function that does that is also in the book's code, but not with the listings: the dataset-export folder contains a script that cleans the results tables and runs all the listings in this chapter with a custom-generated metric-flattening script as the finale. The README documentation has more information on how to configure and run that program.

Account key alignment issues

The code in this section assumes that you can simply link the account IDs on the subscriptions used to create the active periods with the account IDs on the events used to create the metrics. Unfortunately, the subscription database and event data warehouse are often different systems. To keep things simple, this book presents them as residing in a common database and using a common set of account IDs. To prepare you for what you may face in the real world, I will explain some of the practical issues you might face if your subscription (observation) and event (metric) data are in two different systems.

You cannot run a program like listing 4.5 with events and subscriptions on different systems. You must either make the observation dates available to the system with the metrics or the metrics available to the system with the subscriptions and observation dates. Usually, it is easiest to generate the active period data from the system with the subscriptions and load them into the system with the metrics, and then generate observation dates from the active periods on the system with the metrics. This minimizes the amount of data you need to transfer. That's the easy part.

Things get more difficult when the account IDs in the two systems don't match and you need a mapping. A lookup table must be created where each row has the *unique* matching identifiers for an account in both systems. Such a mapping can be used as an additional inner join in listing 4.5. That's not too hard, but the real problem arises when it is not possible to create a perfect mapping, resulting in dropped accounts, duplicates, or both. For example, this might occur when event data is tracked by email, subscriptions are tracked by some kind of database primary key, and there are emails with the subscriptions, but the emails don't reliably match the event data. Another version of the problem can arise in a business context where you have subscriptions at the departmental level, and the event data is tracked by user, but some users are assigned to multiple departments or no department. Unless you have worked on a lot of extract-transform-load (ETL) pipelines, it may surprise you that such mapping problems could occur. I assure you, they are very common. If you find yourself in this situation, at least you have plenty of company!

In any event, there is no trick I can teach you that will always fix these kinds of issues. My approach is to drop incomplete records rather than try to repair them, as long as you end up with enough data to analyze. The good news is, your data doesn't have to be perfect to use it! A small proportion of dropped or duplicated accounts in the

(continued)

analytic dataset does *not* invalidate your dataset. By a small proportion, I mean problematic data should be *much* less than half the total. Data is clean, in my opinion, if it is 90% good; and it can be somewhat messy and still be usable.

It's also important that the affected data is more or less random in terms of the types of customers affected. For example, if all the dropped customers use one particular product feature or come from one sales channel, then your results on those groups will be off. But if a small number of accounts are dropped randomly or duplicated randomly across *all* product features and sales channels, then you should have nothing to worry about. We will review some additional methods to remove problematic records from datasets in later chapters, but your best bet is to get the mapping as correct as possible at the start. Just don't expect it to be perfect.

4.7   *Exporting the current customers for segmentation*

This chapter taught you how to prepare a dataset to analyze your customers. But eventually, you will also want to take some actions to try to reduce churn. As I explained in chapter 1, there are a variety of possible strategies to reduce churn. From a data point of view, all churn-reduction methods have one thing in common: you have to use the data to pick the most appropriate customers to target. This is usually called *segmentation*.

DEFINITION   *Segmentation*—Selecting a set of customers according to a set of criteria.

For now, you will learn a technique that lays the groundwork for segmentation by making a snapshot of current customers. More about segmentation is coming in later chapters.

4.7.1   *Selecting active accounts and metrics*

The first step in segmentation and targeting customers for interventions is to make a snapshot of how your customers are doing right now. That is the same as a dataset of the current set of customers and their metrics, but with no history. This is simpler than constructing the historical dataset.

TAKEAWAY   A dataset containing only current customers is used for customer segmentation.

Listing 4.6 shows a SQL SELECT statement that creates a current customer dataset suitable for segmentation. It uses two tricks: first, a CTE selects the most recent date with metrics using MAX aggregation. You also have the option of simply hardcoding a date, but presumably the most recent date with any metrics would be the last day you updated your data. Then listing 4.6 uses the flattening aggregation trick you learned in the last section. That's all there is to it! Run the SQL and check that the result is similar to that from listing 4.5, but with all the accounts observed on a single date: the most recent.

Listing 4.6 Selecting the currently active accounts

```
with metric_date AS            ←──┐  This CTE selects the most
(                                 │  recent date with metrics.
    SELECT  max(metric_time) AS last_metric_time FROM metric
)
SELECT m.account_id, metric_time,
SUM(CASE WHEN metric_name_id=0 THEN metric_value ELSE 0 END)   ←──┐  This is the
    AS like_per_month,                                             │  flattening
SUM(CASE WHEN metric_name_id=1 THEN metric_value ELSE 0 END)      │  aggregation
    AS newfriend_per_month,                                       │  taught with
SUM(CASE WHEN metric_name_id=2 THEN metric_value ELSE 0 END)      │  listing 4.5.
    AS post_per_month,
SUM(CASE WHEN metric_name_id=3 THEN metric_value ELSE 0 END)
    AS adview_feed_per_month,
SUM(CASE WHEN metric_name_id=4 THEN metric_value ELSE 0 END)
    AS dislike_per_month,
SUM(CASE WHEN metric_name_id=5 THEN metric_value ELSE 0 END)
    AS unfriend_per_month,
SUM(CASE WHEN metric_name_id=6 THEN metric_value ELSE 0 END)
    AS message_per_month,
SUM(CASE WHEN metric_name_id=7 THEN metric_value ELSE 0 END)
    AS reply_per_month,
SUM(CASE WHEN metric_name_id=8 THEN metric_value ELSE 0 END)
    AS account_tenure,                    Selects the metrics for
FROM metric m INNER JOIN metric_date      a single date only
    ON metric_time =last_metric_time   ←──┘
INNER JOIN subscription s                  Joins subscriptions to ensure that
    ON m.account_id=s.account_id   ←──┐    customers are currently active
WHERE s.start_date <= last_metric_time
AND (s.end_date >=last_metric_time or s.end_date is null)
GROUP BY m.account_id, metric_time
ORDER BY m.account_id
```

Listing 4.6 also uses a join on the subscription table to make sure these customers are still within an active subscription. The code that calculated the metrics back in chapter 3 never checked that customers were active, so there can be entries for customers who have already churned but still have events in the time period for the metric. From the point of view of metric calculation, the result is only a few extra records, so I didn't bother showing you how to prevent those metrics from being saved. And in the historical dataset, I took care that every observation corresponded to an active customer. But for the current customer list, you need to make sure you're pulling data only for active subscribers, and the join on the subscription table takes care of that detail.

> **NOTE** In practice, listing 4.6 would have to include account names or emails, or whatever identifiers are necessary to link the accounts with other systems used to make interventions with customers, like email marketing and customer relationship management systems. I omit these details from this simulated example.

4.7.2   *Segmenting customers by their metrics*

Now that you have a list of current customers and all their metrics, the act of segmenting is straightforward. If you gave the output of listing 4.6 to your business colleagues, they would probably know what to do: open it in a spreadsheet and use the filtering features to explore and select customers who match different behavioral profiles based on the metrics. You can also define segments by putting criteria in the SELECT statement of listing 4.6. The hard part is knowing *what to choose* for the values to define the segments and which behaviors to focus on in the first place. To do that in a data-driven way, you need to really understand how the behaviors relate to churn and engagement, and that's the subject of the next chapter.

Summary

- A churn analysis dataset is a table of behavioral snapshots of customers, including both customers who churned and customers who did not churn.
- Churn leading indicators are behaviors that suggest a high likelihood of churn at a time when the customer has not yet made up their mind. Churn leading indicators are usually the focus in fighting churn.
- Churn lagging indicators are behaviors that customers often engage in after they have already decided to churn. Churn lagging behaviors are usually not the underlying cause of churn.
- To focus the analysis on churn leading indicators, a behavioral snapshot of customers who churn is made with a lead time before the actual churn occurred.
- Lead times for observing churn are usually a few weeks in advance of churn for a consumer product and one to three months for a business product.
- It is important to ensure that churns and nonchurns in the dataset are sampled roughly in proportion to the actual churn rate and renewal rate, respectively.
- Behavioral snapshots of customers who renew are made at the same regular interval at which churn is measured: typically monthly for a consumer product and annually for a business product. This ensures that the proportion of churns in the dataset approximately matches the churn rate.
- For subscription products, behavioral snapshots of customers who did not churn are made prior to the renewal or payment dates, also with a lead time.
- The first step in creating the churn analysis dataset is identifying *active periods* for each customer, when the customer had at least one subscription (for subscription products) or at least one event (for nonsubscription products) within a short time.
- For nonsubscription products, events are first aggregated into weeks as a single indicator of whether each account had any events that week. Active periods are found from the active weeks.

- After active periods are found, observation dates are selected for each account in a series based on the start of the active period.
- The dataset is created by merging the observation dates with the previously calculated metrics.
- When the dataset is created, the metrics are *flattened*, meaning they are converted from a format with different metrics all in one column to a format in which different metrics are each in their own column.

Part 2

Waging the war

Now that you have the foundations in place, you can start your fight against churn in earnest. For the data person, that fight mainly means delivering actionable customer metrics to the churn fighters in your organization: product managers, marketers, customer success and support representatives, and so on. Great, actionable customer metrics have a clear relationship to churn and retention and can be used to segment customers to target churn-reducing interventions. A great set of customer metrics also must be concise so that the churn fighters stay on target without getting confused by information overload.

Chapter 5 teaches the methods I use for understanding the relationship between churn and behavior. This chapter shows you which metrics drive customer health and engagement and helps you understand what a healthy customer looks like.

Chapter 6 shows you what to do when you have too many related events and metrics. This issue is important because most online services today have so much data that the result is information overload. When you master the techniques in this chapter, however, there will be no such thing as too much data.

Chapter 7 teaches you how to make advanced customer metrics, bringing everything together. These metrics enable more nuanced kinds of understanding and customer targeting than the simple metrics introduced in chapter 3. What you learn in chapters 5 and 6 makes this understanding possible.

Understanding churn and behavior with metrics

5

This chapter covers

- Showing how churn relates to metrics using cohort analysis
- Summarizing the range of customer behaviors with dataset statistics
- Converting metrics from their normal scale to scores
- Removing invalid observations from a cohort analysis
- Defining customer segments based on metrics and churn

If you need to use statistics to understand your experiment, then you ought to have done a better experiment.

> —Ernest Rutherford, Nobel Prize in Chemistry, 1908, known as
> "The Father of Nuclear Physics" for his discovery of radioactive decay

It's time to do what you came here for: understand why your customers are churning and what keeps them engaged. Although it took a while, the dataset you learned to create in chapters 3 and 4 is the foundation for what comes next. You might expect that now I'm going to dive into some serious statistics or machine learning to do the analysis. Instead, I want to call your attention to the quote at the top of the page, which is my favorite saying by a scientist.

The quote suggests that something is wrong if you are using statistics to analyze an experiment. In the age of big data and data science, that might sound like heresy. But I invite you to hold your judgment and consider what Rutherford was getting at. For one thing, he was a physicist at a time when electrical laboratory equipment was assembled by the scientists. If you had a lot of noise in your experimental apparatus, you could use statistics to deal with it by averaging results over many experiments, but maybe you should have spent more time setting up an experiment with less-noisy equipment. For a twenty-first-century data analyst, that can mean that you should spend a lot of time cleaning your data to get better results, which is completely correct. But does it justify maligning statistics?

Maybe I'm reading too much into Rutherford's advice, but I think there is a deeper level to it. It might also mean that if an experiment shows a result that is *not* obviously a confirmation of the hypothesis, don't bother with statistics to see whether you can make the result look better. Instead, come up with a better hypothesis—one that will really explain the thing you are trying to understand. To achieve that goal, you should design experiments to search for explanations that strongly drive the result, not second-order influences. If such a hypothesis is correct, the *qualitative* results of an experiment can be read from a single look at a plot of the results.

It turns out that the most important results for churn analysis and subscriber engagement are usually this way: you will know it when you see it, and you will not need statistics. It's also important that this property of churn will make it easy to communicate to the nontechnical businesspeople in your organization. In the context of churn analysis and behavioral metrics, look for metrics that show a strong relationship to churn, and if you don't find them, keep looking.

> **TAKEAWAY**   You are looking for behavioral metrics that show a strong relationship to churn. When you find one, you will know it when you see the results, without using statistics.

That said, in the third part of this book, I teach statistical and machine-learning methods for churn. It's not that I think there is no place for statistics and machine learning; the question is emphasis. Also, I won't use statistics and machine learning yet, but I didn't say there won't be math; I teach a small amount of necessary math in this chapter and the chapters that follow.

In terms of the overall themes of the book, the topics of this chapter are highlighted in figure 5.1. This chapter assumes that you measured churn rates with the techniques in chapter 2, made behavioral metrics with the techniques in chapter 3, and created a dataset in chapter 4. This chapter is where everything starts to come together!

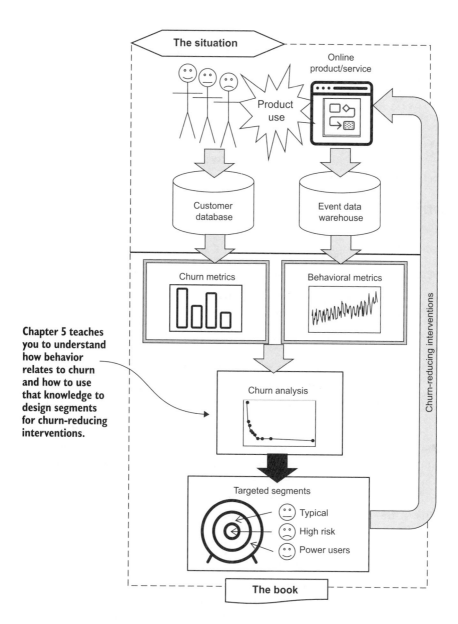

Figure 5.1 This chapter's place in the process of fighting churn with data

Here's how this chapter is organized:

- Section 5.1 teaches you a technique that I call *metric cohorts*, which allows you to investigate the real impact of behaviors that may be related to churn. I demonstrate this technique with examples from case studies to show what typical results look like.

- In section 5.2, I show you how to see the big picture of your customer behaviors by summarizing all the behavior in the dataset. What you find in the dataset summary is useful for refining your cohort analyses.
- Section 5.3 teaches another supporting technique called *scoring*, which is a way to transform customer metrics to improve the quality of analysis. There are no statistics, but the section includes a few equations.
- In section 5.4, I discuss when and how to remove invalid or unwanted data that makes cohort analyses harder to interpret.
- Section 5.5 goes over how to use cohort analysis to define customer segments.

5.1   *Metric cohort analysis*

Cohort analysis is a method of analyzing how churn (and other behaviors) depends on the value of behavioral and subscription metrics, like those taught in chapter 3.

> **DEFINITION**   The following definitions apply throughout the chapter:
>
> - A *cohort* is a group of individuals that are similar (in the specific sense that all those individuals have a particular metric within a relatively small range).
> - A *metric cohort* is a cohort of customers defined by having similar values on a metric.
> - A *cohort analysis* is a comparison of different cohorts on some other measurement (not the one used to define the cohorts)—possibly another metric.
> - A *churn cohort analysis* is a comparison of churn rates in different metric cohorts.

I generally use the term *cohort analysis* for brevity, but it's implied that these analyses are metric cohort analyses of churn unless specified otherwise. You will see a lot of cohort analyses in the rest of the book, so I am going to take the time to introduce the concept before looking at Python code that does the calculation and plots the results. After you've learned the concept and the code, I illustrate the results in some real case studies.

5.1.1   *The idea behind cohort analysis*

Probably the most basic hypothesis of any churn investigation is that people who are using the product a lot are less likely to churn than people who are using the product a little or not at all. A cohort analysis of churn that uses common product behaviors to form the cohorts serves as a test of that hypothesis. Figure 5.2 illustrates the idea. If it is true that active customers churn less than inactive ones, a group of active customers should have a lower churn rate than a group of inactive customers. You can check this hypothesis by dividing the customers into cohorts based on their level of activity and then measure the churn rate in each group. If an activity is related to lower churn, you should find that the churn rate on the most active group is the lowest, a less active group has a higher churn rate, and the least active group has the highest churn rate. Figure 5.2 illustrates this ideal scenario for three groups.

TAKEAWAY   If customers who use a product less churn more, a group of relatively inactive customers should have a higher churn rate than a group of relatively active customers.

An important point to note is that finding relatively higher and lower churn rates in the less and more active groups is more realistic than expecting that *all* active customers don't churn and *all* inactive customers do churn. Churn involves a lot of apparent randomness: sometimes, your best customers quit and your worst stay for reasons that only they will ever know. Comparing churn rates (which are averages) of groups makes sense, but you cannot expect all customers to show exactly the same churn behavior.

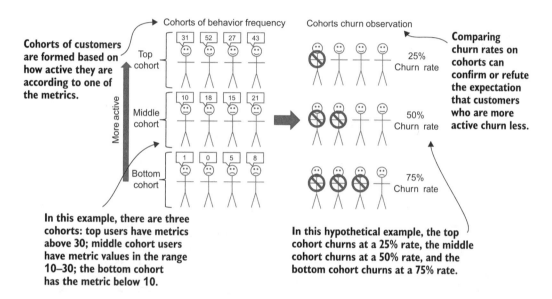

Figure 5.2   The concept of metric cohorts

Next, consider how a cohort analysis is going to work in practice, given the dataset that you created in chapter 4. When you finished that chapter, you created a dataset, which is one big table of data, and on each row, you have one observation of a customer on a particular date, including several metrics and whether the customer churned or renewed on that date. The process of making a metric cohort analysis on a single metric, illustrated in figure 5.3, is as follows:

1 Start from a complete dataset that contains observations of customers, including the metric of interest and whether the customers churn. Some customers can be considered more than once if they renew. The data most likely starts sorted by date and by account ID, assuming that it was created by means of the process described in chapter 4.

2 Using the metric and the variable representing churn or nonchurn, sort those observations by the metric. The identity of the accounts and the observation date are ignored for the rest of the cohort analysis.

3 Group the observations into the cohorts by dividing the observations into a pre-selected number of equal-size groups. In a real cohort analysis, you typically use 10 cohorts, so each cohort contains 10% of the data. (In the simple example shown in figures 5.1 and 5.2, only three cohorts are used.) Note that you do not decide in advance where the boundaries of the cohorts ought to be; the boundaries between cohorts are a result of the analysis.

4 For each cohort, make two calculations:
   - The average value of the metric for all observations in the cohort
   - The percentage of churns in the cohort observations

5 Plot the average metric values and churn rates with the average metric on the x-axis and the churn rate on the y-axis.

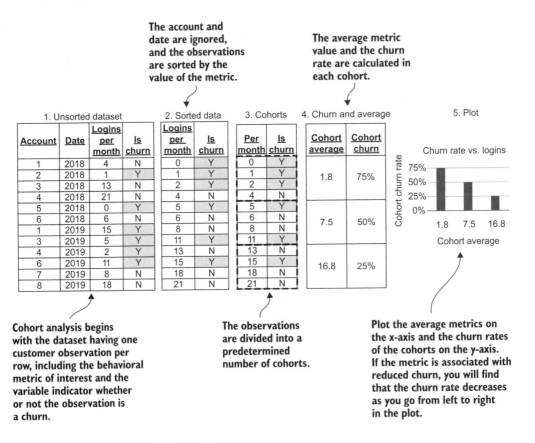

Figure 5.3   Metric cohort analysis example

It might surprise you that the identity of the customers and the date of the observation don't matter for the cohort analysis. Because our dataset is normally formed with multiple observations of most customers, the same customer generally appears many times in your cohorts. Sometimes, a customer appears more than once in one cohort; at other times, the same customer appears in different cohorts. Though this situation may be confusing, it makes sense: you are investigating the hypothesis that the behavior represented by the metric is related to churn, not that the identity of the customer or the timing of the observation is related to churn.

That said, you may not want to explain this detail to your business colleagues, because it can lead to confusion. As discussed in more detail in the sidebar "Analyzing how cohorts change over time" (section 5.1.4), you can test whether both the behavior and the timing of the observation matter, but for now, we continue to explore whether the behavior alone is relevant.

> **TAKEAWAY** Metric cohorts are groups of observations of a customer metric and churn; they are not the same as groups of customers, because one customer can be observed multiple times.

> **WARNING** It is important to understand that one customer can appear multiple times in a cohort analysis, but you probably should not explain this fact to your business colleagues, because they might find it confusing.

5.1.2 Cohort analysis with Python

Figure 5.4 shows a cohort analysis on the simulated dataset that was performed and plotted with Python. The metric is posts per month and is plotted on the x-axis: the cohort averages for the metric range are from near 0 to more than 175. The churn rates are plotted against the y-axis and range from around 0.02 to 0.12. The churn rate decreases dramatically over the cohorts, so behavior has the expected relationship to churn for the simulated social network.

The pattern shown by the simulated data in figure 5.4 is extremely common in real churn case studies. Churn falls rapidly as you move up the bottom cohorts, but the fall in churn rate decelerates and can even level out in the top cohorts. This pattern makes it easy to identify the metric's healthy level. For posts per month in the simulation, above 25 is healthy because at that point, further increases don't have observable effects on the churn rate.

I will show you real case studies in section 5.1.3, but first, let's look at the code to perform cohort analysis. Listing 5.1 shows a Python function that performs a single metric cohort analysis using Pandas `DataFrames`. The function has the following inputs:

- `data_set_path`—A path to a dataset saved in a file, given by a string variable
- `metric_to_plot`—The name of a metric to make the cohort plot, given by a string variable
- `ncohort`—The number of cohorts to use, given by an integer variable

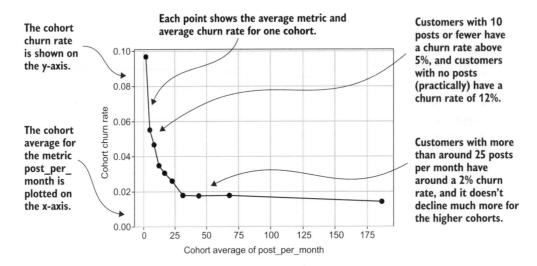

The cohort churn rate is shown on the y-axis.

Each point shows the average metric and average churn rate for one cohort.

Customers with 10 posts or fewer have a churn rate above 5%, and customers with no posts (practically) have a churn rate of 12%.

The cohort average for the metric post_per_month is plotted on the x-axis.

Customers with more than around 25 posts per month have around a 2% churn rate, and it doesn't decline much more for the higher cohorts.

Figure 5.4   Cohort analysis of posts per month for the simulated customer dataset

Given these inputs, the following are the main steps you use to create a cohort plot:

1 Load the dataset into a Pandas `DataFrame` object, and set the `DataFrame` index.
2 Use the `DataFrame` member function `qcut` to divide the observations into cohorts. This function returns a series. The series length is the same as the number of observations, and the series values are integers representing the group assignments.
3 Calculate the average metric and the average churn rate, using the `DataFrame` function `groupby` and passing the `qcut` result (the series of group identifiers) as the parameter.
4 Make a new `DataFrame` from the averages and churn rates.
5 Plot the result, using `matplotlib.pyplot`, and add the appropriate labeling before saving.

Note that this procedure has one important difference from the solution to the example problem in section 5.1.1: rather than sorting the data, forming the cohorts, and calculating the averages by using your logic, the code relies on Pandas `Data-Frame.qcut` and `DataFrame.groupby` functions. `qcut` is short for *quantile-based discretization*, which is a technical term for the kind of cohort groups that we are making, drawing explicitly on the notion of a quantile.

> **DEFINITION**   A *quantile* is a value that results as a dividing point when data is divided into equal groups, each containing the same fraction of the total number of observations. A *decile* is a quantile when the data is divided into 10 groups, with each of the groups containing 10% of the data. A *percentile* is a quantile when the data is divided into 100 groups, each containing 1% of the data.

The first decile is the value of the metric that divides the first 10% of the data from the second 10% of the data when the data is organized by the metric. The second decile is the value of the metric that divides the second 10% of the data from the third 10% of the data, and so on. In a mathematical context, *discrete* means separate (or not continuous). The groups are discrete in the sense that membership in them is all or nothing (not *discreet* in the sense of something secretive or hidden). The qcut function is named quantile-based discretization because the data is divided into discrete groups by the values of the quantiles.

Listing 5.1 Metric cohorts in Python

```python
import pandas as pd
import matplotlib.pyplot as plt
import os

def cohort_plot(data_set_path, metric_to_plot, ncohort=10):
    assert os.path.isfile(data_set_path),
        '"{}" is not a valid path'.format(data_set_path)
    churn_data = pd.read_csv(data_set_path,
        index_col=[0,1])
    groups = pd.qcut(churn_data[metric_to_plot], ncohort,
        duplicates='drop')
    cohort_means =
        churn_data.groupby(groups)[metric_to_plot].mean()
    cohort_churns =
        churn_data.groupby(groups)['is_churn'].mean()
    plot_frame = pd.DataFrame({metric_to_plot: cohort_means.values,
        'churn_rate': cohort_})
    plt.figure(figsize=(6, 4))
    plt.plot(metric_to_plot, 'churn_rate', data=plot_frame,marker='o',
             linewidth=2,label=metric_to_plot)
    plt.xlabel('Cohort Average of  "%s"' % metric_to_plot)
    plt.ylabel('Cohort Churn Rate (%)'
    plt.grid()
    plt.gca().set_ylim(bottom=0)
    save_path = data_set_path.replace('.csv', '_' +
        metric_to_plot + '_churn_corhort.png')
    plt.savefig(save_path)
    print('Saving plot to %s' % save_path)
    plt.close()
```

Checks the dataset path →
Calculates the means of the metric for the cohorts →
Calculates the churn rates of the cohorts →
Makes a new DataFrame from the cohorts →

Loads the dataset into a Pandas DataFrame object and sets the index
Groups into cohorts and returns a series of the group numbers
Opens a new figure
Plots the cohort churn rate vs. the cohort metric average
Adds axes labels
Saves and closes the figure

Writing your own algorithms vs. using off-the-shelf module functions

If you are still in a computer science or programming class, you may think it's cheating to use a function like DataFrame.qcut to implement an algorithm, because normally, a computer science education is about writing your own algorithms. Or maybe you think that in a book like this one, it's cheating to use such a function because books are supposed to teach you to write algorithms. In this context, however, using the Pandas algorithm is the best practice.

(continued)

In case you haven't noticed, there is plenty of work to do in analyzing churn without reinventing the wheel by writing an algorithm to divide data into groups. The same goes for calculating the average and churn rate by using the `DataFrame.groupby` function; there's no reason to write your own logic when a standard module function does exactly what you need to do. I take this approach throughout the book, always trying to achieve goals by using algorithms that are part of a standard module.

Given that the `DataFrame.qcut` and `DataFrame.groupby` functions perform the main steps in the algorithm, half of listing 5.1 is concerned with plotting the result. Because this listing is the first plotting code in this book, I want to briefly mention the importance of clearly labeling all plots and figures that you produce in your analysis.

> **WARNING**   Clearly label all plots produced by your analysis. The business-people with whom you share your analysis won't be familiar with the details, and if you don't label the results clearly, the plots will be difficult for them to follow.

Labeling the results also helps you later, when you come back to your analysis and try to remember what the results mean, especially if you have a lot of events and metrics. You may have to sift through dozens or even hundreds of cohort plots, which will be impossible if you don't build clear annotation into your process.

If you haven't done so already, run listing 5.1 to test it with your own data. Assuming that you have set up your environment (instructions are in the README file in this book's GitHub repository at https://github.com/carl24k/fight-churn) and are using the Python wrapper program, run listing 5.1 with the command

```
fight-churn/listings/run_churn_listing.py --chapter 5 --listing 1
```

The result should be a .png file with a cohort plot that looks like figure 5.4.

5.1.3   *Cohorts of product use*

Figure 5.5 displays a first example of a cohort analysis from a real case study that shows churn in metric cohorts for Broadly's customers. An important event for Broadly's customers is the number of online reviews that are updated, so a metric is calculated for the number of reviews updated per month.

Because this figure illustrates the first real metric cohort churn case study in this book, I need to make an important point that holds true for all other studies in the book that are based on real companies (not simulations): figure 5.5 does not show actual churn rates as percentages on the y-axis. Instead, the y-axis is unlabeled, and the churn rate is described as relative. The actual churn rates are omitted to protect the privacy and business interests of the companies in the case studies, but you can still see the significance of the difference in churn between cohorts because the bottom of the cohort plots is always fixed at zero churn. As a result, the distance of the points from the bottom of the chart shows the *relative* churn rates of the cohorts.

For Broadly's metric, the churn rate is highest in the first cohort and declines over the first five cohorts; the churn rate in the top three cohorts (on the right side of the plot, with the highest metric values) is around half the churn rate in the bottom cohort. You can tell that the churn in the top cohort is around half the churn in the bottom cohort by noting that it is approximately half the distance to the bottom of the graph, using the equally spaced grid lines. (To be precise, the churn in the top cohort of figure 5.5 is a bit more than half the churn rate of the bottom cohort.) Another point worth noting in figure 5.5 is that the reduction in churn rate occurs between the cohorts that have around zero review updates per month and those that have four review updates per month; after four review updates per month, there is no further reduction in churn rate.

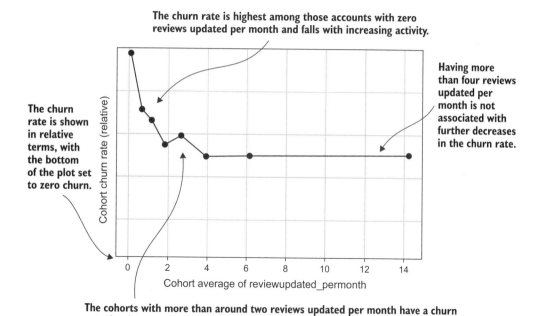

Figure 5.5   Cohort analysis of churn for Broadly's metric (reviews updated per month)

Figure 5.6 shows another example of a metric cohort churn case study for Klipfolio. This figure shows a case study in metric cohort analysis, using the metric dashboard edits per month calculated on Klipfolio's customers. As in figure 5.5, churn rates are shown on a relative scale, with the bottom of the plot fixed to zero churn. In this case, the churn rate of the top cohorts is a fraction of that of the bottom cohorts (about 10%).

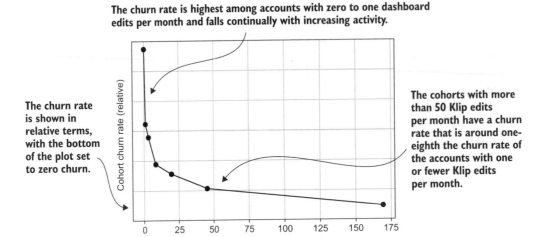

The churn rate is highest among accounts with zero to one dashboard edits per month and falls continually with increasing activity.

The churn rate is shown in relative terms, with the bottom of the plot set to zero churn.

The cohorts with more than 50 Klip edits per month have a churn rate that is around one-eighth the churn rate of the accounts with one or fewer Klip edits per month.

Cohort churn rate (relative)

Cohort average of klip_editor_permonth

Figure 5.6   Cohort analysis of churn for Klipfolio's metric (dashboard edits per month)

Figure 5.7 shows another metric cohort churn example, using Versature's metric for total local-call times per month. This figure depicts another fairly typical relationship between an important behavioral metric and churn. The cohorts with more than 2,500 total local-call times per month churn at around a third the rate of the bottom cohort, which makes practically no calls. The reduction in churn rate happens between zero and 2,500, after which the churn rate seems to increase slightly but not significantly.

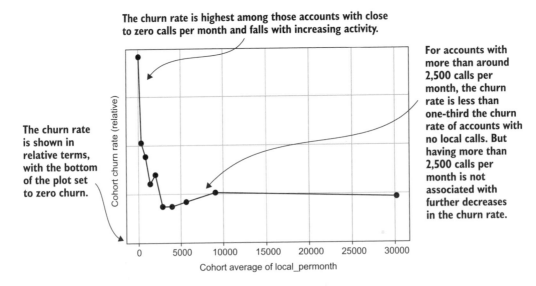

The churn rate is highest among those accounts with close to zero calls per month and falls with increasing activity.

For accounts with more than around 2,500 calls per month, the churn rate is less than one-third the churn rate of accounts with no local calls. But having more than 2,500 calls per month is not associated with further decreases in the churn rate.

The churn rate is shown in relative terms, with the bottom of the plot set to zero churn.

Cohort churn rate (relative)

Cohort average of local_permonth

Figure 5.7   Cohort analysis of churn for Versature's metric local-call times per month

Looking at the distribution of local calls (not churn rates) in figure 5.7, note that most of the cohorts are compressed on the left side of the graph in the low range. In fact, seven cohorts occupy a sixth of the figure (the region between 0 and 5,000 calls). This figure shows that the cohort with the most calls makes a lot more calls than the others, so even the second-highest cohort has less than a third as many calls on average. This example shows a skewed behavioral metric.

> **DEFINITION** A *skewed* metric is one in which the top cohort contains values several times higher than those of the next-closest cohort. Typically, most of the lower cohorts have averages within a relatively small range.

Skew is an important concept in metrics, as I'll explain in section 5.2.1. Skew can cause problems in your analysis, beginning with the fact that figure 5.6 is a bit hard to read. Most of the space is taken up by the top two cohorts; the others are squeezed together. This arrangement is a natural result of skew in the distribution of metric values, because the top cohorts are many multiples above the rest. Skew causes another problem when you try to understand the relationships among metrics, as described in chapter 6. For that reason, I teach the technique known as *scoring metrics* in section 5.3.

I want to call your attention to one more feature of the cohort churn analyses in figures 5.5, 5.6, and 5.7: they all have the same overall shape, with the cohort churn rates falling rapidly in the first couple of cohorts; for higher cohorts, the churn rate is more or less constant. This result is common, and it's the reason why the simulation shown in figure 5.4 was crafted to act that way.

The fact that churn rates fall with behavior and then level off is both useful and a problem. It's useful because it's easy to identify a healthy level for the metric: the level where churn rates stop declining. It's a problem because after a certain point, that metric no longer helps you understand churn or segment customers based on churn risk. In terms of intervening to reduce churn, getting users to take more of certain actions doesn't make a difference past a certain point. If you want to explain differences in the churn rate among customers with high values on those metrics and reduce churn among those customers, you need to do something else. In chapters 6 and 7, you learn techniques to create metrics in which the relationship to churn stays strong, even up to the top cohorts.

5.1.4 Cohorts of account tenure

Another common kind of cohort analysis looks at churn based on the length of time that customers have been customers—a period that I call account tenure. This form of cohort analysis is the most common, so if you have seen a cohort-based churn analysis, it was probably based on tenure.

This type of cohort analysis is the same as metric cohort analysis except that it looks at account tenure instead of behavior. Also, you usually expect to find that customers who have been customers for a long time are less likely to churn and that newer customers are more likely to churn. A cohort analysis using account tenure serves as a test of that hypothesis. Because account tenure is calculated as an account metric, this type of cohort analysis is performed with exactly the same code that was used in the behavioral metric cohort analysis in section 5.1.3.

Figure 5.8 shows the result of a cohort analysis of account tenure for Klipfolio. The results are fairly typical:

- Churn is lower for the newest customers (around a month average tenure) than for customers of longer duration.
- Churn increases in the first half of the year and is about a third higher in the third cohort.
- Churn decreases for customers between a half-year and one year. But churn increases for customers at the end of the first year.
- After the first year (cohorts with average tenure greater than 365 days), churn is lower and declines such that the cohort with the longest tenure (around four years) has about a third less churn as the newest cohort.

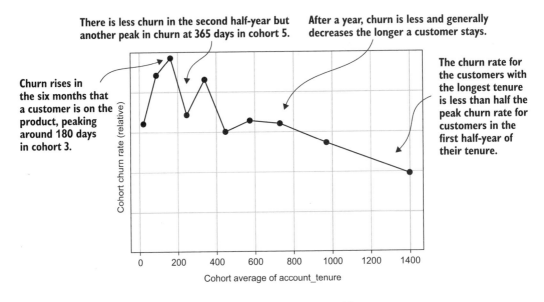

Figure 5.8 Cohort analysis of churn for Klipfolio's account tenure metric

Though tenure-based cohort analysis is the most common form in the literature on churn, the analysis I demonstrated in figure 5.8 is a bit different. The most common way to define account tenure cohorts and perform this analysis is to group customers by the time that they sign up: month, quarter, or year. After that initial cohort assignment, the number of customers remaining in each cohort is tracked over time and used to derive the churn rates for each cohort at different points in time. By contrast, the method I demonstrate observes customers independently on a schedule determined by their own renewals and forms cohorts from all observations that have similar values on the tenure measurement.

One advantage of this approach is that the churn rate for more seasoned (longer-tenure) cohorts is estimated on a larger pool of customers, because the older cohorts combine customers who signed up at different times. A potential disadvantage is that this cohort analysis does not show how the churn rate in cohorts of a given tenure can change over time, because the tenure cohort analysis method blends observations of customers who signed up at different times.

Analyzing how cohorts change over time

Usually, there are no significant differences in churn rates for customers of the same tenure who signed up a few months apart. Any differences may be due to random variation or driven by seasonality. But if you wait a year or more, churn patterns might change considerably.

To check whether any relationship between churn and a metric has changed, I recommend using the methods in chapter 4 to create different datasets for different periods and then comparing the results on separate cohort analyses. You might create one dataset of only observations from the past year and another dataset from observations of the previous year, for example. (Using one-year periods for the datasets should control seasonality.) If you see significant differences between the cohort churn rates for the different datasets, the relationship between churn and tenure changed between those two years. You can use this approach when changes in your product or marketing strategy result in different customer behavior during different time periods. Create a dataset for each time period, and compare your cohort analyses from the different datasets. (See section 5.1.6 for discussion of the minimum number of observations needed.)

5.1.5 *Cohort analysis of billing period*

Metrics based on customer subscriptions can be analyzed with cohort analysis. Figure 5.9 shows an analysis of churn and subscription billing among Broadly customers with monthly or annual billing periods. The figure illustrates two cohorts because there are only two distinct values for the billing period, which appear in the plot as points at 1 and 12 because the billing period is measured in months. Broadly's customers show a typical pattern: customers with annual billing churn at a significantly lower rate than customers with monthly billing.

The result in figure 5.9 is based on monthly churn rates, due to monthly observation. It may seem strange to analyze annual customers this way, however, because an annual customer has the opportunity to churn only once each year. Another possible approach is to do separate metric cohort analyses on annual and monthly customers and then observe the annual customers once a year. That technique can work if you have a lot of annual customers, but it is usually a problem, because you have far fewer observations of annual customers than of monthly customers. As a result, you may not have enough annual customer observations to make a separate behavioral analysis.

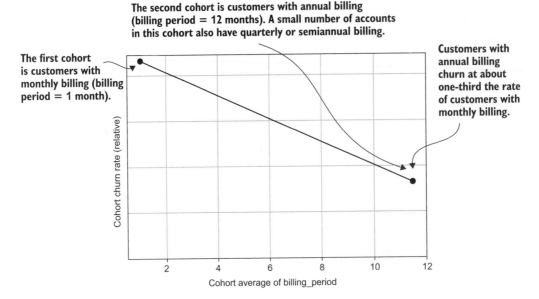

Figure 5.9   Cohort analysis of churn for Broadly's customers having monthly versus annual billing periods

To understand annual customer behavior, it's better to combine annual and monthly customers. You might think it would be a good idea to observe the annual customers once a year and combine them in a single dataset with monthly customers (by changing the logic of dataset construction). But then the annual customers would appear to churn at a *higher* rate; by observing them once a year, you implicitly calculate an annual churn rate on their cohort. Imagine figure 5.9 showing that annual customers churn at a higher rate than monthly customers. If you observe annual billing customers once a year and want to compare them with monthly customers, you have to convert the monthly customer churn rate to annual, thereby showing the true relationship: monthly billing customers have a higher *annual* churn rate. The best choice is to observe mixed populations of monthly and annual customers with monthly observations.

5.1.6   *Minimum cohort size*

An important issue in analyzing churn with cohorts is the number of observations made in each cohort. You need enough observations in each cohort that when you estimate the cohort churn rates, the estimates are likely to be accurate. Remember from the discussion in chapter 1 that churn is affected by a lot of random factors that are outside your knowledge and influence. When you estimate the churn rate in a cohort based on the metric, part of the result is due to the influence of the metric and part is due to all the other things. The idea is that you need a lot of observations to make all those "other things" cancel out and show the influence of the metric. How many is "a lot" depends, but a simple rule of thumb is that you should have 200 to 300 observations in each cohort, and preferably thousands.

TAKEAWAY Every cohort should have at least 200 to 300 observations, and preferably a few thousand.

Note that I am talking about how many *observations* should be in each cohort, not how many *customers*. If you have 500 customers with monthly renewals, and you observe their behavior (metrics and churn) for six months, you will have around 3,000 observations. If you form 10 cohorts, each cohort will have 300 observations, so you should be good. The problem with minimum cohort size comes up with annual renewals: if you have 500 customers with annual renewals, after an entire year, you have only 500 observations.

If you have too few observations in each cohort, the first thing you should do is use fewer cohorts. Given the example of 500 observations, you could form three cohorts of 167, 167, and 166. At least you'd have more than 100 observations in each cohort, if not the few hundred that you want. Then your cohorts would represent low, medium, and high levels of the metric you are analyzing.

WARNING It is more important to have enough observations in a few cohorts than to have a lot of cohorts in a cohort analysis. Reduce the number of cohorts accordingly.

If you still have fewer than 200 observations in each cohort, you are getting into a danger zone where the noise of random events can overwhelm the signal you are looking for in the metric-based cohorts. Around 100 observations might still work if your churn rate is relatively high—well in the double digits (greater than 20%). That is because if the churn rate is fairly high, the influence of random factors on the churn rate is likely to be relatively small. But when the churn rate is low (below 10%), random external factors are more likely to be significant in comparison with the influence of the metric. So if your churn rate is low, you need even more observations to cancel out the noise and reveal the trend. If your churn rate is low, you should not try to do an analysis until you have at least 200 observations per cohort, and preferably a lot more.

Another rule of thumb is to have at least 100 churns in an analysis. For example, if your churn rate is 5%, you should have a total of around 2,000 observations (because to end up with 100 churn observations from a 5% churn rate, you would have to have $100 / 0.05 = 2,000$ observations). Usually, the lower limits on the number of observations and churns aren't a problem; most companies focus initially on customer acquisition and think about churn only when they have been in operation for some time. But a variety of issues can limit the number of observations, such as having a short history of events in the data warehouse, and you should be aware of those limitations.

TAKEAWAY If you have fewer than 100 churns in your data, you should focus on acquiring new customers and understanding their views qualitatively with surveys and focus groups. It will be hard to understand churn from data with so few examples.

These rough guidelines are based more on practical experience than on rigorous statistics. Chapters 8 and 10 discuss some statistics you can use to come up with better answers to questions about sample size.

5.1.7   *Significant and insignificant cohort differences*

So far I have shown you only cases in which a customer metric is clearly related to churn. Inevitably, however, you will test some metrics with cohorts and find no significant result. Figure 5.10 shows one example for the cloud communication services provider Versature. In this case, the metric is the number of extension units that customers purchased. The churn rate does not have any clear trend: the bottom cohort has about the same churn rate as the top cohort, and the churn rates in the middle cohorts bounce around but never differ significantly from the average. This behavior is *not* related to churn.

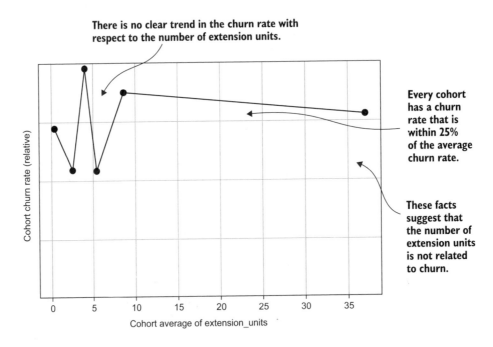

Figure 5.10   Cohort analysis when the difference in churn is not significant

Other cases are less clear-cut but not obviously unrelated. In chapter 8, I go over using statistics to answer these questions more rigorously, but you can often make a reasoned judgment without statistics. If you're trying to decide whether a metric is related to churn, the first question to ask is whether other metrics are much more obviously related to churn.

TAKEAWAY If you are unsure whether a metric is related to churn, first ask whether other obvious metrics have strong relationships to churn. If so, focus on the latter metrics, try to use that knowledge in your retention tactics, and come back to questionable cases later.

The only cases to worry about are borderline cases:

- When you have few metrics that are strongly related to churn
- When a particular metric was expected to relate to churn and a retention or engagement strategy has already been planned based on that expectation

In such cases, you should look at whether the change in churn rates is consistent across cohorts and whether the difference in the lowest and highest churn rate cohorts is significant. If churn generally goes from high to low (or low to high), and the difference between the highest and the lowest is a factor of at least 1.5, it's reasonable to think that you've found a potentially useful relationship to churn.

Finally, you should think about the business reasons for the relationship to churn:

- Does the metric measure something that is closely related to the usefulness or customer enjoyment of the product?
- Or is the metric peripheral to central features of the product?

If you strongly believe that the metric should be important, you can give your analysis the benefit of the doubt and recheck the result when you have more data. On the other hand, if the data doesn't support a pet theory, don't keep trying too long; that's an example of being data driven.

Finally, note that questions of significance are related to sample size, discussed in section 5.1.6: if you have a lot of samples, you are more likely to see a meaningful relationship. More advanced methods are used to look at these questions in chapters 8 and 10.

5.1.8 *Metric cohorts with a majority of zero customer metrics*

Another issue you might face in a cohort analysis is that you can have a lot of observations with no results for the metric of interest, even when you have plenty of observations overall. This situation can happen when an event is rare, even if you measure it over a long period (as described in chapter 3). Figure 5.11 shows an example metric cohort analysis for Klipfolio. Most accounts have zero for the metric in question: the number of orientation switches per month that users make when viewing their dashboards. In this case, only three cohorts are formed by the Python function `Data-Frame.qcut`, even though the parameter for the cohorts was set to 10.

The cohort plot in figure 5.11 still shows a relationship with churn, but the plot does not look quite as expected. If you know the reason, you know that nothing is wrong, but you will have to explain to your business colleagues why there are only three cohorts. In section 5.4, I show you how to improve on this sort of analysis by removing unwanted observations.

More than half of the accounts have zero orientation switches. As a result, only three cohorts are formed, even though there are a large number of observations.

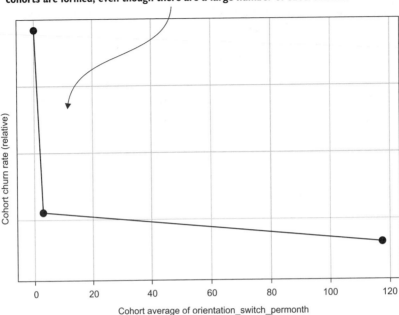

Figure 5.11   Cohort analysis with a majority of zero observations

If an event is rare, and the metric has zero value for most customers, that metric is probably not going to have as significant a relationship to churn as a behavior in which more accounts participate. To some degree, you should ignore rare events and focus on the common ones. There could be exceptional cases, of course, if the behavior in question has an important relationship with churn for the few accounts involved. Another approach to handling rare behavior metrics is to combine them in behavioral groups, as detailed in chapter 6.

5.1.9   *Causality: Are the metrics causing churn?*

Now you know how to discover when behavioral metrics are related to churn, and you have a good sense of when those relationships are significant. But you may be wondering about causality (and if you aren't, now is a good time to start). Causality raises these questions:

- If you see lower churn when a metric is high, do the event and behavior in question cause customer retention?
- Does a low value for a metric (low counts of an event) cause a customer to churn?

Unfortunately, these questions have no simple answers. Advanced statistics can be used to analyze questions of causality, but those techniques are beyond the scope of this book. For that matter, I don't recommend using advanced methods to understand causality for churn due to the need for a parsimonious, agile analysis (chapter 1).

My approach to causality is as follows: customers churn or don't churn because of the utility or enjoyment they get from using the product or service. Here, I mean *utility* in the economic sense of usefulness and subjective pleasure. If the event behind the metric is the act that provides utility to the customer, it is fair to say that the event is causing both retention and churn. If the event is not the one that provides utility but something that happens along the way, it's fair to say that the event and the metric are *associated* with customer engagement and retention, but not the cause.

How do you know which event provides utility to the customer? You should rely on your knowledge of the product and common sense (and if you don't know, try talking to some customers). That said, if you thought that an event provided utility to customers but find that it's related only weakly to churn and retention, you may want to rethink your beliefs—another example of being data driven.

> **TAKEAWAY** You need to rely on your knowledge of the business to decide whether a metric related to churn is *causing* retention and churn or only *associated* with churn and retention. To cause churn, the event must be closely related to customers achieving usefulness from or enjoyment of the product.

The distinction between metrics and events that cause retention or churn and those that are associated with it does not make much difference in the analysis of churn-related data, but it does make a big difference in your strategies to drive retention. If you think an event or metric is associated with retention but not causing it, there is no point in trying to encourage your customers to take that specific action.

> **WARNING** If you do not believe that an event is causing customer retention and churn, do not attempt to encourage customers to take that action, even if it is strongly associated with churn.

5.2 *Summarizing customer behavior*

By now, you know a lot about how to perform metric cohort analyses of churn in relationship to your metrics. You've also seen a few issues that might cause results to be hard to interpret. One issue is that metrics can be skewed, which can make cohort analyses hard to read and hard to compare. Another problem that might come up is having a rare event with most of the account metrics resulting in zero. These problems are fairly typical and not necessarily wrong, but you can do things about them if they are extreme. First, to help diagnose these problems and make sure that you are not surprised when they occur, I am going to show you how to check these kinds of issues by making a summary of your dataset.

A dataset summary helps you check for problems and is also a great way to get a sense of the overall range of behaviors exhibited by your customers. That understanding will help you plan your customer segments and interventions to increase engagement.

5.2.1   *Understanding the distribution of the metrics*

A *summary* of a dataset is a set of measurements of the contents of the dataset—a set of metrics on your metrics. The results in the dataset summary give you a good idea of the range and variety of your customers' behaviors. It can also help you spot many problems in your data before you waste time doing an analysis.

> **TIP**   You should calculate a set of summary statistics and resolve any data problems before you start cohort analysis of churn. I taught you cohort analysis first to show you why you want an initial summary.

The *distribution* of a metric is what statisticians and analysts use to describe these kinds of properties—things like the minimum, maximum, and typical values.

> **DEFINITION**   The *distribution* of a metric refers to the overall set of facts about what values a metric takes for customers. Understanding a distribution means knowing—at an appropriate level of detail—facts such as how many customers have the metric, what the typical values are, and what the minimum and maximum values are.

Figure 5.12 shows such a summary for the simulated social network dataset. Table 5.1 at the end of this section briefly explains the summary statistics, which will be familiar to anyone who has already taken a statistics course. If you want more information, many texts and online resources provide in-depth explanation of these measures.

Following are some key points about the dataset summary in figure 5.12:

1 Most metrics have nonzero values for nearly 100% of accounts except the unfriend_per_month metric, which shows values for only 25% of accounts.

2 Metrics event count means are usually in the hundreds, and the maximum event counts are in the thousands. The exceptions are unfriend and new friend, both of which are rarer.

The table shows statistics of the churns because it is a column in the dataset too.

Metric	count	nonzero	mean	std	skew	min	1pct	25pct	50pct	75pct	99pct	max
is_churn	32316	4.6%	.0459	0.2	4.9	0	0	0	0	0	1	1
like_per_month	32316	99%	93.7	204.7	12.1	0	1	16	39	95	826	6867
newfriend_per_month	32316	90%	6.6	8.1	3.9	0	0	2	4	8	38	136
post_per_month	32316	98%	39.2	72.5	9.8	0	0	8	19	43	315	2148
adview_per_month	32316	98%	38.5	68.9	7.6	0	0	8	19	43	304	1566
dislike_per_month	32316	95%	15.2	22.1	6.4	0	0	4	9	18	102	633
unfriend_per_month	32316	25%	0.30	0.5	1.9	0	0	0	0	1	2	5
message_per_month	32316	98%	60.1	125.9	7.4	0	0	9	24	59	566	2676
reply_per_month	32316	91%	21.8	44.8	6.5	0	0	2	8	22	213	840
account_tenure	32316	100%	61.4	29.6	0.2	18	19	26	54	83	116	116

Most metrics have means in the hundreds and are skewed to some degree.

Unfriend per month is the only metric that has much less than 100% nonzero values.

Account tenure averages 61 days, ranges from 0 to 116 days, and is not skewed.

Figure 5.12   Examples of summary statistics from the social network simulation dataset

3 Most metrics are skewed to varying degrees; events with higher counts have higher skews.

4 The statistics for the account_tenure metric show that all accounts have a measurement because the nonzero measurement (column 2) is 100%. The mean (average) is 61 days, and the skew of account tenure is 0.2, indicating that it is more or less evenly distributed around its mean.

5 The table also shows statistics of churn in the dataset: 4.6% of the observations are churns.

Real churn case study data usually is similar in terms of the distribution and skew of metrics, but real company data typically has many more metrics, for which only a small fraction of accounts have nonzero values. (I deliberately put one in the simulation for you to learn from while still keeping the simulation parsimonious.)

Table 5.1 Metric distribution summary statistics

Summary statistic	Explanation
Percentage nonzero	The percentage of observations in the dataset in which the metric is not zero—an important check on how rare a behavior is.
Mean	The measure of a typical value for a metric (also known as average). It is calculated by summing the metric on all observations and dividing by the number of observations.
Standard deviation	A measure of how varied the values of the metric are in the sense of whether all the values are relatively close to the typical value. A high standard deviation occurs when many values are far from a typical value. Sometimes, it is convenient to refer to a metric value by how many standard deviations the value is from the mean. If the mean is 20 and the standard deviation is 5, for example, a metric observation of 25 is said to be 1 standard deviation above the mean. In that case, 30 would be called 2 standard deviations above the mean, and so on. This terminology is useful because it conveys a sense of how a metric observation compares with typical values without requiring you to remember the typical value for every metric.
Skew	A statistical measure of how symmetric or lopsided the distribution of the metric is. This kind of lopsidedness occurs in the cohort analyses earlier in this chapter. If the skew is zero, the low and high values are symmetrically distributed around the mean. If the skew is positive, there are more observations of the metric that are higher than the mean than observations that are smaller than the mean. If the skew is negative, the opposite is true: more observations are smaller than the mean than those that are greater than the mean. (You are not likely to see that result in typical behavioral metrics.) Generally, skews below 3 or 4 are not significant, but metrics with skews of 5 or greater are significantly skewed.
Quantiles (1%, 5%, and so on)	Quantiles are the metric values required to find a fixed percent of the observations below that value. The 1% quantile, for example, is the metric value that 1% of observations have a value less than; the other 99% of observations have a value greater than the 1% quantile. The 5% quantile is the metric value that 5% of the observations are less than and 95% are greater than. This pattern continues for all the higher quantiles. Looking at the sequence of quantiles in the summary is a good way to get a sense of what percentage of customer values are in what range. If you see that the 25th percentile of logins is 20 and the 75th percentile of logins is 100, 50% of customers (75 − 25 = 50) have between 20 and 100 logins.

Table 5.1   Metric distribution summary statistics *(continued)*

Summary statistic	Explanation
Median (50% quantile)	Another measure of a typical value for a metric, like the mean. The median is the value that half of the observations are greater than and half are less than (same as the 50% quantile). The median is a better measure of the typical value of a metric than the mean when the data includes extreme outliers—when the metric has a high skew. Extreme outliers raise the mean but not the median, so the median always reflects a customer in the middle.
Minimum and maximum	The lowest and highest values observed for any customer.

Normal and fat-tailed distributions

In the famous normal (bell curve) distribution, around two-thirds of all the values are within 1 standard deviation of the mean, and almost all the values are within 3 standard deviations of the mean. If the mean is 20, and the standard deviation is 5, 3 standard deviations means 3 x 5 = 15. In that case, most of the observations have values between 5 and 35 (because 20 − 15 = 5, and 20 + 15 = 35). For a normal distribution, it is extremely rare to have values that are 5 or more standard deviations from the mean.

But behavioral metrics typically have more outliers than a normal distribution, so those relationships probably won't hold in your data. A distribution with more extreme outliers than the normal distribution is often called a *fat-tailed* distribution. The tails of the distribution are the extremes, and if the tails are fat, a lot of observations are extreme. For most of your own metrics, fewer than two-thirds of observations will be within 1 standard deviation of the mean, and more will be farther away; maybe a third of the observations will be within 1 standard deviation of the mean. Having behavioral metric values that are 5 to 10 standard deviations from the mean (or more) is common for most products.

5.2.2 *Calculating dataset summary statistics in Python*

Taking a set of summary measurements on a dataset is a common task in data analysis, so Python's Pandas module already provides a function to do it—DataFrame .describe. This function calculates a set of measurements for every column in the dataset. Recall that each column of the dataset contains the observation values for one metric. Calling the describe function produces a set of summary statistics for each metric.

Listing 5.2 shows a complete program that uses the Pandas function and adds a few fields to the summary, which I find useful for understanding customer behavior. The main steps in listing 5.2 are as follows:

1 Load the dataset into a Pandas `DataFrame`, given a path.

2 Call the Pandas function `DataFrame.describe` to get a basic summary. The basic summary includes the mean, standard deviation, minimum and maximum, and 25th, 50th, and 75th percentiles. The summary data is returned as another Pandas `DataFrame`.

3 Calculate some additional statistics, and add them to the summary result. These additional statistics are

   – The skew, calculated with the Pandas function `DataFrame.skew`

   – The 1st and 99th percentiles, calculated with the Pandas function `DataFrame.quantile`

   – The percentage of nonzero observations of each metric, which is calculated using a little trick: converting the column to a Boolean type and summing it gives the count of nonzero values; then dividing by the number of rows converts it to a percentage

4 The columns of the final results are reordered more logically.

5 The result is saved.

Listing 5.2 will be used again later in this chapter, as some of these summary statistics are needed for further analysis of your dataset.

Listing 5.2 Statistics of a churn analysis dataset

Provides a standard set of summary statistics

```python
import pandas as pd
import os

def dataset_stats(data_set_path):                        # Checks the dataset path
    assert os.path.isfile(data_set_path),
        '"{}" is not a valid path'.format(data_set_path)  # Loads data into a Pandas DataFrame object and sets the index
    churn_data =
        pd.read_csv(data_set_path, index_col=[0,1])

    if 'is_churn' in churn_data:                          # Converts the churn indicator to a float
        churn_data['is_churn'] =
            churn_data['is_churn'].astype(float)

    summary = churn_data.describe()                       # The results are easier to read with the metrics in the rows.
    summary = summary.transpose()

    summary['skew'] = churn_data.skew()                   # Uses the quantile function to measure the 1st percentile
    summary['1%'] = churn_data.quantile(q=0.01)
    summary['99%'] = churn_data.quantile(q=0.99)
    summary['nonzero'] = churn_data.astype(bool).sum(axis=0) /
                         churn_data.shape[0]
```

Uses the quantile function to measure the 99th percentile

Measures the skew with a standard dataset function

Calculates the fraction of values that are not equal to zero

```
summary = summary[ ['count','nonzero','mean','std','skew','min','1%',
                    '25%','50%','75%','99%','max']]
summary.columns = summary.columns.str.replace("%", "pct")      ◁─┐ Reorders
                                                                 └ the columns
save_path = data_set_path.replace('.csv', '_summarystats.csv')
summary.to_csv(save_path,header=True)
print('Saving results to %s' % save_path)
```

You should run listing 5.2 on the simulated dataset yourself. Assuming that you are using the Python wrapper program, change the parameters to

```
fight-churn/listings/run_churn_listing.py --chapter 5 --listing 2
```

A typical result of running listing 5.2 was presented in figure 5.12; your result may be somewhat different because the data is randomly simulated.

5.2.3   Screening rare metrics

After creating the dataset summary statistics, you should check what percentage of accounts have nonzero values on all of your metrics. At this point, you should have already picked longer observation windows for rare metrics, as described in chapter 3. If you still have metrics in which only a small percentage of accounts has a nonzero value, then that's probably the best you can do. If that's the case, I recommend that you remove those metrics with fewer than around 5% nonzero values from your dataset and analysis. The precise cutoff depends on how many "good" metrics you have. If you have a lot of metrics in which most accounts have nonzero values, you should use a higher threshold—maybe 10%. On the other hand, if you have a lot of rare events and metrics with zero values, you may want to use a lower threshold for this kind of screening, such as 1%.

You can make exceptions to this approach if you find that one of these rare metrics is strongly related to churn or if you know it is of particular interest to the business. The principle guiding this approach is parsimony: if a metric applies to only a small percentage of accounts, it is not likely to be useful, even if it has a strong relationship to churn and retention.

5.2.4   Involving the business in data quality assurance

A good time to involve the businesspeople in your organization in quality assurance is after you produce the dataset summary statistics. I recommend that you have one or more meetings with people who represent different parts of your business and review the summary statistics with them. You should do this *before* you show them the results of your cohort analyses. I taught you how to do the cohort analysis first so that you could do some real churn analysis before spending time on more data quality assurance, but you should do the quality assurance first and the churn analysis afterward.

Such a review with the business stakeholders is a chance to confirm with people who should know it well that the data is of good quality. In particular, you want to ask the representatives of the business whether the distribution of metric values meets their expectations. Is the percentage of accounts with a metric lower than they expected or the maximum value higher than they expected? It is important to get this information before you share findings about churn with the business, because your findings may change if you have to make additional corrections or modifications in your dataset.

> **WARNING** Complete your quality assurance checks on the data, including review of the summary statistics with the business, before sharing cohort analysis results. You might lose credibility with the business if you share cohort analyses that you later need to retract due to data quality issues.

5.3 Scoring metrics

One problem we saw when we looked at the cohort analyses in section 5.1 was that for some of the metrics, most of the cohorts occupy only a small portion of the total range of the metric. In section 5.2, you learned that this type of distribution can be identified by looking at the skew statistic of the metrics as part of the dataset summary. In this section, you learn the technique of scoring metrics as a way to improve the interpretability of cohort analysis when your metric is highly skewed. In chapter 6, you learn that metric scores have other important uses, so this section is an introduction.

Scoring vs. normalizing the data

If you are trained in statistics or data science, you probably know the subject I'm calling scoring as the normalization or standardization of data. I have found that businesspeople find those terms intimidating and confusing. I have had better results referring to the whole process as *scoring* and the transformed data as *scores* rather than normalized data. Businesspeople seem to find these terms easier to relate to. For that reason, I describe the process in those terms rather than conventional statistical language.

5.3.1 The idea behind metric scores

The idea behind metric scores is that it is a rescaled version of the metric you started with. In this context, *rescaled* means that the scores will be in a different range of numbers from the original metric.

> **DEFINITION** A *metric score* (or score, for short) is a rescaled version of a metric.

Rescaling also implies that a larger metric observation always converts to a larger score, and two customers with the same metric would end up with the same score. As a result, if the customers are ordered by metric value from greatest to least, and then the same customers are ordered by metric score, the order is exactly the same. The cohorts created from your metric will also be exactly the same as the cohorts based on the score. Figure 5.13 illustrates this process.

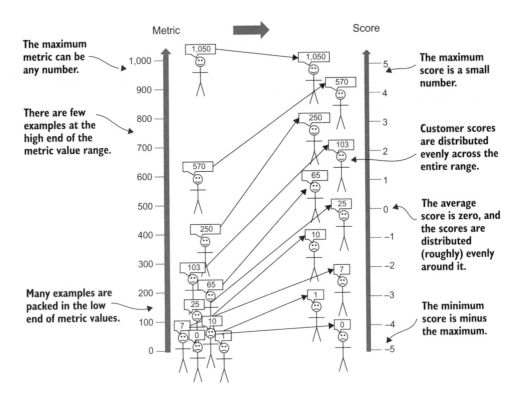

Figure 5.13   Mapping metrics to a score

Scores have some characteristics that make them useful for further analysis of your metrics and churn. Here are a few of those characteristics:

- Whereas metrics can take on any value, scores are always small numbers, positive and negative, but close to zero. Typical scores are –1, 0, or 1. An extreme value for a score might be 3 or 5, so the typical range of a score is around –5 to 5, no matter what the original range of the metric was.
- If the metric is skewed, the score will not be as skewed. Equivalently, the metric can have many observations close to zero and a small number of much larger values, but the score values will be more evenly distributed across the entire range that the scores occupy (approximately –5 to 5).
- The average score is always zero, no matter what the original average of the metric was. You can see at a glance whether a customer is average on the metric by looking at the score, even if you don't know the average value of the metric.
- The standard deviation of a metric score is always 1. This property is useful because you also know how far from the average a given score is. A score of 1 means the customer had an original metric that was 1 standard deviation above

average, and a score of –1 means that the customer had an original metric that was 1 standard deviation below the average.

These properties make scores useful for looking at customer metrics and churn. You learn more useful properties of metric scores later in the book.

5.3.2 *The metric score algorithm*

Now you're going to look at the formula you use to calculate scores from metrics. You can use an algorithm to determine a score formula based on the data, not a single formula. Figure 5.14 illustrates this procedure and is summarized as follows:

1 Determine whether the metric is significantly skewed by checking the skew statistic (section 5.2). A typical threshold considers the skew to be significant when it is above 4, although you can adjust the threshold depending on your preference. Also, you must confirm that the minimum metric value (before any transformation) is zero. If the metric is *not* significantly skewed or has negative values, skip to step 4.

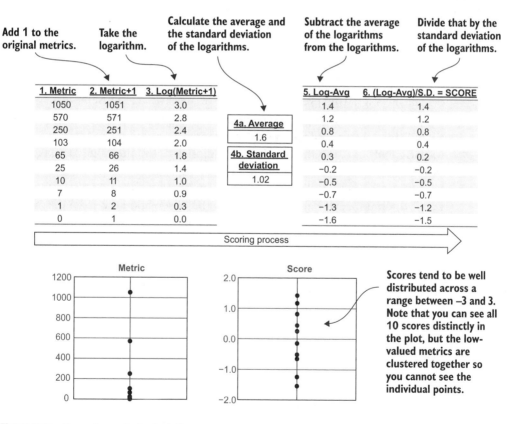

Figure 5.14 Example scoring calculation

2 Add 1 to the skewed customer metrics, so that a customer that has a zero event count now has 1, a customer with 1 now has 2, and so on.

3 Take the logarithm of all the skewed metrics. The natural logarithm (log base *e*) is normally used, but the base of the logarithm does not matter.

4 Calculate the mean and the standard deviation of the metric values at this point in the process. If the metric was not skewed, these values are simply the original metrics. If the metric was skewed, use the logarithm of 1 plus the original customer metrics.

5 Subtract the average from all values.

6 Divide all the values by the standard deviation. The results are the scores.

Taking the logarithm is a key step in making the data less skewed. A difference in order of magnitude between two numbers becomes a small difference in the resulting logarithms of those two numbers. But the logarithm can be taken only on positive numbers, which is why you check that the minimum is zero and then add 1. (An approach for negative metrics is introduced in chapter 7.)

Subtracting the average and dividing the metrics by the standard deviation makes the average of the final scores 0 and the standard deviation 1. The derivation is covered in detail in textbooks on statistics, but you can understand it by noting the following:

- The average is calculated by summing all the metrics and dividing by the number of observations. If you subtract a specific number from every observation, the new average is reduced by the amount you subtracted. If you subtract the original average from every observation, the new average must be zero.

- Suppose that the average is zero and the standard deviation is any number; then divide all the observations by the standard deviation. An observation that was originally equal to the standard deviation now has the value of 1 because it was the standard deviation; then it was divided by the same. In fact, after dividing by the original standard deviation, every observation is converted to a value that is the number of standard deviations the observation was from the average. This result is the same as the metric's having a standard deviation of 1.

Creating a score from an individual metric is the same as calculating the formula in equation 5.1:

$$score(metric) = \frac{m' - \mu_{m'}}{\sigma_{m'}}$$

where

$$m' = ln(metric + 1) \qquad \text{(Equation 5.1)}$$

In equation 5.1, $\mu_{m'}$ indicates the mean of the distribution of m', $\sigma_{m'}$ is the standard deviation of the distribution of m', and ln is the natural logarithm function. If the metric is not skewed, use the original metric instead of m'.

5.3.3 *Calculating metric scores in Python*

Listing 5.3 shows a Python function that implements the score calculation. Note that this function calculates the scores for all the metrics in a dataset, not just one. The function `metric_scores` in listing 5.3 has the following inputs:

- `data_set_path`—A path to a dataset saved in a file, given by a string variable
- `skew_thresh`—The threshold for determining whether a metric should be considered to be skewed

Given these inputs, the following are the main steps to take in calculating the scores:

1 Load the dataset into a Pandas `DataFrame` object, set the `DataFrame` index, and make a copy. The scores are written to the copy.
2 Remove the churn indicator column because it will not be converted to a score; it will be reattached as is after the scores are calculated.
3 Load the dataset stats file saved by listing 5.2.
4 Using the summary stats, determine which columns are significantly skewed by comparing the skew statistics with the threshold.
5 For each column that is significantly skewed, add 1, and take the logarithm.
6 For all columns, subtract the averages, and divide by the standard deviation.
7 Reattach the churn indicator column. The resulting `DataFrame` will be saved.

One thing to note about listing 5.3 is that it does not follow my advice from section 5.1 about using standard Python functions. This listing does not use a standard Python Pandas function to calculate scores; there is one, but listing 5.3 doesn't use it because the standard Pandas function does not include the option to take the logarithm for skewed variables.

Listing 5.3 Calculating metric scores in Python

```
import pandas as pd
import numpy as np
                                                    Checks the
                                                    dataset path
def metric_scores(data_set_path,skew_thresh=4.0):
                                                           Loads the dataset
                                                           into a Pandas
    assert os.path.isfile(data_set_path),                 DataFrame object
        '"{}" is not a valid path'.format(data_set_path)
    churn_data =                                           Works on a copy of
        pd.read_csv(data_set_path,index_col=[0,1])         the data to calculate
    data_scores = churn_data.copy()                        the scores
    data_scores.drop('is_churn',axis=1)
                                             The churn column
                                             should not be converted
    stat_path = data_set_path.replace('.csv',  to a score.
        '_summarystats.csv'))
    assert os.path.isfile(stat_path),
        'You must running listing 5.2 first to generate stats'    Drops the churn row
    stats = pd.read_csv(stat_path,index_col=0)                    from the summary
    stats=stats.drop('is_churn')                                  statistics
```

Checks the summary statistics file

Loads the summary statistics

Makes a Boolean series for which columns are skewed

Iterates over the skewed columns

Removes the entries for columns that were below the threshold

Records the new mean and standard deviation

Converts the skewed columns to the log of 1 plus the original

Subtracts the mean and divides by the standard deviation

Adds back the is_churn column from the original data

Saves the score version of the metrics

```
skewed_columns=(stats['skew']>skew_thresh) &
               (stats['min'] >= 0)
skewed_columns=skewed_columns[skewed_columns]

for col in skewed_columns.keys():
    data_scores[col]=np.log(1.0+data_scores[col])
    stats.at[col,'mean']=data_scores[col].mean()
    stats.at[col,'std']=data_scores[col].std()


data_scores=(data_scores-stats['mean'])/stats['std']
data_scores['is_churn']=churn_data['is_churn']

score_save_path=
    data_set_path.replace('.csv','_scores.csv')
print('Saving results to %s' % score_save_path)
data_scores.to_csv(score_save_path,header=True)
```

If you are following the examples in the chapter, you should run listing 5.3 on the simulated dataset yourself. Assuming that you are using the Python wrapper program, set the parameters to --chapter 5 --listing 3. That action creates the file socialnet_dataset_scores.csv in the output directory. The wrapper program that runs the listings prints the output directory.

If you want to check how the scores dataset differs from the original, one option is to open it in a text editor or spreadsheet. You should be able to see that all the metrics are small numbers (close to zero) and both positive and negative. A better option is to rerun the dataset summary program (listing 5.2) on the new dataset. You can run a second version of the dataset summary listing by adding the argument --version 2 to the Python wrapper program, so run the wrapper program with these arguments:

```
--chapter 5 --listing 2 --version 2
```

The wrapper program saves the result in a file called socialnet_dataset_scores_summary .csv. If you check the result file, all the metrics should be like the one shown in figure 5.15:

- The mean is a small rounding error close to zero. In figure 5.15, the mean is -2.65E-16, which means 10 to the minus 16th power (an extremely small number).
- The standard deviation is 1.
- The minimum and maximum value are around −4 and 4, respectively.
- Although the original metric was heavily skewed (15.5 in figure 5.12), the score has practically no skew.

metric	count	nonzero	mean	std	skew	min	1%	25%	50%	75%	99%	max
like_per_month	32316	100%	-2.65E-16	1	−0.01	−4.42	−2.29	−0.67	0.00	0.68	2.34	4.36

Figure 5.15   Example of summary statistics of a metric in the dataset of *scores* for the simulated dataset

5.3.4 *Cohort analysis with scored metrics*

When you have created the dataset of scores from your original dataset, you do cohort analysis exactly the way that you learned in section 5.1, using the same code. If you look back to listing 5.1 (section 5.1.2), you will find that nowhere in the cohort analysis function does it matter whether the data is original metrics (on their natural scale) or the scored metrics on the transformed scale. Also remember that because converting metrics to scores preserves the order of customers by the metric, the cohorts you find with scores are the same: using scores for the cohort analysis changes only how the data is distributed on the horizontal axis of the cohort plot.

You should run your own cohort analysis on the score metrics from the social network simulation with the Python wrapper program. You can run a second version of the cohort plot (listing 5.1) with these arguments:

```
--chapter 5 --listing 1 --version 2
```

The result looks like figure 5.16, in which the horizontal axis is relabeled as a score ranging from –1.5 to 1.5 (cohort averages). The churn rate in each cohort is the same as shown in figure 5.4. But after converting to scores, the cohort positions are more evenly spread across the figure. At the same time, the churn rate of every point in the scored metric cohort matches the churn rate from one of the original cohorts.

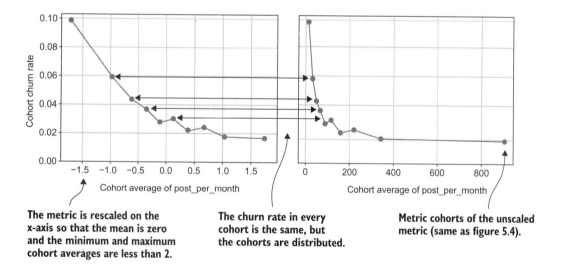

Figure 5.16 Cohort analysis on scored metric from a simulation

Figure 5.17 shows an example comparing the cohort churn plot for one metric on both its natural scale and as a score for Broadly, a service that helps businesses manage

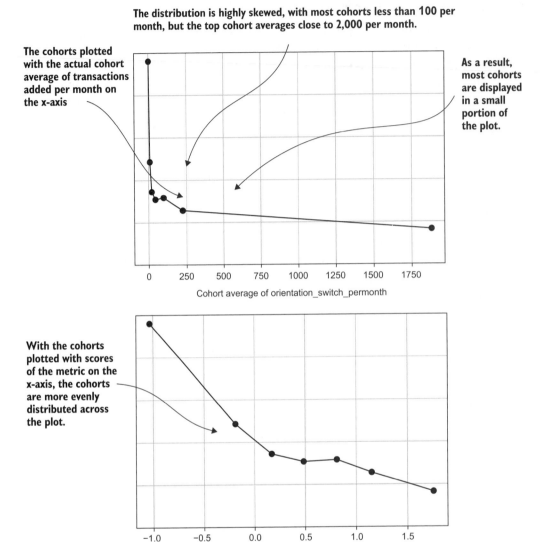

The distribution is highly skewed, with most cohorts less than 100 per month, but the top cohort averages close to 2,000 per month.

The cohorts plotted with the actual cohort average of transactions added per month on the x-axis

As a result, most cohorts are displayed in a small portion of the plot.

Cohort average of orientation_switch_permonth

With the cohorts plotted with scores of the metric on the x-axis, the cohorts are more evenly distributed across the plot.

Cohort average of transactionadded_permonth

Figure 5.17   Scored metric and churn example for Broadly's transactions added per month

their online presence. An important event for Broadly's customers is adding new transactions, and a metric was calculated for the number of transactions added per month. The metric transactions added per month are highly skewed, having a statistic of 23. As a result, when the cohort plot is made using the metric on its natural scale, all the cohorts except one lie in a horizontal range that is around one-eighth of the entire plot. The cohort average values lie between 0 and 250, and the top cohort averages 2,300. By contrast, the cohorts based on the metric scores are distributed more or less evenly between scores of −1.5 and 2.0. Also, it is clear now how the cohorts compare with the average, which is 0. The first three cohorts are below average, and most of the reduction in churn rates goes from the lowest cohort to cohorts near the average.

> **TAKEAWAY** Cohort analysis with scored metric cohorts makes it easy to see how the cohorts relate to the average metric value, which is always the score equal to zero.

5.3.5 *Cohort analysis of monthly recurring revenue*

In chapter 3, you learned that monthly recurring revenue (MRR) should be calculated as a metric, but so far, we have not looked at any cohort analysis results for it. Now I will demonstrate a typical result for MRR cohort analysis, using the metric scores technique introduced in section 5.3.4. I demonstrate a cohort analysis of MRR and churn that uses scores for two reasons:

- MRR is typically highly skewed for business to business (B2B) products because the largest customers, which can be large corporations, typically pay prices many times higher than those paid by the smallest customers, which can be sole proprietorships.
- Presenting this cohort analysis with scores maintains the confidentiality of the pricing information from the case study.

Figure 5.18 shows the results of the scored MRR churn analysis. But before you look at the results, stop to think about what you expect the result to be. (Okay, some of you may remember the answer from chapter 1.) Will cohorts of higher-paying customers have churn rates that are

- A Higher than the churn rates of customers who pay less?
- B Lower than the churn rates of customers who pay less?
- C About the same as the churn rate of customers who pay less?

Figure 5.18 shows that the answer is B: cohorts of customers that pay more on average churn at a lower rate, although the trend is a little bit noisy. The higher-paying customers churn at a rate around one-third to one-half less than that of the lowest-paying cohorts.

This result may surprise you. The usual thinking is that high prices make customers less satisfied, and as a result, they churn at a higher rate. The opposite is usually true, however. On average, customers who pay more usually churn at a lower rate, for multiple reasons. The first reason for lower churn among customers who pay more has to do with *passive* churn. Passive churn (also known as *involuntary* churn) occurs due to a failed payment when the customer has not indicated a choice to churn (hence the term *passive*). The most common scenario for passive churn is an expired payment card or insufficient available balance. Because customers who are paying more sign up at a higher plan level, they generally have more money and, thus, are

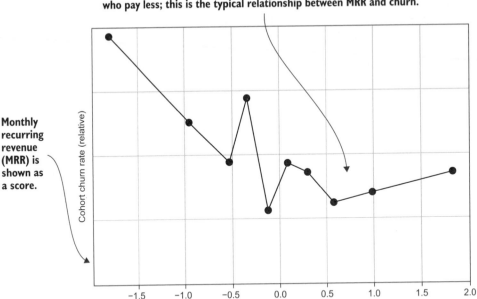

Figure 5.18   Scored MRR and churn example for Versature's MRR scores

less likely to have those kinds of problems. (To reduce passive churn, most companies retry credit cards multiple times until a transaction goes through, but this method of reducing churn is beyond the scope of this book.)

There is a second and usually more important reason customers with higher MRR churn at a lower rate, especially for business products: business products are sold at higher prices to bigger customers, and bigger customers churn less for multiple reasons related to their size. Bigger companies have more employees, so when it comes to product use such as making calls or using software, bigger customers usually use more of the available services. Also, a big business customer invests more to set up a system, so it is less likely to walk away from the investment. You may be surprised to learn that the same pattern often holds for consumer products. Customers who sign up for more expensive plans tend to be more invested and use the product more, and as a result, they churn at a lower rate than customers who signed up for lower-cost plans.

MRR is associated with lower churn, but it's not the cause. If you see a relationship like this one, do not try to raise MRR to reduce churn. This understanding is intuitively unsatisfying, because paying too much for something ought to be a cause for churn, and getting a good deal ought to be a cause for retention. A better way to understand the relationship between what customers pay and churn is to use a different metric—one that reflects the value that customers receive rather than what they pay. These topics are among the main subjects of chapters 6 and 7.

5.4 Removing unwanted or invalid observations

Another useful technique that should be part of your toolkit for cohort analyses is removing unwanted observations from a cohort analysis. Despite your best efforts to do quality assurance and clean your data, some observations may be invalid (bad data), or they may not be invalid but you don't want them because they make your cohort analysis harder to understand. I'm going to show you two motivating case studies in which some observations are removed from a cohort analysis and a Python function that performs the removal.

5.4.1 Removing nonpaying customers from churn analysis

One common scenario in which you may need to remove some observations from your analysis is when you have both paying and nonpaying customers. Customers who don't have to pay may be on temporary free trials, or they may be in some special category of customers, like partners who have permanent free use of the product. You might have a similar situation when some customers pay a nominal amount that is much less than what usual customers pay. The problem with nonpaying (or low-paying) customers is that they tend not to churn because the product doesn't cost them anything, but they don't necessarily use the product much. So nonpaying customers don't have the normal relationship between behavior and churn, and if you have more than a small number of nonpaying customers, they can ruin the results of your analysis.

Figure 5.19 demonstrates the impact of free customers by adding simulated nonpaying customers to Versature's MRR and local-call observations, which are analyzed in section 5.3.5. These nonpaying customers are not real; they are randomly generated observations with $0 MRR. The simulated nonpaying customers were assigned a local-call metric that was also randomly generated to be within the bottom two deciles of the real customers. Enough simulated nonpaying customers were added to make up 15% of the total data. When the cohort plots are regenerated, as shown in figure 5.19, they are significantly distorted by the presence of the nonpaying customers, and the relationships between the metrics and churn appear to be much less significant.

If you have customers who pay and some who do not, you should remove the nonpaying customers before trying to do cohort analysis or the other analyses described in later chapters. Ideally, you might be able to remove such customers when generating your observations (as described in chapter 4) by using some kind of SQL logic based on the plans the customers use. But that approach may be complicated by the presence of multiple subscriptions. A customer might have some $0 MRR subscriptions and others that have a cost attached, so to be sure a customer pays nothing, you must use the MRR metric calculated in chapter 3. This example illustrates why it may be necessary to remove such customers after the dataset has been generated. The Python program in section 5.4.2 shows you how.

In the original data, the lowest-use cohort churns at more than 3 times the rate of the highest.

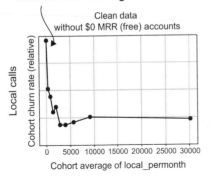

Local calls

In data with free accounts, the lowest-use cohorts churn at a lower rate than the third cohort, but it is artificial.

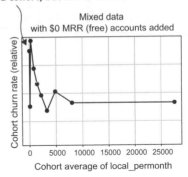

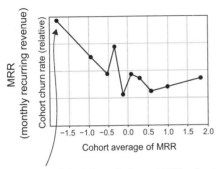

MRR (monthly recurring revenue)

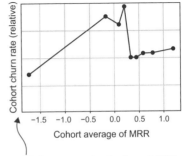

In the original data, the lowest MRR cohort churns at around 2 times the rate of the highest.

In data with free accounts, the lowest MRR cohort churns at a much lower rate, but it is artificial.

Figure 5.19   Impact of $0 MRR (free) trials added to Versature subscription data

5.4.2   *Removing observations based on metric thresholds in Python*

One way to remove observations from a churn analysis is to define a minimum value for a metric, a maximum value for a metric, or both. Any observations in which the metric is below the minimum or above the maximum can be removed, and a new dataset that is a subset of the original is produced.

Listing 5.4 shows a Python function that performs these operations. The function `remove_invalid` has the following inputs:

- `data_set_path`—A path to a dataset saved in a file, given by a string variable.
- `min_valid`—A dictionary containing the minimum valid values of any metric to be screened. Entries are assumed to be key-value pairs, in which the key is the name of a metric (a string), and the value is the minimum to be applied for screening that metric. Any number of criteria can be specified in this way.

- max_valid—A dictionary containing the maximum valid values of any metric to be screened. Entries are assumed to be key-value pairs, in which the key is the name of a metric (a string), and the value is the maximum to be applied for screening that metric. Any number of criteria can be specified in this way.
- save_path—A path to a file in which the scores will be saved.

Given these inputs, following are the main steps to take to create a new dataset with invalid observations removed:

1 Load the dataset into a Pandas DataFrame object, set the DataFrame index, and make a copy. The cleaned data is written to a copy of the DataFrame.
2 For each metric specified in the min_valid dictionary parameter, remove those observations from the DataFrame where the value is below the minimum.
3 For each metric specified in the max_valid dictionary parameter, remove those observations from the DataFrame where the value is above the maximum.
4 Save the resulting DataFrame to a file.

An example of using this algorithm is presented in figure 5.19 earlier in this chapter. The left side of the figure was produced from a dataset cleaned by listing 5.4; the right side of figure 5.19 was made from the original, unclean data.

> **Listing 5.4 Removing invalid observations**

Checks the dataset path

```
import pandas as pd
import os

def remove_invalid(data_set_path,min_valid=None,max_valid=None):
    assert os.path.isfile(data_set_path),
        '"{}" is not a valid path'.format(data_set_path)       Loads data into a
    churn_data =                                               Pandas DataFrame,
        pd.read_csv(data_set_path,index_col=[0,1])             setting the index
    clean_data = churn_data.copy()

    if min_valid and isinstance(min_valid,dict):
        for metric in min_valid.keys():
            if metric in clean_data.columns.values:
                clean_data=clean_data[clean_data[metric] >
                    min_valid[metric]]
            else:
                print('metric %s not in dataset %s' % (metric,data_set_path))

    if max_valid and isinstance(max_valid,dict):
        for metric in max_valid.keys():
            if metric in clean_data.columns.values:
                clean_data=clean_data[clean_data[metric] <
                    max_valid[metric]]
            else:
                print('metric %s not in dataset %s' % (metric,data_set_path))
```

Annotations:
- **Makes a copy of the original DataFrame**
- **Iterates over variables specified for cleaning with a minimum**
- **Confirms that this metric is in the DataFrame**
- **Removes rows in which the metric is less than the minimum**
- **Iterates over variables specified for cleaning with a maximum**
- **Removes rows in which the metric is greater than the maximum**

```
score_save_path=
    data_set_path.replace('.csv','_cleaned.csv')
print('Saving results to %s' % score_save_path)
clean_data.to_csv(score_save_path,header=True)
```
◁─┐ **Saves the resulting**
   │ **DataFrame to a file**

The simulated dataset for this book doesn't contain any free-trial users or other reasons to remove unwanted data, so there is no example on which to run listing 5.4.

5.4.3 *Removing zero measurements from rare metric analyses*

Another situation in which you might want to remove observations from a cohort analysis occurs when a metric measures a rare event and, as a result, most customers have zeros on the metric. This situation is illustrated in section 5.1.7. The function in listing 5.4 provides an easy way to see what the cohorts look like when you consider only those customers who have the event (and a nonzero value on the metric).

Figure 5.20 shows the analysis of Klipfolio's orientation switch event, both with and without customers with zero metric counts.

In the original data, around 80% of the accounts have zero on the metric. As a result, only two cohorts are formed for the nonzero metric customers.

With zeros removed and the analysis set to five cohorts, the trend among the feature users is easier to observe.

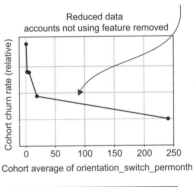
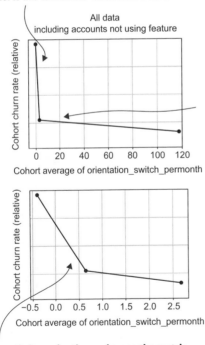
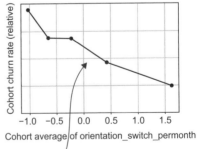

Churn is lower for those who use the metric, but it doesn't distinguish much between those who use the feature in different amounts.

Accounts that use the feature the most have a churn rate that is around one-fourth that of customers who are least active using the feature.

Figure 5.20   Cohorts of rare behaviors for Klipfolio

The version without zero metric customers was created by running listing 5.4 on the dataset to remove customers with zero on the metric and then saving it. Afterward, the cohort analysis was run using five bins because only around 25% of the observations remained.

5.4.4 Disengaging behaviors: Metrics associated with increasing churn

So far, I have showed you cohort analyses of behaviors associated with reduced churn. You may wonder about behaviors associated with increased churn. I call these behaviors *disengaging behaviors.*

> **DEFINITION** A *disengaging behavior* is a customer behavior that leads to an increased risk of churn the more often it is performed.

I have not avoided disengaging behaviors to put a positive spin on the case studies. The fact is that disengaging behaviors are rare in churn case studies and often cannot be detected with simple count and average metrics like the ones you have learned so far. For one thing, it is the product creators' jobs to make features that are engaging, so if the creators are doing their jobs, disengaging behaviors should be rare. Normally, customers who don't even use the product have an even higher churn rate than the customers who perform the disengaging behavior. As a result, if disengaging behaviors exist, their relationship to churn is likely to be weak and can easily be missed.

> **TAKEAWAY** Disengaging behaviors usually show a weak relationship with increasing churn—typically less than the reduction in churn that comes from using the product even a small amount.

An example of a disengaging feature from Klipfolio, an SaaS product for business dashboards, is shown in figure 5.21. The case study shows two versions of the cohort analysis. One version uses all customers, including those who don't use the product or feature, and the other includes only customers who use the feature. If you include all customers, you might miss that the feature is disengaging. The most notable feature of the cohort analysis is that customers who don't use the feature have the highest churn rate. It's easy to miss the fact that customers who use the feature churn at a slightly higher rate the more often they use it. When customers who don't use the feature are removed from the analysis, the increasing churn rate among users of the feature is clearer.

All things considered, the increasing churn among the disengaging feature users shown in figure 5.21 is small compared with the reduced churn associated with using the main product features shown in section 5.1. This result is typical for disengaging behaviors measured with simple metrics. In chapter 7, you learn advanced techniques to create metrics that detect more significant disengaging behaviors.

Your instinct probably is to think that disengaging behaviors must be bad, in the sense of experiences that customers do not like. But I have seen cases in which disengaging behaviors are good, such as when the behavior serves to complete the

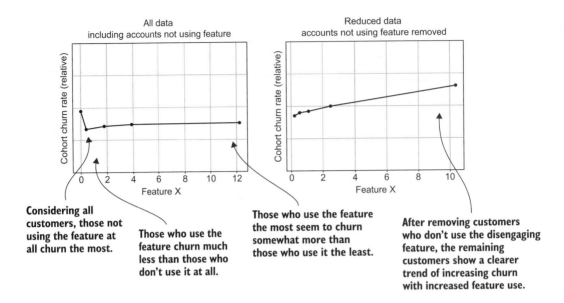

Figure 5.21   Cohorts of a disengaging behavior for Klipfolio

purpose of a product that gave the users exactly what they wanted. Disengaging behavior can also occur when the product has only one purpose for some users and that purpose can be completed. A common example is watching a popular video series. If there is only one popular series, people may churn when they have watched every episode. In that case, watching the best content leads to churn. Creators must make more equally desirable content to change this pattern. To reach that kind of conclusion, you need to use your business knowledge. Usually, people know when a feature or content is good without the churn analysis (but survey users if you're not sure).

5.5   *Segmenting customers by using cohort analysis*

Now you know how to understand customer behavior and churn using a cohort analysis. The next step in fighting churn is using what you've learned to segment your customers and plan interventions. You're going to learn even more about your customers in chapters 6 and 7, but you don't need to wait any longer to get started. As I mentioned in chapter 1, I'm not going to go into details about different types of customer interventions because they are specific to each company's product and situation. But the data-based procedures for creating customer segments based on churn data are pretty much universal.

5.5.1   Segmenting process

Most of the companies I have worked with find segmenting to be pretty straightforward, so this explanation is brief. The main steps are as follows:

1   Use a current customer dataset (which you learned how to create at the end of chapter 4) to create segments. Do *not* use the historical dataset on which you did the cohort analyses.
2   Segmenting is usually performed on spreadsheets by the businesspeople who are going to make the customer interventions. In a large company, a business intelligence system might be used.
3   Define a segment of customers at risk of churn by choosing the metric level based on the result of your cohort analysis. Assuming that the metric is one in which higher values are associated with lower churn, the at-risk customers are those whose metric is below a level that you choose.
4   The resulting customer list can be loaded into another system, such as an email marketing tool or customer relationship management system, if necessary.

This procedure is basic, but there are some nuances in setting the segment criteria.

5.5.2   Choosing segment criteria

You can use a few strategies in setting a metric level to define a segment. One common approach is to set the metric level based on churn risk, such as picking all customers whose churn risk is above a certain level as suggested by the results of the cohort analysis. Suppose that your cohort analysis shows that customers who don't use the product churn at a 20% rate, and at some level of a metric, the risk is reduced to 5%. To define a segment of at-risk customers, you choose the metric level at which churn risk is significantly higher than the lowest churn. You might choose the metric values with a churn rate of 10%, for example. Another strategy is to pick the level of the metric at which most of the churn reduction from increased usage has been achieved (assuming such a level exists, as detailed in section 5.1).

Many companies also have some kind of resource budget or other constraint on the number of customers they will work with for a particular intervention. An alternative way to define a segment is something like picking the 500 customers who have the lowest measure on some behavior. This approach makes sense when the number of customers at risk is greater than your resources, and you need to triage your efforts. To create such a segment, sort the current customer dataset according to the metric of interest and pick a predetermined number of customers from the bottom (or top) of the list.

It is also common to use interventions (such as emails, calls, or training) to target the customers at some intermediate level of risk.

TAKEAWAY   You usually don't intervene to reduce churn with the most disengaged customers.

The reasoning is that the highest-risk (lowest-use) customers can be so disengaged that intervention will have no effect and would be wasted. This consideration is most important when intervention has a cost associated with it or when you think that unwanted communication might disengage customers further.

Summary

- Cohort analysis compares the churn rates on groups of customer observations, with the groups based on measurements of a single metric.
- Metric cohort analysis usually shows that customers who use a product more churn less.
- Each cohort should have at least 200 to 300 observations, and preferably thousands. If you don't have a lot of observations for your customers, use fewer cohorts.
- Cohort analysis can be applied to subscription metrics such as tenure, MRR, and billing period.
- A statistical summary of a dataset consists of a set of measures (such as the average, minimum, and maximum) taken for every metric in a dataset.
- A statistical summary of a dataset is a good quality assurance check on your data and can alert you to conditions for which you need to adjust your cohort analysis. You should check a set of summary statistics *before* you do your cohort analysis.
- You should discuss the dataset summary statistics with people in the business and correct any data issues before performing cohort analyses.
- A metric is skewed when most of the observed values are within a small range but a relatively small number of observations are much larger.
- A score created from a metric is a rescaling of every metric observation so that the rescaled values lie on a small range close to zero. But the order of the observations according to the score is the same as the order according to the metric. (A larger metric value always maps to a higher score.)
- When a metric is skewed, a cohort analysis that uses the metric scores is easier to read than a cohort analysis that uses the untransformed metric.
- If nonpaying users are mixed with paying customers, you should remove the nonpaying users before performing cohort analysis. Nonpaying users tend not to churn, regardless of how much they use the product, and therefore distort the relationships in cohort analyses.
- For metrics based on rare events, you may want to remove the customers with zero metric values so that the cohorts reflect the differences between customers who have events.
- Disengaging behaviors are behaviors where customers who perform the behavior more have higher churn.
- Disengaging behaviors rarely show up in simple behavioral count metrics; often, you must remove nonusers from the cohort analysis to see the trend with cohort analysis on these behaviors.
- You find segments of at-risk customers to target for interventions by choosing a minimum metric level based on the results of cohort analysis.

Relationships between
customer behaviors

For most products and services, analyzing whether individual metrics are related to churn is the beginning but not the end of using your data to reduce churn. This chapter teaches you how to address a common problem: having an *overabundance* of data available for fighting churn. In the age of big data, some companies collect a lot about their customers. That should make it easier to fight churn with data, right? Not quite.

Many customer behaviors are closely related, so metrics based on those behaviors have similar relationships to churn. A cohort churn analysis on a typical company's database of events and metrics probably won't give you just a few cohort churn plots: you probably have dozens or more. This can actually cause more confusion than good. When behaviors measured by metrics are not the specific acts that give enjoyment or utility to the user, then the relationships to churn are just associations and not causal. When you have a lot of metrics that are associated with churn but not causal, you don't have a good way to understand how they act together.

To fight churn effectively with your data, you need to do more than understand how individual customer behaviors are related to churn. You need to understand how customer behaviors are related to each other. When you do that instead of just looking at how single behaviors are related to churn, you can look at how groups of behaviors are related to churn. That way, you turn the problem of having too much data into an asset because groups of behaviors often show a clearer relationship to churn than do individual behaviors alone.

This chapter is organized as follows:

- In section 6.1, the chapter starts with some case studies to demonstrate what it means for behaviors to be correlated and then teaches you how to calculate correlations in your own data with Python and with something called a *correlation matrix*, which is an important way of looking at correlations among a large number of metrics.

- In section 6.2, you'll learn a technique for forming averages of the metric scores of correlated behaviors and then analyze churn using the average score. This is a key technique that you'll use to reduce information overload from having too many metrics associated with churn.

- Last, in section 6.3, you'll learn a technique to automatically find groups of correlated metrics in a large dataset using an algorithm called a *clustering algorithm*. By mastering these techniques, you'll be ready to handle big datasets with lots of correlated metrics and behaviors to be even more effective in your fight against churn.

Grouping behaviors vs. dimension reduction

If you have formal training in data science or statistics, you'll probably recognize that this chapter covers the idea and practice of dimension reduction and is a crash course in linear algebra. But because of the need to communicate the concepts to businesspeople, I refer to it as *behavioral grouping*, which describes the key result in plain English. If you are formally trained, you'll also find that I stick to a basic and intuitive kind of dimension reduction, but I want to caution you against thinking of this as a "dumbed-down" approach. The approach taken is deliberately simple. But while it is not optimal in the usual statistical sense, it is optimized for explainability. It is also excellent for robustness and out-of-sample predictive performance in the face of messy data and a problem that never stops changing (churn is nonstationary). In my experience, extracting the maximum information from a dimension reduction with more complicated methods does not lead to better performance in churn prediction. For interested readers, this chapter ends with a sidebar comparing the results using the methods in this chapter with results obtained from standard dimension reduction using principal component analysis (PCA).

6.1 *Correlation between behaviors*

If you have two customer behaviors that you think are related, start by objectively measuring how they are related. The most practical way to do this is by measuring correlation, which is the subject of this section. You will learn what correlation between customer behaviors means and see demonstrations in customer behavioral data with case studies. Then you'll learn how to calculate and visualize correlations between pairs of metrics as well as between all the metrics in a dataset.

6.1.1 *Correlation between pairs of metrics*

Two metrics or behaviors are said to be *correlated* when a customer who has a high value on the first metric also has a high value on the second metric, and a different customer with a low value on the first metric also has a low value on the second. You can also describe correlation by saying that an *increase* in the first metric is associated with an *increase* in the second metric, in the sense that if a customer increased one behavior, they also tend to increase the other behavior (and the associated metrics).

> **DEFINITION** *Correlation* between a pair of metrics or behaviors is a measure of the consistency with which an increase (or decrease) in one metric or behavior is associated with an increase (or decrease) in the other.

That's the idea of correlation. There is also a measurement of correlation called the *correlation coefficient*, which is also often simply called the correlation.

> **DEFINITION** The *correlation coefficient* is a measurement of correlation that can range from −1.0 to 1.0:

- 1.0 correlation between two metrics means that an increase in one metric is *always* associated with *the same* increase in another metric.
- Negative correlation means that the association is a *decrease* of one metric when the other metric increases.

It is easiest to imagine 1.0 correlation when the increase is 1:1 (an increase of 1 in the first metric corresponds to an increase of 1 in the second metric), but it can also be any ratio (1:2, 2:1, and so forth) when the correlation is the same. That's why the correlation depends on the *consistency* of the association between two metrics but not the exact magnitude of the ratio. Correlation can also be between two metrics with any measurement units or scale (logins, downloads, views, etc.).

> **NOTE** Consistency in the relationship means that a certain amount of increase in one metric results in a proportional amount of increase in the other as given by a specific ratio.

Figure 6.1 shows example pairs of metrics with different degrees of correlation, taken from the case studies of companies introduced in earlier chapters. Scatterplots show the values of two different metrics by plotting each observation as a point with one metric on each axis. Each point in figure 6.1 represents two metrics from a single observation out of the dataset; the complete set of points is all the paired values from those two metrics.

Figure 6.1A shows highly correlated metrics with a correlation above 0.95 (0.98, to be exact). In practice, you'll never see a 1.0 correlation between two metrics (unless you accidentally calculate the same metric twice), but you might see metrics that are highly correlated, like those shown in figure 6.1A. These are closely related metrics from Klipfolio's dashboard editor. (Klipfolio, introduced in chapter 1, is an SaaS product for business dashboards.)

When you plot a set of observations that are highly correlated, they are arranged in an almost diagonal line. At a 1.0 correlation, the points would be precisely on a diagonal line.

Correlation measurements higher than 0.7 are considered a high correlation. Figure 6.1B shows a pair of metrics from Broadly for the number of customers added and the number of asks presented, which have 0.88 correlation. (Broadly, introduced in

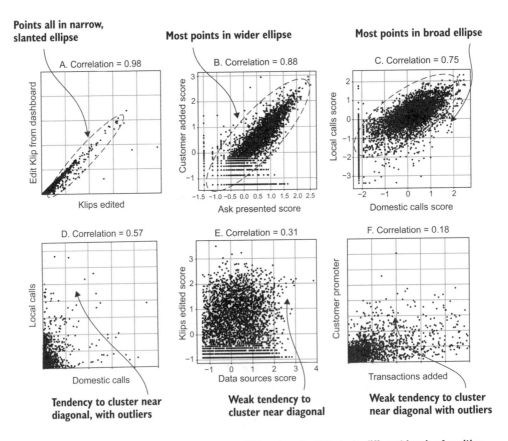

Figure 6.1   Case studies for Klipfolio, Broadly, and Versature that illustrate different levels of positive correlation

chapter 1, helps businesses manage their online presence.) Another metric showing a moderately high degree of correlation (0.75) is shown in figure 6.1C, which is the metric scores for local calls and domestic calls from Versature. (Versature, introduced in chapter 1, provides cloud-based business communication solutions.) For metrics with a relatively high correlation, points in these scatterplots tend to lie in some kind of ellipse or oval that is at a diagonal orientation.

Correlation measurements in the range of around 0.3 to 0.7 are moderately correlated and are illustrated in figures 6.1D and 6.1E. Figure 6.1D is a moderate correlation of 0.57 and shows the same two metrics for local and domestic calls from Versature. In this case, the metrics are shown on their natural scale rather than as scores. Note that the metric scores are significantly more correlated than the underlying metric. This is often the case when metrics are skewed, as described in chapter 5.

TAKEAWAY Metric scores are often more correlated than the underlying metrics on their natural scale, especially when the metrics are heavily skewed. This is another important reason for using metric scores in your analysis.

Figure 6.1E shows two metrics for Klipfolio with weaker but still moderate correlation (0.31). These are the metric scores for the number of data sources and the number of Klips edited. In scatterplots for moderately correlated metrics, the points tend to lie closer to the diagonal than not, but there is much less structure. Figure 6.1F shows two metrics for Broadly that are even more weakly correlated (0.18). These are metrics for the number of transactions added and the number of customer promoters (customers who give positive reviews). Businesses with more transactions tend to have more promoters, but the relationship is weak, and there are many outliers: some observations are high in one metric but low in another, leading to points close to both axes.

Figure 6.2 shows examples of metrics that have zero correlation or close to it; these are commonly called *uncorrelated*. Although scatterplots of metrics with a high correlation usually look similar, there is a lot more variety in metrics with low and near-zero correlations. Figure 6.2A shows two metrics from Broadly that have exactly 0.0 correlation. These metrics are for viewing the customer list and sending follow-up emails. In this case, there is no relationship, and the points tend to lie close to the origin (equally spaced with respect to both axes). Figure 6.2B shows Versature's metric for local calls and account tenure. Account tenure is uniformly distributed across the x-axis up to the maximum, but there is no relationship with the number of local calls. Figure 6.2C shows an example from Klipfolio of near-zero correlation between the metrics for adding templates and switching orientations. The add template metric is rare, so most observations have values near zero on that axis, and there is no relationship to the other metric (orientation switches).

Figure 6.3 shows correlation patterns that you are unlikely to see in your data. No examples were available from case studies, so these were made from simulated data using the code on the book's website (www.manning.com/books/fighting-churn-with-data)

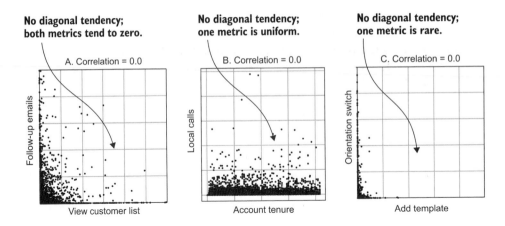

Figure 6.2   Case studies for Klipfolio, Broadly, and Versature that illustrate zero correlation

and in this book's GitHub repository (https://github.com/carl24k/fight-churn/tree/master/data-generation). Figure 6.3A shows an example where two behavioral metrics both lie in a nonzero range with few outliers and no skew and yet still have no correlation. Scatterplots of such metrics have points that tend to lie in a sphere, and this is the classic example of uncorrelated metrics in a statistics textbook. But surprisingly, it is rare to see it in customer behaviors. Usually, when two customer metrics have few zeros and no extreme values, there is some degree of correlation.

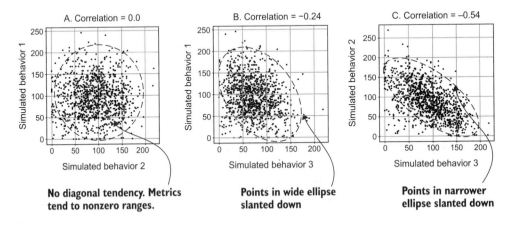

Figure 6.3   Simulations illustrating rare behavioral correlations from simulated data

In the figure, 6.3B and 6.3C show examples of low and moderate negative correlations, respectively. Like positive correlations, the points in a scatterplot tend to lie in an ellipse, but in this case, the ellipse is at a diagonal orientation sloping down to the right rather than up to the left. This shows that an increase in one behavior is associated with a decrease in the other behavior.

It's rare that you'll observe negative correlations between count metrics based on customer events because generally customers with more events do more of everything. That said, there are other types of more advanced behavioral metrics (see the next chapter) that can have negative correlations with other metrics in your dataset.

6.1.2 *Investigating correlations with Python*

Listing 6.1 shows a short Python program to create scatterplots and correlation measurements like the ones shown in the last section. The program assumes a dataset was created and saved using the code in chapter 4 (specifically listings 4.1, 4.2, 4.4, and 4.5). Most of listing 6.1 handles the details of loading the dataset and making the scatterplot with annotations.

The correlation is calculated in a single call to the Pandas function `Series.corr`. If you want to know how the correlation coefficient was calculated, there are many resources online and in statistics textbooks (search for "Pearson" correlation coefficient, for example). The scatterplot is created with a call to the Matplotlib function `pyplot.scatter`. As in previous plot examples, it is important to provide detailed labeling and annotation of the plot, so your business colleagues know what they are looking at (and so you can remember what you plotted when you look at it sometime later).

Figure 6.4 shows the result of running listing 6.1 on the default simulated dataset. You should try it out on a pair of metrics yourself. Assuming you have set up your environment (instructions in the README for the book in the GitHub repository at https://github.com/carl24k/fight-churn), and you are using the Python wrapper program, run listing 6.1 with

```
fight-churn/listings/run_churn_listing.py --chapter 6 --listing 1 --version 1 2
```

That should give you a .png file with a scatterplot between the metrics post_per_month and like_per_month, which looks like figure 6.4. You can also check the results on different pairs of metrics by running the alternative versions by adding the version arguments up to 16:

```
--version 3 4 5 6 7 8 9 10 11 12 13 14 15 16
```

That command generates the pair plots of posts per month as both scores and natural scale metrics. That's just a small number out of all the possible pair plots from the dataset, but it will show you a little variety for possible correlation patterns and the difference it makes when the metrics are converted to scores.

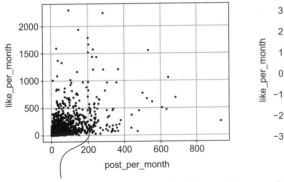

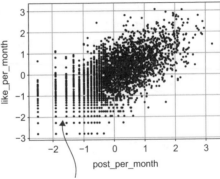

Each point represents a paired observation of likes per month and posts per month. The correlation of 0.5 is moderate.

For scores of the same metrics, the correlation is noticeably higher: 0.66. Discretized scores at the low end represent counts of 0, 1, 2, and so on.

Figure 6.4   Result of running listing 6.1 on the simulated metrics, showing scores for likes per month and posts per month

Listing 6.1   Analyzing correlation in pairs of metrics

```python
import pandas as pd
import matplotlib.pyplot as plt
import os

def metric_pair_plot(data_set_path):
    assert os.path.isfile(data_set_path),
        '"{}" is not a valid path'.format(data_set_path)      # Checks the dataset path
    churn_data =
        pd.read_csv(data_set_path,index_col=[0,1])            # Loads the dataset into a DataFrame

    met1_series = churn_data[metric1]                         # Selects the two metrics
    met2_series = churn_data[metric2]                         # that will be analyzed

    corr = met1_series.corr(met2_series)                      # Calculates the correlation between two series

    plt.scatter(met1_series, met2_series, marker='.')         # Makes a scatterplot from two series

    plt.xlabel(metric1)                                       # Adds axis labels
    plt.ylabel(metric2)
    plt.title('Correlation = %.2f' % corr)                    # Prints the correlation measurement in the title
    plt.tight_layout()                                        # Adjusts the layout to accommodate the labels and title
    plt.grid()
    save_name =
        data_set_path.replace('.csv','_'+metric1+'_vs_'+metric2+'.png')
    plt.savefig(save_name)                                    # Saves the figure in .png format
    print('Saving plot to %s' % save_name)
    plt.close()
```

6.1.3 *Understanding correlations between sets of metrics with correlation matrices*

Scatterplots are useful for understanding the relationships between pairs of metrics that you are interested in, but they are an inefficient way to investigate the correlations between the pairs in a large set of metrics. That's because if you have a moderate number of metrics, there will be a much larger number of combinations (for the mathematically inclined, for N metrics, there are $N \times (N - 1) / 2$ combinations, as illustrated later). You will learn a much more efficient way to look at a large number of correlations in a dataset next; this is called a correlation matrix. A *matrix* is a table (of data) where all of the entries are numbers, and a *correlation matrix* is a table of all the correlations in a dataset. That is, every entry in the correlation matrix is a correlation coefficient between two metrics.

> **DEFINITION** A correlation matrix is a table of all of the pairwise correlation coefficients between the metrics in a dataset.

Figure 6.5 shows an example of creating a correlation matrix from a simple dataset. The dataset was simulated to have five metrics, all counts per month of events (likes, reads, replies, sends, and writes) in a messaging application. The metrics are converted to scores because that can show more of a correlation. Each pair of metrics has its own relationship that can be investigated with a scatterplot and an individual correlation calculation. To display all of the correlations in a single matrix, the metrics are put on *both* the rows and the columns of a table (in the same order). The correlation between each pair is entered at the intersection of that pair of metrics in the table. That way, every correlation can be looked up in a single table.

> **NOTE** Correlation matrices are often color coded by value because it makes it easier to identify high and low correlations visually; a color-coded correlation matrix is often referred to as a *heatmap*.

The correlation matrices in this book are grayscale so they can be printed, but I recommend using full-color heatmaps in all other situations (both for your own analysis and for presentations to your colleagues).

Because metrics are in the rows *and* the columns of the correlation matrix, there are two intersections in the matrix for every pair of metrics. These are in locations that are symmetrical with respect to a diagonal line drawn through the matrix from the top left to the bottom right. There are two options to deal with this redundancy: show every entry twice, or omit half the matrix. The most common approach is to show every entry twice; consequently, the correlation matrix is symmetrical across the diagonal. That can make it easier to find the correlation you are looking for because, whether you start from a row or a column, you find the entry just as fast either way. The alternative approach is to omit half of the matrix either above or below the diagonal. This leads to a cleaner look that is better for presentations. Also, every metric has

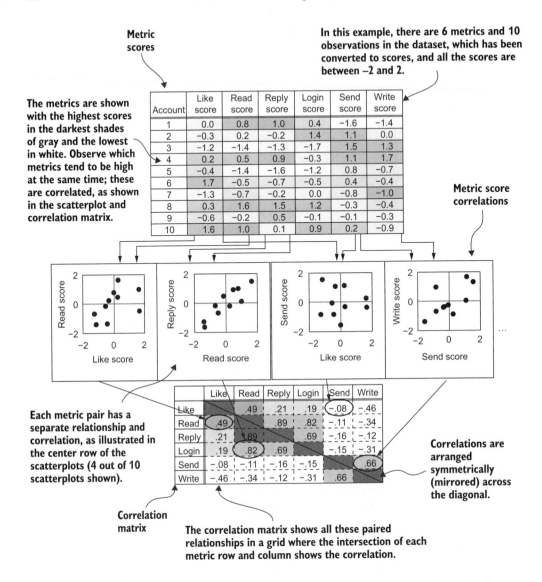

Metric scores

In this example, there are 6 metrics and 10 observations in the dataset, which has been converted to scores, and all the scores are between −2 and 2.

The metrics are shown with the highest scores in the darkest shades of gray and the lowest in white. Observe which metrics tend to be high at the same time; these are correlated, as shown in the scatterplot and correlation matrix.

Account	Like score	Read score	Reply score	Login score	Send score	Write score
1	0.0	0.8	1.0	0.4	−1.6	−1.4
2	−0.3	0.2	−0.2	1.4	1.1	0.0
3	−1.2	−1.4	−1.3	−1.7	1.5	1.3
4	0.2	0.5	0.9	−0.3	1.1	1.7
5	−0.4	−1.4	−1.6	−1.2	0.8	−0.7
6	1.7	−0.5	−0.7	−0.5	0.4	−0.4
7	−1.3	−0.7	−0.2	0.0	−0.8	−1.0
8	0.3	1.6	1.5	1.2	−0.3	−0.4
9	−0.6	−0.2	0.5	−0.1	−0.1	−0.3
10	1.6	1.0	0.1	0.9	0.2	−0.9

Metric score correlations

Each metric pair has a separate relationship and correlation, as illustrated in the center row of the scatterplots (4 out of 10 scatterplots shown).

	Like	Read	Reply	Login	Send	Write
Like		.49	.21	.19	−.08	−.46
Read	.49		.89	.82	−.11	−.34
Reply	.21	.89		.69	−.16	−.12
Login	.19	.82	.69		−.15	−.31
Send	−.08	−.11	−.16	−.15		.66
Write	−.46	−.34	−.12	−.31	.66	

Correlations are arranged symmetrically (mirrored) across the diagonal.

Correlation matrix

The correlation matrix shows all these paired relationships in a grid where the intersection of each metric row and column shows the correlation.

Figure 6.5   A correlation matrix (bottom) summarizes all pairwise correlations among the metrics in a dataset (top).

an intersection with itself in the correlation matrix, and this lies on the diagonal of the matrix because the metrics are in the same order in the rows and columns.

By definition, every metric has a correlation of 1.0 with itself. Although that information is useless, it is mathematically necessary for algorithms involving correlation matrices. But showing the diagonal 1.0s in a matrix can be distracting in a presentation, and therefore it can be omitted.

6.1.4 Case study correlation matrices

Figure 6.6 shows a correlation matrix from Klipfolio's case study as a heatmap. There are around 70 metrics, and they are ordered to show the relationships of high correlation between different types of metrics. Six groups of metrics are highly correlated. The single largest group comprises metrics for the most common ways to use the product. There are also five other smaller groups of metrics that relate to other aspects of the products, and some metrics are not strongly correlated to any other metrics. This structure is fairly typical, although there are not always so many well-defined groups. The technique to produce this order is shown later in listing 6.4.

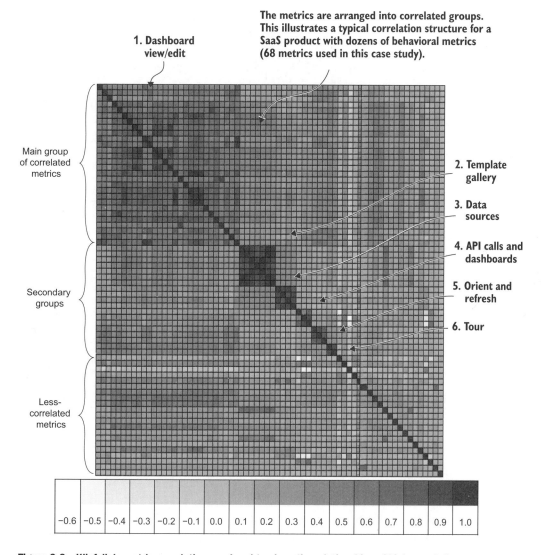

Figure 6.6 Klipfolio's metric correlations, ordered to show the relationships of high correlation

Figure 6.7 shows the correlation matrix from Klipfolio's case study with the metrics organized alphabetically. These are the same metrics as in figure 6.6; only the order is different. The organized matrix in figure 6.6 shows much more structure than the alphabetized matrix in figure 6.7. But something like figure 6.7 is what you are more likely to see the first time you look at your correlations in a heatmap (listing 6.2). Alphabetic ordering of the metrics reveals a structure where metrics that start with the same word are usually related. Still, there are many exceptions, so the related groups are not as evident as in figure 6.6.

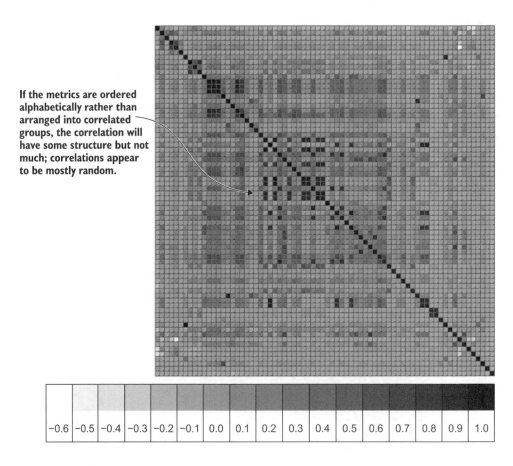

If the metrics are ordered alphabetically rather than arranged into correlated groups, the correlation will have some structure but not much; correlations appear to be mostly random.

-0.6	-0.5	-0.4	-0.3	-0.2	-0.1	0.0	0.1	0.2	0.3	0.4	0.5	0.6	0.7	0.8	0.9	1.0

Figure 6.7   Klipfolio's correlation matrix showing alphabetically arranged metrics

6.1.5   *Calculating correlation matrices in Python*

Listing 6.2 is a short Python program to create correlation matrices like those shown in figures 6.6 and 6.7. The result of running listing 6.2 on the simulated dataset is illustrated in figure 6.8. The program assumes that a dataset was created and saved using the code in chapter 4. Recall that this dataset is a table with one observation of a customer on each row, and one metric in each column. Most of listing 6.1 handles the details of loading a dataset and saving the result. The formatting was done in a free spreadsheet, as described later.

	account_tenure	adview_per_month	dislike_per_month	is_churn	like_per_month	message_per_month	newfriend_per_month	post_per_month	reply_per_month	unfriend_per_month
account_tenure		0.05	0.06	0.00	0.06	0.05	0.09	0.06	0.04	0.06
adview_per_month	0.05		0.34	−0.03	0.56	0.06	0.56	0.56	0.05	0.02
dislike_per_month	0.06	0.34		−0.03	0.37	0.08	0.37	0.34	0.05	0.01
is_churn	0.00	−0.03	−0.03		−0.04	−0.06	−0.08	−0.05	−0.05	0.04
like_per_month	0.06	0.56	0.37	−0.04		0.06	0.57	0.59	0.04	0.01
message_per_month	0.05	0.06	0.08	−0.06	0.06		0.07	0.04	0.93	0.01
newfriend_per_month	0.09	0.56	0.37	−0.08	0.57	0.07		0.57	0.04	0.02
post_per_month	0.06	0.56	0.34	−0.05	0.59	0.04	0.57		0.03	0.02
reply_per_month	0.04	0.05	0.05	−0.05	0.04	0.93	0.04	0.03		0.00
unfriend_per_month	0.06	0.02	0.01	0.04	0.01	0.01	0.02	0.02	0.00	

Metrics are alphabetized.

The grayscale heatmap was applied in a spreadsheet application.

Figure 6.8   Result of running listing 6.2 on the simulated dataset

In listing 6.2, the correlation matrix is calculated with a call to the Pandas `Dataframe.corr` function. Note that listing 6.2 does not attempt to create a heatmap image like the examples in figures 6.6 and 6.7; the function stops after saving the correlation matrix data in a comma-separated (.csv) file. The reason for this is that it's not practical to make a heatmap for a large number of metrics in Python. If there are more than 15 to 20 metrics, either the heatmap image must be enormous, or the metric names and correlation values are too small to read (see figures 6.6 and 6.7 for examples).

TIP It's not practical to explore large correlation heatmaps in *static* images. You should definitely inspect the correlation heatmap closely, but it is usually easier to view it in a spreadsheet application. Fix the metric name row and column to make the matrix scrollable, and use conditional formatting to add the heatmap colors. For presentations, you can export various formatted versions.

Listing 6.2   Calculating the correlation matrix for a dataset in Python

```
import pandas as pd
import os

def dataset_correlation_matrix(data_set_path):

    assert os.path.isfile(data_set_path),
        '"{}" is not a valid path'.format(data_set_path)
    churn_data =
        pd.read_csv(data_set_path,index_col=[0,1])
```

Checks the path

Loads the dataset into a DataFrame and sets the index

Sorts the columns alphabetically

```
churn_data =
    churn_data.reindex(sorted(churn_data.columns), axis=1)

corr_df = churn_data.corr()
save_name = data_set_path.replace('.csv', '_correlation_matrix.csv')
corr_df.to_csv(save_name)
print('Saved correlation matrix to' + save_name)
```

Saves the correlation matrix in .csv format

Calculates the correlation matrix with the Dataframe.corr function

You should run listing 6.2 and confirm that it gives you a similar result on your own dataset. If you are using the wrapper program to run the listings, by now you know that means changing the command-line parameters to `--chapter 6 --listing 2`. The program saves the data in a .csv file (the location of which will be printed by the wrapper program).

6.2   *Averaging groups of behavioral metrics*

Suppose that you have 5 or 10 customer behaviors where the metrics are moderately to highly correlated. What do you do? A foundational technique for handling highly correlated metrics is to average the scores of the correlated metrics together.

6.2.1   *Why you average correlated metric scores*

Handling multiple correlated metrics individually in churn analysis and customer segmentation is problematic for two interrelated reasons:

- The churn relationships you observe in two different cohort analyses are not integrated in the sense that there is no way to understand how customers in different cohorts on different metrics relate to each other. What does it mean if a particular customer is in the third cohort on one metric and the sixth cohort on another in two related activities? Averaging them together is a way to handle this, as will be explained.
- An information overload comes from looking at too many metrics. Remember that behavioral metrics usually do not measure something that is directly causal of churn or retention. It is more common that your behavioral metrics are only associated with churn. Given a large number of metrics associated with churn (but not causal), there is no way to know which metrics and events are most important.

After the correlated metric scores are averaged together, they are often easier to use in a churn cohort analysis for customer segmentation. As explained in the last chapter, averaging together many customers to form the cohorts shows the influence of a metric on churn by averaging away the individual circumstances that shape behavior. In the same way, averaging together groups of metrics further reduces random variation and makes the underlying relationship between churn and a set of behaviors clearer.

What does it mean to average different metric scores together? Remember that different metrics usually mean completely different things, like logging in and editing a document or viewing a video and liking it. Does it even make sense to average logins and edits? Because there are probably going to be a lot more edits than logins, it would be unbalanced. And does it make sense to average views and likes of content? There are going to be a lot more views than likes, so it's not clear such an average is meaningful. The problem is worse if different metrics have units like monetary values or time. Considering the telecommunications context, what would an average of total call duration and overage charges mean? Actually, this is no problem at all; this is another advantage of having converted the metrics to scores.

> **TAKEAWAY** Because each metric score measures the position of the customer with respect to the average, it is okay to average together *scores* of different types of metrics.

It does not make sense to average together different types of metrics when those metrics refer to different things if you are using the original units. But it is okay with scores: the average score describes the overall area of activity that those different metrics relate to. If someone is above average in both logins and edits with an SaaS product, it's fair to call them an above-average user overall. If someone is below average in views and likes on a streaming video product, it makes sense to consider them a below-average user overall. And if someone is below average in calls and above average in overage charges on a telecommunications product, if you average the scores, they are just an average user.

In fact, an average score on a group of metrics is often more useful than the separate scores. That's because different metrics provide different ways of looking at the same area of activity that can substitute for each other. If a customer does not use a particular product feature but instead uses a related one, the average picks it up either way. You would miss the activity for some customers if you relied on a single metric. If a customer is high on one metric and low on another, in one churn cohort they would be in a low-risk cohort, and in the other they would be in a high-risk cohort. By averaging the two together, you get a better picture of the overall activity.

6.2.2 *Averaging scores with a matrix of weights (loading matrix)*

Averaging together groups of correlated metric scores is a straightforward concept, but the implementation is a bit tricky because you may be doing this for a lot of metrics and observations. You are going to use a technique where you encode the groups in a matrix of weights to keep track of which metrics are in which groups and the weights needed to form the averages. Recall that a matrix is just a table where all the entries are numbers. A *weight* in this context means the multiplicative factor, $1/n$, is needed to turn a sum into an average. This matrix of weights is known as a loading matrix.

> **DEFINITION** A *loading matrix* is a table of weights to apply to metrics in order to form averages.

The loading matrix not only keeps track of the metrics in each group but also provides an efficient implementation of the averaging computation (more in the next section). I'm going to walk you through an example with just a small number of metrics. The technique might seem overly complex for a toy problem like the example, but it scales well to dozens or even hundreds of metrics and large datasets.

Figure 6.9 demonstrates the averaging technique for a small dataset with 10 observations and 6 metrics, continuing the example from figure 6.5. Here is how it works:

1. The metrics for login, read, and reply events are averaged into one group because they are highly correlated. The metrics for send and write are averaged into another group, and the metric for like is left alone. These decisions are driven by an inspection of the small correlation matrix. (Later in this chapter,

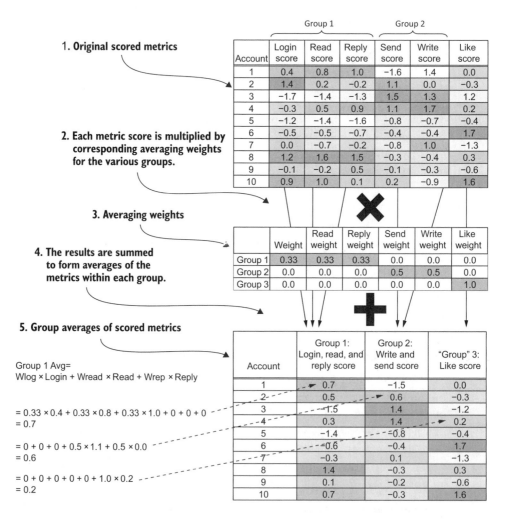

Figure 6.9   The process of grouping related metrics into averages using a matrix of weights

you will learn how to automatically discover groups in datasets with large numbers of metrics.)

2 A loading matrix is defined with a shape that is the number of metrics by the number of groups (three by five, for the example). Also in the example, the weight matrix is shown with the groups arranged on the rows and the metrics in the columns; in practice, it is usually stored the other way (metrics in the rows and groups in the columns), but see the next section for details.

3 Each row for a group contains weights to form an average from the appropriate metrics and zeros for the others. The weight to form an average is one divided by the number of metrics in the group:

  – For the row corresponding to group 1, there are weights of 1/3 (0.33) in each of the three columns for login, read, and reply, and zeros in the others. To form group 1, the weight of 0.33 is applied to the scores for login, read, and reply events. For the other metrics, zeros are shown in their place, indicating these are not used in group 1.

  – For the row corresponding to group 2, there are weights of 1/2 (0.5) in each of the two columns for write and send, and zeros in the other.

  – For the row corresponding to group 3, the likes, there is a 1 in the weight column for it.

4 To calculate the group averages, the metrics for each account are multiplied by the weights for each group, and then the results are added together.

5 The resulting sums are the averages for each group.

6.2.3 Case study for loading matrices

Figure 6.10 shows the loading matrix created for the simulated social network data. Two groups are created:

- A metric group for ad views, likes, and posts: the three most common metrics
- A metric group for messages and replies

If you look at the correlation matrix in figure 6.8, you can easily convince yourself that the metrics in these groups are highly correlated to each other and to the others, less so. (The formal method for discovering groups automatically is coming later in the chapter.)

At this point, I must call your attention to one feature of figure 6.10 that you are not expecting: the weights groups in the real loading matrices are a bit higher than $1/N$, where N is the number of metrics in the group.

The loading matrix still forms an average from the correlated scores, but the weights are boosted slightly above $1/N$. I did not mention this detail earlier because the meaning is the same, and the concept is clearer when explained with $1/N$ weights. For three metric groups, the weights are 0.41 instead of 0.33; and for two metric groups, the weights are 0.62 instead of 0.5. The detail of the reasoning is explained in section 6.3.3 (it has to do with adjusting the standard deviation of the combined score).

Metrics are shown on the rows, and groups are shown on the columns. A nonzero entry indicates group membership.

	Metric	metric_group_1	metric_group_2	account_tenure	dislike_per_month	newfriend_per_month	unfriend_per_month
Main group of correlated metrics	adview_per_month	0.413	0	0	0	0	0
	like_per_month	0.413	0	0	0	0	0
	post_per_month	0.413	0	0	0	0	0
Secondary group	message_per_month	0	0.620	0	0	0	0
	reply_per_month	0	0.620	0	0	0	0
Less-correlated metrics	account_tenure	0	0	1.0	0	0	0
	dislike_per_month	0	0	0	1.0	0	0
	newfriend_per_month	0	0	0	0	1.0	0
	unfriend_per_month	0	0	0	0	0	1.0

There are three metrics in the first group, and the weights are 0.41.

There are two metrics in the second group, and the weights are 0.62.

Four metrics are not grouped.

Figure 6.10 Loading matrix for the simulation case study

Figure 6.11 shows the real loading matrix created in Klipfolio's case study. Now the matrix is shown with the metrics on the rows and the groups in the columns; this is the transposition of the view in figure 6.9. (Figure 6.9 shows the loading matrix transposed so the weights would visually align with the columns of data for illustrative purposes.) The reason for arranging the metrics in the rows and the groups in the columns is clear from figure 6.11: there are typically many more metrics than groups, so it's much easier to read this way. Arranging the metrics along the rows is also the correct orientation for implementation of the averaging calculation, which the next section shows.

In the figure, you can see that the average weights are also not exactly $1/N$: the first group of metrics consists of 28 metrics, so each metric is assigned a weight of 0.041, but $1/28 = 0.0357$. There are five other groups consisting of fewer than 10 metrics each, which all receive weighted entries in the matrix that are a bit above $1/N$. There are also a few dozen other metrics that were not highly correlated enough to be grouped; these are only partially shown in figure 6.11.

6.2.4 *Applying a loading matrix in Python*

Listing 6.3 shows the code that applies a loading matrix to a dataset to calculate the average scores. Most of this listing is the usual reading of the dataset and saving the results, and this time also reading in a loading matrix (created by listing 6.4). The heart of the listing is the following single line:

```
grouped_ndarray = np.matmul(ndarray_2group, load_mat_ndarray)
```

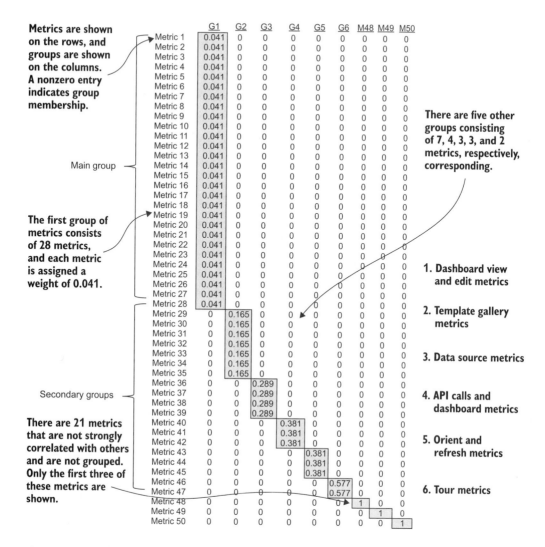

Metrics are shown on the rows, and groups are shown on the columns. A nonzero entry indicates group membership.

Main group

The first group of metrics consists of 28 metrics, and each metric is assigned a weight of 0.041.

Secondary groups

There are 21 metrics that are not strongly correlated with others and are not grouped. Only the first three of these metrics are shown.

There are five other groups consisting of 7, 4, 3, 3, and 2 metrics, respectively, corresponding.

1. **Dashboard view and edit metrics**

2. **Template gallery metrics**

3. **Data source metrics**

4. **API calls and dashboard metrics**

5. **Orient and refresh metrics**

6. **Tour metrics**

	G1	G2	G3	G4	G5	G6	M48	M49	M50
Metric 1	0.041	0	0	0	0	0	0	0	0
Metric 2	0.041	0	0	0	0	0	0	0	0
Metric 3	0.041	0	0	0	0	0	0	0	0
Metric 4	0.041	0	0	0	0	0	0	0	0
Metric 5	0.041	0	0	0	0	0	0	0	0
Metric 6	0.041	0	0	0	0	0	0	0	0
Metric 7	0.041	0	0	0	0	0	0	0	0
Metric 8	0.041	0	0	0	0	0	0	0	0
Metric 9	0.041	0	0	0	0	0	0	0	0
Metric 10	0.041	0	0	0	0	0	0	0	0
Metric 11	0.041	0	0	0	0	0	0	0	0
Metric 12	0.041	0	0	0	0	0	0	0	0
Metric 13	0.041	0	0	0	0	0	0	0	0
Metric 14	0.041	0	0	0	0	0	0	0	0
Metric 15	0.041	0	0	0	0	0	0	0	0
Metric 16	0.041	0	0	0	0	0	0	0	0
Metric 17	0.041	0	0	0	0	0	0	0	0
Metric 18	0.041	0	0	0	0	0	0	0	0
Metric 19	0.041	0	0	0	0	0	0	0	0
Metric 20	0.041	0	0	0	0	0	0	0	0
Metric 21	0.041	0	0	0	0	0	0	0	0
Metric 22	0.041	0	0	0	0	0	0	0	0
Metric 23	0.041	0	0	0	0	0	0	0	0
Metric 24	0.041	0	0	0	0	0	0	0	0
Metric 25	0.041	0	0	0	0	0	0	0	0
Metric 26	0.041	0	0	0	0	0	0	0	0
Metric 27	0.041	0	0	0	0	0	0	0	0
Metric 28	0.041	0	0	0	0	0	0	0	0
Metric 29	0	0.165	0	0	0	0	0	0	0
Metric 30	0	0.165	0	0	0	0	0	0	0
Metric 31	0	0.165	0	0	0	0	0	0	0
Metric 32	0	0.165	0	0	0	0	0	0	0
Metric 33	0	0.165	0	0	0	0	0	0	0
Metric 34	0	0.165	0	0	0	0	0	0	0
Metric 35	0	0.165	0	0	0	0	0	0	0
Metric 36	0	0	0.289	0	0	0	0	0	0
Metric 37	0	0	0.289	0	0	0	0	0	0
Metric 38	0	0	0.289	0	0	0	0	0	0
Metric 39	0	0	0.289	0	0	0	0	0	0
Metric 40	0	0	0	0.381	0	0	0	0	0
Metric 41	0	0	0	0.381	0	0	0	0	0
Metric 42	0	0	0	0.381	0	0	0	0	0
Metric 43	0	0	0	0	0.381	0	0	0	0
Metric 44	0	0	0	0	0.381	0	0	0	0
Metric 45	0	0	0	0	0.381	0	0	0	0
Metric 46	0	0	0	0	0	0.577	0	0	0
Metric 47	0	0	0	0	0	0.577	0	0	0
Metric 48	0	0	0	0	0	0	1	0	0
Metric 49	0	0	0	0	0	0	0	1	0
Metric 50	0	0	0	0	0	0	0	0	1

Figure 6.11   Loading matrix for Klipfolio's case study

That line performs a matrix multiplication of the data by the loading matrix, which does the averaging calculation described in the last section.

DEFINITION *Matrix multiplication* is an operation on two matrices that creates a result matrix. Each element in the first row of the result matrix is given by multiplying the first row of the first matrix by each column of the second matrix and then adding the results for each column; the second row of the result matrix is given by doing the same with the second row of the first matrix and all of the columns of the second matrix in turn, and so on.

Note that for matrix multiplication to work, the number of columns in the first matrix has to equal the number of rows in the second matrix; this condition is met when the loading matrix has the metrics along the rows.

Listing 6.3   Applying a loading matrix to a dataset in Python

```python
import pandas as pd
import numpy as np
import os

def apply_metric_groups(data_set_path):
    score_save_path=
        data_set_path.replace('.csv','_scores.csv')          ◁──  Listing 5.3 saved
    assert os.path.isfile(score_save_path),                        this score data.
        'Run listing 5.3 to save metric scores first'
    score_data =                                             ◁──  Reloads the file into
        pd.read_csv(score_save_path,index_col=[0,1])               a DataFrame and
                                                                   sets the index

    data_2group = score_data.drop('is_churn',axis=1)         ◁──  The churn indicator
                                                                   is removed for now;
                                                                   this returns a copy.
    load_mat_path = data_set_path.replace('.csv', '_load_mat.csv')
    assert os.path.isfile(load_mat_path),
        'Run listing 6.4 to save a loading matrix first'     ◁──  Reads a loading
    load_mat_df = pd.read_csv(load_mat_path, index_col=0)          matrix from a file

    load_mat_ndarray = load_mat_df.to_numpy()               ◁──  Converts the loading
                                                                  matrix to a NumPy array
    ndarray_2group =
        data_2group[load_mat_df.index.values].to_numpy()    ◁──  Rearranges data
    grouped_ndarray =                                             columns to the
        np.matmul(ndarray_2group, load_mat_ndarray)         ◁──  order of the loading
    churn_data_grouped                                            matrix rows
        = pd.DataFrame(grouped_ndarray,
                    columns=load_mat_df.columns.values,           Uses matrix
                    index=score_data.index)                       multiplication on
                                                                  ndarray to do the
    churn_data_grouped['is_churn'] =                              grouping
        score_data['is_churn']
    save_path = data_set_path.replace('.csv', '_groupscore.csv')
    churn_data_grouped.to_csv(save_path,header=True)        ◁──
    print('Saved grouped data to ' + save_path)                   Saves the result
```

Creates a DataFrame from the ndarray result (annotation pointing to `churn_data_grouped = pd.DataFrame(...)`)

Adds back the churn status column (annotation pointing to `churn_data_grouped['is_churn'] = score_data['is_churn']`)

Figure 6.12 illustrates the definition of matrix multiplication in terms of averaging scores. The definition may sound complicated, but it's what you just learned in the last section:

- The first average score for Account 1 is calculated by multiplying the Account 1 row of the data by the first group of loading weights in the first column and summing it together.
- The second average score for Account 1 is calculated by multiplying the Account 1 row of the data by the second group of loading weights in the second column, and so on.

- **In matrix multiplication, two matrices produce a result matrix.**

- **Each element of the result matrix is the sum of the elementwise multiplication of a row of the first matrix and a column of the second.**

- **This implements averaging scores with a loading matrix.**

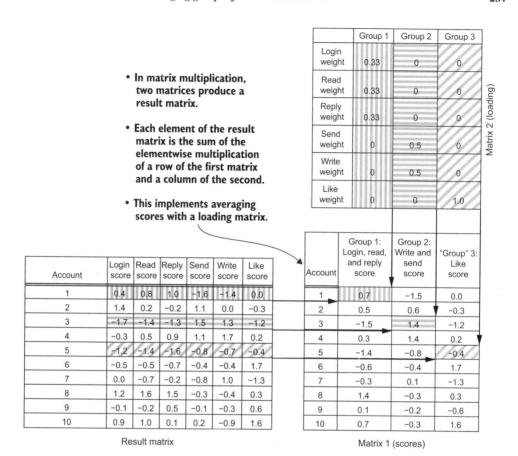

Result matrix

Matrix 1 (scores)

Figure 6.12 Matrix multiplication is an operation that implements the averaging of scores by a loading matrix.

Matrix multiplication is a concise and efficient way to apply the loading weights to calculate averages in large datasets with any number of metrics and groups.

At this point, you probably want to run listing 6.3 on some data and check out the results, but you might be wondering where exactly you get the loading matrix from. You're right to wonder, because I'm teaching you how to use a loading matrix first so you understand its purpose. The next section shows you how to create one from scratch. Be patient: you'll see some case studies to further convince you of the usefulness of grouping metrics with loading matrices, and then in section 6.3, you'll learn how to run the code to make one. Then you can come back and run listing 6.3 using the loading matrix you created.

6.2.5   *Churn cohort analysis on metric group average scores*

Once you have grouped correlated metrics into average scores for the related behaviors, you can perform a churn analysis on the average group. No new code is needed to do so. The procedure is as follows:

1   Use listing 6.3 and save the grouped scores in a new dataset file. It will have the same name as the original dataset except it now ends in group_scores.
2   Use listing 5.1 to create a cohort plot from the grouped dataset by substituting the new filename and the variable name metric_group_1 for the first group, and so forth (see listing 6.3 for details).

Figure 6.13 illustrates the results of a churn cohort analysis for Klipfolio's main group of metrics for viewing and editing dashboards. This is the first group that was illustrated in the correlation matrix of figure 6.6 and in the loading matrix of figure 6.11. Churn cohort analysis was introduced in chapter 5, so I will just briefly summarize the main features. Each point represents the customers in a cohort defined by one decile in the scores. The vertical axis shows the churn rate in the cohort on a relative scale, and the bottom of the graph is fixed at zero. If a cohort is twice as far from the bottom of the plot as another, then it has twice the churn rate.

Figure 6.13 shows that the average of the main group of metric scores for Klipfolio reveals a powerful relationship to churn: the cohort with the highest average scores has a churn rate that is less than one-tenth of the churn rate for the lower cohorts. Another nice property of this relationship is that the churn rate keeps declining, up to the highest cohorts. The average of this group of scores shows a stronger relationship to churn than the individual behaviors that were shown in the last chapter in figure 5.6.

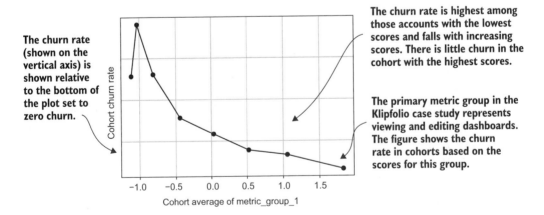

The churn rate (shown on the vertical axis) is shown relative to the bottom of the plot set to zero churn.

The churn rate is highest among those accounts with the lowest scores and falls with increasing scores. There is little churn in the cohort with the highest scores.

The primary metric group in the Klipfolio case study represents viewing and editing dashboards. The figure shows the churn rate in cohorts based on the scores for this group.

Figure 6.13   Cohort analysis of churn for Klipfolio's primary metric group scores

Figure 6.14 shows an example of a churn cohort analysis for the average of the main group of scores for Broadly. The main group of correlated metrics all relate to adding customers and transactions to the system, making requests to customers for reviews and recommendations, and the result of those requests. The cohort analysis based on this group of scores is another example of a strong relationship to churn. In this case, the top cohort has a churn rate around one-seventh the churn rate in the bottom cohorts.

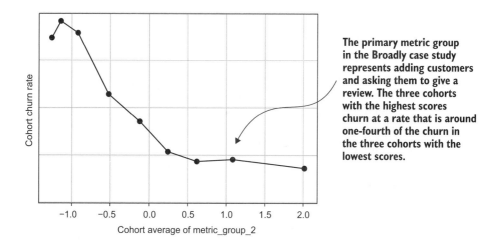

The primary metric group in the Broadly case study represents adding customers and asking them to give a review. The three cohorts with the highest scores churn at a rate that is around one-fourth of the churn in the three cohorts with the lowest scores.

Figure 6.14 Cohort analysis of churn for Broadly's primary metric group scores

Figures 6.13 and 6.14 both show that in real case studies, averages of groups of metric scores often show relationships to churn more effectively than individual metrics alone. Your own results might not show results that are this strong, but it is still preferable to analyze correlated metrics in groups. That's because it avoids information overload from too many metrics.

> **TAKEAWAY**   For correlated metrics, it is better to analyze churn in cohorts using the average score in place of individual metrics.

6.3   *Discovering groups of correlated metrics*

You now know how to average groups of metrics, but there's one last thing: I did not explain how to *find* those groups of metrics in large datasets. For simple cases with just a few metrics, you can probably identify groups of metrics by looking at the correlation matrix. That's the case for the small dataset used in the examples of figures 6.5 and 6.9. But if you have a correlation matrix with dozens of metrics (or more), like the one from the case study (figure 6.7), it's not as simple. Fortunately, there is a standard algorithm that will do it for you.

6.3.1   *Grouping metrics by clustering correlations*

The algorithm that you use to find groups of correlated metrics is called a clustering algorithm.

> **DEFINITION**   A *clustering algorithm* is an automatic procedure for grouping together similar items based on data.

Technically, the procedure of the clustering algorithm is distinct from how similarity between items is measured. To group together metrics, you'll use the correlation coefficient; the higher the correlation, the more similar the metrics. The clustering procedure you'll use is called hierarchical clustering.

> **DEFINITION**   *Hierarchical clustering* is a *greedy, agglomerative* clustering algorithm:
>
> - *Agglomerative* means the algorithm works by combining similar items in a *bottom-up* manner. Groups are formed starting from just two similar elements, and more elements are added to form larger groups of similar items as the algorithm progresses.
> - *Greedy* means that the algorithm works by picking the two elements that appear most similar, and after those two are grouped, the next most similar item is grouped at each stage.
> - *Hierarchical* in this context refers to the fact that greedy agglomeration implies a structure or hierarchy between the items. There are the two most similar items, and after that, there is the next most similar, and so on.

Figure 6.15 illustrates hierarchical clustering, continuing the example of the small dataset that was shown in figures 6.5, 6.9, and 6.12. The algorithm starts with the correlation matrix from figure 6.5 and finds the single highest correlation between any two metrics (figure 6.15.1). The two most correlated metrics form the first group: this is the 0.93 correlation between the metrics for reading and replying to messages.

The second step in the hierarchical clustering algorithm (figure 6.15.2) is to create a loading matrix that converts the original dataset into a new dataset where the two most correlated metrics are grouped, but all the other metrics remain separate. This loading matrix has one fewer column than there are metrics because there is just one group of metrics. The third step in the algorithm (not shown in figure 6.15) is to use the new loading matrix to create a new version of the dataset, following the procedure shown in the last section. The fourth step in the hierarchical clustering algorithm (figure 6.15.3) is to calculate the new correlation matrix for the data after the first two metrics are grouped.

Having a new correlation matrix, the algorithm starts on a new iteration: find the next highest correlation. In the example, the next highest correlation is the 0.77 correlation between the metric for logins and the group metric for reading and replying, created in the last step (figure 6.15.3). The login metric is added to the first group in a new iteration of the loading matrix (figure 6.15.4), leading to a new version of the dataset and correlation matrix (figure 6.15.5), and so on.

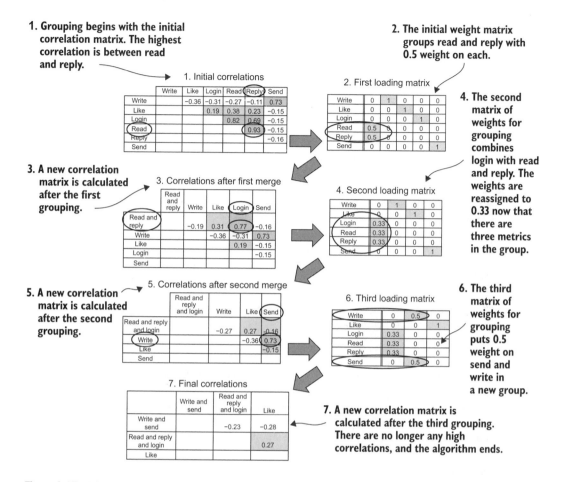

Figure 6.15 Discovering metric groups by clustering correlations

The algorithm stops when enough metrics have been grouped so that nothing is left that is moderately or highly correlated. The exact level of correlation at which the algorithm should stop trying to group things is a parameter that controls the level of grouping. Generally, you set the threshold at a moderate level of correlation. I typically set it in the range of 0.5 or 0.6 in the analyses that I do. I will provide more details about how to set this parameter in section 6.3.3. For now, let's look at how the example in figure 6.15 ends. After login, read, and reply are in one group, and write and send are in another group (figure 6.15.6), the remaining correlations (figure 6.15.7) are all between −.28 and .27; these are only weak correlations, so the algorithm stops. The result of the algorithm is to produce the loading matrix that was first shown in figure 6.9. (Figure 6.15.6 is a transposed and slightly reordered version of the loading matrix in figure 6.9.)

To review, here is the how the hierarchical clustering algorithm works at each step:

1 Identify the highest correlation.
2 Update the loading matrix to group together the two most correlated elements.
3 Create a new grouped dataset using the loading matrix on the original dataset of scores.
4 Calculate a new correlation matrix.
5 Repeat steps 1 through 4 until all of the remaining correlations are below a predetermined threshold.

Efficiency of hierarchical clustering and correlation calculations for large datasets

You might read in other references that hierarchical clustering is inefficient and not suited for big data. But there is a crucial difference here: the correlation matrix is not big data even when your data is big! The size that matters for the run time of hierarchical clustering is the number of metrics in your dataset, not the number of customers (observations). The number of metrics is reduced by one at every step, so the maximum number of iterations is the number of metrics. There is no problem using hierarchical clustering for larger datasets.

If you do have a lot of customers (a lot of observations), you'll find that calculating the correlation matrix is actually the most expensive step. If your data is truly big, you should look at optimization or approximation of the correlation matrix calculation and don't worry about the hierarchical clustering. As you'll see in the next section, you really calculate the correlation matrix only once. My explanation of the algorithm presents it as if you recalculate the correlation matrix at each step, but in practice, the correlation matrix at each step can be deduced using the loading matrix (this detail is beyond the scope of this book).

6.3.2 *Clustering correlations in Python*

Now that you know how hierarchical clustering based on a correlation matrix works, you are ready to learn the Python code that implements it in practice. Listing 6.4 shows the program. Spoiler: the code uses prewritten open source package functions to implement the clustering. Listing 6.4 is mainly concerned with preparing the input to make it ready for the package functions and receiving the output from the package functions and turning those into the loading matrix that you need. The overall process is broken down into three steps that are separate functions in listing 6.4. I explain each one in turn.

The actual clustering in listing 6.4 is in the function `find_correlation_clusters`. SciPy provides an implementation of hierarchical clustering in the package `scipy.cluster.hierarchy` with two functions: `linkage` and `fcluster`. The function `linkage` is the one that really does the work. It can work either on a raw dataset or on a precomputed measurement of the distance between points in a dataset, which is what happens in listing 6.4. But the result of the `linkage` function is not actually the clusters;

instead, the linkage function returns a description of the structure of the distance relationships between the data points, which is the hierarchy of distances referred to in the algorithm name.

I am not going to explain the details of how the hierarchy is represented because there is another function that you can pass the result into to get the clusters you want: that is fcluster. The function fcluster takes the hierarchy description from linkage and a cutoff threshold to form clusters. In our case, this threshold is the correlation cutoff for what we consider to be highly correlated. The result of fcluster is an assigned cluster for each of the original items in the form of a numpy Series.

Listing 6.4   Finding metric groups and creating a loading matrix in Python

```
import pandas as pd
import numpy as np
import os
from collections import Counter
from scipy.cluster.hierarchy import linkage, fcluster        Imports SciPy functions that
from scipy.spatial.distance import squareform                perform hierarchical clustering

def find_correlation_clusters(corr,corr_thresh):
    dissimilarity = 1.0 - corr            Clustering uses dissimilarity,
                                          so invert correlation matrix

    diss_thresh = 1.0 - corr_thresh       The threshold parameter
                                          is also inverted.

    hierarchy = linkage(squareform(dissimilarity),
                        method='single')   Calculates the order of relative
                                           distances between metrics
    labels = fcluster(hierarchy, diss_thresh,
                      criterion='distance')    Determines the groups given
    return labels                              the hierarchy and threshold

def relabel_clusters(labels,metric_columns):
    cluster_count = Counter(labels)       Counts the number of
                                          elements in each cluster

    cluster_order = {cluster[0]: idx for idx, cluster in
                     enumerate(cluster_count.most_common())}   Finds the order of
                                                               the cluster's number
    relabeled_clusters = [cluster_order[l]                     of members
                          for l in labels]
                                                     Makes a new count from
    relabeled_count = Counter(relabeled_clusters)    the relabeled clusters

    labeled_column_df = pd.DataFrame({'group': relabeled_clusters,
        'column': metric_columns}).sort_values(
        ['group', 'column'], ascending=[True, True])     Makes a DataFrame,
    return labeled_column_df, relabeled_count             listing the group for
                                                          each of the metrics

def make_load_matrix(labeled_column_df,metric_columns,relabeled_count, corr):
    load_mat = np.zeros((len(metric_columns),
        len(relabeled_count)))
```

Makes a new series of the cluster labels in order (annotation for `relabeled_clusters = [cluster_order[l] for l in labels]`)

Creates an empty (zero) matrix to hold the averaging weights (annotation for `load_mat = np.zeros(...)`)

Enters the weight for each metric in the loading matrix

Selects those columns in the loading matrix that are groups

Uses equation 6.3 (section 6.3.3) to get the weights

For non-grouped metrics, the weight is simply 1.0.

Makes a Boolean series showing which columns are groups

Makes the names metric_group_n for the groups

Otherwise, the original metric name is entered in the list.

```
for row in labeled_column_df.iterrows():
    orig_col = metric_columns.index(row[1][1])
    if relabeled_count[row[1][0]]>1:
        load_mat[orig_col, row[1][0]] = 1.0/(np.sqrt(corr) *
            float(relabeled_count[row[1][0]])  )
    else:
        load_mat[orig_col, row[1][0]] = 1.0

is_group = load_mat.astype(bool).sum(axis=0) > 1
column_names=
    ['metric_group_{}'.format(d + 1)
        if is_group[d]
        else
            labeled_column_df.loc[
                labeled_column_df['group']==d,'column'].item()
                    for d in range(0, load_mat.shape[1])]
loadmat_df = pd.DataFrame(load_mat,
    index=metric_columns, columns=column_names)

loadmat_df['name'] = loadmat_df.index

sort_cols = list(loadmat_df.columns.values)

sort_order = [False] * loadmat_df.shape[1]

sort_order[-1] = True

loadmat_df = loadmat_df.sort_values(sort_cols,
    ascending=sort_order)

loadmat_df = loadmat_df.drop('name', axis=1)
return loadmat_df

def find_metric_groups(data_set_path,group_corr_thresh=0.5):
    score_save_path=
        data_set_path.replace('.csv','_scores.csv')
    assert os.path.isfile(score_save_path),
        'You must run listing 5.3 to save metric scores first'
    score_data = pd.read_csv(score_save_path,index_col=[0,1])
    score_data.drop('is_churn',axis=1,inplace=True)
    metric_columns = list(score_data.columns.values)

    labels =
        find_correlation_clusters(score_data.corr(), group_corr_thresh)
    labeled_column_df, relabeled_count =
        relabel_clusters(labels,metric_columns)
    loadmat_df = make_load_matrix(labeled_column_df, metric_columns,
        relabeled_count,group_corr_thresh)
    save_path = data_set_path.replace('.csv', '_load_mat.csv')
    print('saving loadings to ' + save_path)
    loadmat_df.to_csv(save_path)

    group_lists=
        ['|'.join(labeled_column_df[labeled_column_df['group']==g]['column'])
                    for g in set(labeled_column_df['group'])]
```

Makes a DataFrame from the weighted matrix

Makes a name column from the DataFrame index column

Makes a list of the columns that sort the rows

Sorts most of the columns in descending order

Sorts the name column in ascending order

Sorts the loading matrix in order for interpretability

Drops the name column because it was used for sorting

Reloads the scores created by listing 5.3

Makes a list of the original metric columns

Calculates the group assignments

Makes a column that lists the metrics in each group

```
save_path = data_set_path.replace('.csv', '_groupmets.csv')
print('saving metric groups to ' + save_path)
pd.DataFrame(group_lists,
            index=loadmat_df.columns.values,
            columns=['metrics']).to_csv(save_path)
```

◁── **Saves the loading matrix**

Getting your data into the cluster algorithm is not that hard. The most important detail is the fact that the linkage function is written to work on data in terms of *dissimilarity*, but so far we have thought about correlation, which is a measure of *similarity*. The solution is as follows: you take 1.0 minus the correlation, and what was a measure of similarity becomes a measure of dissimilarity. What does that mean? Consider: the highest correlation (the most similarity) was 1.0, which becomes 0.0 after being subtracted from 1.0. That is now the *least* dissimilar two items can be. The most dissimilar in terms of correlation would be –1.0, but that becomes 2.0 when subtracted from 1.0 $(1 - -1 = 1 + 1 = 2)$; that is now the most dissimilar. Both the correlation matrix and the correlation threshold are converted by (element-wise) subtraction from 1.0 before they are used in the SciPy functions linkage and fcluster. That's all the preparation needed to run the clustering algorithm.

Unfortunately, the result of the clustering algorithm is not exactly what you want. What you want is a loading matrix and in a particular order. It is easiest to interpret when the largest group comes first, and they are then ordered in descending size. The fcluster function returns the assigned clusters for the groups, but they are not in any particular order sizewise. There are two main parts to the postprocessing after calling linkage and fcluster: first comes sorting and relabeling the clusters, and after that, the creation of the loading matrix.

The second function in listing 6.4, relabel_clusters, is the first step of postprocessing. To sort and relabel the clusters, a Python set is used to find the unique clusters, and a Python Counter is used to count the occurrences of each label in the result of fcluster. The Counter object also has a utility function to iterate through the elements in order from most common to least: that is the function Counter.most_common. After the relabeled cluster names are found, the result is saved in a new Series of labels. Two objects are created to represent the clusters for later: a two-column DataFrame that lists the original metrics and the groups they were placed in, and a new Counter object that counts the new labels.

The third function in listing 6.4, make_load_matrix, is the final step. The loading matrix is initialized as an ndarray of zeros in the right size: the number of rows is the number of metrics, and the number of columns is the number of groups. The function relabel_clusters creates a DataFrame that lists each metric and its group. That is used to iterate over the metrics and fill in an appropriate entry under the right group in the loading matrix. That ndarray is turned into a DataFrame using the metric names as the index.

The weight for each entry in the loading matrix is calculated with 1.0 divided by the number of elements in the group: the number of elements in the group is relabeled_count[row[1][0]] in the code. relabeled_count is a counter object, and row[1][0] selects the appropriate element. But there is also another term in the denominator of the weight calculation, which is the square root of the correlation threshold used for clustering: np.sqrt(corr). That extra term is what makes the weights a bit higher than $1/N$, as I mentioned back when I first showed you the loading matrix in section 6.2.3. I'll explain the reasoning for that choice in the next section, after I finish explaining the algorithm.

The rest of the function make_load_matrix sorts the loading matrix in the order that makes it easiest to read: the largest group comes first and then the second largest, and so forth. Within each group, the metrics are sorted alphabetically by name. This is accomplished using Pandas DataFrame.sort_values with appropriate parameters. The function sort_values takes a list of columns to sort by and a list of Booleans for whether each column is in ascending or descending order. The name of the metrics is added as a column (it was previously the index), and all of the columns are used to sort. The columns for group weights come first and are sorted in descending order, while the column for the name comes last and is sorted in ascending order. Because the columns indicating group membership are in order from largest to smallest, this achieves the desired ordering of the loading matrix: grouped from largest to smallest and sorted alphabetically within each group. Also, the columns are labeled with a label (metric_goup_x, where *x* is the group number for the groups or just the metric name when a group is just a single metric).

The main function that runs all the steps together is at the end of listing 6.4: find_metric_groups. This function loads a dataset and then calls the other steps in the algorithm. find_metric_groups returns the loading matrix as the result, and the default option is to save it to a .csv file. Note that the program outputs only a simple confirmation that it is running and where it saves the result.

If you use the simulated data, then the resulting loading matrix should look like the one figure 6.16 when you open the file in a spreadsheet or text editor. There are two groups of metrics: one for the most common behaviors that are correlated to each

Metric	metric_ group_1	metric_ group_2	account_ tenure	dislike_ per_month	newfriend_ per_month	unfriend_ per_month
adview_per_month	0.413	0	0	0	0	0
like_per_month	0.413	0	0	0	0	0
post_per_month	0.413	0	0	0	0	0
message_per_month	0	0.620	0	0	0	0
reply_per_month	0	0.620	0	0	0	0
account_tenure	0	0	1.0	0	0	0
dislike_per_month	0	0	0	1.0	0	0
newfriend_per_month	0	0	0	0	1.0	0
unfriend_per_month	0	0	0	0	0	1.0

Figure 6.16   Result of running listing 6.4 on the default simulated dataset (a reproduction of figure 6.10)

other (which are posts, viewing ads, and likes) and a smaller group for reading and replying to messages. The metrics for account tenure, disliking, and unfriending are not correlated enough, so they don't enter into any group. Note that the weights are not exactly the $1/N$ for a standard average, but these are modified using equation 6.3 (section 6.3.2) to make the averages work as scores themselves.

Now that you have a loading matrix, you can produce an *ordered* correlation matrix like figure 6.6. For the simulated dataset, this result is shown in figure 6.17. From the ordered correlation heatmap, you can see the higher correlations between the two groups and the lower correlations between other metrics. Figure 6.17 was created by running listing 6.5 and then formatting the resulting data in a spreadsheet.

	adview_ per_ month	like_ per_ month	post_ per_ month	message _per_ month	reply_ per_ month	account_ tenure	dislike_ per_ month	newfriend _per_ month	unfriend _per_ month	
adview_per_month	1.00	0.69	0.69	0.15	0.11	0.08	0.49	0.55	0.02	Groups correspond to the loading matrix in figure 6.16.
like_per_month	0.69	1.00	0.68	0.12	0.09	0.09	0.49	0.55	0.02	
post_per_month	0.69	0.68	1.00	0.11	0.09	0.11	0.49	0.55	0.02	
message_per_month	0.15	0.12	0.11	1.00	0.93	0.09	0.16	0.09	0.01	
reply_per_month	0.11	0.09	0.09	0.93	1.00	0.09	0.13	0.06	0.01	
account_tenure	0.08	0.09	0.11	0.09	0.09	1.00	0.08	0.09	0.06	
dislike_per_month	0.49	0.49	0.49	0.16	0.13	0.08	1.00	0.39	0.01	
newfriend_per_month	0.55	0.55	0.55	0.09	0.06	0.09	0.39	1.00	0.02	
unfriend_per_month	0.02	0.02	0.02	0.01	0.01	0.06	0.01	0.02	1.00	

Group 1   Group 2

The grayscale heatmap was applied in a spreadsheet application.

Figure 6.17   Ordered correlation matrix for the simulated data

Listing 6.5 shows that the code to create the ordered matrix is almost exactly the same as that for creating a regular correlation matrix. The only difference is that you read in the loading matrix and reorder the dataset columns according to the order of the metrics in the loading matrix *before* calculating the correlation matrix. Reordering is a one liner because you already went to the trouble of ordering the loading matrix correctly by groups: just reuse that order.

Listing 6.5   Creating an ordered correlation matrix

```
import pandas as pd
import os

def ordered_correlation_matrix(data_set_path):            Loads the
                                                          saved scores
    churn_data = pd.read_csv(
        data_set_path.replace('.csv','_scores.csv'),index_col=[0,1])
```

```
load_mat_df = pd.read_csv(                                          #B
    data_set_path.replace('.csv', '_load_mat.csv'), index_col=0)
churn_data=churn_data[load_mat_df.index.values]
```
Reorders the dataset columns to the order of the loading matrix rows

Saves the result

```
corr = churn_data.corr()
```
Calculates the correlation matrix

```
save_name =
    data_set_path.replace('.csv', '_ordered_correlation_matrix.csv')
corr.to_csv(save_name)
print('Saved correlation matrix to ' + save_name)
```

6.3.3   *Loading matrix weights that make the average of scores a score*

There is one technical detail about loading matrices that I haven't explained yet, and it has to do with exactly what weights you should use in the loading matrix. The upshot, mentioned in the last section, is that you don't use weights in the loading matrix that are exactly $1/N$. I said $1/N$ when I first taught you the idea of the loading matrix so you would learn the concept easily, and the concept doesn't change: the loading matrix transformation still represents taking an average of the metric scores. But the weights need to be changed a bit.

$1/N$ is the correct weight to make an equally weighted average when all of the numbers in the average have the same scale or unit. But it's a little different with scores because there is no natural unit. (Note that if you don't like equations, this would be a fine time to skip to the next section, after you read the takeaway.)

> **TAKEAWAY**   The weights in the loading matrix will be a bit higher than $1/N$, but the meaning is still the same.

The problem with using $1/N$ weights to make an average of scores is that then the average of the metric scores is not a score anymore. What does that mean? A score was defined as a scaled version of a metric, and it has some particular properties: the average (mean) score is 0, and the standard deviation of the scores is 1. These facts make the scores comparable.

The good news is that if you make an average of scores with any equal weights, the mean (average) of the scores will still be zero. But the bad news is that the standard deviation of the average of scores will not be 1, and instead, it will be less than 1.0. How much less depends on how many metrics you average together and how correlated they are. But I'm going to teach a modification to the weights in the loading matrix that will make the average scores have (almost) the 1.0 standard deviation they are supposed to. That adjustment makes the average still a score regardless of how many metrics you are averaging together.

First I need to remind you what a variance is: the variance is the standard deviation squared. When the standard deviation is 1, the variance is also 1 (because 1 squared is 1). In what follows, I write σ for the standard deviation and σ^2 for the variance; that's the Greek letter sigma, and in math books, it is the usual letter for indicating standard deviation and variance. The thing about standard deviations is that when you sum metrics or other variables and each metric has its own standard deviation, the standard deviation of the sum doesn't stay the same; they sum up scaled by the weight. The relationship is easier to understand in terms of the variance, which is why I reminded you what the variance is. I'll show you how you get the variance for a sum of metrics that all have their own variance. Assuming you multiply each metric by a weight to form an average, the variance of a weighted sum of metrics is given in equation 6.1:

$$\sigma^2(wx_1 + wx_2 + \ldots + wx_N) = \Sigma_{ij}\, w^2 \sigma_i \sigma_j\, c_{ij} \qquad \text{(Equation 6.1)}$$

In equation 6.1, the notation $\Sigma_{ij} \ldots$ is shorthand for the sum of all the different elements' index by the subscripts (in code, that's like adding a sum in a doubly nested loop). What equation 6.1 says is that the variance of a sum of metrics is the sum of the pairwise products of all the standard deviations, multiplied by the pairwise correlation coefficients. That's kind of complicated, and hopefully gives you an idea for why the standard deviation of a sum of metrics will be 1 only under certain conditions. Now I'll show you what those conditions are. First, however, I'm going to make some simplifications:

- In our case, all the standard deviations are 1 because they are all scores, so the terms $\sigma_{i/j}$ drop out.
- You don't know exactly what all the correlations c_{ij} between the metrics are, but you do know this: if you are grouping them together into an average, then they are highly correlated. They probably have individual correlations that are at least as high as your correlation threshold. So instead of using c_{ij}, I approximate it with c_{thresh}, the threshold used to form the clusters.

With those simplifications, equation 6.1 for the variance of the sum is given approximately in equation 6.2:

$$\sigma^2(wx_1 + wx_2 + \ldots + wx_N) \approx N^2 w^2 \qquad \text{(Equation 6.2)}$$

There are N^2 terms in the sum of pairwise correlations; that's where the N^2 in equation 6.2 comes from. Equation 6.2 is an approximation because the correlations aren't really c_{thresh} (most notably the self-correlations for every metric are 1), but it's close enough. The next step is to solve the equation for the weight w that makes the variance (and the standard deviation) equal to 1. The result is shown in equation 6.3:

$$w^2 = \frac{1}{c_{thresh} N^2}$$

$$w = \frac{1}{N}\sqrt{\frac{1}{c_{thresh}}} \qquad \text{(Equation 6.3)}$$

After all the equations, there is a reasonably straightforward change: instead of using $1/N$ as the weights to make the averages in the loading matrix, you multiply $1/N$ by an extra factor, which is the square root of $1/c_{thresh}$, the correlation threshold used in the clustering algorithm. Because the correlation threshold is less than one (typically around 0.5 or 0.6), 1 divided by it is greater than 1 (typically between 1 and 2), and the square root doesn't change that. As a result, the weights you use to average scores will be a bit bigger than the usual $1/N$ in a standard average. It's a technical detail, but keeping your average scores as scores by making this adjustment will make your analysis easier to interpret because the standard deviation of your metric scores will still be 1.

6.3.4   *Running the metric grouping and grouped cohort analysis listings*

Now that you have a loading matrix (produced by running listing 6.4), you can go back and run listing 6.3. Listing 6.3 applies the loading matrix to the dataset of scores to create the grouped average scores. Note that running listing 6.3 produces only a line of output showing it is running, and the real result will be a new .csv dataset (the result prints where it is saved). Figure 6.18 shows a small sample of the dataset saved from running listing 6.3. Instead of metric names, the column headers show group numbers.

account_id	observation _date	metric_ group_1	metric_ group_2	account_ tenure	dislike_ per_month	newfriend_ per_month	unfriend_ per_month	is_churn
1	2/9/20	−0.46	−1.07	−1.19	−0.43	−0.77	0.12	FALSE
16	2/9/20	−2.31	1.22	−1.19	−1.09	−0.91	−0.94	FALSE
37	2/9/20	−2.18	−0.53	−1.19	−0.03	−0.69	−0.94	FALSE
...	...	...	...	...	...	...	...	...
1	3/9/20	−0.45	−0.91	−0.25	−0.29	−0.62	−0.94	FALSE
16	3/9/20	−2.53	1.30	−0.25	−1.30	−0.62	0.12	FALSE
37	3/9/20	−2.15	−0.62	−0.25	−0.07	−0.98	0.12	FALSE
...	...	...	...	...	...	...	...	...
1	4/9/20	−0.54	−1.10	0.70	−0.07	−0.98	−0.94	TRUE
16	4/9/20	−1.96	1.28	0.70	−1.03	−0.55	−0.94	FALSE
37	4/9/20	−1.87	−0.51	0.70	−0.23	−0.84	−0.94	FALSE

The first five metrics were replaced with two group averages.   **Four metrics are not grouped.**

Figure 6.18   Result of running listing 6.3 on the default simulated dataset

With a dataset of grouped metrics, it's also the time to try a cohort analysis (listing 5.1) using a grouped metric. This is the technique that was demonstrated in section 6.2.4. To do this, there is another version of listing 5.1 that you can run by passing the arguments `--chapter 5 --listing 1 --version 3` to the Python wrapper program. Figure 6.19 shows the result of running the cohort analysis on the main group of correlated metrics in the simulated data. The grouped metrics show a strong relationship with churn. (Because the dataset is randomly simulated, your result might not be exactly the same.)

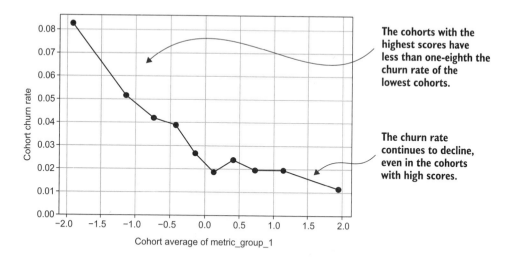

The cohorts with the highest scores have less than one-eighth the churn rate of the lowest cohorts.

The churn rate continues to decline, even in the cohorts with high scores.

Figure 6.19 Result of running listing 5.1 on the first group of metrics generated by the default simulated dataset

6.3.5 *Picking the correlation threshold for clustering*

In explaining the clustering algorithm, I mentioned the threshold for clustering correlations; recall that this threshold determines when metrics should be grouped together or left apart. I did not explain in detail how to set this parameter because I wanted you to learn how the grouping is supposed to work before getting into the technical details. But the clustering threshold parameter is really crucial for the success of behavioral grouping. If you set this parameter at too *low* a value, then you can wind up with every metric grouped together in one big group, even when they are not all related to each other. And if you set the correlation threshold parameter at too *high* a value, then metrics that are strongly related still won't get grouped, and you'll end up with (almost) as many groups as you had metrics to begin with.

Unfortunately, there is no best value that works in every case, so you might have to experiment a bit. I also don't advise any measure of the grouping to evaluate your choice. Rather, I advise you to understand the business (or learn about it from someone who does) and what the correlation matrix tells you about the business. Then ask yourself: do the metrics that are grouped together make sense? Would the grouping make more sense and/or be more useful if a few more metrics were grouped together or split apart?

For example, suppose you *know* that some metrics relate to a product feature or content area normally used together. In that case, it's reasonable to adjust the parameter a bit (if necessary) to break those out into their own group or to keep those from being split. (That's an example of using your prior knowledge to guide the analysis.) On the other hand, if the correlation matrix is telling you some activities are highly correlated, but some of your business colleagues want you to split them to make more groups, it might be their own wishful thinking or office politics dictating that decision. Use your prior knowledge to help decide on close calls, but don't ignore the results of your analysis!

Here are some rules of thumb that I use when setting the correlation levels in my own analyses:

- You should usually end up with the correlation threshold parameter set at the level of a moderate or moderately high correlation in the range between 0.4 and 0.7—never at very high or low correlation, meaning, don't go above 0.8 or below 0.3.
- It's usually better to start out too low, with a threshold value of 0.5 or less, and have all (or most) of the metrics grouped together in one big group:

    If every metric has a high correlation (> 0.7) to at least a few of the other metrics, then you probably should group them all in one group. This might be the case for a small product that does not have a wide variety of features or content, or if the events you track do not vary widely.

- Use a simple binary search on the range of 0.5 to 0.7: if 0.5 looks too low, try 0.6 (halfway between 0.5 and 0.7). If 0.6 still seems too low, try 0.65 (halfway between 0.6 and 0.7); if 0.6 is too high, try 0.55, and so forth. You'll quickly exhaust the plausible range and get a sense of where the best value lies.

    Use a manual search, not an algorithm—I have never found a stopping criterion that works all the time. The search usually doesn't take very long anyway.

- Use color-coded correlation heatmaps and an aesthetic criteria (honestly): a pattern of squares on the diagonal looks well ordered (see figure 6.7), but if you go too far in either direction (too much or too little correlation), it breaks up the symmetry. Once you've done it a few times, this is pretty intuitive.

- The biggest challenge is that sometimes small changes in the correlation can have a highly disproportionate impact on the grouping. This means that a small change of 0.01 or 0.02 in the threshold occasionally has a big impact on how many groups there are, possibly changing from just 1 or 2 groups to 5 or 10.

    In my own studies, I have written an alternative version of the grouping algorithm in listing 6.4, where the parameter is the number of blocks to produce. It uses an algorithmic search to return the grouping with the desired number of groups. This is a nice programming exercise that I leave for you to try; it is helpful if you have a hard time finding a correlation threshold due to irregular responses to small changes. But you can use this approach (choosing a number of blocks) only if you have already experimented enough to have a good idea of what to choose.

In chapter 8, when we look at statistics, you'll learn more about this subject. When you use statistical analysis, there can be some real problems if you group behaviors incorrectly by using too high a correlation threshold. But, for now, you know enough to do a good job on your own data.

6.4 Explaining correlated metric groups to businesspeople

This chapter demonstrated the following:

- The importance of understanding correlation between your metrics
- How to discover groups of related metrics
- How to perform churn analysis on metric group average scores

This chapter got pretty technical, and you might have learned some new terms: correlation matrix, loading matrix, and clustering (not to mention the real monster, hierarchical agglomerative clustering!). Now let's take a deep breath and think about how you are going to explain all this to your business colleagues. This isn't an issue if you are reading this book for educational purposes only, but this is a very big issue if you are trying to apply these techniques in a business context.

The concepts in this chapter are not that hard to understand, but there are a lot of technical details and jargon. I recommend starting simply and making sure to explain each concept with actual data from your own company. You can leave out the details of how everything gets done and just communicate the final results.

> **TAKEAWAY** Your job is to shield your business colleagues from as much of the jargon as possible. So do not try to impress them with technical terms! Rather, try to simplify things to a common language.

Here is how I usually handle it when I present case study results to a business audience for the first time:

1   Before you begin, ask the businesspeople how much statistics they know. You should adapt your explanations based on their level of knowledge. In what follows, I'll explain how to go through the concepts, assuming an average group of business users who do not have any statistics training but also aren't scared of statistics.

2   Teach (or remind) everyone what correlations are by showing them scatterplots (like the ones in figure 6.1) that you created from the business's own data. It's fine (and necessary) to use the term *correlation* with the business, but you should probably drop the term *coefficient*. Even nonmathematical people understand correlations easily when they know which product behaviors go together. Showing them scatterplots and the correlation number is giving them a nice new way to look at something they already know.

3 Show the heatmap, organized (after you have formed the groups) and formatted more or less like the one in figure 6.5 (except use full color). I try to avoid the term *matrix* with businesspeople, so I usually just describe it as a correlation heatmap and not a correlation matrix. After they have learned about individual correlations, they usually understand the overall pattern shown by the heatmap too. Again, this is showing something they already know intuitively, so they like it (and heatmaps look cool!).

4 Show them the metrics that form the groups, both by outlining them in the heatmap (see figure 6.5) and by giving them a list of what metrics are in each group. You need to explain that the groups are formed *automatically* and *based on the data* (they must understand you did not choose the groups). Do not attempt to explain the details of the algorithm. but you can mention it is a clustering algorithm if there are relatively technical people in the group:

They might debate the grouping, and that's healthy. If they challenge the grouping in a sensible way, you might want to try adjusting the threshold as described in section 6.3.4. But make sure they realize that you cannot (or at least should not) manually choose the groups.

5 Show them the behavioral cohort analysis that was done on the grouped metrics and how it compares to the cohort analysis on the individual metrics (just a selection of individual metrics, if there are a lot).

That's it! You're done. In particular, you do not need to discuss the following terms or algorithms with businesspeople:

- Matrix (either for the correlation matrix or the loading matrix)
- Loading
- Matrix multiplication
- Clustering (or even worse, hierarchical agglomerative clustering)

Hierarchical clustering vs. principal component analysis

If you studied statistics or data science, there is a good chance you learned a technique called *principal component analysis* (PCA). PCA is similar to *hierarchical clustering* (HC) in that it reduces the number of metrics in a dataset by multiplication with a loading matrix. But the loading matrix from PCA is derived using a different technique than HC. PCA has some nice properties that statisticians like, but it is beyond the scope of this book because it's not very useful for churn, and the loadings it produces are too difficult to interpret for most people. However, the loadings produced by HC and PCA have a lot in common, which this figure illustrates.

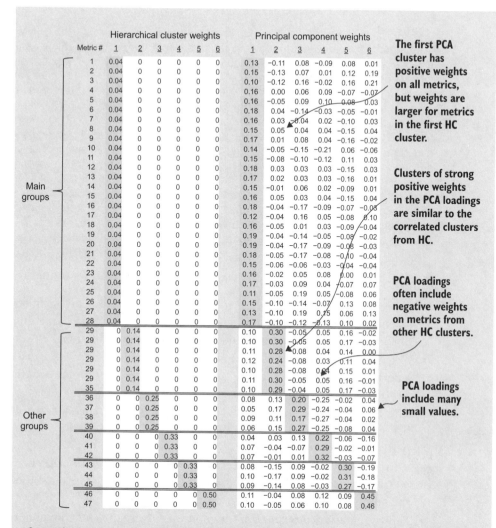

Comparison of the loading matrices for hierarchical clustering (HC) and principal component analysis (PCA)

This figure was created by calculating a PCA loading matrix and ordering the metrics in the same order as the HC groups. When run on the same data, the blocks discovered by HC are usually similar to clusters of high weights in the PCA loading matrix. You can see that the two algorithms are capturing some of the same underlying properties of the data. But the PCA loading matrix has both positive and negative weights, and every entry in the loading matrix is nonzero. Details of how to interpret a PCA loading matrix are beyond the scope of this book.

(continued)

One important point to note is that because the PCA matrix has negative as well as positive weights, the resulting grouped metrics are not simply averages but also differences between the (scored) metrics. A *difference* between two subscriber metrics means a derived metric that is high when one metric is high and the other is low, in contrast to an average or total, which is high when both metrics are high. Differences between scored subscriber metrics are not very intuitive but can be important because they measure how much one behavior exceeds another. For example, if you had scored metrics for local calls and international calls on a telecommunications service, the difference would show whether a subscriber is more or less an international or local caller. Differences like that can be important for understanding engagement, but differences between scored metrics produced by loading matrices with negative entries are difficult to interpret. The next chapter teaches techniques to capture information about differences between behaviors in a way that is easily understandable by businesspeople and data people alike.

Summary

- Correlation in the positive sense refers to when a high value on one metric is consistently associated with a high value on another metric, or when an increase in one metric is consistently associated with an increase in another.

- Negative correlation refers to when an increase in one metric is associated with a decrease in another. Negative correlation is rare in customer behavioral metrics on events.

- The correlation coefficient is a statistical measure of correlation that ranges between −1 and 1, where 1 means perfect positive correlation, and −1 means perfect negative correlation.

- Correlation coefficients measure the *consistency* of the relationship between two metrics but are insensitive to the ratio implied by the relationship. Equivalently, the units or scale of the metrics is irrelevant to correlation.

- Pairwise metric scatterplots are a good way to visualize individual correlations in your data, but there can be too many pairs to look at them all.

- A correlation matrix is a table of all the pairwise correlation coefficients in a dataset and is an efficient way to explore a large number of correlations.

- When metrics are highly correlated, you can improve a churn analysis by averaging together the scores of the correlated metrics.

- A loading matrix is a table of the weights used to average metrics. It is used in the calculation of the average scores.

- Matrix multiplication of the loading matrix by the dataset is the operation that efficiently performs the averaging of grouped metrics.

- After averaging metric scores together with a loading matrix, you can do behavioral cohort analysis of churn using the averaged scores. This often gives stronger results than the individual metrics.

- Clustering means to group together related items based on some measure of similarity among their data.
- Hierarchical clustering is an algorithm that can be used to group together correlated metrics. The algorithm stops at a threshold in the correlation level so that all strongly correlated metrics become grouped.
- After running hierarchical clustering, you use the result to create a loading matrix.

Segmenting customers
with advanced metrics

You've learned a lot about understanding churn with metrics derived from events and subscriptions. You've seen that simple behavioral measurements can be powerful for segmenting customers who may be at risk for churn and who have different levels of engagement. But you've also seen some of the limitations of simple behavioral metrics.

Many simple metrics are correlated, and correlations arise because customers who have a lot of product-related events tend to have a lot of other events as well. Correlations make it harder to tell which types of behaviors are most important.

The problem is deeper than a lack of refinement. In this chapter, you'll learn that correlation between metrics can make you misread the influence of a behavior. A behavior that's negative (in the sense that it takes utility and enjoyment away from customers) can appear to enhance engagement when it's correlated with other behaviors that provide utility and enjoyment.

Also, you may have been wondering about relationships among behaviors. Many common hypotheses about churn ask whether combinations of behaviors have an effect that is greater than the sum of their parts. You may wonder, for example, whether it's better for users of a document-editing and file-sharing app to create a lot of documents even if they don't share, or whether it's better for users to share everything they create, even if they don't create a lot. Another question not yet addressed is whether changes in behavior over time tell you anything. Is a surge in use a sign that a customer is getting more engaged, for example, or having one last binge before they churn? If you think that the simple behavioral metrics you learned in chapter 3 cannot answer these questions, you're right.

In terms of the themes outlined at the start of the book, this chapter relates to all the areas shown in figure 7.1. Behavioral metrics and churn analysis are presented together, which can generate ideas about segmenting your customers for churn-reduction strategies.

In this chapter, you are going to create a type of metric that allows you to understand complex combinations of behaviors and see what they tell you about churn and retention of your customers. I call this metric a *ratio metric*.

> **DEFINITION** A *ratio metric* is any customer metric calculated by taking the ratio of one metric to another; equivalently, one metric is divided by the other.

Here's how this chapter is organized:

- Section 7.1 teaches you the main ratio metric technique and includes several case studies to motivate their use and illustrate typical results.
- Section 7.2 teaches you how to make metrics that are ratios from a part to a whole, which makes the ratio a percentage of a total.
- Section 7.3 covers ratios between one metric at two different points in time, which measures change in behavior, typically as a percentage. This section also covers a metric for the amount of time a customer has been inactive.
- Section 7.4 changes gears to non-ratio advanced metrics: this section covers scaling the metric-measurement time period just like a churn rate. That allows you to estimate metrics quickly, using a shorter measurement window for new customers but still makes better estimates for seasoned users.
- Section 7.5 teaches you how to make measurements for multiuser systems (when multiple individuals share one subscription or account with a product).

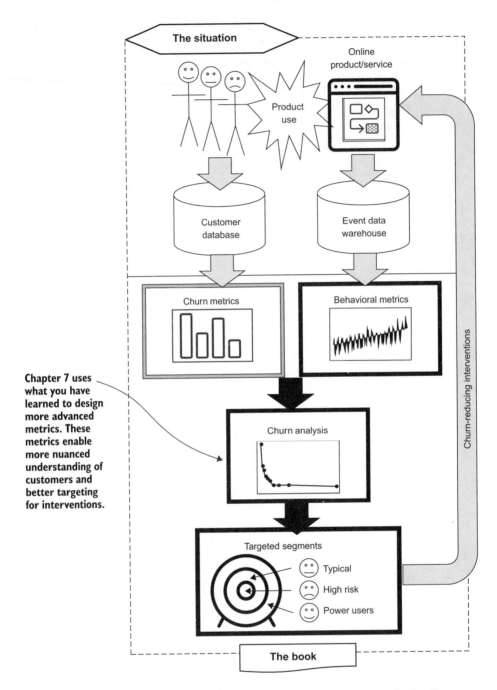

Chapter 7 uses what you have learned to design more advanced metrics. These metrics enable more nuanced understanding of customers and better targeting for interventions.

Figure 7.1   Themes in chapter 7 include behavioral metrics, churn analysis, and subscriber segments.

7.1   *Ratio metrics*

You're about to learn the single most important technique in the book (if I had to pick only one): using metrics that are ratios of other behavioral measurements. These metrics provide powerful, easy-to-understand explanations of customer behavior.

7.1.1   *When to use ratio metrics and why*

Figure 7.2 provides a case study illustrating when you need to look more closely at the relationship between two metrics. The figure reproduces some cohort analyses from chapter 5 for Versature, a provider of integrated cloud communication services. In the figure, churn is somewhat lower for customers who pay higher monthly fees for their service. This figure probably defies your intuition that paying more is a bad thing for customer engagement. At the same time, figure 7.2 shows that paying more is highly correlated with making more calls—something you learned to analyze in chapter 6. And, of course, customers who make a lot of calls churn less than customers who don't, which is a stronger relationship with churn than monthly recurring revenue (MRR).

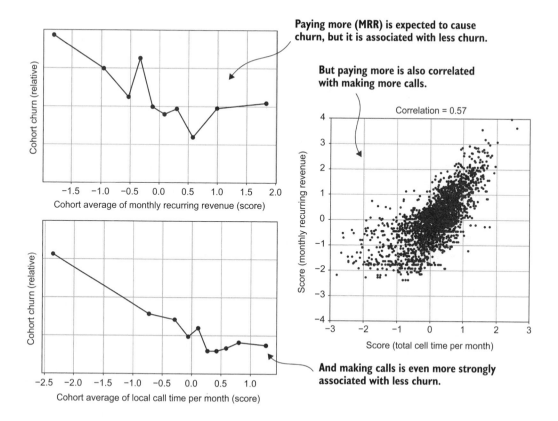

Figure 7.2   Case study that motivates a ratio metric

The reason paying more (higher MRR) looks like it reduces churn is that, typically, customers who pay more also make more calls—enough to justify paying the higher MRR. But what about a customer who pays more but *doesn't* make enough calls to justify the higher MRR? Those customers probably are most at risk for churn, but they don't show up in your metrics that look at MRR and calls separately. To find the customers who pay more but don't make a lot of calls (and see whether they churn at a higher rate), you need to create a third metric that captures the relationship between the first two: the ratio of the first two metrics.

> **DEFINITION**   A *ratio metric* is a metric that is made by taking the ratio of the values of two other metrics. Each value of the new metric is a value of one metric divided by the value of another metric.

In the following sections, I'll explain the details of how you calculate such a metric and why, and try to persuade you that this way is the best way. For now, let's start with the results.

If you take a metric that is the amount a customer pays (MRR) and divide it by the amount of calls they make, the result is the *average cost per call*—a measure of the unit cost the customers pay, similar to price per gallon of gasoline or liter of milk. The difference is that the ratio of MRR to calls is an effective recurring unit cost, not a contractual one, because the product is not priced and packaged for customers to pay by the call.

Figure 7.3 shows the churn cohort analysis performed for Versature's customers, using MRR per call as the metric. This metric shows a strong relationship with increasing churn following increasing values of the metric. It's true that customers who pay more churn more, but you have to measure the effective unit cost with a ratio metric to see that result. Figure 7.3 also shows the correlations of the MRR per call metric with the MRR and call metrics that were used to create it. MRR per call is correlated weakly (negatively) with calls and is practically uncorrelated with MRR. All these facts make MRR per call a great metric for understanding customer engagement and churn. In section 7.1.2, you'll learn how to calculate a ratio metric like this one and practice doing so with the churn simulation data you've used throughout the book.

> **TAKEAWAY**   An effective recurring unit cost metric is created from the ratio of MRR to some outcome achieved by the customers. A recurring unit cost metric usually shows increasing churn with increasing unit cost. By contrast, a simple recurring cost metric (MRR) usually shows decreasing churn with increasing cost due to correlation with the utility or enjoyment derived from using the product.

Figure 7.4 shows a situation in the social network simulation case study similar to the ones in figures 7.2 and 7.3. You expect one metric—ads viewed per month—to be bad because most people don't like viewing ads. But when you run a churn cohort analysis, you find that the more ads people watch, the less they churn. At the same time, you find that viewing ads is correlated with making posts, and customers who make a lot of posts churn at a low rate.

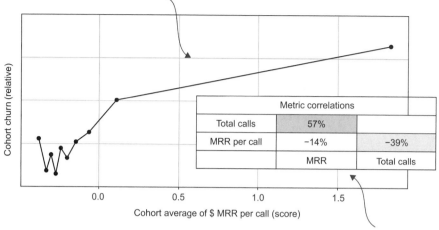

The metric cost per call created by dividing MRR by calls per month is strongly associated with increasing churn.

Metric correlations		
Total calls	57%	
MRR per call	−14%	−39%
	MRR	Total calls

Cost per call is less correlated with MRR and total calls than those metrics are with each other.

Figure 7.3 Case study churn cohort analysis of cost per call for Versature

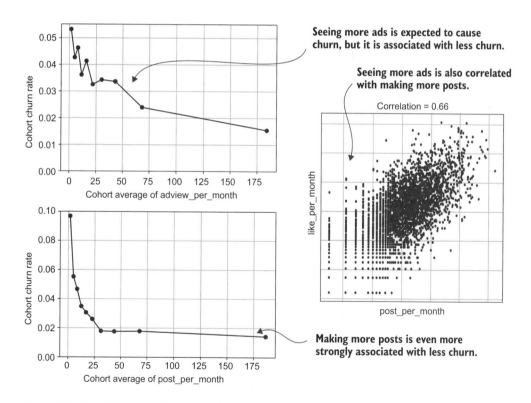

Seeing more ads is expected to cause churn, but it is associated with less churn.

Seeing more ads is also correlated with making more posts.

Correlation = 0.66

Making more posts is even more strongly associated with less churn.

Figure 7.4 Simulation case study scenario motivating a ratio metric

Before going on to the next section, you should reproduce the results in figure 7.4, using the simulated churn data and the code in this book's GitHub repository (https:// GitHub.com/carl24k/fight-churn). This task is the first step in the code exercises for this chapter. By reproducing the plots in figure 7.4, you will confirm that your data and metrics are ready for what comes next.

You should have calculated the metrics for ads viewed per month and posts per month back in chapter 3. If you did *not* calculate the metrics then, after setting up your environment as explained in the repository's README file, you can calculate all the metrics with the Python wrapper program by using the following command:

```
fight-churn/listings/run_churn_listing.py --chapter 3 --listing 3 4 --version
    1 2 3 4 5 6 7 8
```

If you ran the listing code in chapter 5, you should already have created a cohort analysis of posts per month like the one shown in figure 7.4. If you did not, you can do it now by running the Python wrapper program with the parameters `--chapter 5` `--listing 1`. To create a new cohort analysis for ads viewed per month, you can run another version of listing 5.1 by adding the argument `--version 3`. All together, the parameters to add are `--chapter 5 --listing 1 --version 3`.

The same goes for recreating the metric pair scatterplot in chapter 6 (listing 6.1). You can rerun the Python wrapper program with the parameters `--chapter 6 --listing 1` `--version 2` to recreate a scatterplot like the one in figure 7.4.

7.1.2 *How to calculate ratio metrics*

Now that you know what a ratio metric is, it's time to get into the details of how to calculate it. The calculation of a ratio metric is illustrated with a little sample data (figure 7.5). When I said that you divide one metric by the other, I meant it literally. You start with two metrics that were already saved in the database. To calculate the ratio metric, you match the two metrics, account by account and date by date; it is assumed that you calculated and saved the other two metrics at all the same dates, as demonstrated in chapter 3. For every account and date, the ratio is the value of one metric for that date and account divided by the other metric for the same date and account. There's not much to the process, although you need to watch out for the following two "gotchas":

- The denominator metric (the metric you are dividing by) must be greater than zero.
- The numerator metric can be zero but should not be negative. We have not looked at metrics that can be negative so far, but you'll see some in section 7.3. You might already have metrics that can be negative if you make metrics from event properties in your own data, like sums of currency amounts that can be both positive or negative.

Metrics for ad views and posts are
already calculated in the database.

Account ID	Date	adview_per_month
1	1/1/20	75
1	2/1/20	50
2	1/1/20	30
2	2/1/20	20
3	1/1/20	100
3	2/1/20	90

Account ID	Date	post_per_month
1	1/1/20	60
1	2/1/20	45
2	1/1/20	50
2	2/1/20	45
3	1/1/20	80
3	2/1/20	110

To calculate the ratio:

1. **Match the two metrics for each account.**

2. **Divide one by the other.**

3. **The result of the division is the ratio.**

Account ID	Date	Division	Ratio
1	1/1/20	= 75/60 =	1.25
1	2/1/20	= 50/45 =	1.67
2	1/1/20	= 30/50 =	1.50
2	2/1/20	= 20/45 =	1.67
3	1/1/20	= 100/80 =	0.94
3	2/1/20	= 90/110 =	0.68

Figure 7.5 Mechanics of calculating a ratio metric

If the metric in the denominator of the ratio is zero for an account, the ratio is undefined. You'll get an error if you try to divide by zero in any program language. And if either metric can be negative sometimes, the ratio is mathematically okay, but it lacks the usual meaning of a ratio of two other measurements: a unit cost or a rate of an event relative to another event. Otherwise, calculating ratios is pretty straightforward.

Listing 7.1 provides a short SQL program that calculates a ratio metric, and figure 7.6 illustrates a few lines of the output. The short SQL program shown in listing 7.1 also returns the numerator and denominator of the metric for illustrative purposes. Otherwise, the calculation strategy in listing 7.1 closely mirrors figure 7.5: two common table expressions (CTEs) select the results for the two metrics that are going to form the ratio. The final SELECT statement is a LEFT OUTER JOIN with the denominator in the left position. As a result, the ratio metric will be calculated for any account on a date when the denominator is available. Let's look at the figure first.

account_id	metric_time	num_value	den_value	metric_value
3491	5/10/20	15	13	1.15
3490	5/10/20	5	8	0.63
3489	5/10/20	11	18	0.61
3488	5/10/20	11	8	1.38
3487	5/10/20	20	18	1.11

The metric value is the ratio of the numerator and denominator.

The SELECT shows numerator and denominator of the metric for illustrative purposes.

Figure 7.6   Output of running listing 7.1

The SQL uses a CASE statement as part of the calculation to guard against a zero metric in the denominator. If you use count metrics as in chapter 3, you don't store zeros, but it's a best practice to guard against dividing by zero in case you work with metrics imported from other systems. When you use a CASE statement, a zero denominator metric produces a zero ratio. That result would be the same as the result of a zero numerator, which is mathematically fine and produces zero. That said, if you didn't store the zeros for the numerator metric, you won't produce the ratio, but you'll still fill the result with zero in your churn analysis dataset for any account that doesn't get the ratio (as described in chapter 4).

> **NOTE**   Accounts that are missing the values or have zeros for either metric in a ratio get zeros for the metric in the churn analysis dataset.

You should run listing 7.1 and confirm that your result is similar to figure 7.6. If you are using the wrapper program to run the listings, use the parameters `--chapter 7 --listing 1` like so:

```
fight-churn/listings/run_churn_listing.py --chapter 7 --listing 1
```

Listing 7.1   SQL ratio metric calculation

```
WITH num_metric AS (
    SELECT account_id, metric_time, metric_value AS num_value
    FROM metric m INNER JOIN metric_name n ON
      n.metric_name_id=m.metric_name_id          Picks the metric
    AND n.metric_name = 'adview_per_month'        for the numerator
    AND metric_time BETWEEN '2020-04-01' AND '2020-05-10'
), den_metric AS (
    SELECT account_id, metric_time, metric_value AS den_value
    FROM metric m INNER JOIN metric_name n ON
      n.metric_name_id=m.metric_name_id          Picks the metric for
    AND n.metric_name = 'post_per_month'          the denominator
    AND metric_time BETWEEN '2020-04-01'          Matches the date range for the
        AND '2020-05-10'                          numerator and denominator
)
```

```
SELECT d.account_id, d.metric_time,
    num_value, den_value,
    CASE WHEN den_value > 0
        THEN COALESCE(num_value,0.0)/den_value
        ELSE 0
    END AS metric_value
FROM den_metric d  LEFT OUTER JOIN num_metric n
    ON n.account_id=d.account_id
    AND n.metric_time=d.metric_time;
```

The ratio is undefined when the denominator is not positive.

Calculates the ratio; coalesces for zero null numerator

Fills with zeros when the denominator is missing

Selects the numerator and denominator value for illustration

LEFT OUTER JOIN makes a result whenever the denominator is available.

You also need to save the result to the database to continue with the examples, but because listing 7.1 selects the numerator and denominator of the metric for illustrative purposes, it's not suitable for inserting a metric into the database. A prewritten SQL statement in the listing framework does this: insert_7_1_ratio_metric.sql (which is the same as listing_7_1_ratio_metric.sql except for insert rather than listing in the SQL filename). To run the version of listing 7.1 designed for inserting the result, add the --insert flag to the arguments for the script that runs the listing. If you are using the Python wrapper program to run the listings, the command follows:

```
fight-churn/listings/run_churn_listing.py --chapter 7 --listing 1 --insert
```

That insert shows you the SQL it uses, but it won't print any result. You should make your own SELECT statement to verify the result or, better, run the metric quality assurance query from chapter 3 (listing 3.6) to look at a summary of the result over time. This pattern of learning and then inserting metrics into your database will repeat throughout the chapter:

- The listings shown in the book include extra columns for illustrative purposes.
- If the metric needs to be saved in your database to follow the examples, a second version of the listing in the repository performs the insert. You run it by adding the --insert flag to the wrapper script command.
- The illustrative version of the listing has a path like listings/chap7/listing_7_, and the version of the listing written to insert into the database has a path like listings/chap7/insert_7_.

After saving the new ads per post metric to the database, you should analyze it for correlations and the relationship to churn. Remember that to run the cohort analysis, you first need to reexport your churn dataset with SQL. The code that exports the dataset with your new metric (and all the other metrics you create in this chapter) is shown in listing 7.2, which is an update of listing 4.5.

You should run listing 7.2 to save a new dataset that allows you to run the cohort analysis on the new metric ads per post. Review chapter 4, and specifically listing 4.5, if you don't remember how listing 7.2 works; it is exactly the same. Don't worry that you haven't yet created all the metrics in listing 7.2; you will create them throughout the chapter. For now, any metric you didn't create will be filled with zeros in the dataset.

Listing 7.2 Exporting the dataset with chapter 7 metrics

```
WITH observation_params AS                    ◁         This listing starts the
(                                                        same as listing 4.5.
    SELECT  interval '7' AS metric_period,
    '2020-03-01'::timestamp AS obs_start,
    '2020-05-10'::timestamp AS obs_end
)
SELECT m.account_id, o.observation_date, is_churn,
SUM(CASE WHEN metric_name_id=0 THEN metric_value ELSE 0 END)
    AS like_per_month,
SUM(CASE WHEN metric_name_id=1 THEN metric_value ELSE 0 END)
    AS newfriend_per_month,
SUM(CASE WHEN metric_name_id=2 THEN metric_value ELSE 0 END)
    AS post_per_month,
SUM(CASE WHEN metric_name_id=3 THEN metric_value ELSE 0 END)
    AS adview_per_month,
SUM(CASE WHEN metric_name_id=4 THEN metric_value ELSE 0 END)
    AS dislike_per_month,
SUM(CASE WHEN metric_name_id=5 THEN metric_value ELSE 0 END)
    AS unfriend_per_month,
SUM(CASE WHEN metric_name_id=6 THEN metric_value ELSE 0 END)
    AS message_per_month,
SUM(CASE WHEN metric_name_id=7 THEN metric_value ELSE 0 END)
    AS reply_per_month,
SUM(CASE WHEN metric_name_id=8 THEN metric_value ELSE 0 END)
    AS account_tenure,
SUM(CASE WHEN metric_name_id=21 THEN metric_value ELSE 0 END)
    AS adview_per_post,                              ◁    New metrics
SUM(CASE WHEN metric_name_id=22 THEN metric_value ELSE 0 END)   begin here.
    AS reply_per_message,
SUM(CASE WHEN metric_name_id=23 THEN metric_value ELSE 0 END)
    AS like_per_post,
SUM(CASE WHEN metric_name_id=24 THEN metric_value ELSE 0 END)
    AS post_per_message,
SUM(CASE WHEN metric_name_id=25 THEN metric_value ELSE 0 END)
    AS unfriend_per_newfriend,
SUM(CASE WHEN metric_name_id=27 THEN metric_value ELSE 0 END)
    AS dislike_pcnt,
SUM(CASE WHEN metric_name_id=28 THEN metric_value ELSE 0 END)
    AS unfriend_per_newfriend_scaled,
SUM(CASE WHEN metric_name_id=30 THEN metric_value ELSE 0 END)
    AS newfriend_pcnt_chng,
SUM(CASE WHEN metric_name_id=31 THEN metric_value ELSE 0 END)
    AS days_since_newfriend,
SUM(CASE WHEN metric_name_id=33 THEN metric_value ELSE 0 END)
    AS unfriend_28day_avg_84day_obs,
SUM(CASE WHEN metric_name_id=34 THEN metric_value ELSE 0 END)
    AS unfriend_28day_avg_84day_obs_scaled
FROM metric m INNER JOIN observation_params
ON metric_time BETWEEN obs_start AND obs_end
```

```
INNER JOIN observation o ON m.account_id = o.account_id
    AND m.metric_time > (o.observation_date - metric_period)::timestamp
    AND m.metric_time <= o.observation_date::timestamp
GROUP BY m.account_id, metric_time, observation_date, is_churn
ORDER BY observation_date, m.account_id
```

After creating the new version of the dataset, you can run a cohort analysis to see how it relates to churn. The listing version is --chapter 5 --listing 1 --version 5. Run the Python wrapper program with those arguments to create the cohort plot.

Figure 7.7 shows the typical result of these analyses: a higher ratio of ads per post is associated with higher churn, not higher retention. That result confirms the intuition that seeing more ads exacts a price in terms of customer satisfaction (or, rather, confirms that the simulation was crafted so that more ad viewing reduces satisfaction). But to see the negative effect of seeing more ads, you have to disentangle the metric from the correlation with other behaviors that lead to customer satisfaction. Figure 7.7 also shows the correlations between the new adview_per_post metric and the original ads per month and post per month. Ads per post has a weak positive correlation with viewing ads and a moderate negative correlation with viewing posts. (You can check by rerunning listing 6.2 on your new dataset.)

The correlations in figure 7.7 are typical for many ratio metrics. It is natural for the ratio to have positive correlation with the numerator metric because the ratio tends to be larger when the numerator is larger. It is also normal for the ratio to have negative correlation with the denominator metric because all else being equal, a larger denominator leads to a lower ratio. The precise results depend on the nature of the relationship between the two metrics themselves, however. If you look at real case studies, you'll find results that vary widely from the typical scenarios shown in figure 7.3 and figure 7.7.

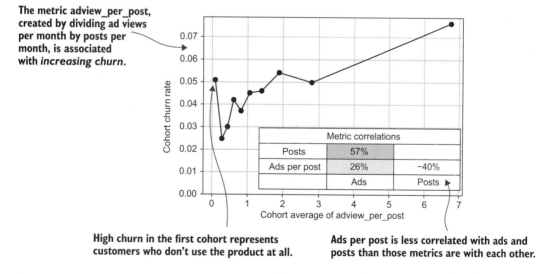

The metric adview_per_post, created by dividing ad views per month by posts per month, is associated with *increasing churn*.

Metric correlations		
Posts	57%	
Ads per post	26%	–40%
	Ads	Posts

High churn in the first cohort represents customers who don't use the product at all.

Ads per post is less correlated with ads and posts than those metrics are with each other.

Figure 7.7 Simulation case study of the metric adview_per_post, churn, and correlation analysis

7.1.3   *Ratio metric case study examples*

Ratio metrics are useful not only when you have a metric that you think causes disengagement but also when you have two behaviors whose interaction is relevant to customer engagement and churn. By *interaction,* I mean a situation in which the relationship between the two metrics matters—not whether the two metrics are big or small, but which one is bigger or smaller than the other. This section contains a few more examples from case studies to show this interaction.

One scenario in which the ratio of two metrics matters deals with *efficiency.* Many behaviors have a relationship in which one event leads to the other in a process, and the more events that occur at the end of the process, the better. Figure 7.8 shows an example for the SaaS service Broadly, which helps businesses manage their online presence. Broadly keeps track of both customers and transactions, and transactions always follow a customer signup, so it's natural that numbers of customers and numbers of transactions are correlated (at 0.93). A high ratio of transactions per customer is usually good for a business; it can also be relevant for engagement and success on the Broadly platform. Figure 7.8 shows that businesses on Broadly with above-average transactions per customer (score greater than 0.0) churn at a significantly lower rate than businesses with below-average transactions per customer. Such businesses are probably more successful, so they are less likely to be more engaged with Broadly, leading to higher customer engagement and lower churn.

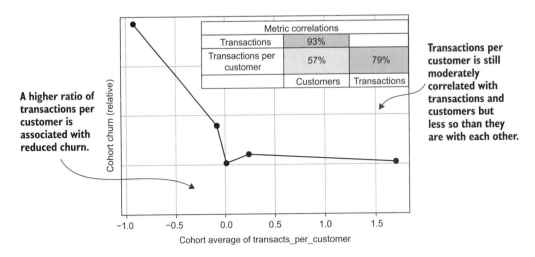

Figure 7.8   Case study showing a cohort analysis of the ratio metric transactions per customer for Broadly

TAKEAWAY   If one event is downstream from another in a process, the ratio of a metric on the downstream event to a metric on the precursor event can be viewed as an efficiency measurement for the process.

Figure 7.9 shows a case study of churn with another ratio from Broadly: the review-ask acceptance rate. Asking for reviews from customers is one of the most important uses of Broadly, and the rate at which customers accept such requests is a measure of efficiency in using the product. This rate can also be seen as a *success rate*, because each attempt at the activity either succeeds or fails.

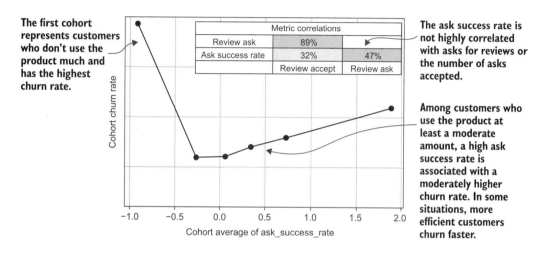

The first cohort represents customers who don't use the product much and has the highest churn rate.

The ask success rate is not highly correlated with asks for reviews or the number of asks accepted.

Among customers who use the product at least a moderate amount, a high ask success rate is associated with a moderately higher churn rate. In some situations, more efficient customers churn faster.

Figure 7.9   Case study showing a cohort analysis of the review-ask acceptance rate for Broadly

Figure 7.9 might surprise you because it shows that other than the bottom cohort, which has the highest churn, increasing success rate shows a modest relationship with increasing churn. This pattern is typical for a disengaging behavior (introduced in chapter 3). The bottom cohorts are those with zero metrics because they don't have one behavior or both. But for customers who use the product, a higher review-ask acceptance rate is associated with increased churn probability, which can be surprising, because you would expect that more successful customers would churn less. But this result can happen with products that have a specific purpose. If a customer is more successful faster, it could hasten their churn. In this case, most businesses using Broadly need a certain number of reviews to make themselves look good. When it has enough reviews, a business may be at heightened risk of churn because it achieved its goal and no longer sees Broadly as being useful. The highest risk of churn for Broadly's customers comes when customers don't use the product much (the bottom cohorts).

> **TAKEAWAY**   The ratio of two event metrics, in which one event represents a successful result of the first event, defines a *success rate* metric.

Klipfolio is an SaaS company that allows businesses to create online dashboards of their key metrics. Figure 7.10 shows a case study of another kind of efficiency rate from Klipfolio: the number of dashboard edits per month divided by the number of saves. In this case, the rate is probably better described as an *inefficiency rate*, because a lot of editing without a lot of saving probably indicates that it takes the user more effort to achieve acceptable results that they want to save. Figure 7.10 shows that customers with this kind of inefficiency (a high score on the ratio) are, in fact, at higher risk of churn than Klipfolio users who are more efficient in this regard.

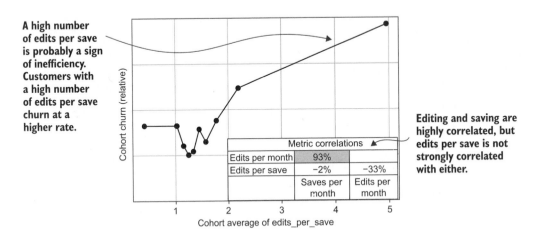

A high number of edits per save is probably a sign of inefficiency. Customers with a high number of edits per save churn at a higher rate.

Editing and saving are highly correlated, but edits per save is not strongly correlated with either.

Metric correlations		
Edits per month	93%	
Edits per save	-2%	-33%
	Saves per month	Edits per month

Figure 7.10   Case study showing a cohort analysis of edits_per_save ratio for Klipfolio

I hope that these examples have given you some idea of the wide range of situations in which you can use ratio metrics. They are powerful tools! The next sections teach you some different, more specialized ratios. Near the end of the chapter, I return to the question of when all these types of ratios are appropriate and how to find ratio metrics that are useful for your particular situation.

7.1.4   Additional ratio metrics for the simulated social network

Before you move on, try a few more ratio metrics on the simulated social network. I'll say more about how to choose ratios when you have a lot of metrics in section 7.6. For now, I'll say only that the following group of metrics tests some interesting relationships:

- Replies per message
- Likes per post
- Posts per message
- Unfriends per new friend

All these metrics have prepared versions of listing 7.1 that you can run with the following command in the Python wrapper program:

```
run_churn_listing.py --chapter 7 --listing 1 --insert --version  2 3 4 5
```

IMPORTANT You must have already calculated the underlying metrics for the ratios, as explained in section 7.1.2.

Then, as an exercise, check how these new ratio metrics relate to churn with additional versions of the metric cohort plots with the following command in the Python wrapper program:

```
run_churn_listing.py --chapter 5 --listing 1 --version 11 12 13 14 15 16
```

You see more about how these additional metrics help you analyze and predict churn in chapter 8.

7.2 *Percentage of total metrics*

A *percentage* is a specialized case of a ratio: a measurement of a part of something for the numerator divided by the whole amount of that something in the denominator. *Percentage metrics* can be used to make a more interpretable version of a ratio when only two outcomes are possible. A *set* of percentage metrics can be used to analyze the relationship between a group of correlated metrics in which each metric measures one specific type of a general behavior.

7.2.1 *Calculating percentage of total metrics*

Figure 7.11 illustrates a fictional streaming service and a typical situation in which you would want to make metrics that measure percentage of a total. The service has four types of content: Action, Comedy, Drama, and Romance. For any product with one main activity and subcategories, a count per period metric on each activity area is generally highly correlated with the other activity areas; customers who use the service a lot tend to use it more in all areas. The way to understand whether the relative amount of the activities is relevant to customer engagement and churn is to calculate an additional ratio metric for each category: activity in that category divided by total activity in all categories. As shown in figure 7.11, the total in all categories is exactly the number of events in all the categories, and the percentages are the relative proportions of activities in each category.

Percentage of total is a special kind of ratio metric, in that it is calculated like any other kind of ratio metric (refer to listing 7.1). What makes a percentage metric different is that the denominator in the ratio is a total of the other metrics that represent the categories. To make these ratios, the only thing you need (in addition to listing 7.1) is a suitable total to use as the denominator.

TAKEAWAY Percentage of total metrics reveals the relative balance between a set of closely related, highly correlated activities.

You've been introduced to the idea of calculating a metric from other metrics in a ratio calculation, and here is another area in which this trick comes in handy. If you need to calculate a metric that is the total of different categories to use as the denominator in a ratio, you can sum the values of all the metrics you are going to use in the

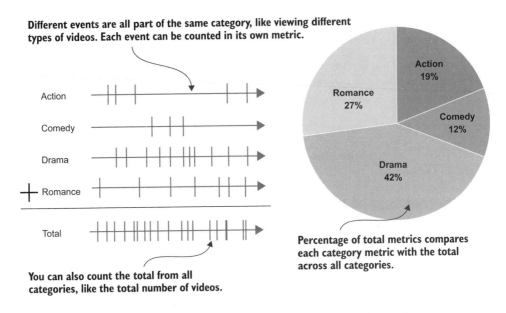

Different events are all part of the same category, like viewing different types of videos. Each event can be counted in its own metric.

You can also count the total from all categories, like the total number of videos.

Percentage of total metrics compares each category metric with the total across all categories.

Figure 7.11   The percentage of total metrics for a fictional content-streaming service

numerator. This calculation strategy, summarized in figure 7.12, is similar to the calculation of a ratio metric in that the accounts and dates of calculation for the other metrics must be matched. One important difference is that the sum of other metrics can operate on multiple other metrics. Figure 7.11 shows four metrics for four content areas, and there could be more in a real streaming service. Other examples could be total purchases in different categories and calls in different regions; see the example in section 7.2.2.

The SQL statement to calculate a total of other metrics is shown in listing 7.3, which shows the total likes and dislikes for accounts in the churn simulation from the GitHub repository. Figure 7.13 shows typical output. Note that listing 7.3 selects a string aggregation of the metrics being summed for illustrative purposes. The SQL statement for the total metric is simpler than the calculation in figure 7.12: the SQL statement uses a SUM aggregation grouped by date and account when the metrics are provided in a list. This approach is easier than using CTEs for the ratio metric (implied by figure 7.12). The simpler approach is possible because the metric order does not matter, and SQL provides a standard SUM aggregation.

You may be wondering whether you can calculate the total of other metrics directly by making a total of the events that go into the other metrics—making a SELECT to count multiple event types rather than adding separate counts of the different event types. The answer is that you can do that and get the same result. The advantage of adding precalculated category metrics is that it can be much faster than recounting the total underlying events if your dataset is big. That said, adding precalculated

Metric for different types of video views are already calculated in the database.

Acct ID	Date	action_view_ per_month
1	1/1/20	3
1	2/1/20	5
2	1/1/20	6
2	2/1/20	6
3	1/1/20	4
3	2/1/20	2

Acct ID	Date	comedy_view _per_month
1	1/1/20	7
1	2/1/20	8
2	1/1/20	2
2	2/1/20	1
3	1/1/20	NULL
3	2/1/20	4

Acct ID	Date	drama_view_ per_month
1	1/1/20	NULL
1	2/1/20	1
2	1/1/20	4
2	2/1/20	8
3	1/1/20	3
3	2/1/20	1

To calculate the total:
1. Select the metrics for all accounts and categories.
2. Group the metrics by account and date.
3. Aggregate by summing the category metric values.

Account ID	Date	Add	Total
1	1/1/20	= 3+7 =	10
1	2/1/20	= 5+8+1 =	14
2	1/1/20	= 6+2+4 =	12
2	2/1/20	= 6+1+8 =	15
3	1/1/20	= 4+3 =	7
3	2/1/20	= 2+4+1 =	7

Figure 7.12 Percentage of total metrics calculation

account_id	metric_time	metric_sum	metric_total
1	4/5/20	224 + 46	270
2	4/5/20	17 + 38	55
3	4/5/20	242 + 46	288
4	4/5/20	41 + 254	295
7	4/5/20	99 + 10	109

The SUM aggregation result is the value for the new metric.

The SELECT shows sum terms as a string for illustrative purposes.

Figure 7.13 Output of running listing 7.3 on the default simulated dataset from the GitHub repository

metrics introduces a dependency into the order of your metric calculation. You'll have to decide what makes the most sense in your particular case.

Listing 7.3 Total of metrics

```
SELECT account_id, metric_time,
    STRING_AGG(metric_value::text,'+') AS metric_sum,
SUM(metric_value) AS metric_total
FROM metric m INNER JOIN metric_name n
    ON n.metric_name_id=m.metric_name_id
AND n.metric_name in
    ('like_per_month', 'dislike_per_month)
WHERE metric_time BETWEEN '2020-01-01' AND '2020-02-01'
GROUP BY metric_time, account_id
```

STRING shows metrics being summed for illustration.

Calculates the total with a GROUP BY aggregation

Uses an INNER JOIN; available metrics will be part of the sum.

Lists the metrics that contribute to the total

Aggregates the results by date and account

You should run listing 7.3 on the simulated dataset created with the code in this book's GitHub repository. If you are using the Python wrapper program, run it with the following parameters:

```
--chapter 7 --listing 3
```

Your output won't be exactly the same, because the simulated data is randomly generated. Note that listing 7.3 selects a string aggregation of the metrics being summed for illustrative purposes. To calculate such a metric and save it in a database, you would have to remove that part of the SELECT and select the metric's ID in an insert statement.

A prewritten SQL version of listing 7.3 in the listing code folder performs the insert. (The insert version has the same path but a filename beginning with insert_7_3 instead of listing_7_3.) Run the insert SQL statement by adding the --insert flag to arguments for the script that runs the listing; you'll need the saved result to continue with the examples. That listing shows you the SQL it uses but won't print a result. You should make your own SELECT statement to verify the result or run the metric_qa code from chapter 3 (listing 3.6).

After saving the total metric, you still need to create the ratio metric that will be a percentage of the total. To do so, use listing 7.1 (the ratio metric) again. An additional version of listing 7.1 with the parameters is already prepared: the numerator metric is the metric named dislikes_per_month, and the denominator is the new metric created with the insert version of listing 7.3 (named total_opinions). Run that insert statement by adding the arguments --version 2 --insert when you run listing 7.1. All together, the arguments are as follows:

```
fight-churn/listings/run_churn_listing.py --chapter 7 --listing 1 --version 2
    --insert
```

7.2.2 Percentage of total metric case study with two metrics

After creating the total metric for total likes and dislikes in the simulation and a new metric for the simulation customer percentage of dislikes, you should complete a new churn cohort analysis for the metric. To perform the cohort analysis for the dislike percentage, follow these steps:

1 Rerun listing 7.2 to export a version of the dataset to a .csv file with your new metric using the arguments `--chapter 7 --listing 2`.

2 Rerun listing 5.1 to create the new cohort analyses using the version arguments 6, 7, and 8: `--chapter 5 listing 1 --version 6 7 8`. That code will run the cohort analyses for three metrics: likes per month, dislikes per month, and dislike percent. All together, the arguments are

```
--chapter 5 --listing 1 --version 6 7 8.
```

Figure 7.14 shows a typical result of this analysis. The number of likes per month and the number of dislikes per month are associated with reduced churn and correlated

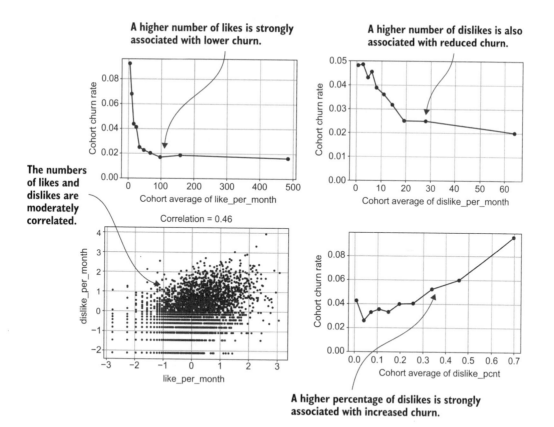

Figure 7.14 Percent dislike simulation case study illustrating the use of a percentage of total metric

with each other, but the dislike percentage shows increasing churn risk for a higher percentage of dislikes. The result of this analysis is similar qualitatively to the analysis of ad views presented in section 7.1.1. In that analysis, a behavior-reducing engagement was correlated with a behavior that increases engagement, and a ratio metric made this fact apparent. The difference is that, this time, you used a percentage rather than a simple ratio.

If you think that the results would not have been that different if you used the simple ratio (of dislikes and likes), you are right. So why bother with the percentage? The reason I recommend using a percentage rather than a simple ratio in cases like this one is interpretability. Because likes and dislikes form a category, it's more intuitive to describe this kind of relationship with a percentage. My advice is to use a percentage ratio when the two metrics are related as parts of a whole (likes and dislikes, for example) and to use a simple ratio when two metrics are not two parts of a whole (ad views and posts, for example).

> **TAKEAWAY**   When two metrics are two parts of a whole, a percentage ratio is
> more interpretable than a simple ratio.

A similar case study occurs for Broadly. Illustrated in figure 7.15, this case study shows the results for the metrics customer promoter per month, customer detractor per month, and percentage of detractors. A customer *promoter event* occurs when a customer leaves a positive review, so this event is expected to provide value to a business that uses Broadly and make the customer less likely to churn, which it appears to do in figure 7.15. A *detractor event* occurs when a customer leaves a bad review, which is expected to displease the business that uses Broadly, but it appears to be associated with reduced churn as well. Figure 7.15 also shows the churn cohort result for the percentage of detractors, which is the ratio made by dividing the number of detractors by the total number of promoters and detractors. Higher percentages of detractors are strongly associated with churn, and businesses with the lowest percentage of detractors—around 2%—had virtually no churn during the study period.

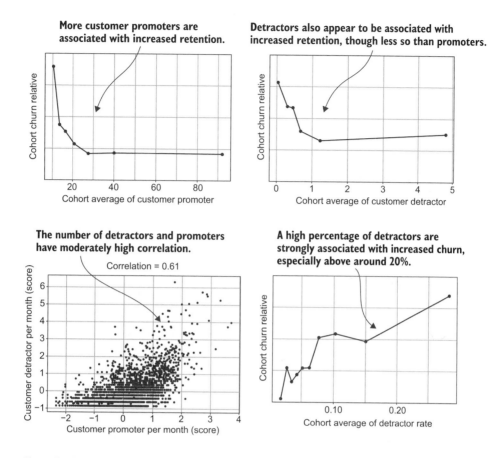

Figure 7.15   Detractor percentage case study

7.2.3   *Percentage of total metrics case study with multiple metrics*

Percentage of total metrics is useful for making a ratio from two categories more interpretable. But percentage of total metrics really shines when you have many subcategories that together form a total. Figure 7.16 shows an example for Versature, an integrated telecommunications provider. Versature provides service in four geographical regions, labeled 1 through 4 in figure 7.16. The correlation matrix in figure 7.16 shows that the numbers of calls per month in all four regions are moderately to highly correlated.

As a result of the correlation between the numbers of calls in the four regions, trying to analyze churn by using simple count metrics tells you only one thing: more calls by customers reduces churn. But the percentage of total metrics (shown on the right side of figure 7.16) can provide some more information. In region 1, lowest churn occurs when the percentage is high but not the highest. Region 1 has the most calls, but when customers make calls only in region 1, those calls seem to lead to less engagement.

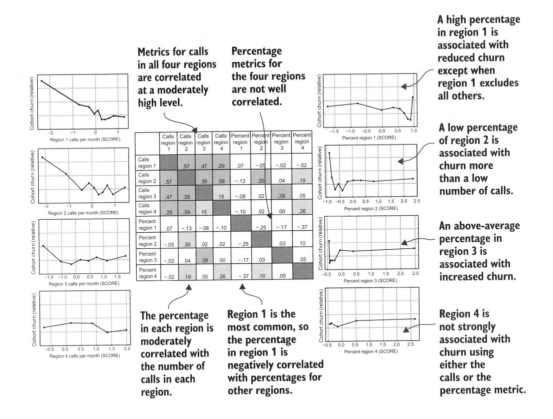

Figure 7.16 Regional percentages case study for Versature

Regions 2 and 3 show a relationship to churn in which a moderate percentage of calls in the region is optimal; either too few or too many lead to higher churn.

Also as shown in figure 7.16, the correlations between the percentage of total metrics in all four regions are weakly correlated. Because region 1 has the most calls overall, the percentage in region 1 shows weak to moderate negative correlation with the other percentage metrics: a high percentage in region 1 generally leaves few calls in the other regions. The other three regional percentages of total metrics are correlated weakly with one another and with the call amount metrics, indicating that these metrics provide new information for understanding customer engagement and churn (distinct from the information in the call amounts).

7.3 *Metrics that measure change*

So far, you have looked at measurements of customer behavior around the time the measurements are made. But change in behavior can give you additional clues to engagement. To understand how change in customer behavior relates to engagement and churn, you'll create a few more metrics specifically for this purpose and then analyze the change measurements, using the same techniques you've already learned.

7.3.1 Measuring change in the level of activity

Because you've calculated metrics on sequences of dates, it's easy to see whether the behavior of a customer is changing by looking at their metrics and comparing the current value with the previous value. If the metric has gone up, you know that the behavior is increasing; if the metric has gone down, the behavior is decreasing. That result is one reason why you calculate metrics at different points over time. But if you want to understand how change relates to churn and engagement, you need to look at change as another natural experiment and compare customers whose behavior has increased with customers whose behavior has decreased. To do so, you need metrics that represent change; then you can apply the cohort analysis technique that you've learned.

A metric that represents change is a derived metric representing the change in a primary metric you are interested in. Because you've already learned about making metrics from other metrics, this idea should not seem as strange to you as it might have before you picked up this book. Figure 7.17 illustrates a hypothetical scenario for measuring change in the number of logins for two accounts and introduces the concept of percentage change as a metric.

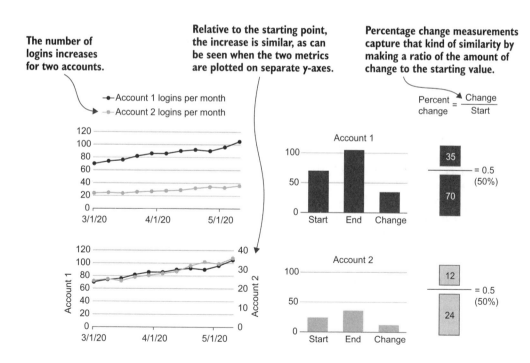

Figure 7.17 Using percentage change metrics for two imaginary accounts

DEFINITION   The *percentage change* is a ratio that takes the change in a metric over time and divides that change by the value of the metric at the start of the period.

Suppose that two accounts have different amounts of logins; one account logs in much more than the other. Also suppose that both accounts' logins per month are increasing. If you look at how much the number of logins changes over time, you'll probably find that the size of the change is larger for the account that had more logins to begin with. That is, the size of change in a metric is correlated with the level of the metric. Because the size of change is often correlated with the starting level of a metric, a simple difference is not the best metric for representing change. You can see this result if you look at the change in the number of logins in a chart where each account gets its own y-axis scale. The relative change can be seen as the same if you allow each account its own scale. Because you've learned that using ratios is a way to rescale metrics to emphasize relative amounts, you can probably see where this example is going.

This ratio calculation makes a measurement of change that is less correlated to how high the level of the metric was at the beginning. Figure 7.17 shows that for those two accounts, the percentage change is the same, which shows the similarity in their increase despite the big difference in the starting points. Equation 7.1 shows the definition of the percentage change in a mathematical formula.

$$\text{Percentage Change} = \frac{Metric_{@end} - Metric_{@start}}{Metric_{@start}} = \frac{Metric_{@end}}{Metric_{@start}} - 1.0 \quad \textbf{(Equation 7.1)}$$

In equation 7.1, $Metric_{@start}$ means the metric at the start of the measurement window, and $Metric_{@end}$ means the metric at the end. Equation 7.1 also shows a simplification: the percentage change is actually the *ratio* of the metric at the start to the metric at the end, minus 1.0, because the fraction is separable into the ratio of the end metric to the start metric, minus the ratio of the start metric to itself. This simplification is based on the fact that any number divided by itself is 1.0.

TAKEAWAY   Use percentage change metrics to see whether behavior has changed. Do not include either the (old) metric start values or the absolute change values in your analysis directly; those values are correlated with the overall level of activity captured by the ending metric value.

To make this example more concrete, figure 7.18 shows the details of the calculation of the percentage change as a metric. This figure continues the imaginary example of logins from figure 7.17, with one important difference: like every other metric, this one is calculated repeatedly on a sequence of dates. This type of calculation is sometimes called a *rolling percentage change* calculation.

In figure 7.18, a period of four weeks is used. For each week, the calculation applies equation 7.1 on the metric for that week (as the end metric) and the metric from four weeks earlier (as the start metric). As shown on the right of figure 7.18, the resulting rolling percentage change measurements are not constant; they fluctuate, depending on the precise ups and downs of the underlying metric. For the period of illustration in which both metrics are fairly consistent, an increase in the four-week percentage change ranges from around 5% to around 25%.

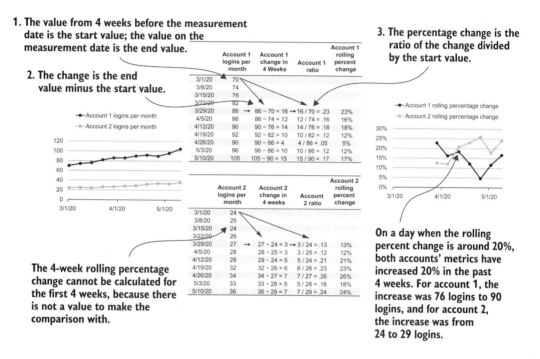

Figure 7.18 Calculation of rolling percentage change metrics

Figure 7.19 displays the sample output of the SQL statement to calculate percentage change (listing 7.4). The figure shows that this metric has something new to this book: negative values. If you were familiar with percentage change before reading this book, that fact comes as no surprise. If the term is new to you, *negative percentage change* means that the metric in question has gone down over the measurement period. Recall from equation 7.1 that the percentage change is

$$\frac{Metric_{@end}}{Metric_{@start}} - 1.0$$

when the end metric is less than the start metric and the fraction is less than 1.0, so after subtracting 1, the percentage change becomes negative.

account_id	metric_date	start_value	end_value	percent_change	
1	4/5/20	9	11	22%	The ratio percentage change result is the value for the new metric.
1	4/12/20	7	10	43%	
1	4/19/20	7	10	43%	
...	...	...	...	...	
2	4/5/20	9	4	−56%	
2	4/12/20	11	1	−91%	
2	4/19/20	10	NaN	−100%	

The **SELECT** shows the start and end value of the underlying metric for illustration.

Figure 7.19 Output of running listing 7.4, showing negative results

Because the percentage change is a ratio metric minus 1.0, listing 7.4 is similar to calculating a regular ratio metric. The differences between listing 7.4 and a regular ratio calculation are

- The numerator and denominator are from the same metric instead of two different metrics.
- The denominator metric (the start value) is selected from sometime earlier than the end value (four weeks, in the example). (This selection has to be accounted for in both the JOIN and SELECT statements.)
- In listing 7.4 (the percentage change), the number 1 is subtracted from the ratio in the final calculation.

Listing 7.4 Percentage change in a metric

```
WITH end_metric AS (                                    ◁──────  This CTE selects all
    SELECT account_id, metric_time, metric_value AS end_value       the metrics for the
    FROM metric m INNER JOIN metric_name n                          numerator.
        ON n.metric_name_id=m.metric_name_id
    AND n.metric_name = 'new_friend_per_month'          This CTE selects all
    AND metric_time BETWEEN '2020-04-01' AND '2020-05-10'    the metrics for the
), start_metric AS (                                    ◁──────  denominator.
    SELECT account_id, metric_time, metric_value AS start_value
    FROM metric m INNER JOIN metric_name n
        ON n.metric_name_id=m.metric_name_id            Uses the same metric for both
    AND n.metric_name = 'new_friend_per_month'   ◁──    numerator and denominator
    AND metric_time BETWEEN                      ◁──    Offsets the dates for
        ('2020-04-01'::timestamp -interval '4 week')           the denominator by
        AND ('2020-05-10'::timestamp -interval '4 week')       the change period
)
SELECT s.account_id, s.metric_time + interval '4 week',
    start_value, end_value,
    COALESCE(end_value,0.0)/start_value - 1.0     The percentage change
        AS percent_change               ◁──      according to equation 7.1
```

Uses the time from the more recent metric for the ratio

```
FROM start_metric s LEFT OUTER JOIN end_metric e          ◁──┐  LEFT OUTER JOIN; if the
    ON s.account_id=e.account_id                                 end metric is NULL, the
    AND e.metric_time                                            change is –100%.
        =(s.metric_time + interval '4 week')      ◁──────
WHERE start_value > 0      ◁──┐  Guards against              The JOIN adjusts for the
                              │  divide-by-zero              offset between the start
                              │  errors                      and end.
```

Also note that listing 7.4 selects the start and end values used in the calculation for illustrative purposes. If you calculate the percentage change as a metric to save in the database, you have to leave out the illustration columns and include an INSERT statement with a metric ID. You should run listing 7.4 with the Python wrapper program in the usual way to see the output like figure 7.19 and then rerun listing 7.4 with the --insert flag to save it to the database like this:

```
fight-churn/listings/run_churn_listing.py --chapter 7 --listing 4 --insert
```

You may be wondering whether it would make more sense to use start_value as the second argument in the COALESCE in listing 7.4 so that the result of the calculation returns 0 when end_value is null. But note that start_value has to be greater than 0 due to the WHERE clause. Then, if there is no end_value, the change is defined –100% because you went from something (the nonzero start_value) to nothing, so that the COALESCE around the end_value gives the correct result.

   You should run a cohort analysis on your new metric for percentage change in new friends. The steps are similar to those you saw in section 7.1:

1 Rerun listing 7.2 to reexport the dataset, including the new metric.
2 Run listing 5.1 with the argument --version 9 to plot the cohort analysis of percentage change in new friends. All together, the arguments are

```
--chapter 5 --listing 1 --version 9
```

Figure 7.20 shows a typical result for this analysis. Cohorts with a significant drop in new friends per month are found to be at elevated risk of churn.

7.3.2 Scores for metrics with extreme outliers (fat tails)

A problem with percentage change metrics is that these metrics can have extreme values. This problem is not apparent in the simulated data because it tends to be less extreme than real human behavior. Actually, any ratio can have extreme values when the denominator is small (less than 1) because then the value of the ratio becomes quite large. But for most common ratios, this problem doesn't exist because things like unit costs and efficiency measurements such as transaction per customer are constrained by the nature of the business, and percentages must be between 0% and 100% by design. When a customer has a low value in a metric, and their next measurement is large, the percentage change can be huge. But if a customer goes from a high metric value to zero (or near zero), will the metric go extremely negative? Not quite:

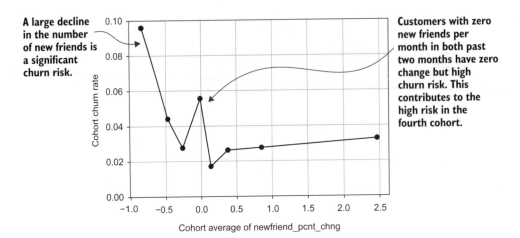

A large decline in the number of new friends is a significant churn risk.

Customers with zero new friends per month in both past two months have zero change but high churn risk. This contributes to the high risk in the fourth cohort.

Figure 7.20   Simulation percentage change in friends per month for the churn cohort case study

the lowest possible percentage change measurement is –100% because that's the percentage change when any nonzero metric goes to zero.

Figure 7.21 shows measurements of the distribution of percentage change metrics from the social network simulation and from the case study of Versature. To reproduce the statistics for the case study, use the Python wrapper program as follows:

1 Rerun listing 7.2 to export a version of the dataset to a CSV file with your new metric with the arguments --chapter 7 --listing 2.

2 Rerun listing 5.2 to save a table of the dataset summary statistics with the arguments --chapter 5 --listing 2 --version 2.

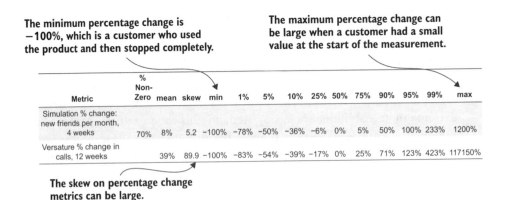

The minimum percentage change is –100%, which is a customer who used the product and then stopped completely.

The maximum percentage change can be large when a customer had a small value at the start of the measurement.

Metric	% Non-Zero	mean	skew	min	1%	5%	10%	25%	50%	75%	90%	95%	99%	max
Simulation % change: new friends per month, 4 weeks	70%	8%	5.2	–100%	–78%	–50%	–36%	–6%	0%	5%	50%	100%	233%	1200%
Versature % change in calls, 12 weeks	39%	89.9		–100%	–83%	–54%	–39%	–17%	0%	25%	71%	123%	423%	117150%

The skew on percentage change metrics can be large.

Figure 7.21   Versature percentage change in calls statistics

Your results will include the stats from the simulation metric percentage change in new friends shown in the first row of figure 7.21. The values from the simulation aren't too extreme, because the percentage change is for a four-week period, and the simulated customers don't change that much. Still, the maximum is 1,200%, indicating that at least one customer went from one new friend per month to 12 new friends per month; the minimum is –100%, as promised.

The Versature case study metric is more like what you should expect in real customer data: the minimum is also –100%, and the maximum is 117,150%. That's an 11,000 times increase! Somewhere in the dataset is a customer who went from one call per month three months ago to 11,715 calls 12 weeks later—an extreme case of a big customer that started the service at the start of the percentage change measurement. The 99th percentile of the change is 423%, meaning that 99% of the customers had increases less than 4.23 times.

Another important point to note is that the median change is 0% (the 50th percentile shown in the 50% column in figure 7.21). About as many customers increased their number of calls as decreased their number of calls. This result usually occurs for a percentage change metric. You may not realize that fact if you look at the average, which is usually greater than 0%. This is the case for both the simulation percentage change metric and Versature's percentage change metric in figure 7.20. The reason that the average is greater than 0% when equal numbers of customers have positive and negative change metrics is that the positive percent change measurements may be much greater in magnitude than negative percent change measurements.

Something else to notice in figure 7.21 is the skew around 5 for the simulation and nearly 90 for the real data. As you may recall from chapter 5, skew means that most of the metric values are packed together, but a few are way out there. A skew of 5 qualifies as moderately skewed; a skew of 90 is highly skewed. When a metric is highly skewed, you should turn it into a score to make it easier to understand your cohort analysis (see chapter 5).

But there is a problem. You can't use the skewed metric version of the scoring transformation if a metric is zero or negative, but percentage change is often zero and negative. To solve this problem, you can use another scoring formula, which I call the *fat-tails* formula because it transforms a metric into a score when there are extreme outliers in both negative and positive directions. The condition of having both positive and negative extreme values is called *fat tails* because *tails* refer to the extremes of the distribution. When a distribution is normal or has thin tails, the most extreme values aren't too extreme relative to the middle of the distribution. If the distribution of a metric has fat tails, the extreme values are farther from the middle of the range, and there are more extreme values.

Equation 7.2 shows the fat-tails score formula:

$$score(metric) = \frac{m' - \mu_{m'}}{\sigma_{m'}}$$

where

$$m' = \ln(m + \sqrt{m^2 + 1})$$ **(Equation 7.2)**

Equation 7.2 has the same format as the score formula in chapter 5 (equation 5.1): you are going to transform the metric and then subtract the mean and divide by the standard deviation of the transformed metric. In equation 7.2, $\mu_{m'}$ stands for the mean of the distribution of the transformed metric m', and $\sigma_{m'}$ stands for the standard deviation of the transformed metric.

The metric transformation in the fat-tails score formula is only a little bit different from the regular score formula: the second part of equation 7.2 says that the transformed metric m' is created by taking the logarithm of the original metric m plus the square root of the original metric squared plus 1. Recall that in the chapter 5 score formula, you used the logarithm of the original metric plus 1 (without squaring or taking the square root).

The fat-tails score formula works for negative values because when the original metric m is negative, the term in the square root is always positive and a little bit greater in absolute value then the negative term. Negative values end up as small numbers closer to zero, and positive values get pushed out. After applying the log function, subtract the mean and divide by the standard deviation of the transformed variable.

The second half of equation 7.2 with the logarithm is also known to scientists and mathematicians as the *inverse hyperbolic sine transform*, which is a mouthful that you don't have to remember. This transform is used in certain types of engineering and geometry calculations. Regardless of what you call it, the fat-tails score transform is a great trick for transforming metrics with extreme values.

> **TAKEAWAY**   Use the fat-tails transformation to create scores from metrics with extreme values that are both positive and negative.

Listing 7.5 updates listing 5.3 to include the fat-tails score transform. (I skipped this added complication in chapter 5 because we weren't looking at metrics that needed it.) The expanded listing does all the same things, and it makes an additional check for skewed columns with negative values. If there are any such columns, the score formula defined by equation 7.2 is applied, in addition to the regular score transformations for skewed and nonskewed columns.

> **NOTE**   Another test for fat-tailed metrics is to check for a high value on the statistic called *kurtosis*, a measurement designed to detect fat-tailed distributions. I am omitting it for simplicity because in churn cases, the fat-tailed metrics are also skewed.

Listing 7.5 Scoring metrics with fat tails

```
import pandas as pd
import numpy as np                                    ◁─── Wraps the skewed
import os                                                   data transform
                                                            from listing 5.3
def transform_skew_columns(data,skew_col_names):    ◁───
    for col in skew_col_names:                          The transform for
        data[col] = np.log(1.0+data[col])          ◁─── skewed scores

def transform_fattail_columns(data,fattail_col_names):  ◁───  A new transform
    for col in fattail_col_names:                             for fat-tailed data
        data[col] = np.log(data[col] +
                    np.sqrt(np.power(data[col],2) + 1.0))  ◁───  Applies the fat-tails
                                                                 score formula
def fat_tail_scores(data_set_path,                               (equation 7.2)
                    skew_thresh=4.0,**kwargs):  ◁───
                                                   Uses kwargs to
    churn_data =                                   ignore the default
        pd.read_csv(data_set_path,index_col=[0,1]) listing parameters
    data_scores = churn_data.copy()
    data_scores.drop('is_churn',inplace=True, axis=1)

    stat_path = data_set_path.replace('.csv', '_summarystats.csv')
    assert os.path.isfile(stat_path),'You must running listing 5.2 first to
      generate stats'
    stats = pd.read_csv(stat_path,index_col=0)
    stats.drop('is_churn',inplace=True)

    skewed_columns=(stats['skew']>skew_thresh) & (stats['min'] >= 0)
    transform_skew_columns(data_scores,skewed_columns[skewed_columns].keys())

    fattail_columns=(stats['skew']>skew_thresh)
        & (stats['min'] < 0)                     ◁───  Fat-tails score when
                                                       skew is high and negative
                                                       values are present
    transform_fattail_columns(data_scores,
                        fattail_columns[fattail_columns].keys())

    mean_vals = data_scores.mean()               ◁───  This rescaling is the
    std_vals = data_scores.std()                       same as listing 5.3.
    data_scores=(data_scores-mean_vals)/std_vals
    data_scores['is_churn']=churn_data['is_churn']

    score_save_path=data_set_path.replace('.csv','_scores.csv')
    data_scores.to_csv(score_save_path,header=True)

    print('Saving results to %s' % score_save_path)
    param_df = pd.DataFrame(
        {'skew_score': skewed_columns,          ◁───  Saves what columns are
         'fattail_score': fattail_columns,            transformed and the
         'mean': mean_vals,                           parameters
         'std': std_vals}
    )
```

Annotations (left margin):
- Loops over all columns with fat tails →
- Most of this code is the same as listing 5.3. →

```
param_save_path=data_set_path.replace('.csv','_score_params.csv')
param_df.to_csv(param_save_path,header=True)
print('Saving params to %s' % param_save_path)
```

You can try listing 7.5 on your own data by making the following calls to the Python wrapper program:

1 If you have not done so already, run listing 7.4 with the `--insert` flag to save the new metric.

2 Rerun listing 7.2 to recreate your saved dataset, using the arguments `--chapter 7 --listing 2`. This dataset includes your new percentage change metric.

3 Run listing 7.5 to create the dataset of scores, using the arguments `--chapter 7 --listing 5`.

4 Rerun listing 5.2, version 2, to check the statistics on the scores, using the arguments `--chapter 5 --listing 2 --version 2`.

Figure 7.22 shows the analysis of the percentage change in calls with data from Versature. For this case study, the metric is the percentage change in the number of calls per month, measured over the past 12 weeks. The cohort with the greatest reduction in calls shows an elevated churn risk. Because the metric is measured over a longer period than the lead time before churn, with which the observation is made, this indicator probably is not a churn leading indicator, as discussed in chapter 4. That is, if two weeks before a customer comes up for renewal, you see that their use is way down from three months earlier, there is a good chance that they have already made up their mind to churn. On the other hand, with two weeks left before the actual renewal, there may be time to resolve an issue, if there is one.

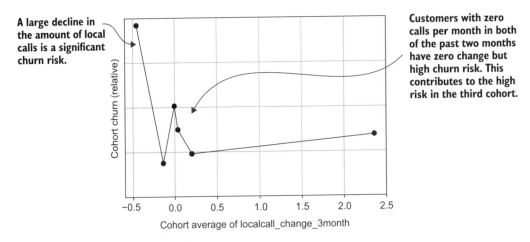

Figure 7.22   Churn cohort case study for Versature's percentage change in calls

7.3.3   *Measuring the time since the last activity*

Percentage changes are a good way to know whether a user's behavior has dropped or increased. A useful related measurement is time since last activity. Time since last activity is not a measurement of change in behavior, but it relates how a customer's current behavior compares with their past behavior. In particular, time since last activity distinguishes customers who are newly inactive from those who may have been inactive for a long time.

Figure 7.23 illustrates the concept with a simple example on the event series for one account. Any time you calculate the metric, time since last activity is the time difference between the most recent event before the measurement date and the measurement date. If a customer has an event on the day of the measurement, the metric is zero. If the customer has no events for an extended period, the metric increases by one every day until another event occurs.

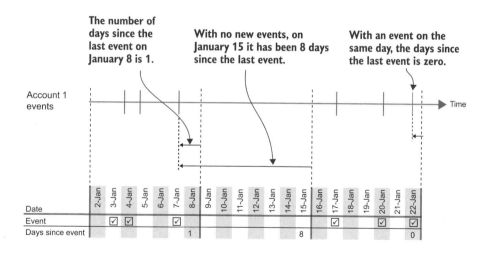

Figure 7.23   Measuring the time since the last activity: an event

Like all the metrics we use, time since last activity would be tedious to calculate by hand. Fortunately, that calculation isn't hard to make with SQL CTEs and aggregations. Figure 7.24 shows a sample of the typical output from SQL that calculates the days since the last event. Note that this output includes the date of the last event in the SELECT statement for illustrative purposes.

Listing 7.6 gives the SQL program to calculate the time since the last event. The basic strategy is to use a MAX aggregation on the event times (constrained to events before the measurement date) to find all the most recent events. The most recent event dates are stored in a CTE. After that, the metric is the difference between that event date and the measurement date. The only thing that makes this calculation a bit

account_id	metric_date	last_date	days_since_event
0	5/3/20	2/14/20	79
0	5/10/20	2/14/20	86
1	5/3/20	5/3/20	0
1	5/10/20	5/10/20	0
2	5/3/20	3/20/20	44
2	5/10/20	5/6/20	4
3	5/3/20	5/3/20	0
3	5/10/20	5/10/20	0

The days since the last event is the value for the new metric.

The SELECT shows the last event date for illustrative purposes.

Figure 7.24 Output of running listing 7.4. For each account and date, the date of the last event is selected for illustration; the metric value is the number of days from the last event to the date of the measurement.

complicated is that, as for all the metrics, the calculation is performed simultaneously for a series of measurement dates. The query is not finding only one last event date per account but a whole series of last event dates for every account.

You should run listing 7.6 on the simulated dataset, following the usual pattern with the Python wrapper program, and confirm that the output looks similar to figure 7.24. Also following the usual pattern, to insert the metric in the database, you need to remove the illustrative (extra) column and include the metric name ID in an insert statement. The GitLab repository has a version of the listing that you can run by passing the --insert flag as an argument to the program that runs the listings as follows:

```
fight-churn/listings/run_churn_listing.py --chapter 7 --listing 6 --insert
```

Listing 7.6 SQL for measuring time since an event

```
WITH date_vals AS (              ←┤  CTE for a sequence of dates on
  SELECT i::date AS metric_date       which to calculate the metrics
    FROM generate_series('2020-05-03', '2020-05-10', '7 day'::interval) i
),
last_event AS (                  ←┤  CTE for a temporary result:
    SELECT account_id, metric_date,     the date of the last event
        MAX(event_time)::date AS last_date   ←┐  SELECTs the last date
    FROM event e INNER JOIN date_vals d        │  with a MAX aggregation
    ON e.event_time::date <= metric_date  ←┐
    INNER JOIN event_type t                Use the date of the last event
                                           up to each measurement date.
```

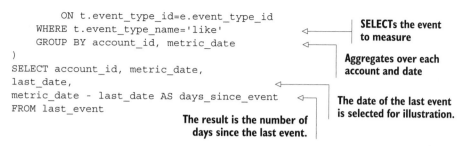

```
        ON t.event_type_id=e.event_type_id
    WHERE t.event_type_name='like'
    GROUP BY account_id, metric_date
)
SELECT account_id, metric_date,
last_date,
metric_date - last_date AS days_since_event
FROM last_event
```

SELECTs the event to measure

Aggregates over each account and date

The date of the last event is selected for illustration.

The result is the number of days since the last event.

After running the version of listing 7.6 that inserts the metric, you can regenerate the dataset and run a cohort churn analysis on it. All together, the runs of the Python wrapper program are

1. Run listing 7.6 with the insert flag to save the new metric: `--chapter 7 --listing 6 --insert`.
2. Rerun listing 7.2 to reexport the dataset: `--chapter 7 --listing 2`.
3. Run a new cohort analysis using listing 5.1, version 10: `--chapter 5 --listing 1 --version 10`.

Figure 7.25 shows the output of the cohort analysis. A gap of more than around five days since the last new friend event is associated with an increasing risk of churn. The increase in risk is gradual but becomes fairly significant for the cohort with the longest time since the event.

Figure 7.26 shows a churn cohort analysis for the number of days since the last dashboard edit for Klipfolio. In the real case study, days since last edit is a significant

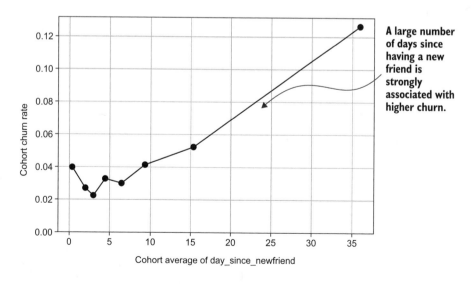

A large number of days since having a new friend is strongly associated with higher churn.

Figure 7.25 Case study of churn and days since the last new friend event

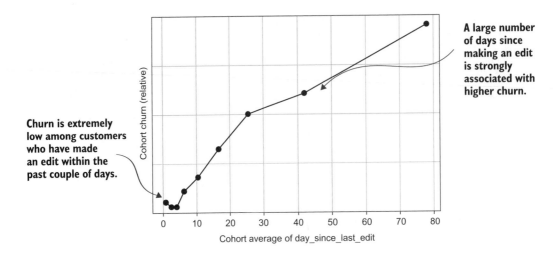

Figure 7.26   Case study of churn and days since last dashboard edit for Klipfolio

predictor of churn risk: risk increases substantially over the first month. Unlike in the simulated data, the risk increases only modestly in the cohorts with the longest time since activity.

When a customer has been inactive for a long time, they can forget about the subscription. At that point, some practitioners argue, the best churn-reducing strategy is to do nothing and let sleeping dogs lie by not reminding the customer that they have the subscription. It is a plausible hypothesis, although a somewhat dubious business strategy, to depend on people forgetting about you to boost your retention. In any event, figure 7.26 does *not* suggest that churn risk decreases when the time since the last action gets longer. The question of whether interventions with people that far gone have positive return on investment is one that must be answered empirically by any company that is considering such an approach.

7.4   *Scaling metric time periods*

In chapter 3, when you learned how to calculate behavioral metrics, I recommended that you scale the metric measurement window for simple metrics based on the frequency of the event, using longer measurement windows for rarer events. That advice is good, but it introduces a couple of problems:

- Choosing different measurement windows for different events is going to be confusing.
- If you use a long measurement period for rare events, you have to wait a long time to observe your customers properly. This problem is compounded if you want to make percentage change metrics like the ones introduced in section 7.3.

This section teaches scaling techniques that address both these issues by scaling measurements from one time frame to another. These techniques are similar to the scaling of churn rates you learned in chapter 2, but they work a bit differently for metrics than for churns.

7.4.1 Scaling longer metrics to shorter quoting periods

Using different measurement periods for different metrics can be confusing, especially if you have a lot of events. It's easier to compare behaviors when all the measurements are on the same scale.

> **WARNING** Reporting a lot of metrics measured on different time scales will confuse people.

How can you reconcile that advice with the advice in chapter 3 to use long time frames to measure rare events? It's easy: you can describe your behavioral measurements on a different time scale than the window you used to make the measurement. Figure 7.27 illustrates this concept. In essence, you are going to describe the metric as an average count of something per month rather than a total count measured over multiple months.

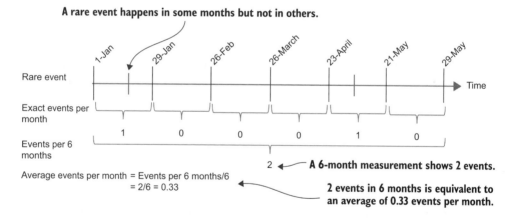

Figure 7.27 Quoting a long-period count metric as a short-period average

You can measure behavior over a one-year period, for example, but convert it to a monthly value by dividing the number you measured over the year by 12, because the average number of events per month is the number of events per year divided by 12. This idea is the same as scaling churn measurements (chapter 2) but with simpler math. You don't need any complicated reasoning about survival rates to scale standard behavioral metrics in time. This time, the technique is straight multiplication and division.

TAKEAWAY   Do not confuse the time period over which you make an average behavioral measurement with the time period with which you choose to describe the behavior. The time periods don't have to be the same. You can describe all your metrics on one time scale, even if the metrics are measured over different-length time windows.

Equation 7.3 shows the multiplication and division necessary to convert an event count taken during any time period of measurement (*TMeasure*) to an average at any other time period for describing the behavior (*TDescribe*).

$$Average_{TDescribe} = \frac{T_{Describe}}{T_{Measure}} Count_{TMeasure} \qquad \text{(Equation 7.3)}$$

Plugging the formula into the simple example of annual measurement with a monthly description, the ratio is four weeks description period divided by 52 weeks measurement period, or one-thirteenth. Or if you like to do this calculation in days, that's 30.4 (the average number of days in a month) divided by 365 days in a year, or one-thirteenth. Remember that you have to use the same units for the time period of both the description and the count, whether those units are days, months, or years.

Better yet, how about calculating the scaling on the fly with your measurement? Listing 7.7 shows an event per period behavior measurement (like listing 3.2) that automatically scales the measurement to a monthly description period average.

Equation 7.3 also applies to metrics that are totals of event properties, such as the total time spent on some activity. But scaling is not necessary; in fact, it's incorrect if the metric is an average of an event property. If the events are in-app purchases, for example, and you want to make a metric of the average purchase amount, this metric doesn't depend on the length of time for which you make the measurement because the average of an event property is defined as a per-event measurement, even though you can measure it over a longer time frame.

WARNING   Do not time-scale metrics that are averages of the value of event properties. Only metrics that are counts or sums should be scaled.

You should run listing 7.7 by using the Python wrapper program as usual (with the arguments --chapter 7 --listing 7). Figure 7.28 shows a typical result.

Listing 7.7   Scaling a number of events per account metric

```
WITH date_vals AS (              ◁──┐  This SQL is mostly the
    SELECT i::timestamp AS metric_date │  same as listing 3.2.
    FROM generate_series('2017-12-31', '2017-12-31', '7 day'::interval) i
)
SELECT account_id, metric_date,  COUNT(*) AS total_count,
(28)::float/(84)::float * COUNT(*) AS n      ◁──┐
FROM event e INNER JOIN date_vals d             │  The count is scaled from an 84-day
ON e.event_time <= metric_date                  │  to 28-day period (equation 3.1).
```

```
AND e.event_time > metric_date - interval '84 day'
INNER JOIN event_type t ON t.event_type_id=e.event_type_id
WHERE t.event_type_name='unfriend'
GROUP BY account_id, metric_date
GROUP BY account_id, metric_date;
```

Counts over 84 days

account_id	metric_date	total_count	unfriend_28day_avg_84day_obs
0	4/1/20	2	0.67
1	4/1/20	4	1.33
5	4/1/20	1	0.33
8	4/1/20	2	0.67
10	4/1/20	2	0.67
14	4/1/20	1	0.33

The total count divided by 3 (84/28) is the value for the metric.

The SELECT shows the total count for illustrative purposes.

Figure 7.28   Sample output from listing 7.7

Note that listing 7.7 includes a total count column that is shown for illustrative purposes. To insert metrics like this one into the database, you need to remove that column, replace it with a metric name ID, and add an INSERT statement. As usual, the repository also contains an insertable version of the metric that you can run by adding the --insert flag to the execution command as follows:

```
fight-churn/listings/run_churn_listing.py --chapter 7 --listing 7 --insert
```

After you've inserted the unfriend_per_month metric from listing 7.7 into the database, perform the following steps to check your result:

1 Regenerate the dataset by rerunning listing 7.2 with the arguments: --chapter 7 --listing 2.
2 Rerun the dataset summary statistics by rerunning listing 5.2 with these arguments: --chapter 5 --listing 2 --version 1.

Figure 7.29 shows a typical result for the summary statistics of the original unfriend_per_month metric and the new averaged unfriend per month measured over 84 days (unfriend_28day_avg_84day_obs). The average covers 50% of accounts with a non-zero measurement, but the original count covered only 26% of accounts. At the same time, the mean value and the percentiles are similar, not three times larger, because the metric was measured over a time frame three times as long. In fact, the new metrics

metric	count	non-zero	mean	std	skew	min	1pct	25pct	50pct	75pct	99pct	max
unfriend_per_month	25168	26%	0.31	0.56	1.78	0	0	0	0	1	2	4
unfriend_28day_avg 84day_obs	25168	50%	0.24	0.29	1.27	0	0	0	0.33	0.33	1	2

The metric with the long observation window produces nonzero results for more accounts.

For the 84-day metric, the minimum value above zero is 0.33, corresponding to one event in the 84-day observation period.

Figure 7.29   Statistics comparing rare simulation events measured at short and long time periods

are somewhat lower: not only is the mean lower, but so are the quantiles of the distribution. Think about why that is. (You'll find out the answer in section 7.4.2.)

Another benefit of using metrics with longer observation periods than description periods is that metrics estimated this way are robust when temporary changes in customer activity occur. If you measure some behavior with a one-month period, for example, a customer taking a two-week vacation can appear to have a low level of activity. Similarly, some customers can go through a brief and intense period of activity. In either case, if you measure the average behavior over a three-month period, these temporary variations won't make as much of an impact.

But one downside of using long observation periods for metrics is that the metric is no longer up to date as to the latest changes in behavior. With a long observation period, when behavior changes, it takes longer for the change to register in the metric. The best way to handle this situation is to use the long-observation window metrics for most behaviors in combination with a few metrics that measure percentage change in behaviors. That way, you have stable estimates of the average level of behavior but also a few indicators that will rapidly reveal recent changes.

One other important problem with measuring behavioral metrics over long time frames is taking measurements of new accounts. The problem exists for any measurement window, but it is exacerbated when the measurement window is long. If an account has been using the service for only a short duration (a tenure shorter than the measurement period), the measurement is not valid. Suppose that an old customer has only one login per month, so they are a light user of the product and at risk for churn. A new customer who joined yesterday can also have only one login in the past month, but that's not the same as the old customer having only one login per month.

NOTE Event count measurements made on new customers are not comparable with normal accounts that have been around for the entire measurement period.

This situation typically applies to customers measured at the time of their first renewal. For a monthly renewal subscription, the first measurement of customers in your dataset is made after two to three weeks, due to the lead time used in observing customers before renewal (as described in chapter 4). If you use four-week metric measurement periods, new customers had only one-half to three-quarters of the full period, and their metrics are probably underestimated. This problem is amplified if you use metric observation periods longer than one month. The first renewal is critical, so you don't want to make this kind of mistake.

7.4.2 Estimating metrics for new accounts

As described previously, any metric you measure over a period of several weeks or months is not valid for new accounts that have not been using the product that long. Fortunately, you have a straightforward way to handle this problem that is consistent with the averaging technique you learned in section 7.4.1: you can estimate an average by using a shorter time period than you are describing the average for. This technique is similar to calculating an average over a long time period and describing it as a shorter time period but in reverse. Figure 7.30 illustrates the concept.

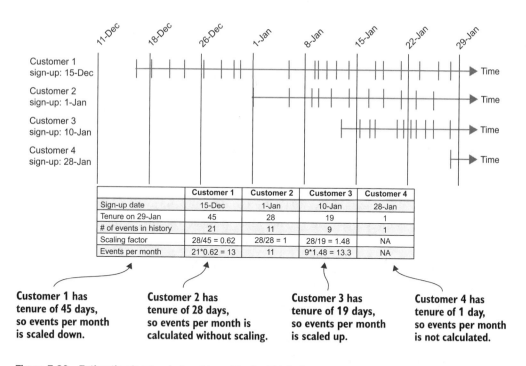

Figure 7.30 Estimating long-period metrics with short histories

The idea is as follows: Suppose that an account has been on a product for two weeks and has 10 logins per month. You don't know how many logins it will have after four weeks, but you can make an educated guess—after four weeks, there should be twice as many logins as after two weeks. This idea can be extended to scale a measurement over any shorter time period to make an estimate of what the average measured over a longer time period would be.

One important caveat is for new customers: if an account has one login after one day, does it make sense to estimate that it will have 28 logins after 28 days? Superficially, yes, but in practice, no. The problem is that if you estimate starting from a short length of time, such as one day, the estimate will be unstable and jump around. Suppose that after one day and one login for a customer, you estimate 28 logins per month. But on day two, the customer doesn't log in, so your estimate becomes 14. (One login in two days implies 14 logins in 28 days.) That activity is a big jump in the estimate of logins_per_month metric in one day. That kind of volatility is normal in estimates made from only a few days' worth of data; it usually takes at least 5 to 10 days of data for this kind of estimate to settle down. In chapter 3, you learned that most customer behaviors follow weekly cycles, so in general, you should use the following rules:

- Do not make estimates for one-month averages until you've observed at least one week of behavior, and preferably two.
- Similarly, if you are making averages to estimate quarterly or annual counts and totals, you should not estimate a metric until you've observed a month or more of the behavior of interest.

Equation 7.4 provides the math and logic for estimating count metrics for new accounts, which also includes the kind of scaling of an average count that you learned in section 7.4.1. The term $Count_{Tmeasure}$ in equation 7.4 refers to the actual trailing count of events, and there are three time-period parameters in equation 7.3:

- *Tmin* is the minimum tenure for an account to receive an estimate of this metric (one to two weeks for a monthly metric and two to three months for an annual metric).
- *Tdescribe* is the time period that's used to describe the average (four weeks).
- *Tmeasure* is the time period that's used to make the measurement (for an old customer).

Also in equation 7.4, there are three cases based on the subscriber tenure:

- If the tenure is less than *Tmin*, no metric value is calculated.
- If the tenure is greater than *Tmin* but less than the time period for describing the metric, the count is scaled up by the ratio of the description period to the account tenure. This count is the estimated average.
- If the tenure is greater than the description period, the count is scaled down by the ratio of the description period to the measurement period. This count is an average calculated over a longer period.

If tenure < Tmin

$$Average_{TDescribe} = NULL$$

Else If Tmin <= tenure <= Tdescribe

$$Average_{TDescribe} = \frac{Tdescribe}{tenure} Count_{Tmeasure}$$

Else

$$Average_{TDescribe} = \frac{Tdescribe}{Tmeasure} Count_{Tmeasure} \qquad \textbf{(Equation 7.4)}$$

The third case in equation 7.4 is the same as in equation 7.3. This equation adds the logic in the second case, using account tenure.

Listing 7.8 gives the SQL that implements equation 7.4 as a metric. This metric is a little different from any you've seen before: it uses the account tenure metric (assumed to be saved in the database already), and, at the same time, it makes a count of events. The saved account tenure metric defines the sequence of dates for which the new event count metric will be calculated, and the tenure value enters into the logic and scaling.

You might expect there to be an `IF` or `CASE` statement in listing 7.8 to implement the case logic from equation 7.4. Instead, this logic is implemented in two separate places:

- The case that there should be no result for accounts with tenure below the minimum is implemented with the `WHERE` clause constraint that the tenure metric value must be above a minimum.
- The difference between the cases in which the tenure is below the description period and those in which the tenure is above the description period is implemented by using the `LEAST` function in the denominator of the scaling:
  - When tenure is below the description period, it is the result of the `LEAST` function, and the tenure is the denominator for the scaling (the second case).
  - When the tenure is above the description period, the description period is the result of the `LEAST` function, and the description period is the denominator of the scaling term.

This logic works as long as the description period is longer than the minimum tenure, which should be the case when you use this kind of metric.

Listing 7.8 Scaled count metric with new account estimates

```
SELECT m.account_id, metric_time,
    m.metric_value AS tenure_metric,
    COUNT(*) AS count_unscaled,
    (28/ LEAST(84,m.metric_value)) AS scaling,
    (28/ LEAST(84,m.metric_value)) * COUNT(*)
        AS message_permonth_84day_avg
FROM event e INNER JOIN metric m
    ON m.account_id = e.account_id
    AND event_time <= metric_time
```

COUNTs the number of events → `COUNT(*) AS count_unscaled,`

SELECTs the previously calculated tenure metric

Calculates the scaling multiplier (equation 3.2)

The scaling multiplied by the raw count

JOINs on account ID

INNER JOIN calculates only the metric for accounts with tenure.

```
        AND event_time >  metric_time-interval '84 days'
    INNER JOIN event_type t ON t.event_type_id=e.event_type_id
    INNER JOIN metric_name  n ON m.metric_name_id = n.metric_name_id
    WHERE t.event_type_name='unfriend_per_month'
        AND n.metric_name='account_tenure'
        AND metric_value >= 14
    GROUP BY m.account_id, metric_time, metric_value
    GROUP BY m.account_id, metric_time, metric_value
```

Limits the events to the appropriate time range

The event for which the metric is calculated

Sets the minimum tenure of accounts for which to calculate

Includes nonaggregated parts of the SELECT statement (required)

The metric ID for the account tenure metric

You should run listing 7.8 by using the code in the GitHub repository for the Python wrapper program with the arguments `--chapter 7 --listing 8` to calculate a new scaled version of the unfriend_per_month metric. Figure 7.31 shows typical output from listing 7.8 on the default simulated dataset. Note that listing 7.8 outputs the count and scaling factor in addition to the final metric value for illustrative purposes. Figure 7.31 also illustrates accounts that fall into the different cases of equation 7.4:

- An older account (ID 21) starts with a tenure of 58 days, which is above the description period and below the measurement period. The scaling factor is always below 1.0, and it reaches a minimum of 0.33 after the tenure is greater than the measurement period of 84 days.
- Account 12371 appears in the result when it reaches 14 days' tenure; at this point, the scaling factor is 2.0 to produce an estimate of a 28-day average from

The SELECT shows the account tenure, the count, and the scaling factor for illustrative purposes.

The product of the count and the scaling is the value for the metric.

account_id	metric_time	tenure_ metric	count_ unscaled	scaling	unfriend_28day_avg_ 84day_obs_scaled
21	3/29/20	58	1	0.48	0.48
21	4/5/20	65	4	0.43	1.72
21	4/12/20	72	4	0.39	1.56
21	4/19/20	79	5	0.35	1.77
21	4/26/20	86	5	0.33	1.67
21	5/3/20	93	5	0.33	1.67
...	...	...	..	...	...
12371	4/5/20	14	1	2	2
12371	4/12/20	21	1	1.33	1.33
12371	4/19/20	28	1	1	1
12371	4/26/20	35	1	0.8	0.8
12371	5/3/20	42	1	0.67	0.67

For seasoned accounts, the scaling is greater than 1, so the metric is an average.

For new accounts, the scaling is greater than 1, so the metric is an estimate.

Figure 7.31   Sample output for listing 7.8 on the default simulated dataset

14 days of data. As the tenure increases, the scaling factor falls. At 28 days' tenure, the scaling factor is 1.0; at this point, the metric is equivalent to an exact 28-day count. After the tenure increases above 28 days. the scaling factor falls below 1.0.

To save the metric in the database, you need to remove the unscaled count and scaling columns and then supply the metric name ID as part of an INSERT statement. A version of the listing that has these changes is in the GitHub repository and can be run by adding the --insert argument to the script executable statement. You should take the following steps:

1 Save the result of listing 7.8 to the database with the arguments --chapter 7 -- listing 8 --insert.
2 Regenerate the dataset by rerunning listing 7.2 with the arguments --chapter 7 --listing 2.
3 Rerun the dataset summary statistics by rerunning listing 5.2 with the arguments --chapter 5 --listing 2 --version 1.

Figure 7.32 shows typical results of the summary statistics. The summary statistics show that the new metric (labeled unfriend_28day_avg_84day_obs_scaled) has the same account coverage as the 12-week period metric (unfriend_28day_avg_84day_obs) taught in section 7.4.1, but the metric values are somewhat higher, and, in general, they are a better match for the simple count metric. The reason is that the unscaled metric increases coverage by using a long observation period but does not correct for the fact that not all accounts have sufficient tenure to cover that observation period. The new metric corrects for this situation with scaling on new accounts.

metric	count	nonzero	mean	std	skew	min	1pct	25pct	50pct	75pct	99pct	max
unfriend_per_month	25168	26%	0.31	0.56	1.78	0	0	0	0	1	2	4
unfriend_28day_avg _84day_obs	25168	50%	0.24	0.29	1.27	0	0	0	0.33	0.33	1	2
unfriend_28day_avg _84day_obs_scaled	25168	50%	0.31	0.40	1.61	0	0	0	0.33	0.54	1.56	4

In comparison with the metric without scaling, the average value is greater.

The metric with scaling also results in higher values for the percentiles.

Figure 7.32 Statistics comparing rare simulation events measured at short and long time periods

Because you have the final unfriend_per_month metric, you should also recalculate the ratio metric it was used in—unfriend per new friend—and recheck the cohort analysis. Following are the additional versions of the program arguments to use:

1 Calculate a new unfriend_per_new_friend metric (--chapter 7 --listing 1 --version 7 --insert).

2 Regenerate the dataset by rerunning listing 7.2 (`--chapter 7 --listing 2`).

3 Run the cohort analyses for unfriend per month and unfriend per new friend by rerunning listing 5.1, versions 14 and 16 (`--chapter 5 --listing 1 --version 14 16`).

Now that you know about scaled metrics based on account tenure, you're probably expecting a case study showing this new technique used in a company. I hate to disappoint you, but I don't have a new company case study to add—because *every* company case study in the book uses metrics with this type of scaling. I didn't mention this fact until now because it would have been too much information for you before you learned all the other techniques.

I always use metrics with the form like listing 7.8 for my case studies because these metrics have so many advantages, including highest possible coverage of accounts and robust estimation of the metric, without sacrificing the best possible estimate for new accounts. The only modest downside is that the metric calculation is a bit complicated, which means that you tell your businesspeople it is an average (without going into details).

> **TAKEAWAY** To understand churn, you should use average metrics with longer observation periods than the description periods and scaling to make comparable estimates of the averages for new accounts. Simple count metrics should be used only to measure use of a contracted quantity, in which case the exact count in the contract period matters.

I use the following standard metrics for churn studies, depending on whether the product uses primarily monthly or annual subscriptions:

- For monthly subscriptions, scaled count metrics with the following parameters:
  - *Tmin* = 14 days (2 weeks)
  - *Tdescribe* = 28 days (4 weeks)
  - *Tmeasure* = 84 days (12 weeks)
- For annual subscriptions, scaled count metrics with the following parameters:
  - *Tmin* = 28 days (1 month)
  - *Tdescribe* = 28 days to 84 days (4–12 weeks, 1 month to 1 quarter)
  - *Tmeasure* = 365 days (1 year)

7.5 *User metrics*

One final area of behavioral measurement you should know about is how to handle products with multiple users. These products include multiseat licenses for enterprise software and family plans for consumer products.

7.5.1 Measuring active users

The first thing to understand about multiuser products is that it's still best to understand churn at the subscription or account level because all the users share one subscription; if the subscription is not renewed, all the users churn together.

> **NOTE** Churn does not occur when individual users become inactive on a multiuser product.

If you are interested in analyzing user health, you can perform an analysis of user activity and inactivity by modifying the techniques for activity-based churn analysis from chapter 4. The goal is still to understand churn at the account level, not the user level, and to take advantage of the information about the behavior of individual users.

To understand how individual user behavior affects churn, the first important question to answer is how many active users there are. This question can be answered with a metric based on events, as illustrated in figure 7.33. It's similar to making a metric by counting events in a time period, but, instead, you count the number of distinct users who produced the events. To count the number of active users programmatically, you have to have user identifiers stored with the events in the database or data warehouse, which requires one additional field in comparison with the standard event

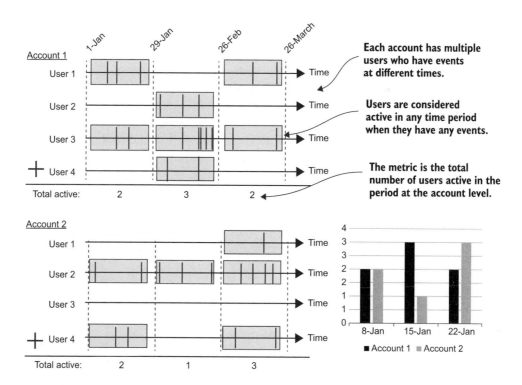

Figure 7.33 Calculating the number of active users from events

table schema (table 7.1). You may recall from chapter 3 that, in general, events can contain optional fields with additional event information, so this situation is not too different.

Table 7.1   Event table with user IDs

Column	Type
account_id	Integer or char
event_type_id	Integer or char
event_time	Timestamp
user_id	Integer or char

Listing 7.9 shows a short SQL program that counts the number of active users as a metric. This listing is practically identical to the simple event count metric in chapter 3 with one crucial difference: instead of counting the number of events, the aggregation is on the number of DISTINCT user IDs. Another difference between this metric and standard event count metrics is that this one does not specify the type of event: any event indicates user activity. (That option is available, of course, and if you want to determine user activity only from certain events, that change is easy to make.)

> **TAKEAWAY**   Counting the number of active users is easy to do with a DISTINCT aggregation on the user IDs.

One subtle difference between the active user count metric and event count metric is that the count of active users should not be scaled by the tenure or anything having to do with the tenure or measurement period. The number of distinct active users is an example of an aggregate metric that does not scale in that way. If an account has two active users in the first two weeks of a four-week period, it doesn't follow that there will be four active users in four weeks. Mathematically, the DISTINCT aggregative is not additive, like a COUNT aggregation.

Listing 7.9   Counting the number of active users

```
WITH date_vals AS (                                    ◁─┤ This CTE defines the dates on
    SELECT i::timestamp AS metric_date                      which users will be counted.
    FROM generate_series('2018-12-01', '2018-12-31', '7 day'::interval) i
)
SELECT account_id, metric_date,                                 Counts the number of
    COUNT(DISTINCT user_id) AS n_distinct_users      ◁─┤  users with a COUNT
FROM event e INNER JOIN date_vals d                            DISTINCT aggregation
ON e.event_time <= metric_date                     ◁─
AND e.event_time > metric_date - interval '84 days'       SELECT limits the query to
GROUP BY account_id, metric_date      ◁─┐                 any events within 12 weeks.
GROUP BY metric_date, account_id;

                                        GROUP BY so the number of users
                                        is measured at account level.
```

The default churn simulation on GitHub does not include users in the simulation, but it's possible to extend the simulation framework to include users. If you are interested in the subject, consider extending the framework this way as an exercise.

7.5.2   Active user metrics

Figure 7.34 shows a case study in measuring the number of active users for Klipfolio. The product is sold in multiseat licenses, so there is a metric for the number of active users as in listing 7.9, as well as a metric for the number of seats sold, using the unit quantity metric pattern as described in chapter 3. Figure 7.34 shows that the number of active users is strongly related to churn in a pattern that should be familiar by now: churn falls rapidly between one and four active users, but then the decrease in risk slows, and there is little difference in the churn for customers with dozens of users or more. At the same time, the number of licensed users does not appear to be strongly related to churn.

License utilization is a metric that is defined as the ratio of the number of users to the maximum number of allowed users. Sometimes, the number of users is measured by creation of user accounts, but for churn, I prefer to measure the actual or active license use by making a ratio of the active users divided by the number of licensed users. Figure 7.34 also shows the churn cohort analysis for license utilization defined

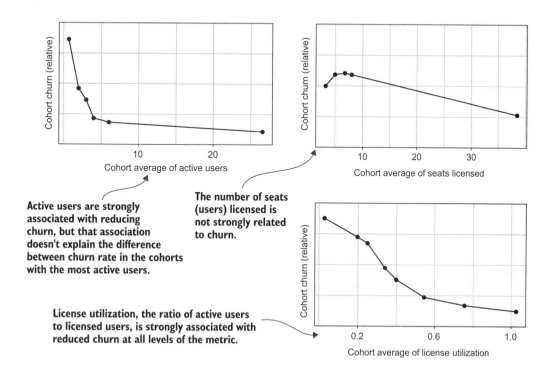

Figure 7.34   Cohort analysis of churn for Klipfolio's active users per month metric

this way for Klipfolio. License utilization shows a strong relationship to churn—stronger than active users alone. The decrease in churn risk with increasing license utilization is fairly continuous for every cohort. License utilization is clearly a useful metric for measuring customer engagement.

> **TAKEAWAY**   License utilization is a ratio of the number of active users to the number of users allowed, and it usually is an important measure of engagement for products sold by the user or seat.

Figure 7.34 illustrates another type of user metric with another example from the Klipfolio case study: dashboard views per user per month. This ratio is made from the measurement of dashboard views per month and the number of active users. Many metrics of this type are possible. Pretty much any behavior you've measured at the account level can be divided by the number of active users to form a per user ratio. Because the total amount of most behaviors is correlated to total number of active users, this type of ratio can result in useful metrics that are less correlated to the number of active users, the overall behavior of users, or both.

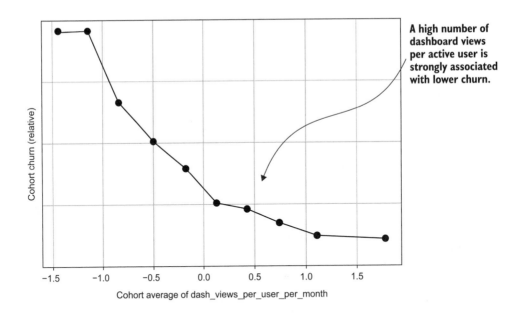

Figure 7.35   Cohort analysis of churn for Klipfolio's dashboard views per user metric

7.6   Which ratios to use

You now know a lot about the design and interpretation of customer metrics and case studies in customer churn and behavior. In this section, I will tie together a few themes and answer a few common questions.

7.6.1 *Why use ratios, and what else is there?*

I have spent a lot of time in this chapter on metrics that are ratios and not much time on anything else. I taught you that ratio metrics are a great way to understand the relationships between customer behaviors, but are there any other options? There are other options, but in my experience, none is as useful. If you have a statistics or data science background, you probably have heard of an *interaction* measurement. This concept is similar to a ratio, but instead of dividing one metric by another, you multiply the two metrics.

> **DEFINITION** An *interaction metric* is the product (multiplication) of two other metrics.

Interaction measurements, like ratios, are ways to understand the relationships between behaviors. In fact, in classical statistics, this method is the main one for understanding the relationships between measurements. To have a high measurement on the interaction term, for example, you must have a high value on *both* underlying metrics. As in a ratio, a zero in either metric means a zero in the interaction.

An interaction term is a bit like an and operation in computer science. If you have a computer science background, you may be thinking that you could make metrics with a Boolean operation like "Assign a 1 when two metrics are both above a certain level." You can think of a multiplicative interaction as being a more nuanced alternative. An interaction isn't just 0 or 1 when both metrics are high; it measures how high both metrics are as a real value. Interaction terms also have interesting statistical properties when applied to scores or metrics that can take negative values, because when either one metric or the other is negative, the interaction measurement takes on a negative value.

If interaction measurements are so interesting and widely used in statistics, you may be wondering why I don't recommend them for churn analysis. The simple answer is that no one in the business world understands interaction terms, but ratios are easy to understand. That is, metrics that result from the multiplication of two other metrics usually have unintuitive units in comparison to ratios. The ratio of the amount paid and the number of calls (or videos viewed, and so on) is the amount paid per call (or video, and so on), but the multiplication of an amount paid and the number of calls (or any behavior) does not have a conventional meaning.

If you took a physics class, you may remember that the multiplication of different types of quantities, such as mass (kilograms) and distance (meters), results in combined units like kilogram meters. Usually, these units are not too understandable. (What's a dollar call?) The exception that proves the rule is when one of the metrics is time and the other metric is a measure of intensity, like a kilowatt hour in electricity sales. I have never found a cognitive study that explains why ratio units are easy to understand and multiplicative units are not, but that fact is clear from everyone's experience. My advice is to use multiplicative interaction metrics only when you already have a business case that gives it an obvious meaning.

Another alternative that is familiar to data scientists and statisticians is making metrics from differences (subtraction) of *scores* rather than ratios (of natural scale metrics). In the sidebar in chapter 6 on principal component analysis (PCA), I pointed out that PCA does such subtractions implicitly. The idea is that if you want to understand the relationship between two metrics, you can look at the difference by subtracting one from the other in the same way as taking the ratio. This method is not really logical if the metrics are for different things. You don't get a meaningful metric by subtracting the calls someone makes on a telco product from the MRR paid, but it is okay to do so after converting the metrics to unitless scores. You saw that trick used in chapter 6 for taking average groups: scores show whether someone is above average (greater than zero), average (near zero), or less than average (a negative number).

The difference (subtraction) of a calls score and an MRR score is a measure of propensity to make calls in relation to the amount paid. So differences between metric scores can work like ratios, but once again, the problem is in the interpretation. You can tell your businesspeople that you made a metric for dollars per call, and they think that's great; it's not as easy to explain a metric for the subtraction of the calls per month score from the MRR score. When it comes to understandable metrics that capture the relationship between two behaviors, ratios are the only option. The only exception is if you have technical businesspeople who understand the less-intuitive approaches.

7.6.2 *Which ratios to use?*

I hope that at this point, you are convinced that ratio metrics are useful for understanding the relationships between different behaviors and how they relate to churn and customer engagement. Now is the time to think more generally about what ratios to investigate.

First, note that not all metrics can form useful ratios. One requirement is that both of the metrics should be nonzero for most customers (and they should have no negative values, which is less of a problem). One simple criterion is whether a lot of customers have nonzero values for both metrics. Even if you find a strong relationship to churn and engagement, a metric that applies to a small number of customers is not as useful as one that applies to a lot of customers.

A lot of metrics could define ratios in a typical dataset that has dozens of event types. If you are familiar with probability and combinatorics, you may recall that the number of possible pairs chosen from N items is $N \times (N-1)$. If you have N possible metrics, you could choose the numerator of the ratio with N different metrics and have $N-1$ left over to go in the denominator. That result is a lot of combinations, and it raises an additional question: which metric should go into the numerator, and which should go into the denominator? The first important thing to realize is that you should not try every possible combination.

> **WARNING** Do not create every possible pair of metrics for a possible ratio to check the relationship to churn.

The reason is that, typically, there are too many combinations, and most will not be meaningful. Even so, you risk finding a spurious relationship to churn and engagement by checking a lot of metrics.

> **DEFINITION** A *spurious relationship* between a metric and an outcome is a relationship that occurred due to random chance, not due to a repeatable, causal relationship. As a result, the relationship is not likely to recur.

If you are new to data analysis, it may sound strange to hear that you can see a relationship in your data that is somehow not true, but this problem is well known in data science. If you check enough metrics, eventually, you'll find some that appear to be related even though they are not. The problem can be helped by using strict criteria to decide when a relationship is strong or weak, which is the subject of chapter 8. But the best practice is to not consider relationships that don't seem to be intuitive to begin with.

> **TAKEAWAY** You mainly consider ratio metrics that make intuitive sense to someone in the business.

As you can see, no rule always works; you'll need to use your knowledge of the situation. The same answer goes for which metric should be in the numerator and which should be the denominator: whichever one makes more sense. You can try the two following approaches:

- Sometimes, interesting relationships (and good ratio metrics) can exist when two metrics are in different parts of a related set of activities. Try looking at the ratios of the most common metrics in a correlated group (as described in chapter 6); ignore the group members that are less common.
- Sometimes, there are interesting relationships between different areas of activity. Try testing a ratio of the most common metrics in one correlated group with the most common metric in another correlated group. Again, don't bother with any less common metrics.

Table 7.2 summarizes the most common cases for engagement and churn that are covered in this chapter.

Table 7.2 Summary of ratio metrics for customer engagement

Name	Ratio	Correlation	Information
Unit cost	MRR/Use	Customers on more expensive plans typically use the product more.	Unit cost shows whether the per unit price is high or low in comparison to other customers.
Unit value	Use/MRR	Customers on more expensive plans typically use the product more.	Unit value shows whether use is high or low relative to the price paid.

Table 7.2   Summary of ratio metrics for customer engagement *(continued)*

Name	Ratio	Correlation	Information
Utilization	Use/Allowance	Customers on a plan that allows a lot of use usually use more.	Utilization shows whether use is close to the limit.
Success rate (or efficiency)	Successes/ Total attempts	Customers who attempt something a lot succeed more by sheer persistence.	Success rate shows whether the customer is relatively successful or efficient at an activity.
Percent of total	Part/Whole	Assume that some activity falls into mutually exclusive categories: customers who use the product a lot use a lot in all categories.	Percent of total shows whether a customer is relatively high or low in the categories, apart from the overall level of use.
Percentage change	(Current metric/ Past metric) –1.0	If a customer uses the product a lot now, they probably used it a lot in the past.	Percentage change shows whether use is high or low relative to the customer's own history.

A lot of interesting ratio metrics are not listed in table 7.2, so think of this table as being illustrative rather than exhaustive. But the table should be enough to get you going.

Summary

- Metrics created from ratios of other metrics can reveal how the balance between behaviors is related to churn and engagement.
- Ratio metrics are usually less correlated with the numerator and denominator metrics than those metrics are with each other.
- A recurring unit cost metric is the ratio of some cost of using the product (such as paying MRR or watching ads) to an outcome of using the product (such as making calls or viewing content).
- Churn usually increases with increasing values of a recurring unit cost metric, even when the nonunit recurring cost metric itself (plain MRR or number of ads) does not show increasing churn.
- The ratio of a downstream event in some process to an upstream event can be viewed as an efficiency measure. Examples include transactions per customer or saves per edit of a document.
- The ratio of the completion, or successful outcome, of a process to the number of attempts is a success rate. An accepted request rate is an example of such a metric.
- Churn can increase or decrease with increased values on efficiency and success ratio metrics, depending on the characteristics of the business.
- A percent of total ratio is a special case of a ratio in which the numerator is part of an overall total represented by the denominator. Examples include percentage

of calls made to different regions and percentage of shows viewed in different categories (Action, Comedy, Drama, and so on).

- Percent of total metrics can be used to understand how the balance of behavior in different categories relates to churn and engagement when the level in all categories is correlated.

- A percentage change metric is the ratio of the change in a metric value over some period of time to the value of the metric at the start of the time period. An example is the percentage change in the number of logins from one month to the next.

- Percentage change metrics can be used to analyze whether increases or decreases in any behavior predict future churn and engagement.

- Time since last event is a metric for understanding how periods of inactivity relate to future churn.

- Active users can be measured when a product tracks multiple user IDs.

- Active users can be used to form a variety of ratio metrics, such as license utilization, which is the ratio of active users to the number of users allowed.

- Any count metric measured on a time period can be described as an average for a shorter time period or as an estimate for a longer time period.

- A single scaled metric can combine estimates for new accounts with averages for mature accounts. This method is the best way to calculate count and total metrics for analyzing churn and engagement.

Part 3

Special weapons and tactics

I call the techniques in this part "special" weapons and tactics because not all companies need to use them. In my opinion, however, all companies fighting churn need a great set of customer metrics. To someone who trained as a data scientist, this may be a surprise because the subjects in this part include what most people think of as the heart of data science: prediction! But I explained back in chapter 1 that churn is different: predicting churn has only a few use cases, whereas there are many more use cases for great customer metrics. Nevertheless, prediction can be an important weapon in your arsenal, with a few wrinkles unique to churn.

If you have never worked on any predictive analytics before, you might find that chapters 8 and 9 have a steep learning curve. That said, these chapters do cover all the basics, and I think anyone who learned the techniques in parts 1 and 2 can master the part 3 techniques as well. But if you have no experience in predictive analytics, you may need to put in a little extra time and use some of the recommended online resources.

Chapter 8 teaches you how to forecast churn probability with logistic regression. With this technique, you can see the combined influence of all factors that affect churn and rank them in importance. Regression also gives you a forecast that you can use to calculate customer lifetime value.

Chapter 9 goes over how to measure the accuracy of churn forecasts; the usual rules don't apply to churn. This chapter also introduces machine learning, which you can use to get the most accurate forecasts possible. But you'll also see that the great customer metrics you worked so hard on in part 2 begin to pay off in forecasting accuracy.

Chapter 10 is a standalone chapter on using demographics and firmographics in the fight against churn. You can't change a customer into someone different from who they are, but you may be able to find more customers similar to your best ones. This chapter shows you how.

Forecasting churn

8

This chapter covers

- Predicting the probability of customer churn with logistic regression
- Understanding the relative influence of different behaviors on churn
- Checking the calibration of your forecasts
- Using churn forecasts to estimate customer lifetime and lifetime value

At this point, you know all the steps necessary to analyze churn and to design great customer metrics. Those metrics will allow businesspeople to make targeted interventions that should reduce the churn on their product. And those things are the most important for most products, so that's why the techniques beginning in this chapter (part 3 of the book) can be considered to be special or extra tactics: you can use them if you need to, but they are not always necessary. The most important thing in fighting churn is that the business should make data-driven decisions when segmenting customers and making targeted interventions.

This chapter is devoted to the topic of forecasting how likely customers are to churn, given the combination of all their behaviors. So far, I have showed you only how to evaluate customer health, one behavior at a time, by looking at churn rates in metric cohorts. But how do you integrate these multiple views of the customer? What if a customer is in a top cohort with a low churn risk for one behavior but in one of the bottom cohorts with a much higher churn risk for another behavior? Given the usual correlations between customer behaviors, what I've described is an edge case, but it still would be good to know how to handle it.

A related question that would be good to know the answer to is which behavior makes the most difference for customer health and churn. The relative importance of different behaviors can be an important piece of information in deciding which churn-reducing interventions or product modifications to pursue. So far, you know only how to look at this information qualitatively by comparing the relationships in cohort plots. That approach can work for a few metrics (or groups of metrics), but if you have a lot of metrics, you need a more systematic approach. This chapter teaches you how to use the statistical model known as logistic regression to answer these questions.

> **DEFINITION**   *Logistic regression* is a statistical model that forecasts the probability of an event occurring, given multiple factors that can influence the outcome.

Logistic regression is frequently used to evaluate medical data to discover the cause of disease. It is appropriate for churn because you are discovering the causes of good and bad customer health. Because logistic regression is the only regression model covered in this book, I sometimes use the term *regression* for short. This chapter is designed as follows:

- The first section (section 8.1) shows you the concepts behind logistic regression.
- Section 8.2 reviews all the data-preparation steps that you have used throughout the book to make sure you are ready to run the logistic regression algorithm.
- Section 8.3 shows you how to run the regression algorithm and interpret the results.
- Section 8.4 teaches you how to make forecasts using the model you created.
- Section 8.5 explains some pitfalls and problems you may encounter along the way.
- The final section (section 8.6) is devoted to customer lifetime estimation and measuring customer lifetime value, which are derived from churn probability forecasts.

8.1   Forecasting churn with a model

I start with a summary of the theory of logistic regression for readers who are not familiar with it. The explanations are for the specific case of predicting churn and retention.

8.1.1   Probability forecasts with a model

When I talk about a customer churn- or retention-probability forecast, I am talking about an estimate that is made individually for each customer, like a metric. But unlike a metric, a churn-probability forecast is not a measurement of something that happened: it's an estimate of the probability that something will happen in the future, namely, churn.

> **DEFINITION** A *churn probability forecast* for a customer is a prediction that if you have a cohort of customers with that same forecast, you expect the percentage given by the probability to churn. A churn probability forecast never tells you whether a single customer definitively will or won't churn.

Given that the forecast is specific to an individual customer, like a metric, it is a bit counterintuitive that the definition of the forecast probability is not about whether the individual customer will be retained or will churn. Understand that for an individual customer, things can always go either way. Although I won't mention this fact most of the time, a time horizon is implied in the forecast. To be precise, the forecast is the probability a customer will churn during the lead time before their next renewal (defined in chapter 4). This timing is implied because that is how the historical dataset was designed, and that dataset will be used to determine the forecast.

A forecast is a statement about how a group of similar customers would behave. Even if a customer is forecast to have a 99% chance to churn, it doesn't mean that they will definitely churn. It means that in a group of 100 such customers, you expect 99 to churn during the lead time before their next renewal. The point is that if you are looking at an individual customer, that customer may turn out to be the one who stays. (If you forecast a 99% chance of churn, there may be problems with your data; see section 8.5.) The same applies for retention: if you forecast a retention probability, and you have a hypothetical cohort of customers with a 90% retention probability, you expect 90% of the cohort to be retained.

I'm going to teach you everything in terms of forecasting retention probabilities because that context is easier to understand. Churn probabilities will be found from 100% minus the retention probability. I'll point out why forecasting retention is easier in section 8.1.2.

You're going to learn to make forecasts with a mathematical forecasting model: logistic regression. A model in this context means something that works like the real thing, but I want to caution you against thinking that the model is real. The model assumes that customer engagement and retention work a certain way, but it does so because the assumptions work for the purpose of forecasting, not because the world is that way. Suspend your disbelief. Remember that the model is a construct that closely matches reality, but not every part of it is real, and not every part needs to be perfect for the model as a whole to be useful.

8.1.2 Engagement and retention probability

The first concept of logistic regression in forecasting retention is that increasing customer engagement leads to increasing chance of retention. By *engagement*, I mean a subjective state that cannot be measured. Different people have different ideas, but following is my working definition of engagement.

DEFINITION   *Engagement* is a state of involvement and commitment.

For this discussion, *involvement* means use of the product, and *commitment* means likelihood of renewal. It makes sense that more engagement should lead to a higher chance of retention. For now, don't worry that engagement itself is a subjective state.

A key feature of the model for forecasting churn and retention is that the relationship between engagement and retention is subject to diminishing returns on the effect of the engagement. Even the most engaged customer has a chance of churning. A consequence (or requirement) is that the more engaged a customer is, the less difference additional engagement makes in further increasing retention probability. The converse should also be true: the less engaged a customer is, the less likely they are to be retained. But even the least-engaged customers still have a chance of being retained. Also, the less engaged a customer is, the less difference further decreases in engagement make in the probability of retention. Figure 8.1 illustrates this concept.

The diminishing relationship between engagement and retention at both the high and low ends makes an S curve like the one shown in figure 8.1. The rate of change of the probability must peak in the middle ranges of engagement and flatten at the extremes.

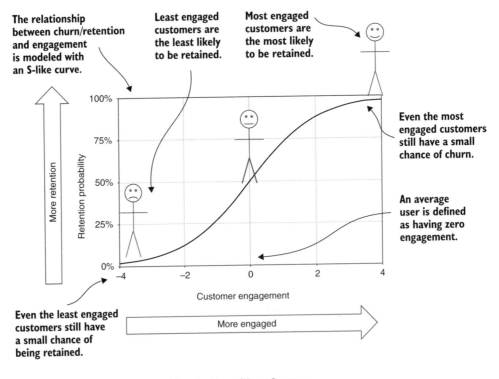

Figure 8.1   Mapping engagement to retention with an S curve

8.1.3 Engagement and customer behavior

In my explanation of the relationship between engagement and retention, I spoke of a customer's engagement as though it were measurable, like any other behavioral metric. That definition is a good one for a model because the way I framed it, engagement is the underlying driver of retention and churn. But engagement still is not measurable. Logistic regression solves the problem this way: you believe that engagement exists, even if you cannot measure it, so you assume that engagement can be estimated from behavioral measurements and churn observations.

> **TAKEAWAY** Customer engagement cannot be measured directly, but you can estimate it from customer metrics for the purpose of predicting churn probability by matching the observed churn with the S curve.

If that explanation seems like circular reasoning, you have to accept that it is a model; you'll see in a moment that it works. The process of estimating churn and retention probabilities has intermediate steps for estimating engagement for each customer. The model assumes that engagement measurement takes a form like a metric score. Engagement estimates will be numbers, mostly in the range of –4 to 4, and the average engagement of your customers will be set at zero. As in a metric score, a positive number means above-average engagement, and a negative number means below-average engagement. This definition is arbitrary, given that you can't measure engagement, but it is convenient for making forecasts.

Figure 8.2 illustrates the model for estimating engagement from behavior and turning it into a retention-probability estimate. The key concept is that each behavioral metric score is multiplied by an engagement strength, which I call a *weight*, that captures how much the behavior contributes to engagement. The weight can also be negative, indicating that the behavior is associated with disengagement and an increase in churn rather than retention. Overall engagement is the sum of the contribution of each behavior.

> **TAKEAWAY** Customer engagement is estimated from a model in which engagement weights are multiplied by the scores for each metric and then added together.

The forecasting model in figure 8.2 consists of the following steps:

1. Begin with scores for all your metrics.
2. Assume that each metric has a weight that represents how strongly the values of the metric score contribute to engagement.
   - The engagement contribution of each metric score is the engagement weight for that metric multiplied by the score value.
   - The total engagement estimate is the sum of all the contributions from each metric.
3. After calculating the total engagement, get the retention probability by applying the S curve to the engagement estimate.

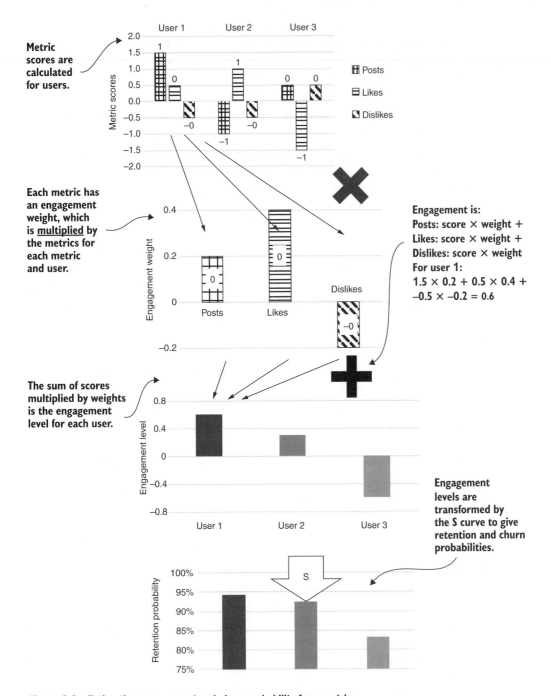

Metric scores are calculated for users.

Each metric has an engagement weight, which is <u>multiplied</u> by the metrics for each metric and user.

Engagement is:
Posts: score × weight +
Likes: score × weight +
Dislikes: score × weight
For user 1:
1.5 × 0.2 + 0.5 × 0.4 +
−0.5 × −0.2 = 0.6

The sum of scores multiplied by weights is the engagement level for each user.

Engagement levels are transformed by the S curve to give retention and churn probabilities.

Figure 8.2   Estimating engagement and churn probability from metrics

The weights are also referred to as *coefficients* because a coefficient is a number that multiplies another number. The Python packages use the term *coefficient*, but I prefer *weight* because it is a more functional description (keeping with the goal of communicating with businesspeople in plain English).

This approach of estimating engagement from behavior sidesteps the problem that engagement can't be measured by assuming engagement follows a simple model. But a new problem is that you don't know what the engagement weight of your various metrics ought to be. I suggest that you replace one thing you can't measure—the level of engagement of a customer—with another thing that you can't measure—the engagement weights of behaviors.

If this approach seems like cheating, I want to remind you (again) that this scenario isn't real; it's a model that's going to work as though it's real. The problem of finding the engagement weights is solved by the logistic regression algorithm itself (see section 8.3). But before you learn how to run the algorithm and find the weights, you need to learn more about matching the prediction model to the details of your data. Section 8.1.4 shows how the regression model exactly fits the churn rate of your customers.

8.1.4 An offset matches observed churn rates to the S curve

One important detail to understand about the model is how the S curve can match products with a particular churn rate. First, recall that the average on each metric score is 0 because that's how the metric scores were defined. As a result, a perfectly average user has zero engagement in the model. Because engagement comes from multiplying weights by scores, and all the scores are 0, the engagement must also be zero. Figure 8.3 illustrates this concept.

As shown in the figure, a default version of an S curve would match 0 engagement with 50% retention probability (and 50% churn probability) because it is defined symmetrically. But that result would be correct only if the average user of a product really had a 50% retention probability. There has to be a way to adjust the model so that an average user has a realistic probability forecast for retention and churn.

The solution to this problem comes from another feature of the model. The S relationship between engagement and retention probability can include an offset so that an average user maps to an average probability of retention. The offset means that the S curve is shifted to the left or right relative to the default. The offset is also referred to as an intercept because the offset determines where the S curve intersects the zero engagement line. (*Intercept* means the value at an intersection. The Python packages use the term *intercept*, but I use *offset* because it describes what the quantity does, not only what it is.)

In figure 8.3, it is assumed that the retention probability is around 90%. In that case, the S curve must be offset by around 2 so that a user with 0 (average) engagement ends up with a retention probability forecast around 90%.

> **TAKEAWAY** The logistic regression model includes an offset that allows a standard S curve to match any average retention probability.

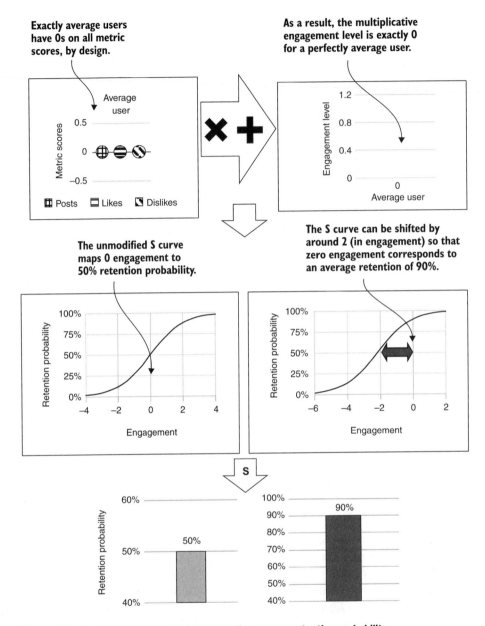

Figure 8.3   An offset matches the S curve to the average retention probability

Once again, you may be wondering how to come up with the correct value for this new variable. This problem is also taken care of by the logistic regression algorithm. Together, the engagement weights and the S-curve offset are the main outputs of the algorithm, and that's all you need to make a realistic churn- and retention-probability forecast for your customers.

8.1.5 *The logistic regression probability calculation*

Now that I've explained all the concepts, I will show you the set of equations that define the mathematical model. Like the rest of the math in this book, this math is designed to help the mathematically inclined in their understanding. If that's not you, don't worry. If you have understood the concepts explained up to now, you'll be ready to do your forecasting whether or not you study the equations in this section.

These equations use vectors, in the sense of a list of numbers, to represent the metrics and the engagement weights. A bar above the variable indicates that it is a vector, so I will use $\overline{m}$ to stand for the vector of all the metric scores for one account and $\overline{w}$ to represent the vector of all the engagement weights. In that case, the engagement (E) of an account is given by equation 8.1:

$$E = \overline{m} \cdot \overline{w} \qquad \text{(Equation 8.1)}$$

The dot ($\cdot$) indicates the dot product operation, which is the element-by-element multiplication of the two vectors followed by the summing of the results of those multiplications. The dot product is the procedure that I described when explaining how the metric scores are combined with the engagement weights to get the total engagement for an account. Given the engagement, the rest of the model for the retention probability, P, is

$$P_{retain} = S(E + \mathit{off}) \qquad \text{(Equation 8.2)}$$

where E is the engagement, *off* is the offset, and $S(...)$ is the S-curve function. The S-curve function referenced in equation 8.2 is given by equation 8.3:

$$S(x) = \frac{1}{1 + e^{-x}} \qquad \text{(Equation 8.3)}$$

Note that the little e in equation 8.3 stands for the number known as the base of the natural logarithm, or $e \approx 2.72$. But you don't need to learn what the natural logarithm is to understand equation 8.3. To understand it, first remember the following facts about exponentiation (or taking a number to a power):

- For any positive number greater than 1.0, if you exponentiate it with a positive value, it gets bigger. (The only thing you need to know about e is that it is a positive number greater than 1.0.)
- If you exponentiate such a number with a negative value, it gets smaller because exponentiation with a negative value is 1 divided by the number exponentiated with a positive power: $x^{-y} = 1.0 / x^{y}$.

In equation 8.3, x represents the engagement plus the offset, and x has a negative sign on the variable for the exponentiation of e. The negative sign reverses the usual effect of exponentiation so that when *x* gets bigger, the *e* term gets smaller, and when *x* is negative, the *e* term gets bigger. As a result:

- When *x* (engagement) is positive and the *e* term is small, the denominator gets close to 1 and the fraction also goes toward 1, which corresponds to retention going to 100% when engagement is high.
- When *x* (engagement) is negative and the *e* term is large, the denominator gets large and the fraction goes toward 0, which corresponds to retention going to 0% when engagement is low.

Understanding equation 8.3 doesn't have anything to do with using *e* and natural logarithms. There is a reason why equation 8.3 uses the base of the natural logarithm and not some other number, and that reason has to do with technical details in the logistic regression algorithm, not because it is necessary to produce the S curve.

This section completes the explanation of the model for churn-probability forecasting going from metric scores to forecasting retention probabilities. The next thing you need to know is how to come up with the engagement weights for the metrics and the offset to use in the S curve. That task is handled by the logistic regression algorithm when you run it on your data.

8.2   *Reviewing data preparation*

Before I show you the details of running the logistic regression algorithm, let's review all the steps that you took to produce the data. This review will ensure that your data is ready for what comes next, and having these steps fresh in your mind will help you when it comes time to make your probability forecasts.

The first step in preparation is exporting a slightly modified version of the dataset. In chapter 7, you experimented with a few versions of the metric for the rare event unfriend_per_month. To avoid confusion, you will now export a version of the dataset that has only the final scaled version of the unfriend_per_month metric. In a case study of a real company, you will also experiment with different metric versions and then choose a subset for your dataset. This final dataset also omits the account_tenure measurement. In a real service, you should include account_tenure in your analysis, but it is not meaningful for the simulation. Because you have already seen the dataset export several times (in listings 4.5, 4.6, and 7.2), I do not present this SQL in the book. The code is in the chapter 8 listings folder, if you want to take a look. To match the results presented in this chapter, you should extract the new version of the dataset with the following command line for the Python wrapper program:

```
fight-churn/listings/run_churn_listing.py --chapter 8 --listing 0
```

Figure 8.4 shows a summary of all the functions used to prepare the data after it is exported from the database. The steps are as follows:

1 Calculate a set of summary statistics about the data. Those summary statistics are saved in a table (listing 5.2).

2 Use the summary statistics to convert the metrics from their natural scale to scores. This step saves the second version of the dataset and another table of the mean and standard deviations used to create the scores, as well as the metrics transformed for skew and fat tails (listing 7.5).

3 Find correlated metrics that are combined in groups, and save a loading matrix that explains the groupings. This matrix is used to implement the averaging of scores (listing 6.4).

4 Use the loading matrix to create the third and final version of a dataset in which correlated metric scores are averaged (listing 6.3; I taught this before listing 6.4 so that you would understand what the loading matrix was before you set out to create one).

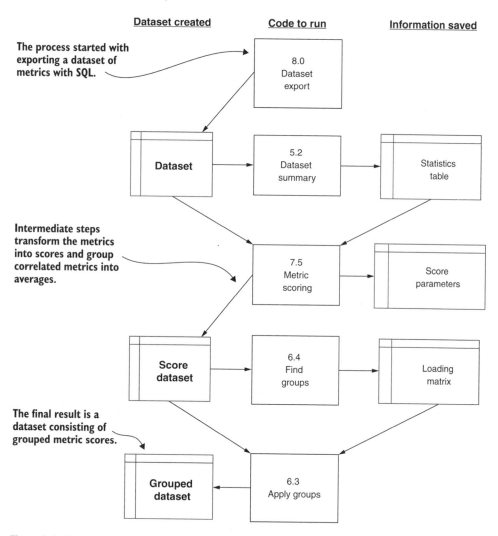

Figure 8.4 Data preparation steps for churn analysis and forecasting

Listing 8.1 shows all the steps in the data preparation, and you can use listing 8.1 to prepare your own data if you have not taken all these steps already. Chapter 7 did not explicitly tell you to rerun your statistics, scores, or grouping. If you were following the instructions as they were given, this listing is for you. Running listing 8.1 creates several items in your output directory: two additional versions of the dataset, and three tables of statistics and derived parameters used in the process.

Listing 8.1 Data preparation listings combined

```
from listing_5_2_dataset_stats import dataset_stats
from listing_7_5_fat_tail_scores import fat_tail_scores
from listing_6_4_find_metric_groups import find_metric_groups
from listing_6_3_apply_metric_groups import apply_metric_groups
from listing_6_5_ordered_correlation_matrix
    import ordered_correlation_matrix


def prepare_data(data_set_path='',group_corr_thresh=0.55):      ◁──┐ Finds the average,
    dataset_stats(data_set_path)                                     skew, and percentiles
    fat_tail_scores(data_set_path)                                   of the distribution
    find_metric_groups(data_set_path,group_corr_thresh)        ◁──┐ Finds what metrics are
    apply_metric_groups(data_set_path)        ◁────────┐            correlated, and decides
    ordered_correlation_matrix(data_set_path)          │            which to group
```

Converts the data from metrics to scores

Creates a dataset with grouped
metrics averaged together

If you have not performed all these steps, run listing 8.1 with the Python wrapper program and these arguments:

```
fight-churn/listings/run_churn_listing.py --chapter 8 --listing 1
```

When you learned about advanced metrics in chapter 7, the focus was on the motivation and code for the new metrics and testing the relationships to churn. I never demonstrated the final result for correlations and metric groups with all the chapter 7 metrics using the techniques of chapter 6. Figure 8.5 shows the result you should have for the loading matrix, which summarizes the grouping.

If you run the metric grouping algorithm on the dataset from chapter 7 with the default parameters, you should find two multimetric groups, with several metrics remaining independent. The first metric group consists of three metrics representing the most common behaviors: posting, liking, and viewing ads. The second group averages the metrics for messaging, including replies. The metrics that were not correlated enough to go into groups were the metric for unfriending, the advanced metrics for adviews_per_post, days_since_new_friend, and the percentage change in the rate of new friend events.

If running your code returned something that looks like figure 8.5, you are ready to run the examples of logistic regression in section 8.3.1. If you have something else, the most likely explanation is that you did not create all the new metrics in chapter 7.

	metric_group_1	metric_group_2	newfriend_per_month	dislike_per_month	unfriend_per_month	adview_per_post	reply_per_message	like_per_post	post_per_message	unfriend_per_newfriend	dislike_pcnt	newfriend_pcnt_chng	days_since_newfriend
adview_per_month	0.4134	0	0	0	0	0	0	0	0	0	0	0	0
like_per_month	0.4134	0	0	0	0	0	0	0	0	0	0	0	0
post_per_month	0.4134	0	0	0	0	0	0	0	0	0	0	0	0
message_per_month	0	0.6202	0	0	0	0	0	0	0	0	0	0	0
reply_per_month	0	0.6202	0	0	0	0	0	0	0	0	0	0	0
newfriend_per_month	0	0	1.0	0	0	0	0	0	0	0	0	0	0
dislike_per_month	0	0	0	1.0	0	0	0	0	0	0	0	0	0
unfriend_per_month	0	0	0	0	1.0	0	0	0	0	0	0	0	0
adview_per_post	0	0	0	0	0	1.0	0	0	0	0	0	0	0
reply_per_message	0	0	0	0	0	0	1.0	0	0	0	0	0	0
like_per_post	0	0	0	0	0	0	0	1.0	0	0	0	0	0
post_per_message	0	0	0	0	0	0	0	0	1.0	0	0	0	0
unfriend_per_newfriend	0	0	0	0	0	0	0	0	0	1.0	0	0	0
dislike_pcnt	0	0	0	0	0	0	0	0	0	0	1.0	0	0
newfriend_pcnt_chng	0	0	0	0	0	0	0	0	0	0	0	1.0	0
days_since_newfriend	0	0	0	0	0	0	0	0	0	0	0	0	1.0

Basic metrics from chapter 3 (rows adview_per_month through dislike_per_month)

Advanced metrics from chapter 7 (rows unfriend_per_month through days_since_newfriend)

There are two multimetric groups.

Other metrics remain separate.

Figure 8.5 Result of running the metric grouping algorithm (listing 6.4) on the simulation dataset with the additional metrics created in chapter 7

To make sure that you have all the metrics, you can use the following two sets of arguments to run the Python wrapper program and generate them now.

The first run of the wrapper program creates the days_since_new_friend, newfriend_pcnt_chng, tenure-scaled version of unfriend_per_month, and metric for the total number of likes and dislikes (labeled as the number of opinions):

```
run_churn_listing.py --chap 7 --listing 3 4 6 8 --insert
```

The second command runs all the versions of the ratio metric to create the adview_per_post, reply_per_message, like_per_post, unfriend_per_newfriend, and dislike_pcnt metrics:

```
run_churn_listing.py --chap 7 --listing 1 --version 1 2 3 4 5 6 --insert
```

After creating all the metrics, you should be able to run listing 8.1 and get the loading matrix shown in figure 8.5.

8.3   *Fitting a churn model*

Now that your data is ready and you know how a regression forecasting model works, it's time to run the algorithm that gives you the weights and the offset to match your data. Finding the weights and offset that match the data is called *fitting* the model.

> **DEFINITION**   Fitting a statistical model means finding the values for the key parameters that make the model match the sample data as closely as possible. Fitting a model is also sometimes called training a model.

I'll show you how to read the results and then how to create them.

8.3.1   *Results of logistic regression*

Figure 8.6 shows the weights and offset resulting from fitting logistic regression on the simulated churn dataset. (This result will be in a file after you run listing 8.2.) Each row in the file shows the result for one metric or group of metrics. The result consists of the following two numbers:

- The engagement weight
- A measurement of the impact of the metric on the retention (churn) probability, which I call the retention impact

The engagement weights are small numbers, typically less than 1, as I suggested earlier. That makes sense, because the multiplication of the engagement weights and the metric scores is going to add up to the total engagement, which has a scale similar to a score. A positive weight indicates that the metric (or group) is associated with increasing engagement, and a negative weight indicates that the metric is associated with reduced retention (increased churn). For this reason, setting up the model to predict retention makes it easier to interpret: a positive number to represent something good is more intuitive than a negative number, and if you had set up the model to predict churn, all the things that increase engagement would have had negative weights.

> **TAKEAWAY**   Forecasting retention probabilities is easier to interpret than forecasting churn probabilities because that way, positive weights in the numeric sense associate with positive outcomes in the sense of engagement.

The measurement of a metric's impact on churn is shown as a percentage change in the retention probability. I will show you the details of the calculation in a moment, but first, I will explain what it means.

> **DEFINITION**   The *retention impact* of a metric or group of metrics is the difference that it makes to the retention probability for a customer to be one standard deviation above the average in this metric, assuming that all the other metrics are exactly average.

If the retention impact for a metric is 2%, a customer who is one standard deviation above average on that metric and average in all the other metrics has a forecast retention probability 2% higher than the average retention probability. That probability is 2% less than the average churn probability, so you can describe it either way, as long as you keep track of the direction of the impact. The churn impact is not a standard metric taught in statistics classes, but I have found it useful in explaining logistic regression models to businesspeople.

> **TAKEAWAY**   The impact of a metric on retention and churn probability is important for communicating regression results to businesspeople.

Remember two other things when you interpret churn and retention impacts:

- If a metric is below average rather than above average, it has approximately an equal and opposite effect on churn rate.

- The cumulative effect of multiple metrics that are above (or below) average has a diminishing effect on churn rate due to the way that the S curve shapes the probability forecast. The same goes for a metric that is more than one standard deviation above average: a metric two standard deviations above average will have less than two times the churn impact shown in the result.

The result for the offset is an extra row at the bottom of figure 8.6: the number in the weight column for the offset is not a weight but the amount of the offset.

Each group (or single metric) gets a weight for engagement impact. The offset is shown last.

The *retain_impact* is how much difference in the retention probability it would make to be one standard deviation above average in this area, assuming a customer was average in all other respects.

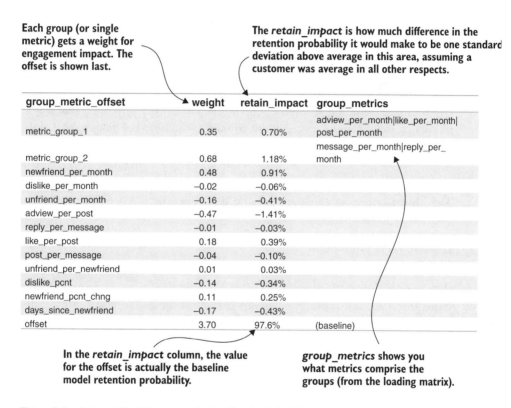

group_metric_offset	weight	retain_impact	group_metrics
metric_group_1	0.35	0.70%	adview_per_month|like_per_month|post_per_month
metric_group_2	0.68	1.18%	message_per_month|reply_per_month
newfriend_per_month	0.48	0.91%	
dislike_per_month	−0.02	−0.06%	
unfriend_per_month	−0.16	−0.41%	
adview_per_post	−0.47	−1.41%	
reply_per_message	−0.01	−0.03%	
like_per_post	0.18	0.39%	
post_per_message	−0.04	−0.10%	
unfriend_per_newfriend	0.01	0.03%	
dislike_pcnt	−0.14	−0.34%	
newfriend_pcnt_chng	0.11	0.25%	
days_since_newfriend	−0.17	−0.43%	
offset	3.70	97.6%	(baseline)

In the *retain_impact* column, the value for the offset is actually the baseline model retention probability.

group_metrics shows you what metrics comprise the groups (from the loading matrix).

Figure 8.6 Output of logistic regression for the simulated dataset

I previously suggested that the offset would be about 2 for around a 90% retention rate. In figure 8.6, you see an offset of 3.7 for the simulation retention rate, which is around 95.4%. The number in the retain_impact column for the offset is the retention probability forecast for a perfectly average customer. Recall that a perfectly average customers has zero on all the metric scores, so in equation 8.2, for the probability ($P_{retain} = S(E + off)$), the only term is the offset.

Note that the forecast probability for the perfectly average customer is 2.4% (100% − 97.6%, the retention rate in figure 8.6), but the churn rate in the simulation is around

4.6% (see chapter 5, figure 5.12). You probably would expect a perfectly average customer to have a churn probability equal to the overall or average churn rate, but this is not quite the case.

NOTE   The forecast churn probability for a perfectly average customer normally is close to the overall churn rate but not equal to it.

Here is how the churn impact is calculated. If a customer is perfectly average, they have zero in all scores, and the probability of retention becomes equal to equation 8.4:

$$P_{retain} = S(off) = \frac{1}{1 + e^{-off}} \qquad \textbf{(Equation 8.4)}$$

On the other hand, if a customer is perfectly average in all respects except for being one standard deviation above average on a single metric or group, the multiplication of the weights by the scores reduces to exactly the weight for the one score on which they are one standard deviation above average. In that case, if the variable w stands for the value of the one weight in the engagement equation, equation 8.4 leads to equation 8.5:

$$P_{retain} = S(w + off) = \frac{1}{1 + e^{(-w - off)}} \qquad \textbf{(Equation 8.5)}$$

The churn impact is calculated as the difference between equation 8.4 and 8.5 for each engagement weight.

8.3.2 *Logistic regression code*

Listing 8.2 provides the code for logistic regression analysis. This listing is a lot more than simply fitting the regression, which is only two lines. The rest of the code prepares the data, does some analysis of the result, and saves everything. The listing is divided into seven functions, described here in the order in which they are called:

- `logistic_regression_analysis` *(the main function)*—After calling a helper function to create the data, the function creates the sklearn `LogisticRegression` object and calls the `fit` method to run the model fitting. Then it calls more helper functions to analyze and save the results.
- `prepare_data`—The function loads the saved dataset of grouped scores and separates the columns indicating churn. The churn indicator is reversed so that it indicates retention. Using the grouped scores is an option controlled by a default argument because (in chapter 9) it is used to load other files.
- `save_regression_summary`—The function makes a `DataFrame` where one column is the regression model weights and offset, and the other column is the one standard deviation impact. Note that this method (and the following two) have an optional extension argument that is used to save additional versions in chapter 9; this is the table of data illustrated in figure 8.6. It calls `calculate_impacts` to get the churn impact numbers and then takes the weights from the `Logistic-Regression` object; these values are stored in a field called `coef_`. (coef is short

for *coefficient*, which is a generic term for a number that multiplies another number.) These results are combined with the names of metrics and groups in a DataFrame and then saved.

- calculate_impacts—This function calculates the impact of a one standard deviation score on the retention probability, using the equations described earlier. It calls the s_curve function on the offset, which is the variable intercept_ of the regression object, to get the baseline retention probability. It also calls the s_curve function on the difference between the offset and the weights, which is stored in the variable coef_ of the regression object. The result of the function is both the vector of retention impacts and the baseline retention probability.
- s_curve—This function implements equation 8.2.
- save_regression_model—This function saves the regression object to a pickle file so that it can be reloaded and used to forecast later.
- save_dataset_predictions—This function calculates what the churn and retention probabilities would have been on the observations in the dataset used to create the model. It calls the predict_proba function on the regression object with the dataset as the parameter. The results are saved in a .csv file, which is explained further in section 8.3.5.

You should run listing 8.2, using the Python wrapper program in the usual way with these arguments:

```
fight-churn/listings/run_churn_listing.py --chapter 8 --listing 2
```

The program prints a few lines of output telling you where it saved the three results, which are

- The file containing the weights and one standard deviation impact
- The file containing the pickle of the model
- The file containing the historical churn and retention probabilities

You should open the summary file, churnsim_logreg_summary.csv, and confirm that it is similar to figure 8.5. It won't be exactly the same because the data is randomly simulated. I talk more about the results in the historical probability file in section 8.3.5 and how to use the pickle file in section 8.4.

Listing 8.2 Logistic regression analysis

```
import pandas as pd
import numpy as np
import os
from sklearn.linear_model import LogisticRegression
from math import exp
import pickle

def logistic_regression_analysis(data_set_path=''):
  X,y = prepare_data(data_set_path)          Calls the helper
                                             function prepare_data
```

Creates the object for the right kind of regression

Puts data into the form needed for the regression

Loads the dataset, setting the index

```
retain_reg = LogisticRegression(fit_intercept=True,
    solver='liblinear', penalty='l1')
retain_reg.fit(X, y)
save_regression_summary(data_set_path,retain_reg)
save_regression_model(data_set_path,retain_reg)
save_dataset_predictions(data_set_path,retain_reg,X)
```

Fits the model coefficients based on the churn data

Calls save_regression _summary to save a summary of the result

Calls save_dataset_predictions to make predictions

Calls save_regression_model to save the regression object

```
def prepare_data(data_set_path,ext='_groupscore',
                     as_retention=True):
    score_save_path = data_set_path.replace('.csv', '{}.csv'.format(ext))
    assert os.path.isfile(score_save_path), 'You must run listing 6.3 first'
    grouped_data =
        pd.read_csv(score_save_path,index_col=[0,1])
    y = grouped_data['is_churn'].astype(np.bool)
    if as_retention: y=~y
    X = grouped_data.drop(['is_churn'],axis=1)
    return X,y
```

Separates the outcome and converts it to True for retention

Separates the metrics

The churn of a perfectly average customer

```
def calculate_impacts(retain_reg):
    average_retain=s_curve(-retain_reg.intercept_)
    one_stdev_retains=np.array(
        [ s_curve(-retain_reg.intercept_-c)
         for c in  retain_reg.coef_[0]])
    one_stdev_impact =
        one_stdev_retains - average_retain
    return one_stdev_impact, average_retain

def s_curve(x):
    return 1.0 - (1.0/(1.0+exp(-x)))
```

The impact of being one standard deviation above average

For every coefficient, calculates the impact

Impact is probability difference for one standard deviation above average.

Reuses the metrics in each group in the summary

Creates a DataFrame combining the results

```
def save_regression_summary(data_set_path,
                            retain_reg,ext=''):
    one_stdev_impact,average_retain =
        calculate_impacts(retain_reg)
    group_lists = pd.read_csv(
                        data_set_path.replace('.csv', '_groupmets.csv'),
                        index_col=0)
    coef_df = pd.DataFrame.from_dict(
        {'group_metric_offset':  np.append(group_lists.index,'offset'),
         'weight': np.append(retain_reg.coef_[0],retain_reg.intercept_),
         'retain_impact' : np.append(one_stdev_impact,average_retain),
         'group_metrics' : np.append(group_lists['metrics'],'(baseline)')})
    save_path =
        data_set_path.replace('.csv', '_logreg_summary{}.csv'.format(ext))
    coef_df.to_csv(save_path, index=False)
    print('Saved coefficients to ' + save_path)
```

Saves the object by pickling it

```
def save_regression_model(data_set_path,retain_reg,ext=''):
    pickle_path =
        data_set_path.replace('.csv', '_logreg_model{}.pkl'.format(ext))
    with open(pickle_path, 'wb') as fid:
        pickle.dump(retain_reg, fid)
    print('Saved model pickle to ' + pickle_path)
```

```
def save_dataset_predictions(data_set_path,
                                retain_reg, X,ext=''):
    predictions = retain_reg.predict_proba(X)
    predict_df = pd.DataFrame(predictions,
                              index=X.index,
                              columns=['churn_prob','retain_prob'])
    predict_path =
        data_set_path.replace('.csv', '_predictions{}.csv'.format(ext))
    predict_df.to_csv(predict_path,header=True)
    print('Saved dataset predictions to ' + predict_path)
```

Makes a new DataFrame and saves the predictions → `predict_df = pd.DataFrame(predictions,`

`predict_proba` **predicts both churn and retention** ← `predictions = retain_reg.predict_proba(X)`

The `LogisticRegression` object in listing 8.2 takes a few parameters. `fit_intercept` `=True` tells the logistic regression that you are going to include an offset in the model. It's optional because there are other uses of logistic regression in which you would not include an offset. The other parameters, `solver='liblinear'` and `penalty='l1'`, control what method is used to find the weights and the offset. You can use different methods to fit the model, but this book focuses on the application of logistic regression to fighting churn (and I won't go into details). These parameters correspond to the method known as ridge regression (also known as Tikhonov regularization), and it is easy to find additional explanations of this in statistics textbooks or online.

> **DEFINITION** *Ridge regression* is a modern method of fitting regression parameters that performs well when many metrics can have correlation.

The fact that ridge regression works well when a large number of metrics can be somewhat correlated makes it suitable for the typical data used for customer churn. You learn more about ridge regression and the parameters for the `LogisticRegression` object in chapter 9. But first, let's talk about how to explain the regression results to your business colleagues.

8.3.3 Explaining logistic regression results

The regression result shows you which metric or group of related metrics has the biggest impact on churn and retention. This finding is an important one to share with your business colleagues because it is an objective estimate of what behaviors or aspects of the product cause the most engagement (and disengagement) with your customers. The results for both the weight estimate and the retention probability impact show the relative importance; both tell the same story about what has the biggest impact. This result is illustrated in figure 8.7, which shows the weights and impact on retention ordered from most positive for retention to most negative for retention.

In figure 8.7, you can sort by either weight or retention impact, and the order is the same, which makes sense if you consider the shape of the S curve. More engagement always leads to higher retention probability, so the bigger the impact on engagement (which is what the weight represents), the more impact on retention probability.

It's important to understand the weights from the regression, but I don't recommend talking about them with businesspeople. To explain the impact of the different behaviors on retention to your business colleagues, I recommend that you use only

group_metric_offset	weight	retain_impact
metric_group_2	0.68	1.18%
newfriend_per_month	0.48	0.91%
metric_group_1	0.35	0.70%
like_per_post	0.18	0.39%
newfriend_pcnt_chng	0.11	0.25%
unfriend_per_newfriend	0.01	0.03%
reply_per_message	−0.01	−0.03%
dislike_per_month	−0.02	−0.06%
post_per_message	−0.04	−0.10%
dislike_pcnt	−0.14	−0.34%
unfriend_per_month	−0.16	−0.41%
days_since_newfriend	−0.17	−0.43%
adview_per_post	−0.47	−1.41%

You can sort the metrics by either weight or retention impact, and the order is the same.

Figure 8.7   Comparison of regression coefficients and retention probability impact

the impact on retention probability. The engagement and weights used by the regression are abstract concepts but don't exist, and this can be confusing. The benefit of using the impact on retention probability is that the probability of retention is a concrete business metric that people already understand from the retention rate.

Before you explain the impact of the metrics on retention and churn, you need to make sure that the businesspeople understand the following concepts:

- What a probability is and what your product's churn and retention rates are. In this area particularly, make sure that people understand the following:
  - The churn rate is equivalent to a probability.
  - The churn and retention probabilities add up to 100%.
- What a standard deviation is, in a general sense. Most people have heard of standard deviation but don't have a concrete working knowledge of it. They need to understand that someone who is one standard deviation above average is noticeably above average but not extremely so. They also need to understand that you can talk about being below average in standard deviations too.

Figure 8.8 demonstrates a good way to present this result to businesspeople: a bar chart. Putting the retention impact in a bar chart makes seeing the relative importance easy. I also recommend sorting the metrics and groups by importance from most positive to most negative. Label the metric groups with descriptive names.

The reason I like to show a bar chart to businesspeople to explain retention probability is that a metric or behavior that is good for engagement is shown as a positive number, whereas a metric or behavior that is bad for engagement is shown as a negative number. At the same time, it's convenient to talk in terms of the impact on the churn probability for individual customers. If you find that being one standard deviation above average in social feeds use leads to a 2% increase in retention probability,

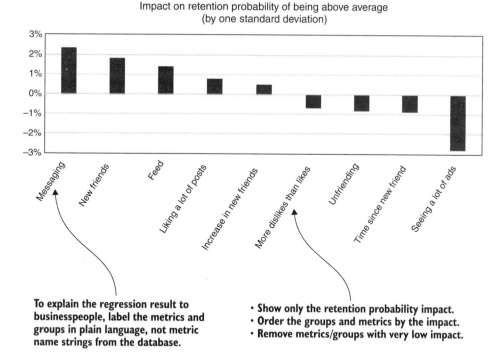

Figure 8.8 Bar chart explaining the impact of behaviors on churn probability

you're more likely to say that it decreases a customer's churn probability from 10% to 8%, rather than increasing the retention probability from 90% to 92%. The impact is more tangible in terms of the churn probability, which is a smaller number.

After you have shown the businesspeople the bar chart demonstrating the impact of being above average in behavior, you should make sure to explain the following additional facts to them:

- Being below average has approximately the equal and opposite effect as being above average. It's not exactly equal and opposite, but the relative impact of the different metrics will be the same.
- If a customer is multiple standard deviations above average, there are diminishing returns, meaning that each additional standard deviation above average has less impact on the churn or retention probability.
- The same diminishing returns goes for being above average in multiple respects: the combined churn probability reduction will be lower than the sum of the quoted retention probability impacts.

Usually, these points cover most of the questions people have and should give them a good idea of how impactful the different behaviors are for retention and churn.

8.3.4   *Logistic regression case study*

Figure 8.9 shows an example result from the logistic regression case study for Broadly, an SaaS product that helps businesses manage their online presence. About 80 metrics were analyzed in the case study. The two largest groups contain about 20 metrics each, and both groups received strong positive weights in the regression. Five smaller groups and nine metrics remained separate in the grouping, and some of those metrics appeared in earlier case studies in the book, including account_tenure, billing_period, and detractor_rate.

As you can see in figure 8.9, a real case study can have a lot more metrics than a simulation. Although grouping correlated metrics may seem to be unnecessary in the simulation, in a real case study, it is important to group the correlated metrics; otherwise, the result would have too many metrics to make sense. In section 8.4, you'll see another way in which grouping is essential for understanding churn with a large number of metrics.

> **TAKEAWAY**   Grouping correlated metrics helps reduce information overload when there are many metrics in regression analysis.

Another feature of the weights in the Broadly case study is that several metrics and groups have weights that are small, such as 0.01 or 0.03. By comparison, the strongest engagement weights in the table are around 0.6, so those small weights are 1/20th or less of the strong metrics, which is insignificant for engagement. These small weights correspond to metrics where the cohort analysis would have shown no significant relationship to churn as well. You're not going to use those kinds of metrics for segmenting your customers or making any interventions to reduce churn. If the small weights were removed, the result in figure 8.9 would be more manageable but still as meaningful. In chapter 9, you learn how to remove the small and insignificant weights from the regression by using a technique that also maximizes the accuracy of the model.

> **TAKEAWAY**   It's normal for many of your metrics to show relatively small engagement weights, and they correspond to customer metrics that are not significant for churn and retention.

If your data produces a table that looks like figure 8.9, you should definitely remove the low-weight metrics before you make a bar chart. Chapter 9 shows you the best way.

8.3.5   *Calibration and historical churn probabilities*

One other output from listing 8.2 is the regression analysis, which is the result of applying the churn probability forecast model to the dataset. This isn't forecasting because there's no point in making a forecast for something that has already happened; the customers represented by the dataset have already either churned or been retained. I will refer to these outputs for the dataset as being *churn probabilities* rather than forecasts. In any event, it's instructive to look at this output so that you know what to expect when you forecast active customers.

group or metrics	weight	group metrics
metric_group_1	0.16	Customers and Messages: 22 metrics
metric_group_2	0.55	Reviews: 22 metrics
metric_group_3	0.1	6 metrics
metric_group_4	−0.01	3 metrics
metric_group_5	−0.07	3 metrics
metric_group_6	−0.01	2 metrics
metric_group_7	0.07	2 metrics
metric_group_8	0.03	2 metrics
metric_group_9	−0.1	2 metrics
metric_group_10	0.18	2 metrics
metric_group_11	0.06	2 metrics
account_tenure	0.63	
...	0.06	
billing_period	0.34	
...	−0.01	
...	−0.05	
...	0.2	
...	0.01	
...	0.21	
detractor_rate	−0.07	
...	−0.03	
...	0.11	
...	−0.07	
...	−0.19	

The top two groups have around 20 metrics each and strong positive engagement weights.

There are nine other groups, but some have engagement weights only around 0.01.

With 24 metrics and weights, many of them insignificant, a table like this has too much information.

Figure 8.9   Example results from logistic regression for Broadly

Figure 8.10 shows a small sample, which is like the dataset in that each row is for one account and one observation date. But instead of having metrics for the rest of the columns, the figure has one column for churn probability and one column for retention probability. Also, because the dataset is made up of historical observations, a single account can appear more than once on different dates until it churns.

These historical probabilities are also useful for checking the model. One important check of a forecasting model is that the forecasts it produces should correspond closely to the real observed churn rate from your product. This check is called model calibration.

DEFINITION   *Calibration* refers to the degree of correspondence between the estimated probabilities of churn and retention produced by the model and the actual churn experienced by the customers.

Results are ordered by date and account.	account_id	observation _date	churn_prob	retain_prob	Predictions include both churn and retention probabilities.
	12	3/1/20	0.117346	0.882653	
	35	3/1/20	0.026151	0.973848	
	...	...	...	...	
The average is shown for illustration; it is not part of the data file.	12	4/1/20	0.108008	0.891992	
	35	4/1/20	0.015863	0.984136	
	...	...	...	...	
	12	5/1/20	0.070167	0.929832	
	35	5/1/20	0.013329	0.986670	
	...	...	...	...	
		Average	0.0459452	0.9540548	

Figure 8.10   Historical churn probability estimates for the simulated dataset. The average is calculated in a spreadsheet or analysis program (not saved with the dataset).

In section 8.6.2, you'll see how to use churn-probability forecast to estimate customer lifetime value, which can be an important metric in deciding on interventions. As the name implies, customer lifetime value measures how much a customer is worth to you over their lifetime. The customer lifetime value estimates will be accurate only if the model is well calibrated. The same goes for any reasoning about the impacts of behaviors on churn: if the model isn't calibrated, the retention impacts aren't as useful.

The most important check of calibration is that the average churn rate predicted by the model should match the churn rate in the data. Figure 8.11 repeats the churn-rate measurement for the simulated dataset, which was produced from listing 5.2 by running the dataset summary function with the following arguments:

```
run_churn_listing.py --chap 5 --listing 2
```

Comparing the average historical probability from figure 8.10 with the churn rate in figure 8.11, you can see that these figures are close, within 1/100 of a percentage. You should make a similar comparison with your own simulated dataset and with any dataset you work on for a real case study. For datasets with a reasonable number of observations of both churn and retention and without extreme outliers or missing values in the metrics, you should find that the dataset churn rate and the average predicted forecast are always close.

	count	nonzero	mean	The churn rate in the sample dataset is very close to the average forecast from the regression.
is_churn	32316	4.59%	0.04591	

Figure 8.11   Historical churn probability estimates for the simulated dataset produced by using listing 5.2

In figure 8.6, you saw that the churn probability of the average customer was 2.4% (from 100% minus the retention rate, shown to be 97.6% in the figure), not 4.6%; the average customer did not have a churn probability equal to the average churn rate. That's fine. For calibration, you need the average predicted churn probability to match the true churn rate, but the average customer doesn't have to match the average churn rate. In fact, the presence of outlier churn probabilities usually guarantees that the average customer will not have an average churn probability: the average customer usually has a churn probability that is a bit lower than the churn rate, as in the social network simulation.

There are also more advanced ways to measure calibration. As you divided the customers into deciles when making churn cohort plots, for example, you can test calibration in deciles. With that approach, you would order the customers by the predicted cohort average forecast, divide them into 10 cohorts, and then check how the true churn rate in each cohort compares with the cohort average forecast. The result would tell you whether your prediction model is well calibrated to forecast probabilities for customers who are likely or unlikely to churn (customers far from the average). I don't recommend that you do that kind of calibration check routinely, but this technique is a good one to be aware of.

You may want to check calibration with that level of detail if you are planning expensive interventions specifically for high- or low-churn-probability customers. Then it's particularly important to know whether your model was accurate in estimating the churn probability for those customers. As you see in chapter 9, a model can still identify the most and least at-risk customers when the calibration is not perfect.

One last thing to note: calibration is only one measure of how well your model matches the data. Other important measures of the quality of your model are introduced in chapter 9.

8.4 Forecasting churn probabilities

Forecasting means making a prediction about something that hasn't happened yet. In the context of churn, forecasting means taking all of your customers who are currently active and predicting their probability of churning before their next renewal. This section also covers how to prepare data for segmenting with grouped metrics, a topic that was not covered in chapter 6.

8.4.1 Preparing the current customer dataset for forecasting

The first step in forecasting for your current customers is creating a dataset of those customers who are active at the present time, including the most recent measurement of all their metrics. You saw how to do this in chapter 4 when you learned how to extract such a dataset for segmenting the active customers. Then, in chapter 7, you updated the dataset to include more metrics, so you need to update the code to extract the current dataset, as you updated the code to extract the historical dataset at the beginning of this chapter.

Listing 8.3 provides the code to extract the dataset with all the metrics created in chapter 7. This listing is almost like listing 4.6 but has more metrics. The short common table expression at the beginning of the query selects the most recent available date; then the main SELECT statement uses the flattening aggregation trick that you learned in chapter 4 (section 4.6).

There is one new element in listing 8.3: the SELECT is limited to accounts with more than 14 days of tenure. The CTE account_tenures selects all accounts with at least 14 days' tenure, and an inner join in the main SELECT limits the dataset to those customers. This constraint makes sure that customers have been observed for at least a few weeks before their metrics are used. Otherwise, most new customers will have low metrics due to the short observation period.

In chapter 7, you learned that customers with short tenure can get more accurate first-month metric forecasts through scaling. You used that technique to make more accurate estimates of the rare metric unfriend_per_month. For your own case studies, I recommended that you use this pattern for all metrics, and in that case, you would match the two-week minimum for observations. (I did not ask you to recalculate all those metrics to save time.)

Listing 8.3   Revised current dataset

```
WITH metric_date AS          ←┐  This CTE selects the
(                              │  most recent date.
    SELECT  max(metric_time) AS last_metric_time FROM metric
),
account_tenures AS (
    SELECT account_id, metric_value AS account_tenure
    FROM metric m INNER JOIN metric_date ON metric_time =last_metric_time
    WHERE metric_name_id = 8
    AND metric_value >= 14
)                                                          Selects the basic
SELECT s.account_id, metric_time,                          metrics with the
SUM(CASE WHEN metric_name_id=0   THEN metric_value ELSE 0 END)  flattening
    AS like_per_month,                              ←┘     aggregation
SUM(CASE WHEN metric_name_id=1   THEN metric_value ELSE 0 END)
    AS newfriend_per_month,
SUM(CASE WHEN metric_name_id=2   THEN metric_value ELSE 0 END)
    AS post_per_month,
SUM(CASE WHEN metric_name_id=3   THEN metric_value ELSE 0 END)
    AS adview_per_month,
SUM(CASE WHEN metric_name_id=4   THEN metric_value ELSE 0 END)
    AS dislike_per_month,                                  This is the scaled
SUM(CASE WHEN metric_name_id=27 THEN metric_value ELSE 0 END)  metric from
    AS unfriend_per_month,                         ←┘     listing 7.7.
SUM(CASE WHEN metric_name_id=6   THEN metric_value ELSE 0 END)
    AS message_per_month,
SUM(CASE WHEN metric_name_id=7   THEN metric_value ELSE 0 END)
    AS reply_per_month,                                   This is the ratio
SUM(CASE WHEN metric_name_id=21 THEN metric_value ELSE 0 END)  metric from
    AS adview_per_post,                            ←┘     listing 7.1.
SUM(CASE WHEN metric_name_id=30 THEN metric_value ELSE 0 END)
```

```
            AS reply_per_message,
   SUM(CASE WHEN metric_name_id=31 THEN metric_value ELSE 0 END)
            AS like_per_post,
   SUM(CASE WHEN metric_name_id=32 THEN metric_value ELSE 0 END)
            AS post_per_message,
   SUM(CASE WHEN metric_name_id=33 THEN metric_value ELSE 0 END)
            AS unfriend_per_newfriend,
   SUM(CASE WHEN metric_name_id=23 THEN metric_value ELSE 0 END)
            AS dislike_pcnt,
   SUM(CASE WHEN metric_name_id=24 THEN metric_value ELSE 0 END)
            AS newfriend_pcnt_chng,
   SUM(CASE WHEN metric_name_id=25 THEN metric_value ELSE 0 END)
            AS days_since_newfriend
   FROM metric m INNER JOIN metric_date d
         ON m.metric_time =d.last_metric_time
   INNER JOIN subscription s ON m.account_id=s.account_id
   WHERE s.start_date <= d.last_metric_time
   AND (s.end_date >=d.last_metric_time OR s.end_date IS null)
   GROUP BY s.account_id, d.last_metric_time
   ORDER BY s.account_id
```

> This is the percentage change metric from listing 7.4.

> This is the percentage metric from listing 7.1, version 2.

> Selects the metrics for the most recent date

> This is the days_since_event metric from listing 7.6.

> JOIN on subscription to ensure only active accounts.

> **The GROUP BY** aggregation completes the flattening.

You should run listing 8.3, using the Python wrapper program and these arguments:

```
run_churn_listing.py --chap 8 --listing 3
```

Running listing 8.3 saves a dataset of current customers and their metrics in a file. This chapter doesn't contain an example of the output because, by now, you know what a dataset looks like.

In section 8.1, you reviewed all the steps to prepare a dataset before using it in the regression (in particular, see figure 8.4). Those steps were as follows:

1 Calculate statistics on the dataset.
2 Convert metrics to scores using the statistics.
3 Save a score parameter table summarizing the parameters used to make the scores.
4 Find groups using the correlation matrix, and create a loading matrix.
5 Calculate average scores for all the groups, using the loading matrix.

But there is a key difference when repeating the process for the current customer dataset: you don't want to calculate new statistics to convert the metrics into scores. Neither do you want to create a new loading matrix to group the correlated metrics. For the current dataset, you want to repeat the process using the same statistics and loading matrix that you derived from the historical customer dataset when you analyzed it in chapters 5 and 6. You have to reuse the same parameters and loading matrix for the current customers to ensure that every column in the current customer dataset that you put in the regression has the same meaning that the same column had in the historical dataset.

Consider what would happen if you calculated a new loading matrix on the current customer dataset and found a different number of groups. That could happen if the current dataset metrics had correlations different from the historical dataset metrics. You would have no way to map the current customers' grouped metrics to those that the regression expected from fitting on the historical dataset. Even the mean and standard deviation used for scoring should be those calculated on the historical data. Because the mean and standard deviation used for the scaling were not derived from the current customer data, for the current customer scores, the mean may not be exactly zero, and the standard deviation may not be exactly one. But this result is correct as long as those differences reflect the true difference between the current customers and the historical customers. The scoring process for the current customer dataset involves the following four steps:

1 Reload the score parameters saved from the historical customer dataset.
2 Convert the current customer metrics to scores, using the historical dataset statistics.
3 Reload the loading matrix created from the historical dataset.
4 Calculate average group scores for the current customers, using the reloaded loading matrix.

Now you can see a second reason why the listing that made the scores saved all those details in a table: the same information will be needed again if you are going to make churn and retention probability forecasts.

> **TAKEAWAY**   When you prepare the current customer dataset for forecasting, you need to reuse the scoring parameters and loading matrix that you created when you originally analyzed the historical dataset.

Listing 8.4 gives the code to score the current customer dataset. (Again, this chapter does not show an example of the output.) Because listing 8.4 has to reload so much data created by the earlier listings, it contains a function to reload an individual dataset by name and listing number. After loading the current customer dataset and the old score parameters and loading matrix, listing 8.4 performs the following main steps:

1 Validates the inputs by making sure that the metric columns named in the dataset, score parameters, and loading matrix match. These inputs could become out of sync if you are iterating on creating different versions of a dataset and calculating statistics and different versions of the grouping.
2 Transforms the skewed and fat-tailed columns on columns indicated in the score parameter table, using the transforms from listing 7.5.
3 Subtracts the mean from the metrics and divides by the standard deviation, using the mean and standard deviation from the score parameter table. This task is done in the new helper function `score_current_data`.
4 Multiplies the scaled data by the loading matrix to calculate averages for the metric groups. This step happens in the new helper function `group_current_data`.
5 Saves the results.

A final helper function call prepares a version of the dataset for segmenting, which is described after the listing.

Listing 8.4 Rescoring the current dataset

```python
import pandas as pd
import numpy as np
import os
from listing_7_5_fat_tail_scores import
    transform_fattail_columns, transform_skew_columns


def rescore_metrics(data_set_path=''):

    load_mat_df = reload_churn_data(data_set_path,
        'load_mat','6.4',is_customer_data=False)
    score_df = reload_churn_data(data_set_path,
        'score_params','7.5',is_customer_data=False)
    current_data = reload_churn_data(data_set_path,
        'current','8.3',is_customer_data=True)
    assert set(score_df.index.values)==set(current_data.columns.values),
        "Data does not match score params"
    assert set(load_mat_df.index.values)==set(current_data.columns.values),
        "Data does not match load matrix"

    transform_skew_columns(current_data,
        score_df[score_df['skew_score']].index.values)
    transform_fattail_columns(current_data,
        score_df[score_df['fattail_score']].index.values)
    scaled_data = score_current_data(current_data,score_df,data_set_path)
    grouped_data = group_current_data(scaled_data, load_mat_df,data_set_path)
    save_segment_data(grouped_data,current_data,load_mat_df,data_set_path)


def score_current_data(current_data,score_df, data_set_path):
    current_data=current_data[score_df.index.values]
    scaled_data=(current_data-score_df['mean']) /
        score_df['std']
    score_save_path=data_set_path.replace('.csv','_current_scores.csv')
    scaled_data.to_csv(score_save_path,header=True)
    print('Saving score results to %s' % score_save_path)
    return scaled_data


def group_current_data(scaled_data,load_mat_df,data_set_path):
    scaled_data = scaled_data[load_mat_df.index.values]
    grouped_ndarray = np.matmul(scaled_data.to_numpy(),
                               load_mat_df.to_numpy())
    current_data_grouped = pd.DataFrame(grouped_ndarray,
                              columns=load_mat_df.columns.values,
                              index=current_data.index)
    score_save_path=
        data_set_path.replace('.csv','_current_groupscore.csv')
    current_data_grouped.to_csv(score_save_path,header=True)
    print('Saving results to %s' % score_save_path)
    return current_data_grouped
```

Annotations (left and right margins):

- **Imports the transform functions defined in listing 7.5**
- **Reloads the parameters saved during scoring**
- **Reloads the loading matrix using reload_churn_data**
- **Loads the current customer data created with listing 8.3**
- **Checks for consistency between data and scoring parameters**
- **Checks for consistency between data and loading matrix**
- **Transforms any columns that were determined to be skewed**
- **Transforms any columns that were determined to be fat tailed**
- **Subtracts the mean and divides by the standard deviation**
- **Makes sure the dataset columns match the score param column**
- **Ensures the dataset columns match the loading matrix order**
- **Applies the loading matrix to calculate average group scores**
- **Converts the result to a DataFrame**
- **Saves the result**

Determines
columns for
grouped
metrics

Makes a
version of the
dataset for
segmenting

Customer
data files have
two columns
for the index.

Determines
columns for
metrics that are
not grouped

Wraps the steps to verify and
load previously saved data

Ensures that the file
exists, and prints a
message if it doesn't

```
def save_segment_data(current_data_grouped,
                      current_data, load_mat_df, data_set_path):
    group_cols =
        load_mat_df.columns[load_mat_df.astype(bool).sum(axis=0) > 1]
    no_group_cols =
        load_mat_df.columns[load_mat_df.astype(bool).sum(axis=0) == 1]
    segment_df =
        current_data_grouped[group_cols].join(current_data[no_group_cols])
    segment_df.to_csv(data_set_path.replace('.csv',
                      '_current_groupmets_segment.csv'),header=True)

def reload_churn_data(data_set_path, suffix,
                      listing,is_customer_data):
    data_path = data_set_path.replace('.csv', '_{}.csv'.format(suffix))
    assert os.path.isfile(data_path),
        'Run {} to save {} first'.format(listing,suffix)
    ic = [0,1] if is_customer_data else 0
    churn_data = pd.read_csv(data_path, index_col=ic)
    return churn_data
```

You should run listing 8.4 in the usual way, using the Python wrapper program, so that you can be ready to calculate the current customer forecast for your own data. Here are the arguments:

```
run_churn_listing.py --chap 8 --listing 4
```

8.4.2 *Preparing the current customer data for segmenting*

One subject that was not covered when you learned about grouping metrics was how to create a dataset of current customers with metrics grouped into average scores. That's what you need to do if the businesspeople in your organization are going to plan interventions based on averages of metric scores. If you read section 8.4.1, you can see the reason why I waited to explain it until now: the process is not completely straightforward. Now that you have reprocessed the current dataset for forecasting, you can reuse the work you did there (which is why the technique is included in the last section of listing 8.4). But I don't recommend that you use your forecasting dataset for segmenting. Rather, I recommend the following hybrid version of the dataset:

- Use scores for all metric groups.
- Use regular (natural scale) metrics for any metrics that were not grouped.

The advantage of this approach is that it's much easier for businesspeople to use. Groups are useful for reducing the number of metrics, and if you explained scores and metric groups by following my advice in chapter 6 (section 6.4), the businesspeople should be ready to interpret and use the metric scores and groups. It's usually not easy to segment with a metric when it is not on its natural scale, however, so if you don't have to convert a metric to a score for segmenting, it's probably better not to.

Given the current dataset of metrics, the scores, and the loading matrix, the helper function in listing 8.4, save_segment_data, takes the columns for the groups and then adds the original unscaled metrics. The function is a few lines of Pandas manipulation, but it can make life much easier for your business colleagues who are trying to reduce churn.

You may be thinking that for the simulated dataset that has fewer than 10 events and not many more metrics, the idea of using grouped metrics for segmenting doesn't make much sense. Regular metrics are easier to understand, and grouping removes only a few metrics. For the simulated dataset, you're probably right. But if you work on a product or service with dozens (or hundreds) of events and metrics, your business colleagues may really need to use the average scores to cut down on information overload from so many metrics.

8.4.3 Forecasting with a saved model

In this section, you'll learn the code to make forecasts on the current customers. Figure 8.12 shows an example of what this output will look like. It's similar to the forecast outputs for the historical customer dataset, except now, you have only one observation date and a single observation for every customer.

Forecasts for the current dataset have one forecast per account, all on the same date.	account_id	observation _date	churn_prob	retain_prob
	1	5/10/20	0.114500	0.885499
	2	5/10/20	0.005148	0.994851
	3	5/10/20	0.027381	0.972618
	4	5/10/20	0.003928	0.996071
	6	5/10/20	0.037595	0.962404
	...	...	...	...

Figure 8.12 Output of forecasting on the current customer dataset (listing 8.5)

A second output of listing 8.5 is a visual display of the distribution of churn forecasts in a plot known as a histogram (figure 8.13). A *histogram* helps you visualize a distribution by dividing the distribution into ranges and showing the number of observations in each range with the height of a bar on the plot. Unlike in the cohort plots, the ranges used to divide the customer observations in a histogram are fixed, and the number of customers within each range varies. Instead of showing you the average churn rate for groups of fixed size, a histogram shows you the size of the group that has a particular (forecast) churn rate.

In figure 8.13, you can see that the range of churn forecasts with the most customers is between 0% and 5%. Most customers have a churn probability that is less than 20%, but a small number have higher churn probabilities (between 20% and 50%).

You learned the term for the tail of a distribution when you saw fat-tailed distributions in chapter 7. The narrow strip of customers with higher churn probabilities in figure 8.13 is referred to as the *tail of the churn* probability distribution.

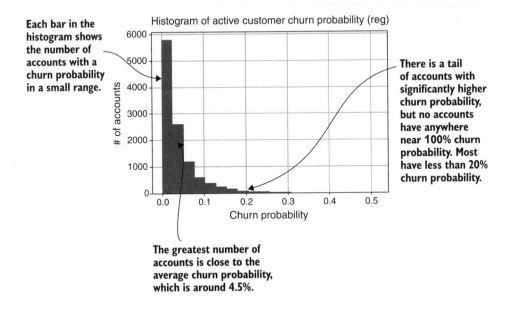

Figure 8.13   Distribution of a simulation forecast and churn probabilities

Listing 8.5 gives the code to make the forecast. These are the main steps:

1. Load the pickle of the logistic regression object that was saved by listing 8.2.
2. Load the dataset of grouped scores for the current customers that was saved by listing 8.4.
3. Call the predict_proba function on the logistic regression object, passing in the customer dataset as a NumPy ndarray. The result is a two-column ndarray of predictions for churn and retention probability.
4. Save the forecasts in a file like the one shown in figure 8.12.
5. Create and save a churn probability histogram like the one shown in figure 8.13. The histogram is created in a separate function. The histogram function calls the matplotlib.pyplot package function hist and then adds appropriate annotation before saving the result as an image. The counts from the histogram are also saved in a file.

The listing for forecasting is similar to the listing for fitting the regression model, in the sense that the algorithmic tasks take a single function call to the package object. But much of the work is preparing the data and analyzing and saving the results.

Listing 8.5 Forecasting on the current customer dataset

```
import pandas as pd
import os
import pickle
import matplotlib.pyplot as plt                        Reuses the data
                                                        loading function
                                                        from listing 8.4
from listing_8_4_rescore_metrics
    import reload_churn_data          ◁
                                                Reloads the model
                                                saved as an object
def churn_forecast(data_set_path=''):           using pickle
    pickle_path =
        data_set_path.replace('.csv', '_logreg_model.pkl')
    assert os.path.isfile(pickle_path),
        'You must run listing 8.2 to save a logistic regression model first'
    with open(pickle_path, 'rb') as fid:
        logreg_model = pickle.load(fid)
                                                        Reloads current
                                                        customer group scores
    current_score_df = reload_churn_data(data_set_path,  created with listing 8.4
                        'current_groupscore','8.4',is_customer_data=True)

    predictions =
        logreg_model.predict_proba(current_score_df.to_numpy())

    predict_df =
        pd.DataFrame(predictions, index=current_score_df.index,
                    columns=['churn_prob', 'retain_prob'])
    forecast_save_path =
        data_set_path.replace('.csv', '_current_predictions.csv')

    print('Saving results to %s' % forecast_save_path)       Calls the
    predict_df.to_csv(forecast_save_path, header=True)        helper function
    forecast_histogram(data_set_path,predict_df)       ◁     forecast_histogram

def forecast_histogram(data_set_path,predict_df,ext='reg')
    plt.figure(figsize=[6,4])
    n, bins,_ = plt.hist(predict_df['churn_prob'].values,  ◁
                        bins=20)                                Creates a histogram
    plt.xlabel('Churn Probability')                            plot, and returns the
    plt.ylabel('# of Accounts')                                resulting data
    plt.title(
        'Histogram of Active Customer Churn Probability ({})'.format(ext))
    plt.grid()
    plt.savefig(
        data_set_path.replace('.csv', '_{}_churnhist.png'.format(ext)),
        format='png')
    plt.close()
    hist_df=pd.DataFrame({'n':n,'bins':bins[1:]})
    hist_df.to_csv(data_set_path.replace('.csv', '_current_churnhist.csv'))
```

- **Reuses the data loading function from listing 8.4**
- **Reloads the model saved as an object using pickle**
- **Reloads current customer group scores created with listing 8.4**
- **predict_proba uses the model to make the predictions.**
- **Saves the predictions in a new DataFrame**
- **Calls the helper function forecast_histogram**
- **Creates a histogram plot, and returns the resulting data**
- **Provides annotation on the plot**
- **Saves the histogram results in a file for closer inspection**

You should run listing 8.5 on your own simulated dataset and confirm that you get results like those shown in figures 8.12 and 8.13. Assuming that you have created the current customer grouped metric scores (using listing 8.4), you can create the forecast from listing 8.5 by using this command:

```
run_churn_listing.py --chap 8 --listing 5
```

8.4.4   *Forecasting case studies*

Figure 8.14 shows some example histograms of predicted churn probabilities from the case studies you have seen throughout the book. These histograms have basic features in common with the result in figure 8.13 from simulation: a small peak representing a range with most of the churn probabilities and a tail made up of customers with higher churn probabilities.

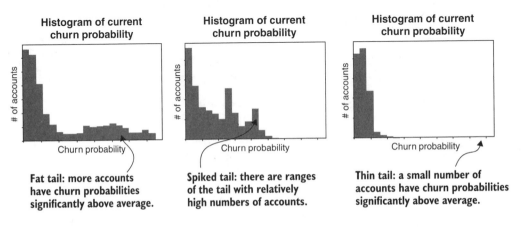

Figure 8.14   Case study distributions of forecast churn probabilities

In figure 8.14, the three case studies show three fairly common variations on how the tail of a churn probability distribution can appear:

- A *fat tail* in the churn probability distribution is when the number of customers with higher churn probabilities is large enough to show up clearly in the histogram.
- A *spiked tail* in the churn probability distribution is when there are certain ranges of churn probabilities in the tail with abnormally high numbers of customers. Sometimes, these numbers are related to identifiable behaviors such as lacking a particular behavior or having monthly versus annual billing.
- A *multipeak distribution* is another way to describe this type of distribution, although you usually describe the churn probability distribution as multipeak only when two or more peaks in the histogram shape have similar height. No case study example of this type was available.
- A *thin tail* is when most of the customers are packed in a narrow probability range, but there is a small number of customers with much higher churn probability.

In a thin tail, the number is so small that these customers are not visible in the histogram; that's when you look at the saved .csv file to see exactly how many such customers there are.

In fact, the churn probability distributions resulting from real case studies are usually less smooth and regular looking than the distribution resulting from the simulation (shown in figure 8.13).

8.4.5 Forecast calibration and forecast drift

When you first fit the regression model, I showed you how to check the calibration by comparing the average churn probability prediction to the churn rate in the historical dataset. You should also check the calibration of the forecasts made for your current customer dataset. But in this case, you can't compare the average with the churn rate in the current customer data because no customers in the current customer dataset have churned yet (of course). Instead, you can compare the average forecast on the current customer dataset with the churn rate in the historical dataset, or with a churn measurement made on recent customers, by using the methods you learned in chapter 2.

> **TAKEAWAY** Check the forecast calibration by comparing the average forecast churn with the historical dataset churn probability or a recent churn rate measurement (keeping in mind possible seasonality in the timing of a recent measurement).

The top of figure 8.15 shows an example of such a comparison for the simulated dataset. In this case, it shows that the average churn probability forecast on the current dataset is about three-tenths of a percent less than the average churn forecast and churn rate in the historical dataset (4.3% compared with 4.6%). That difference may not seem like much, but it is noticeable, especially considering that the historical average and forecast are so close.

When you find that the current forecasts are noticeably different from the historical numbers, you should investigate a little further to make sure that you understand what caused the difference. What could cause this kind of difference? The churn probability model is based on customer metrics, so if the current forecasts are different from the historical forecast, the current metrics must be different in some way from the historical metrics.

> **TAKEAWAY** If the current customer churn probability forecast doesn't match the historical churn probability forecast, it must be because of differences between current and historical metrics.

When you find this type of difference, you can investigate it by comparing the current metrics with the historical metrics. The easiest way is to use the dataset summary statistics that you already know how to create. The bottom of figure 8.15 illustrates a comparison of the summary statistics from the historical dataset with the summary statistics from the current dataset. This comparison was made in a simple spreadsheet. You can do the same thing or write a short script of your own. To create the summary statistics in the current dataset, you can run an extra version of the summary statistics listing with the arguments `--chapter 5 --listing 2 --version 4` in the Python wrapper program.

The comparison of metrics in figure 8.15 shows that the average values of the customer metrics in the current dataset are a little higher than the average values of customer metrics in the historical dataset (by around 5% in most cases). The metric for percent change in new friends shows a big change because it is estimated as zero in a new account, due to the requirement to have history for calculating the change. The current sample has more tenants with the required history, leading to the difference in the average. Because most of the customer metrics have a positive impact, higher metrics in the current dataset explain lower churn probability forecast for the current dataset.

In the case of the simulated dataset, the difference between the average metric in the current and historical datasets is correct but not meaningful. In the simulation, the service came into existence a short time ago, so the average tenure of the customers is increasing. At the same time, most of the metrics are not corrected for recent sign-ups, and as a result, new customers (on average) have slightly lower metrics. From those considerations, it is fair to say that the average churn forecast on the current dataset is reasonable, and the difference with the historical forecasts is not something to be concerned about.

For analysis of churn on a real product, if you find that the metrics for current customers are significantly different from historical dataset customers, you should do some additional quality assurance to make sure that the results are correct. If you have legitimate metric differences between the current dataset and historical dataset, it is reasonable to conclude that the churn rates for your current customers may be different from the churn rates you saw in the past. On the other hand, if the behavior of your current customers is substantially different from the historical customers due to material changes in the product or your market environment, you should be skeptical of the reliability of the churn forecasts. You may have to wait until you can form a new historical dataset under the current conditions to forecast churn probabilities reliably.

Another issue is that outliers in the current dataset can cause some churn probabilities to be different from the historical dataset, altering the average. You can assess differences in extreme outliers in the metrics by comparing the maximum and higher percentiles in the summary statistics (not shown in figure 8.15). This area is another one in which you have to use your judgment in evaluating the differences.

8.5   *Pitfalls of churn forecasting*

You now know how to fit a churn probability model and how to forecast for active customers under normal circumstances. This section covers a few pitfalls you should be aware of, because they can prevent you from getting the best possible results in some circumstances.

Comparison of churn rates:

measurement of churn	average
current forecasts	0.04334235
historical forecasts	0.04594520
historical average	0.04590566

The average forecast on the current dataset is different from the historical forecasts by a noticeable amount in the second significant figure 0.043, as compared to .046.

The average forecast on the historical dataset matches the sample churn rate out to three significant figures.

Comparison of metrics:

metric	historical mean	current mean	current/ historical
like_per_month	95.6	98.9	103%
newfriend_per_month	6.72	7.14	106%
post_per_month	40.1	41.7	104%
adview_per_month	39.3	40.7	103%
dislike_per_month	15.5	16.2	105%
unfriend_per_month	0.31	0.31	102%
message_per_month	61.6	64.4	104%
reply_per_month	22.4	23.5	105%
adview_per_post	1.63	1.65	101%
reply_per_message	0.39	0.40	103%
like_per_post	3.75	3.83	102%
post_per_message	3.81	3.66	96%
unfriend_per_newfriend	0.09	0.08	97%
dislike_pcnt	0.23	0.23	101%
newfriend_pcnt_chng	0.19	0.24	129%
days_since_newfriend	7.43	8.12	109%

The current dataset for the simulation has higher average values for the metrics than the historical data, and these are mostly associated with increased engagement. This explains the difference in the churn rate forecast.

Figure 8.15 Calibration and forecast drift

8.5.1 Correlated metrics

You have learned about grouping correlated metrics and that you should do this grouping as part of metric cohort churn analysis before you use customer datasets for forecasting. So far, I have taught you that grouping correlated metrics is desirable because it makes your results easier to understand. But using a regression model adds a new imperative for using grouping: the regression algorithm is designed under the assumption that the metrics you use in it are not highly correlated. Because regression is not intended for high correlation between metrics, the result might not be sensible if they are.

TAKEAWAY   Regression is designed for uncorrelated or moderately correlated metrics. Do not use highly correlated metrics in a regression.

One reason not to use highly correlated metrics in regression is that it makes the engagement weights harder to interpret. Highly correlated metrics make the engagement weights harder to interpret because when you think about the churn probability impact of a correlated metric, you have to remember that it is typically paired with impacts from the other correlated metrics. Suppose that two metrics have a correlation of 0.75. In that case, if a customer is one standard deviation above average on one metric, they are expected to be well above average on the other. You need to think about these relationships when you reason about the impact of different behaviors on retention. This fact remains true, even when metrics are weakly or moderately correlated; the impact is smaller, so ignoring it isn't as problematic.

If you learned about regression in the past, you may remember a condition called *collinearity*. Collinearity is related to correlation; it is a condition of perfect correlation between two metrics or between the sum of some group of metrics in the data. (Summing is in the sense of metrics such as totals, but collinearity refers to the condition when the addition of some metrics *could* result in correlated pairs, not that you make the metric sums.) Collinearity is a serious problem with some regression algorithms and can cause them to fail. But newer regression algorithms, like the ridge regression you used in listing 8.2, generally do not suffer from that kind of failure, even when the data includes correlated or collinear metrics.

A more subtle problem occurs in the regression if you use highly correlated metrics. Sometimes, if you use multiple highly correlated metrics and do not average them into groups, you may find that the weights produced by the regression have nonsensical relationships to engagement and churn. Some of the metrics are assigned weights that are good for retention, and some are assigned weights that are bad for retention, but clearly, all should have a similar influence.

Figure 8.16 is an example from a real case study of Klipfolio, an SaaS tool for creating and sharing dashboards of company metrics. The case study had four versions of metrics that measured dashboard views in slightly different ways: dashboard views per day, dashboard views per month calculated with a fixed period, dashboard views per month calculated with account-tenure-scaled metric periods, and dashboard views per user per month. These four metrics are highly correlated.

All four metrics showed strong relationships to retention in cohort analysis in the same way. Normally, such metrics should be grouped into an average score, but if that grouping is not done and the four metrics are put into regression as independent metrics, a strange result occurs: two of the metrics receive positive weights, indicating that the behavior increases engagement, and two of the metrics receive negative weights, suggesting that the behaviors reduce engagement. These weights are not meaningful, however.

Strangely, such models generally forecast as well as, and sometimes better than, the models when all the engagement weights are meaningful. The opposing weights result from the correlations and imbalance between the engagement strength of the correlated metrics that are the real patterns in the data. But it is usually not a good

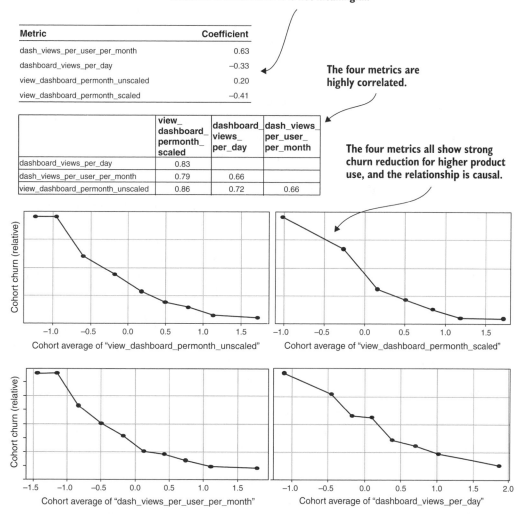

If correlated metrics are used in a regression without averaging scores, they may receive *both* positive coefficients and negative coefficients. But this assignment of positive and negative influence is an artifact: it is not meaningful.

Metric	Coefficient
dash_views_per_user_per_month	0.63
dashboard_views_per_day	−0.33
view_dashboard_permonth_unscaled	0.20
view_dashboard_permonth_scaled	−0.41

The four metrics are highly correlated.

	view_dashboard_permonth_scaled	dashboard_views_per_day	dash_views_per_user_per_month
dashboard_views_per_day	0.83		
dash_views_per_user_per_month	0.79	0.66	
view_dashboard_permonth_unscaled	0.86	0.72	0.66

The four metrics all show strong churn reduction for higher product use, and the relationship is causal.

Figure 8.16 Misleading regression weights from correlated metrics

idea to create this kind of model. You learn about accuracy comparison and machine learning models that are not interpretable in chapter 9.

This situation happens if you use a high correlation threshold in the metric grouping algorithm from chapter 6. The motivation typically is to keep correlated metrics separate to try to determine the relative importance of churn and retention by seeing which regression weight is the largest. It is ironic that an analysis like this can result in nonsensical weights that prevent you from seeing a meaningful relationship. The solution is to use the methods described in chapter 6 and 7 to group the correlated metrics into averages and then investigate whether the relationships between the metrics are significant by forming a ratio of the two metrics and checking the ratio's relationship with churn and retention. If the ratio is not correlated with either part of the original pair, it can be tested in regression.

8.5.2   *Outliers*

Another pitfall that can prevent you from getting the best results in churn forecasting occurs when you have extreme outliers in your data. In chapter 3, when you were learning to create metrics, I showed you some techniques for detecting and removing records that contain incorrect or inappropriate data. Now you're going to learn about something a little different: how to deal with data when it is a correct measurement but so extreme that it causes problems in some aspect of churn forecasting. This situation is not too common if you are converting all your metrics to scores by using the transforms for skewed and fat-tailed data. Those transforms reduce problems with outliers because the transformed scores have less extreme values than the original distribution. Also, extreme outliers are incredibly common if you do not use those transforms, which is why I recommended using them as a standard practice. Still, I'm going to alert you to two potential problems so that you'll know the signs and what to do about them.

Outliers can cause problems with fitting the model and forecasting after the model has been fit. Many statistics and data science classes emphasize the problem that outliers cause with fitting the model. But for most churn use cases, I have seen more problems with outliers when forecasting. Outliers can cause severe problems in fitting a model when few observations are used in the regression. If you have fewer than 100 observations in a regression, and there are extreme outliers, your results can be severely affected by the outliers. But most churn scenarios have thousands of data points. If you have tens of thousands of observations, a few outliers usually have little impact on the regression.

In any event, you are likely to notice the presence of extreme outliers in your forecasting, and you will probably see them when you have forecast churn or retention probabilities that are close to 0% or close to 100%. Figure 8.17 illustrates what I'm talking about.

I mentioned previously that it is rare to have accounts with churn probability close to 100%, so if any account receives a churn probability forecast that is above 99% (or even 100%), that result is probably due to some extreme outlier on one or more of the metrics. The same goes for accounts that are forecast to have a churn probability that's exactly 0%. Churn probabilities that are exactly 0% or 100% don't make sense because in the real world, there is always a chance that a customer will churn or be retained.

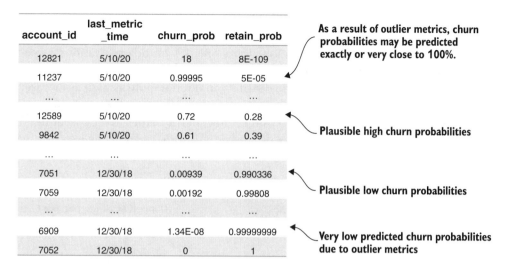

account_id	last_metric _time	churn_prob	retain_prob
12821	5/10/20	18	8E-109
11237	5/10/20	0.99995	5E-05
...	...	...	...
12589	5/10/20	0.72	0.28
9842	5/10/20	0.61	0.39
...	...	...	...
7051	12/30/18	0.00939	0.990336
7059	12/30/18	0.00192	0.99808
...	...	...	...
6909	12/30/18	1.34E-08	0.99999999
7052	12/30/18	0	1

As a result of outlier metrics, churn probabilities may be predicted exactly or very close to 100%.

Plausible high churn probabilities

Plausible low churn probabilities

Very low predicted churn probabilities due to outlier metrics

Figure 8.17 Churn probabilities resulting from outliers

If you know that these extreme probabilities are probably not accurate, the simplest thing to do is ignore them. Remember that an account shown with 100% churn probability is not that likely to churn, but it's probably still significantly at risk, which is good to know. The problem I usually have with extreme forecasts is that they can be distracting to businesspeople. Businesspeople can become obsessed with knowing why some accounts have such high or low churn probabilities, and it may cause them to doubt the otherwise reasonable predictions of the model.

> **TAKEAWAY** Forecasts for extreme outliers can cause confusion and doubt for businesspeople when you present the model results to them.

The problem with extreme outliers when they are real customers in your current dataset is that you cannot remove them as you would when you are constructing the historical dataset. Often, the context for making churn probability forecasts on the current customers is segmentation or some other analysis in which you need forecasts for all customers who are currently active. Often, the extreme outliers are high- or low-risk customers; the modeling can exaggerate the true level of risk. The solution that keeps the customers and allows you to make more reasonable forecasts for them is called outlier clipping.

> **DEFINITION** *Outlier clipping* means reducing the value of extreme outliers so that they are still near the high (or low) end of possible values but not quite as extreme.

Outlier clipping is different from the related concept of outlier removal in that the outliers are kept in the data at a reduced level. Figure 8.18 illustrates the most common approach to outlier clipping. Outlier clipping modifies the observations of a metric that are above the 99th percentile by setting them equal to the 99th percentile value. By definition, this transformation affects only 1% of the observations for each metric you apply it to. The values that formerly were above the 99th percentile are still high in comparison with most of the distribution but not quite as high as they were before. Usually, outlier trimming is for high metric values, but the same approach can be used for low metric values. Extremely low metric values are unusual in count metrics, in which the minimum is usually zero, but they can occur in ratios or percentage change metrics.

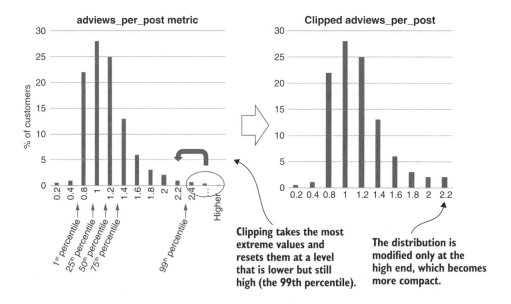

Figure 8.18   Outlier clipping

Listing 8.6 shows an example of code you can use to perform outlier clipping on a dataset. In listing 8.6, clipping is performed as part of the process of transforming the current customer dataset into group scores, so listing 8.6 is a variant of listing 8.4. The clipping thresholds used are the 1st and 99th percentiles of all the metrics, which are in the saved dataset summary statistics. Clipping occurs after the data is loaded and before the metrics are converted to scores. Otherwise, listing 8.6 is the same as listing 8.4.

Note that listing 8.6 clips all the variables, but it's not hard to create a similar function that clips only a select group of variables that you specify in a parameter. In general, it is better to clip data only when necessary when outliers are extreme enough to cause unreasonable forecasts. That said, in some real datasets with many events and metrics, it can be difficult to identify precisely which extreme metrics are causing the unreasonable forecasts. In that case, the quick solution is to proceed as shown in listing 8.6 and clip everything.

Listing 8.6 Clipping scores in Python

```
import pandas as pd
import numpy as np
from listing_7_5_fat_tail_scores
    import transform_fattail_columns, transform_skew_columns
from listing_8_4_rescore_metrics
    import reload_churn_data

def clip_hi_cols(data, hi_vals):
    for col in hi_vals.index.values:
        data.loc[data[col] > hi_vals[col],col]
            = hi_vals[col]


def clip_lo_cols(data, lo_vals):
    for col in lo_vals.index.values:
        data.loc[data[col] < lo_vals[col],col]
            = lo_vals[col]


def rescore_metrics(data_set_path):

    current_data =
        reload_churn_data(data_set_path,'current','8.2',is_customer_data=True)
    load_mat_df = reload_churn_data(data_set_path,
        'load_mat','6.4',is_customer_data=False)
    score_df = reload_churn_data(data_set_path,
        'score_params','7.5',is_customer_data=False)
    stats = reload_churn_data(data_set_path,
        'summarystats','5.2',is_customer_data=False)
    stats.drop('is_churn',inplace=True)
    assert set(score_df.index.values)==set(current_data.columns.values),
        "Data does not match transform params"
    assert set(load_mat_df.index.values)==set(current_data.columns.values),
        "Data does not match load matrix"
    assert set(stats.index.values)==set(current_data.columns.values),
        "Data does not match summary stats"

    clip_hi_cols(current_data, stats['99pct'])
    clip_lo_cols(current_data, stats['1pct'])

    transform_skew_columns(current_data,
        score_df[score_df['skew_score']].index.values)

    transform_fattail_columns(current_data,
        score_df[score_df['skew_score']].index.values)

    current_data=current_data[score_df.index.values]
    scaled_data=(current_data-score_df['mean'])/score_df['std']

    scaled_data = scaled_data[load_mat_df.index.values]
    grouped_ndarray = np.matmul(scaled_data.to_numpy(),
                                load_mat_df.to_numpy())
```

Reuses the fat-tails and skew transform functions

Reuses the helper function for loading churn data

Clips values in the data above those in the hi_vals parameter

Sets values above the threshold to the threshold

Sets values below the threshold to the threshold

Clips values in the data below those in the lo_vals parameter

This function is similar to that in listing 8.4.

Reloads saved data, loading matrix, parameters, and stats

Don't use the churn measurement in the summary stats!

Clips values above the 99th percentile

Clips values below the 1st percentile

The rest of this listing is the same as listing 8.4.

```
current_data_grouped = pd.DataFrame(grouped_ndarray,
                                    columns=load_mat_df.columns.values,
                                    index=current_data.index)

score_save_path=data_set_path.replace('.csv','_current_groupscore.csv')
current_data_grouped.to_csv(score_save_path,header=True)
print('Saving results to %s' % score_save_path)
```

If you need to use clipping because you had some extreme forecasts, you may also want to check whether the outliers have made a significant difference in fitting the regression itself. To do so, you should use the clipping functions in listing 8.6 in the function that creates the scores for the historical dataset.

8.6   *Customer lifetime value*

Now that you know how to forecast churn probabilities, I will introduce you to one great application of churn forecasting: estimating customer lifetime value (CLV). Estimates of CLV let you know how much a customer is worth to you over their entire lifetime. This information is crucial for evaluating the return on investment of your acquisition and retention efforts. It may surprise you, but the key to estimating CLV is the churn rate. Customer churn probability forecasts (like the ones you have learned how to make) allow you to tailor CLV estimates individually to each customer.

8.6.1   *The meaning(s) of CLV*

The first thing to understand is that CLV is a forecast about expected customer values, not only the sum of past payments from particular customers.

> **DEFINITION**   *Customer lifetime value* is the amount you expect a customer to be worth to your business, including the revenue and costs you foresee, over the customer's entire lifetime. This forecast includes future payments.

CLV needs to include both the revenue that a customer is expected to bring in and the cost of acquiring and keeping them as a customer, as illustrated in figure 8.19.

> **DEFINITIONS**   *Customer acquisition cost* (CAC) is the total amount spent on marketing and sales per customer acquired. CAC usually depends on the channel or campaign through which the customer was acquired. *Cost of goods sold* (COGS) is the total amount spent to maintain the service for existing customers, including things like cloud computing costs and the cost of providing customer support. COGS can depend on the type of customer.

> **NOTE**   In this section, it is assumed that you know the CAC and COGS for your customers. The focus in this section is on the recurring part of CLV, which depends on the churn rate.

The revenue from the customer is recurring over their lifetime, which you were previously introduced to as monthly recurring revenue (MRR). For now, I will refer to the

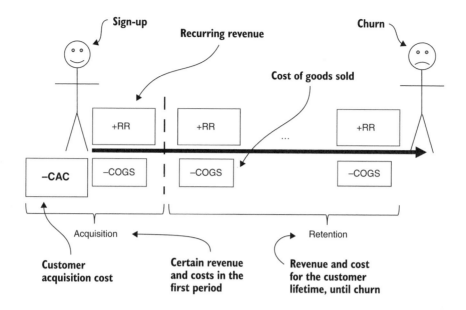

Figure 8.19 Components of CLV

revenue generically as *recurring revenue* (RR) without respect to the time period, which could be monthly or annually. Recurring revenue can include subscription payments and also any revenue generated by ads, in-app purchases, or use charges.

The name customer lifetime value implies that it combines all the costs and recurring revenue over the customer's expected lifetime. You can write CLV as shown in equation 8.6:

$$CLV = -CAC + \sum_{lifetime} RR - COGS \qquad \textbf{(Equation 8.6)}$$

In the equations in this section, the Σ symbol stands for summation of all of the terms indicated by the subscript beneath it, so $\Sigma_{lifetime}$ means all the revenue and costs over the entire customer lifetime, summed together.

That's CLV. Next, I need to teach you about a second lifetime value related to CLV that ignores acquisition costs and the first period's revenue and costs.

DEFINITION   *Future lifetime value (FLV)* is the sum of the recurring payments and maintenance costs, at any time after the first period.

You want to use FLV (without acquisition costs and the first period revenue and cost) when you are evaluating customers who have already signed up and are trying to decide how much it is worth to retain them. If you are trying to decide how much a customer is worth after they have signed up, the acquisition cost is irrelevant (a *sunk cost* in financial terminology). Similarly, the payment from the sign-up was never at risk for churn, so you ignore the first period payment (and costs). Instead, you care only about the expected *future* recurring revenue and costs after sign-up, as shown in equation 8.7

$$FLV = \sum_{future} RR - COGS, \qquad \text{(Equation 8.7)}$$

where the sum Σ_{future} ... means all the payments expected in the future. For the payment and cost sequence shown in figure 8.19, the future payments are those after the sign-up period. But this valuation stays the same throughout the customer lifetime, without regard to past periods of recurring revenue and costs.

> **TAKEAWAY**   At any point in a customer's lifetime, FLV is based only on expected future payments, and all costs and revenue in the past are seen as a sunk costs or benefits.

FLV is especially relevant to churn; you're going to use it to evaluate return on investment on churn interventions. Also note that the difference between CLV and FLV is only the acquisition cost and one period of recurring revenue (RR in the equations) and one period of costs (COGS in the equations). The difference between the two lifetime value calculations is not an estimate or a forecast, because those are known quantities in the sense that you can calculate them from the data in your accounting system. By contrast, FLV is a forecast or an estimate of the future because the future lifetime of the customer is not known with certainty. For this reason, when you are talking about CLV, the emphasis is often on FLV.

> **TAKEAWAY**   FLV emphasizes the future view of CLV for retention, which ignores acquisition and past revenue and costs.

Because FLV is the hard part to estimate and is closely related to churn and retention, FLV is going to be the focus for the rest of the chapter. As I've mentioned, you can always get CLV from FLV by subtracting CAC and one period of COGS and then adding RR (equation 8.8):

$$CLV = FLV - CAC - COGS + RR \qquad \text{(Equation 8.8)}$$

One last thing to note about the definition is that COGS is usually summarized by the margin defined in equation 8.9:

$$m = \frac{RR - COGS}{RR} \qquad \text{(Equation 8.9)}$$

Most companies summarize their costs with a margin, and it is assumed that you know the margin for your customers. With that definition, you can rewrite the FLV formula by combining equations 8.8 and 8.9 to get equation 8.10:

$$FLV = m \sum_{future} RR \qquad \textbf{(Equation 8.10)}$$

NOTE If you don't know the margin for your customers, don't worry, because all the rest of the instruction on CLV and FLV applies, and you can always add the margin when you know it.

8.6.2 *From churn to expected customer lifetime*

To calculate the expected sum of a customer's RR to use in the FLV formula (equation 8.11), you need to estimate the expected future lifetime of a customer. You might expect that estimating a customer's expected lifetime would be complicated, and you would have to do something like go back to the database and measure the average account tenures at the time of churn. But estimating customer lifetime is simple as long as you know a customer's churn probability. I'll tell you the answer first and then persuade you that it's right. If you know that a customer has a certain churn probability, the expected future lifetime of the customer is given in equation 8.11:

$$L = \frac{1}{churn} \qquad \textbf{(Equation 8.11)}$$

Note that in equation 8.11, the units for the lifetime are the same as the time period for measuring churn: months or years (typically).

TAKEAWAY In plain English, equation 8.11 says that if the churn probability is a monthly period forecast, the expected lifetime of a customer is 1 divided by the churn probability in months. If the churn probability is an annual period forecast, the expected lifetime of a customer is 1 divided by the churn probability in years.

If the churn probability is 5% per month, the expected customer lifetime is $1.0/0.05 =$ 20 months. If the churn probability is 30% per year, the expected customer lifetime is $1.0/0.30 = 3.33$ years.

That sounds simple, and it is, as long as you have the churn probabilities for your customers. Here is why equation 8.11 makes sense:

- What would the churn rate be if every customer had a lifetime of 20 months? If every customer churns once every 20 months, the churn rate would be 1/20, or 5% per month.
- What would the churn rate be if every customer had a lifetime of three years? If every customer churns once every three years, the churn rate would be one-third, or 33% per year.

Those examples show that (in an average sense) the churn rate is 1 divided by the lifetime, and equation 8.11 is turning that relationship around. In reality, not every customer has the same lifetime, even if they have exactly the same churn probability. Many factors external to the service and missing information prevent you from estimating churn probability perfectly. But for every customer, *expected* lifetime in the sense of an estimate or a forecast is 1 divided by churn probability.

If you want to read more details about why the expected lifetime is 1 divided by the churn rate, you should read about exponential decay models, which are where the approximations are derived from.

> **NOTE** If you don't make individual customer churn probability forecasts, you can use the average churn rate in equation 8.11 and estimate the average customer lifetime.

8.6.3   CLV formulas

The next step isn't exactly FLV or CLV but an intermediate step: the expected total profit over the customer's lifetime, not including CAC. Combine the expected lifetime (equation 8.11) with the margin equation for profit (equation 8.10) to get equation 8.12:

$$m \sum_{future} RR = \frac{mRR}{churn}$$

(Equation 8.12)

The expected lifetime profit (excluding acquisition) is the margin multiplied by RR divided by the churn rate. Note that *mRR* here is the margin (m) multiplying recurring revenue (*RR*), not MRR for monthly recurring revenue. (This notation is unfortunate but standard.) Note that the expected lifetime from the churn probability can be a number that is uneven, and usually, it will be. If the churn rate is 12% per month, the expected lifetime is $1/.12 = 8.3$ months. But you multiply that lifetime by the per-period profit to get the expected lifetime profit. This result is okay because an estimate is an average. In the example of an expected 8.3-month lifetime, no customer will pay for 8.3 periods, but some may pay for 8, and some pay for 9, so the average is 8.3.

Also note that FLV doesn't depend on the account tenure or how long that customer has been a customer. It doesn't matter whether a customer completed their first period after they were acquired or their hundredth: the expected future lifetime profit depends only on churn probability. (It may be true that the churn probability forecast depends on account tenure, so there can be a second-order, indirect effect.) As a result, FLV is forward-looking in that account tenure matters only to the extent that it affects the churn probability forecast, which is also forward-looking.

> **TAKEAWAY** FLV does not depend directly on the length of time a customer has been a customer. It is a forward-looking estimate. Only expected future revenue matters when evaluating how much it is worth to save a customer.

In any event, equation 8.12 is not FLV yet because it is the profit from the recurring payments over the entire lifetime. But FLV is supposed to ignore the payments in the first payment period (because those payments form part of the certain cost and payment from each customer). The answer is to subtract one period's worth of RR (and COGS) to get equation 8.13:

$$FLV = mRR\left(\frac{1}{churn} - 1\right)$$

(Equation 8.13)

On the other hand, to get the CLV from equation 8.12, you need to subtract the acquisition cost, which leads to equation 8.14:

$$CLV = \frac{mRR}{churn} - CAC$$

(Equation 8.14)

WARNING Many people use equation 8.12 alone for CLV because it is an easy simplification. But equation 8.12 alone is not the correct formula for either CLV or FLV! Equation 8.12 is an overestimate in both cases because both equations 8.13 and 8.14 subtract from it. Because it is an overestimate, equation 8.12 is sometimes used for reporting CLV to outside investors but not for evaluating the return on investment of acquisition or retention of customers.

You should be aware of an additional form of FLV necessary only for companies with low churn. If churn is less than 20% per year, customers are expected to have lifetimes longer than five years. If customers are expected to stay that long, it's not reasonable to assume that their FLV is the full amount suggested by their expected lifetime. With such a long lifetime, there are more risks to the customer's making all those payments than churn alone. A recession might occur, or a new competitor may change the market, or any number of things could happen over five or more years.

The way to handle this uncertainty is to add a cash-flow discount factor like the kind that is used in evaluating capital investment projects. Explaining the formula is beyond the scope of the book, but it looks like equation 8.15:

$$FLV = mRR \frac{retention}{(1 + discount - retention)}$$

(Equation 8.15)

The formula in equation 8.15 uses the retention rate instead of the churn rate, and the *discount* variable in the denominator is the discount rate that your company uses to evaluate long-term investments. (If your company does not have such a discount rate, you probably don't need to use this formula.) For details on this long-customer-lifetime version of FLV and CLV, I recommend "Customers as Assets," by Sunil Gupta and Donald Lehman, in the *Journal of Interactive Marketing*. The article is available for download at www0.gsb.columbia.edu/mygsb/faculty/research/pubfiles/721/gupta_customers.pdf.

Summary

- Forecasting churn probabilities is done with a model known as logistic regression.
- Logistic regression models retention as an S-shaped function of engagement.
- For the purpose of forecasting, engagement is modeled as the multiplication of a set of engagement weights by the scores for each metric.
- The logistic regression algorithm determines the engagement weights that best fit the data.
- A churn forecasting model is calibrated if the probabilities of churn that it predicts are in agreement with the churn rates observed on real customers.
- You check the calibration of forecasts by comparing the average forecast with the churn rate in the dataset used to create the model.
- To make forecasts on currently active customers, you must transform the current customer dataset in the same way that the historical customer dataset was transformed before fitting the model.
- The expected lifetime for any customer is 1 divided by their predicted churn probability with the same units as the churn probability (months or years).
- The expected lifetime can be used to estimate customer lifetime value (CLV).

Forecast accuracy
and machine learning

9

You know how to forecast the probability of customer churn, and you also know how to check the calibration of your forecasts. Another important measurement of a forecasting model is whether the customers predicted to be highly at risk are really more at risk than those predicted to be safe. This type of predictive performance is generally known as *accuracy*, although as you will see, there is more than one way to measure accuracy.

Back in chapter 1, I told you that forecasting churn with a predictive model was not the emphasis of this book because it isn't helpful in many situations. The focus of this book is on having a good set of metrics that segment customers into healthy and unhealthy populations based on behavior. But there are a few reasons why it's good to have accurate predictive churn forecasts, so this chapter will round out your skill set and ensure that you can forecast accurately when necessary.

One time when it can be useful to forecast churn risk accurately is when an intervention is particularly expensive. An onsite training session with a product expert will be more expensive to deliver than an email, for example. If you're selecting customers for onsite training with the intention of reducing churn risk, it makes sense to select only customers who have a high churn risk so that you enroll only customers with a suitable risk profile. Alternatively, you might not select the most at-risk customers because they may be beyond saving; it is often better to select customers with above-average but not maximum risk. (Also, you probably would screen the customers by particular metrics to make sure that they would benefit from this hypothetical training.)

Another reason it is worth your time to forecast churn accurately is that doing so validates your entire data and analytic process; you can compare the accuracy of your predictions with known benchmarks, as I explain in this chapter. If you find that the performance of your process is below typical, that result suggests that you need to correct some aspect of your data or process. You may need to improve the way you clean your data by removing invalid examples, for example, or you might need to calculate better metrics. On the other hand, if you find that the performance of your analysis is in the high range of the benchmark, you can be confident that you have done a thorough analysis and there may not be much more to discover. You may even find that your accuracy is impossibly high, which might suggest the need for corrections and improvements in your data preparation, such as increasing the lookahead period you use to make your observations (chapter 4).

This chapter is organized as follows:

- Section 9.1 explains ways to measure forecasting accuracy and teaches you some accuracy measurements that are particularly useful for churn.
- Section 9.2 teaches you how to calculate accuracy measurements using a historical simulation.
- Section 9.3 returns to the regression model from chapter 8 and explains how you can use an optional control parameter to control the number of weights that the regression uses.
- Section 9.4 teaches you how to pick the best value of the regression control parameter based on the accuracy test results.
- Section 9.5 teaches you how to predict churn risk by using a machine learning model called XGBoost, which is usually more accurate than regression. You also learn about some of the pitfalls of the machine learning approach and see benchmark results from real case studies.

- Section 9.6 covers some practical issues involved in forecasting with the machine learning model.

The sections build on one another, so you should read them in order.

9.1 *Measuring the accuracy of churn forecasts*

To start, you learn what accuracy means in the context of churn forecasting and how to measure it. In fact, measuring the accuracy of churn forecasts is not straightforward.

9.1.1 *Why you don't use the standard accuracy measurement for churn*

When you're talking about the accuracy of a forecast (such as churn probability predictions), the word accuracy has both a general and a specific meaning. First, the general definition.

> **DEFINITION** *Accuracy* (in the general sense) means the correctness or truthfulness of forecasts.

All methods of measuring the accuracy of churn forecasting involve comparing the predictions of risk with actual churn events, but there are many ways to measure accuracy. To make matters more confusing, one particular measurement of forecasting accuracy is called *accuracy*. This measurement is specific, but it is not a useful measurement for churn, as you're about to see. I am going to start with that measurement, which I will call the standard accuracy measurement to prevent confusion with the more general meaning of accuracy. (When I say accuracy, I mean the word in the general sense.)

Figure 9.1 illustrates the standard accuracy measurement. In chapter 8, you learned how to assign a churn or retention forecast probability to each customer. The standard accuracy measurement further assumes that on the basis of those forecasts, you divide the customers into two groups: those who are expected to be retained and those who are expected to churn. I will return to the question of how you might divide customers into those two groups when I finish explaining the standard accuracy measurement.

After customers are divided into expected retention and expected churn groups, the assigned categories are compared with what really happened. To define the standard accuracy measurement, you need to use the following terms:

- A *true-positive (TP)* prediction is a predicted churn that churns.
- A *true-negative (TN)* prediction is a predicted retention that stays.
- A *false-positive (FP)* prediction is a predicted churn that stays instead of churning.
- A *false-negative (FN)* prediction is a predicted retention that churns.

Using these definitions, the standard accuracy measurement is defined as follows.

> **DEFINITION** The *standard accuracy* is the percentage of forecasts that are either true positives or true negatives. In an equation, this would be *Standard Accuracy* = (#*TP* + #*TN*) / (#*Total*).

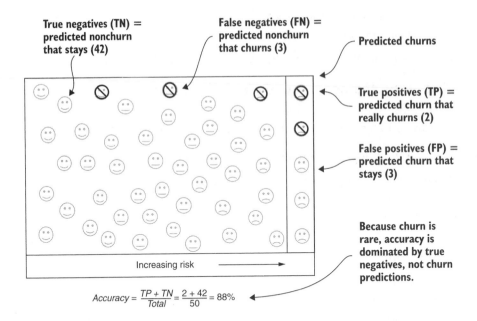

Figure 9.1   The standard accuracy measurement

Standard accuracy is meant to represent the percentage of predictions that were correct in a particular literal sense: the percentage of the category assignments that came true. That sounds reasonable, but in fact, standard accuracy is inappropriate for measuring the validity of churn forecasts. Standard accuracy has two problems when it comes to churn:

- Churn is rare, so standard accuracy is dominated by nonchurns.
- The basic assumption of the standard accuracy measurement is that you divide customers into two groups: expected churns and expected retentions. But that division isn't a useful portrayal of customer segmentation use cases.

I will explain each of these problems in detail.

Standard accuracy is dominated by nonchurns because churns are rare, so true positives cannot possibly have much impact on the numerator in the standard accuracy ratio. As a result, the measurement doesn't always do a good job of showing whether forecasts are appropriate. To make this point, note that there is an easy way to get a high standard accuracy measurement, as illustrated in figure 9.2. If you were to predict that no customers would churn (all customers in the nonchurn group), you would have true-negative predictions for the majority. If you have all the true negatives correctly assigned, the resulting accuracy is the retention rate, and you would have a high standard accuracy measurement without having predicted anything about churn.

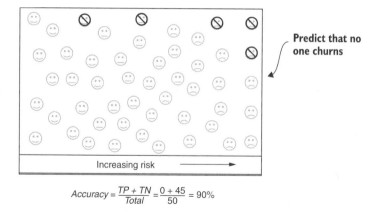

$$Accuracy = \frac{TP + TN}{Total} = \frac{0 + 45}{50} = 90\%$$

Figure 9.2 Gaming the standard accuracy measurement for churn

TAKEAWAY The standard accuracy measurement is inappropriate for churn because churn is rare, so the measurement can be gamed by predicting that no one will churn. More generally, accuracy on churned customers makes only a small contribution to the measurement.

One possible remedy for this weakness in the standard accuracy measurement is to augment it with measurements based on not only true positives and true negatives but also false positives and false negatives. I don't recommend this approach either, however, because there is another way in which standard accuracy measurement is inappropriate for churn use cases. Calculating standard accuracy relies on the assumption that you divided the customers into two groups: expected churns and expected retentions. Dividing predictions into two exclusive groups is standard for some forecasting use cases, but it is rarely done that way for customer churn.

As mentioned at the start of the chapter, the most common use case for churn and retention forecasts is to select customers for relatively expensive interventions to reduce churn. In that case, the churn or retention probability is used like any other segmenting metric, in that the department organizing the intervention orders the customers by the metric and then uses its own criteria to pick the most appropriate customers. If the intervention has a specific budget, for example, the department might pick a fixed number of customers who are most at risk for churn or a fixed number of customers who are not most at risk. A common strategy is to select customers with above-average risk who still use the product a little because the most at-risk customers who do not use the product may not be savable. You (the data person) aren't dividing the customers into expected churns and nonchurns as presumed by the standard accuracy measurement.

TAKEAWAY Churn forecasting use cases rely on using the ranking provided by the churn forecast as a segmenting metric but do not involve categorizing the customers into two groups: expected churns and nonchurns.

Because real churn use cases depend on the model's ability to rank customers by risk but not divide them into two groups per se, it makes more sense to turn to alternative (nonstandard) measurements of accuracy that better reflect the situation. As described in section 9.1.2, these measurements also remedy the problems in the standard accuracy measurement caused by the rarity of churn.

9.1.2   *Measuring churn forecast accuracy with the AUC*

The first accuracy measurement that you should use for churn is *area under the curve* (AUC), where *the curve* refers to an analytic technique known as the receiver operating curve. This naming is unfortunate, because AUC is a technical description of the way in which the metric is calculated but doesn't convey clearly what it means. But everyone uses this name, so we have no choice but to stick with it; I won't refer to the receiver operating curve anymore because it is not necessary for understanding or applying the metric. As you will see, my advice is not to even mention this measurement to your business colleagues. If you want more details, it is easy to find resources online.

The meaning of AUC is simpler than the name, as summarized in figure 9.3. As in the standard accuracy measurement, you start with a dataset in which you made a forecast for every customer and know which customers churned. Consider the following test. Take one customer who churned and one customer who didn't churn. If your model is good, it should have forecast a higher churn risk for the customer who churned than for the one who didn't. If the model did so, consider that comparison to be a success. Now consider the same test for every possible comparison. One by one, compare every churn with every nonchurn to see whether the model predicted higher churn risk for true churn. The overall proportion of successful predictions is the AUC.

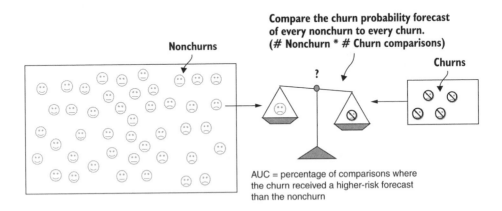

Figure 9.3   Measuring accuracy with the AUC

> **DEFINITION**   *AUC* is the percentage of comparisons in which the model forecasts higher churn risk for a churn than for a nonchurn, considering pairwise comparisons of all churns and nonchurns.

AUC avoids the problem in standard accuracy, which is that prediction on churns doesn't matter much because churns are such a small percentage of the population. In the AUC calculation, accurate prediction of churns is central because every comparison involves one churn, even if churns are only a small percentage of the data. At the same time, AUC is based on the ranking of risks and doesn't require an artificial categorization of customers into two groups.

If you think about the definition of AUC, that measurement could involve a lot of comparisons. The total number of pairwise comparisons is the product of the number of churned customers and the number of nonchurned customers. Fortunately, there is a more efficient way to do the calculation, involving that receiver operating curve, but I'm not going to teach you how to use it. Instead, you will use an open source package to do the calculation (listing 9.1). It's true that AUC is more expensive to calculate than the standard accuracy metric, but the difference is not enough to cause concern.

If you run listing 9.1, you'll see the short output in figure 9.4—a first demonstration. You will be using the AUC measurement throughout this chapter.

```
Running 9 listing listing_9_1_regression_auc on schema socialnet7
Regression AUC score=0.766
```
Listing 9.1 produces only one line of output: the AUC measurement for the forecasts.

Figure 9.4 Output of listing 9.1 for calculating the forecast model AUC

To demonstrate the AUC, listing 9.1 reloads the logistic regression model that you saved in chapter 8; it also reloads the dataset used to train the model (the historical dataset with labeled churns and retentions, not the current customer dataset). The model's `predict_proba` function is used to create forecasts, and these forecasts are passed to the function `roc_auc_score` from the sklearn.metrics package. You should run listing 9.1 on your own saved data and regression model with the following standard command and these arguments:

```
fight-churn/listings/run_churn_listing.py --chapter 9 --listing 1
```

Listing 9.1 Calculating the forecast model AUC

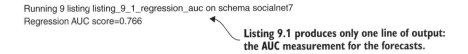

Reloads the regression model pickle

sklean has a function to calculate the AUC.

Reuses the prepare_data function from listing 8.2

```
import os
import pickle
from sklearn.metrics import roc_auc_score
from listing_8_2_logistic_regression import prepare_data

def reload_regression(data_set_path):
    pickle_path = data_set_path.replace('.csv', '_logreg_model.pkl')
    assert os.path.isfile(pickle_path), 'Run listing 8.2 to save a log reg model'
```

```
                     with open(pickle_path, 'rb') as fid:
                         logreg_model = pickle.load(fid)
                     return logreg_model

                 def regression_auc(data_set_path):
                     logreg_model = reload_regression(data_set_path)
                     X,y = prepare_data(data_set_path)
                     predictions = logreg_model.predict_proba(X)
                     auc_score = roc_auc_score(y,predictions[:,1])
                     print('Regression AUC score={:.3f}'.format(auc_score))
```

Calls the reload_regression function

Calls the prepare_data function from listing 8.2

predict_proba returns probability predictions.

Calls the function to calculate the AUC

You should find that the regression model has an AUC of around 0.7, which raises the question of whether 0.7 is good. AUC is a percentage, like accuracy, and 100% is the best possible. If you had 100% AUC, all the churns were ranked higher in risk than all the nonchurns. But you will never find a real churn-prediction system that has an AUC anywhere near that high.

 On the other hand, consider the worst you could possibly do. Zero percent sounds bad, but that result would mean that you had all the nonchurns ranked as a higher risk than the churns. If you think about it, that result would be fine, because then you could use your model as a perfect predictor of retention. Probably, though, something went wrong in your model setup to make it predict backward.

 In fact, the worst AUC would be 0.50, which would mean that your predictions were like coin flips: right half the time and wrong half the time. If a forecast model has an AUC of 0.5, it has the worst possible performance—the same as random guessing.

> **TAKEAWAY**   AUC ranges from 0.5, which is equivalent to random guessing (no predictive power), to 1.0, which is perfect ranking of churns versus nonchurns.

Table 9.1 shows a list of benchmarks for what you can consider to be healthy and unhealthy AUC. Generally, churn forecasting AUC is healthy in the range from around 0.6 to 0.8. If it's less than 0.6 or greater than 0.8, something is probably wrong, and you need to check the data in your model. You may not think that high accuracy would be cause for concern, but it could be. I'll say more about that subject in section 9.2.3.

Table 9.1   Churn forecasting AUC benchmarks

AUC result	Diagnosis
< 0.45	Something is wrong! The model is predicting backward. Check your data and the code calculating the AUC; is it using the wrong column of the predict_proba result?
0.45–0.55	No different from random guessing (0.5). Check your data.
0.55–0.6	Better than random guessing but not good. Check your data, collect better events, or make better metrics.
0.6–0.7	Healthy range for weakly predictable churn.
0.7–0.8	Healthy range for highly predictable churn.

Table 9.1 Churn forecasting AUC benchmarks *(continued)*

AUC result	Diagnosis
0.8–0.85	Extremely predictable churn. This result is suspicious for a consumer product and usually is possible only for a business product with informative events and advanced metrics.
> 0.85	Something probably is wrong. Normally, churn is not this predictable, even for business products. Check your data to make sure that you're not using too short of a lead time to construct the dataset and that there are no lookahead events or customer data fields (described in section 9.2.3).

NOTE The AUC benchmarks in table 9.1 apply only to customer churn. For other problem domains, the expected range of forecasting AUC can be higher or lower.

AUC is used throughout the rest of this chapter, but first, you should be aware of one other nonstandard accuracy measurement: the lift.

9.1.3 *Measuring churn forecast accuracy with the lift*

AUC is a useful metric, but it has one downside: it is abstract and hard to explain. I recommend a different metric for churn accuracy, primarily because it is easy for businesspeople to understand. In fact, this metric, known as the *lift*, originated in marketing. I'll explain first the general use of lift in marketing and then its specific application to churn.

DEFINITION *Lift* is the relative increase in responses due to some treatment relative to the baseline.

If 1% of people who visit a website sign up for the product, and a promotion increases the sign-up rate to 2%, the lift caused by the promotion is 2.0 (2% divided by 1%). According to that definition, a lift of 1.0 means no improvement. One thing to notice about lift is that it emphasizes improvement over the baseline, so it is suitable for measuring improvement in things that are rare to begin with. For measuring the accuracy of prediction models, you can use a more specific version of lift called the top decile lift.

DEFINITION The *top decile lift* of a predictive churn model is the ratio of the churn rate in the top decile of customers predicted to be most at risk to the overall churn rate.

Figure 9.5 illustrates this definition. The top decile lift is like a regular lift measurement, but the baseline is the overall churn rate, and the treatment is that you picked the 10% most at-risk customers according to the model.

IMPORTANT Because this definition is the most common definition of lift for churn forecasting, when I use the term *lift*, you should be aware from the context that I mean top decile lift.

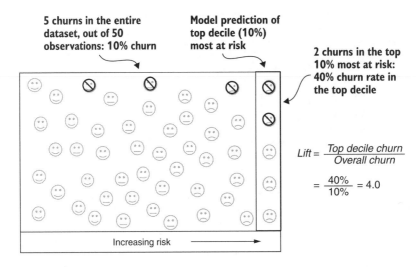

5 churns in the entire dataset, out of 50 observations: 10% churn

Model prediction of top decile (10%) most at risk

2 churns in the top 10% most at risk: 40% churn rate in the top decile

$$Lift = \frac{Top\ decile\ churn}{Overall\ churn}$$

$$= \frac{40\%}{10\%} = 4.0$$

Increasing risk

Figure 9.5   Measuring accuracy with the lift

Why is the overall churn rate the baseline? That's how accurate you would be in predicting churn if you were randomly guessing. If you have a 5% churn rate, you will find churns 5% of the time if you pick customers at random. If you can do better than random guessing (lift greater than 1.0), your result improves. You might respond that you could do better than guessing randomly, and you probably could, especially if you use segments based on data-driven metrics like the ones you learn how to make in this book. But the point is that the overall churn rate is a reasonable baseline at all companies, regardless of whatever else you might be doing.

TAKEAWAY   Top decile lift is good for measuring accuracy because it emphasizes improvement from a low baseline level of prediction.

Listing 9.2 shows how to calculate the lift with Python, assuming that you have a model saved (as in listing 9.1). Again, the output, as shown in figure 9.6, is a simple printout of the results and only a demonstration.

Running 9 listing listing_9_2_top_decile_lift on schema socialnet7
Regression Lift score=4.284

Listing 9.1 produces only one line of output: the lift measurement for the forecasts.

Figure 9.6   Output of listing 9.2 (lift)

Listing 9.2 doesn't use an open source package to calculate the lift. At the time of this writing, no open source package makes this calculation, so I have made an implementation for you in the function `calc_lift`. The steps to calculate the lift are as follows:

1 Validate the data to make sure you have a sufficient number of distinct forecasts.
2 Calculate the overall churn rate in the sample.
3 Sort the predictions by the churn risk forecast.
4 Locate the position of the top decile.
5 Calculate the number of churns in the top decile and the top decile churn rate. The result is the top decile churn rate divided by the overall churn rate.

The lift calculation I provide requires at least 10 unique values or levels for the forecasts. Not enough forecasts can be a problem with bad data or a misspecified model. The most common manifestation of bad data or a bad model is that all accounts get the same forecast, but other variants are possible. The criteria of 10 is a rule of thumb, not a hard rule. (In principle, the forecasts should allow you to select exactly 10% of the customers who are most at risk for the comparison. For example, it would be okay for the purpose of calculating lift to have just two distinct predictions coming from the model as long as exactly 10% of the population gets one prediction or the other. The 10-unique-values rule of thumb catches the most egregious model or data failures, and matching the condition precisely is not really necessary anyway.)

> **Listing 9.2 Calculating the forecast model lift**

Uses the prepare_data function from listing 8.2

Uses the reload_regression function from listing 9.1

Parameters are series of true churn outcomes and predictions.

Checks to make sure that the predictions are valid

Calculates the overall churn rate

Sorts the predictions

Counts the churns in the top decile

Calculates the index of the 90th percentile

Returns the ratio of the top decile churn to the overall churn

Calculates the top decile churn rate

Loads the model, and generates predictions as in listing 8.1

Loads the data but doesn't invert the outcome to retention

Calls the lift calculation function

```python
from listing_8_2_logistic_regression
    import prepare_data
from listing_9_1_regression_auc
    import reload_regression
import numpy

def calc_lift(y_true, y_pred):
    if numpy.unique(y_pred).size < 10:
        return 1.0
    overall_churn = sum(y_true)/len(y_true)
    sort_by_pred=
        [(p,t) for p,t in sorted(zip(y_pred, y_true))]
    i90=int(round(len(y_true)*0.9))
    top_decile_count=
        sum([p[1] for p in sort_by_pred[i90:]])
    top_decile_churn =
        top_decile_count/(len(y_true)-i90)
    lift = top_decile_churn/overall_churn
    return lift


def top_decile_lift(data_set_path):
    logreg_model = reload_regression(data_set_path)
    X,y = prepare_data(data_set_path,as_retention=False)
    predictions = logreg_model.predict_proba(X)
    lift = calc_lift(y,predictions[:,0])
    print('Regression Lift score={:.3f}'.format(lift))
```

You should run listing 9.2 with the following arguments to check the result yourself:

```
fight-churn/listings/run_churn_listing.py --chapter 9 --listing 2
```

You should find that the regression model achieves a lift of around 4.0 on the simulated data. I've already mentioned that the minimum lift is 1.0, which indicates that your model is no better than random guessing because it can't find more churns than the overall churn rate. A lift less than 1.0 is akin to an AUC less than 0.5, which means that your model is predicting risk in reverse because the top decile has fewer churns than the overall sample.

You can also deduce the maximum possible lift if the top decile of customers most at risk contained only customers who churned. The lift would be 100% divided by the overall churn rate. So the maximum lift depends on the overall churn rate. Here are some examples:

- If the churn rate is 20%, the maximum possible lift would occur if the top decile of forecasts were all churns. Then the lift would be 5 (100%/20% = 5).
- If the churn rate is 5%, the maximum lift would be if all those 5% churns were in the top decile forecast group. Then the top decile churn rate would be 50%, and the lift would be 10 (50%/5% = 10).

The pattern is that the higher the overall churn rate is, the lower the maximum possible lift. You are not going to get anywhere close to those maximums, but the relationship between churn rates and more typical lift values is the same.

TAKEAWAY   The higher the overall churn rate, the lower the lift you should expect from a predictive model.

Table 9.2 lists benchmarks for what you can expect to find for lift in real churn prediction use cases. Unlike for the AUC, the reasonable range of lift values depends on the churn rate. If the churn rate is low, it's easier to get a somewhat greater lift. If the churn rate is high (greater than 10%), the lift is likely to be lower. As explained in the preceding paragraph, the maximum lift is reduced when the churn rate is high. That property carries over to expecting lower lift scores generally because you're not likely to find so many churns in the top decile. For low-churn products, a healthy lift is in the range from 2.0 to 5.0, whereas for high-churn products, the healthy range is around 1.5 to 3.0.

Table 9.2   Churn forecasting lift benchmarks

Low churn (< 10%) lift result	High churn (> 10%) lift result	Diagnosis
< 0.8	< 0.8	Something is wrong! The model is predicting backward. Check your data and the code calculating the lift. Is it using the wrong column of the predict_proba result?
0.8–1.5	0.8–1.2	Random guessing (1.0), or not very different from random guessing. Check your data.

Table 9.2 Churn forecasting lift benchmarks (continued)

Low churn (< 10%) lift result	High churn (> 10%) lift result	Diagnosis
1.5–2.0	1.2–1.5	Better than random guessing but not good. Check your data, collect better events, or make new metrics.
2.0–3.5	1.5–2.25	Healthy range of weakly predictable churn.
3.5–5.0	2.25–3.0	Healthy range of highly predictable churn.
5.0–6.0	3.0–3.5	Extremely predictable churn. This result is suspicious for a consumer product and usually is possible only for a business product with good events and metrics.
> 6.0	> 3.5	Something probably is wrong. Normally, churn is not this predictable, even for business products. Check your data to make sure you're that not using too short of a lead time to construct the dataset and that there are no lookahead events or customer data fields (described in section 9.2.3).

I like to use the lift when I explain accuracy to businesspeople because the term is intuitive and related to metrics that they already understand. But there is one problem with the lift: it can be unstable, particularly with small datasets. Small changes in the metrics or model you use to predict may create big changes in the result.

> **WARNING** The lift can be unstable, especially for small datasets. The result can vary significantly, comparing different time periods and forecasting models. To measure lift, you should have thousands of observations and hundreds of churns in the dataset (or more). The lower the churn rate, the more observations you need to make the lift measurement stable.

Suppose that you have only 500 customer observations and a 5% churn rate, so you have only 25 churns. In that case, the lift is based on how many of those 25 are in the top 10% forecast at risk, with the baseline being an expected (average) 2.5. The addition or removal of a few churns from the top decile will make big swings in the lift. Generally, you should use the lift when you have thousands of observations or more. The AUC avoids this type of problem because it always uses every churn in the dataset and maximizes their use (by comparing every churn with every nonchurn).

> **TAKEAWAY** Use the AUC to evaluate your model accuracy for your own understanding. Use the lift to explain the churn accuracy to businesspeople.

Another nice property of the lift is that it makes the imprecise business of forecasting churn sound more impressive. Compare these two statements:

- This model is three times better than the baseline.
- This model ranks a customer who churns 70% of the time as more risky than a customer who doesn't.

Even though both statements imply the same level of improvement above random guessing, three times is a more impressive statistic than 70%.

9.2   *Historical accuracy simulation: Backtesting*

Now you know the right way to measure accuracy of churn forecasts and what is typical in churn forecasting. But I ignored an important detail: the observations on which you should measure accuracy. As with many parts of the analysis, the situation is a little different for churn.

9.2.1   *What and why of backtesting*

Earlier, I demonstrated the accuracy measurements you learned by calculating the accuracy of the forecast on the dataset with which you created the model. This demonstration is not the best practice, however; it's like testing a student on questions that they have already seen in the sense that the same customer observations were used to fit the model. The best practice in forecasting is to test the accuracy of a model on observations that were not used to fit the model. This type of testing is known as *out-of-sample* testing because it tests observations that were not in the data sample given to the algorithm for determining the model.

In general, accuracy is lower for new customer observations than for the ones used in the model fitting. How different in-sample and out-of-sample accuracy are depends on many factors. For regression on churn problems, the difference is usually slight; for the machine learning model shown in section 9.5, using in-sample observations for testing can create a large overestimate of accuracy.

> **TAKEAWAY**   Forecasting models should be tested on out-of-sample data that was not used to fit the model.

Do you need to wait to see how well the model predicts new churns on live customers to see how accurate it is? Waiting would work, and you should do that, but there's an easier way: hold back some of the observations from the data when you fit the model and then test the accuracy on those held-back observations. Then you can see how accurate the model would be on new customers it hasn't seen without waiting to get fresh new customers. After testing, you refit the model on all the data without holding anything back and use that final version to make the real new forecasts on active customers.

The next question is which data to use and how much you should hold back for testing. The most realistic way to test the accuracy of a churn-forecasting model is to use a historical simulation. This procedure is called backtesting and is illustrated in figure 9.7.

> **DEFINITION**   *Backtesting* is the historical simulation of a forecasting model's accuracy, as though it had been repeatedly fit and then used to forecast out of sample for consecutive periods in the past.

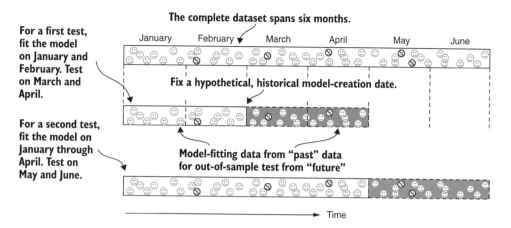

Figure 9.7 **The backtesting process for measuring forecasting performance**

Here's how backtesting works:

1 Decide on a point in time in the past that is somewhere around one-half to one-third of the time in the period spanned by your dataset.

2 Use all the observations that correspond to points in time before that date to fit your model.

3 Use the observations in the time from one to three months after the date you chose to test. This procedure tests what the accuracy of your model would have been if it were forecasting churn in the past but still forecasts on customer data that came in after the model was fit.

4 Assuming that you have more data, advance the target date to the end of your test period.

5 Repeat the process by refitting the model on all the data from the first fit, plus the observations you used to test on, and test the next one to three months.

My advice for churn forecasting is a bit different from what is taught in most data science and statistics courses, which rarely mention backtesting. Students usually learn a random shuffling procedure to create out-of-sample tests that don't pay attention to timing. The procedure of backtesting originated in financial forecasting on Wall Street. Backtesting was created due to the observation that markets are changing all the time, so predictive models perform differently on randomly shuffled accuracy tests than on live forecasting. Accuracy tests based on a realistic historical simulation do the best job of estimating how a model would have done if had been live at the time.

The reason why live-prediction accuracy can differ from a shuffled data test is that if economic conditions change, such as at the start of a recession, a live model fit before the recession probably won't predict as well under the new recession conditions. For the model to do better, the new conditions have to be observed for some time; then the model could be refit. But with a shuffled data test, it is as though you fit a model that knows about the recession by observing the future before it happened. Such a model can appear to forecast well, but the real results will likely be worse than the test.

The same reasoning applies to churn forecasting. If your market, product, or competition changes during the time spanned by your dataset, it might be hard to forecast churn accurately in the time after the change. If you shuffle the data, you can get a different result than you would have if you had been forecasting for your customers at that time. The most realistic simulation is to have your model run through the data and forecast out of sample in the order in which events happened. You may not know whether the conditions driving your customer churn behavior changed during your period of observation. But what you don't know can hurt you, so backtesting is the best practice. Although the historical simulation I described sounds complicated, open source packages take care of all the details for you.

9.2.2   Backtesting code

Open source Python packages provide functions that run historical simulations like the one described in section 9.2.1. You provide the package your data and the type of model you're fitting and tell it how many tests you want to divide your data into.

Figure 9.8 shows example output from a historical simulation, including the lift and the AUC for each out-of-sample test as well as the averages. For the simulated dataset, you will probably find that the AUC and lift in the backtest are similar to the AUC and lift from the in-sample data, but that will not necessarily be the case for a real product dataset.

mean _fit_ time	std_ fit_ time	mean_ score_ time	std_ score_ time	param _C	par- ams	split0 _test _lift	split1 _test _lift	mean _test _lift	std_ test_ lift	rank_ test_ lift	split0 _test _AUC	split1 _test _AUC	mean _test _AUC	std_t est_A UC	rank_ test_ AUC
0.0447	0.0135	0.0127	0.0003	1	{'C': 1}	4.028	4.027	4.027	0.000	1	0.7386	0.7432	0.7409	0.0023	1

Timing statistics   See sections 9.3. and 9.4   The lift in each test   Statistics of the lift   The AUC in each test   Statistics of the AUC

Figure 9.8 Output of backtesting (listing 9.3)

In figure 9.8, each testing period is known as a split, in reference to the fact that the data is split into a dataset for fitting the model and a holdout dataset for testing.

> **DEFINITION** *Split* is a generic term for the division of a dataset into separate parts for model fitting and testing.

Listing 9.3 contains the Python code that produced the output shown in figure 9.8. This listing contains many of the same elements as the regression fitting code in chapter 8 and the accuracy measurements discussed in section 9.1. But there are three important new classes from the sklearn.model_selection package:

- GridSearchCV—A utility that performs a variety of tests on forecasting models. The name of the class derives from the fact that it specializes in searching for the best models through a process known as *cross-validation* (the CV in Grid-SearchCV). You'll learn more about cross-validation in section 9.4; for now, you use the object to test a single model.
- TimeSeriesSplit—A helper object that tells GridSearchCV that the testing should be performed by historical simulation, rather than another type of test (typically, random shuffling). The name of the class is TimeSeriesSplit, but I recommend that you stick with the original Wall Street term that your business colleagues are most likely to understand: backtesting.
- scorer—An object that wraps a scoring function. When you use a nonstandard scoring function with GridSearchCV, you must wrap it in such an object. This task is easy: call the make_scorer function, provided by the package for this purpose. You pass your scoring function as a parameter when making the scorer object. In listing 9.3, this technique is used for the top decile lift calculation.

Other than TimeSeriesSplit, the parameters required to create GridSearchCV are the regression model object and a dictionary containing the two accuracy measurement functions. The lift measurement function is passed with the scorer object, and the AUC scoring function is passed as a string (naming it because this scorer object is a Python standard).

Other parameters that control the details of the test include the following:

- return_train_score—Controls whether to also test for in-sample accuracy (also known as training accuracy)
- param_grid—Tests parameters to find a better model (a subject you learn more about in section 9.4)
- refit—Tells the model to refit a final model on all the data (which you will do in section 9.4)

In other respects, listing 9.3 combines elements you have already seen: loading and preparing data, creating a regression model, and saving results. One thing to note is that the test is triggered by calling the fit function on GridSearchCV rather than on the regression object itself.

Listing 9.3 Backtesting with Python time-series cross-validation

```
import pandas as pd
from sklearn.model_selection
    import GridSearchCV, TimeSeriesSplit      ◁—  These classes
from sklearn.metrics import make_scorer              run the tests.
from sklearn.linear_model import LogisticRegression
```

These classes run the tests.

Defines a custom score function: the lift score

Reuses listing 8.2 to reload data →

Reuses listing 9.2 to calculate the lift ←

Loads the data, keeping the outcome as a churn flag ←

Creates an object that controls the splits →

Creates a scorer object that wraps the lift function ←

Creates a dictionary that defines the scoring functions ←

Creates a new Logistic-Regression object →

Creates a GridSearchCV object →

Runs the test ←

Saves the results in a DataFrame ←

```
from listing_8_2_logistic_regression
    import prepare_data
from listing_9_2_top_decile_lift
    import calc_lift

def backtest(data_set_path,n_test_split):

    X,y = prepare_data(data_set_path,as_retention=False)

    tscv = TimeSeriesSplit(n_splits=n_test_split)

    lift_scorer =
        make_scorer(calc_lift, needs_proba=True)
    score_models =
        {'lift': lift_scorer, 'AUC': 'roc_auc'}

    retain_reg = LogisticRegression(penalty='l1',
                        solver='liblinear', fit_intercept=True)

    gsearch = GridSearchCV(estimator=retain_reg,
                    scoring=score_models, cv=tscv,
                    return_train_score=False,  param_grid={'C' : [1]},
        refit=False)

    gsearch.fit(X,y)

    result_df = pd.DataFrame(gsearch.cv_results_)
    save_path = data_set_path.replace('.csv', '_backtest.csv')
    result_df.to_csv(save_path, index=False)
    print('Saved test scores to ' + save_path)
```

You should run listing 9.3 on your own data from the social network simulation (chapter 8) and confirm that your result is similar to the one in figure 9.8. With the Python wrapper program, the command to run is the following:

```
fight-churn/listings/run_churn_listing.py --chapter 9 --listing 3
```

9.2.3 *Backtesting considerations and pitfalls*

For the simulation, only two tests were used because the entire dataset spans only six months. If more tests were specified for a larger dataset, the additional results would appear as additional columns in the same file. But in backtesting for churn prediction, it is typical to test with a few splits. By contrast, the procedure you may have learned for randomly shuffled tests usually calls for 10 random tests or more. You should pick the number of splits based on the length of time spanned by your data sample and how often you would be likely to refit the model.

Although you may optimistically think you would refit a new model every month, in reality, many companies "set it and forget it." Even if you are very determined, you will probably refit your own model only a few times a year after you finish the initial development. (Refitting the simulation model every two months may be overly optimistic; I use this example for demonstration purposes.) Also, frequent model changes are confusing to businesspeople. In fact, some companies mandate an annual refitting of production models to prevent "moving the goal posts" when business metrics are tied to the model outputs. For example, if customer support representative compensation is linked to reducing churn probability, then the model must remain fixed for the fiscal year.

If you're worried that using a few splits for the test is not as rigorous as using 10 tests, don't worry. These measurements should be made with the spirit of agility and parsimony that I advocated in chapter 1. Using a few tests will tell you whether you are predicting well or have work to do on your model; doing more tests wastes time. Also, if a high number of test splits implies an unrealistic rate of refitting your model when it is live, your test may overestimate the accuracy you would achieve in the real world, where you refit less often.

One other pitfall to be aware of in backtesting for accuracy is the possibility of adverse effects due to mistakes in how times are recorded in your database or data warehouse. This problem occurs mainly if events, subscriptions, or other customer data records were backdated when they were added to your database. In that case, you would calculate historical metrics and run your test with information that may not be available in real time for live forecasting on active customers. This type of error is known as a lookahead error or bias in forecasting.

> **DEFINITION** A *lookahead bias* is an error that occurs when you estimate accuracy in a historical simulation using information that would not be available in real time for forecasting on active customers.

> **WARNING** Backdated records for events, subscriptions, or other customer data can lead to lookahead bias in your forecasts and cause the backtest to appear more accurate than what you would achieve in real-time forecasting.

The fix for lookahead bias is to be aware of any backdating of records in your database and, if necessary, to correct it with custom lags in the event selection when you calculate metrics. If you know that all events are loaded into the data warehouse with a one-week delay and backdated to the time the event occurred, for example, you should include this delay when you calculate your metrics. The trick is that you won't notice the one-week delay when you run your historical analysis, but you will when you try to forecast churn probabilities in real time and find that all your metrics are a week old.

9.3 *The regression control parameter*

After measuring the accuracy of your forecasts, you're probably wondering whether there is any way to be more accurate. Another problem I've mentioned is that a regression can result in many small weights on unimportant metrics. You have a way to adjust the regression that can help with both issues.

9.3.1   *Controlling the strength and number of regression weights*

In chapter 8, I mentioned that regression models can have too many small weights and that you can remove them. This technique is illustrated in figure 9.9, which shows the relative size of the regression weights from the social network simulation (figure 8.7 in chapter 8). Most of the weights are greater than 0.1, one weight is 0.00, and two weights are 0.01; those 0.01 weights are extraneous. Two small weights may not seem like a problem, but remember that real data can have a dozen or more smaller weights, which can make it harder for you and the businesspeople to understand the result.

Group/metric	Weight	|Weight|	
metric_group_2	0.68	0.68	
newfriend_per_month	0.48	0.48	Weaker weights may be removed when they make a trivial contribution to the regression.
adview_per_post	−0.47	0.47	
metric_group_1	0.35	0.35	
like_per_post	0.18	0.18	In this case, weights below around 0.1 could be removed.
days_since_newfriend	−0.17	0.17	
unfriend_per_month	−0.16	0.16	
dislike_pcnt	−0.14	0.14	
newfriend_pcnt_chng	0.11	0.11	
post_per_message	−0 04	0 04	?
dislike_per_month	−0.02	0.02	
reply_per_message	−0.01	0.01	
unfriend_per_newfriend	0.01	0.01	

Figure 9.9   Regressions result in small weights that can be removed.

It might seem that the simplest thing to do would be to set those very small weights to zero. But the decision about which weights to keep and which to remove may not be so clear-cut. Also, if some weights are removed, others should be readjusted. The regression algorithm has a more principled way to handle this situation with a parameter controlling the total weight available for the algorithm to distribute across all the metrics.

When the control parameter is set to a high value, the regression weights tend to be larger, and there will be fewer zeros. When the control parameter is set to a low value, the weights tend to be lower, and the lower the parameter is set, the more weights will be zero. The precise weights are optimized by the algorithm. Unfortunately, this controlling parameter has no good, generally accepted name. Because there is only one relevant parameter for the regression, I will call it the control parameter. Conveniently, the Python code refers to the parameter as (capital) C, so calling it the control parameter is clear.

DEFINITION The *regression control parameter* sets the size and number of weights that result from a regression. Higher C settings yield more and higher weights, and lower C settings yield fewer and lower weights.

The Python nomenclature C derives from something called a *cost parameter* in the regression algorithm. It's called a cost because the algorithm includes a penalty cost for the size of the weights. But the documentation states that the cost is $1/C$, so C is the inverse or reciprocal of the cost. It is confusing to have a parameter that you call the cost, but where the cost is higher for lower parameter values, so I stick with calling it a control parameter, or C.

9.3.2 *Regression with the control parameter*

Listing 9.4 shows a new version of the regression using the control parameter. This listing reuses all the helper functions from listing 8.2 (chapter 8), so there's not much to it. The only difference is that listing 9.4 takes a value for C in the function call, passes it in when it creates the object, and then passes it as an extension to the output files. The output files are the same as those produced by listing 8.2.

You should run listing 9.4 on your simulated data. To see the effect of setting the C parameter, you can run three versions. These three versions have the C parameter set to 0.02, 0.01 and 0.005, respectively. Run these versions with the Python wrapper program, using the version argument as follows:

```
fight-churn/listings/run_churn_listing.py --chapter 9 --listing 4 --version 1 2 3
```

The results of running the two versions of listing 9.4 are compared in figure 9.10, along with the result from the original regression (listing 8.2):

- In the original listing, all but one weight is nonzero, and the highest-magnitude weight is 0.68.
- With the C parameter set to 0.02, four weights are zero, and the highest-magnitude weight is 0.61.
- With the C parameter set to 0.005, eight weights are zero, and the highest magnitude weight is 0.42.

This overall pattern is what happens as the C parameter is reduced.

Listing 9.4 Regression using the control parameter C

```
from sklearn.linear_model import LogisticRegression
from listing_8_2_logistic_regression
    import prepare_data, save_regression_model
from listing_8_2_logistic_regression
    import save_regression_summary, save_dataset_predictions

def regression_cparam(data_set_path, C_param):
    X,y = prepare_data(data_set_path)
```

This listing uses all the helper functions from listing 8.2.

There is an additional parameter, C, for the regression.

Passes the parameter when the regression is created

```
retain_reg = LogisticRegression( C=C_param,
                                  penalty='l1',
                                  solver='liblinear', fit_intercept=True)
retain_reg.fit(X, y)
c_ext = '_c{:.3f}'.format(C_param)
save_regression_summary(data_set_path,retain_reg,ext=c_ext)
save_regression_model(data_set_path,retain_reg,ext=c_ext)
save_dataset_predictions(data_set_path,retain_reg,X,ext=c_ext)
```

Fits the regression, as in listing 8.2

Adds the parameter to the result filename

Calls the save functions

Group/Metric	C=1	C=0.02	C=0.01	C=0.005
metric_group_1	0.35	0.31	0.30	0.28
metric_group_2	0.68	0.61	0.54	0.42
newfriend_per_month	0.48	0.27	0.14	0
dislike_per_month	−0.02	0	0	0
unfriend_per_month	−0.16	−0.11	−0.06	0
adview_per_post	−0.47	−0.36	−0.27	−0.18
reply_per_message	−0.01	0	0	0
like_per_post	0.18	0.08	0	0
post_per_message	−0.04	0	0	0
unfriend_per_newfriend	0.01	0	0	0
dislike_pcnt	−0.14	−0.15	−0.14	−0.08
newfriend_pcnt_chng	0.11	0.08	0.04	0
days_since_newfriend	−0.17	−0.17	−0.16	−0.14

When the regression is run with the C parameter set to a low level, lower weights are used overall and more weights are set to zero by the regression.

The zeroed weights are not exactly those that had the lowest contribution in the original regression: the C parameter is not an explicit cutoff.

Figure 9.10   Comparison of regression weights resulting from different values of the control parameter, C

Note that the response of the algorithm to the C parameter setting is irregular. Changing the C parameter from 1 to 0.02 removes two additional metrics from the regression results, and a further reduction from point 0.02 to 0.005 removes three more. The way that the parameter is defined in the algorithm, you need to consider values of the control parameter that vary in a range below 1.0 (the default) and above zero, but the impact varies on a logarithmic scale as the parameter gets smaller.

When I say that the impact varies on a logarithmic scale, I mean that changes in the parameter must be significantly different in the logarithm of the parameter to make a big difference in the algorithm. The impact of going from 1.0 to 0.9 is not going to be much, and the impact of going from 1 to 0.1 is likely to be about the same as going from 0.1 to 0.01. It is inefficient to test the range of parameters between 1 and 10 on a linear scale like [1, 0.9, 0.8, ..., 0.1] because the best value can be below 0.1, and you will probably not see that much change between values like 0.9 and 0.8. Instead, you should test parameters decreasing by a divisive factor, such as dividing by 10: [1, 0.1, 0.01, 0.001]. How small you have to go to see the right impact depends on your data. If you want to do a more detailed search of the parameter space, divide by a smaller factor like 2, as in [0.64, 0.32, 0.16, ...].

> **TAKEAWAY** When you check smaller values of C, you must check values that are orders of a magnitude smaller than 1.0. Usually, a C parameter around 1.0 assigns weights to all (or most) of the metrics that are even a little bit related to churn. To reduce the number of nonzero weights, try values of C like 0.1, 0.01, and 0.001.

9.4 Picking the regression parameter by testing (cross-validation)

At this point, you should be wondering how low you should go with the control parameter. It makes sense to remove metrics with small weights, but at what point should you stop? This decision is best made by looking at the accuracy that results from each parameter setting.

9.4.1 Cross-validation

It should come as no surprise that you can remove metrics with small weights from a regression, and it won't make much difference in the accuracy. (Because these weights are the small weights, they don't make much difference.) A logical approach is to remove weights until you find that doing so harms accuracy. What can be more surprising is that removing some metrics *improves* accuracy.

You're going to take different values of the C parameter and run a backtest with the parameter to see how accurate the resulting models are. At the same time, you can check how many metrics get zero and nonzero weights in the regression. Figure 9.11 illustrates this process. The general term for this type of procedure in machine learning and statistics is cross-validation.

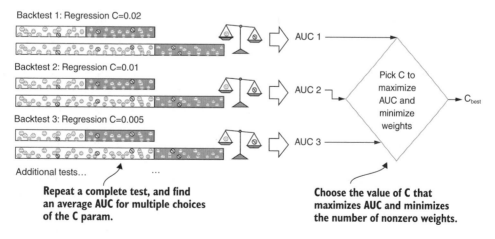

Figure 9.11 Cross-validation to select the regression parameter

> **DEFINITION** *Cross-validation* is the process of optimizing a forecasting model by comparing the accuracy and other characteristics of models created with different parameters.

Cross-validation is a common task in data science and machine learning, and what the CV means in the GridSearchCV object you were introduced to earlier. The GridSearch part of the name refers to the fact that a typical cross-validation works on a sequence or multiple sequences of parameters. If there were two parameters, each with its own sequence of values, the combinations of those two sequences would define a grid. In fact, there can be any number of parameters. For the regression model, you will do a cross-validation of one parameter. Later, you use higher-dimensional cross-validation for a machine learning model.

9.4.2 Cross-validation code

Figure 9.12 shows the main result of cross-validation, which plots the AUC, the lift, and the number of weights that you get when running the regression for a sequence of values from the C parameter. This result confirms that small-weight metrics can be removed, and accuracy will not suffer: the number of metrics can be reduced from 13 to 9 before any noticeable change in accuracy occurs. In the simulation, there was a slight gain in the lift, but no gain in the AUC when the less important metrics were removed.

Listing 9.5 contains the code that produced figure 9.12. The listing contains multiple function definitions, but note that much of the code is for plotting and analysis. The Python open source package takes care of the cross-validation in a few lines. The functions in listing 9.5 follow:

- crossvalidate_regression—This main function performs cross-validation, and it is almost the same as that in listing 9.4. The most important difference is that a sequence of C parameter values is passed instead of a single value. The other difference is that after the fit function on the GridSearchCV object returns, helper functions are called to perform additional analysis and to save the results.

- test_n_weights—The GridSearchCV object tests each parameter for the accuracy of the model on the backtest, but it doesn't test the number of weights returned by the regression. A separate loop is called to fit a regression at each C parameter in the sequence, and the number of nonzero weights is counted. This is done on the full dataset, so it is not a backtest but a measurement of the final model.

- plot_regression_test—This function creates the plot shown in figure 9.12 by combining the results for AUC, lift, and the number of metrics with nonzero weights.

- one_subplot—This helper function creates and formats each subplot.

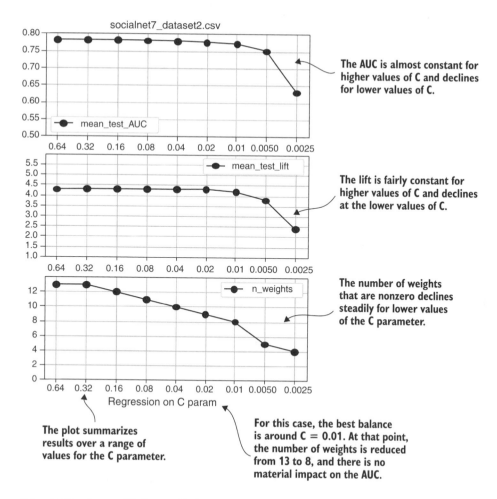

Figure 9.12   Cross-validation result plot

Listing 9.5 also saves the results from figure 9.12 in a .csv file, shown in figure 9.13. This result is the output from GridsearchCV (as in section 9.2), but instead of a single row, there is one row in the table per value of the C parameter that was tested. There is also an extra column with the result from testing the number of weights. The output from the cross-validation with multiple parameters shows that the columns labeled rank_test_lift and rank_test_AUC refer to the ranking of the models fit with the different parameter values on the accuracy metrics. (Some of these columns may have seemed extraneous when you first saw them in section 9.2.)

You should run listing 9.5 with the following command-line arguments to generate your own plot like figure 9.12 and a .csv file like figure 9.13:

```
fight-churn/listings/run_churn_listing.py --chapter 9 --listing 5
```

Each row summarizes tests with a different C parameter (timing information omitted).

param _C	params	split0_ test_ lift	split1_ test_ lift	mean_ test_ lift	std_ test_ lift	rank_ test_ lift	split0_ test_ AUC	split1_ test_ AUC	mean_ test_ AUC	std_ test_ AUC	rank_ test_ AUC	n_ weights
0.64	{'C': 0.64}	3.969	4.586	4.278	0.308	6	0.7720	0.7896	0.7808	0.0088	1	13
0.32	{'C': 0.32}	3.969	4.621	4.295	0.326	2	0.7719	0.7895	0.7807	0.0088	2	13
0.16	{'C': 0.16}	3.969	4.621	4.295	0.326	2	0.7717	0.7894	0.7805	0.0088	3	12
0.08	{'C': 0.08}	3.969	4.621	4.295	0.326	2	0.7710	0.7890	0.7800	0.0090	4	11
0.04	{'C': 0.04}	3.995	4.586	4.291	0.296	5	0.7692	0.7882	0.7787	0.0095	5	10
0.02	{'C': 0.02}	3.995	4.621	4.308	0.313	1	0.7648	0.7863	0.7756	0.0107	6	9
0.01	{'C': 0.01}	3.842	4.517	4.180	0.338	7	0.7595	0.7821	0.7708	0.0113	7	8
0.005	{'C': 0.005}	3.206	4.379	3.793	0.587	8	0.7225	0.7790	0.7507	0.0282	8	5
0.0025	{'C': 0.0025}	1.000	3.793	2.397	1.397	9	0.5000	0.7604	0.6302	0.1302	9	4

Parameter   The lift in each test   Statistics of the lift   Rank of the lift   The AUC in each test   Statistics of the AUC   Rank of the AUC   Number of regression weights

Differences in the AUC are pretty small until the final row.

Figure 9.13   Cross-validation result table

Listing 9.5   Regression C parameter cross-validation

```
import pandas as pd
import ntpath
import numpy as np
from sklearn.model_selection import GridSearchCV, TimeSeriesSplit
from sklearn.metrics import make_scorer
from sklearn.linear_model import LogisticRegression
import matplotlib.pyplot as plt

from listing_8_2_logistic_regression import prepare_data
from listing_9_2_top_decile_lift import calc_lift

def crossvalidate_regression(data_set_path,
                             n_test_split):          ◁── The number of test
                                                          splits is a parameter.

    X,y = prepare_data(data_set_path,as_retention=False)
    tscv = TimeSeriesSplit(n_splits=n_test_split)        The score function wraps
    score_models = {                                ◁── the lift in a scorer object.
        'lift': make_scorer(calc_lift, needs_proba=True),
        'AUC': 'roc_auc'
    }
    retain_reg = LogisticRegression(penalty='l1',
                             solver='liblinear', fit_intercept=True)
    test_params = {'C' : [0.64, 0.32, 0.16, 0.08,
                          0.04, 0.02, 0.01, 0.005, 0.0025]}
    gsearch = GridSearchCV(estimator=retain_reg,          ◁── Creates the cross-
                    scoring=score_models, cv=tscv,            validation object,
                    verbose=1,return_train_score=False,       and calls the fit
                    param_grid=test_params, refit=False)      method
    gsearch.fit(X,y)
```

Instead of one C parameter, tests a list ──▷

Puts the result in a DataFrame

Makes a plot with plot_regression_test

```
result_df = pd.DataFrame(gsearch.cv_results_)
result_df['n_weight']=
    test_n_weights(X,y,test_params)
result_df.to_csv(data_set_path.replace('.csv', '_crossval.csv'),
    index=False)
plot_regression_test(data_set_path,result_df)
```

Adds another column with the result of the weight test

Loops over the parameters

Fits the model

```
def test_n_weights(X,y,test_params):
    n_weights=[]
    for c in test_params['C']:
        lr = LogisticRegression(penalty='l1',C=c,
                    solver='liblinear', fit_intercept=True)
        res=lr.fit(X,~y)
        n_weights.append(
            res.coef_[0].astype(bool).sum(axis=0))
    return n_weights
```

Tests the number of weights for different C parameters

Creates a logistic regression with one value of C

Counts the number of nonzero weights

String version of C parameter to use as the x-axis

Adds a title above the first of three subplots

Calls a helper function to plot the number of nonzero weights

```
def plot_regression_test(data_set_path, result_df):
    result_df['plot_C']=result_df['param_C'].astype(str)
    plt.figure(figsize=(4,6))
    plt.rcParams.update({'font.size':8})
    one_subplot(result_df,1,'mean_test_AUC',
            ylim=(0.6,0.8),ytick=0.05)
    plt.title(
        ntpath.basename(data_set_path).replace(
                    '_dataset.csv',' cross-validation'))
    one_subplot(result_df,2,'mean_test_lift',
            ylim=(2, 6),ytick=0.5)
    one_subplot(result_df,3,'n_weight',
            ylim=(0,int(1+result_df['n_weights'].max())),ytick=2)
    plt.xlabel('Regression C Param')
    plt.savefig(data_set_path.replace('.csv', '_crossval_regression.png'))
    plt.close()
```

Makes a plot from the result of the regression tests

Calls a helper function to plot the AUC

Calls a helper function to plot the lift

Adds an x-label after the third subplot

Starts the subplot given by the parameter

```
def one_subplot(result_df,plot_n,var_name,ylim,ytick):
    ax = plt.subplot(3,1,plot_n)
    ax.plot('plot_C', var_name,
            data=result_df, marker='o', label=var_name)
    plt.ylim(ylim[0],ylim[1])
    plt.yticks(np.arange(ylim[0],ylim[1], step=ytick))
    plt.legend()
    plt.grid()
```

Sets the y-limits based on the parameters

Sets the ticks based on the parameters

Plots the named variable against the string version of C

9.4.3 *Regression cross-validation case studies*

Figure 9.14 shows examples of regression cross-validation from real company case studies. The number of nonzero weights is shown as a percentage rather than a count; otherwise, these results are read the same way as figure 9.12.

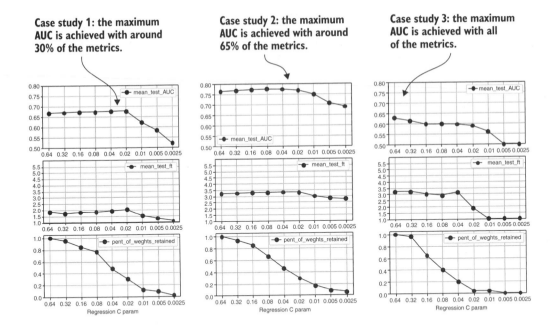

Figure 9.14   Cross-validation case study results

Following are some interesting features of the case study results:

- The forecasts have AUC in the range 0.6 to 0.8.
- The forecasts have lift in the range 2.0 to 3.5.
- For two of the three case studies, a noticeable improvement in AUC and lift occurs when many metrics get zero weight from the regression. (This result is a clear example of simplicity also benefiting accuracy.) In these cases, the optimal values of the C parameter are in the range of around 0.02 to 0.08. The improvement over including all the features is a few percentage points of AUC.
- For the third simulation, the optimal AUC is achieved with all the metrics; removing any metrics results in significant loss of accuracy.

These results are typical, but you may see more diversity in real case studies than I can present here.

9.5   *Forecasting churn risk with machine learning*

So far, you have learned about forecasting churn with a regression in which predictions are made by multiplying metrics by a set of weights. You can also predict churn with other kinds of forecasting models that are collectively known as machine learning. There is no official definition of what constitutes a machine learning model, but for the purpose of this book, I use the following.

> **DEFINITION** A *machine learning model* is any predictive algorithm that has the following two characteristics: (1) the algorithm learns to make the prediction by processing sample data (as compared with making predictions with rules set by a human programmer), and (2) the algorithm is not the regression algorithm.

The second condition may seem strange because the regression algorithm certainly meets the first condition. The distinction is historical because the regression approach predates machine learning methods by decades.

9.5.1 The XGBoost learning model

This book covers only one machine learning algorithm—XGBoost—but the same techniques for fitting the model and forecasting apply to most other algorithms you may consider. The XGBoost algorithm is based on the concept of a decision tree, illustrated in figure 9.15.

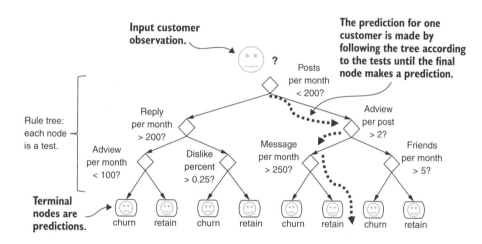

Figure 9.15 Making predictions with a tree of rules

> **DEFINITION** A *decision tree* is an algorithm for predicting an outcome (such as a customer's churning or not churning) that consists of a binary tree made up of rules or tests.

Each test in a decision tree takes a single metric and checks whether it is greater than or less than a predetermined cut point. The prediction for an observation (of a customer) is determined by starting at the root of the tree and performing the first test. The result of the test determines which of the two branches to follow from the node leading to one of the second-level tests. The result of all the tests determines a path through the tree, and each leaf of the tree has a designated prediction.

Small decision trees seem to be simple, and they were once considered to be easy-to-interpret machine learning models. But in practice, large decision trees for datasets with many metrics become hard to interpret. Fortunately, no one has to read the rules in the tree to make a prediction.

An algorithm is used to test metrics and decide on the cut points to optimize performance when making predictions using the sample data. If a backtest shows that the results are accurate, you can make predictions by using a decision tree without being too concerned about the substance of the rules. Methods to interpret a decision tree exist, but they are beyond the scope of this book. If you have more than a few metrics, understanding the influence of metrics on the likelihood of churn is best done through the grouping and regression methods shown in earlier chapters, so I won't spend time on interpreting decision trees.

Apart from being difficult to interpret, decision trees are no longer state of the art in terms of prediction accuracy. But decision trees are actually the building blocks for more accurate machine learning models. One example is a random forest, illustrated in figure 9.16.

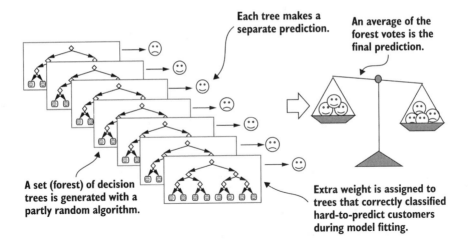

Figure 9.16   **Making predictions with a forest of rule trees**

DEFINITION   A *random forest* is an algorithm for predicting an outcome such as a customer's churning by randomly generating a large set of decision trees (a forest). All the trees try to predict the same outcome, but each does so according to a different set of learned rules. The final prediction is made by averaging the predictions of the forest.

The random forest is an example of what is called an ensemble prediction algorithm because the final prediction is made from the combination of a group of other machine learning algorithms. *Ensemble* means a group evaluated as a whole rather than individually. A random forest is a simple type of ensemble in that each tree gets an equal vote in the outcome, and additional trees are added at random. Boosting is a name for machine learning algorithms that make some important improvements over ensembles such as random forest.

> **DEFINITION**   *Boosting* is a machine learning ensemble in which the ensemble members are added so that they correct the errors of the existing ensemble.

Rather than randomly adding decision trees, as in a random forest, you create each new tree in a boosting ensemble to correct wrong answers made by the existing ensemble, rather than repredicting on the correct examples. Internal to the boosting algorithm, successive trees are generated to correct the observations that were not correctly classified by earlier trees. Also, the weight assigned to successive trees in the vote is made to best correct the mistakes, not an equal vote like in random forests. These improvements make boosted forests of decisions trees more accurate than a truly random forest of decision trees.

XGBoost (short for *extreme gradient* boosting) is a machine learning model that (at the time of this writing) is the most popular and successful model for general-purpose prediction. XGBoost is popular because it delivers state-of-the-art performance, and the algorithm to fit the model is relatively fast (compared with other boosting algorithms, but not as fast as regression). Details about the XGBoost algorithm are beyond the scope of this book, but there are many excellent free resources online.

9.5.2   *XGBoost cross-validation*

Machine learning algorithms like XGBoost can make accurate predictions, but this accuracy comes with some additional complexity. One area of complexity is that the algorithms have multiple optional parameters that you must choose correctly to get the best results. The optional parameters for XGBoost include ones that control how the individual decision trees are generated, as well as parameters that control how the votes of different decision trees are combined. Here are a few of the most important parameters for XGBoost:

- `max_depth`—The maximum depth of rules in each decision tree
- `n_estimator`—The number of decision trees to generate
- `learning_rate`—How heavily to emphasize the weight of votes from the best trees
- `min_child_weight`—The minimum weight of each tree in the vote, regardless of how well it did

Because there is no straightforward way to select the values for so many parameters, the values are set by out-of-sample cross-validation. You used this approach for the control parameter on the regression in section 9.4.

> **TAKEAWAY**   State-of-the-art machine learning models have so many parameters that the only way to make sure you pick the best values is to cross-validate

a large number of them. That is, you test a sequence of plausible values for each parameter and choose the ones that have the best values on a cross-validation test.

Figure 9.17 shows an example of such a cross-validation result.

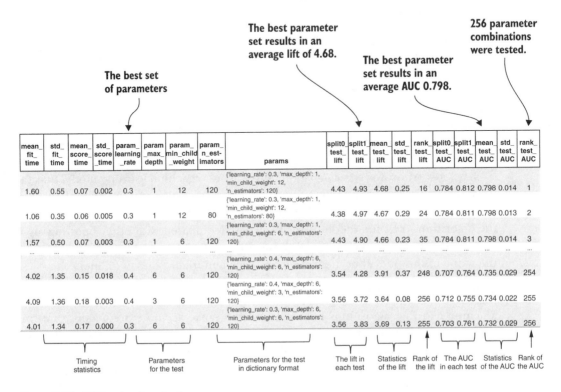

Figure 9.17 XGBoost code output

Figure 9.17 was created by running listing 9.6 on the simulated social network dataset used in earlier chapters. It is similar to the cross-validation results you saw for picking the regression C parameter, but it has both more columns and more rows:

- There are four columns of parameters because four parameters were part of the test: max_depth, n_estimator, learning_rate, and minimum_child_weight.
- There are many more rows in the output table—256 parameter combinations, to be precise. The reason for 256 parameter combinations becomes clear when you inspect listing 9.6: the test is made over four parameters, and the sequence of values for each parameter has four entries. The total number of combinations is the product of the number of values for each parameter—in this case, $4 \times 4 \times 4 \times 4 = 256$.

You should run listing 9.6 on your own simulated data, using the following usual Python wrapper program command with these arguments:

```
fight-churn/listings/run_churn_listing.py --chapter 9 --listing 6
```

Do not be surprised if the cross-validation for the XGBoost model takes a lot longer than it did for the regression. There are a lot more parameter combinations to test, and each time a model is fit, the process takes significantly longer. The precise time can vary (depending on your hardware), but for me, the XGBoost model takes about 40 times longer to fit in comparison with the regression model. As shown in figure 9.8, the regression takes only a few hundredths of a second to fit on average; figure 9.17 shows that the XGBoost fits take around 1 to 4 seconds.

NOTE XGBoost is in its own Python package, so if you have not used it before, you need to install it before running listing 9.6.

Listing 9.6 XGBoost cross-validation

```
import pandas as pd
import pickle
from sklearn.model_selection import GridSearchCV, TimeSeriesSplit
from sklearn.metrics import make_scorer
import xgboost as xgb                    ◁─── Imports XGBoost, which
                                              is in a separate package

from listing_8_2_logistic_regression import prepare_data
from listing_9_2_top_decile_lift import calc_lift


def crossvalidate_xgb(data_set_path,n_test_split):

   X,y = prepare_data(data_set_path,ext='',as_retention=False)
   tscv = TimeSeriesSplit(n_splits=n_test_split)
   score_models = {'lift': make_scorer(calc_lift, needs_proba=True), 'AUC':
      'roc_auc'}

   xgb_model = xgb.XGBClassifier(objective='binary:logistic')   ◁
   test_params = { 'max_depth': [1,2,4,6],
                   'learning_rate': [0.1,0.2,0.3,0.4],
                   'n_estimators': [20,40,80,120],
                   'min_child_weight' : [3,6,9,12]}

   gsearch = GridSearchCV(estimator=xgb_model,n_jobs=-1,
       scoring=score_models,
                cv=tscv, verbose=1, return_train_score=False,
                      param_grid=test_params,refit='AUC')
   gsearch.fit(X.values,y)    ◁
```

Most of this function is the same as listing 9.5: the regression cross-validation. → `X,y = prepare_data(...)`

Tests tree depths from 1 to 6 → `test_params = { 'max_depth': [1,2,4,6],`

Tests learning rates from 0.1 to 0.4 → `'learning_rate': [0.1,0.2,0.3,0.4],`

Creates an XGBClassifier object for a binary outcome

Tests the number of estimators from 20 to 120

Tests minimum weights from 3 to 12

Refits the best model according to AUC after cross-validation

Creates the GridSearchCV object with the XGBoost model object, and tests parameters

Passes as values, not a DataFrame, to avoid a known package issue at the time of this writing

Transfers the results to a DataFrame

```
result_df = pd.DataFrame(gsearch.cv_results_)
result_df.sort_values('mean_test_AUC',ascending=False,inplace=True)
save_path = data_set_path.replace('.csv', '_crossval_xgb.csv')
result_df.to_csv(save_path, index=False)
print('Saved test scores to ' + save_path)
```

Sorts the result so the best AUC is first

```
pickle_path = data_set_path.replace('.csv', '_xgb_model.pkl')
with open(pickle_path, 'wb') as fid:
    pickle.dump(gsearch.best_estimator, fid)
print('Saved model pickle to ' + pickle_path)
```

Creates a pickle of the best result

The best result is in the best_estimator field of the GridSearchCV object.

The code in listing 9.6 is similar to the one for cross-validating the regression (listing 9.5). The main steps are

1 Prepare the data.
2 Create a model instance (in this case, an XGBoost model).
3 Define the accuracy measurement functions to use (lift and AUC).
4 Define the sequences of parameters to test.
5 Pass the prepared parameters to the GridSearchCV object and call the fit function.
6 Save the results (with no additional analysis, as in the regression cross-validation).

One important and slightly subtle difference between listing 9.6 and the regression cross-validation in listing 9.5 is that the dataset is created from the original unscaled metrics, and it doesn't use scores or groups as you do for the regression. There is no reason to rescale metrics for XGBoost (or decision trees generally) because the cut points in the rules operate as well on the metrics, regardless of scale or skew. Also, grouping correlated metrics doesn't provide any benefit; in fact, it can hurt the performance of this type of machine learning model. Grouping correlated metrics is beneficial for interpretation and averts the problems that correlated metrics can cause in regression.

On the other hand, for XGBoost, a diversity of metrics is beneficial, and correlation does no harm. (If two metrics are correlated, either can make a suitable rule node in a tree.) For these reasons, the prepare_data function from chapter 8 is called with an empty extension argument so that it loads the original dataset rather than the grouped scores (the default behavior).

9.5.3   *Comparison of XGBoost accuracy to regression*

Because XGBoost takes much longer to fit the larger number of parameters, you should expect that it provides some improvement in forecasting accuracy. This expectation is confirmed in figure 9.18, which compares the AUC and lift achieved by regression and the XGBoost models for the simulation, as well as three real company

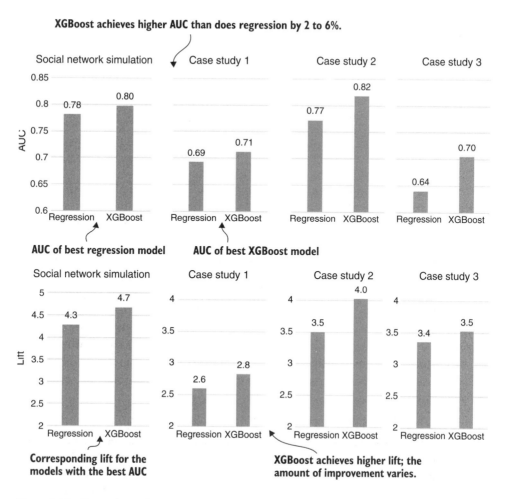

Figure 9.18 Comparison of regression and XGBoost lift

case study datasets for the companies introduced in chapter 1. The AUC improvement ranges from 0.02 to 0.06, and XGBoost always produces more accurate forecasts than does regression. In terms of lift, the improvement is 0.1 to 0.5.

Are those improvements significant? Remember that the full range of AUCs you're likely to see in churn forecasting is around 0.6 to 0.8. The maximum AUC, therefore, is 0.2 more than the minimum, and in relative terms, an improvement of 0.02 in AUC represents a 10% improvement in terms of overall possible range. By the same token, a 0.05 improvement in AUC represents 25% of the difference between worst and best in class, so these improvements are significant. Still, the forecasting is not perfect, even with machine learning, which why I advised in chapter 1 that predicting churn with machine learning is not likely to live up to some of the hype in the machine learning field.

> **TAKEAWAY** Though machine learning algorithms can produce forecasts that are significantly more accurate than regression, churn will always be hard to predict due to factors such as subjectivity, imperfect information, rarity, and extraneous factors that influence the timing of churn.

9.5.4 *Comparison of advanced and basic metrics*

Another important question is how much improvement in accuracy can be attributed to the work you did to create advanced metrics back in chapter 7. So far, you may have assumed that because the advanced metrics showed a relationship to churn in cohort analysis, they must have improved the model. But as you want to validate your data and modeling by showing that your model can predict out of sample, it makes sense to confirm that the work you did creating more metrics contributed something empirically.

To make the comparison on the simulated social network datasets, you can run additional versions of the cross-validation testing command on the original dataset from chapter 4. That is, you run the dataset without the advanced metrics from chapter 7—you use only the basic metrics from chapter 3. To run the regression cross-validation on the basic metric dataset, use the following:

```
fight-churn/listings/run_churn_listing.py --chapter 9 --listing 5 --version 1
```

The result is a cross-validation table like one shown in figure 9.13. You will probably find that the maximum accuracy of any model is somewhat less for data with basic metrics than for data with advanced metrics. As illustrated in the bar chart in figure 9.19, the maximum accuracy that I got on my regression simulation with basic metrics was 0.63; for the regression on the simulated data with advanced metrics, the maximum AUC was 0.75. The time spent creating advanced metrics was well spent. In fact, the regression accuracy with advanced metrics is significantly better than when using XGBoost with basic metrics, and the additional improvements for the machine learning algorithm when it uses advanced metrics are relatively small.

You can perform the same check on the XGBoost model by running the second version of the XGBoost cross-validation command with these arguments:

```
fight-churn/listings/run_churn_listing.py --chapter 9 --listing 6 --version 1
```

In this case, you will probably find that the XGBoost forecasts did a bit better with the advanced metrics. I got an AUC of 0.774 by using XGBoost with basic metrics compared with 0.797 for XGBoost with advanced metrics; the improvement attributable to advanced metrics is 0.023.

Figure 9.18 also contains similar comparisons for forecasts made on three real company case studies introduced in chapter 1. These comparisons show different

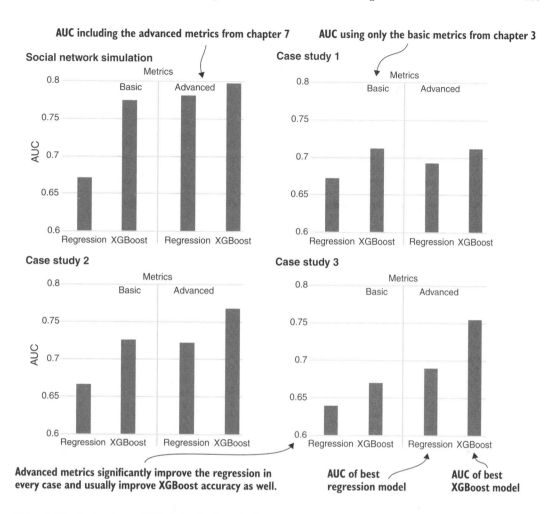

Figure 9.19 Comparison of AUC using basic and advanced metrics

relationships between accuracy with and without advanced metrics. These three cases illustrate the range of scenarios you may encounter in your own case studies:

1 In the first case study, the regression accuracy is significantly improved by the advanced metrics, but XGBoost doesn't get any improvement, and XGBoost is best overall. This result shows that you can't always expect advanced metrics to improve machine learning.

2 In the second case study, both the regression and XGBoost are significantly improved by the addition of advanced metrics. The regression accuracy with advanced metrics is about the same as the XGBoost accuracy with basic metrics. The XGBoost accuracy with advanced metrics is the highest of all by a significant amount: around 0.1 more than regression with basic metrics.

3   In the third case study, the regression using advanced metrics has higher accuracy than XGBoost without advanced metrics. But the highest accuracy of all is achieved by XGBoost using advanced metrics: more than 0.1 improvement over basic metrics and regression. This case study is most similar to the social network simulation.

These cases demonstrate that if high accuracy on churn forecasts is a high priority for you, both machine learning and advanced metrics are important. In my experience, advanced metrics usually improve the accuracy of churn forecasts for both regression and machine learning models like XGBoost.

9.6   *Segmenting customers with machine learning forecasts*

Listing 9.6 found a set of parameters that produces a machine learning model with high accuracy. The program also saved the best model in a pickle file. If you want to use the model to forecast on your active customers, you need to reload the saved model and use it on an active customer list. The code is demonstrated in listing 9.7. Listing 9.7 is practically the same as listing 9.5, which you used to make forecasts with the saved regression model. The listing does the following:

1   Reloads the saved model pickle
2   Loads the current customer dataset
3   Calls the `predict_proba` function on the model, passing the data as a parameter
4   Saves the results as a DataFrame of predictions and a histogram summarizing the result

As in the XGBoost classification in listing 9.6, the data is kept in its original form, unscaled and ungrouped. The preparation of the data for forecasting must match the way the data was prepared when the model was trained.

Listing 9.7   XGBoost forecasting

```
import pandas as pd
import os
import pickle
from listing_8_4_rescore_metrics import reload_churn_data
from listing_8_5_churn_forecast import forecast_histogram

def churn_forecast_xgb(data_set_path):
    pickle_path =
        data_set_path.replace('.csv', '_xgb_model.pkl')      ◁──┐ Reloads the XGBoost
    assert os.path.isfile(pickle_path),                          model saved in the
        'Run listing 9.6 to save an XGB model'                   pickle file
    with open(pickle_path, 'rb') as fid:
        xgb_model = pickle.load(fid)                          ◁──┐ Reloads the
                                                                  current customer
    curren_df = reload_churn_data(data_set_path,             ◁──┘ metric data
                        'current','8.3',is_customer_data=True)
```

Makes the predictions →

```
predictions =
    xgb_model.predict_proba(current_df.values)
predict_df = pd.DataFrame(predictions,
                          index=current_df.index,
                          columns=['retain_prob','churn_prob'])

forecast_save_path =
    data_set_path.replace('.csv', '_current_xgb_predictions.csv')
print('Saving results to %s' % forecast_save_path)
predict_df.to_csv(forecast_save_path, header=True)

forecast_histogram(data_set_path,
                   predict_df,ext='xgb')
```

← **Makes a DataFrame from the predictions**

← **This function from listing 8.5 makes a histogram.**

Listing 9.7 also creates a histogram of the XGBoost churn forecasts on current customers. It's not shown because it is similar to the plot that you made for the churn probability forecasts with the regression model (made with the same function).

NOTE You should check the calibration and distribution of XGBoost forecasts as you learned to do for the regression forecasts in chapter 8.

For the social network simulation, the distribution and calibration of XGBoost forecasts turned out to be similar to the regression, but this result is a coincidence, not something you can always expect. You can't expect XGBoost forecasts to be calibrated and distributed like the regression forecasts because the XGBoost forecast probabilities are not probabilities in the same sense as the regression forecast probabilities.

Recall that calibration refers to the property that your forecasts are in accordance with the true probability of the events occurring. On the other hand, accuracy measured by the AUC and lift depends on the ordering or ranking of the forecasts, not the precise values. The regression model is designed so that the forecast probabilities are calibrated to the sample data, as well as being as accurate as the model allows. When the XGBoost model gives a forecast probability, it is the weighted voted of the ensemble decision trees. Those votes are optimized to rank the risk of churn—something at which XGBoost is successful, as shown by the accuracy results. But the vote of the ensemble decision trees is not designed to produce forecasts calibrated to actual churn rates.

TAKEAWAY XGBoost doesn't necessarily give calibrated churn probability forecasts. The XGBoost model is optimized for accuracy as measured by the classification of churns, not matching observed churn rates.

As a consequence of the forecasts from the XGBoost model's not being reliably calibrated, the XGBoost forecasts are not suitable to use for estimating customer lifetime value, as was demonstrated in chapter 8.

WARNING Do not use XGBoost for predicting customer lifetime value or any other use case that depends on the churn probability forecasts matching real churn probabilities. The same applies to most machine learning models: read the literature for the model you're using to confirm whether it produces fore-casts that are calibrated in addition to being accurate.

Summary

- Because of the rarity of churn, the accuracy of churn forecasts cannot be mea-sured with the standard accuracy measurements.
- The area under the curve (AUC) is the percentage of times that the model ranks a churn as having higher risk than a nonchurn, considering all pairs of churns and nonchurns.
- The lift is the ratio of the churn rate in the top decile of churn risk forecasts to the overall churn rate.
- The AUC and lift are good measurements for the accuracy of churn forecast.
- Accuracy should be measured on samples that were not used to train the model.
- For churn, accuracy should be measured in a backtesting (historical) simulation that reflects the fact that product and market conditions may change over time.
- The regression model taught in this book includes a control parameter that sets the overall size of the weights and the number of nonzero weights.
- The best value to use for the regression control parameter can be found by test-ing the accuracy of versions of the model using different values of the regres-sion parameter.
- Setting a forecasting model parameter by testing is known as cross-validation.
- For regression, you choose the value of the control parameter that minimizes the number of nonzero weights and helps or doesn't harm accuracy.
- Usually, a significant fraction of the metrics can be assigned zero weights in a regression; the accuracy either improves or doesn't get worse.
- A machine learning model is a forecasting model that is fit from the data (not programmed) and is not the regression model.
- A decision tree is a simple machine learning model that forecasts by analyzing customers with a tree of metric comparison rules.
- XGBoost is a state-of-the-art machine learning model that uses an ensemble of decision trees and weights their predictions together to maximize accuracy.
- XGBoost and other machine learning models have many parameters that must be set using cross-validation.
- The accuracy of XGBoost forecasts generally exceeds the accuracy of regression forecasts.
- Using advanced metrics in addition to basic metrics usually makes forecasts more accurate for both regression and machine learning models.
- XGBoost churn probability forecasts are not calibrated to actual churn rates, so XGBoost churn forecasts should not be used for customer lifetime value or other use cases that depend on matching the actual churn probabilities.

Churn demographics
and firmographics

10

This chapter covers

- Creating a dataset that includes demographic or firmographic information
- Converting date information to intervals and analyzing the relationship to churn
- Analyzing text categories for the relationship to churn
- Forecasting churn probability with demographic or firmographic information
- Segmenting customers with demographic or firmographic information

You now know all about using customer behavior data to segment your customers for the purpose of creating interventions to increase engagement. These strategies are the most important ones for increasing customer engagement and retention, which is why they are the focus of the book. But one other way to reduce your customer churn is not about intervening with your existing customers: find new customers who are more likely to be engaged to begin with. Identify facts about customers who tend to be more engaged, and then focus your customer acquisition efforts on finding more customers like them. Such facts are generally known as demographic data (data about individuals) and firmographic data (data about companies). For the purpose of this discussion, I use the following definitions.

> **DEFINITION**   *Demographics* are facts about individual customers, and *firmographics* are facts about customers that are companies (firms).

Demographics and firmographics generally are unchanging facts about the customer or facts that change only rarely. Demographics and firmographics do not include product use or subscription-derived metrics, but they can include facts about how the customer signed up or about the hardware a customer uses to access an online service. Normally, a business-to-consumer (B2C) or direct-to-consumer (D2C) company uses demographic data, whereas a business-to-business (B2B) company uses firmographic data. As you will see, demographics and firmographics differ in the specific pieces of information that are normally available. But the characteristics of that information are similar in either case, and for that reason, the techniques for handling demographics and firmographics are the same.

> **NOTE**   This chapter uses the example of the social network simulation from the GitHub repository for the book (https://github.com/carl24k/fight-churn), which is a consumer product. For that reason, I generally speak about demographics, but the same techniques apply to firmographics.

It is worth noting at the outset that targeting demographics is the least direct method of reducing churn because it doesn't help your existing customers become more engaged. You can sometimes influence your customer's behavior, but you cannot change the demographic or firmographic facts about them! Also, targeting acquisitions usually has limited impact because most products and services cannot get all the customers they would like from only one or a few preferred channels. Still, this approach can move the needle on churn over time, and it is worth your while to try every means at your disposal.

This chapter is organized as follows:

- Section 10.1 describes typical demographic and firmographic data types and database schemas that contain it and teaches you how to extract such data as part of a dataset.
- Section 10.2 shows you how to individually analyze textual demographic data fields with category cohort analysis, which is a bit different from metric cohort analysis because it uses a new concept: confidence intervals.
- Section 10.3 teaches you to handle large numbers of demographic categories by combining them.
- Section 10.4 demonstrates analyzing a date field for its relationship to churn (the same as metric cohort analysis after the date has been converted to a time interval).
- Section 10.5 teaches you the techniques necessary to fit churn probability models like regression and XGBoost when your data includes demographic data fields.

- Section 10.6 extends the modeling in section 10.5 to forecasting and segmenting active customers by using demographic fields.

NOTE No real personal information was used to create this chapter. All examples are created from simulated data, designed to be similar to real case studies I have worked on.

10.1 Demographic and firmographic datasets

First, I will explain what exactly I mean by demographic and firmographic data and how it differs from the metrics you have looked at throughout most of this book. Then I will use a social network simulation to demonstrate a typical method for creating a dataset that includes demographic data along with metrics.

10.1.1 Types of demographic and firmographic data

Table 10.1 provides examples of demographic and firmographic data. Although this table covers the most common examples, there are many more possibilities. As you can see, some types of data are common to both consumers and firms in slightly different forms. An individual has a birthdate, and a company has a founding date, for example; a household has a number of members, and a company has a number of employees. Other items are specific to a consumer or businesses, such as a person's education level or the company's industry. Table 10.1 also shows the data type for the items listed.

Table 10.1 Examples of demographic and firmographic data

Demographic	Firmographic	Data type
Date of birth	Founding date	Date
Sales channel	Sales channel	String
Place of residence	Company domicile or geography	String
Occupation	Industry or vertical	String
Hardware and OS information	Technology stack information	String
Number of household members	Number of employees	Number
Education level attained	Company stage (start-up, funding round, or public)	String
Gender	B2B or B2C business model	String

In principle, there isn't much difference between using demographic facts and metrics to understand churn and segment customers.

> **TAKEAWAY** To understand churn and form customer segments with demographic data, you form cohorts of customers based on the values of the demographic fields and compare the churn rates in each cohort.

The non-numeric types are the reason why separate techniques are needed for demographic and firmographic data in comparison with metrics. If you are looking at numeric demographic data, the technique is the same as for metrics except for where the data comes from.

10.1.2 *Account data model for the social network simulation*

Because demographic data is tied to each account and rarely changes, it is standard to store it in a single database table indexed by account ID, as shown in table 10.2. Table 10.2 includes some of the demographic fields that are part of the social network simulation:

- *Channel (short for the sales channel)*—The sales channel refers to how the customer found the product and signed up. All users sign up through one method, so the channel is a required field with no null values in the social network simulation. In the simulated social network dataset, the different sales channels are as follows:
  - App store 1
  - App store 2
  - Web sign-up
- *Date of birth*—Many products require a customer to enter their date of birth as a statement that they are of (or older than) the minimum age to use the product. Because all users are required to enter something, the date of birth is a required field with no null values for the social network simulation.
- *Country*—The country in which the user lives can often be derived from the user's payment information or their localization choices in the software. In the social network simulation, users come from more than 20 countries, which are represented by two-character codes (from the International Standards Organization ISO 3166-1 alpha-2 standard). For the social network simulation, the country field can include missing values (null values in the database). It is assumed that this setting is an optional setting; some users don't bother to set it.

These three fields represent the minimal set necessary to demonstrate the techniques in this chapter. In a real product, there probably would be more fields, although the number varies considerably by product area. Many B2B companies know a great deal about their customers, but demographics can be sparse for consumer products with minimal sign-up requirements.

Table 10.2 Typical account data schema

Column	Type	Notes
account_id	integer or char	The account ID linking to subscriptions, events, and metrics
channel	char	The channel through which the customer purchased the app
date_of_birth	date	The birthdate entered by the customer for age verification when they signed up

Table 10.2   Typical account data schema *(continued)*

Column	Type	Notes
country	char	The country in which the user lives, represented by a two-character string
. . .	. . .	...
optional fields	char, float, int, or date	Optional; platform specific

In the rest of this section, I'll show you how to put the data in such a schema to work fighting churn.

10.1.3 Demographic dataset SQL

Given a schema of demographic data keyed by the account ID, the first step is exporting it from the database along with the dataset you usually create for the metrics. This way, you reuse all the existing code you have, showing when accounts renew and who has churned. Also, you will eventually combine the demographic data with the metrics in a single forecasting model, and by exporting the metrics and demographic fields together, you start with everything you are going to need.

Figure 10.1 shows a typical result of such a data extraction. As in the dataset you have used since chapter 4, each row starts with the account ID, the observation date, and the churn indicator. The demographic fields come after those fields and before the metrics.

account _id	observation _date	is_churn	channel	country	customer _age	like_per _month	...
36	3/1/20	FALSE	appstore2	DE	49.7	36	...
92	3/1/20	TRUE	appstore1	BR	17.8	31	...
103	3/1/20	FALSE	appstore1	CN	20.1	51	...
112	3/1/20	FALSE	appstore2	CA	63.9	69	...
115	3/1/20	TRUE	web	BR	21.2	5	...
127	3/1/20	FALSE	web	JP	71.9	178	...
...	...	...	...	...	...	...	...

The demographic fields are between the fields identifying the observation and the metrics. The date_of_birth field has been converted to customer_age at the time of the observation date.

Figure 10.1   Social network simulation dataset with demographic fields (result of listing 10.1)

Listing 10.1 shows the SQL statement that creates a dataset like the one shown in figure 10.1. Instead of the date_of_birth field, which was in the database, the dataset contains a field called customer_age. The one new technique listing 10.1 introduces is the conversion of the date field for the birthdate to a time interval in years: the customer's age.

> **TAKEAWAY** You convert demographic date fields to time intervals because then the numeric interval can be used for customer analysis and segmentation in the same way as a metric.

At a high level, the conversion is accomplished by subtracting the demographic date from the observation date, or vice versa:

- When the demographic date is in the past (such as a birthdate), you subtract the demographic date from the observation date, and the result is a positive interval representing the time since the demographic field at the time of the observation.
- If the demographic date is in the future (such as the day of college graduation), subtract the observation date from the future date to keep the interval positive. Then the interval represents the time from the observation date until the date from the demographic data.

Because the birthdate is in the past, listing 10.1 subtracts the birthdate from the observation date to get the customer's age. In PostgreSQL, the interval is converted to an age in years by using the date_part function with the 'days' parameter to get the interval length in days and then dividing by 365 (taking care with type conversions).

Listing 10.1   Exporting a dataset with demographic data fields

```
WITH observation_params AS          ◁─┤ Most of this listing is the
(                                        same as listings 7.2 and 4.5.
    SELECT  interval '%metric_interval' AS metric_period,
    '%from_yyyy-mm-dd'::timestamp AS obs_start,      The channel string from
    '%to_yyyy-mm-dd'::timestamp AS obs_end           the account table
)
SELECT m.account_id, o.observation_date, is_churn,
a.channel,                                           The country string from
a.country,                                           the account table
date_part('day',o.observation_date::timestamp        Subtracts the date
        - a.date_of_birth::timestamp)::float/365.0 AS customer_age,  of birth from the
SUM(CASE WHEN metric_name_id=0 THEN metric_value else 0 END)         observation date
    AS like_per_month,
SUM(CASE WHEN metric_name_id=1 THEN metric_value else 0 END)
    AS newfriend_per_month,
SUM(CASE WHEN metric_name_id=2 THEN metric_value else 0 END)
    AS post_per_month,
SUM(CASE WHEN metric_name_id=3 THEN metric_value else 0 END)
    AS adview_per_month,
SUM(CASE WHEN metric_name_id=4 THEN metric_value else 0 END)
    AS dislike_per_month,
SUM(CASE WHEN metric_name_id=34 THEN metric_value else 0 END)
    AS unfriend_per_month,
```

```
      SUM(CASE WHEN metric_name_id=6 THEN metric_value else 0 END)
          AS message_per_month,
      SUM(CASE WHEN metric_name_id=7 THEN metric_value else 0 END)
          AS reply_per_month,
      SUM(CASE WHEN metric_name_id=21 THEN metric_value else 0 END)
          AS adview_per_post,
      SUM(CASE WHEN metric_name_id=22 THEN metric_value else 0 END)
          AS reply_per_message,
      SUM(CASE WHEN metric_name_id=23 THEN metric_value else 0 END)
          AS like_per_post,
      SUM(CASE WHEN metric_name_id=24 THEN metric_value else 0 END)
          AS post_per_message,
      SUM(CASE WHEN metric_name_id=25 THEN metric_value else 0 END)
          AS unfriend_per_newfriend,
      SUM(CASE WHEN metric_name_id=27 THEN metric_value else 0 END)
          AS dislike_pcnt,
      SUM(CASE WHEN metric_name_id=30 THEN metric_value else 0 END)
          AS newfriend_pcnt_chng,
      SUM(CASE WHEN metric_name_id=31 THEN metric_value else 0 END)
          AS days_since_newfriend
FROM metric m INNER JOIN observation_params
ON metric_time BETWEEN obs_start AND obs_end
INNER JOIN observation o ON m.account_id = o.account_id
      AND m.metric_time > (o.observation_date - metric_period)::timestamp
      AND m.metric_time <= o.observation_date::timestamp
INNER JOIN account a ON m.account_id = a.id
GROUP BY m.account_id, metric_time, observation_date,
          is_churn, a.channel, date_of_birth, country
ORDER BY observation_date,m.account_id
```

JOINs with the account table → points to `INNER JOIN account a ON m.account_id = a.id`

Includes the demographic fields in the GROUP BY clause ← points to `GROUP BY ... is_churn, a.channel, date_of_birth, country`

Most of listing 10.1 is the same as the previous listings you've used to extract a dataset: observation dates are selected from the observation table and joined with metrics by using an aggregation to flatten the data. The other new aspects of listing 10.1 follow:

- The query makes an INNER JOIN on the account table (table 10.1) to select the fields for the channel, country, and date of birth.
- Because these demographic fields are one per account in the account table, there is no need to aggregate these fields. Instead, the demographic fields are included in the GROUP BY clause.

You should run listing 10.1 on the social network simulation to create the dataset that will be used throughout the rest of the chapter. Assuming that you are using the Python wrapper program to run the listings, the command is

```
fight-churn/listings/run_churn_listing.py --chapter 10 --listing 1
```

The result of listing 10.1 (saved in the output directory) should appear similar to figure 10.1 at the start of this section.

Tracking demographic and firmographic data changes and avoiding looka-head biases

In this section, I describe storing demographic data as a single, unchanging value. But not all demographic or firmographic fields are truly unchanging: people and companies can move, companies can achieve new stages of development, people can achieve higher levels of education, and so on. To model such changes better, some companies track demographic data in a time-sensitive manner, either by adding effective-date timestamps to the account table or by tracking demographic fields in separate tables from the account itself (known as *slowly changing dimensions* in data warehouse terminology). Because these more advanced methods are not common, I don't cover them in this book. If that situation is your situation, listing 10.1 is modi-fied to join the demographic data effective dates to the observation date.

The reason why the more complicated approach can be advantageous is that in some scenarios, treating demographic fields as static when they are not can result in a kind of lookahead bias in predicting churn using the demographic field. You see something about a customer in your historical dataset paired with a churn or renewal status in the past, but in a nonhistorical context (at the time of the observation timestamp), you would not have known that information. To make an example from firmographics, consider the company stage at a start-up or public company. Start-ups that go public must be successful and are less likely to go out of business and churn. If the data includes start-ups that went public in the past, the firmographic data identifies them as public companies because that was the current status when you created the data-set. But only successful start-ups go public, so the data becomes biased.

Such a bias can also confer unrealistic forecasting accuracy to a model. That said, this type of scenario is usually a second-order effect, which justifies the usual prac-tice of ignoring the time-changing component of demographic and firmographic data.

10.2 Churn cohorts with demographic and firmographic categories

Now that you've got a dataset with demographic data, you will compare the demo-graphic cohorts by their churn rates to see how the demographic data is related to churn. At the start of the chapter, I told you that there are three types of demograph-ics fields: dates, numbers, and strings. Earlier, I showed you that you should convert the dates to numeric intervals. In the cohort analysis, there are only two types: num-bers and strings.

Churn cohort analysis with numeric demographic data is exactly the same as cohorts based on metrics, as I will show briefly in section 10.4. This section is about the new subject of comparing churn rates in cohorts by using demographic informa-tion described by strings.

10.2.1 Churn rate cohorts for demographic categories

The section is about demographic categories, so I start with a definition.

> **DEFINITION** For the purposes of this book, a *category* is one possible value of a demographic field described by a string.

In the social network simulation, the categories associated with the channel field are appstore1, appstore2, and web. The categories associated with the country field are two-character codes such as BR, CA, and CN. It is possible for a value to be missing in a demographic field, so you can consider no value (null in the database) to be one additional category for every field.

> **NOTE** For each demographic field, a customer can belong to only one category or have no value as a category.

In principle, churn cohort analysis for demographic categories is simple: define a cohort with each category, and calculate the churn rates. But there are important differences between cohorts made from categories and cohorts made from metrics. As a result, you need to be more careful in how you compare the churn rates in cohorts defined by categories. Following are some important differences between cohorts based on metrics and cohorts based on categories:

- With metrics, the cohorts have a natural order given by the metrics. In most cases, categories do not have a meaningful order. Category-based cohorts, therefore, are harder to interpret because you cannot use the trend you see across categories as a guide for interpreting the differences in the churn rates.
- For metrics of product use, you have natural expectations, such as "More use leads to lower churn" and "More cost for use leads to higher churn." But there is no obvious expectation with categories.
- When you define metric cohorts, you guarantee that each cohort has a significant portion of the observations—typically, 10% or more. With category-based cohorts, there is no guarantee of the minimum or maximum percentage of the data that might be captured in each cohort.

Based on my own experience, cohorts from demographics have weaker relationships to churn than cohorts based on product-use metrics.

> **TAKEAWAY** You must be more careful making comparisons of churn rates in cohorts based on demographic categories than in cohorts based on metrics.

By *careful*, I mean that you need to rely on strong evidence to make sure that the difference is significant. For that reason, you will use a new technique known as confidence intervals to make the comparison.

10.2.2 *Churn rate confidence intervals*

To be more careful with churn rate comparisons between demographic cohorts, you should not simply calculate the churn rates in each cohort; you should also estimate best- and worst-case scenario churn rates in each cohort. This process is known as calculating confidence intervals.

> **DEFINITION** *Confidence intervals* for a metric like the churn rate are the range from the best-case (lowest) estimate of the churn rate to the worst-case (highest) estimate for the churn rate.

Understanding confidence intervals starts with realizing that the churn rate you calculate on your customers is not the churn rate you want to measure. Consider the following:

- What you want to know is what the churn rate would be on all the possible customers in the world who would match your cohort demographic category. That estimate would be the best estimate of future churn for that type of customer.
- You can measure only the churn rate you have seen for the customers you have had.

This scenario is illustrated in figure 10.2. You can't be sure that the churn rate you have seen in past customers is what the churn rate is going to be for future customers. You may see a different churn rate in the future. Maybe you got lucky in the past and got better-than-average customers, or maybe the opposite is true; you never know. But you can expect two things:

- The churn rate you would see in the full universe of customers should be close to what you have seen in the past, assuming that you observed a reasonable number of customers in each cohort.
- The more customers you see, the closer the churn rate you have seen in the past should be to the churn rate in the entire universe. Put another way, the more customers you see, the less uncertainty exists about the range of possible churn rates for the universe.

For this reason, people usually talk about confidence intervals as the range around the measured churn rate, which is known to be near the center of the best- and worst-case scenarios (but, as you will see, not necessarily at the center). To describe the measured churn and the best-case and worst-case estimates, we'll use the following definitions.

> **DEFINITION** The measured churn rate on past customers is referred to as the *expected value*, and it is considered to be the most likely value for the universal churn rate. The *upper confidence interval* is the range from the expected churn rate to the worst-case estimate, described by the size of that range, or the worst-case churn minus the expected churn. The *lower confidence interval* is the range from the best-case estimate to the expected churn, described by the size of that range, or the expected churn minus the worst-case estimate.

Figure 10.2 illustrates the differences among the universal churn rate, your estimate, and the upper and lower confidence intervals for the estimate.

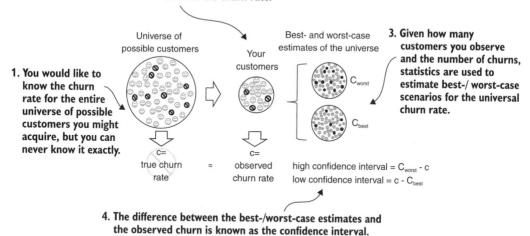

2. You acquire a smaller set of customers that is representative of the universe and observe the churn rate.

Universe of possible customers

Your customers

Best- and worst-case estimates of the universe

3. Given how many customers you observe and the number of churns, statistics are used to estimate best-/ worst-case scenarios for the universal churn rate.

1. You would like to know the churn rate for the entire universe of possible customers you might acquire, but you can never know it exactly.

C_{worst}

C_{best}

c= true churn rate

≈

c= observed churn rate

high confidence interval = C_{worst} - c
low confidence interval = c - C_{best}

4. The difference between the best-/worst-case estimates and the observed churn is known as the confidence interval.

Figure 10.2   Confidence intervals assess best- and worst-case scenarios.

I said the churn rate in each cohort should be close to the universal churn rate for such customers, assuming that you observed enough of them. How many is enough was discussed at length in chapter 5: ideally, you want to observe thousands of customers in each category, but hundreds may be enough.

When you use confidence intervals, the number of customers you use translates to the size of the confidence intervals. The more customers you measure the churn on, the narrower is the range of uncertainty around the churn rate. In section 10.2.3, you will learn how to calculate confidence intervals and compare them.

> **TAKEAWAY**   Because you can't calculate the universal churn rate measurement, you will instead calculate best- and worst-case estimates for the universal churn rate, given the available data.

10.2.3   *Comparing demographic cohorts with confidence intervals*

Figure 10.3 shows an example of comparing demographic cohorts with confidence intervals, which is the result for the channel category in the social network simulation. The basic idea is the same as the metric cohort plots you saw in earlier chapters, but there are a few significant differences:

- The data is displayed in a bar chart instead of a line chart. The churn rate in each cohort is shown by the height of each bar.

- Each bar has a pair of lines above and below the main bar, showing the extent of the confidence intervals. The lines showing the confidence intervals in a plot are often known as *error bars* or *whiskers.*
- The x-axis still identifies the cohort, but now it is a string label showing the category that the cohort represents.

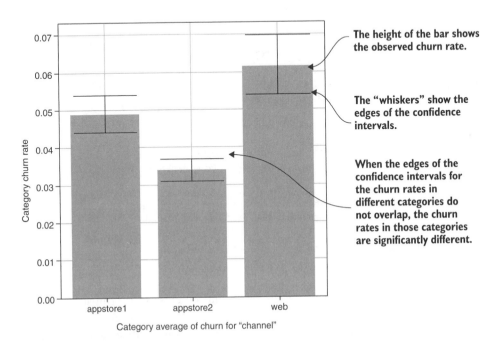

Figure 10.3   Channel churn rates with confidence intervals (output of listing 10.2)

In the category cohort plot, you are looking at not only the expected universal churn rates but also the best- and worst-case estimates, so you should use the confidence intervals as a guide to compare the significance of the difference between the category churn rates. This technique is known as *statistical significance.*

> **DEFINITION**   The difference between the churn rates in two different categories is statistically significant if the best-case churn rate (lower confidence interval) for one category is greater than the worst-case churn rate (upper confidence interval) for the other category. In that case, the two confidence intervals do not overlap.

Considering figure 10.3, you would say that the difference between the churn rates for the appstore1 and appstore2 categories is statistically significant because the confidence intervals are far apart. The worst-case churn rate for appstore2 is around 3.5%, and the best-case churn rate for appstore1 is around 4.5%, so the two are not touching.

But the difference between the churn rates for the appstore1 and the web customers is on the borderline for statistical significance because the confidence intervals are practically touching. The best-case churn for the web channel is around 5.4%, and the worst-case churn for appstore1 is also around 5.4%. According to a strict definition, you might say that the difference is not statistically significant. But in practice, statistical significance is not applied as a hard rule. If you have some reason to think that a difference is significant, you might still act on a difference in churn rates when there is a little overlap in the confidence intervals. In this case, I would say the fact that appstore2 is so different lends credibility to differences between the channels and, by extension, the differences between web and appstore1. As you will see in figure 10.4, the confidence intervals for the web and appstore2 churn rates are not touching by just 0.02%, which you can't tell in the figure. But whether confidence intervals overlap or don't by such a small amount shouldn't make a difference in your interpretation.

TAKEAWAY   In practice, whether a difference in churn rates is statistically significant or not is not black and white when the edges of the confidence intervals are nearly touching or overlap a little bit.

Listing 10.2 shows the code that produces figure 10.3. Listing 10.2 consists of a main function, `category_churn_cohorts`, that calls three helper functions:

- `prepare_category_data`—Loads the data and fills any missing categories with the string `'-na-'`. This string clearly marks any customers that are missing a category.
- `category_churn_summary`—Calculates the churn rates and the confidence intervals and puts all the results in a `DataFrame`, which is saved as a .csv file. (Details on the calculation follow the listing.)
- `category_churn_plot`—Plots the results in a bar chart, showing the confidence intervals and adding annotations. Confidence intervals are added by setting the yerr param of the bar function, which stands for y error bar.

Listing 10.2   Analyzing category churn rates with confidence intervals

```
import pandas as pd
import matplotlib.pyplot as plt
import os
import statsmodels.stats.proportion as sp

def category_churn_cohorts(data_set_path, cat_col):
    churn_data = \
        prepare_category_data(data_set_path,cat_col)
    summary = \
        category_churn_summary(churn_data,cat_col,data_set_path)
    category_churn_plot(cat_col, summary, data_set_path)

def prepare_category_data(data_set_path, cat_col):
    assert os.path.isfile(data_set_path), \
        '"{}" is not a valid dataset path'.format(data_set_path)
    churn_data = pd.read_csv(data_set_path,index_col=[0,1])
```

Main function for the category analysis and plot

Helper function prepare_category_data reads the dataset.

Calls category_churn_summary to perform the analysis

Calls category_churn_plot to make the plot

```
    churn_data[cat_col].fillna('-na-',inplace=True)          ◄─────   Fills any missing
    return churn_data                                                 values with a
                                                                      string '-na-'

def category_churn_summary(churn_data,                       ◄──────
                           cat_col, data_set_path):                   Uses category_churn_
    summary = churn_data.groupby(cat_col).agg(    ◄─────               summary to analyze
        {                                                             the categories
            cat_col:'count',
            'is_churn': ['sum','mean']                       Uses the Pandas
        }                                                    aggregation function to
    )                                                        group data by the category


    intervals = sp.proportion_confint(summary[('is_churn','sum')],     Calculates the
                              summary[ (cat_col,'count')],             confidence
                              method='wilson')          ◄──────        intervals
```

Copies the
results
into the
summary
DataFrame

```
    summary[cat_col + '_percent'] = (                ◄─────   Divides the category
        1.0/churn_data.shape[0]) * summary[(cat_col,'count')]    count by the total
                                                                number of rows
    summary['lo_conf'] = intervals[0]
    summary['hi_conf'] = intervals[1]
                                        Lower confidence interval = mean
                                        minus lower confidence bound
    summary['lo_int'] =
        summary[('is_churn','mean')]-summary['lo_conf']
    summary['hi_int'] =
        summary['hi_conf'] - summary[('is_churn','mean')]     Saves the result
    save_path =                                       ◄─────
        data_set_path.replace('.csv', '_' + cat_col + '_churn_category.csv')
    summary.to_csv(save_path)
    return summary
```

Upper
confidence
interval =
upper
confidence
minus mean

```
                                                Uses category_churn_plot
                                                to plot the result
def category_churn_plot(cat_col,         ◄─────
                        summary, data_set_path):
    n_category = summary.shape[0]                      Scales the size of
                                                       the plot based on the
    plt.figure(figsize=(max(4,.5*n_category), 4))   ◄─   number of categories
    plt.bar(x=summary.index,
            height=summary[('is_churn','mean')],
            yerr=summary[['lo_int','hi_int']].transpose().values,
            capsize=80/n_category)            ◄─────
    plt.xlabel('Average Churn for  "%s"' % cat_col)    The Y error bar is
    plt.ylabel('Category Churn Rate')                  given by confidence
    plt.grid()                                         intervals.
    save_path =
        data_set_path.replace('.csv', '_' + cat_col + '_churn_category.png')
    plt.savefig(save_path)
    print('Saving plot to %s' % save_path)
```

The
percentage
of churns
is the bar
height.

Annotates
the figure
and saves it

You should run the Python wrapper program to produce your own plot like figure 10.3 for the simulated dataset. The command and its arguments to the wrapper program are

```
fight-churn/listings/run_churn_listing.py --chapter 10 --listing 2
```

Turning to the details of the calculation of the cohort churn rates in listing 10.2, the average churn rate is calculated in the category_churn_summary function, using the Pandas DataFrame groupby and agg functions:

```
summary = churn_data.groupby(cat_col).agg({cat_col:'count','is_churn':
    ['sum','mean']})
```

The following breaks down the details of this dense line:

1. The groupby function is called with the category as the grouping variable. The result of this function is a specialized DataFrameGroupBy object that can be used to retrieve different results based on the grouping.
2. After grouping, the desired measures are found by calling the aggregation function agg on DataFrameGroupBy. The results to be created by DataFrameGroupBy are specified in a dictionary where each dictionary key is a column to calculate aggregate functions and the value for the keys are one or more aggregate functions. In this case, you use the following:

```
{
cat_col :'count',
'is_churn': [
'sum',
'mean']
}
```

   - The first entry in the dictionary indicates that the column containing the category (the variable cat_col) should be aggregated with a count. For every category, show the number of rows in the dataset that had the category.
   - The second entry in the dictionary indicates that the column containing the churn indicator should be aggregated by summing the number of churns and also calculating the mean, which results in the observed churn rate for the category.

The result of the call to the function is a DataFrame with one row per category and columns containing the three aggregation results. The columns are labeled by tuples, combining the column and the aggregation. The column labeled cat_col,'count' contains the row count for the categories, for example, and the column labeled 'is_churn','mean' contains the mean of the churn indicator, which is the churn rate.

The function category_churn_summary in listing 10.2 uses the statsmodels module to calculate the confidence intervals. The function used is statsmodels.stats .proportion.proportion_confint, which is for calculating confidence intervals on measurements of percentages resulting from binary trials (which is what measuring churn rates amounts to, from a statistician's point of view). The function proportion _confint takes as parameters the count in each category and the number of churn observations (passed by selection from the aggregation result DataFrame using the tuple labels I've described).

As mentioned early in the chapter, the number of observations and number of churns form the basis for calculation of the confidence intervals using statistics. The call to `proportion_confint` also passes the optional method parameter `method=`
`'wilson'`. The Wilson method for calculating confidence intervals is the best choice for churn because it is known to produce the most accurate results when the proportion of events (in this case, churns) in the binary trials is small. I won't go into details on how the Wilson method calculates confidence intervals, but there are many good resources online.

Figure 10.4 shows the data file output from the category churn cohort analysis with confidence intervals. This output contains all the information used to produce the channel cohort bar chart (figure 10.3) and more details. One important piece of information available in this file and not in the bar chart is the percentage of observations from each channel. Most organizations that acquire customers through different channels already have a good idea of the percentage of customers acquired through each channel. In such a case, you should compare the number in your dataset with the number measured by the sales department for quality assurance (to make sure that there are no problems in the data feed and so on).

The file output of listing 10.2 also shows the size of the low- and high-confidence intervals. In figure 10.4, you can see that the high interval is a little larger than the low interval. This asymmetry occurs because the churn probability is a small percentage. If the churn rate were 50%, the size of the confidence intervals would be symmetric.

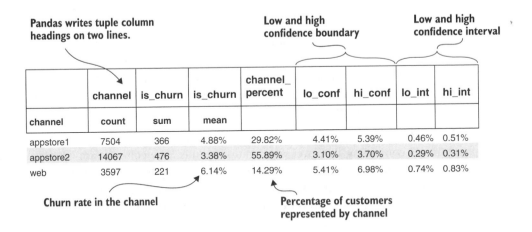

Pandas writes tuple column headings on two lines.				Low and high confidence boundary		Low and high confidence interval	
channel	is_churn	is_churn	channel_ percent	lo_conf	hi_conf	lo_int	hi_int
channel	count	sum	mean				
appstore1	7504	366	4.88%	29.82%	4.41%	5.39%	0.46%	0.51%
appstore2	14067	476	3.38%	55.89%	3.10%	3.70%	0.29%	0.31%
web	3597	221	6.14%	14.29%	5.41%	6.98%	0.74%	0.83%

Churn rate in the channel

Percentage of customers represented by channel

Figure 10.4 Data output of category churn cohorts for the channel field

The other demographic field with categories in the simulated social network is the country. Figure 10.5 shows the churn cohort plot for the country categories. The churn cohort results for the country are different from the plot of the churn cohorts for the channel because there are many more countries. Because some of the countries have only a small percentage of the customers, some of the confidence intervals are large compared with the churn rates. In fact, as a result of the large confidence intervals, there are no statistically significant churn rate differences among the countries. All the confidence intervals in the country categories overlap the confidence intervals of the other categories by a large amount. (Figure 10.5 shows no cases in which the confidence intervals overlap by a bit.)

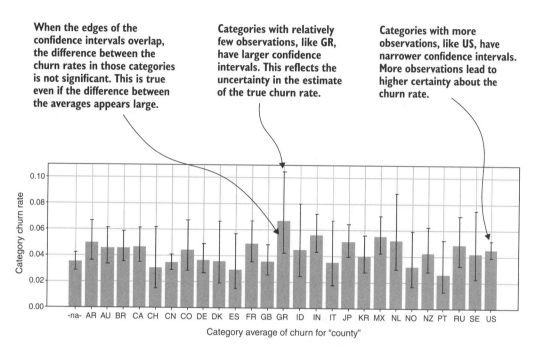

Figure 10.5 contains three callout annotations:

When the edges of the confidence intervals overlap, the difference between the churn rates in those categories is not significant. This is true even if the difference between the averages appears large.

Categories with relatively few observations, like GR, have larger confidence intervals. This reflects the uncertainty in the estimate of the true churn rate.

Categories with more observations, like US, have narrower confidence intervals. More observations lead to higher certainty about the churn rate.

Axis labels: Category churn rate (y-axis, 0.00 to 0.10); Category average of churn for "county" (x-axis with categories -na- AR AU BR CA CH CN CO DE DK ES FR GB GR ID IN IT JP KR MX NL NO NZ PT RU SE US)

Figure 10.5   Country cohort churn rates with confidence intervals (output of listing 9.2)

Figure 10.6 displays the data file output for the country cohort churn analysis. It shows that most countries have less than 10% of the data and that some have as little as 1%. The countries with the smallest number of customer observations have the largest confidence intervals for the churn rate. SE had just 1% of the observations (236 observations), and with a measured churn of 5.9%, the lower end of the confidence interval is 3.6% and the upper end is 9.7%: a span of around 6%. US, on the other hand, represents 15% of the observations (3,710 observations) with a similar observed churn rate of 5.3%, and the confidence intervals range from 4.7% to 6.1%—a span of only 1.5%.

The results in figures 10.5 and 10.6 show that having too many categories is a problem for doing an effective churn cohort analysis. Section 10.3 teaches you a simple and effective way to deal with this problem.

	country	is_churn	is_churn	country_ percent	lo_conf	hi_conf	lo_int	hi_int
country	count	sum	mean					
-na-	2837	99	3.5%	11.3%	2.9%	4.2%	0.6%	0.7%
AR	786	39	5.0%	3.1%	3.7%	6.7%	1.3%	1.7%
AU	876	40	4.6%	3.5%	3.4%	6.2%	1.2%	1.6%
BR	1269	58	4.6%	5.0%	3.6%	5.9%	1.0%	1.3%
...	...	...	...	...	...	...	...	...
RU	495	24	4.8%	2.0%	3.3%	7.1%	1.6%	2.3%
SE	239	10	4.2%	0.9%	2.3%	7.5%	1.9%	3.3%
US	3890	175	4.5%	15.5%	3.9%	5.2%	0.6%	0.7%

Categories with more observations, like US, have narrower confidence intervals. More observations leads to higher certainty about the churn rate.

Categories with relatively few observations, like SE, have larger confidence intervals. This reflects the uncertainty in the estimate of the true churn rate.

Figure 10.6   Data output of category churn cohorts for the country field

The significance level of the confidence intervals

The function `proportion_confint` has another parameter: the significance level, which I leave at the default value in my code. If you check the documentation for `proportion_confint`, you will find that the default significance level is 0.05. This parameter corresponds to what people call the 95% confidence level and represents the degree of certainty that the true universal churn rate is within the range defined by the best- and worst-case estimates.

Like most things in statistics, the best- and worst-case churn rates are estimates, and the significance level determines the possibility that these estimates are also wrong. When people say "95% confidence," they're saying 100% minus this significance level. In other words, there is a 5% chance that the true universal churn rate is not within the stated bounds and a 95% chance that the universal churn rate is within the bounds.

Lowering the significance-level parameter less than 0.05 results in larger confidence intervals, or a large difference between the best-case and worst-case estimates. If you use a lower significance level, it takes a larger difference between the churn rates for two categories to qualify as statistically significant (by having the confidence intervals that do not touch). On the other hand, a higher significance level (greater than 0.05) makes smaller confidence intervals, and it will be easier to say that differences are statistically significant, but you will be less sure that the universal churn rate for the category was within the stated bounds.

Choosing the significance level and interpreting confidence intervals is a controversial topic in statistics, and I'm trying to give you some simple best practices. My advice is to leave the significance parameter as the default. In principle, you should use a lower significance level for a demographic field that has a large number of categories (more than a few dozen). That way, you would apply more stringent criteria in determining which differences are significant.

In section 10.3, I will teach you another way of handling a large number of categories: grouping those that are less common. Overall my advice is to leave this parameter unchanged. I mention it here only because you might be asked what significance level you use to calculate the confidence intervals. (The answer is that you use the standard 0.05 significance level.)

10.3 Grouping demographic categories

In section 10.2.3, I showed you that if you have a lot of categories, you run the risk that the number of observations in the rare categories will be too small to produce useful results. With few observations, the confidence intervals can become large, depending on the amount of data you have to work with. If you have millions of customers, you can have statistical significance for the results in even the rarest categories. Still, information overload can be a problem, and it can be desirable to look at fewer categories for that reason as well.

10.3.1 Representing groups with a mapping dictionary

The solution to the problem of having a lot of categories that represent small fractions of the data is grouping rare categories that are related. Countries can be grouped into regions, for example. Figure 10.7 illustrates mapping countries into regions by using a Python dictionary. The dictionary in figure 10.7 is literally a mapping from regions to lists of countries because that mapping is a more efficient way to express the relationship.

```
{
    "APac" :    ["AU","ID","IN","JP","KR","NZ"],
    "Eur"  :    ["CH","DE","DK","ES","FR","GB","GR","IT","NL","NO","PT","RU","SE"],
    "LaAm" :    ["AR","BR","CO","MX"],
    "NoAm" :    ["US","CA"]
}
```

Keys in the mapping represent the groups for the categories, which in this case are geographic and cultural regions: APac = Asia and Pacific; Eur = Europe; LaAm = Latin America; NoAm = North America

The values in the mapping are lists of countries that should map to the region. It is assumed that each country appears once or not at all; countries not listed will remain separate from any group. In this case, CN will be kept separate.

Figure 10.7   Mapping group-simulated country categories into regions

The code on which figure 10.7 is based is in the GitHub repository for this book, in the file fight-churn/listings/conf/socialnet_listings.json; look for the chapter 10 section and the key listing_10_3_grouped_category_cohorts. I'll say more about how and why this particular mapping was chosen later, but for now, I will show you how this kind of grouping helps with the category cohort analysis.

10.3.2 *Cohort analysis with grouped categories*

Figure 10.8 shows the result of rerunning the cohort analysis based on regions instead of countries. As a result of the grouping, there are six categories. If you look at the data output that goes with the plot (not shown in the figure), you will see that every one of the new categories represents no less than 10% of the data; the smallest category is now the customers who do not have any country (-na-), which is 11%. As a result of the larger number of observations, the size of the confidence interval on every category in figure 10.8 is smaller than when the countries were separate (figure 10.5).

> **TAKEAWAY**   If your demographics include rare categories, you can simplify by grouping related categories. This approach reduces the churn rate confidence intervals and information overload.

Despite the smaller confidence intervals, figure 10.8 shows no statistically significant differences between the churn rates in any region. The confidence intervals around the churn rate in every region overlap significantly with all the others. The fact that there is no statistically significant difference in this simulated dataset doesn't mean that you won't find important relationships in your own product or service.

Listing 10.3 provides the code for performing the grouping and rerunning the category cohort analysis. This listing uses all the helper functions from the category cohort

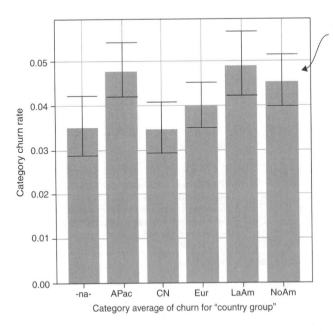

After grouping the countries into regions, the confidence intervals are all reasonably narrow. Still, the confidence intervals overlap, so there is not a statistically significant difference among the groups.

Figure 10.8   Churn cohorts for country categories grouped in regions

churn analysis (without grouping), and it adds only one new function to perform the grouping: `group_category_column`. This function has two main parts:

- The first part inverts the mapping dictionary so that it is a mapping from country to region rather than from region to country. Inverting a dictionary can be done in a Python one-liner, using a double list comprehension. The first list comprehension iterates over the keys that were the regions, and the second list comprehension iterates over the values in each key, which were the countries. A dictionary mapping the old values to the old keys (country to region) is formed from the results.

- After the mapping dictionary has been inverted, a new column is created in the DataFrame, using the `DataFrame apply` function. The `apply` function takes another function as a parameter, and that function is applied to all the elements in the column. In this case, the purpose is to look up the value in the inverted dictionary if one is present; otherwise, it returns the original value. The result of applying this function to the column is that every country that is part of one of the region groups will be mapped, and any country that is not will be copied as is. After this mapping, the code in listing 10.3 uses the analysis and plotting functions from listing 10.2, which did category cohort analysis on ungrouped categories.

The `group_category_column` function makes a name for the new column by prepending the word *group* to the original column name and dropping the original column from the result.

Listing 10.3 Grouped category cohort analysis

```
import pandas as pd
import os                                  This listing reuses the helper
                                           functions from listing 10.2.

from listing_10_2_category_churn_cohorts import category_churn_summary,
    category_churn_plot, prepare_category_data

def grouped_category_cohorts(data_set_path,                The main function
                             cat_col, groups):             is mostly the same
    churn_data = prepare_category_data(data_set_path,cat_col)   as the regular
    group_cat_col =                                        category plot.
        group_category_column(churn_data,cat_col,groups)
    summary =
        category_churn_summary(churn_data,group_cat_col,data_set_path)
    category_churn_plot(group_cat_col, summary, data_set_path)
                                                  This function maps the
                                                  categories into groups
def group_category_column(df, cat_col, group_dict):   with mapping dict.
    group_lookup = {
                   value: key for key in group_dict.keys()
                             for value in group_dict[key]
                   }
    group_cat_col = cat_col + '_group'
```

Calls helper function to map the category column to groups

Helper function from listing 10.2 analyzes the categories.

Inverts the dictionary

Makes a new name for the group column

```
df[group_cat_col] = df[cat_col].apply(lambda x:
                              group_lookup[x] if x in group_lookup else x)

df.drop(cat_col,axis=1,inplace=True)
return group_cat_col
```

Drops the original category column

Returns the new column name as the result

Transforms data with the DataFrame apply method and lambda

You should run listing 10.3 to create your own cohort analysis where the countries are grouped into regions. Do this with the usual command to the Python wrapper program and these arguments:

```
fight-churn/listings/run_churn_listing.py --chapter 10 --listing 3
```

You should get a result that is qualitatively similar to figure 10.8, but don't expect to get the specific churn rates in each group when you create your own version. The reason is that in the simulation, the countries have no relationship to churn and engagement and thus are random. (Believe me: I know because I created the simulation.) Although you should get confidence intervals of similar size to those in figure 10.8, don't expect to get the same churn rates.

> **NOTE** For the most part, this book has avoided having you analyze anything in the simulation that did not relate to churn in some way, to save you the time of generating and exploring meaningless data. But in real data from actual products and services, you should expect to find both events and demographic information that are unrelated to customer retention and churn.

> **WARNING** Do not take the results from the social network simulation from the book's GitHub repository as a guide to what you can expect from your own product or service. The examples are a realistic-looking set of data for the purpose of demonstrating the methods to use on real data, but nothing more. The simulated results cannot be expected to predict the results for any real product or service.

10.3.3 *Designing category groups*

Now that you know how to implement category groupings for a cohort analysis, I will give you some advice on how to pick such groupings. First, consider the scenario that you do not have a lot of data, so you are grouping categories to find enough observations in your cohorts (so that you end up with reasonable-size confidence intervals around the churn rates). If this situation is your situation, you don't have the option to do something that is data driven based on your own data; you don't have enough data to analyze the differences between the categories, and that's the problem. In this case, you should group categories based on your knowledge of how the categories relate to one another. Apart from the country region example, some sensible groupings you may want to use include the following:

- If you have a lot of categories for operating system versions, you can group them by major releases.

- If you have categories for industry sectors, you can group related ones such as banking and finance in one group and consumer products and retail in another.

- If you have categories for occupations, you can group related fields such as doctors and dentists in one group and software engineers and data scientists in another.

- If you have categories for education levels, you can group rare ones such as master's degrees, doctorates, and so on.

Remember that your goal is to group the rare categories in a reasonable way and try to get a sense of any relationships. If you find some relationships, you can always revise your grouping to take advantage of the structure you discovered (as described later in this section).

Also note that you don't have to slavishly follow standard definitions of groups: you should customize them based on the details of your product or service. In my own mapping from country to region, I made the following editorial decisions:

- I didn't include China (CN) in the Asia Pacific (APac) group because China alone represented more than 10% of the data samples, which is enough on its own.

- I chose to include Mexico (MX) with Latin America (LaAm) and not North America (LaAm) because if this were a real social network, I would expect that language and culture would be more significantly related to engagement than geography is related to engagement. (If my product or service had to do with industrial manufacturing and transportation, I probably would have focused on geographical rather than cultural relationships.)

These are examples of some of the considerations you might want to use. My last piece of advice on the subject follows.

> **WARNING** Do not overthink your category groups or spend too much time on them. Remember the need for agility in your analysis. Do something that gives you a manageable result for a first pass, take feedback from your business colleagues, and iterate from there.

On the other hand, consider that you have enough data to have narrow confidence intervals around every churn rate, and your problem is the information overload from too many categories (or after your first attempt at grouping, you achieved a similar result). Then you can take a more data-driven approach:

- Run the category cohort analysis on the ungrouped categories; then use the churn rates you see from the first iteration to decide on groups to use in a second iteration:
  - Group categories that are related according to your knowledge and that have similar churn rates.

- In this context, a similar churn rate means that the two categories *do not* have a statistically significant difference in their churn rates. (Confidence intervals overlap.)
- If the two churn rates are different by a statistically significant amount (confidence intervals do *not* overlap), do not group them, even if you know that the categories are related.

- You should still use groups based on knowledge as described. Do not group categories only on the grounds that the two categories have similar churn rates or other metrics.

You can also use the correlation analysis described in section 10.5 as an additional way to assess the similarity between your groups based on their relationship to other metrics. But as you will see, the grouping algorithm you used for metrics does not work for categories, and I do not recommend using an automated method for this kind of grouping.

If you have too many categories to handle by designing a grouping scheme from your knowledge (hundreds or thousands of categories), chances are that the information is not going to be helpful in your fight against churn. The businesspeople probably wouldn't segment customers into such confusing categories.

10.4   *Churn analysis for date- and numeric-based demographics*

As I mentioned earlier, you should look at numeric demographic information with cohorts the same way that you do metrics. In section 10.1, I taught you that date type demographic and firmographic information can easily be converted to numeric intervals, so you can also use metric-style cohort analysis with date type demographic data. Because you learned how to analyze numeric customer data in chapter 5, this section is going to be a short demonstration.

The demographic information for the social network simulation includes the date of birth that the customer entered when they signed up, and listing 10.1 converted this date to a numeric field in the social network simulation dataset: customer_age. Figure 10.9 shows the result of running a standard metric cohort analysis on customer age. The figure shows that in the social network simulation, the higher customer age is associated with higher churn. The lowest age cohort, with an average age around 15 years, has a churn rate around 4%, whereas the higher age cohorts (older than 60 years) have an average churn rate around 5.5%. The change in churn rates across cohorts is a little irregular, but it is consistent with the finding that older customers churn more (the effect is weak compared with the influence of their behavior that was demonstrated in chapters 5 and 7).

To create your own version of figure 10.9 from the data you simulated, you must reuse the metric cohort listing 5.1 (with the filename listing_5_1_cohort_plot.py). The configuration already has a version that you run as follows:

```
run_churn_listing.py --chapter 5 --listing 1 --version 17
```

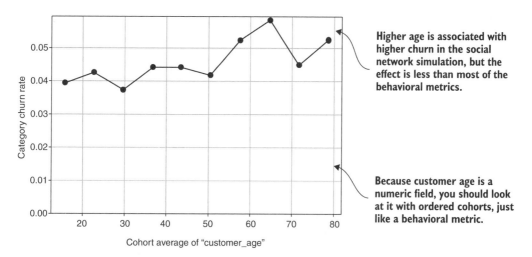

Higher age is associated with higher churn in the social network simulation, but the effect is less than most of the behavioral metrics.

Because customer age is a numeric field, you should look at it with ordered cohorts, just like a behavioral metric.

Figure 10.9 Customer demographic age cohort analysis

Your result can be somewhat different from figure 10.9 because the relationship is not strong and the data is randomly simulated. This example demonstrates that after you extract demographic information in numeric format in your dataset, you can analyze it with cohorts the same way that you would a metric.

Confidence intervals for metric cohorts

I interpret metric cohorts based on the consistency of the trend, but by now, you have probably realized that you could add confidence intervals around every point in a metric cohort plot. I don't do this normally because it makes the plots too cluttered to show to businesspeople, and it's usually not necessary for interpretation of the relationship to churn. But confidence intervals can help interpret metric cohort plots when the trend and significance are weak. Here's one strategy I have used:

1 Divide the metric into three cohorts. You are comparing customers who are low versus medium versus high in the metric. Large groups help make narrow confidence bounds.

2 Plot the cohort averages with confidence bounds, and see whether the confidence bounds overlap. If the confidence intervals overlap, statistically significant differences exist between customers who are low versus medium versus high in the metric.

I leave this exercise to interested readers.

10.5   *Churn forecasting with demographic data*

You have learned the techniques to analyze single demographic fields for their relationship to customer churn and retention. As with metrics, you may want to look at the influence on churn for all your demographic fields together to see how the combination predicts churn. Also, you should test forecasting with the demographic or firmographic data combined with your metrics. To do that, you need to convert demographic information in strings to an equivalent form as numeric information because the regression and XGBoost forecasting algorithms that you learned require only numeric inputs.

10.5.1   *Converting text fields to dummy variables*

To use your string-type demographic information for forecasting, you will convert it to numeric data by using a technique known as dummy variables.

> **DEFINITION**   A *dummy variable* is a binary variable that represents membership in a category, with 1 representing all customers in the category and 0 representing all customers that are not in the category.

If you studied data science in a computer science or engineering program, you may have learned about this technique, called *one-hot encoding.*

Figure 10.10 shows the process of creating dummy variables. Using dummy variables is similar to flattening metric data to create a dataset. In this case, a string demographic field is a tall data format in the sense that all the possible categories are stored in one column (using strings). To replace the column of strings with numeric data, you add one dummy variable column per unique string in the original data. Each columns is the dummy variable for one string category: all the customers who had a

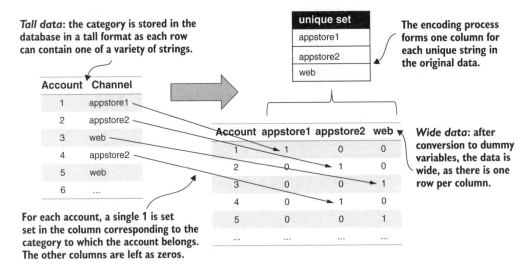

Figure 10.10   Flattening a string variable to dummy variable columns

particular string get 1 in the column for that category and 0 in all the other columns. Then you drop the original string column and are left with a purely numeric dataset that still represents the same category information as the dataset that included strings.

Figure 10.11 shows the result of creating dummy variables for the social network simulation. You can see that the string category labels for the channel and country are removed from the dataset. Instead, a set of new columns containing only zeros and ones represents the categories. Figure 10.11 also shows dummy variable columns for the country field grouped into regions, as they were earlier. The countries are still grouped because the same concerns about an overabundance of sparsely populated

In the extracted data, the demographic data is stored as strings after the observation identifiers.

account _id	observation _date	is_churn	channel	country	customer _age	like_per_ month	....
8	3/1/20	TRUE	web	BR	79.7	8	...
10	3/1/20	FALSE	appstore2	US	39.7	2	...
115	3/1/20	FALSE	appstore2	AU	22.5	23	...
135	3/1/20	FALSE	appstore2	CO	42.3	35	...
137	3/1/20	FALSE	appstore2	MX	39.2	65	...
148	3/1/20	FALSE	appstore1	NZ	16.5	81	...
...	...	...	...	...	...	...	...

In the transformed data, the demographic data is converted to dummy variable columns.

As part of creating the dummy variables, the countries were grouped into regions using a mapping.

account _id	obser- vation _date	channel_ appstore1	channel_ appstore2	channel _web	country _group _APAC	country _group _CN	country _group _EUR	country _group _LaAm	country _group _NoAm	is_ churn
8	3/1/20	0	0	1	0	0	0	1	0	TRUE
10	3/1/20	0	1	0	0	0	0	0	1	FALSE
115	3/1/20	0	1	0	1	0	0	0	0	FALSE
135	3/1/20	0	1	0	0	0	0	1	0	FALSE
137	3/1/20	0	1	0	0	0	0	1	0	FALSE
148	3/1/20	1	0	0	1	0	1	0	0	FALSE
...	...	...	...	...	...	...	...	...	...	...

The churn column is included so this dataset can be used to forecast without the metrics.

Figure 10.11 Result of creating dummy variables for the simulated social network dataset

categories apply to forecasting, the same way that they did when you were looking at the country alone.

Listing 10.4 provides the code to create a dataset with dummy variables like the one in figure 10.11. Creating dummy variables is a standard function of a Pandas DataFrame (called get_dummies). This function automatically detects all the string-type columns in your dataset and replaces them with appropriate binary dummy variables. The names for the dummy variable columns are created by concatenating the original column name with the category string.

Listing 10.4   Creating dummy variables

```
import pandas as pd                          Imports the group category
                                             mapping function from listing 10.3

from listing_10_3_grouped_category_cohorts import group_category_column   ◁─┘

def dummy_variables(data_set_path, groups={},current=False):
    raw_data = pd.read_csv(data_set_path,           Reads in the raw data
                    index_col=[0, 1])         Keys of the mapping
                                              dictionary are the
                                              categories to be mapped.
    for cat in groups.keys():                  ◁──
        group_category_column(raw_data,cat,groups[cat])   ◁──  Calls the group
                                                                mapping function
    data_w_dummies =
        pd.get_dummies(raw_data,dummy_na=True)    ◁──  Uses the Pandas
                                                        get_dummies function
    data_w_dummies.to_csv(
        data_set_path.replace('.csv', '_xgbdummies.csv'))
                                              Determines the dummy variable
                                              columns by set difference
    New_cols = sorted(list(set(
                data_w_dummies.columns).difference(set(raw_data.columns))))
    cat_cols = sorted(list(set(
                raw_data.columns).difference(set(data_w_dummies.columns))))

    dummy_col_df =                                 ◁──  Saves a list of
        pd.DataFrame(new_cols,index=new_cols,columns=['metrics'])   columns for
    dummy_col_df.to_csv(                                            consistency with
        data_set_path.replace('.csv', '_dummies_groupmets.csv'))   grouped datasets

    if not current:                                Saves a dataset with
        new_cols.append('is_churn')                only dummy variables
    dummies_only = data_w_dummies[new_cols]    ◁──
    save_path =                                    ◁──
        data_set_path.replace('.csv', '_dummies_groupscore.csv')
    print('Saved dummy variable (only) dataset ' + save_path)   Names the dataset
    dummies_only.to_csv(save_path)                               consistently with a
                                                                 regular dataset

    raw_data.drop(cat_cols,axis=1,inplace=True)    ◁──  Saves the dataset
    save_path = data_set_path.replace('.csv', '_nocat.csv')   with no demographic
    print('Saved no category dataset ' + save_path)           categories
    raw_data.to_csv(save_path)
```

Annotations (left margin):
- **Reads in the raw data**
- **This version of the dataset is for XGBoost forecasting.**
- **Determines the original category columns by set difference**
- **Includes churn if not being used for current customers**

Calling the package function get_dummies is not all that happens in listing 10.4. First, listing 10.4 applies the optional grouping of categories that you learned in section 10.2.

Then it is saved in three versions: the part with the original metrics and any numeric demographic information, a part with only the dummy variables, and everything together. Each version has a purpose, as follows:

- The metrics and numeric demographic information must be converted to scores and run through the metric grouping algorithm. This process should happen without the dummy variables.
- Saving the dummy variables by themselves facilitates running a regression analysis on the dummy variables alone.
- The version with everything together is for XGBoost, which uses the untransformed metrics together with the dummy variables.

These points will be explained further throughout the rest of this chapter, but for now, I will focus on explaining the rest of listing 10.4. This code is mostly a mechanical use of the Pandas library, separating out the parts of the dataset. The only trick is using sets and operations related to the differences between sets to figure out which columns were added by making the dummy variables.

Listing 10.4 saves multiple versions of the dataset with different filename extensions:

- The file with the postfix .dummies is the dataset with only the dummy variables. This file is also saved with the postfix .groupscore because that convention will be expected when you use the regression code on it. A listing of the columns is also saved with the postfix .groupmets because that also will be expected by the regression code, even though for the dummy variables, there will be no groups.
- The file with the postfix .nocat is the file with numeric metrics and demographic fields. This file is simply saved and will be run through the usual scoring and grouping.
- The file with the postfix .xgbdummies will be reloaded by the XGBoost cross-validation.

You should run listing 10.4 to create your own version of the dataset with the string categories replaced by dummy variables (and the files described previously). If you are using the Python wrapper program, use the usual form of the command and these arguments:

```
fight-churn/listings/run_churn_listing.py --chapter 10 --listing 4
```

Your results should look similar to figure 10.11, although the precise accounts and their demographics will be different because the data is randomly generated.

10.5.2 *Forecasting churn with categorical dummy variables alone*

Now that you have a dataset with demographic dummy variables, it is instructive to try churn forecasting in a regression model with the demographic data alone. This exercise is intended to increase your understanding of the combined influence of the demographic variables on churn probabilities. As you will see, if you want to forecast churn as accurately as possible, use the demographic dummy variables and the metrics together, as described in section 10.5.4.

If you run a regression cross-validation and then fit the model at the optimal C parameter, the results that you get are shown in figure 10.12. The results show that the demographic dummy variables are weakly predictive of churn. The best AUC measurement found in the cross-validation is around 0.56, and the maximum lift is around 1.5. If you recall from chapter 9, the regression using metrics resulted in an AUC higher than 0.7 and a lift higher than 4.0. A low value of the C parameter can be used and then most of the dummy variables removed without affecting the AUC significantly, but the lift is best with a higher value of the C parameter: 0.32 or greater.

Figure 10.12 also shows the regression coefficients and impact on retention probability with the C parameter set to 0.32. The dummy variables for the two app-store channels are assigned fairly large weights, which translates into a positive retention impact of 1.2% and 2.8%, respectively (churn reducing). The web channel gets zero weight, which reflects the fact that it has the highest churn because both of the other two channels were shown to have a positive impact. In this sense, the zero weight means that it is like the default, or baseline, and the other categories represent improvements.

The get_dummies function also created a variable for a channel not available (nan), and this channel also got zero weight, because in this dataset, all customers have the channel assigned. (Pandas makes a nan column for every variable when the na_default parameter is set.) These effects are in line with the churn-rate differences you saw in the category cohort plot (figure 10.3).

Figure 10.12 also shows much smaller coefficients and retention impacts for the country group dummy variables. In this case, CN, Eur, and the missing data have a slight positive retention impact (churn rate lower), and LaAm and APac have a negative retention impact (churn rate higher). Again, these results are in line with what you saw in the cohort plot for the country groups (figure 10.8).

Figure 10.12 was created from the listings from previous chapters, and there are already versions of the configuration prepared for you to do this. To create the regression cross-validation chart from figure 10.12, use the command for regression cross-validation, version 4, as follows:

```
fight-churn/listings/run_churn_listing.py --chapter 9 --listing 5 --version 2
```

To find the coefficients with the C parameter fixed at 0.32, use the command to run the regression with a fixed value of C:

```
fight-churn/listings/run_churn_listing.py --chapter 9 --listing 4 --version 4
```

Your result for cross-validation should be similar to figure 10.12, and so should your result for coefficients on the channels, which are randomly assigned to customers but in such a way that they produce consistent results in the simulation. You may get

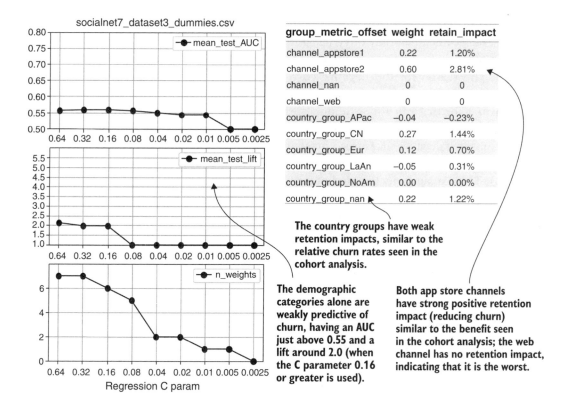

group_metric_offset	weight	retain_impact
channel_appstore1	0.22	1.20%
channel_appstore2	0.60	2.81%
channel_nan	0	0
channel_web	0	0
country_group_APac	−0.04	−0.23%
country_group_CN	0.27	1.44%
country_group_Eur	0.12	0.70%
country_group_LaAn	−0.05	0.31%
country_group_NoAm	0.00	0.00%
country_group_nan	0.22	1.22%

The country groups have weak retention impacts, similar to the relative churn rates seen in the cohort analysis.

The demographic categories alone are weakly predictive of churn, having an AUC just above 0.55 and a lift around 2.0 (when the C parameter 0.16 or greater is used).

Both app store channels have strong positive retention impact (reducing churn) similar to the benefit seen in the cohort analysis; the web channel has no retention impact, indicating that it is the worst.

Figure 10.12 Regression results with a dummy category variable dataset

different results for the small weights and impact of the country group because in the simulation they are random.

10.5.3 Combining dummy variables with numeric data

In earlier sections, I mentioned that you cannot use the type of grouping that you use for metrics when you are working with dummy variables derived from categories. Instead, I suggested separating the dummy variables from the metrics and processing the metrics as usual. In this section, I provide details on the reason and this process. I start by explaining some facts about correlations involving dummy variables because that will help make it clear why you do not group categorical dummy variables along with the metrics.

Figure 10.13 shows the portion of the correlation matrix from the social network simulation that relates the demographic categories for channel and country to one another and to the metrics. (You haven't run the code to create this correlation matrix yet, but you will soon.) The portion of the correlation matrix with metric-to-metric correlations is omitted in figure 10.13. One distinctive feature that might surprise you is the categories; dummy variables from each field are negatively correlated with the other dummy variables from the same field. This is especially true for the channel field, which had only three categories where the correlation is as low as –0.74. For the country groups, the negative correlations between the regions are around –0.2.

The reason for the negative correlations between the categories is due to the exclusive nature of category membership: if a customer is in one category, it gives them 1 for that category's dummy variable, and it requires that they have 0 for the other dummy variables from the same field. That exclusivity for the binary indicator results in a negative measured correlation from the definition of the correlation coefficient: when one dummy variable takes a high value (1), the others take low values (0). This explains why the kind of grouping you used for the metric variables will not group demographic categories from the same demographic field. That algorithm uses a high correlation to indicate that the variables should form group members.

Considering the rest of figure 10.13, the demographic category dummy variables are mostly uncorrelated with the metrics, but there are a few exceptions:

- The channels appstore1 and web have negative correlation with messages and replies.
- The channel appstore2 has positive correlation with messages and replies.
- The channel web also has positive correlation with posts.

When you use demographic categories to understand customer churn and retention, it can be worthwhile to look at the correlation matrix using the dummy variables, because it can reveal things about how different groups of your customers use the product. But you should not group the demographic dummy variables with your metric groups, even when they are correlated.

> **TAKEAWAY**   The correlations between demographic dummy variables and other metrics can help you understand your customers better, but you should not group dummy variables with other dummy variables or with metrics.

Back in chapter 6, I advised you to use correlation between metrics as a way of assessing the relatedness of the metrics and determining which should be grouped. But there are a few reasons why this same approach doesn't carry over with dummy variables created from demographic categories:

- You can calculate correlation coefficients for 0/1 binary variables, but correlation coefficients are not meant for this purpose. In statistics, other metrics are better for measuring relatedness between binary variables. When you calculate correlation coefficient with your dummy variables, it's not as good a measure of relatedness as correlation between metrics.
- The demographic categories are not related in the same way as behaviors that you group by using correlation. When two behaviors (such as using two product features) are correlated, usually they are part of a single activity or process. Therefore, it is reasonable to represent the overall process with an average of the scores, which is not normally the case for a demographic category and any other metric.

**The dummy variables within each category
are always *negatively* correlated.**

	channel_appstore1	channel_appstore2	channel_web	country_group_APac	country_group_CN	country_group_Eur	country_group_LaAm	country_group_NoAm	country_group_nan
channel_appstore1		−0.72	−0.27	0.0	0.0	0.0	0.0	0.0	0.0
channel_appstore2	−0.72		−0.47	0.0	0.0	0.0	0.0	0.0	0.0
channel_web	−0.27	−0.47		0.0	0.0	0.0	0.0	0.0	0.0
country_group_APac	0.0	0.0	0.0		−0.20	−0.26	−0.19	−0.23	−0.17
country_group_CN	0.0	0.0	0.0	−0.20		−0.23	−0.17	−0.21	−0.15
cocountry_group_Eur	0.0	0.0	0.0	−0.26	−0.23		−0.21	−0.26	−0.19
country_group_LaAm	0.0	0.0	0.0	−0.19	−0.17	−0.21		−0.19	−0.14
country_group_NoAm	0.0	0.0	0.0	−0.23	−0.21	−0.26	−0.19		−0.17
country_group_nan	0.0	0.0	0.0	−0.17	−0.15	−0.19	−0.14	−0.17	
adview_per_post	0.0	0.0	0.0	0.0	0.0	0.0	0.0	0.0	0.0
customer_age	0.0	0.0	0.0	0.0	0.0	0.0	0.0	0.0	0.0
days_since_newfriend	0.0	0.0	0.0	0.0	0.0	0.0	0.0	0.0	0.0
dislike_pcnt	0.0	0.1	−0.1	0.0	0.0	0.0	0.0	0.0	0.0
dislike_per_month	0.0	0.0	0.0	0.0	0.0	0.0	0.0	0.0	0.0
is_churn	0.0	0.0	0.1	0.0	0.0	0.0	0.0	0.0	0.0
like_per_post	0.0	0.0	0.0	0.0	0.0	0.0	0.0	0.0	0.0
metric_group_1	0.0	0.10	0.18	0.0	0.0	0.0	0.0	0.0	0.0
metric_group_2	−0.21	0.49	−0.42	0.0	0.0	0.0	0.0	0.0	0.0
newfriend_pcnt_chng	0.0	0.0	0.0	0.0	0.0	0.0	0.0	0.0	0.0
newfriend_per_montn	0.0	−0.1	0.1	0.0	0.0	0.0	0.0	0.0	0.0
reply_per_message	−0.29	0.44	−0.24	0.0	0.0	0.0	0.0	0.0	0.0
unfriend_per_month	0.0	0.0	0.0	0.0	0.0	0.0	0.0	0.0	0.0
unfriend_per_newfriend	0.0	0.0	0.0	0.0	0.0	0.0	0.0	0.0	0.0

**There are correlations between the channels and some
of the service features, like messaging and replying:
appstore 2 customers have more messages and replies;
appstore 1 and web customers have somewhat less.
Web customers also post somewhat more.**

**In the simulated dataset, the country
and channel are not correlated
with most of the metrics.**

Figure 10.13   Correlation matrix for the social network simulation demographic categories

For these reasons, my advice is that if you want to use demographic dummy variables
to forecast churn, you should keep all dummy variables separate from the groups.

TAKEAWAY   Run the metrics and numeric demographic fields through a standard preparation process without demographic dummy variables, and then
combine them with dummy variables at the end.

account_id	observation_date	metric_group_1	metric_group_2	customer_age	dislike_per_month	unfriend_per_month	adview_per_post	reply_per_message	like_per_post	post_per_message	unfriend_per_newfriend	dislike_pcnt	newfriend_pcnt_chng	days_since_newfriend	is_churn	channel_appstore1	channel_appstore2	channel_nan	channel_web	country_group_APac	country_group_CN	country_group_Eur	country_group_LaAm	country_group_NoAm	country_group_nan
36	3/1/20	−0.57	1.95	0.16	−0.45	1.78	−0.50	0.15	0.32	−0.91	1.38	−0.50	2.04	−0.20	FALSE	0	0	0	0	0	0	1	0	0	0
92	3/1/20	−0.37	−0.31	−1.41	−0.31	1.78	−1.01	−0.51	−0.97	0.30	3.90	−0.31	−0.94	0.89	TRUE	1	0	0	0	0	0	0	1	0	0
103	3/1/20	−0.95	−1.89	−1.30	1.22	−0.76	−1.21	−1.50	−0.25	1.17	0.40	0.88	−0.19	−0.65	FALSE	1	0	0	0	0	1	0	0	0	0
...	...	...	...	...	...	...	...	...	...	...	...	...	...	...	...	...	...	...	...	...	...	...	...	...	...

The combined dataset starts with the metric group averages and metric scores.

Categorical dummy variables are included at the end of each row.

Figure 10.14   Metric groups, metric scores, and categories in one dataset

This result is illustrated in figure 10.14.

To create your own dataset like the one in figure 10.13, the first step is running the data-preparation process that you learned in earlier chapters on the version of the dataset that has the metrics and numeric demographic information. There is a version of the listing configuration prepared for you to do that with one command. Recall that listing 8.1 (with the filename listing_8_1_prepare_data.py) was the combined data-preparation function, and this is the third use of it (version 3):

```
fight-churn/listings/run_churn_listing.py --chapter 8 --listing 1 --version 3
```

After processing the metrics, combine them with the dummy variables. A new function shown in listing 10.5 is a straightforward application of a Pandas `DataFrame` manipulation. The group scores produced from the metrics are merged with the file for the dummies. The merge is performed with the Pandas `DataFrame` `merge` function, using the indices of both `DataFrame`s to perform an `INNER JOIN`. The final step in listing 10.4 combines the `DataFrame` that lists the group metrics with the names of the dummy variables; such a file will be expected by the code that runs the regression on the combined dataset.

Listing 10.5   Merging dummy variables with grouped metric scores

```
import pandas as pd

def merge_groups_dummies(data_set_path):

    dummies_path =                                    ← Loads the file containing
        data_set_path.replace('.csv', '_dummies_groupscore.csv')    the dummy variable
                                                                    dataset
```

```
                 dummies_df =pd.read_csv(dummies_path,index_col=[0,1])
                 dummies_df.drop(['is_churn'],axis=1,inplace=True)          ◁─┐  Drops the
                                                                               churn column
Loads the    ─▷ groups_path =
metric            data_set_path.replace('.csv', '_nocat_groupscore.csv')
group            groups_df = pd.read_csv(groups_path,index_col=[0,1])           Merges the dummy
scores                                                                          variables and metric
                 merged_df =                                              ◁──   group scores
                     groups_df.merge(dummies_df,left_index=True,right_index=True)
Saves the    ─▷ save_path =                                                    Loads the
merged file       data_set_path.replace('.csv', '_groupscore.csv')            group metric
under the        merged_df.to_csv(save_path)                                   listing from
name for         print('Saved merged group score + dummy dataset ' + save_path)  the metric-
the group                                                                      only data
scores           standard_group_metrics = pd.read_csv(                    ◁──
                     data_set_path.replace('.csv', '_nocat_groupmets.csv'),index_col=0)
             ─▷ dummies_group_metrics = pd.read_csv(
                     data_set_path.replace('.csv', '_dummies_groupmets.csv'),index_col=0)
                 merged_col_df =                                          ◁──┐
                     standard_group_metrics.append(dummies_group_metrics)    │
                 merged_col_df.to_csv(data_set_path.replace('.csv', '_groupmets.csv'))
```
Loads the listing of the   **Combines the two**
dummy variables   **metric lists and saves it**

You should run listing 10.5 on your own simulated social network dataset to prepare
for forecasting in section 10.5.4. Issue the usual command to the Python wrapper program with these arguments:

```
fight-churn/listings/run_churn_listing.py --chapter 10 --listing 5
```

After running listing 10.5, one of the results should be a dataset like the one you saw
in figure 10.14. Also, now that you have created the combined dataset, you can make a
correlation matrix like the one I showed you at the start of this section (figure 10.13).
Use a version of the correlation matrix listing configuration by issuing the following
command with these arguments:

```
fight-churn/listings/run_churn_listing.py --chapter 6 --listing 2 --version 3
```

Running listing 6.2 with parameter configuration version 3 creates the raw data for a
correlation matrix like the one shown in figure 10.13. The formatting for figure 10.13
was done in a spreadsheet program (as explained in chapter 6).

10.5.4 Forecasting churn with demographic and metrics combined

Now that you have created a dataset combining the group metric scores and the demographic category dummy variables, you can run a regression or machine learning model
to forecast churn probabilities. Figure 10.15 shows the result of the regression.

   The cross-validation of the C parameter shows that many of the variables can be
assigned zero weight before accuracy is affected. Figure 10.15 also shows the weights
resulting from the regression when the C parameter is set to 0.04. Nearly all the

demographic dummy variables have zero weight and retention impact (and a few of the metrics as well).

Figure 10.15 was created by using listings from chapter 9. To run your own regression on the dataset with dummy variables and metrics combined, you can use prepared versions of the configuration. To run the cross-validation of the regression C parameter (listing 9.5) shown in figure 10.15, use the following command:

```
fight-churn/listings/run_churn_listing.py --chapter 9 --listing 5 --version 3
```

To run the regression with the C parameter fixed (listing 9.4) at 0.04 on the combined dummy variables and metrics dataset, use the command

```
fight-churn/listings/run_churn_listing.py --chapter 9 --listing 4 --version 5
```

Those commands produce results similar to figure 10.15, although you may have different weights on the country group dummy variables because they are assigned randomly in the simulation.

You may wonder why the regression coefficients in figure 10.15 show that the channel demographic variable had no influence on the churn prediction, but early in the chapter, both the cohort churn analysis with confidence intervals and the regression on the dummy variables showed that the channel was strongly predictive of churn (and retention). What's going on here? Is something wrong in the regression?

Nothing is wrong. When taken together with the behavioral metrics, the channel provides no additional information about churn, and the regression discovers this fact. The customer channels are correlated with certain behaviors, and behavior causes customer churn and retention in the simulation. When you look at the channel alone, it is related to churn rates, but when combined with the behavioral metrics in a regression, the regression algorithm automatically determines the most explanatory factors and removes the others. The regression correctly determines that customer engagement is most predictable by watching the metrics and not the channels.

> **TAKEAWAY**   Demographic categories are often related to churn and engagement because customers from different demographics behave differently. But if you use detailed behavioral metrics, you will usually find that behaviors are the underlying drivers of retention in a predictive forecast.

I told you that understanding demographics and firmographics is a secondary method of fighting churn because behavior can (sometimes) be modified by interventions but demographics cannot (ever). The fact that demographics are not usually helpful in predicting churn is another reason why I emphasize understanding behavior with metrics when fighting churn. But even if a demographic field is not useful for predicting churn, it does not detract from the primary use of demographics in fighting churn.

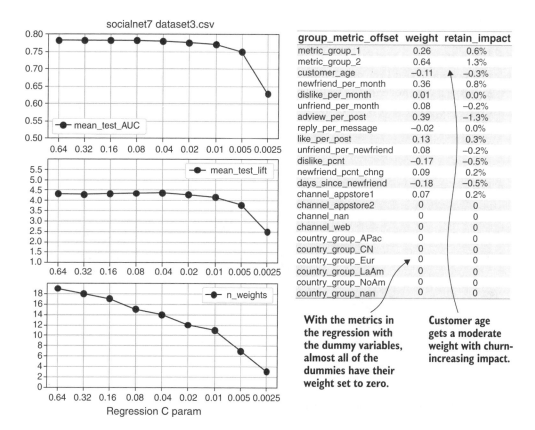

Figure 10.15 Regression result for dataset combining metric scores and category dummy variables

TAKEAWAY If you see a strong relationship between demographics and retention in your cohort analysis, you should try to emphasize your best demographics in your acquisition efforts. It doesn't matter if those same demographics are not predictive of engagement in a regression with behavioral metrics.

WARNING Do not assume that your own product or sevice's churn data will show exactly the same result as I presented here from the simulation. The social network simulation was designed to mimic the result that I have most commonly seen when studying customer churn, but there can always be exceptions, and your product may be one of them.

If you find that your own demographics are strongly predictive of churn, even when you have factored in behavioral metrics, you should check your data to see whether it can be improved. Make sure that all relevant customer behaviors are represented by your events and that your metrics adequately capture the relationships between your events and churn. Demographic correlations with unmeasured behaviors can lead to a result in which demographics predict churn, even when including metrics. If that's the case, you would be better off figuring out what those behaviors are so that you can measure them and attempt to influence them for the better.

You can also test how much improvement demographic variables make for prediction with a machine learning model like XGBoost. The result of such an experiment is shown in figure 10.16. The demographic variables add around 0.005 to the AUC of XGBoost, or one-half of 1%. Figure 10.16 also shows the improvement in the regression AUC, which is even smaller (but an improvement nonetheless).

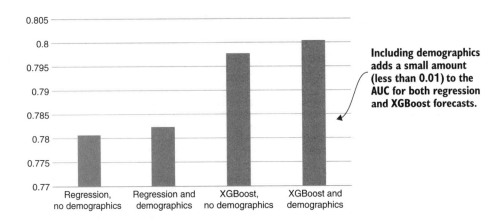

Figure 10.16   Accuracy comparison with demographic data

TAKEAWAY   The highest predictive accuracy comes from XGBoost using demographic data combined with detailed customer metrics. XGBoost may find demographics more helpful in prediction than regression does.

To reproduce the XGBoost result in figure 10.16, you can run a version of the XGBoost cross-validation listing configuration with the following command (listing_9_6_crossvalidate_xgb.py):

```
fight-churn/listings/run_churn_listing.py --chapter 9 --listing 6 --version 2
```

Note that the listing and configuration create the results for XGBoost with demographic variables. If you have been following along, you should have already found the accuracy for the other models and datasets.

10.6   *Segmenting current customers with demographic data*

The final subject for this chapter is how to use demographic information as part of the effort to segment customers. As the data person, you're not responsible for defining the segments or intervening with customers, but you do need to provide the data so that the businesspeople can do their jobs effectively. The final dataset for segmenting customers should include the following elements:

- All customers active on the most recently available date
- Scores for metric groups
- The original (unscaled) metric values for metrics that were not grouped
- Categorical demographic information in string format
- Categories grouped where appropriate
- Churn forecast probabilities (optional)

Figure 10.17 is an example of a dataset that has all those features.

account _id	observation _date	metric_ group_1	metric_ group_2	customer _age	newfriend _per_ month	days_ since_ newfriend	...	channel	country
2	5/10/20	0.092	0.081	53.7	2	12	...	appstore1	AR
5	5/10/20	−0.018	−1.704	22.2	4	5	...	appstore1	NZ
7	5/10/20	1.228	−1.861	22.9	14	2	...	appstore1	US
8	5/10/20	−0.253	−0.529	57.9	7	2	...	web	AU
10	5/10/20	1.408	−0.367	70.9	12	4	...	web	
11	5/10/20	0.621	0.517	42.2	10	4	...	appstore2	DE
14	5/10/20	−0.464	1.606	23.4	7	0	...	appstore2	CA
15	5/10/20	−0.042	−0.009	23.3	4	5	...	appstore1	DE

The metric groups are scores, scaled to be small numbers averaging to zero.   **Ungrouped metrics are on their natural scales.**   **Demographic categories are included as a string.**

Figure 10.17   Dataset to segment customers with metric group scores, metrics, and demographic information

Creating such a dataset requires a few steps:

1. Extract all the metrics and demographic information for current customers from the database.
2. Reprocess the metric information to form groups, using the score parameters and loading matrix from the historical data.
3. Save a version of the dataset that has all the desired features.

Note that this process also creates a dataset ready for churn probability forecasting on active customers. That version combines scores for all the metrics and numeric demographic data but dummy variables for the demographic categories.

Listing 10.6 provides the SQL statement to extract demographic data along with all metrics for currently active customers. This listing is almost the same as similar listings in chapters 4 and 8, so I'll explain it only briefly. The main portion of the SQL program is the aggregation to flatten the metrics. The new feature is to join on the account table and also select the channel country and the date of birth. The date of birth is converted to a time interval representing the customer's age in years (following the pattern used to create the historical dataset with demographic data presented earlier in this chapter).

Listing 10.6   Exporting metrics and demographic data for currently active customers

```
WITH metric_date AS                                    ⊲──┤  Most of this listing is the
(                                                          same as listings 4.6 and 8.3.
    SELECT  max(metric_time) AS last_metric_time FROM metric
),
account_tenures AS (
    SELECT account_id, metric_value AS account_tenure
    FROM metric m INNER JOIN metric_date ON metric_time =last_metric_time
    WHERE metric_name_id = 8
    AND metric_value >= 14
)
SELECT s.account_id, d.last_metric_time AS observation_date,
a.channel,
a.country,
date_part('day',d.last_metric_time::timestamp
    - a.date_of_birth::timestamp)::float/365.0 AS customer_age,
SUM(CASE WHEN metric_name_id=0 THEN metric_value else 0 END)
    AS like_per_month,
SUM(CASE WHEN metric_name_id=1 THEN metric_value else 0 END)
    AS newfriend_per_month,
SUM(CASE WHEN metric_name_id=2 THEN metric_value else 0 END)
    AS post_per_month,
SUM(CASE WHEN metric_name_id=3 THEN metric_value else 0 END)
    AS adview_per_month,
SUM(CASE WHEN metric_name_id=4 THEN metric_value else 0 END)
    AS dislike_per_month,
SUM(CASE WHEN metric_name_id=34 THEN metric_value else 0 END)
    AS unfriend_per_month,
SUM(CASE WHEN metric_name_id=6 THEN metric_value else 0 END)
    AS message_per_month,
SUM(CASE WHEN metric_name_id=7 THEN metric_value else 0 END)
    AS reply_per_month,
SUM(CASE WHEN metric_name_id=21 THEN metric_value else 0 END)
    AS adview_per_post,
SUM(CASE WHEN metric_name_id=22 THEN metric_value else 0 END)
    AS reply_per_message,
SUM(CASE WHEN metric_name_id=23 THEN metric_value else 0 END)
    AS like_per_post,
SUM(CASE WHEN metric_name_id=24 THEN metric_value else 0 END)
    AS post_per_message,
SUM(CASE WHEN metric_name_id=25 THEN metric_value else 0 END)
    AS unfriend_per_newfriend,
SUM(CASE WHEN metric_name_id=27 THEN metric_value else 0 END)
    AS dislike_pcnt,
```

The channel string from the account table →

The country string from the account table ⊲

Subtracts the date of birth from the observation date

```
SUM(CASE WHEN metric_name_id=30 THEN metric_value else 0 END)
    AS newfriend_pcnt_chng,
SUM(CASE WHEN metric_name_id=31 THEN metric_value else 0 END)
    AS days_since_newfriend
FROM metric m INNER JOIN metric_date ON m.metric_time =d.last_metric_time
INNER JOIN account_tenures t ON t.account_id = m.account_id
INNER JOIN subscription s ON m.account_id=s.account_id
INNER JOIN account a ON m.account_id = a.id            ◁─┤ JOINs with the
WHERE s.start_date <= d.last_metric_time                   account table
AND (s.end_date >=d.last_metric_time OR s.end_date IS null)
GROUP BY s.account_id, d.last_metric_time,
    a.channel, a.country, a.date_of_birth       ◁─┐ Includes the demographic
ORDER BY s.account_id                               fields in the GROUP BY clause
```

You can run listing 10.6 on your own simulated social network dataset to create your own dataset file for the current customers by running the following command and these arguments:

```
fight-churn/listings/run_churn_listing.py --chapter 10 --listing 6
```

The Python program that converts the raw data for current customers to versions that can be used for forecasting and segmenting is shown in listing 10.7. Much of listing 10.7 is similar to the transformation that you saw in chapter 8, and it includes several helper functions from chapters 7, 8, and 10. But listing 10.7 also includes a few new steps to accommodate the demographic data.

The one important new technique in listing 10.7 is what I call *aligning* the dummy variables in the historical and current datasets. The Pandas get_dummies function (called from listing 10.4 dummy_variables) creates dummy variable columns for every category in the data frame, but the categories in the historical dataset and the current dataset may not match. Typically, the historical dataset has enough customer observations that you will see a rare category in a few customers, but the current dataset will have fewer customers and may not include any examples of the rare category. The result in that case would be that the historical dataset has a column that the current dataset does not have. This situation would cause a failure when you try to forecast churn probabilities on the current dataset.

The same problem would happen if a category goes out of use historically and is no longer present in the current dataset. The reverse problem would occur if a new category comes into use: the historical dataset may lack the category, and only the current dataset includes it. In summary, aligning the categories does two things:

- Adds to the current dataset, for any category in the historical data that is missing, a new dummy variables column containing zeros. This way, the current dataset is equivalent in its columns to the historical dataset, and zeros are the correct categorical value for a category of which no one is part.
- Drops any categories from the dummy variables for the current dataset that were missing in the historical dataset. Again, this step aligns the columns in the

historical and current datasets. If the category was not available in the historical dataset, you don't know whether or how it's predictive of churn, so removing it is correct for the purpose of forecasting.

Overall, the main steps in listing 10.7 are

1 Run the `dummy_variables` creation listing from earlier in this chapter (listing 10.4), using the path to the current dataset. This code saves three versions of the data:
   — Only the numeric fields for further processing by scoring and grouping
   — Only the dummy variables to merge back together with the scores and groups later
   — The numeric fields and dummy variables together, which is used by XGBoost (this file is saved from within the `dummy_variables` function)
2 Load the dummy variables derived from the current dataset.
3 Run the `align_dummies` helper function that takes care of inconsistencies between the two sets of dummy variables.
4 Load the dataset with only numeric fields that were created from the current data by the `dummy_variables` function. Also load the loading matrix and score parameters created from the historical dataset. Run this current dataset through the reprocessing steps you learned in chapter 8:
   a Transform any skewed columns.
   b Transform any columns with fat tails.
   c Rescale the data so all fields are scores with a mean near 0 and a standard deviation near 1.
   d Combine any correlated metrics by using the loading matrix created on the historical data.
5 Merge the dummy variables with the metric group and score data, and save this version of the dataset. This version can be used for forecasting churn probabilities for current customers.
6 Create the version of the dataset designed to be used by businesspeople for segmenting. This version of the dataset combines the following elements:
   — Scores for the grouped metrics
   — The original (untransformed) metrics for those that are not grouped
   — The original strings (not the dummy variables) for the demographic categories

Listing 10.7   Preparing a current customer dataset with demographic fields

```
import pandas as pd

from listing_7_5_fat_tail_scores
    import transform_fattail_columns, transform_skew_columns
from listing_8_4_rescore_metrics
    import score_current_data, group_current_data, reload_churn_data
from listing_10_4_dummy_variables import dummy_variables
```

```
def rescore_wcats(data_set_path,categories,groups):

    current_path = data_set_path.replace('.csv', '_current.csv')

    dummy_variables(current_path,groups, current=True)
    current_dummies = reload_churn_data(data_set_path,
        'current_dummies_groupscore', '10.7',is_customer_data=True)
    align_dummies(current_dummies,data_set_path)

    nocat_path =
        data_set_path.replace('.csv', '_nocat.csv')
    load_mat_df = reload_churn_data(nocat_path,
                            'load_mat','6.4',is_customer_data=False)
    score_df = reload_churn_data(nocat_path,
                            'score_params','7.5',is_customer_data=False)
    current_nocat =
        reload_churn_data(data_set_path,'current_nocat','10.7',is_customer_data=
        True)
    assert set(score_df.index.values)==set(current_nocat.columns.values),
            "Data to re-score does not match transform params"
    assert set(load_mat_df.index.values)==set(current_nocat.columns.values),
            "Data to re-score does not match loading matrix"
    transform_skew_columns(current_nocat,
        score_df[score_df['skew_score']].index.values)
    transform_fattail_columns(current_nocat,
        score_df[score_df['fattail_score']].index.values)
    scaled_data = score_current_data(current_nocat,score_df,data_set_path)
    grouped_data = group_current_data(scaled_data, load_mat_df,data_set_path)

    group_dum_df =
        grouped_data.merge(current_dummies,left_index=True,right_index=True)
    group_dum_df.to_csv(
        data_set_path.replace('.csv','_current_groupscore.csv'),header=True)

    current_df = reload_churn_data(data_set_path,
                            'current','10.7',is_customer_data=True)
    save_segment_data_wcats(
        grouped_data,current_df,load_mat_df,data_set_path, categories)


def align_dummies(current_data,data_set_path):

    current_groupments=pd.read_csv(
        data_set_path.replace('.csv','_current_dummies_groupmets.csv'),
        index_col=0)

    new_dummies = set(current_groupments['metrics'])
    original_groupmets =
        pd.read_csv(data_set_path.replace('.csv','_dummies_groupmets.csv'),
                    index_col=0)

    old_dummies = set(original_groupmets['metrics'])
    missing_in_new = old_dummies.difference(new_dummies)
    for col in missing_in_new:
        current_data[col]=0.0
```

Runs the function dummy_variables on the current dataset

Calls helper function to align current dummies with historical ones

Prepares the current data without categories

Merges the group score data with the dummy data

Saves the result using the original dataset name

Uses the function to prepare the data for use in segmenting

Makes a set from the file listing current dummy variables

Makes a set from the file listing original dummy variables

For any dummy missing in the new data, adds a column of zeros

Set difference finds dummy columns in original but not current.

Drops dummy columns in current but not original

Group columns have more than one loading matrix entry.

Makes the segmenting data

```
missing_in_old = new_dummies.difference(old_dummies)
for col in missing_in_old:
    current_data.drop(col,axis=1,inplace=True)


def save_segment_data_wcats(current_data_grouped, current_data,
                            load_mat_df, data_set_path, categories):
    group_cols =
        load_mat_df.columns[load_mat_df.astype(bool).sum(axis=0) > 1]
    no_group_cols =
        list(load_mat_df.columns[load_mat_df.astype(bool).sum(axis=0) == 1])
    no_group_cols.extend(categories)
    segment_df =
        current_data_grouped[group_cols].join(current_data[no_group_cols])

    segment_df.to_csv(
        data_set_path.replace('.csv','_current_groupmets_segment.csv'),
        header=True)
```

Set difference finds dummy columns in current but not original.

Standard metric columns have one loading matrix entry.

Adds the category variable names to the list

You can run listing 10.7 with the Python wrapper program with the following command and these arguments:

```
fight-churn/listings/run_churn_listing.py --chapter 10 --listing 7
```

This code creates three files for the current customer data for the purposes described previously:

- Forecasting with regression
- Forecasting with XGBoost
- Segmenting by businesspeople

If you want to forecast with the regression model, use listing 8.5 (with the filename listing_8_5_churn_forecast.py) with the following command and these parameters:

```
fight-churn/listings/run_churn_listing.py --chapter 8 --listing 5 --version 2
```

If you want to forecast with the XGBoost model (with the filename listing_9_7_churn _forecast_xgb.py), use

```
fight-churn/listings/run_churn_listing.py --chapter 9 --listing 7 --version 2
```

Regarding the dataset for segmenting customers that your business colleagues will use, it is important to realize that for businesspeople, demographic data is important even when it does not relate to churn and retention. The marketing department, for example, will need to write different copy for engagement campaigns targeting customers in different countries or regions. In a large organization, the marketing department probably has access to all of that kind of information through its own system, but I include everything here for the sake of completeness.

TAKEAWAY   Demographic information can be relevant to designing interventions with customers, even when it is not related to engagement and retention.

Summary

- Demographic and firmographic data are facts about the customers that do not change over time, like metrics. The type of demographic/firmographic fields can be date, numeric, or string.
- Date type information about customers can be converted to intervals and analyzed using the same techniques as metrics.
- To compare the churn rate in cohorts defined by demographic category strings, you use confidence intervals that are best- and worst-case estimates for the churn rate.
- Churn rates in different categories are said to be different by a statistically significant amount when the confidence intervals around their churn rates do not overlap.
- If you have many categories representing small percentages of the customer population, you should group related categories before analyzing them.
- Grouping demographic categories is usually done using previous knowledge, and the mapping can be efficiently represented by using a dictionary.
- To use demographic categories in regression or machine learning forecasting, convert them to columns of binary dummy variables.
- Dummy variables are not grouped with metric scores, but investigating the correlation between dummy variables in metrics can provide useful information.
- Using demographic information can improve forecasting accuracy, but it is usually a secondary contribution compared with behavior-based metrics.

Leading the fight against churn

This chapter covers

- Planning to go from data to data-driven churn reduction
- Loading your own data and running the book code on it
- Migrating the book listings to work in your own production environment

I want to start this last chapter by thanking you for sticking with me and making it to this point. I hope that what you learned in the preceding chapters was interesting and that you feel like you learned a lot that you will be able to apply. In this short final chapter, I am going to try to give you some advice to help you put what you learned into practice.

In section 11.1, I tie together the strategic churn-fighting advice that was distributed throughout the book and give you a checklist of steps to take to pursue the various strategies.

Then I'll go over the practical steps you need to take to use the techniques from the book on your own data. You can take two paths, which are the subjects of the next two sections:

- Section 11.2 goes over the steps to take if you want to load your own data into the PostgresSQL schema used in the book and then run the book listings on your own data.

- Section 11.3 describes the alternative, which is to take the book's listings (SQL, Python, or both) and port them to your own production environment.

After that, there is not much more I can teach you; it will be up to you to put your knowledge to use and find more resources to help along the way. Section 11.4 describes some of the resources available for learning more.

11.1 Planning your own fight against churn

This book covered a lot of different techniques and provided advice that would apply in many scenarios. But the truth is that you can make a big difference in churn for a typical product or service by using only some of the techniques in the book. I'm going to back out to a higher level now and give you some advice about which techniques to use and how to apply them.

Throughout the book, I've mentioned a variety of churn-reducing strategies, which I summarize here:

- *Product improvement*—Most companies already use data to improve their products, typically collected in surveys or focus groups. Although surveys typically capture the views of only a small number of participants, churn is effectively a survey of all users, who vote with their feet. Product managers and content producers can take the churn analysis results as valuable new insights into the preferences of customers (without running a survey or focus group).

- *Engagement marketing*—If a company uses email marketing, it can send engagement emails to customers. Use the result of churn data to target customers and encourage them to use product features they aren't using already, provide advanced tips to power users, and so on. The point is to use the data to make the communication valuable to the customers who receive it.

- *Pricing and packaging*—For products that charge a fee, pricing and packaging are crucial. A company that produces such products should use advanced metrics to understand the value that customers receive (or don't) and how that value relates to churn. This information helps when the company devises new pricing and packaging that satisfy the various customer segments.

- *Customer success and support*—Larger companies probably have a customer support function that helps customers who report difficulty. A greater impact on churn is a data-driven, proactive customer success function that helps customers before they ask for it. Track your churn versus account tenure, and try to make sure that customers get an onboarding experience before it's too late.

- *Channel targeting*—If you find your customers through multiple channels, it may be worthwhile to understand which channel delivers the best customers in terms of engagement and retention.

Table 11.1 summarizes the most common churn-reduction strategies and how they relate to the techniques you learned in this book.

Table 11.1   Data-driven churn reduction

Churn-reducing strategy	Core concepts/customer metrics	Chapter(s)
Product improvement Make more of the best features. Make the best features easy to find.	Metric cohorts based on product-use events identify engaging and disengaging product features.	3, 5, 8
Engagement marketing Promote the best features. Use targeted product insights.	Metric cohorts provide benchmarks for healthy levels of product use. Segment customers with metrics for targeting.	3, 5, 7
Pricing and packaging Differentiate pricing to provide value without discounting. Understand relationships between the use of different features/content.	Unit cost and unit value metrics identify customers who are getting good/bad value from the product. Consider monetizing valued groups of product features.	6, 7
Customer success and support Help customers in need. Identify failing customers proactively.	Metric cohorts benchmark healthy use levels. Forecast customer risk level with regression or machine learning.	3, 5, 8, 9
Channel targeting Identify your best customer channels. Find lookalikes.	Cohort churn rates with confidence intervals identify the best (worst) sales channels and demographic/firmographic indicators of success.	10

But don't be intimidated by the long list of strategies and the fact that some of them require several techniques to put into practice. I want to stress that you don't need to use every churn-reducing strategy in this book. Also, it's better to start with something small than to get overwhelmed and do nothing. This book taught a large number of techniques because I wanted to cover a variety of common scenarios and pitfalls. But you don't necessarily need to tackle all of them to have a big impact on your company's churn.

> **TAKEAWAY**   It's better to start small and deliver something than to try everything and not deliver anything. The techniques in the book are front-loaded so that you don't have to use most of them to get most of the benefits.

I don't want to sell short the more advanced techniques, because they can be useful, but the benefits are front-loaded in the sense that most of the benefit is derived from the techniques taught in the beginning of the book. I estimate that your company can get almost half the benefit of using data to reduce churn if you can make it through chapter 3 and deliver a correct churn rate and a well-designed set of customer metrics to your company. By *half the benefit*, I mean half the benefits realized by a company that uses all the advanced techniques in later chapters. (Achieving the full benefit also requires various business units to use the metrics in their decision-making, of course.)

If you can make it through chapter 5 and deliver an analysis of basic metrics by using metric cohorts, your company probably will get two-thirds of the total possible benefit of using data to drive churn-reduction initiatives. Section 11.1.2 lays out the steps you need to take.

11.1.1 Data processing and analysis checklist

When teaching these techniques, I sometimes teach some steps out of order to make the concepts easier to follow. Table 11.2 shows you the steps to take to achieve what I call the *foundation* level of data-driven churn fighting, including all the steps up to delivering a current customer list with customer metrics based on event data. If you can take these steps and communicate the results to the businesspeople in your company (as explained in section 11.1.3), you will achieve almost half the benefit of data-driven churn reduction.

Table 11.2   Checklist for the foundation level of data-driven churn fighting

Step	Step description	Chapter	Section(s)
1	Churn rates	2	2.4 for B2C subscription 2.5 for no subscription 2.6 for B2B subscription
2	Event-data quality assurance (QA)	3	3.8
3	Standard behavioral metrics	3	3.5, 3.6, 3.10, 3.11
4	Metrics QA	3	3.7
5	Current customer metrics dataset	4	4.5

If you complete all the foundation steps in table 11.2, you are ready to go on to using the more advanced techniques in the book. Table 11.3 lists the steps for *advanced* data-driven churn-fighting techniques, beginning with creating the analytic dataset and analyzing the basic metrics for their relationship to churn. The goal is the creation of advanced metrics that reveal more important information about engagement and retention.

Table 11.3   Checklist for advanced data-driven churn fighting

Step	Step description	Chapter	Section(s)
6	Dataset creation	4	4.1–4.4
7	Dataset summary statistics and QA	5	5.2
8	Metric cohort analyses	5	5.1
9	Churn behavioral grouping and analysis	6	All
10	Advanced behavioral metrics creation and analysis	7	7.1–7.4

Table 11.3 Checklist for advanced data-driven churn fighting *(continued)*

Step	Step description	Chapter	Section(s)
11	Advanced metrics QA	3	3.7
12	Current customer advanced metrics dataset	8	8.4

The forecasting techniques in chapters 8 and 9 of this book usually provide only a little additional benefit beyond those in the first two parts. Those techniques are most likely to be applied by experienced statisticians, data scientists, or machine learning engineers in a company that is accustomed to using advanced analytics. For that reason, I'll call these techniques the *extreme* level of data-driven churn fighting. Table 11.4 provides a checklist of the steps to take.

Table 11.4 Checklist for extreme data-driven churn fighting with forecasting

Step	Step description	Chapter	Section(s)
13	Cross-validate regression model to find best parameter.	9	9.4
14	Run regression on full dataset at optimal parameter.	9	9.3
15	Create current customer list with churn forecast and lifetime value.	8	8.4, 8.6
16	Cross validate XGBoost model to find best parameters.	9	9.5
17	Create current customer XGBoost forecasts.	9	9.6

Last are the techniques for reducing churn by identifying the best channels or demographic and firmographic categories. All those techniques are discussed in chapter 10 and don't require you to use any of the advanced techniques: you can use demographic/firmographic techniques separately or in combination with the other techniques in the book. Table 11.5 lists the steps for using demographics or firmographics, starting from step 1. The steps in table 11.5 restart from step 1 because these steps do not depend on the steps in tables 11.2, 11.3 and 11.4.

Table 11.5 Checklist for fighting churn with demographics/firmographics

Step	Step description	Chapter	Sections
1	Export historical dataset with demographic/firmographic information.	10	1
2	Categorical cohort analysis for demographic/firmographic categories.	10	2
3	Metric cohort analysis for numeric demographic/firmographic data.	5	1
4	Create current customer list with demographic/firmographic information.	10	6
5	Optional: demographic/firmographic data for forecasting.	10	5

11.1.2 Communication to the business checklist

Section 11.1.1 provides a checklist of technical steps in a data-driven fight against churn. But what about the business context? In this section, I'll review and summarize how you should be collaborating with your business colleagues and what outcomes you should try to achieve.

Table 11.6 lists the suggested points of business involvement corresponding to each step in achieving the foundation of data-driven churn fighting. These steps align with the technical steps described in table 11.2. Each stage of the data processing and analysis has one or more deliverables to the business. You should make sure that these discussions lead to action that reduces churn (because the data person can't do that job alone)!

Table 11.6 Checklist for the foundations of communicating churn data to the business

Step(s)	Step description	Business involvement
1	Churn rates	Discuss churn rate calculation method.
		Present monthly and annual churn rates.
		If the business has an existing churn calculation, compare the results, and come to an agreement on the best method to measure churn for your product or service.
2	Event-data QA	Present daily event count plots for major events.
		Present a summary of events per account per month.
		Come to an agreement with businesspeople that these events properly reflect the business and are not excessively affected by bad data. Decide on any steps to improve data collection.
3, 4	Metrics and QA	Present choices for metric time window and reasoning.
		Present metric time series QA.
		Present metric summary statistics.
		Come to an agreement that these metrics are an acceptable summary of customer behaviors.
		Agree on simple criteria for customer health. (Example: healthy customers are those who are above average on the most common customer metrics.)
		Decide on any steps to improve data collection or metric formulas.
5	Current customer metrics dataset	Deliver the customer list with metrics.
		Review samples of high-, typical-, and low-use accounts.

I'm not a presentation coach, so I'm not going to attempt to go into detail about how you should communicate with businesspeople. Remember my advice to label the data you present clearly and make sure that the data is legible. As for the level of effort involved, I estimate that it would take a typical data person about a day to take the results described in table 11.6 and assemble them into an acceptable presentation (document or slide deck). It will probably take about an hour to review them with a group of businesspeople, and you should plan on having at least one follow-up discussion to answer questions and agree on the next steps.

TAKEAWAY   The most important outcome from the interaction with the business is to get the businesspeople using the metrics to evaluate customer health with simple criteria.

If you have read all the techniques in this book, you may think that it's not very data-driven to decide on customer health criteria without having done cohort analysis. I agree that it is better to understand customer health with metric cohorts. But the point I am trying to make (again) is that it's better to do something than nothing. If you can achieve only the foundation results described in table 11.6, you have accomplished a lot. If you followed the reasoning in the cohort and correlation analysis portion of the book, you should expect that every major customer behavior will be associated with increased engagement and churn reduction. (All the major behaviors are likely to be highly correlated.) So the most important thing is to get the businesspeople thinking about the metrics and how to improve customer engagement. That's why having the metrics can be so powerful.

That said, I encourage you to take your churn fighting to the next level if possible. Table 11.7 summarizes the business involvement required to take on more advanced data-driven churn fighting. Preparing for these meetings will probably be more time consuming than preparing for the meetings about the basic level of data-driven churn fighting. You have more results to show, and you need to prepare to explain some statistical concepts, such as correlation, scores, and averaging. If you don't have a lot of experience in communicating technical results to nontechnical audiences, I recommend that you practice.

Table 11.7   Checklist for advanced communication of churn data to the business

Step	Step description	Business involvement
6	Dataset creation	Explain the lead time concept and how you chose the lead time for your company data. Explain the dataset concept. Show how many observations and how much churn were in your dataset.
7	Optional: dataset summary statistics and QA	Skip presenting these statistics if the summary statistics in step 4 (Metric QA) were acceptable.
8	Metric cohort analyses	Present metric cohort churn charts for the major event-based metrics and subscription-based metrics (if any). Agree on healthy target levels for metrics. Discuss which behaviors cause engagement and retention, and how well they are reflected by the available data. Discuss the churn-reducing strategies suggested by the results. (Examples: product features to promote or produce more of and customer segments to target for training.)

Table 11.7 Checklist for advanced communication of churn data to the business *(continued)*

Step	Step description	Business involvement
9	Churn behavioral grouping and analysis	Present examples of correlated metric scatterplots, and explain correlation.
		Present a metric correlation heatmap for basic metrics.
		Present the groups of metrics you found with the clustering algorithm.
		Present metric cohorts for grouped average metric cohorts.
11	Advanced behavioral metrics creation and analysis	Discuss choices made when designing advanced metrics.
		Present metric cohort analyses for advanced metrics.
		Update the behavioral grouping results for metric groups, if necessary. (Example: present the new correlation matrix and any changes to metric groups.)
		Discuss the churn-reducing strategies suggested by the results. (Examples: segments to target for engagement or training based on efficiency or success metrics.)
		Discuss alternative pricing strategies suggested by unit cost metric analysis.
12	Current customer advanced metrics dataset	Deliver the customer list with metrics.
		Review samples of high-. typical-, and low-use accounts.

If you can achieve the results in table 11.7, you will be getting 90% of the benefit of data-driven churn fighting (by my estimate). As it was at the foundation level, the most important thing is getting the businesspeople to look at well-designed customer metrics, understand them, and use them to make decisions.

As for the forecasting techniques in part 3 of the book, these techniques require still more effort to explain to your business colleagues. Despite my best efforts to keep this material accessible by providing background information, explaining concepts such as regression forecasts and gradient boosting to your business colleagues is a talent that you'll need to develop (if you haven't done so already). If you're a data scientist or machine learning engineer for a company that already uses advanced analytics in other areas, you should present the churn analysis methods with your existing predictive analytics as a reference and explain how the situation changes for churn.

11.2 Running the book listings on your own data

Running the book listings on your own data (loaded into the book schema) is probably the fastest way to get to your own results. This method will work if the data from your product is in a format similar to the schema described in this book and if the number of customers you have is small enough for an available PostgresSQL database.

11.2.1 Loading your data into this book's data schema

Two main types of underlying data are used in this book:

- Customer subscriptions (chapter 2)
- Product-use events (chapter 3)

You should consult tables 2.1 and 3.1, which show the table schemas for subscriptions and events to check that your data has the required fields. Remember that the fields may not have the same names in your own system.

The first step is creating a new PostgreSQL schema with a name of your choice. The GitHub repository contains a script that will do this job for you: fight-churn/data-generation/py/churndb.py. (If you created the simulated dataset and ran the listings in the book, you must have run this script way back at the beginning.) The most up-to-date details on how to run that script are in the README file of the book's GitHub repository: www.github.com/carl24k/fight-churn.

After you have created the schema, you need to get your data into it. There are many ways to import data into a PostgreSQL database. I favor GUI tools and have had successful experiences with the free tool PGAdmin (www.pgadmin.org). More details are available in the README file of the book's GitHub repository.

> **WARNING** All database import tools are finicky and will fail if the data has unexpected characteristics. Things to look out for are date and time formats, separators, and null specifiers.

Don't be surprised if it takes several frustrating attempts to load the data for each data source. The good news is that after you figure out the idiosyncrasies of your own data, loading should be easier. But you might have to repeat this process if you plan to redo your analysis in the future. In that case, you probably should go with a scripted method of loading your data.

> **TIP** Write a script to automate any transforms you have to make to your data to load it into PostgreSQL. Avoid manual approaches such as search/replace, because you may have to load the data into the database more than once.

11.2.2 Running the listings on your own data

After you have your data loaded, you need to run the listings with parameters that you specify. There are two straightforward approaches:

- Use the Python wrapper program that came with the book in the GitHub repository.
- Write your own wrapper program that imports the book listings as modules.

If you use the book's wrapper program, you need to create a configuration that specifies the parameters to provide each listing when you run it from the wrapper program. Such a file was used to configure the code to run for the social network simulation: fight-churn/listings/conf/socialnet_listings.json. If you are not familiar with JSON (JavaScript Object Notation), all you need to know is that it is a simple format for storing key-value pairs. JSON is not meant for storing parameters but is often used for this purpose. It has the advantage of a direct and simple mapping to a Python dictionary.

If you look in the file socialnet7_listings.json, you will find a key for each chapter: chap1, chap2, and so on. Each chapter key maps to a nested object of parameters for that chapter. Within each chapter object, each listing is specified with a string object, such as "list1," "list2," and so on. Each such key maps to an object that contains fields for the listing name and the various parameters. The object for each listing also contains the additional version parameters that you have been running throughout the book. To run the Python wrapper program on your own data, you need to make a JSON configuration file for your own schema, with the schema name in the filename (as in the social network simulation); then fill it with the parameter definitions suitable for your data. This approach is very useful if you have multiple schemas on which you want to run the listings. (While writing this book, I ran the listings on multiple versions of the simulation, as well as the company case studies.)

Because you probably have only one schema to run the data on, another good approach is to write your own wrapper program in Python to call all the listing functions you want to use. Because every Python listing in the book consists of a function in its own file, it is straightforward to start a new Python code file and import the book listing functions. (There are numerous examples of the book listings importing other listings in chapters 8, 9, and 10.) Because you are writing your own program, you can store all your own parameters in your program as variables or have that program fetch them from any other database or key-value store that you are already using.

> **TAKEAWAY** Writing a custom Python wrapper program is probably the best choice for most companies trying to use the book listings with a minimal number of modifications.

The advantage of writing your own wrapper program is that you can combine any other custom processing you need for your data as well as your own controls for different steps in the process. But with this approach, you will also have to write your own methods to bind variables into the SQL listings and send them to your database schema or refactor the examples in the wrapper program that I wrote. (I have no doubt that many of my readers could do a better job than I did!)

One other thing you have to do to, whether you run the book listings directly or write a wrapper program, is write your own version of the data-extraction SQL (listing 4.5). That example is hardcoded to the metrics in the book. For an example script that automatically generates SQL for all the metrics in a schema, see the script that I used for my customer case studies: fight-churn/dataset-export/py/observe_churn.py.

11.3 Porting this book's listings to different environments

There are a lot of good reasons why you may not want to use the code provided with the book but want to reuse the techniques. In that case, you are looking at porting the book listings to work in different environments. This subject is big, and I must admit to not being an expert. The best I can do is try to give you some guidelines. That said, this kind of work is the bread and butter of professional software developers, and many other resources are available to you. You could search for books or online resources about porting code to the system of your choice or hire a contractor or consultant, for example.

11.3.1 *Porting the SQL listings*

If you have a lot of data in a database other than PostgresSQL, you should consider doing whatever is necessary to port the book listings to your database. Because the book's SQL code makes heavy use of common table expressions (CTEs), this process will be a lot easier if the other database supports CTEs as well.

You may not want to use PostgresSQL because of its performance limitations. If you have not already chosen your database, I recommend checking out Presto, an open source distributed SQL engine for big data (https://prestodb.io). Presto supports CTEs, and porting the SQL code from this book to run on it would be a low-effort task.

If you need to port the book's SQL code to run on a database that does not support CTEs, changes in the code will be necessary. If possible, you could replace the CTEs with temporary tables, which would allow you to keep the layout and flow of the code. If your system does not allow temporary tables, a port of the code may be accomplished with subqueries. Again, this subject is a big one; I recommend searching for resources specific to the system you are working on.

11.3.2 *Porting the Python listings*

Another option you may want to consider is refactoring the Python listings to work as part of your own software framework. The code listings in this book were written with the primary goal of teaching the subject clearly in a series of small increments. For that reason, this code is admittedly suboptimal in almost every other respect, and I certainly won't take offense if you don't choose to use it in its current form.

If you want to port the code, it will certainly be easiest to keep it in Python. That process would be like writing your own wrapper program plus doing some refactoring (moving the code around without changing the core logic). If you want to port the code to a different language, you have a bigger task. Whether you are refactoring or porting the code to another language, this type of thing can be tricky.

> **WARNING**   Porting analytic code involves risk; seemingly minor differences in calculations or analytic functions can make a significant difference in the results. The greatest risk is from results that look correct superficially but contain a calculation error that alters the meaning of a metric or analytic result.

I recommend that you test each function by rerunning the analysis on the social network simulation data as you port the code or as you refactor each function in Python. Make sure that you can reproduce the results with your own code or that you have a good understanding of the reason for any differences.

> **TAKEAWAY**   Use your results of the social network simulation as a regression test for porting the code.

11.4 Learning more and keeping in touch

Before I leave you to your own fight against churn, I will give you some pointers to more information.

11.4.1 Author's blog site and social media

I maintain my own blog, where I post information and updates about churn fighting:

https://fightchurnwithdata.com

By now, you should know that all the code from the book is available in my GitHub repository:

https://github.com/carl24k/fight-churn

I stream demonstrations of churn analysis on Twitch:

https://www.twitch.tv/carl24k

Also, please keep in touch with me on social media:

- Twitter: @carl24k
- LinkedIn: in/carlgold

I would love to hear about your own experiences and results fighting churn with data!

11.4.2 Sources for churn benchmark information

I did not provide any information in this book about real company churn rates. Such information can be useful for benchmarking your own churn rate against your peers. At the time of this writing, I know of a few online resources that provide average churn rates based on data:

- *Zuora's Subscription Economy Index*—https://www.zuora.com/resource/subscription-economy-index (Disclaimer: I work for Zuora and am the principal author of the index.)
- *Profitwell average churn rate benchmarks*—https://www.profitwell.com/blog/average-revenue-churn-rate-benchmarks
- *Recurly churn rate benchmarks*—https://info.recurly.com/research/churn-rate-benchmarks

All these reports are free, but don't be surprised if you have to provide your email address to download the documents. (If you provide a corporate email address, you may receive follow-up contacts from salespeople, but they are smart enough not to bother people who register to download the report with a personal email address.)

> **WARNING** Typical benchmark churn rates vary widely by the type of product or service, so make sure that your company's product is similar to the ones in a benchmark before comparing your churn rate with the benchmark.

Benchmarks can be useful, but they are not perfect. The reports cover somewhat different types of companies, so don't be surprised if you find differences in the benchmark churn rates between reports. Read the reports carefully, learn about the kinds of companies and products covered in each report, and pick the benchmarks that most closely match your own company and product.

11.4.3 *Other sources of information about churn*

If you do an online search for churn, you are going to find a lot of links, because nowadays, many people know that churn is a big problem. But the truth is, most of the information at these links is basic compared with the information in this book, and many of the articles you will find are thinly disguised advertisements for products that you have to pay for. That said, at the time of this writing, there is one free resource I recommend that may not come up in your search (or may be buried under the ads): ChurnFM (https://www.churn.fm), a podcast devoted to churn.

Please contact me on social media if you know of any other free resources for fighting churn.

11.4.4 *Products that help with churn*

Not surprisingly, some products are specifically designed to help with different aspects of fighting churn. The focus of the book is on understanding churn by using open source tools and your own data, but you should know that the following product categories exist:

- *Customer support platforms*—Software that helps organize onboarding and retention tactics
- *Credit card retry automation*—Software that retries failed credit cards to minimize involuntary churn
- *Exit survey and offer automation*—Software that surveys users about their reasons for canceling and offers them one last chance to keep their subscriptions

You can easily find more information about all these product categories by searching by category name.

Summary

- The benefit of the techniques in the book are front-loaded, so you don't have to use all of them to get most of the benefit.
- A typical company gets the most benefit of fighting churn with data from using a good set of data-driven customer metrics.
- Sharing the results of churn analysis with business colleagues is an important part of the churn-fighting process—if the businesspeople don't take action, there won't be any reduction in churn.

- The fastest way to run the listings in the book on your own data is to load your own data into a PostgresSQL schema like the one used in the book and create a configuration to run the book's wrapper program.
- For a company wishing to reuse the code listings in a production process, the best practice is usually to write your own wrapper program that imports and runs the listings.
- If you want to port the book's code to run in your own production environment, use the social network simulation described in the book as a regression test.
- Most of the information online about churn is advertising for products, but there are a few free resources, including the author's own website, churn rate benchmarks, and podcasts.

index

D

RELATED MANNING TITLES

Succeeding with AI
by Veljko Krunic

ISBN 9781617296932
288 pages, $49.99
March 2020

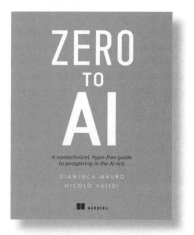

Zero to AI
by Nicolò Valigi and Gianluca Mauro

ISBN 9781617296062
264 pages, $49.99
April 2020

Machine Learning for Business
by Doug Hudgeon, Richard Nichol

ISBN 9781617295836
280 pages, $39.99
December 2019

For ordering information go to www.manning.com

The Manning Early Access Program

Don't wait to start learning! In MEAP, the Manning Early Access Program, you can read books as they're being created and long before they're available in stores.

Here's how MEAP works.

- **Start now.** Buy a MEAP and you'll get all available chapters in PDF, ePub, Kindle, and liveBook formats.

- **Regular updates.** New chapters are released as soon as they're written. We'll let you know when fresh content is available.

- **Finish faster.** MEAP customers are the first to get final versions of all books! Pre-order the print book, and it'll ship as soon as it's off the press.

- **Contribute to the process.** The feedback you share with authors makes the end product better.

- **No risk.** You get a full refund or exchange if we ever have to cancel a MEAP.

Explore dozens of titles in MEAP at www.manning.com.